# WELCOME TO DINGBURG

## ZIPPY'S HOME TOWN



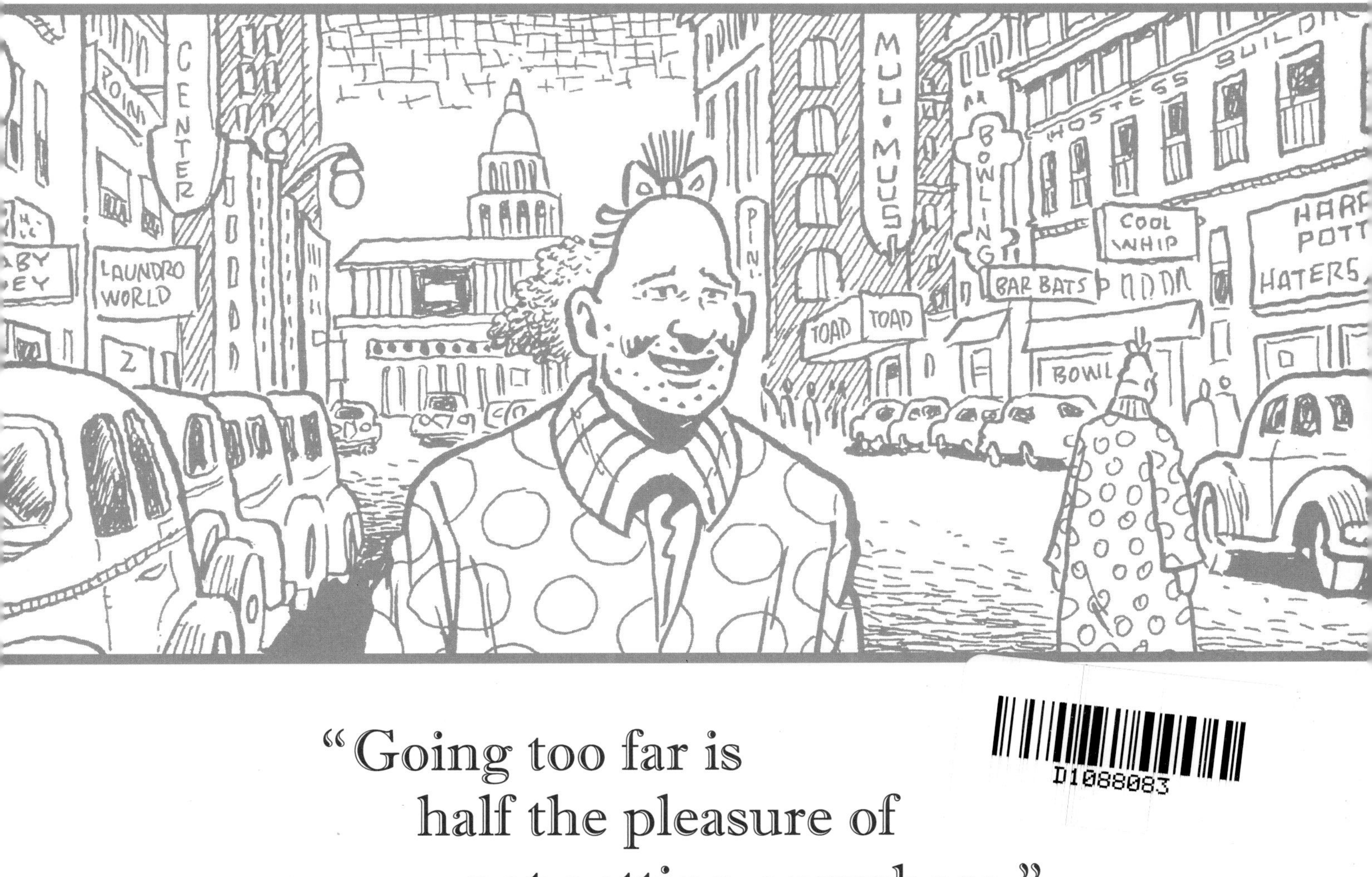
CENTER
LAUNDRO WORLD
Z
MUU-MUUS
BOWLING
HOSTESS BUILDING
COOL WHIP
BAR BATS
TOAD
TOAD
BOWL
HATERS



"Going too far is
half the pleasure of
not getting anywhere."

– Official Dingburg City Motto

# ZIPPY

## WELCOME TO DINGBURG

The City inhabited entirely by Pinheads

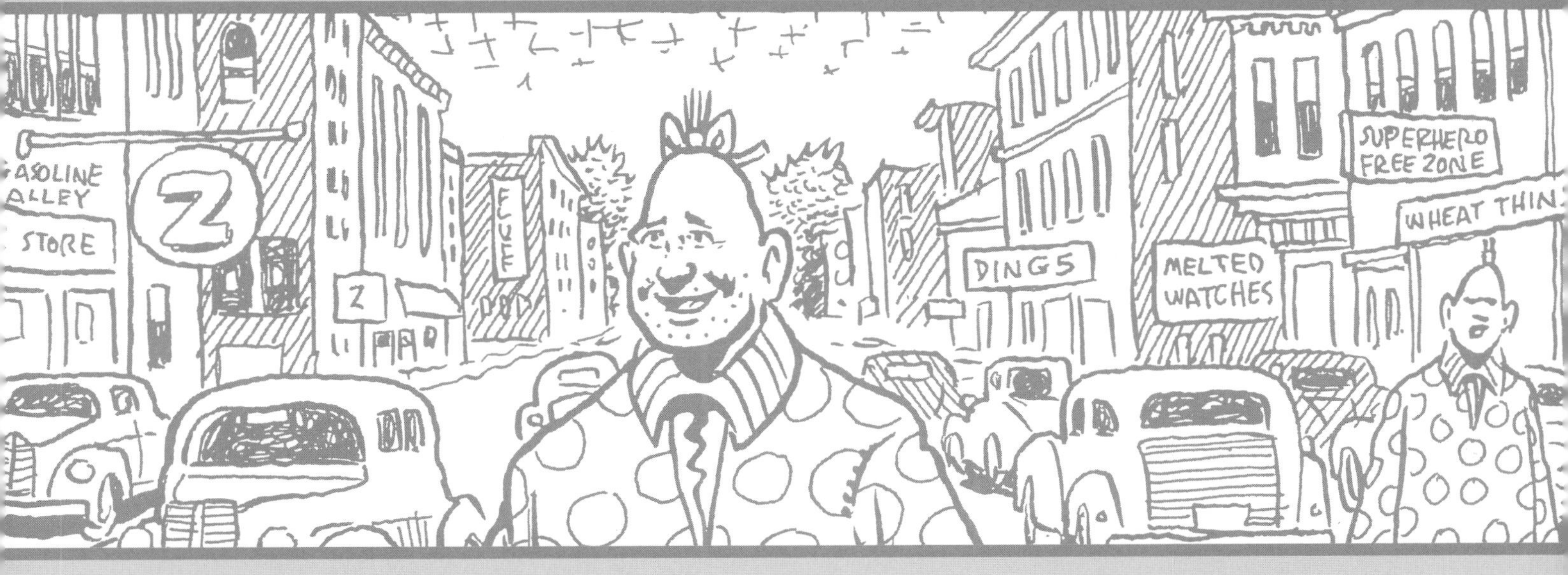

ASOLINE ALLEY STORE
Z
Z
FLUFF
DINGS
MELTED WATCHES
SUPERHERO FREE ZONE
WHEAT THIN


## AUGUST 2007 – AUGUST 2008

**ZIPPY / Welcome to Dingburg**
Zippy Annual – Volume 9
Copyright © 2007, 2008 Bill Griffith
All rights reserved, including the right to reproduce
this book or portions thereof in any form.

# FANTAGRAPHICS BOOKS

7563 Lake City Way NE, Seattle WA 98115
www.fantagraphics.com
Call 1-800-657-1100 for a full color catalog of fine comics publications.
First Edition: November 2008
Designed by Bill Griffith
Production managed by Kim Thompson
Production by Paul Baresh
Cover production by Paul Baresh
Published by Gary Groth and Kim Thompson
Promotion by Eric Reynolds

Printed in Malaysia
ISBN: 978-1-56097-963-0

The comic strips in this book have appeared in newspapers and on
newspaper websites in the United States and abroad, distributed by
King Features Syndicate, 300 W. 57th St., New York NY 10019.
www.kingfeatures.com

For more on Zippy (including the Zippy Store, Zippy Strip Search,
Letters page, Newsroom and extensive free Zippy Archives), visit:
www.zippythepinhead.com

Thanks and a tip o' th' pin to: American Color, Gary Groth, Kim Thompson, Jon Buller,
and Diane Noomin.

Books by Bill Griffith:
*Zippy Stories* • *Nation of Pinheads* • *Pointed Behavior* • *Pindemonium*
*Are We Having Fun Yet?* • *Kingpin* • *Pinhead's Progress* • *Get Me A*
*Table Without Flies, Harry* • *From A To Zippy* • *Zippy's House Of Fun*
*Griffith Observatory* • *Zippy Annual #1* • *Zippy Annual 2001*
*Zippy Annual 2002* • *Zippy Annual 2003* • *ZIPPY: From Here To*
*Absurdity* • *ZIPPY: Type Z Personality* • *ZIPPY: Connect The Polka Dots*
*ZIPPY: Walk A Mile In My Muu-Muu*

To contact Bill Griffith:
Pinhead Productions, LLC, P.O. Box 88, Hadlyme CT 06439
Griffy@zippythepinhead.com

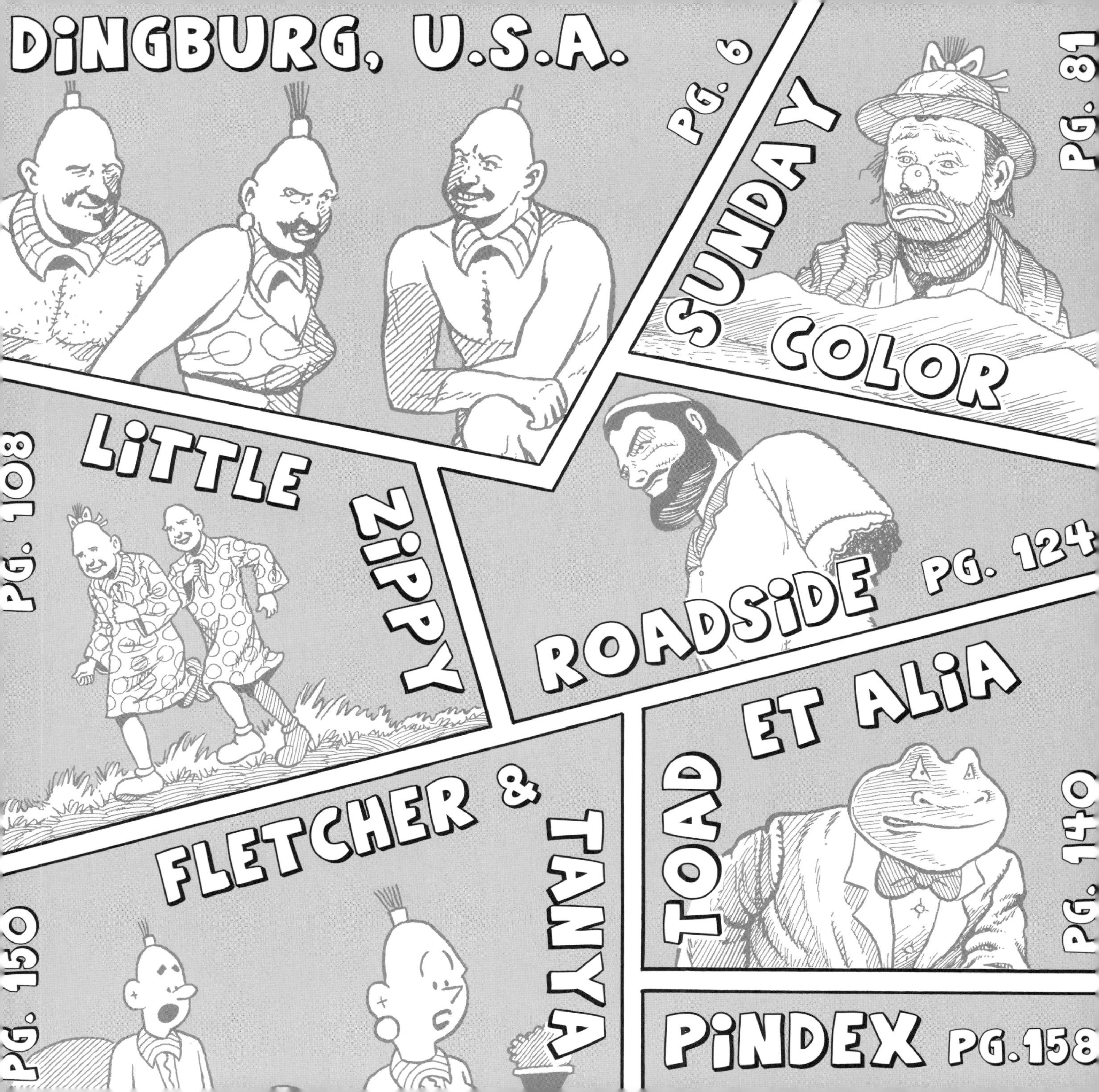
DiNGBURG, U.S.A.
PG. 6
SUNDAY COLOR
PG. 81
LiTTLE ZiPPY
PG. 108
ROADSiDE
PG. 124
TOAD ET ALiA
PG. 140
FLETCHER & TANYA
PG. 150
PiNDEX PG. 158

# DINGBURG, U.S.A.

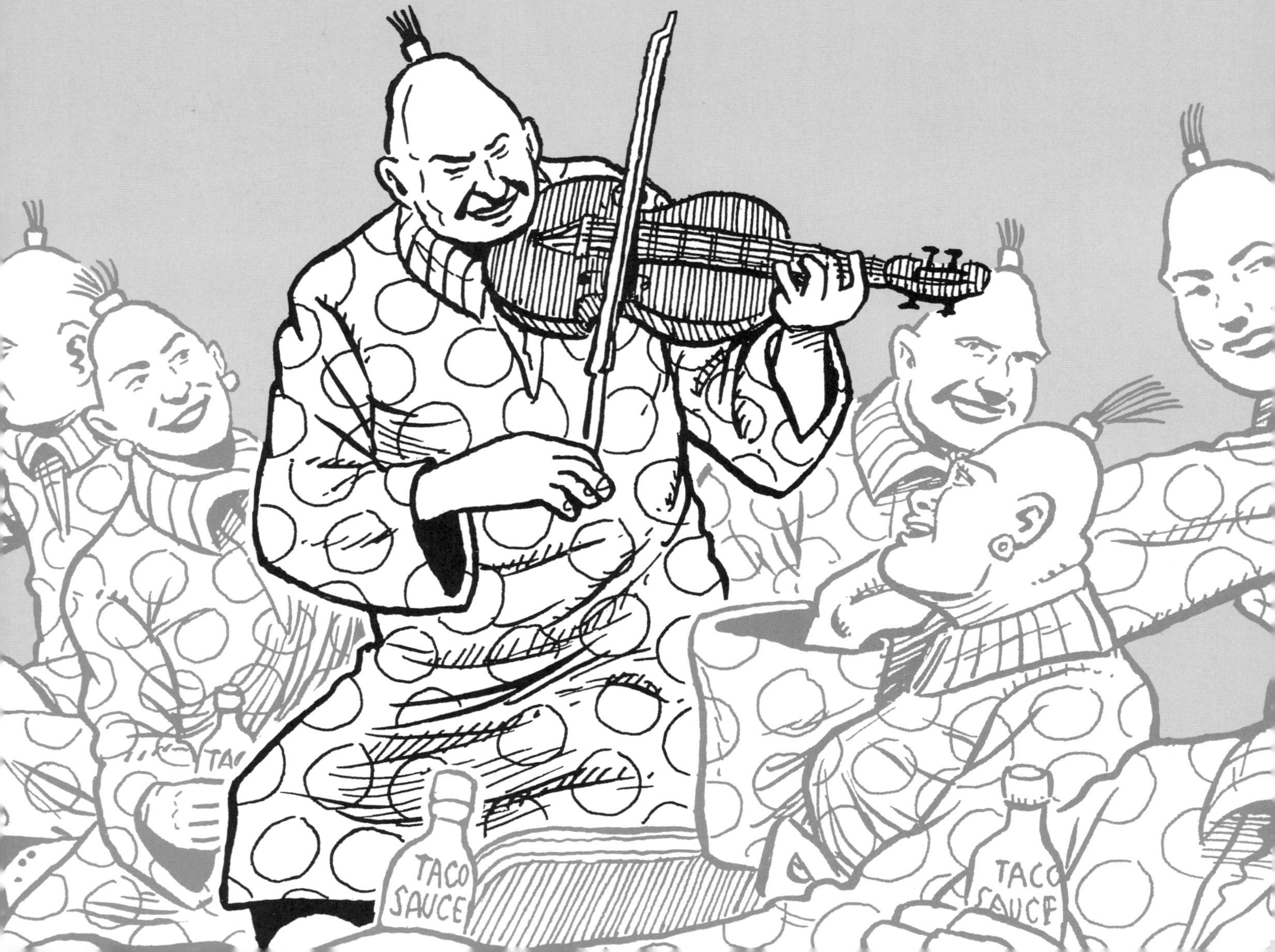
TACO SAUCE
TACO

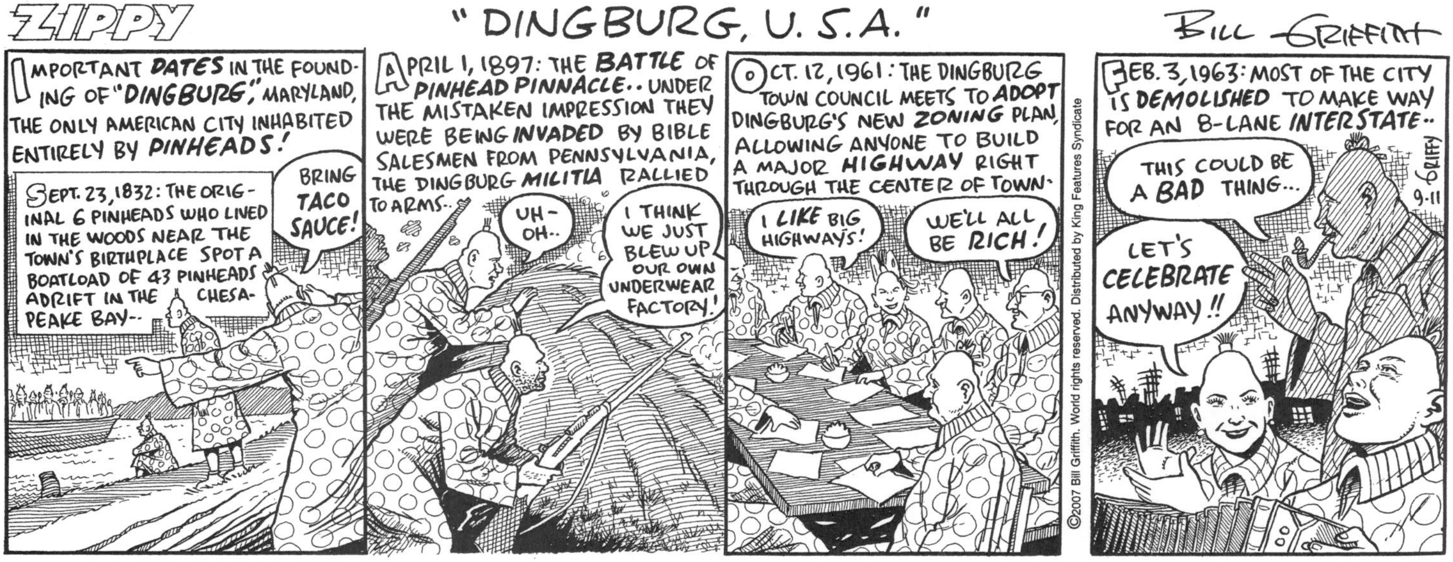
ZIPPY
"DINGBURG, U.S.A."
BILL GRIFFITH
IMPORTANT DATES IN THE FOUNDING OF "DINGBURG," MARYLAND, THE ONLY AMERICAN CITY INHABITED ENTIRELY BY PINHEADS!
SEPT. 23, 1832: THE ORIGINAL 6 PINHEADS WHO LIVED IN THE WOODS NEAR THE TOWN'S BIRTHPLACE SPOT A BOATLOAD OF 43 PINHEADS ADRIFT IN THE CHESAPEAKE BAY..
BRING TACO SAUCE!
APRIL 1, 1897: THE BATTLE OF PINHEAD PINNACLE.. UNDER THE MISTAKEN IMPRESSION THEY WERE BEING INVADED BY BIBLE SALESMEN FROM PENNSYLVANIA, THE DINGBURG MILITIA RALLIED TO ARMS..
UH-OH..
I THINK WE JUST BLEW UP OUR OWN UNDERWEAR FACTORY!
OCT. 12, 1961: THE DINGBURG TOWN COUNCIL MEETS TO ADOPT DINGBURG'S NEW ZONING PLAN, ALLOWING ANYONE TO BUILD A MAJOR HIGHWAY RIGHT THROUGH THE CENTER OF TOWN.
I LIKE BIG HIGHWAYS!
WE'LL ALL BE RICH!
©2007 Bill Griffith. World rights reserved. Distributed by King Features Syndicate
FEB. 3, 1963: MOST OF THE CITY IS DEMOLISHED TO MAKE WAY FOR AN 8-LANE INTERSTATE..
THIS COULD BE A BAD THING...
LET'S CELEBRATE ANYWAY!!
GRIFFY 9-11

1

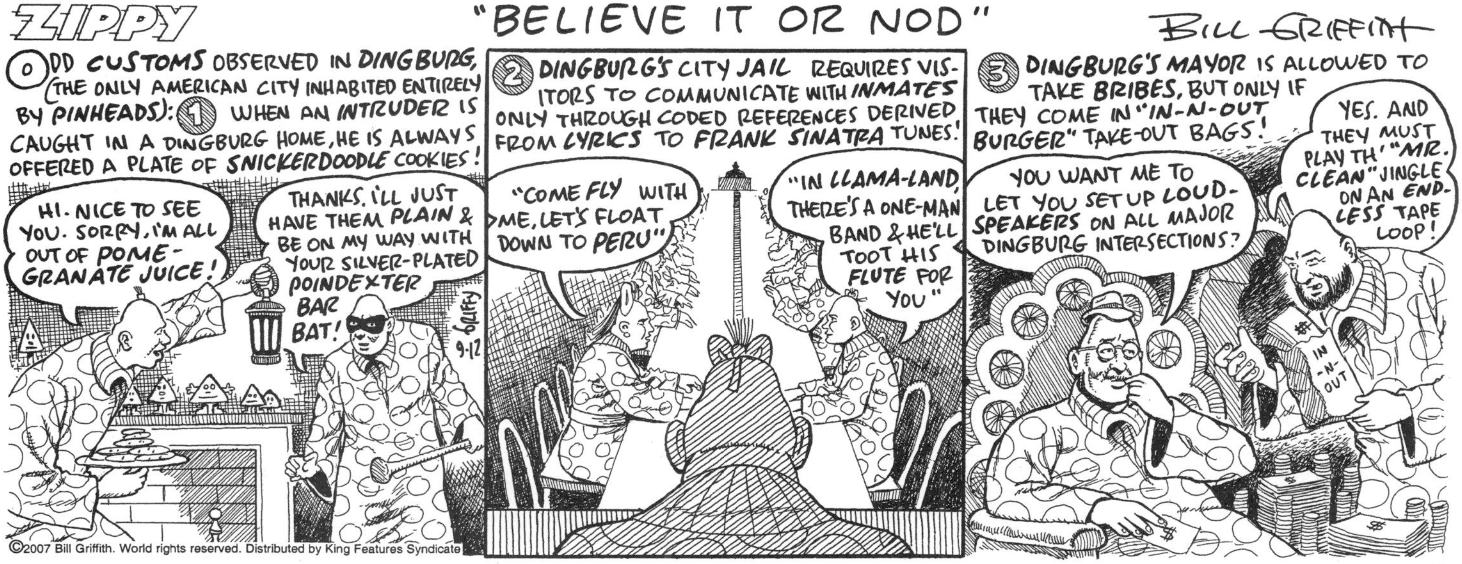
ZIPPY
"BELIEVE IT OR NOD"
BILL GRIFFITH
ODD CUSTOMS OBSERVED IN DINGBURG, (THE ONLY AMERICAN CITY INHABITED ENTIRELY BY PINHEADS): 1 WHEN AN INTRUDER IS CAUGHT IN A DINGBURG HOME, HE IS ALWAYS OFFERED A PLATE OF SNICKERDOODLE COOKIES!
HI. NICE TO SEE YOU. SORRY, I'M ALL OUT OF POMEGRANATE JUICE!
THANKS. I'LL JUST HAVE THEM PLAIN & BE ON MY WAY WITH YOUR SILVER-PLATED POINDEXTER BAR BAT!
GRIFFY 9-12
©2007 Bill Griffith. World rights reserved. Distributed by King Features Syndicate
2 DINGBURG'S CITY JAIL REQUIRES VISITORS TO COMMUNICATE WITH INMATES ONLY THROUGH CODED REFERENCES DERIVED FROM LYRICS TO FRANK SINATRA TUNES!
"COME FLY WITH ME, LET'S FLOAT DOWN TO PERU"
"IN LLAMA-LAND, THERE'S A ONE-MAN BAND & HE'LL TOOT HIS FLUTE FOR YOU"
3 DINGBURG'S MAYOR IS ALLOWED TO TAKE BRIBES, BUT ONLY IF THEY COME IN "IN-N-OUT BURGER" TAKE-OUT BAGS!
YOU WANT ME TO LET YOU SET UP LOUDSPEAKERS ON ALL MAJOR DINGBURG INTERSECTIONS?
YES. AND THEY MUST PLAY TH' "MR. CLEAN" JINGLE ON AN ENDLESS TAPE LOOP!
IN-N-OUT

2

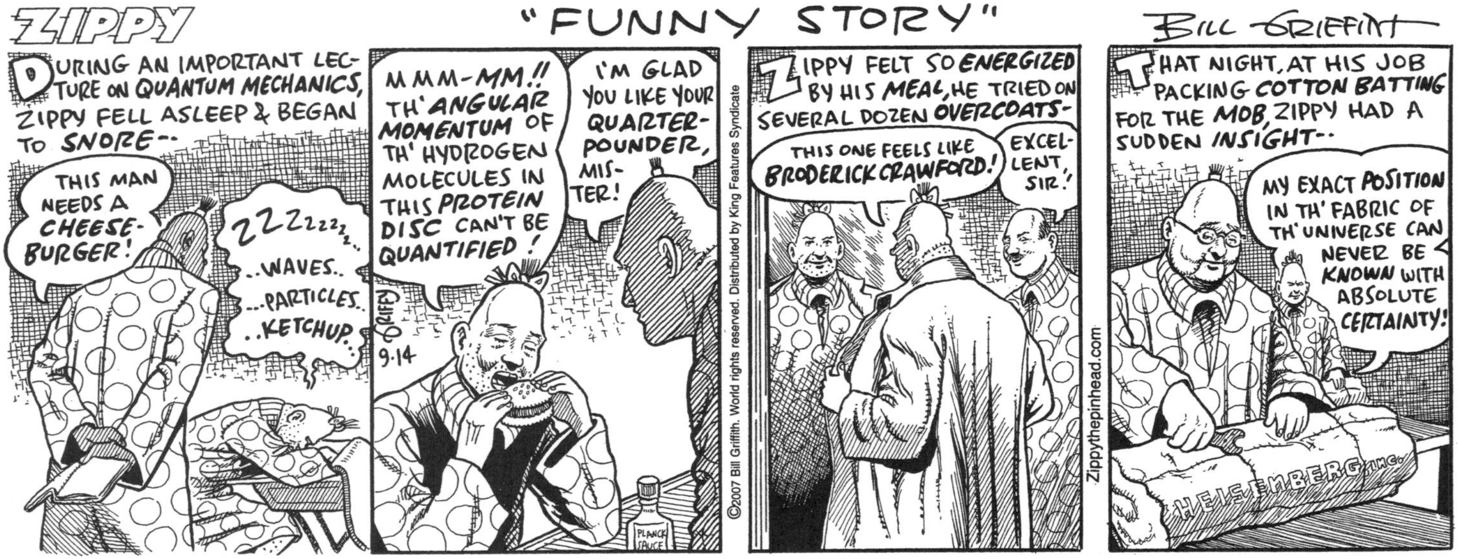
ZIPPY
"FUNNY STORY"
BILL GRIFFITH
DURING AN IMPORTANT LECTURE ON QUANTUM MECHANICS, ZIPPY FELL ASLEEP & BEGAN TO SNORE--
THIS MAN NEEDS A CHEESEBURGER!
ZZZzzzz.. ..WAVES.. ...PARTICLES.. ..KETCHUP..
MMM-MM!! TH' ANGULAR MOMENTUM OF TH' HYDROGEN MOLECULES IN THIS PROTEIN DISC CAN'T BE QUANTIFIED!
I'M GLAD YOU LIKE YOUR QUARTER-POUNDER, MISTER!
GRIFFY 9.14
PLANCK SAUCE
©2007 Bill Griffith. World rights reserved. Distributed by King Features Syndicate
ZIPPY FELT SO ENERGIZED BY HIS MEAL, HE TRIED ON SEVERAL DOZEN OVERCOATS-
THIS ONE FEELS LIKE BRODERICK CRAWFORD!
EXCELLENT, SIR!
Zippythepinhead.com
THAT NIGHT, AT HIS JOB PACKING COTTON BATTING FOR THE MOB, ZIPPY HAD A SUDDEN INSIGHT--
MY EXACT POSITION IN TH' FABRIC OF TH' UNIVERSE CAN NEVER BE KNOWN WITH ABSOLUTE CERTAINTY!
HEISENBERG INC.

3

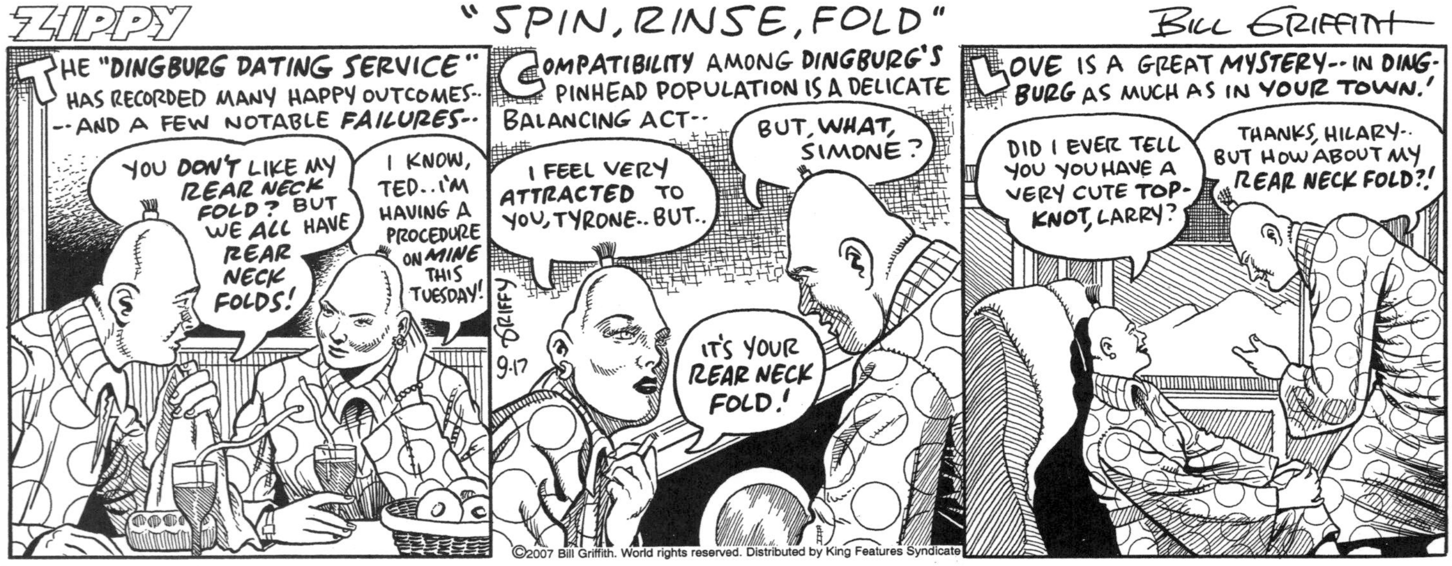
ZIPPY
"SPIN, RINSE, FOLD"
BILL GRIFFITH
THE "DINGBURG DATING SERVICE" HAS RECORDED MANY HAPPY OUTCOMES-- --AND A FEW NOTABLE FAILURES--
YOU DON'T LIKE MY REAR NECK FOLD? BUT WE ALL HAVE REAR NECK FOLDS!
I KNOW, TED.. I'M HAVING A PROCEDURE ON MINE THIS TUESDAY!
COMPATIBILITY AMONG DINGBURG'S PINHEAD POPULATION IS A DELICATE BALANCING ACT--
I FEEL VERY ATTRACTED TO YOU, TYRONE.. BUT..
BUT, WHAT, SIMONE?
IT'S YOUR REAR NECK FOLD!
GRIFFY 9.17
©2007 Bill Griffith. World rights reserved. Distributed by King Features Syndicate
LOVE IS A GREAT MYSTERY-- IN DINGBURG AS MUCH AS IN YOUR TOWN.
DID I EVER TELL YOU YOU HAVE A VERY CUTE TOP-KNOT, LARRY?
THANKS, HILARY.. BUT HOW ABOUT MY REAR NECK FOLD?!

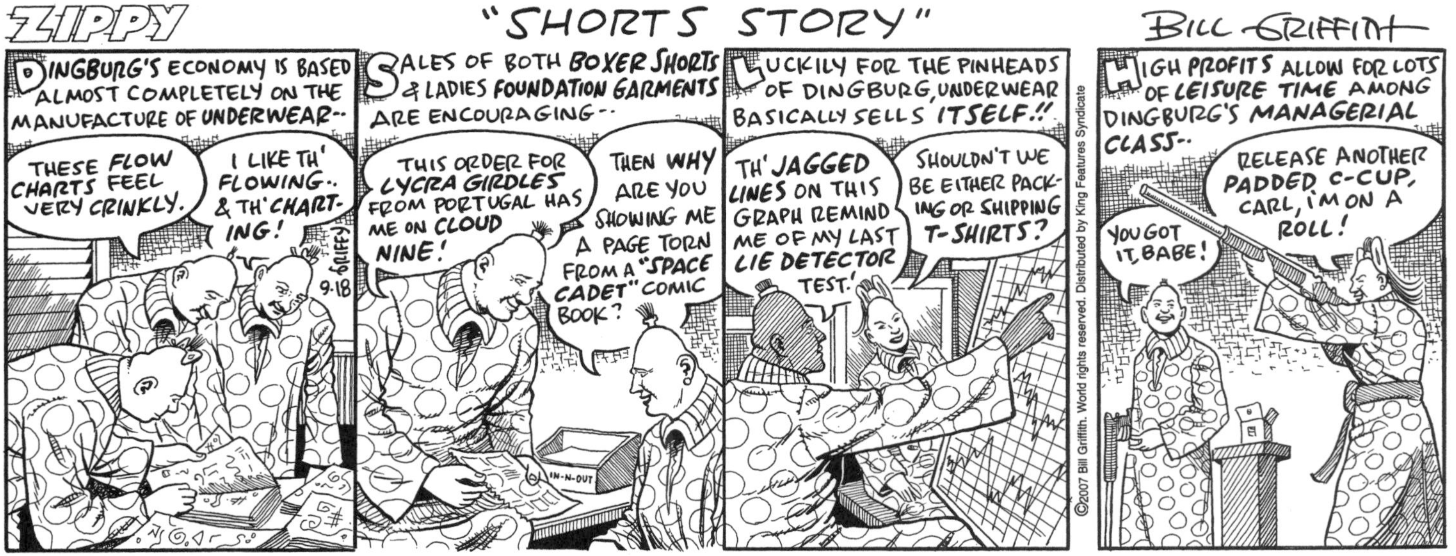
ZIPPY
"SHORTS STORY"
BILL GRIFFITH
DINGBURG'S ECONOMY IS BASED ALMOST COMPLETELY ON THE MANUFACTURE OF UNDERWEAR--
THESE FLOW CHARTS FEEL VERY CRINKLY.
I LIKE TH' FLOWING.. & TH' CHARTING!
GRIFFY 9.18
SALES OF BOTH BOXER SHORTS & LADIES FOUNDATION GARMENTS ARE ENCOURAGING--
THIS ORDER FOR LYCRA GIRDLES FROM PORTUGAL HAS ME ON CLOUD NINE!
THEN WHY ARE YOU SHOWING ME A PAGE TORN FROM A "SPACE CADET" COMIC BOOK?
IN-N-OUT
LUCKILY FOR THE PINHEADS OF DINGBURG, UNDERWEAR BASICALLY SELLS ITSELF!!
TH' JAGGED LINES ON THIS GRAPH REMIND ME OF MY LAST LIE DETECTOR TEST!
SHOULDN'T WE BE EITHER PACKING OR SHIPPING T-SHIRTS?
©2007 Bill Griffith. World rights reserved. Distributed by King Features Syndicate
HIGH PROFITS ALLOW FOR LOTS OF LEISURE TIME AMONG DINGBURG'S MANAGERIAL CLASS--
YOU GOT IT, BABE!
RELEASE ANOTHER PADDED C-CUP, CARL, I'M ON A ROLL!

4

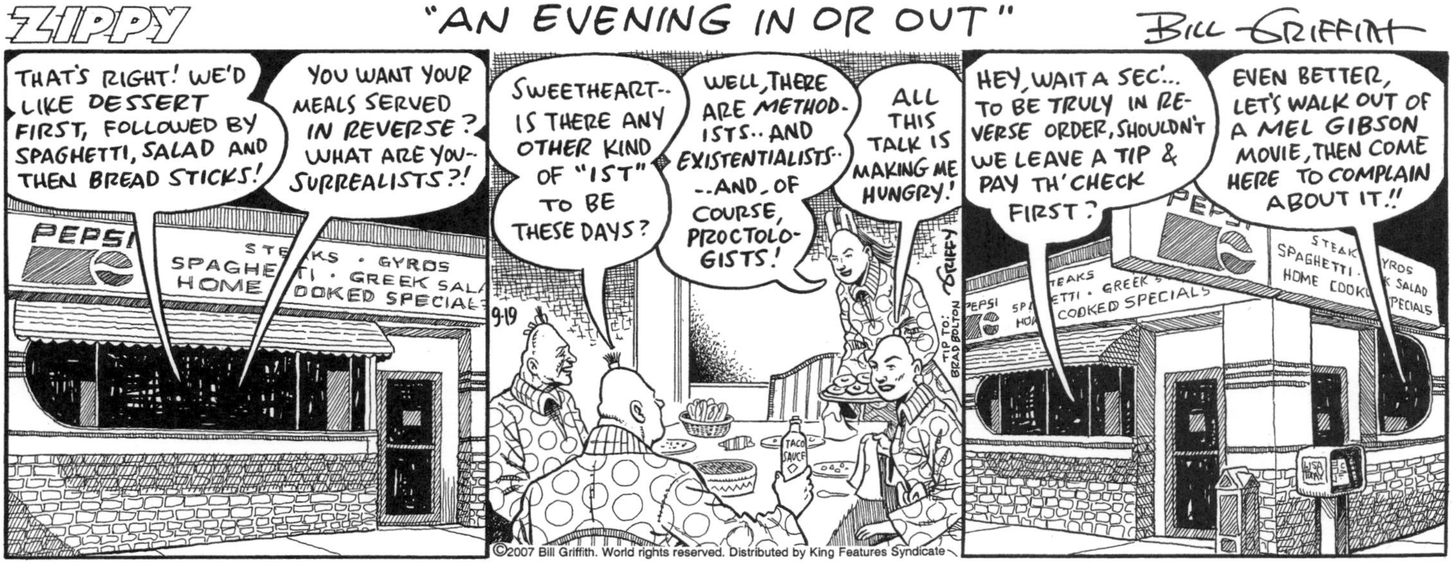
ZIPPY
"AN EVENING IN OR OUT"
BILL GRIFFITH
THAT'S RIGHT! WE'D LIKE DESSERT FIRST, FOLLOWED BY SPAGHETTI, SALAD AND THEN BREAD STICKS!
YOU WANT YOUR MEALS SERVED IN REVERSE? WHAT ARE YOU-- SURREALISTS?!
PEPSI
STEAKS • GYROS
SPAGHETTI • GREEK SALAD
HOME COOKED SPECIALS
SWEETHEART-- IS THERE ANY OTHER KIND OF "IST" TO BE THESE DAYS?
WELL, THERE ARE METHODISTS.. AND EXISTENTIALISTS.. --AND, OF COURSE, PROCTOLOGISTS!
ALL THIS TALK IS MAKING ME HUNGRY!
9.19
GRIFFY
TIP TO: BRAD BOLTON
TACO SAUCE
HEY, WAIT A SEC!.. TO BE TRULY IN REVERSE ORDER, SHOULDN'T WE LEAVE A TIP & PAY TH' CHECK FIRST?
EVEN BETTER, LET'S WALK OUT OF A MEL GIBSON MOVIE, THEN COME HERE TO COMPLAIN ABOUT IT!!
©2007 Bill Griffith. World rights reserved. Distributed by King Features Syndicate

5

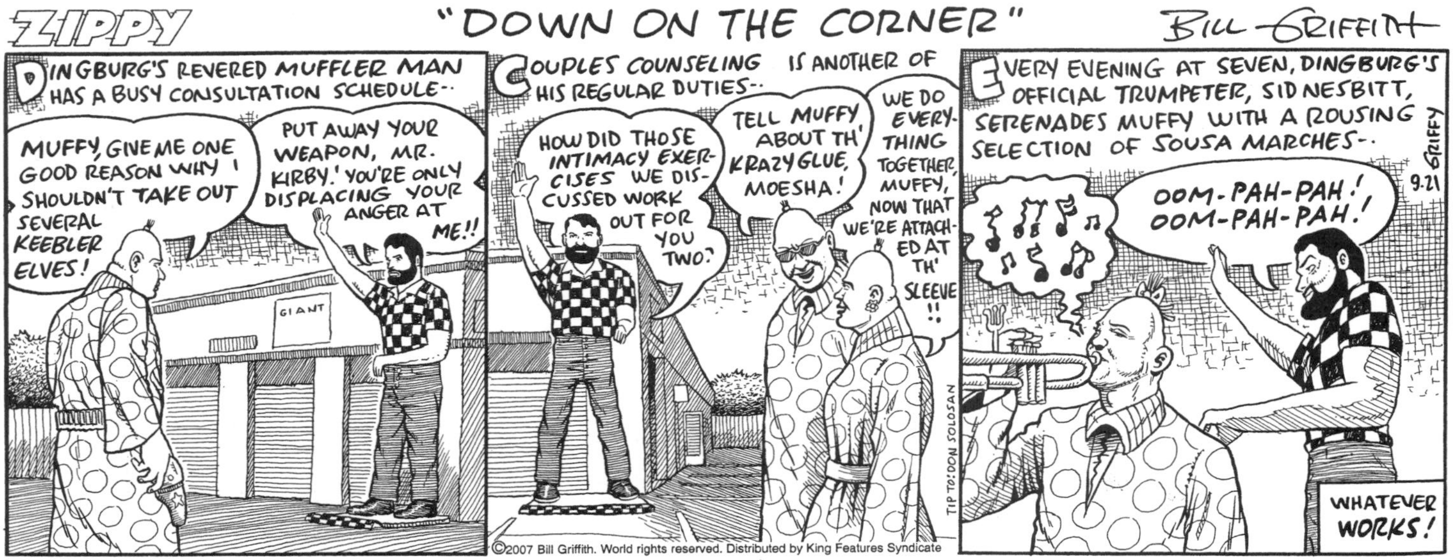
ZIPPY
"DOWN ON THE CORNER"
BILL GRIFFITH
DINGBURG'S REVERED MUFFLER MAN HAS A BUSY CONSULTATION SCHEDULE--
MUFFY, GIVE ME ONE GOOD REASON WHY I SHOULDN'T TAKE OUT SEVERAL KEEBLER ELVES!
PUT AWAY YOUR WEAPON, MR. KIRBY! YOU'RE ONLY DISPLACING YOUR ANGER AT ME!!
GIANT
COUPLES COUNSELING IS ANOTHER OF HIS REGULAR DUTIES--
HOW DID THOSE INTIMACY EXERCISES WE DISCUSSED WORK OUT FOR YOU TWO?
TELL MUFFY ABOUT TH' KRAZY GLUE, MOESHA!
WE DO EVERYTHING TOGETHER, MUFFY, NOW THAT WE'RE ATTACHED AT TH' SLEEVE!!
TIP TO: DON SOLOSAN
EVERY EVENING AT SEVEN, DINGBURG'S OFFICIAL TRUMPETER, SID NESBITT, SERENADES MUFFY WITH A ROUSING SELECTION OF SOUSA MARCHES--
GRIFFY 9.21
OOM-PAH-PAH! OOM-PAH-PAH!
WHATEVER WORKS!
©2007 Bill Griffith. World rights reserved. Distributed by King Features Syndicate

6

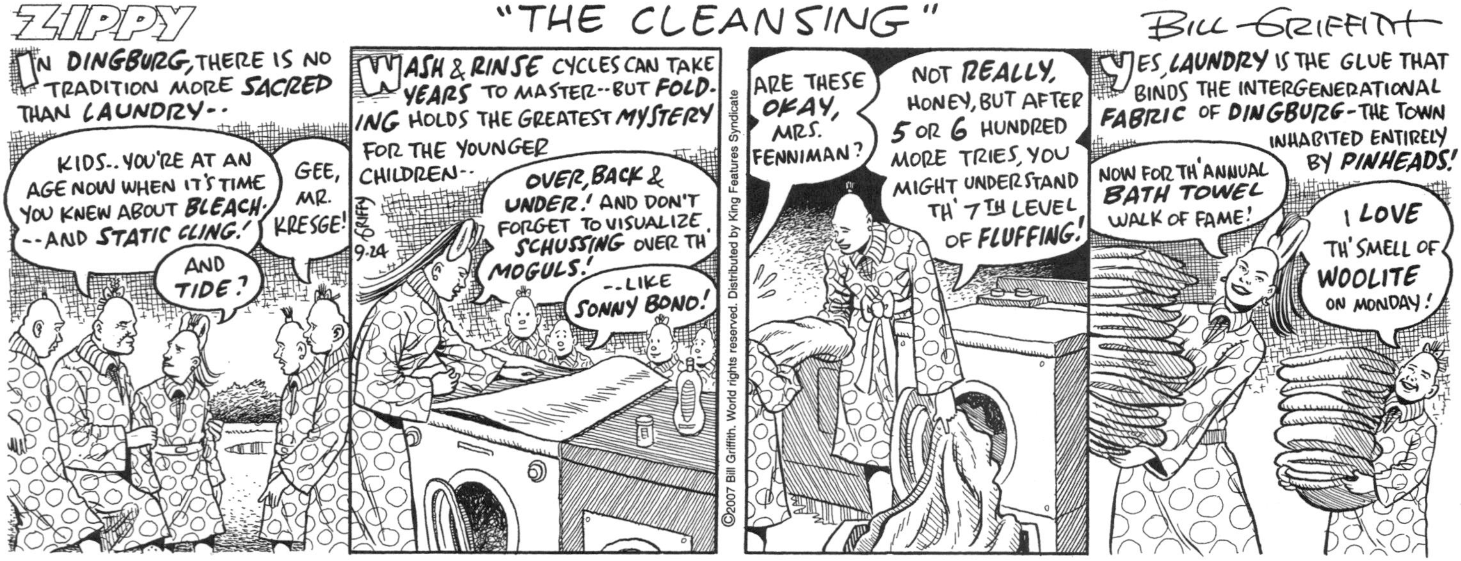
ZIPPY
"THE CLEANSING"
BILL GRIFFITH
IN DINGBURG, THERE IS NO TRADITION MORE SACRED THAN LAUNDRY--
KIDS.. YOU'RE AT AN AGE NOW WHEN IT'S TIME YOU KNEW ABOUT BLEACH! --AND STATIC CLING!
GEE, MR. KRESGE!
AND TIDE?
WASH & RINSE CYCLES CAN TAKE YEARS TO MASTER--BUT FOLDING HOLDS THE GREATEST MYSTERY FOR THE YOUNGER CHILDREN--
GRIFFY 9.24
OVER, BACK & UNDER! AND DON'T FORGET TO VISUALIZE SCHUSSING OVER TH' MOGULS!
--LIKE SONNY BONO!
©2007 Bill Griffith. World rights reserved. Distributed by King Features Syndicate
ARE THESE OKAY, MRS. FENNIMAN?
NOT REALLY, HONEY, BUT AFTER 5 OR 6 HUNDRED MORE TRIES, YOU MIGHT UNDERSTAND TH' 7TH LEVEL OF FLUFFING!
YES, LAUNDRY IS THE GLUE THAT BINDS THE INTERGENERATIONAL FABRIC OF DINGBURG--THE TOWN INHABITED ENTIRELY BY PINHEADS!
NOW FOR TH' ANNUAL BATH TOWEL WALK OF FAME!
I LOVE TH' SMELL OF WOOLITE ON MONDAY!

7

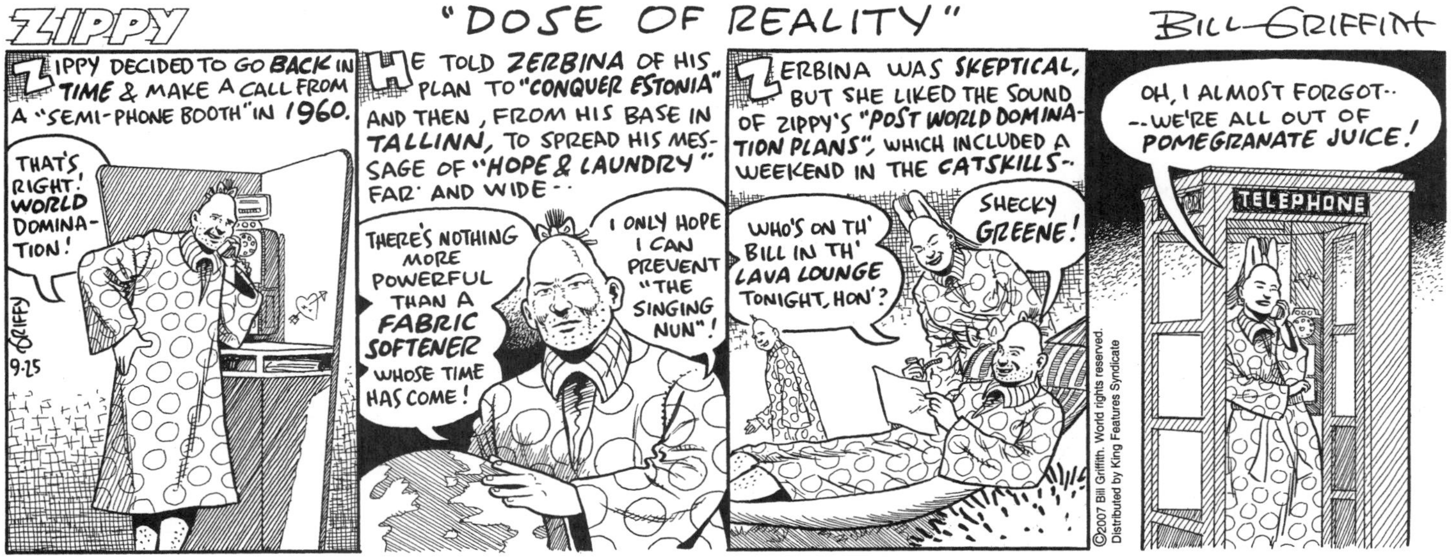
ZIPPY
"DOSE OF REALITY"
BILL GRIFFITH
ZIPPY DECIDED TO GO BACK IN TIME & MAKE A CALL FROM A "SEMI-PHONE BOOTH" IN 1960.
THAT'S RIGHT! WORLD DOMINATION!
GRIFFY 9·25
HE TOLD ZERBINA OF HIS PLAN TO "CONQUER ESTONIA" AND THEN, FROM HIS BASE IN TALLINN, TO SPREAD HIS MESSAGE OF "HOPE & LAUNDRY" FAR AND WIDE--
THERE'S NOTHING MORE POWERFUL THAN A FABRIC SOFTENER WHOSE TIME HAS COME!
I ONLY HOPE I CAN PREVENT "THE SINGING NUN"!
ZERBINA WAS SKEPTICAL, BUT SHE LIKED THE SOUND OF ZIPPY'S "POST WORLD DOMINATION PLANS", WHICH INCLUDED A WEEKEND IN THE CATSKILLS--
WHO'S ON TH' BILL IN TH' LAVA LOUNGE TONIGHT, HON'?
SHECKY GREENE!
©2007 Bill Griffith. World rights reserved. Distributed by King Features Syndicate
OH, I ALMOST FORGOT-- --WE'RE ALL OUT OF POMEGRANATE JUICE!
TELEPHONE

8

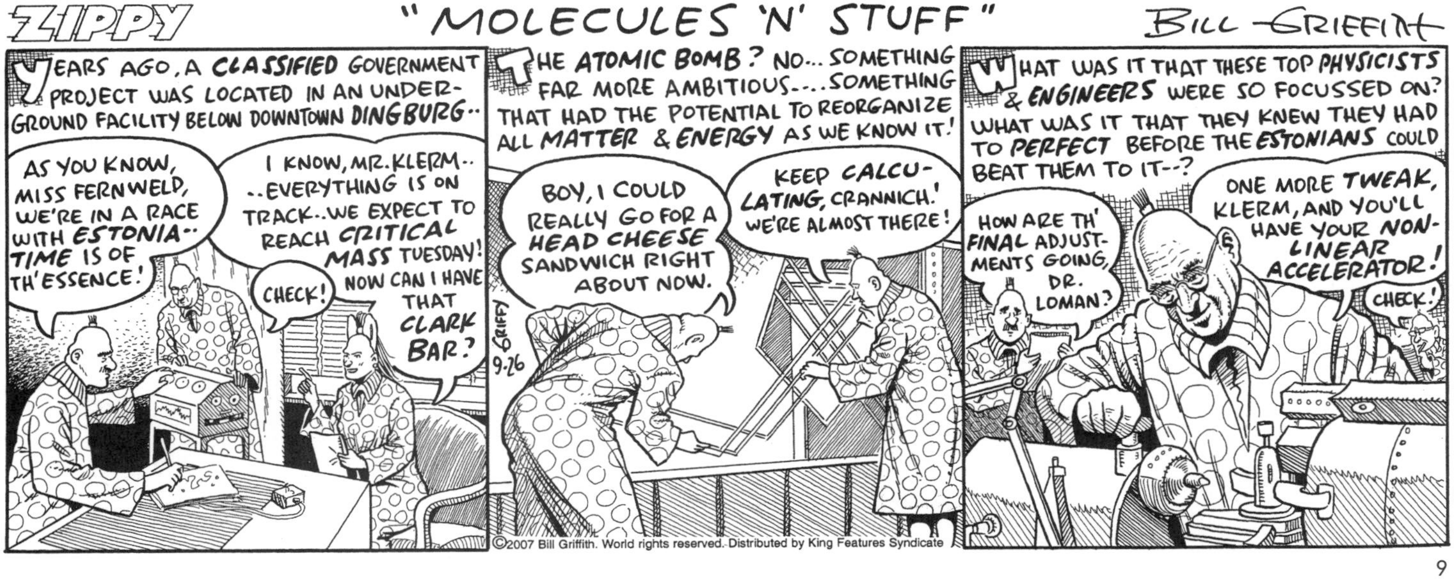
ZIPPY
"MOLECULES 'N' STUFF"
BILL GRIFFITH
YEARS AGO, A CLASSIFIED GOVERNMENT PROJECT WAS LOCATED IN AN UNDERGROUND FACILITY BELOW DOWNTOWN DINGBURG--
AS YOU KNOW, MISS FERNWELD, WE'RE IN A RACE WITH ESTONIA-- TIME IS OF TH' ESSENCE!
I KNOW, MR. KLERM-- --EVERYTHING IS ON TRACK--WE EXPECT TO REACH CRITICAL MASS TUESDAY! NOW CAN I HAVE THAT CLARK BAR?
CHECK!
GRIFFY 9-26
THE ATOMIC BOMB? NO... SOMETHING FAR MORE AMBITIOUS.... SOMETHING THAT HAD THE POTENTIAL TO REORGANIZE ALL MATTER & ENERGY AS WE KNOW IT!
BOY, I COULD REALLY GO FOR A HEAD CHEESE SANDWICH RIGHT ABOUT NOW.
KEEP CALCULATING, CRANNICH! WE'RE ALMOST THERE!
©2007 Bill Griffith. World rights reserved. Distributed by King Features Syndicate
WHAT WAS IT THAT THESE TOP PHYSICISTS & ENGINEERS WERE SO FOCUSSED ON? WHAT WAS IT THAT THEY KNEW THEY HAD TO PERFECT BEFORE THE ESTONIANS COULD BEAT THEM TO IT--?
HOW ARE TH' FINAL ADJUSTMENTS GOING, DR. LOMAN?
ONE MORE TWEAK, KLERM, AND YOU'LL HAVE YOUR NON-LINEAR ACCELERATOR!
CHECK!

9

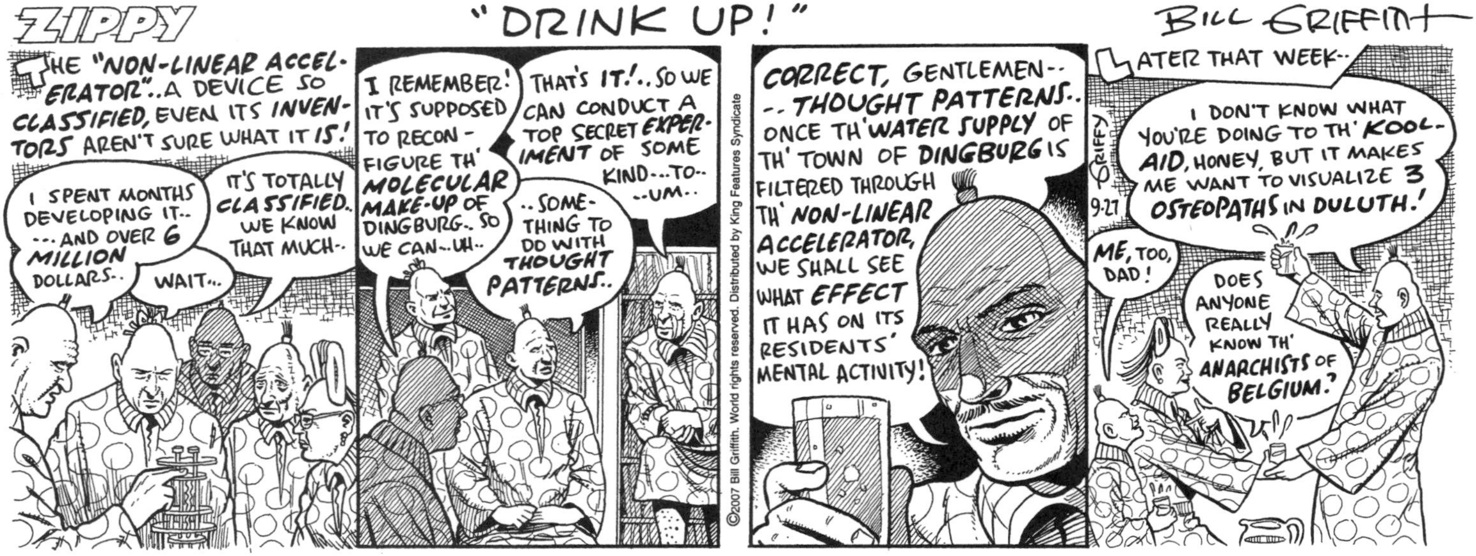
ZIPPY
"DRINK UP!"
BILL GRIFFITH
THE "NON-LINEAR ACCELERATOR"..A DEVICE SO CLASSIFIED, EVEN ITS INVENTORS AREN'T SURE WHAT IT IS!
I SPENT MONTHS DEVELOPING IT.. ...AND OVER 6 MILLION DOLLARS..
IT'S TOTALLY CLASSIFIED.. WE KNOW THAT MUCH..
WAIT...
I REMEMBER! IT'S SUPPOSED TO RECONFIGURE TH' MOLECULAR MAKE-UP OF DINGBURG.. SO WE CAN..UH..
THAT'S IT!..SO WE CAN CONDUCT A TOP SECRET EXPERIMENT OF SOME KIND...TO.. ..UM..
..SOMETHING TO DO WITH THOUGHT PATTERNS..
©2007 Bill Griffith. World rights reserved. Distributed by King Features Syndicate
CORRECT, GENTLEMEN-- --THOUGHT PATTERNS.. ONCE TH' WATER SUPPLY OF TH' TOWN OF DINGBURG IS FILTERED THROUGH TH' NON-LINEAR ACCELERATOR, WE SHALL SEE WHAT EFFECT IT HAS ON ITS RESIDENTS' MENTAL ACTIVITY!
GRIFFY 9-27
LATER THAT WEEK..
I DON'T KNOW WHAT YOU'RE DOING TO TH' KOOL-AID, HONEY, BUT IT MAKES ME WANT TO VISUALIZE 3 OSTEOPATHS IN DULUTH!
ME, TOO, DAD!
DOES ANYONE REALLY KNOW TH' ANARCHISTS OF BELGIUM?

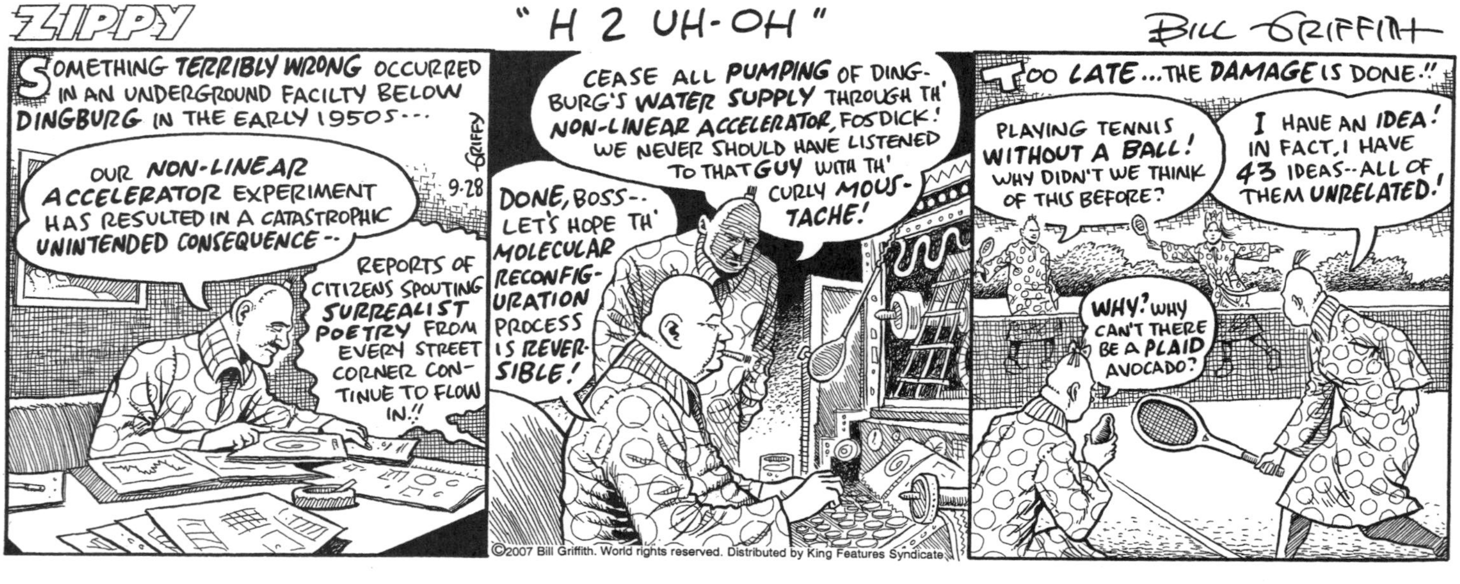
ZIPPY
"H 2 UH-OH"
BILL GRIFFITH
SOMETHING TERRIBLY WRONG OCCURRED IN AN UNDERGROUND FACILTY BELOW DINGBURG IN THE EARLY 1950S---
GRIFFY 9-28
OUR NON-LINEAR ACCELERATOR EXPERIMENT HAS RESULTED IN A CATASTROPHIC UNINTENDED CONSEQUENCE--
REPORTS OF CITIZENS SPOUTING SURREALIST POETRY FROM EVERY STREET CORNER CONTINUE TO FLOW IN!!
CEASE ALL PUMPING OF DINGBURG'S WATER SUPPLY THROUGH TH' NON-LINEAR ACCELERATOR, FOSDICK! WE NEVER SHOULD HAVE LISTENED TO THAT GUY WITH TH' CURLY MOUSTACHE!
DONE, BOSS-- LET'S HOPE TH' MOLECULAR RECONFIGURATION PROCESS IS REVERSIBLE!
©2007 Bill Griffith. World rights reserved. Distributed by King Features Syndicate
TOO LATE...THE DAMAGE IS DONE!!
PLAYING TENNIS WITHOUT A BALL! WHY DIDN'T WE THINK OF THIS BEFORE?
I HAVE AN IDEA! IN FACT, I HAVE 43 IDEAS--ALL OF THEM UNRELATED!
WHY? WHY CAN'T THERE BE A PLAID AVOCADO?

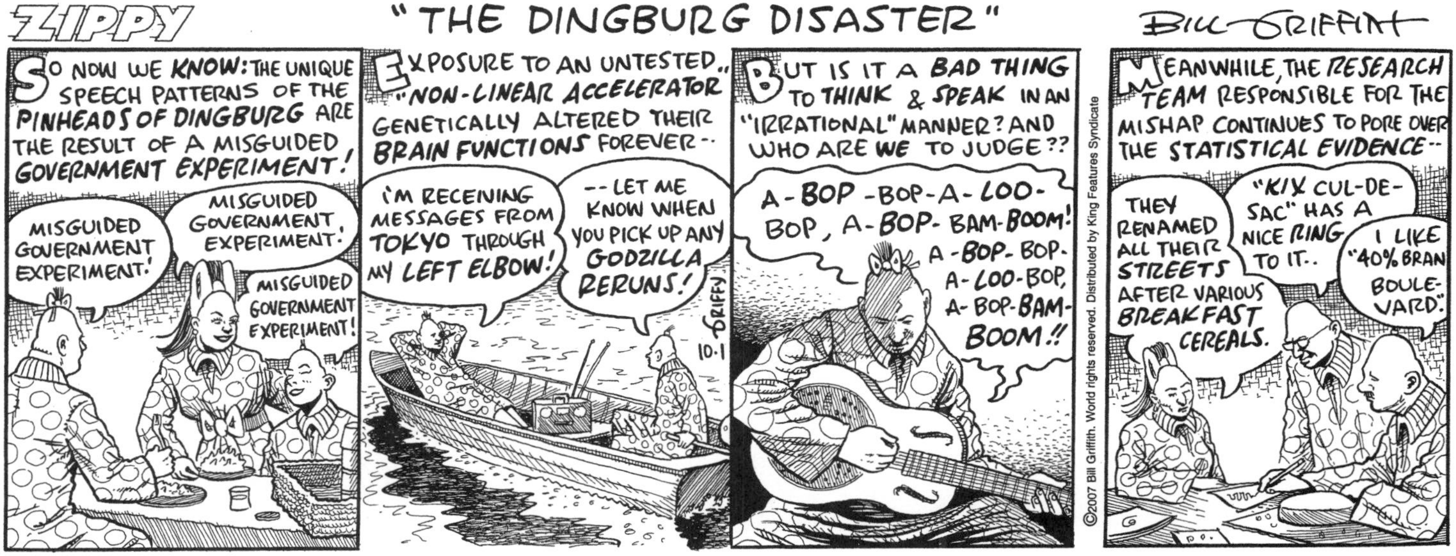
ZIPPY
"THE DINGBURG DISASTER"
BILL GRIFFITH
SO NOW WE KNOW: THE UNIQUE SPEECH PATTERNS OF THE PINHEADS OF DINGBURG ARE THE RESULT OF A MISGUIDED GOVERNMENT EXPERIMENT!
MISGUIDED GOVERNMENT EXPERIMENT!
MISGUIDED GOVERNMENT EXPERIMENT!
MISGUIDED GOVERNMENT EXPERIMENT!
EXPOSURE TO AN UNTESTED "NON-LINEAR ACCELERATOR" GENETICALLY ALTERED THEIR BRAIN FUNCTIONS FOREVER--
I'M RECEIVING MESSAGES FROM TOKYO THROUGH MY LEFT ELBOW!
--LET ME KNOW WHEN YOU PICK UP ANY GODZILLA RERUNS!
GRIFFY 10.1
BUT IS IT A BAD THING TO THINK & SPEAK IN AN "IRRATIONAL" MANNER? AND WHO ARE WE TO JUDGE??
A-BOP-BOP-A-LOO-BOP, A-BOP-BAM-BOOM! A-BOP-BOP-A-LOO-BOP, A-BOP-BAM-BOOM!!
©2007 Bill Griffith. World rights reserved. Distributed by King Features Syndicate
MEANWHILE, THE RESEARCH TEAM RESPONSIBLE FOR THE MISHAP CONTINUES TO PORE OVER THE STATISTICAL EVIDENCE--
THEY RENAMED ALL THEIR STREETS AFTER VARIOUS BREAKFAST CEREALS.
"KIX CUL-DE-SAC" HAS A NICE RING TO IT..
I LIKE "40% BRAN BOULEVARD".

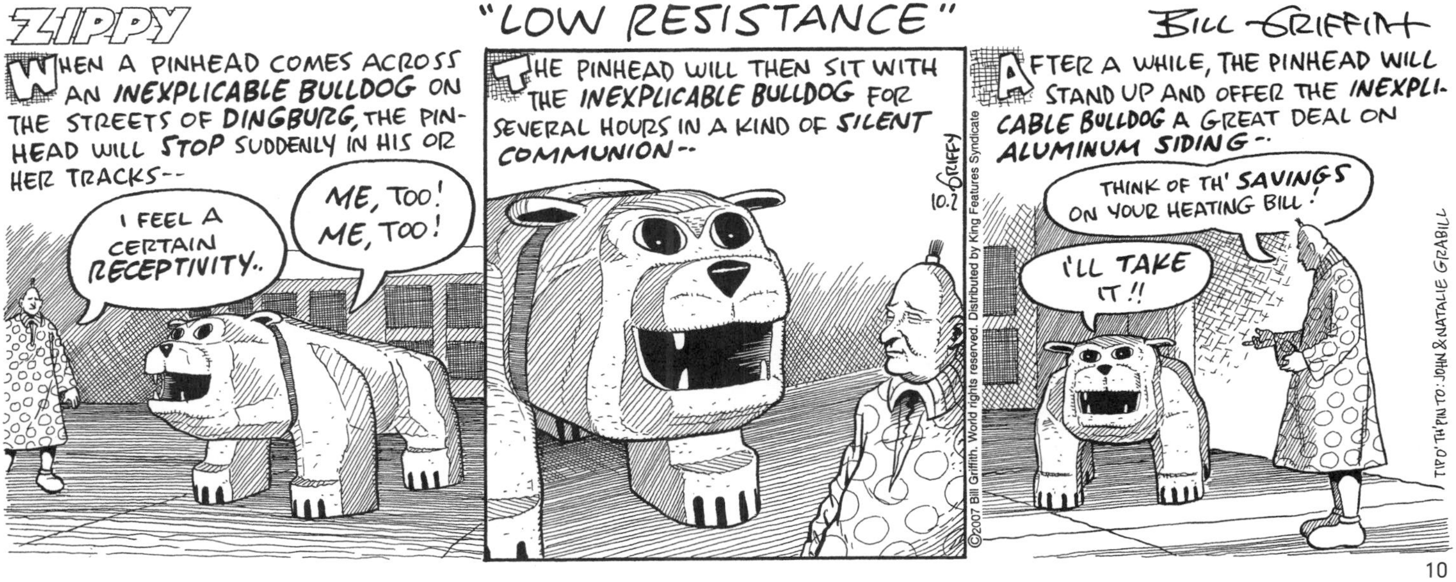
ZIPPY
"LOW RESISTANCE"
BILL GRIFFITH
WHEN A PINHEAD COMES ACROSS AN INEXPLICABLE BULLDOG ON THE STREETS OF DINGBURG, THE PINHEAD WILL STOP SUDDENLY IN HIS OR HER TRACKS--
I FEEL A CERTAIN RECEPTIVITY..
ME, TOO! ME, TOO!
THE PINHEAD WILL THEN SIT WITH THE INEXPLICABLE BULLDOG FOR SEVERAL HOURS IN A KIND OF SILENT COMMUNION--
GRIFFY 10.2
©2007 Bill Griffith. World rights reserved. Distributed by King Features Syndicate
AFTER A WHILE, THE PINHEAD WILL STAND UP AND OFFER THE INEXPLICABLE BULLDOG A GREAT DEAL ON ALUMINUM SIDING--
THINK OF TH' SAVINGS ON YOUR HEATING BILL!
I'LL TAKE IT!!
TIP O' TH' PIN TO: JOHN & NATALIE GRABILL
10

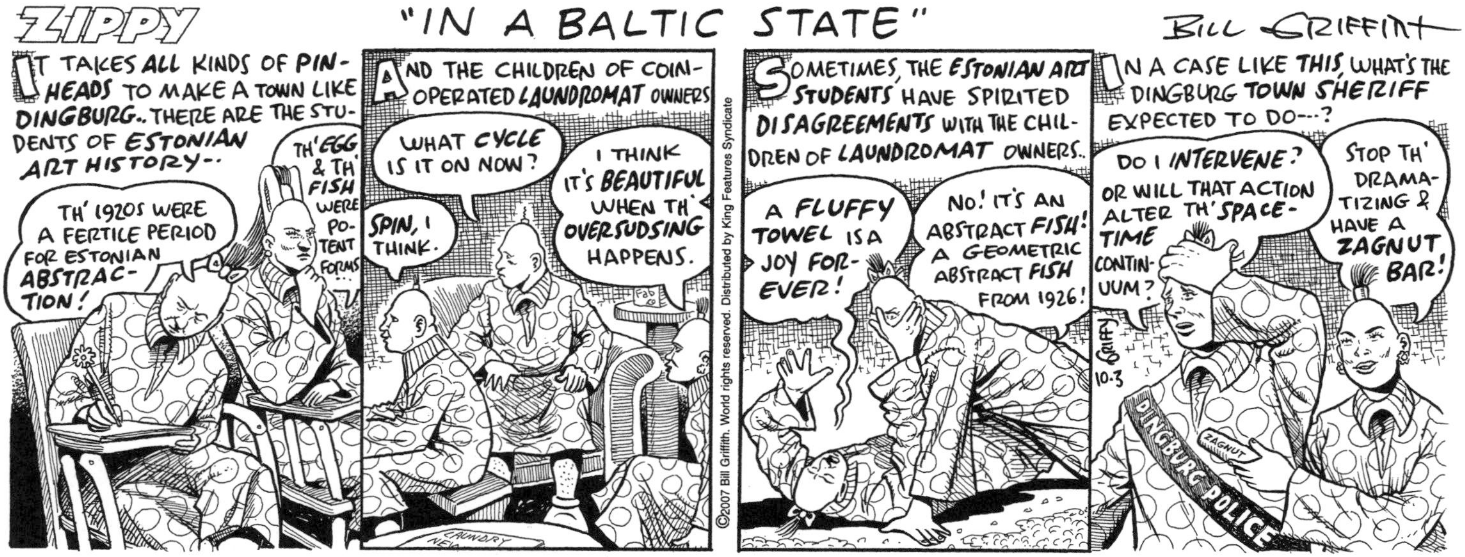
ZIPPY
"IN A BALTIC STATE"
BILL GRIFFITH
IT TAKES ALL KINDS OF PINHEADS TO MAKE A TOWN LIKE DINGBURG.. THERE ARE THE STUDENTS OF ESTONIAN ART HISTORY--
TH' 1920S WERE A FERTILE PERIOD FOR ESTONIAN ABSTRACTION!
TH' EGG & TH' FISH WERE POTENT FORMS...
AND THE CHILDREN OF COIN-OPERATED LAUNDROMAT OWNERS
WHAT CYCLE IS IT ON NOW?
SPIN, I THINK.
I THINK IT'S BEAUTIFUL WHEN TH' OVERSUDSING HAPPENS.
©2007 Bill Griffith. World rights reserved. Distributed by King Features Syndicate
SOMETIMES, THE ESTONIAN ART STUDENTS HAVE SPIRITED DISAGREEMENTS WITH THE CHILDREN OF LAUNDROMAT OWNERS..
A FLUFFY TOWEL IS A JOY FOREVER!
NO! IT'S AN ABSTRACT FISH! A GEOMETRIC ABSTRACT FISH FROM 1926!
GRIFFY 10-3
IN A CASE LIKE THIS, WHAT'S THE DINGBURG TOWN SHERIFF EXPECTED TO DO---?
DO I INTERVENE? OR WILL THAT ACTION ALTER TH' SPACE-TIME CONTINUUM?
STOP TH' DRAMATIZING & HAVE A ZAGNUT BAR!
ZAGNUT
DINGBURG POLICE

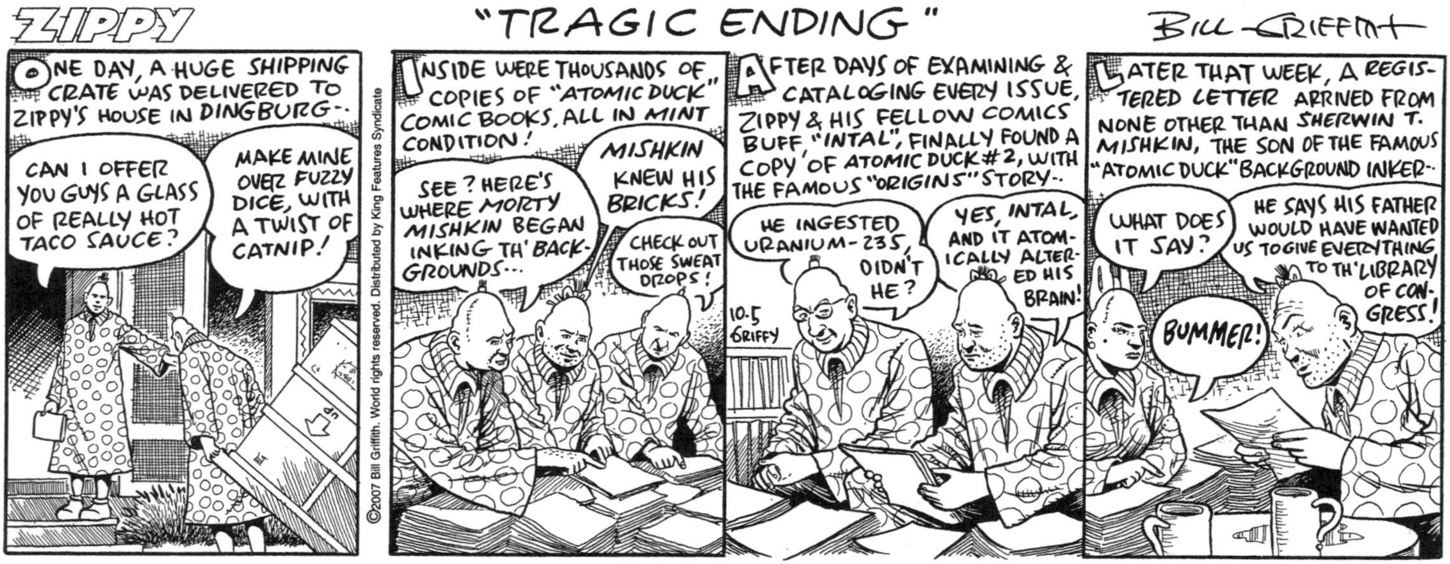
ZIPPY
"TRAGIC ENDING"
BILL GRIFFITH
ONE DAY, A HUGE SHIPPING CRATE WAS DELIVERED TO ZIPPY'S HOUSE IN DINGBURG--
CAN I OFFER YOU GUYS A GLASS OF REALLY HOT TACO SAUCE?
MAKE MINE OVER FUZZY DICE, WITH A TWIST OF CATNIP!
©2007 Bill Griffith. World rights reserved. Distributed by King Features Syndicate
INSIDE WERE THOUSANDS OF COPIES OF "ATOMIC DUCK" COMIC BOOKS, ALL IN MINT CONDITION!
SEE? HERE'S WHERE MORTY MISHKIN BEGAN INKING TH' BACKGROUNDS...
MISHKIN KNEW HIS BRICKS!
CHECK OUT THOSE SWEAT DROPS!
AFTER DAYS OF EXAMINING & CATALOGING EVERY ISSUE, ZIPPY & HIS FELLOW COMICS BUFF, "INTAL", FINALLY FOUND A COPY OF ATOMIC DUCK #2, WITH THE FAMOUS "ORIGINS" STORY--
HE INGESTED URANIUM-235, DIDN'T HE?
YES, INTAL, AND IT ATOMICALLY ALTERED HIS BRAIN!
10.5 GRIFFY
LATER THAT WEEK, A REGISTERED LETTER ARRIVED FROM NONE OTHER THAN SHERWIN T. MISHKIN, THE SON OF THE FAMOUS "ATOMIC DUCK" BACKGROUND INKER--
WHAT DOES IT SAY?
HE SAYS HIS FATHER WOULD HAVE WANTED US TO GIVE EVERYTHING TO TH' LIBRARY OF CONGRESS!
BUMMER!

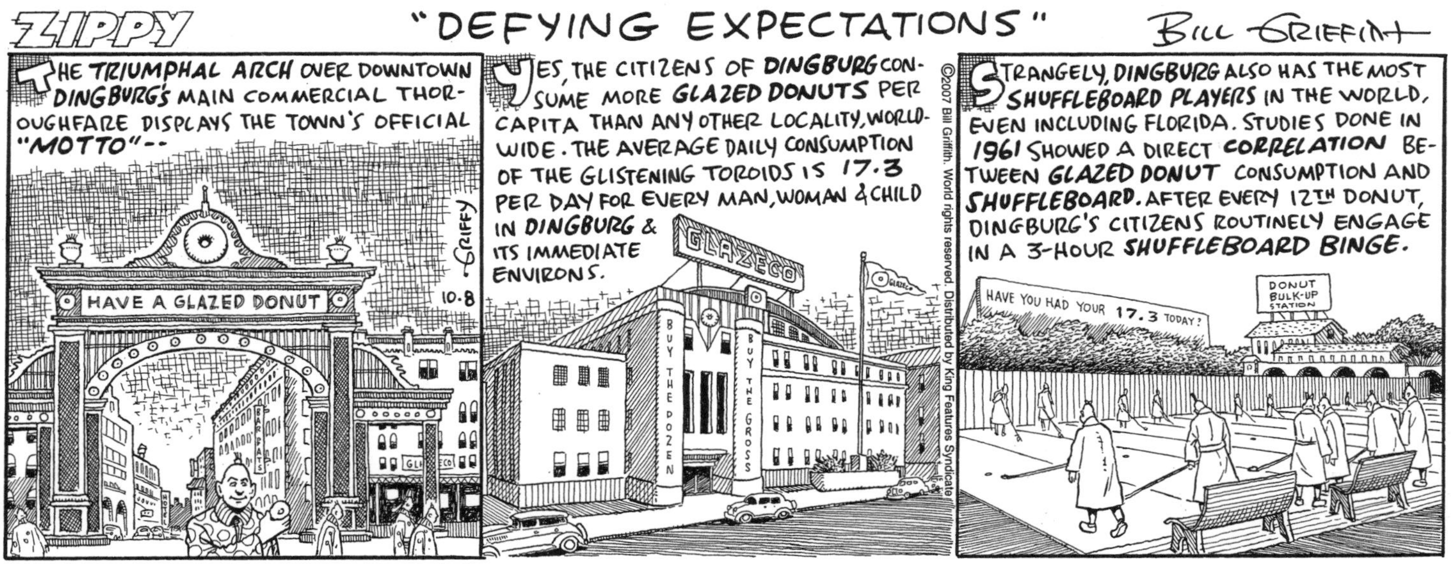
ZIPPY
"DEFYING EXPECTATIONS"
BILL GRIFFITH
THE TRIUMPHAL ARCH OVER DOWNTOWN DINGBURG'S MAIN COMMERCIAL THOROUGHFARE DISPLAYS THE TOWN'S OFFICIAL "MOTTO"--
HAVE A GLAZED DONUT
GRIFFY
10-8
YES, THE CITIZENS OF DINGBURG CONSUME MORE GLAZED DONUTS PER CAPITA THAN ANY OTHER LOCALITY, WORLD-WIDE. THE AVERAGE DAILY CONSUMPTION OF THE GLISTENING TOROIDS IS 17.3 PER DAY FOR EVERY MAN, WOMAN & CHILD IN DINGBURG & ITS IMMEDIATE ENVIRONS.
GLAZECO
BUY THE DOZEN
BUY THE GROSS
©2007 Bill Griffith. World rights reserved. Distributed by King Features Syndicate
STRANGELY, DINGBURG ALSO HAS THE MOST SHUFFLEBOARD PLAYERS IN THE WORLD, EVEN INCLUDING FLORIDA. STUDIES DONE IN 1961 SHOWED A DIRECT CORRELATION BETWEEN GLAZED DONUT CONSUMPTION AND SHUFFLEBOARD. AFTER EVERY 12TH DONUT, DINGBURG'S CITIZENS ROUTINELY ENGAGE IN A 3-HOUR SHUFFLEBOARD BINGE.
HAVE YOU HAD YOUR 17.3 TODAY?
DONUT BULK-UP STATION

12

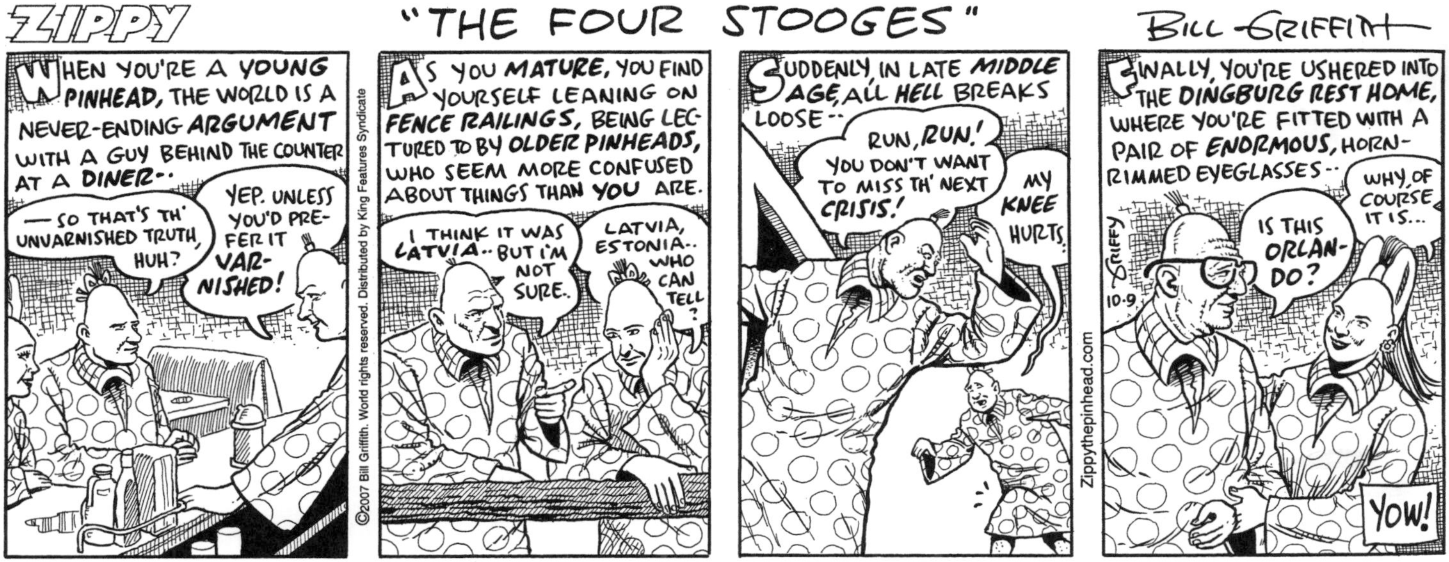
ZIPPY
"THE FOUR STOOGES"
BILL GRIFFITH
WHEN YOU'RE A YOUNG PINHEAD, THE WORLD IS A NEVER-ENDING ARGUMENT WITH A GUY BEHIND THE COUNTER AT A DINER--
—SO THAT'S TH' UNVARNISHED TRUTH, HUH?
YEP. UNLESS YOU'D PREFER IT VARNISHED!
©2007 Bill Griffith. World rights reserved. Distributed by King Features Syndicate
AS YOU MATURE, YOU FIND YOURSELF LEANING ON FENCE RAILINGS, BEING LECTURED TO BY OLDER PINHEADS, WHO SEEM MORE CONFUSED ABOUT THINGS THAN YOU ARE.
I THINK IT WAS LATVIA.. BUT I'M NOT SURE.
LATVIA, ESTONIA.. WHO CAN TELL?
SUDDENLY, IN LATE MIDDLE AGE, ALL HELL BREAKS LOOSE--
RUN, RUN! YOU DON'T WANT TO MISS TH' NEXT CRISIS!
MY KNEE HURTS.
Zippythepinhead.com
FINALLY, YOU'RE USHERED INTO THE DINGBURG REST HOME, WHERE YOU'RE FITTED WITH A PAIR OF ENORMOUS, HORN-RIMMED EYEGLASSES--
GRIFFY
10-9
IS THIS ORLANDO?
WHY, OF COURSE IT IS...
YOW!

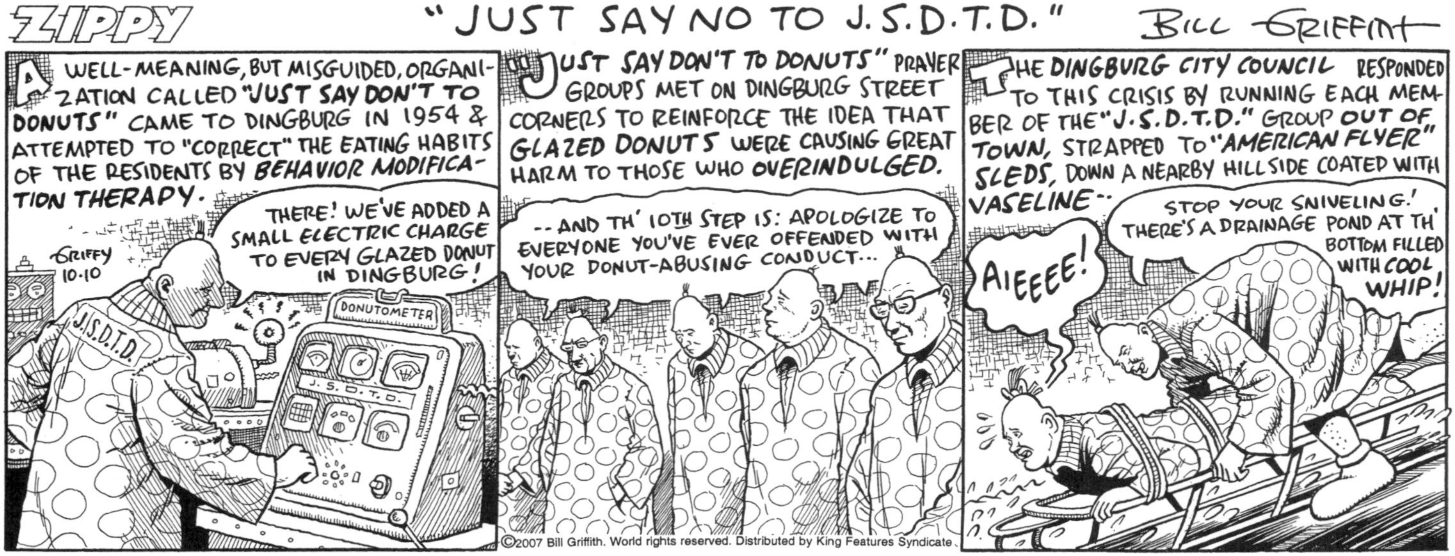
ZIPPY
"JUST SAY NO TO J.S.D.T.D."
BILL GRIFFITH
A WELL-MEANING, BUT MISGUIDED, ORGANIZATION CALLED "JUST SAY DON'T TO DONUTS" CAME TO DINGBURG IN 1954 & ATTEMPTED TO "CORRECT" THE EATING HABITS OF THE RESIDENTS BY BEHAVIOR MODIFICATION THERAPY.
THERE! WE'VE ADDED A SMALL ELECTRIC CHARGE TO EVERY GLAZED DONUT IN DINGBURG!
GRIFFY 10-10
J.S.D.T.D.
DONUTOMETER
J. S. D. T. D.
"JUST SAY DON'T TO DONUTS" PRAYER GROUPS MET ON DINGBURG STREET CORNERS TO REINFORCE THE IDEA THAT GLAZED DONUTS WERE CAUSING GREAT HARM TO THOSE WHO OVERINDULGED.
--AND TH' 10TH STEP IS: APOLOGIZE TO EVERYONE YOU'VE EVER OFFENDED WITH YOUR DONUT-ABUSING CONDUCT...
THE DINGBURG CITY COUNCIL RESPONDED TO THIS CRISIS BY RUNNING EACH MEMBER OF THE "J.S.D.T.D." GROUP OUT OF TOWN, STRAPPED TO "AMERICAN FLYER" SLEDS, DOWN A NEARBY HILLSIDE COATED WITH VASELINE--
AIEEEEE!
STOP YOUR SNIVELING! THERE'S A DRAINAGE POND AT TH' BOTTOM FILLED WITH COOL WHIP!



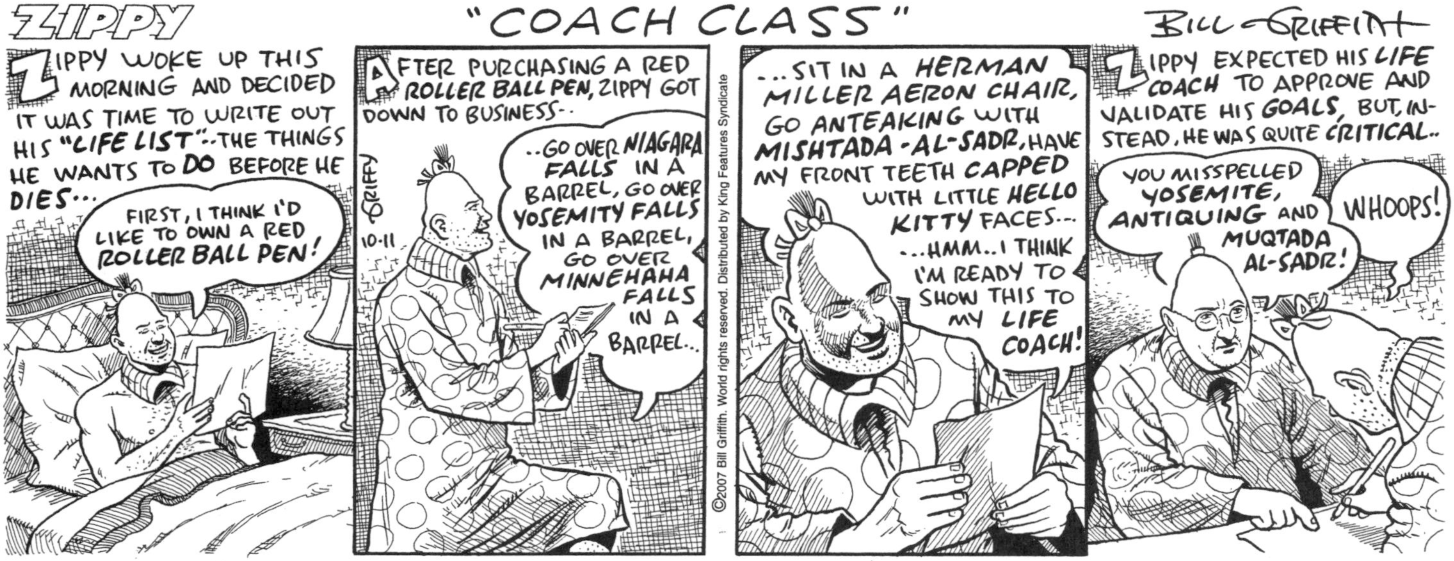
ZIPPY
"COACH CLASS"
BILL GRIFFITH
ZIPPY WOKE UP THIS MORNING AND DECIDED IT WAS TIME TO WRITE OUT HIS "LIFE LIST"--THE THINGS HE WANTS TO DO BEFORE HE DIES...
FIRST, I THINK I'D LIKE TO OWN A RED ROLLER BALL PEN!
AFTER PURCHASING A RED ROLLER BALL PEN, ZIPPY GOT DOWN TO BUSINESS--
GRIFFY 10-11
..GO OVER NIAGARA FALLS IN A BARREL, GO OVER YOSEMITY FALLS IN A BARREL, GO OVER MINNEHAHA FALLS IN A BARREL...
...SIT IN A HERMAN MILLER AERON CHAIR, GO ANTEAKING WITH MISHTADA-AL-SADR, HAVE MY FRONT TEETH CAPPED WITH LITTLE HELLO KITTY FACES--
...HMM..I THINK I'M READY TO SHOW THIS TO MY LIFE COACH!
ZIPPY EXPECTED HIS LIFE COACH TO APPROVE AND VALIDATE HIS GOALS, BUT, INSTEAD, HE WAS QUITE CRITICAL..
YOU MISSPELLED YOSEMITE, ANTIQUING AND MUQTADA AL-SADR!
WHOOPS!



13

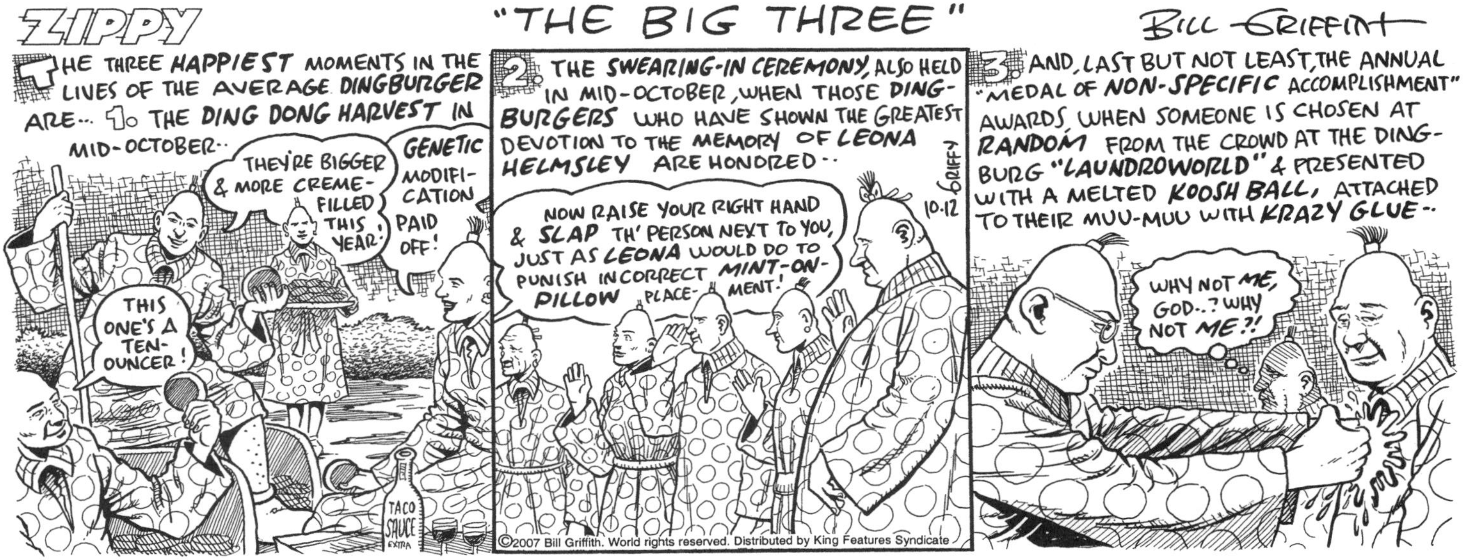
ZIPPY
"THE BIG THREE"
BILL GRIFFITH
THE THREE HAPPIEST MOMENTS IN THE LIVES OF THE AVERAGE DINGBURGER ARE-- 1. THE DING DONG HARVEST IN MID-OCTOBER--
THEY'RE BIGGER & MORE CREME-FILLED THIS YEAR!
GENETIC MODIFICATION PAID OFF!
THIS ONE'S A TEN-OUNCER!
TACO SAUCE EXTRA
2. THE SWEARING-IN CEREMONY, ALSO HELD IN MID-OCTOBER, WHEN THOSE DINGBURGERS WHO HAVE SHOWN THE GREATEST DEVOTION TO THE MEMORY OF LEONA HELMSLEY ARE HONORED--
NOW RAISE YOUR RIGHT HAND & SLAP TH' PERSON NEXT TO YOU, JUST AS LEONA WOULD DO TO PUNISH INCORRECT MINT-ON-PILLOW PLACE-MENT!
GRIFFY 10.12
©2007 Bill Griffith. World rights reserved. Distributed by King Features Syndicate
3. AND, LAST BUT NOT LEAST, THE ANNUAL "MEDAL OF NON-SPECIFIC ACCOMPLISHMENT" AWARDS, WHEN SOMEONE IS CHOSEN AT RANDOM FROM THE CROWD AT THE DINGBURG "LAUNDROWORLD" & PRESENTED WITH A MELTED KOOSH BALL, ATTACHED TO THEIR MUU-MUU WITH KRAZY GLUE--
WHY NOT ME, GOD--? WHY NOT ME?!

14

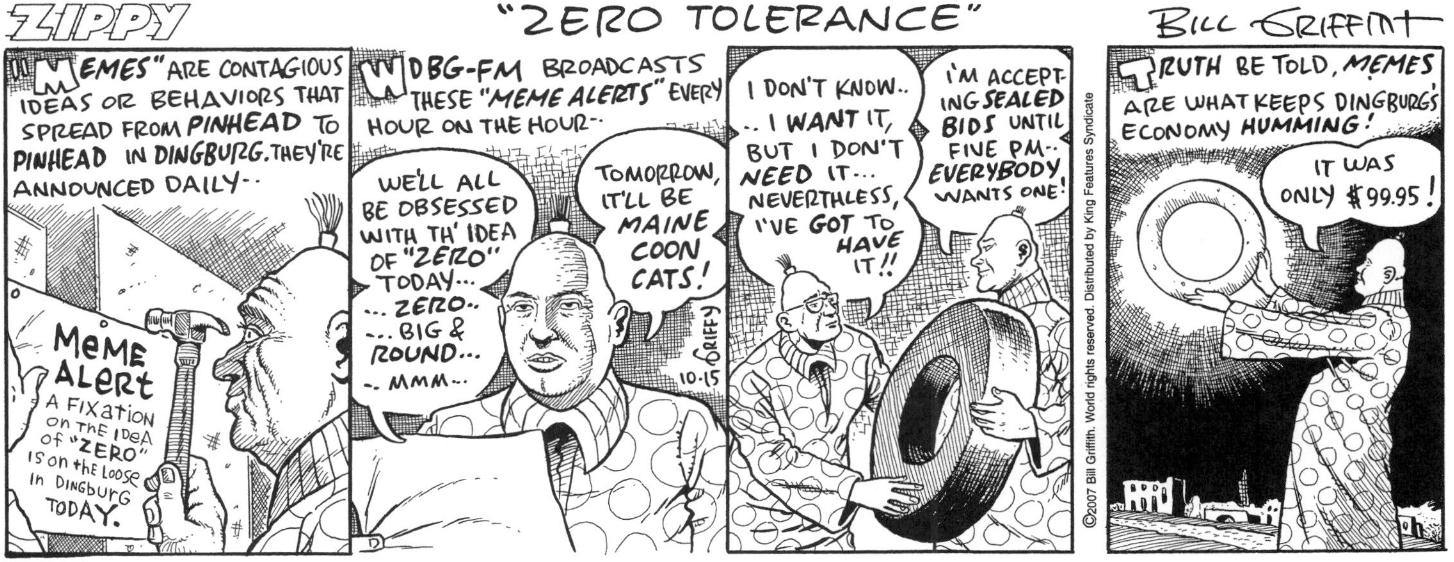
ZIPPY
"ZERO TOLERANCE"
BILL GRIFFITH
"MEMES" ARE CONTAGIOUS IDEAS OR BEHAVIORS THAT SPREAD FROM PINHEAD TO PINHEAD IN DINGBURG. THEY'RE ANNOUNCED DAILY--
MeME ALert
A FIXation on THE IDEA of "ZERO" is on the Loose in DingburG TODAY.
WDBG-FM BROADCASTS THESE "MEME ALERTS" EVERY HOUR ON THE HOUR--
WE'LL ALL BE OBSESSED WITH TH' IDEA OF "ZERO" TODAY... ...ZERO-- ...BIG & ROUND... --MMM--
TOMORROW, IT'LL BE MAINE COON CATS!
GRIFFY 10.15
I DON'T KNOW-- --I WANT IT, BUT I DON'T NEED IT... NEVERTHLESS, I'VE GOT TO HAVE IT!!
I'M ACCEPTING SEALED BIDS UNTIL FIVE PM-- EVERYBODY WANTS ONE!
©2007 Bill Griffith. World rights reserved. Distributed by King Features Syndicate
TRUTH BE TOLD, MEMES ARE WHAT KEEPS DINGBURG'S ECONOMY HUMMING!
IT WAS ONLY $99.95!

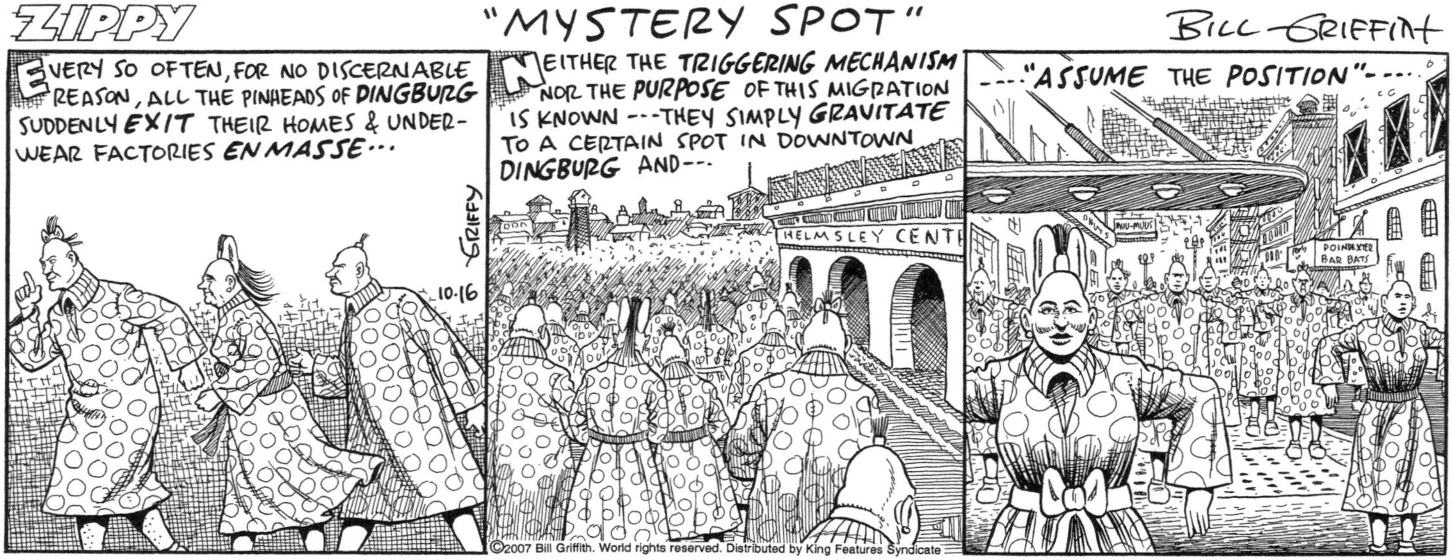
ZIPPY
"MYSTERY SPOT"
BILL GRIFFITH
EVERY SO OFTEN, FOR NO DISCERNABLE REASON, ALL THE PINHEADS OF DINGBURG SUDDENLY EXIT THEIR HOMES & UNDERWEAR FACTORIES EN MASSE...
GRIFFY
10.16
NEITHER THE TRIGGERING MECHANISM NOR THE PURPOSE OF THIS MIGRATION IS KNOWN---THEY SIMPLY GRAVITATE TO A CERTAIN SPOT IN DOWNTOWN DINGBURG AND---
HELMSLEY CENT
---"ASSUME THE POSITION"----
MUU-MUUS
POINDEXTER BAR BATS
©2007 Bill Griffith. World rights reserved. Distributed by King Features Syndicate

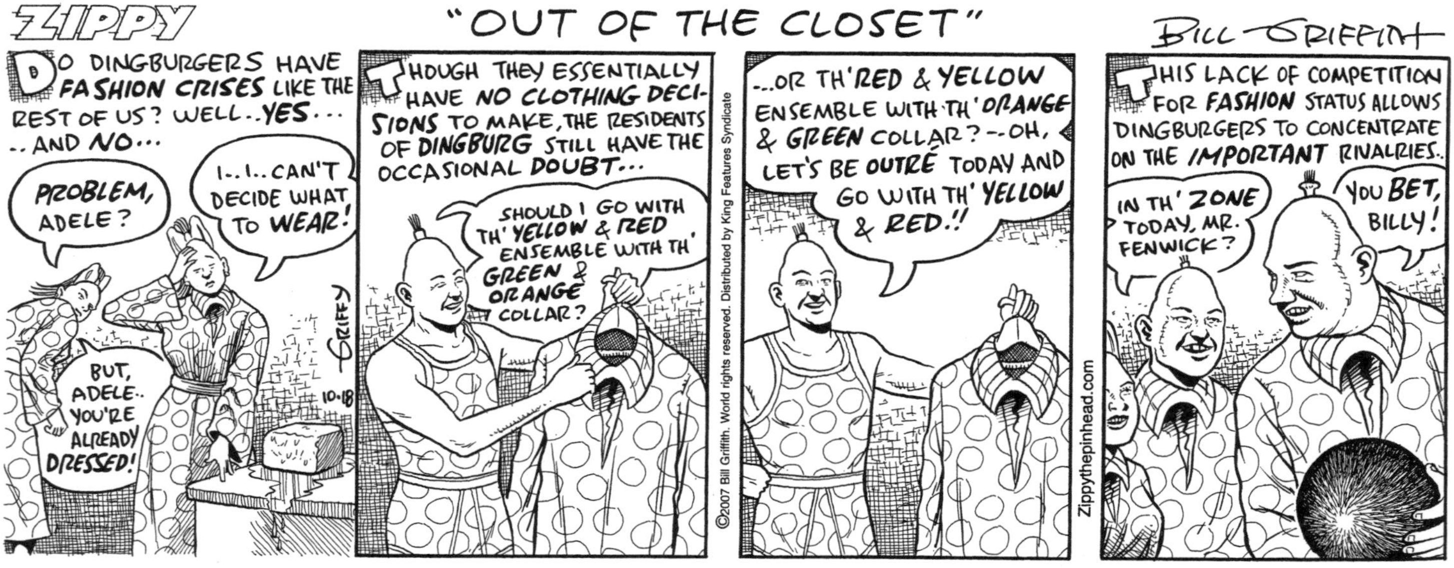
ZIPPY
"OUT OF THE CLOSET"
BILL GRIFFITH
DO DINGBURGERS HAVE FASHION CRISES LIKE THE REST OF US? WELL..YES... ..AND NO...
PROBLEM, ADELE?
I..I..CAN'T DECIDE WHAT TO WEAR!
BUT, ADELE.. YOU'RE ALREADY DRESSED!
GRIFFY
10.18
THOUGH THEY ESSENTIALLY HAVE NO CLOTHING DECISIONS TO MAKE, THE RESIDENTS OF DINGBURG STILL HAVE THE OCCASIONAL DOUBT...
SHOULD I GO WITH TH' YELLOW & RED ENSEMBLE WITH TH' GREEN & ORANGE COLLAR?
©2007 Bill Griffith. World rights reserved. Distributed by King Features Syndicate
...OR TH' RED & YELLOW ENSEMBLE WITH TH' ORANGE & GREEN COLLAR? --OH, LET'S BE OUTRÉ TODAY AND GO WITH TH' YELLOW & RED.!!
Zippythepinhead.com
THIS LACK OF COMPETITION FOR FASHION STATUS ALLOWS DINGBURGERS TO CONCENTRATE ON THE IMPORTANT RIVALRIES..
IN TH' ZONE TODAY, MR. FENWICK?
YOU BET, BILLY!

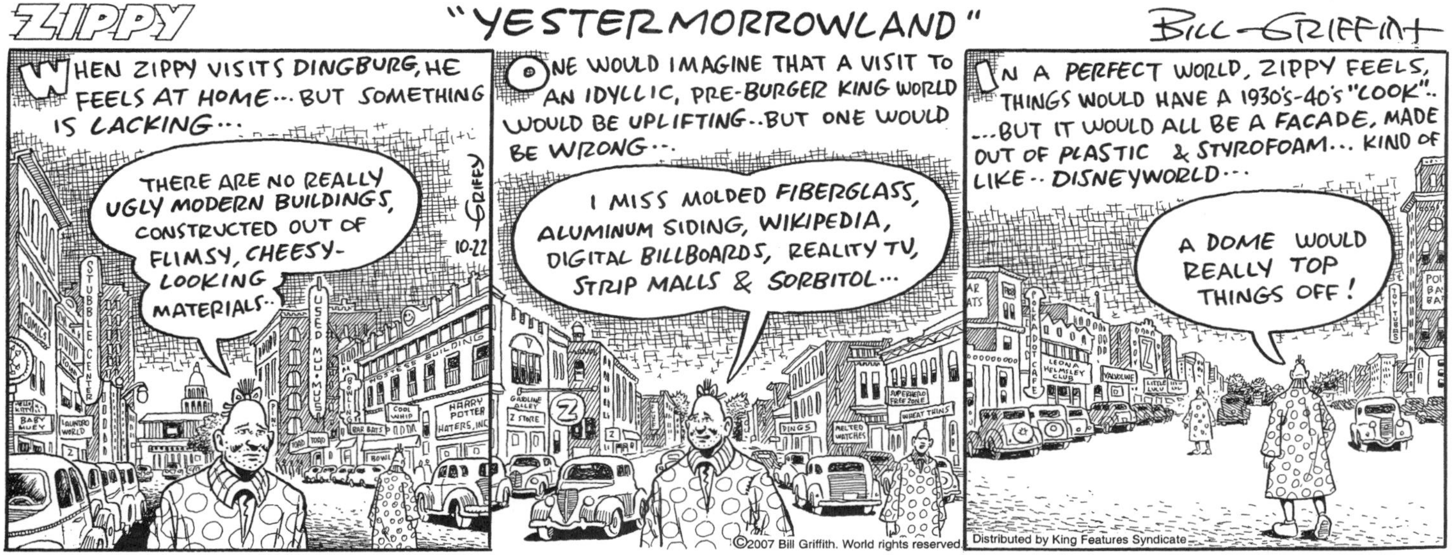
ZIPPY
"YESTERMORROWLAND"
BILL GRIFFITH
WHEN ZIPPY VISITS DINGBURG, HE FEELS AT HOME... BUT SOMETHING IS LACKING...
THERE ARE NO REALLY UGLY MODERN BUILDINGS, CONSTRUCTED OUT OF FLIMSY, CHEESY-LOOKING MATERIALS..
GRIFFY 10-22
ONE WOULD IMAGINE THAT A VISIT TO AN IDYLLIC, PRE-BURGER KING WORLD WOULD BE UPLIFTING..BUT ONE WOULD BE WRONG..
I MISS MOLDED FIBERGLASS, ALUMINUM SIDING, WIKIPEDIA, DIGITAL BILLBOARDS, REALITY TV, STRIP MALLS & SORBITOL...
IN A PERFECT WORLD, ZIPPY FEELS, THINGS WOULD HAVE A 1930'S-40'S "LOOK".. ...BUT IT WOULD ALL BE A FACADE, MADE OUT OF PLASTIC & STYROFOAM... KIND OF LIKE.. DISNEYWORLD...
A DOME WOULD REALLY TOP THINGS OFF!
©2007 Bill Griffith. World rights reserved.
Distributed by King Features Syndicate

15

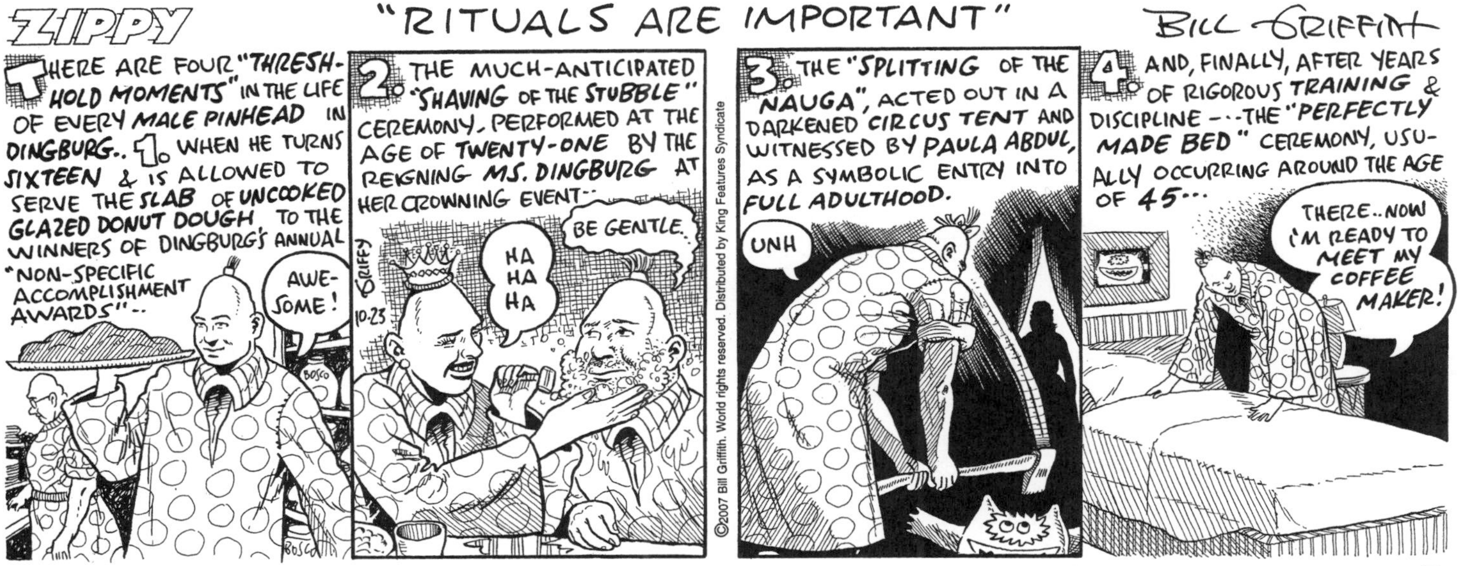
ZIPPY
"RITUALS ARE IMPORTANT"
BILL GRIFFITH
THERE ARE FOUR "THRESHHOLD MOMENTS" IN THE LIFE OF EVERY MALE PINHEAD IN DINGBURG.. 1. WHEN HE TURNS SIXTEEN & IS ALLOWED TO SERVE THE SLAB OF UNCOOKED GLAZED DONUT DOUGH TO THE WINNERS OF DINGBURG'S ANNUAL "NON-SPECIFIC ACCOMPLISHMENT AWARDS"..
AWE-SOME!
2. THE MUCH-ANTICIPATED "SHAVING OF THE STUBBLE" CEREMONY, PERFORMED AT THE AGE OF TWENTY-ONE BY THE REIGNING MS. DINGBURG AT HER CROWNING EVENT..
GRIFFY 10-23
HA HA HA
BE GENTLE.
©2007 Bill Griffith. World rights reserved. Distributed by King Features Syndicate
3. THE "SPLITTING OF THE NAUGA", ACTED OUT IN A DARKENED CIRCUS TENT AND WITNESSED BY PAULA ABDUL, AS A SYMBOLIC ENTRY INTO FULL ADULTHOOD.
UNH
4. AND, FINALLY, AFTER YEARS OF RIGOROUS TRAINING & DISCIPLINE -- THE "PERFECTLY MADE BED" CEREMONY, USUALLY OCCURRING AROUND THE AGE OF 45...
THERE..NOW I'M READY TO MEET MY COFFEE MAKER!

16

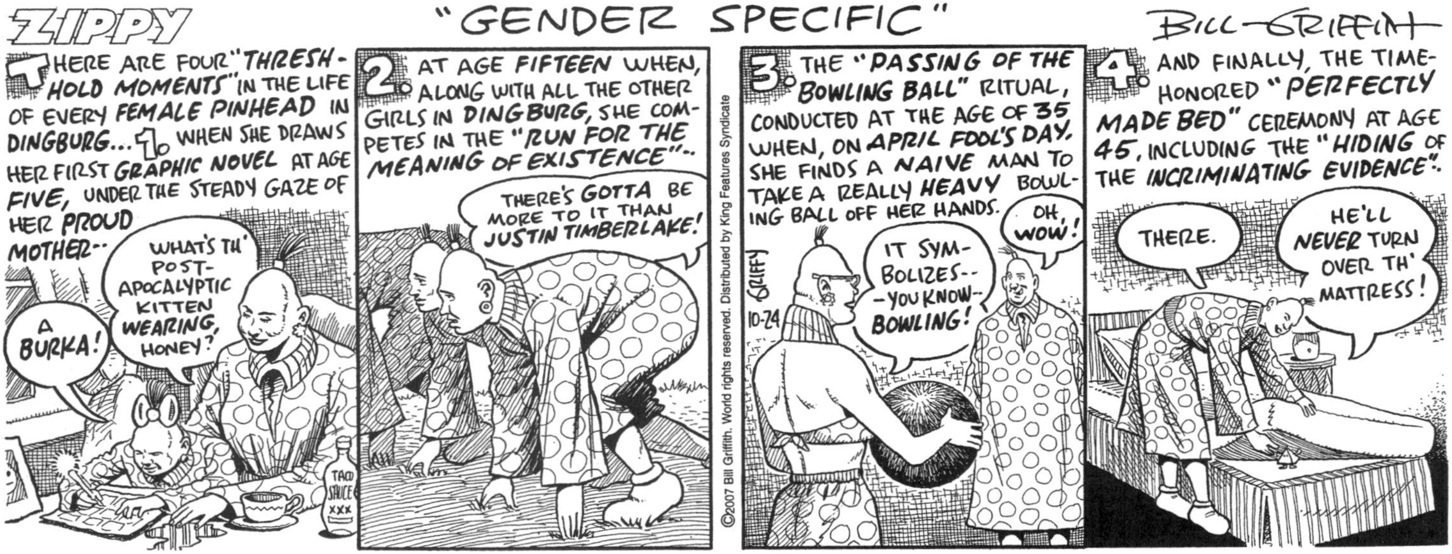
ZIPPY
"GENDER SPECIFIC"
BILL GRIFFITH
THERE ARE FOUR "THRESH-HOLD MOMENTS" IN THE LIFE OF EVERY FEMALE PINHEAD IN DINGBURG... 1. WHEN SHE DRAWS HER FIRST GRAPHIC NOVEL AT AGE FIVE, UNDER THE STEADY GAZE OF HER PROUD MOTHER--
WHAT'S TH' POST-APOCALYPTIC KITTEN WEARING, HONEY?
A BURKA!
TACO SAUCE XXX
2. AT AGE FIFTEEN WHEN, ALONG WITH ALL THE OTHER GIRLS IN DINGBURG, SHE COMPETES IN THE "RUN FOR THE MEANING OF EXISTENCE"--
THERE'S GOTTA BE MORE TO IT THAN JUSTIN TIMBERLAKE!
©2007 Bill Griffith. World rights reserved. Distributed by King Features Syndicate
GRIFFY
10-24
3. THE "PASSING OF THE BOWLING BALL" RITUAL, CONDUCTED AT THE AGE OF 35 WHEN, ON APRIL FOOL'S DAY, SHE FINDS A NAIVE MAN TO TAKE A REALLY HEAVY BOWLING BALL OFF HER HANDS.
IT SYMBOLIZES-- --YOU KNOW-- BOWLING!
OH, WOW!
4. AND FINALLY, THE TIME-HONORED "PERFECTLY MADE BED" CEREMONY AT AGE 45, INCLUDING THE "HIDING OF THE INCRIMINATING EVIDENCE".
THERE.
HE'LL NEVER TURN OVER TH' MATTRESS!

17

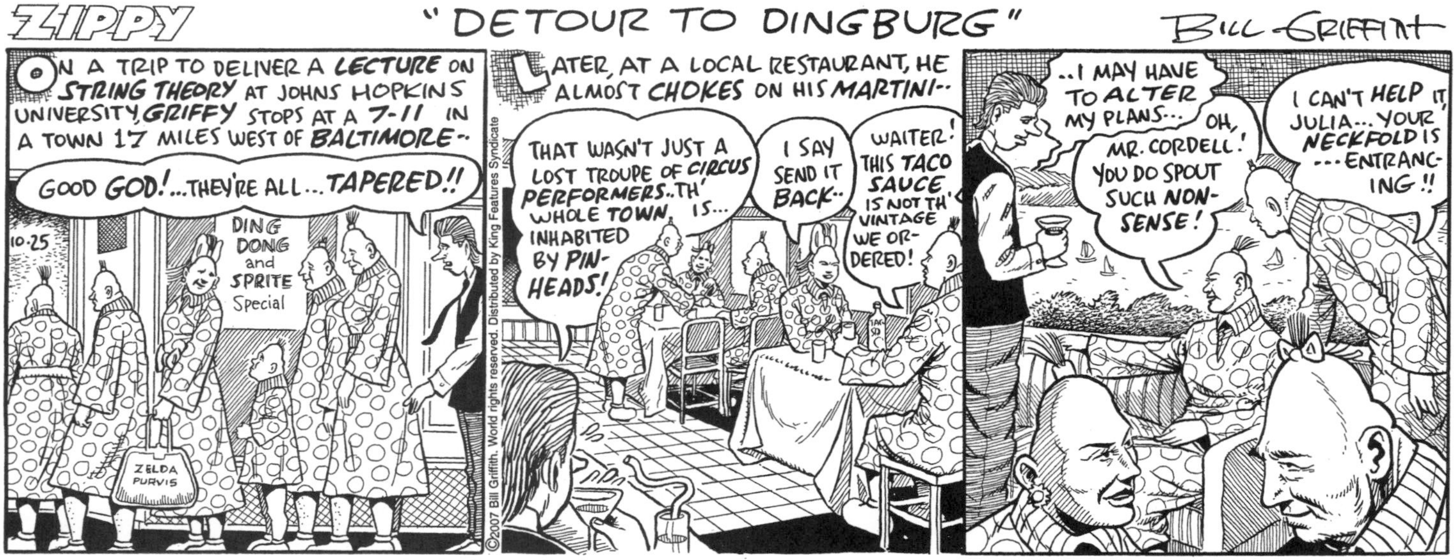
ZIPPY
"DETOUR TO DINGBURG"
BILL GRIFFITH
ON A TRIP TO DELIVER A LECTURE ON STRING THEORY AT JOHNS HOPKINS UNIVERSITY, GRIFFY STOPS AT A 7-11 IN A TOWN 17 MILES WEST OF BALTIMORE--
GOOD GOD!...THEY'RE ALL...TAPERED!!
10-25
DING DONG and SPRITE Special
ZELDA PURVIS
©2007 Bill Griffith. World rights reserved. Distributed by King Features Syndicate
LATER, AT A LOCAL RESTAURANT, HE ALMOST CHOKES ON HIS MARTINI--
THAT WASN'T JUST A LOST TROUPE OF CIRCUS PERFORMERS..TH' WHOLE TOWN IS... INHABITED BY PINHEADS!
I SAY SEND IT BACK--
WAITER! THIS TACO SAUCE IS NOT TH' VINTAGE WE ORDERED!
..I MAY HAVE TO ALTER MY PLANS...
OH, MR. CORDELL! YOU DO SPOUT SUCH NONSENSE!
I CAN'T HELP IT, JULIA... YOUR NECKFOLD IS ...ENTRANCING!!

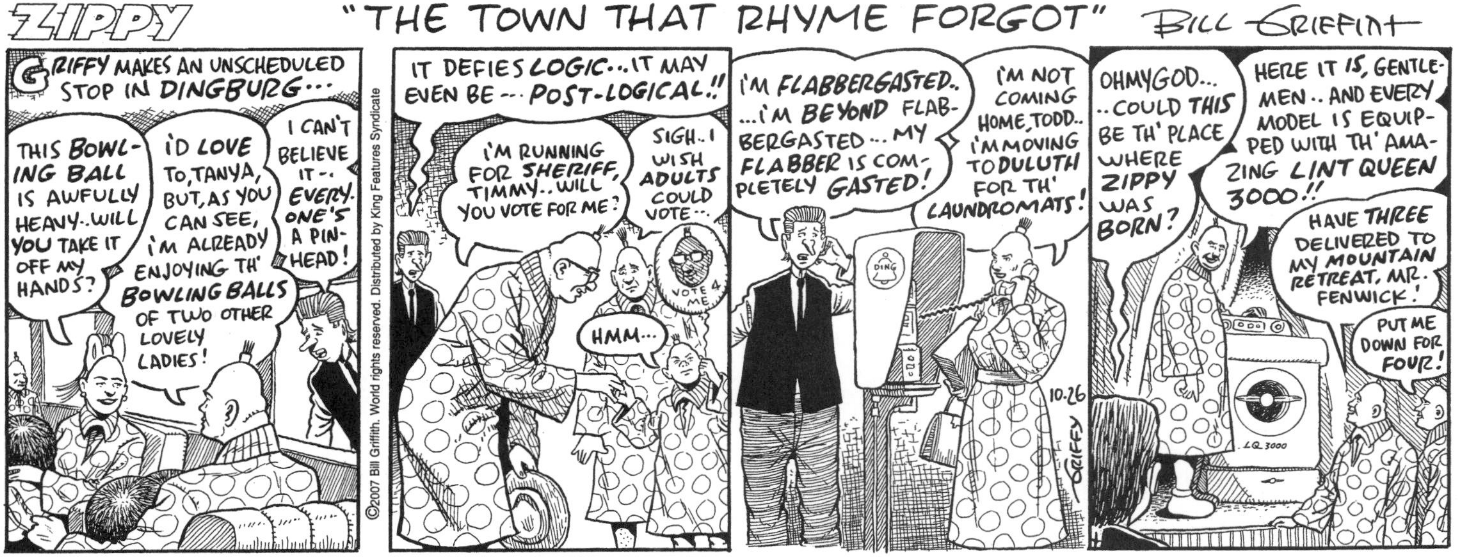
ZIPPY
"THE TOWN THAT RHYME FORGOT"
BILL GRIFFITH
GRIFFY MAKES AN UNSCHEDULED STOP IN DINGBURG...
THIS BOWLING BALL IS AWFULLY HEAVY..WILL YOU TAKE IT OFF MY HANDS?
I'D LOVE TO, TANYA, BUT, AS YOU CAN SEE, I'M ALREADY ENJOYING TH' BOWLING BALLS OF TWO OTHER LOVELY LADIES!
I CAN'T BELIEVE IT-. EVERY-ONE'S A PIN-HEAD!
©2007 Bill Griffith. World rights reserved. Distributed by King Features Syndicate
IT DEFIES LOGIC...IT MAY EVEN BE -- POST-LOGICAL!!
I'M RUNNING FOR SHERIFF, TIMMY..WILL YOU VOTE FOR ME?
SIGH..I WISH ADULTS COULD VOTE...
VOTE 4 ME
HMM...
I'M FLABBERGASTED.. ...I'M BEYOND FLAB-BERGASTED... MY FLABBER IS COM-PLETELY GASTED!
I'M NOT COMING HOME, TODD.. I'M MOVING TO DULUTH FOR TH' LAUNDROMATS!
DING
10-26
GRIFFY
OHMYGOD... ..COULD THIS BE TH' PLACE WHERE ZIPPY WAS BORN?
HERE IT IS, GENTLE-MEN.. AND EVERY MODEL IS EQUIP-PED WITH TH' AMA-ZING LINT QUEEN 3000!!
HAVE THREE DELIVERED TO MY MOUNTAIN RETREAT, MR. FENWICK!
PUT ME DOWN FOR FOUR!
LQ 3000

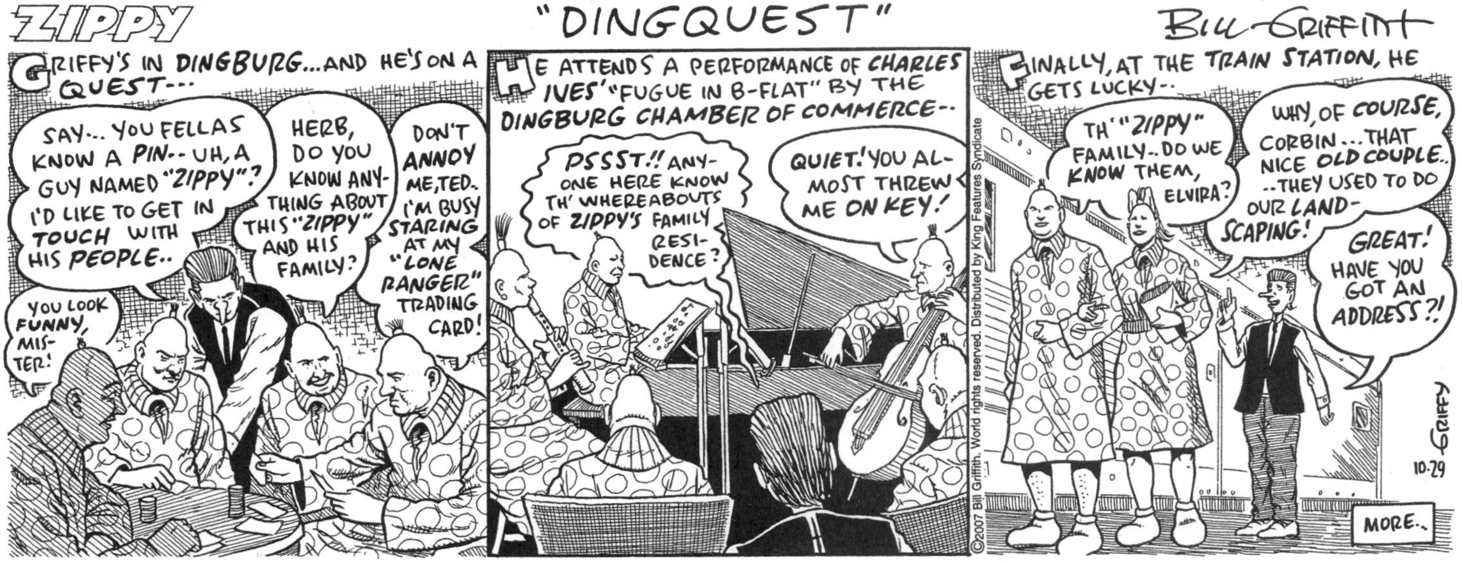
ZIPPY
"DINGQUEST"
BILL GRIFFITH
GRIFFY'S IN DINGBURG...AND HE'S ON A QUEST...
SAY... YOU FELLAS KNOW A PIN-- UH, A GUY NAMED "ZIPPY"? I'D LIKE TO GET IN TOUCH WITH HIS PEOPLE..
HERB, DO YOU KNOW ANY-THING ABOUT THIS "ZIPPY" AND HIS FAMILY?
DON'T ANNOY ME, TED.. I'M BUSY STARING AT MY "LONE RANGER" TRADING CARD!
YOU LOOK FUNNY, MIS-TER!
HE ATTENDS A PERFORMANCE OF CHARLES IVES' "FUGUE IN B-FLAT" BY THE DINGBURG CHAMBER OF COMMERCE..
PSSST!! ANY-ONE HERE KNOW TH' WHEREABOUTS OF ZIPPY'S FAMILY RESI-DENCE?
QUIET! YOU AL-MOST THREW ME ON KEY!
©2007 Bill Griffith. World rights reserved. Distributed by King Features Syndicate
FINALLY, AT THE TRAIN STATION, HE GETS LUCKY..
TH' "ZIPPY" FAMILY.. DO WE KNOW THEM, ELVIRA?
WHY, OF COURSE, CORBIN... THAT NICE OLD COUPLE.. ..THEY USED TO DO OUR LAND-SCAPING!
GREAT! HAVE YOU GOT AN ADDRESS?!
GRIFFY
10-29
MORE..

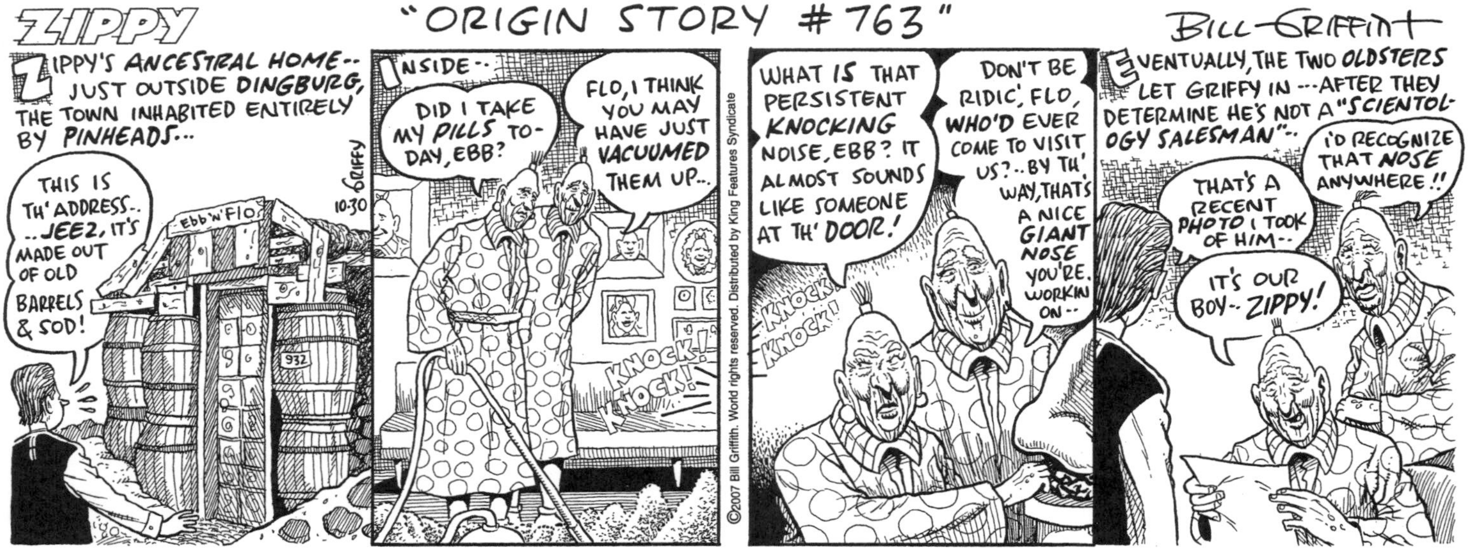
ZIPPY
"ORIGIN STORY #763"
BILL GRIFFITH
ZIPPY'S ANCESTRAL HOME-- JUST OUTSIDE DINGBURG, THE TOWN INHABITED ENTIRELY BY PINHEADS...
THIS IS TH' ADDRESS-- ..JEEZ, IT'S MADE OUT OF OLD BARRELS & SOD!
EBB 'N' FLO
932
GRIFFY 10-30
INSIDE--
DID I TAKE MY PILLS TO-DAY, EBB?
FLO, I THINK YOU MAY HAVE JUST VACUUMED THEM UP...
KNOCK! KNOCK!
©2007 Bill Griffith. World rights reserved. Distributed by King Features Syndicate
WHAT IS THAT PERSISTENT KNOCKING NOISE, EBB? IT ALMOST SOUNDS LIKE SOMEONE AT TH' DOOR!
DON'T BE RIDIC', FLO, WHO'D EVER COME TO VISIT US?..BY TH' WAY, THAT'S A NICE GIANT NOSE YOU'RE WORKIN ON--
KNOCK KNOCK!
EVENTUALLY, THE TWO OLDSTERS LET GRIFFY IN ---AFTER THEY DETERMINE HE'S NOT A "SCIENTOLOGY SALESMAN"--
I'D RECOGNIZE THAT NOSE ANYWHERE!!
THAT'S A RECENT PHOTO I TOOK OF HIM--
IT'S OUR BOY-- ZIPPY!

18

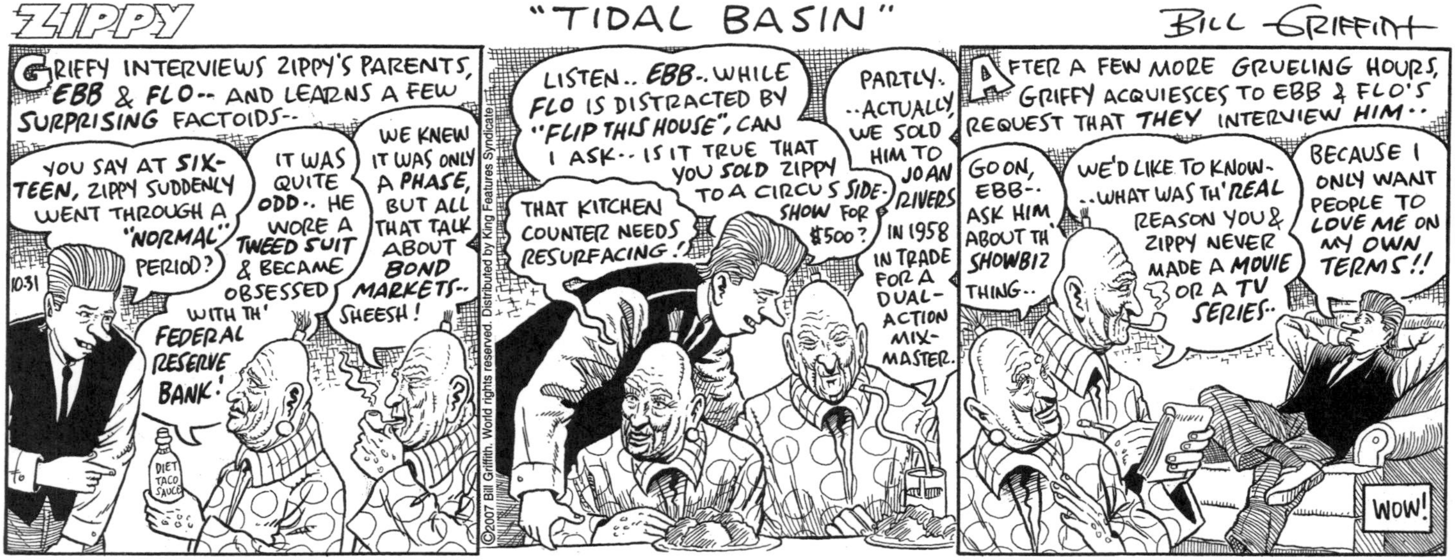
ZIPPY
"TIDAL BASIN"
BILL GRIFFITH
GRIFFY INTERVIEWS ZIPPY'S PARENTS, EBB & FLO-- AND LEARNS A FEW SURPRISING FACTOIDS--
YOU SAY AT SIXTEEN, ZIPPY SUDDENLY WENT THROUGH A "NORMAL" PERIOD?
10-31
IT WAS QUITE ODD-- HE WORE A TWEED SUIT & BECAME OBSESSED WITH TH' FEDERAL RESERVE BANK!
WE KNEW IT WAS ONLY A PHASE, BUT ALL THAT TALK ABOUT BOND MARKETS-- SHEESH!
DIET TACO SAUCE
©2007 Bill Griffith. World rights reserved. Distributed by King Features Syndicate
LISTEN.. EBB-- WHILE FLO IS DISTRACTED BY "FLIP THIS HOUSE", CAN I ASK-- IS IT TRUE THAT YOU SOLD ZIPPY TO A CIRCUS SIDE-SHOW FOR $500?
PARTLY. ..ACTUALLY WE SOLD HIM TO JOAN RIVERS IN 1958 IN TRADE FOR A DUAL-ACTION MIX-MASTER.
THAT KITCHEN COUNTER NEEDS RESURFACING!
AFTER A FEW MORE GRUELING HOURS, GRIFFY ACQUIESCES TO EBB & FLO'S REQUEST THAT THEY INTERVIEW HIM--
GO ON, EBB-- ASK HIM ABOUT TH' SHOWBIZ THING--
WE'D LIKE TO KNOW- ..WHAT WAS TH' REAL REASON YOU & ZIPPY NEVER MADE A MOVIE OR A TV SERIES--
BECAUSE I ONLY WANT PEOPLE TO LOVE ME ON MY OWN TERMS!!
WOW!

19

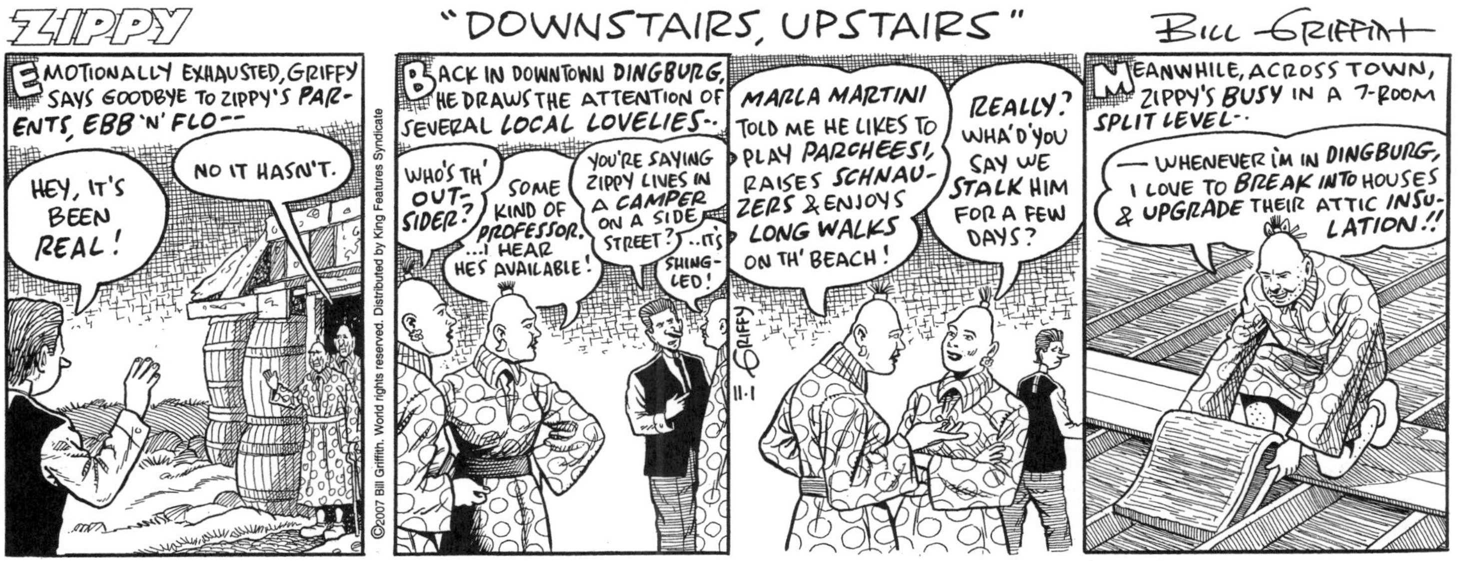
ZIPPY
"DOWNSTAIRS, UPSTAIRS"
BILL GRIFFITH
EMOTIONALLY EXHAUSTED, GRIFFY SAYS GOODBYE TO ZIPPY'S PARENTS, EBB 'N' FLO--
HEY, IT'S BEEN REAL!
NO IT HASN'T.
©2007 Bill Griffith. World rights reserved. Distributed by King Features Syndicate
BACK IN DOWNTOWN DINGBURG, HE DRAWS THE ATTENTION OF SEVERAL LOCAL LOVELIES..
WHO'S TH' OUTSIDER?
SOME KIND OF PROFESSOR. ...I HEAR HE'S AVAILABLE!
YOU'RE SAYING ZIPPY LIVES IN A CAMPER ON A SIDE STREET?
..IT'S SHINGLED!
GRIFFY 11.1
MARLA MARTINI TOLD ME HE LIKES TO PLAY PARCHEESI, RAISES SCHNAUZERS & ENJOYS LONG WALKS ON TH' BEACH!
REALLY? WHA'D'YOU SAY WE STALK HIM FOR A FEW DAYS?
MEANWHILE, ACROSS TOWN, ZIPPY'S BUSY IN A 7-ROOM SPLIT LEVEL..
—WHENEVER I'M IN DINGBURG, I LOVE TO BREAK INTO HOUSES & UPGRADE THEIR ATTIC INSULATION!!

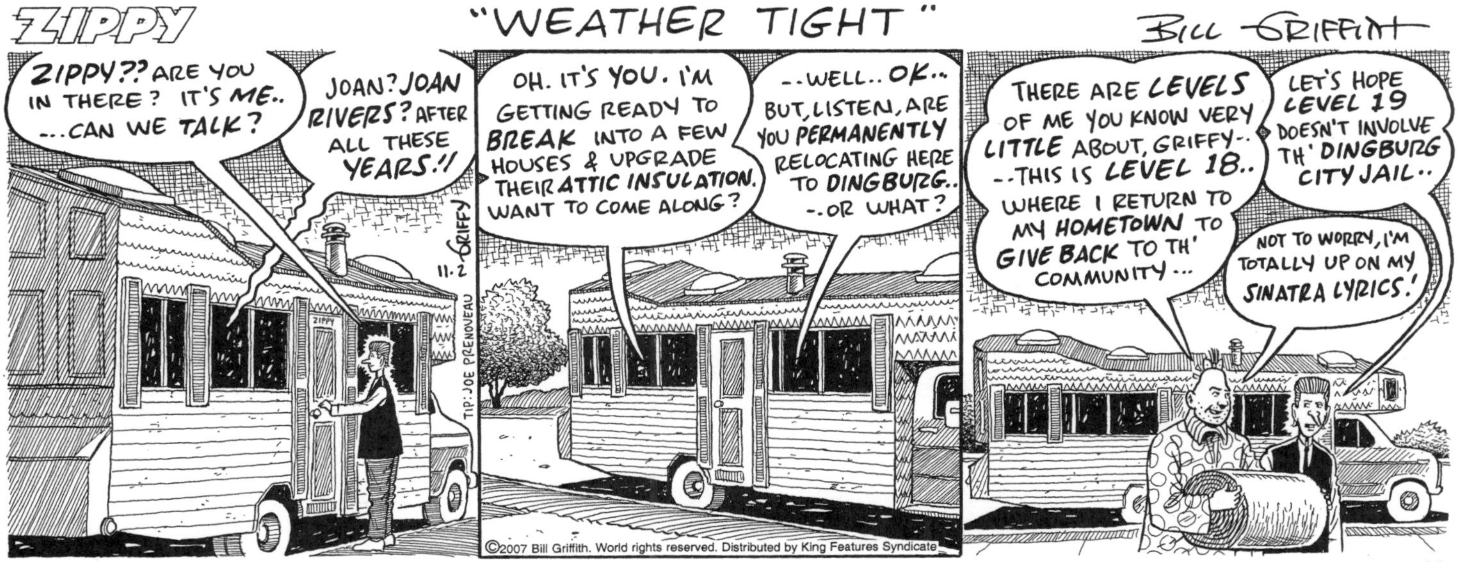
ZIPPY
"WEATHER TIGHT"
BILL GRIFFITH
ZIPPY?? ARE YOU IN THERE? IT'S ME.. ...CAN WE TALK?
JOAN? JOAN RIVERS? AFTER ALL THESE YEARS!!
GRIFFY 11.2
TIP: JOE PRENOVEAU
OH. IT'S YOU. I'M GETTING READY TO BREAK INTO A FEW HOUSES & UPGRADE THEIR ATTIC INSULATION. WANT TO COME ALONG?
--WELL.. OK.. BUT, LISTEN, ARE YOU PERMANENTLY RELOCATING HERE TO DINGBURG.. --OR WHAT?
©2007 Bill Griffith. World rights reserved. Distributed by King Features Syndicate
THERE ARE LEVELS OF ME YOU KNOW VERY LITTLE ABOUT, GRIFFY.. --THIS IS LEVEL 18.. WHERE I RETURN TO MY HOMETOWN TO GIVE BACK TO TH' COMMUNITY...
LET'S HOPE LEVEL 19 DOESN'T INVOLVE TH' DINGBURG CITY JAIL..
NOT TO WORRY, I'M TOTALLY UP ON MY SINATRA LYRICS!

20

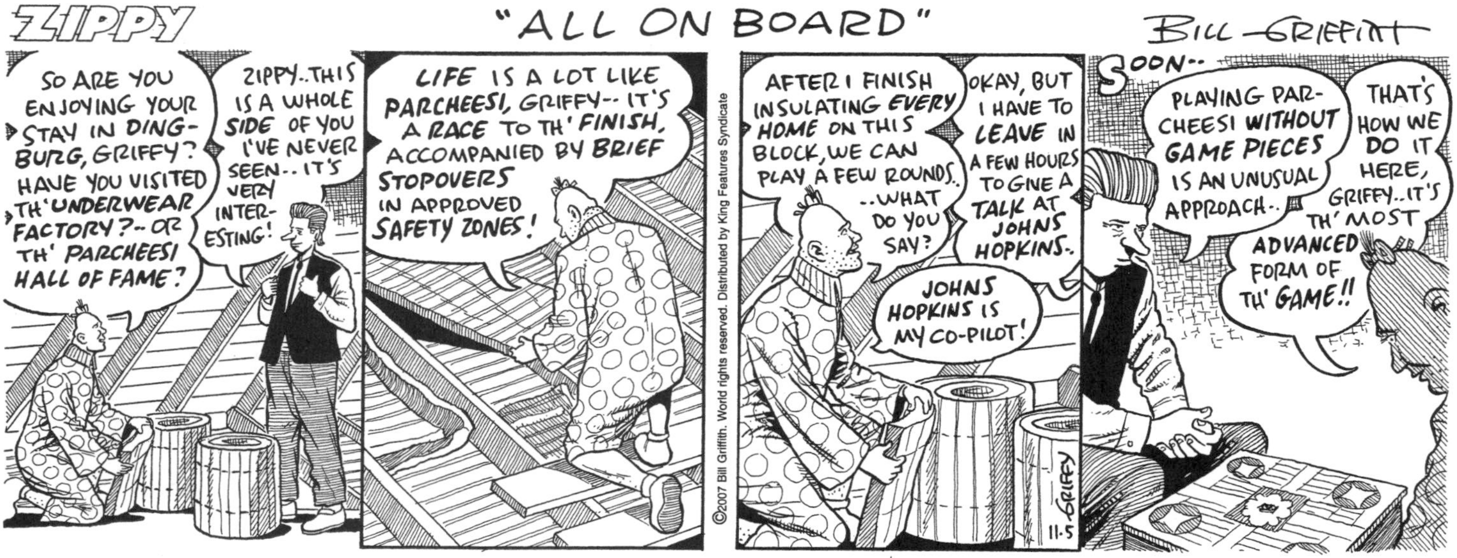
ZIPPY
"ALL ON BOARD"
BILL GRIFFITH
SO ARE YOU ENJOYING YOUR STAY IN DINGBURG, GRIFFY? HAVE YOU VISITED TH' UNDERWEAR FACTORY?-- OR TH' PARCHEESI HALL OF FAME?
ZIPPY..THIS IS A WHOLE SIDE OF YOU I'VE NEVER SEEN..IT'S VERY INTERESTING!
LIFE IS A LOT LIKE PARCHEESI, GRIFFY-- IT'S A RACE TO TH' FINISH, ACCOMPANIED BY BRIEF STOPOVERS IN APPROVED SAFETY ZONES!
©2007 Bill Griffith. World rights reserved. Distributed by King Features Syndicate
AFTER I FINISH INSULATING EVERY HOME ON THIS BLOCK, WE CAN PLAY A FEW ROUNDS.. ..WHAT DO YOU SAY?
OKAY, BUT I HAVE TO LEAVE IN A FEW HOURS TO GIVE A TALK AT JOHNS HOPKINS..
JOHNS HOPKINS IS MY CO-PILOT!
GRIFFY 11-5
SOON..
PLAYING PARCHEESI WITHOUT GAME PIECES IS AN UNUSUAL APPROACH..
THAT'S HOW WE DO IT HERE, GRIFFY..IT'S TH' MOST ADVANCED FORM OF TH' GAME!!

21

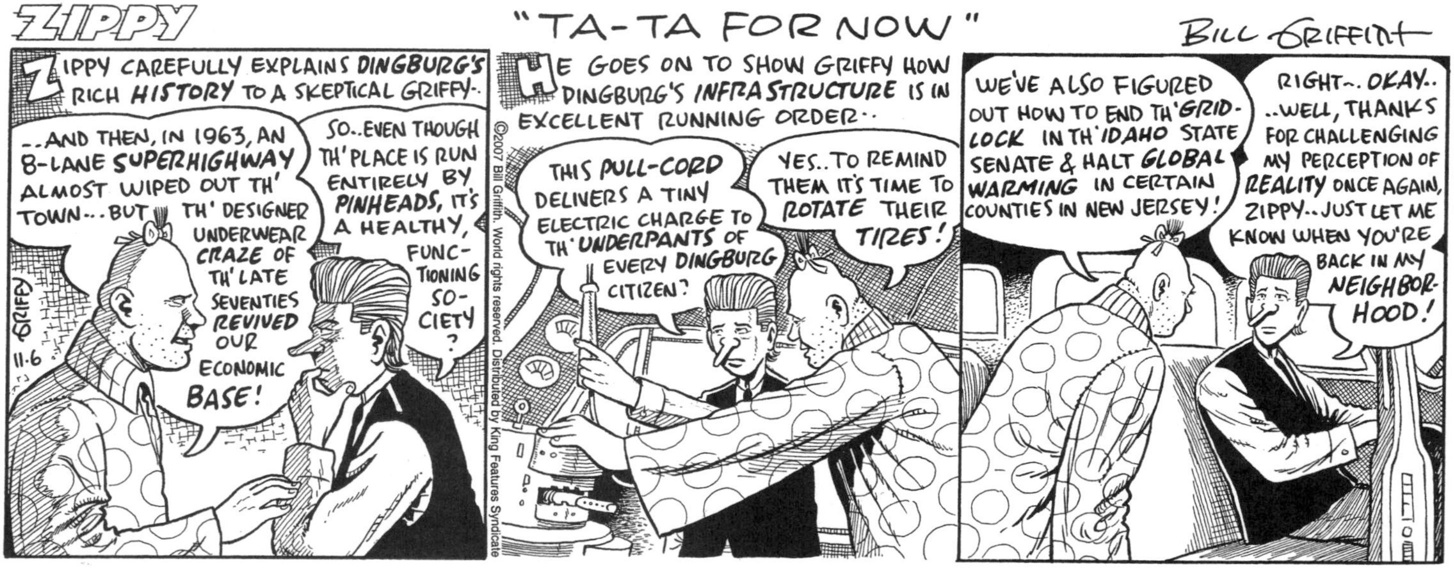
ZIPPY
"TA-TA FOR NOW"
BILL GRIFFITH
ZIPPY CAREFULLY EXPLAINS DINGBURG'S RICH HISTORY TO A SKEPTICAL GRIFFY..
..AND THEN, IN 1963, AN 8-LANE SUPERHIGHWAY ALMOST WIPED OUT TH' TOWN...BUT TH' DESIGNER UNDERWEAR CRAZE OF TH' LATE SEVENTIES REVIVED OUR ECONOMIC BASE!
SO..EVEN THOUGH TH' PLACE IS RUN ENTIRELY BY PINHEADS, IT'S A HEALTHY, FUNCTIONING SOCIETY?
GRIFFY 11-6
©2007 Bill Griffith. World rights reserved. Distributed by King Features Syndicate
HE GOES ON TO SHOW GRIFFY HOW DINGBURG'S INFRASTRUCTURE IS IN EXCELLENT RUNNING ORDER..
THIS PULL-CORD DELIVERS A TINY ELECTRIC CHARGE TO TH' UNDERPANTS OF EVERY DINGBURG CITIZEN?
YES..TO REMIND THEM IT'S TIME TO ROTATE THEIR TIRES!
WE'VE ALSO FIGURED OUT HOW TO END TH' GRIDLOCK IN TH' IDAHO STATE SENATE & HALT GLOBAL WARMING IN CERTAIN COUNTIES IN NEW JERSEY!
RIGHT-..OKAY.. ..WELL, THANKS FOR CHALLENGING MY PERCEPTION OF REALITY ONCE AGAIN, ZIPPY..JUST LET ME KNOW WHEN YOU'RE BACK IN MY NEIGHBORHOOD!

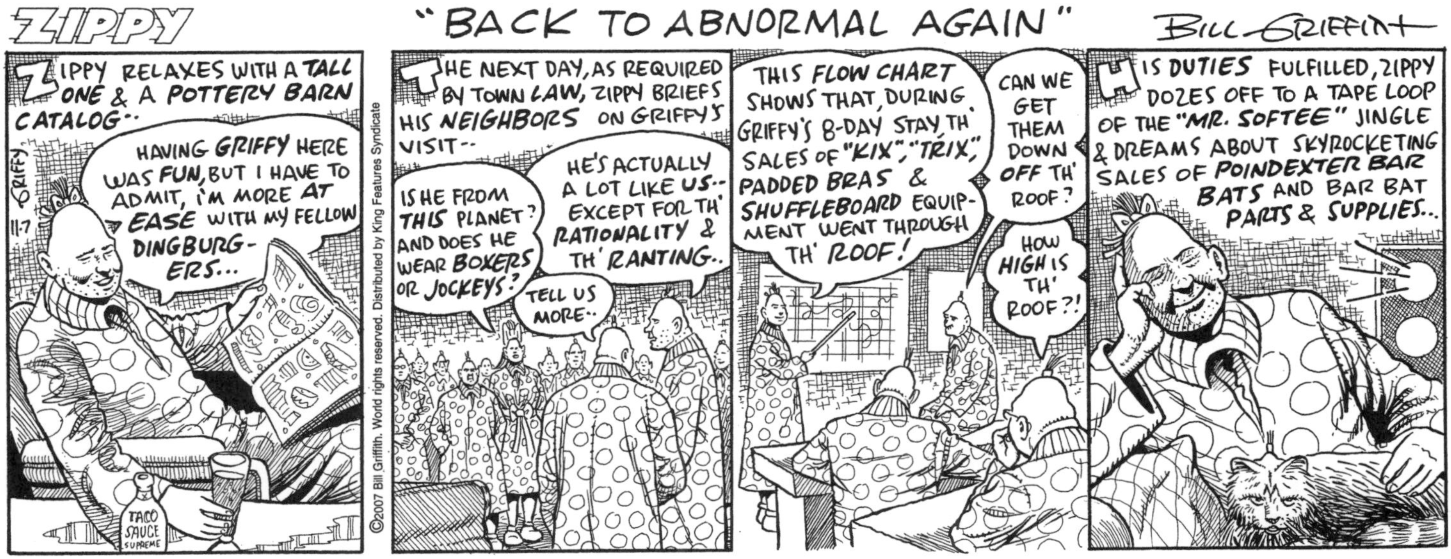
ZIPPY
"BACK TO ABNORMAL AGAIN"
BILL GRIFFITH
ZIPPY RELAXES WITH A TALL ONE & A POTTERY BARN CATALOG..
HAVING GRIFFY HERE WAS FUN, BUT I HAVE TO ADMIT, I'M MORE AT EASE WITH MY FELLOW DINGBURG-ERS...
GRIFFY
11-7
TACO SAUCE SUPREME
©2007 Bill Griffith. World rights reserved. Distributed by King Features Syndicate
THE NEXT DAY, AS REQUIRED BY TOWN LAW, ZIPPY BRIEFS HIS NEIGHBORS ON GRIFFY'S VISIT--
IS HE FROM THIS PLANET? AND DOES HE WEAR BOXERS OR JOCKEYS?
HE'S ACTUALLY A LOT LIKE US.. EXCEPT FOR TH' RATIONALITY & TH' RANTING..
TELL US MORE..
THIS FLOW CHART SHOWS THAT, DURING GRIFFY'S 8-DAY STAY, TH' SALES OF "KIX", "TRIX," PADDED BRAS & SHUFFLEBOARD EQUIPMENT WENT THROUGH TH' ROOF!
CAN WE GET THEM DOWN OFF TH' ROOF?
HOW HIGH IS TH' ROOF?!
HIS DUTIES FULFILLED, ZIPPY DOZES OFF TO A TAPE LOOP OF THE "MR. SOFTEE" JINGLE & DREAMS ABOUT SKYROCKETING SALES OF POINDEXTER BAR BATS AND BAR BAT PARTS & SUPPLIES...

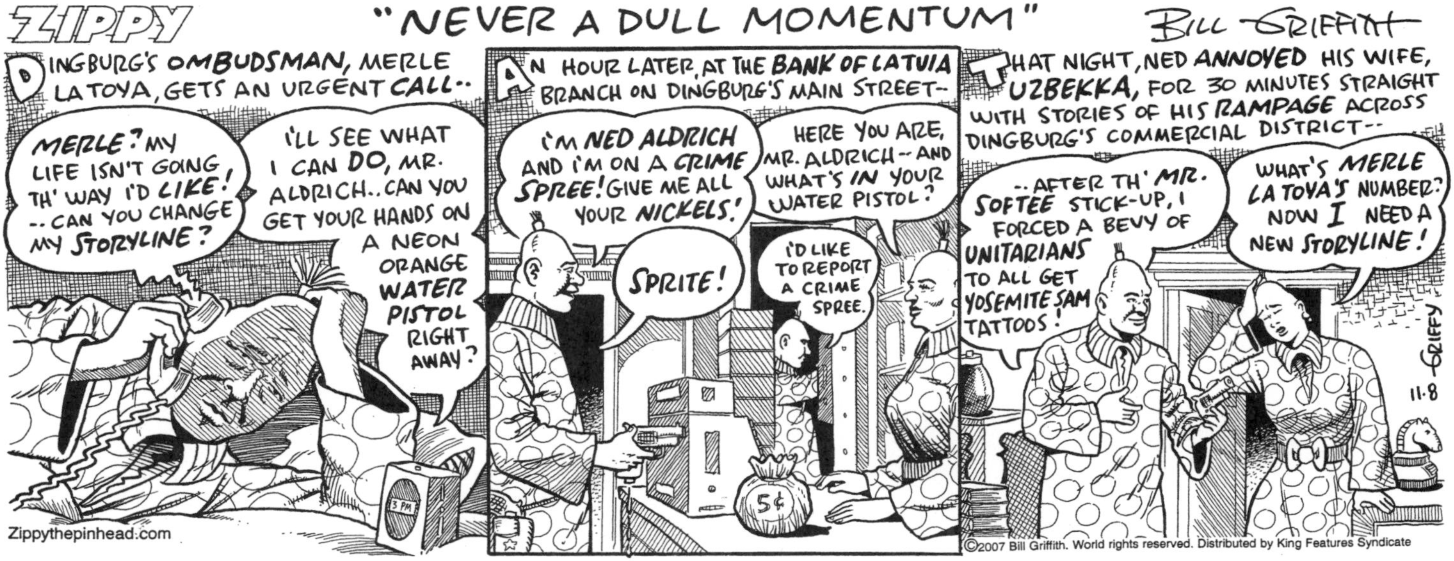
ZIPPY
"NEVER A DULL MOMENTUM"
BILL GRIFFITH
DINGBURG'S OMBUDSMAN, MERLE LATOYA, GETS AN URGENT CALL..
MERLE? MY LIFE ISN'T GOING TH' WAY I'D LIKE! -- CAN YOU CHANGE MY STORYLINE?
I'LL SEE WHAT I CAN DO, MR. ALDRICH.. CAN YOU GET YOUR HANDS ON A NEON ORANGE WATER PISTOL RIGHT AWAY?
3 PM
Zippythepinhead.com
AN HOUR LATER, AT THE BANK OF LATVIA BRANCH ON DINGBURG'S MAIN STREET--
I'M NED ALDRICH AND I'M ON A CRIME SPREE! GIVE ME ALL YOUR NICKELS!
HERE YOU ARE, MR. ALDRICH -- AND WHAT'S IN YOUR WATER PISTOL?
SPRITE!
I'D LIKE TO REPORT A CRIME SPREE.
5¢
THAT NIGHT, NED ANNOYED HIS WIFE, UZBEKKA, FOR 30 MINUTES STRAIGHT WITH STORIES OF HIS RAMPAGE ACROSS DINGBURG'S COMMERCIAL DISTRICT--
-- AFTER TH' MR. SOFTEE STICK-UP, I FORCED A BEVY OF UNITARIANS TO ALL GET YOSEMITE SAM TATTOOS!
WHAT'S MERLE LATOYA'S NUMBER? NOW I NEED A NEW STORYLINE!
GRIFFY
11-8
©2007 Bill Griffith. World rights reserved. Distributed by King Features Syndicate

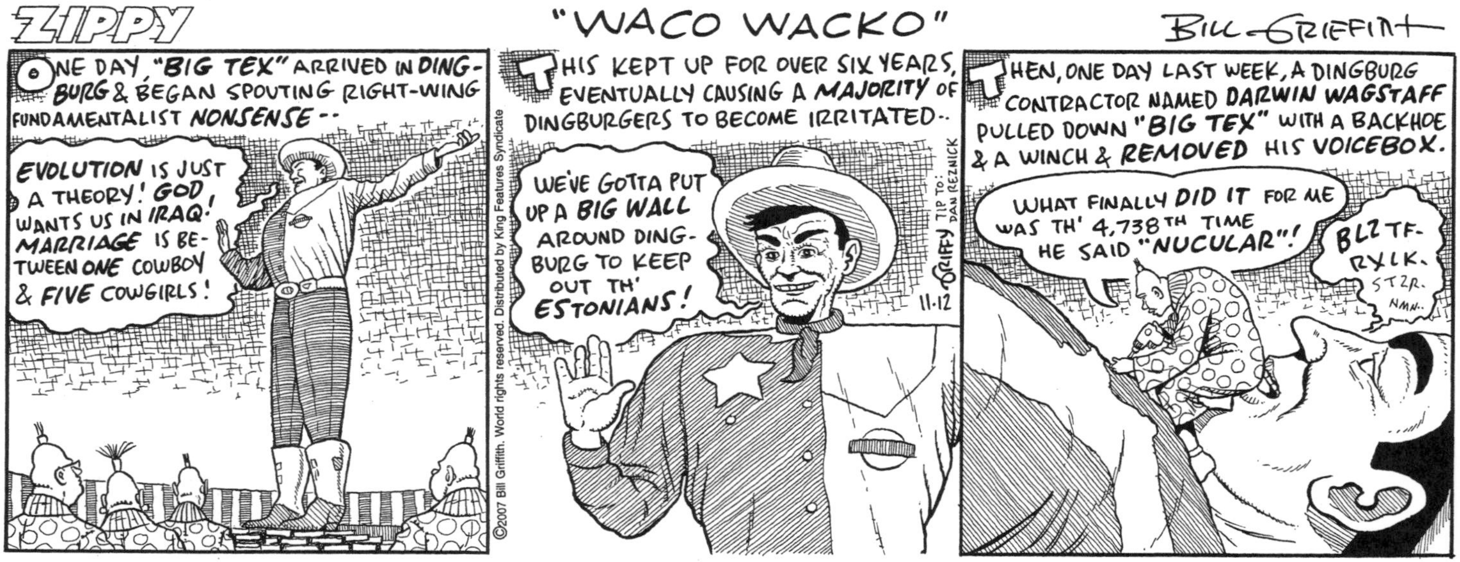
ZIPPY
"WACO WACKO"
BILL GRIFFITH
ONE DAY, "BIG TEX" ARRIVED IN DINGBURG & BEGAN SPOUTING RIGHT-WING FUNDAMENTALIST NONSENSE--
EVOLUTION IS JUST A THEORY! GOD WANTS US IN IRAQ! MARRIAGE IS BETWEEN ONE COWBOY & FIVE COWGIRLS!
©2007 Bill Griffith. World rights reserved. Distributed by King Features Syndicate
THIS KEPT UP FOR OVER SIX YEARS, EVENTUALLY CAUSING A MAJORITY OF DINGBURGERS TO BECOME IRRITATED--
WE'VE GOTTA PUT UP A BIG WALL AROUND DINGBURG TO KEEP OUT TH' ESTONIANS!
TIP TO: DAN REZNICK
GRIFFY
11-12
THEN, ONE DAY LAST WEEK, A DINGBURG CONTRACTOR NAMED DARWIN WAGSTAFF PULLED DOWN "BIG TEX" WITH A BACKHOE & A WINCH & REMOVED HIS VOICEBOX.
WHAT FINALLY DID IT FOR ME WAS TH' 4,738TH TIME HE SAID "NUCULAR"!
BLZTF-RXLK. STZR. NMN..

22

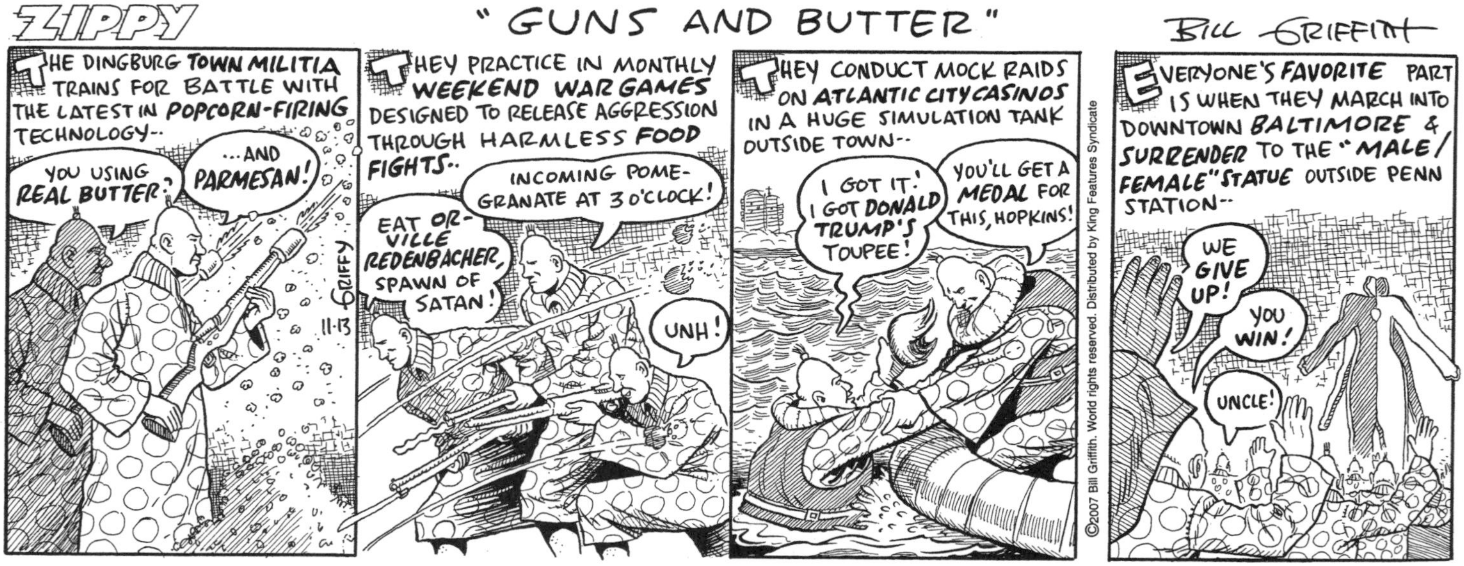
ZIPPY
"GUNS AND BUTTER"
BILL GRIFFITH
THE DINGBURG TOWN MILITIA TRAINS FOR BATTLE WITH THE LATEST IN POPCORN-FIRING TECHNOLOGY--
YOU USING REAL BUTTER?
...AND PARMESAN!
GRIFFY
11-13
THEY PRACTICE IN MONTHLY WEEKEND WAR GAMES DESIGNED TO RELEASE AGGRESSION THROUGH HARMLESS FOOD FIGHTS..
INCOMING POMEGRANATE AT 3 O'CLOCK!
EAT ORVILLE REDENBACHER, SPAWN OF SATAN!
UNH!
THEY CONDUCT MOCK RAIDS ON ATLANTIC CITY CASINOS IN A HUGE SIMULATION TANK OUTSIDE TOWN--
I GOT IT! I GOT DONALD TRUMP'S TOUPEE!
YOU'LL GET A MEDAL FOR THIS, HOPKINS!
©2007 Bill Griffith. World rights reserved. Distributed by King Features Syndicate
EVERYONE'S FAVORITE PART IS WHEN THEY MARCH INTO DOWNTOWN BALTIMORE & SURRENDER TO THE "MALE/FEMALE" STATUE OUTSIDE PENN STATION--
WE GIVE UP!
YOU WIN!
UNCLE!

23

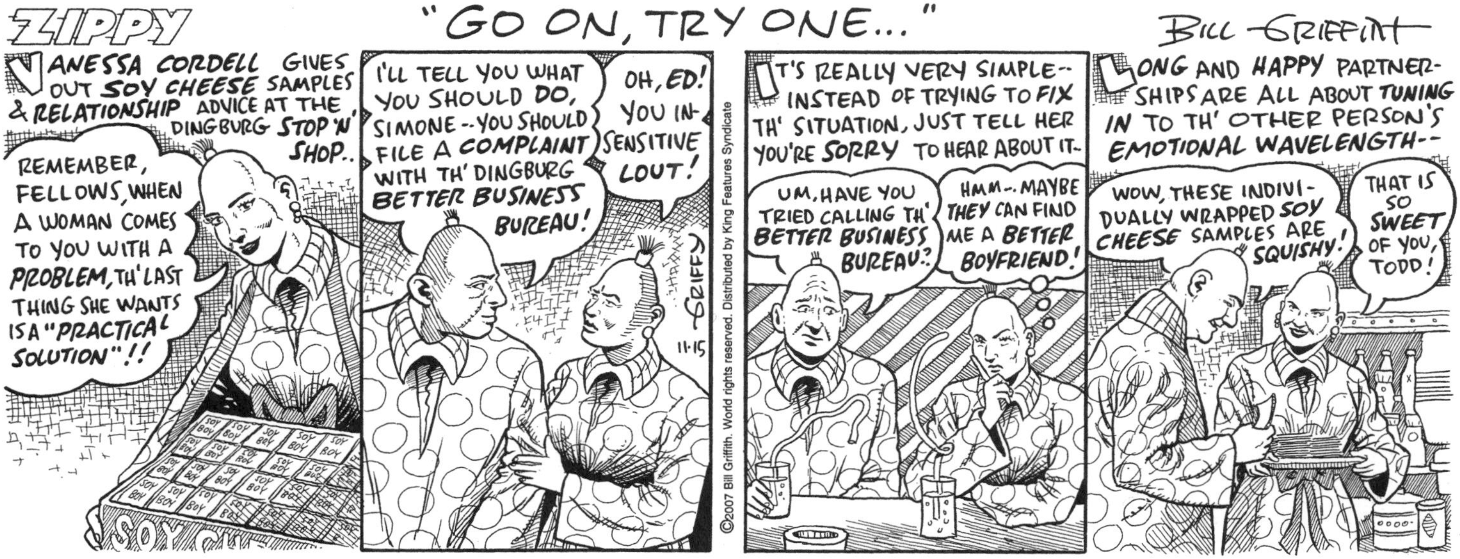
ZIPPY
"GO ON, TRY ONE..."
BILL GRIFFITH
VANESSA CORDELL GIVES OUT SOY CHEESE SAMPLES & RELATIONSHIP ADVICE AT THE DINGBURG STOP 'N' SHOP..
REMEMBER, FELLOWS, WHEN A WOMAN COMES TO YOU WITH A PROBLEM, TH' LAST THING SHE WANTS IS A "PRACTICAL SOLUTION"!!
I'LL TELL YOU WHAT YOU SHOULD DO, SIMONE -- YOU SHOULD FILE A COMPLAINT WITH TH' DINGBURG BETTER BUSINESS BUREAU!
OH, ED! YOU INSENSITIVE LOUT!
IT'S REALLY VERY SIMPLE-- INSTEAD OF TRYING TO FIX TH' SITUATION, JUST TELL HER YOU'RE SORRY TO HEAR ABOUT IT-
UM, HAVE YOU TRIED CALLING TH' BETTER BUSINESS BUREAU?
HMM-- MAYBE THEY CAN FIND ME A BETTER BOYFRIEND!
LONG AND HAPPY PARTNERSHIPS ARE ALL ABOUT TUNING IN TO TH' OTHER PERSON'S EMOTIONAL WAVELENGTH--
WOW, THESE INDIVIDUALLY WRAPPED SOY CHEESE SAMPLES ARE SQUISHY!
THAT IS SO SWEET OF YOU, TODD!
GRIFFY 11-15
©2007 Bill Griffith. World rights reserved. Distributed by King Features Syndicate

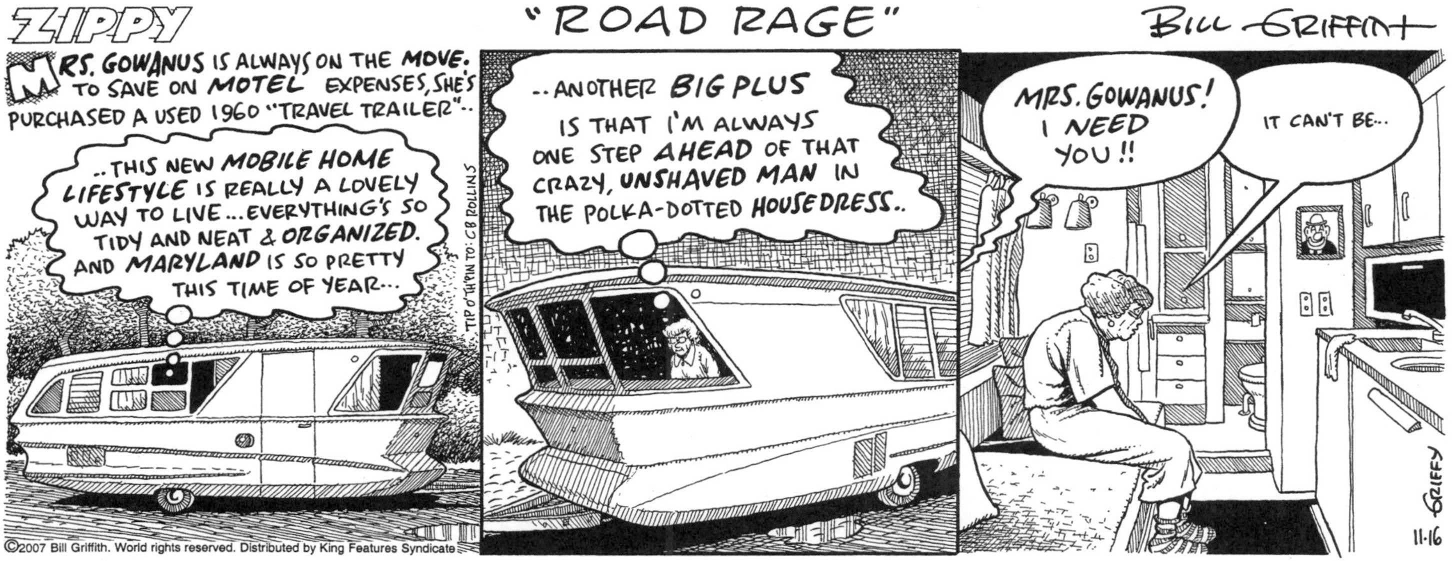
ZIPPY
"ROAD RAGE"
BILL GRIFFITH
MRS. GOWANUS IS ALWAYS ON THE MOVE. TO SAVE ON MOTEL EXPENSES, SHE'S PURCHASED A USED 1960 "TRAVEL TRAILER"..
..THIS NEW MOBILE HOME LIFESTYLE IS REALLY A LOVELY WAY TO LIVE...EVERYTHING'S SO TIDY AND NEAT & ORGANIZED. AND MARYLAND IS SO PRETTY THIS TIME OF YEAR...
TIP O' TH' PIN TO: C.B. ROLLINS
..ANOTHER BIG PLUS IS THAT I'M ALWAYS ONE STEP AHEAD OF THAT CRAZY, UNSHAVED MAN IN THE POLKA-DOTTED HOUSEDRESS..
MRS. GOWANUS! I NEED YOU!!
IT CAN'T BE..
GRIFFY 11-16
©2007 Bill Griffith. World rights reserved. Distributed by King Features Syndicate

24

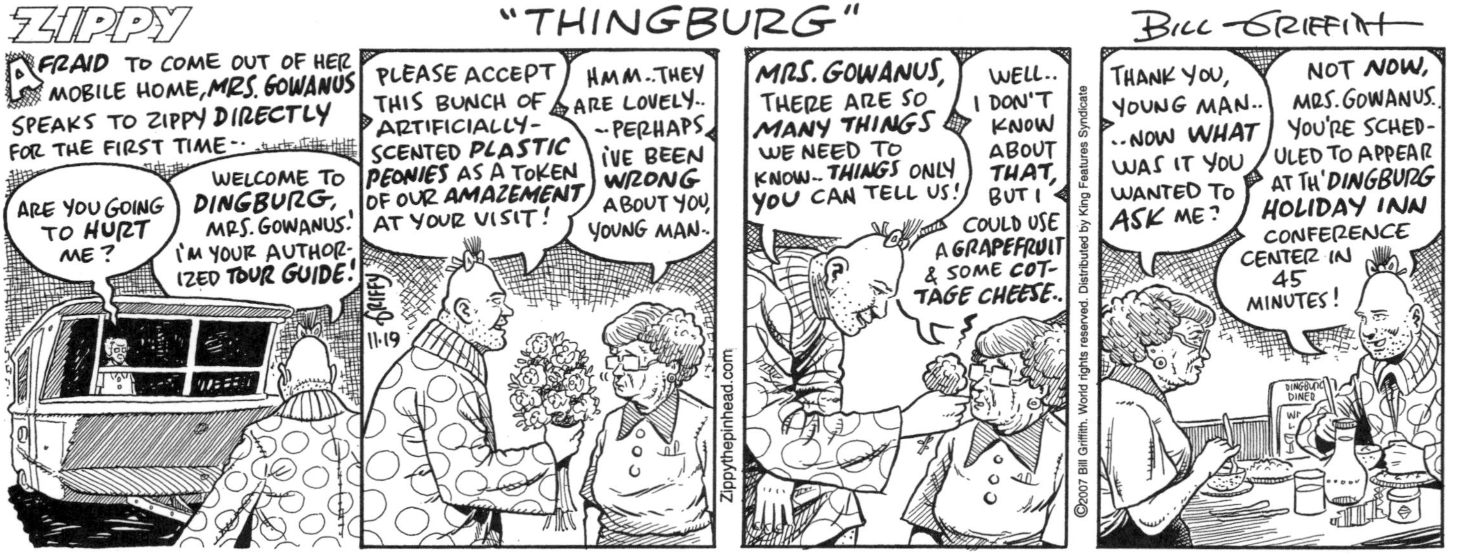
ZIPPY
"THINGBURG"
BILL GRIFFITH
AFRAID TO COME OUT OF HER MOBILE HOME, MRS. GOWANUS SPEAKS TO ZIPPY DIRECTLY FOR THE FIRST TIME--
ARE YOU GOING TO HURT ME?
WELCOME TO DINGBURG, MRS. GOWANUS! I'M YOUR AUTHORIZED TOUR GUIDE!
PLEASE ACCEPT THIS BUNCH OF ARTIFICIALLY-SCENTED PLASTIC PEONIES AS A TOKEN OF OUR AMAZEMENT AT YOUR VISIT!
HMM..THEY ARE LOVELY.. --PERHAPS I'VE BEEN WRONG ABOUT YOU, YOUNG MAN..
GRIFFY 11-19
Zippythepinhead.com
MRS. GOWANUS, THERE ARE SO MANY THINGS WE NEED TO KNOW.. THINGS ONLY YOU CAN TELL US!
WELL.. I DON'T KNOW ABOUT THAT, BUT I COULD USE A GRAPEFRUIT & SOME COTTAGE CHEESE..
©2007 Bill Griffith. World rights reserved. Distributed by King Features Syndicate
THANK YOU, YOUNG MAN.. ..NOW WHAT WAS IT YOU WANTED TO ASK ME?
NOT NOW, MRS. GOWANUS. YOU'RE SCHEDULED TO APPEAR AT TH' DINGBURG HOLIDAY INN CONFERENCE CENTER IN 45 MINUTES!
DINGBURG DINER

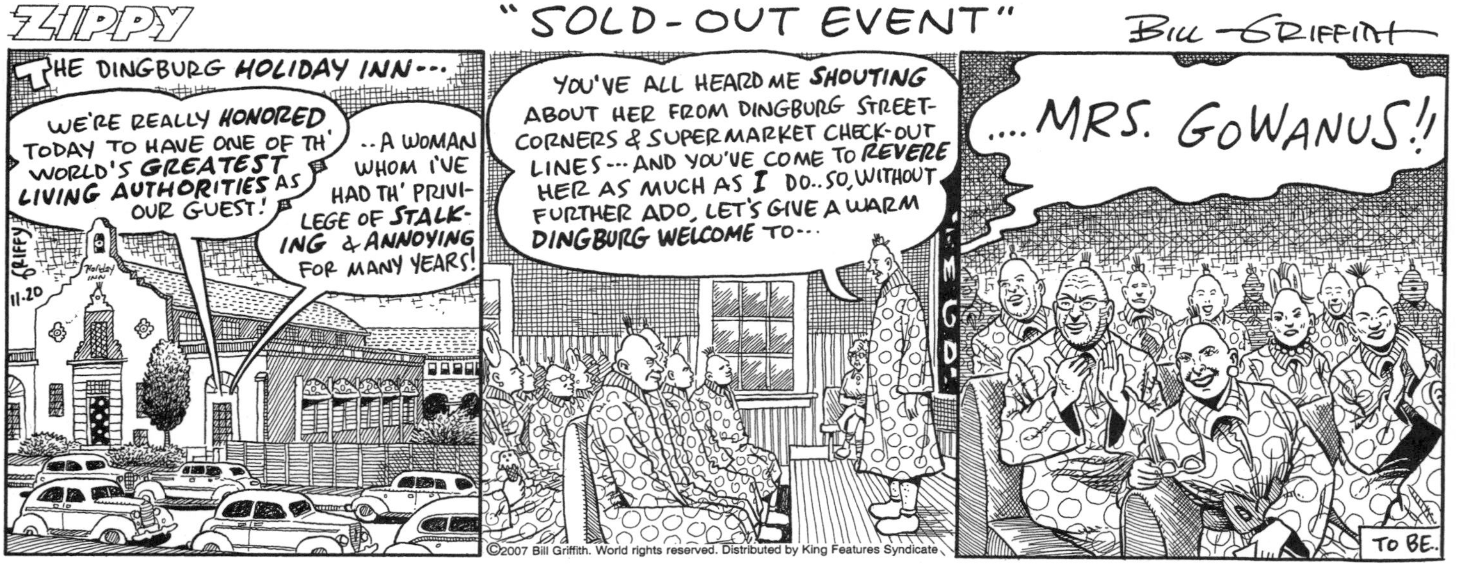
ZIPPY
"SOLD-OUT EVENT"
BILL GRIFFITH
THE DINGBURG HOLIDAY INN---
WE'RE REALLY HONORED TODAY TO HAVE ONE OF TH' WORLD'S GREATEST LIVING AUTHORITIES AS OUR GUEST!
..A WOMAN WHOM I'VE HAD TH' PRIVILEGE OF STALKING & ANNOYING FOR MANY YEARS!
GRIFFY 11-20
YOU'VE ALL HEARD ME SHOUTING ABOUT HER FROM DINGBURG STREET-CORNERS & SUPERMARKET CHECK-OUT LINES--- AND YOU'VE COME TO REVERE HER AS MUCH AS I DO.. SO, WITHOUT FURTHER ADO, LET'S GIVE A WARM DINGBURG WELCOME TO--
©2007 Bill Griffith. World rights reserved. Distributed by King Features Syndicate
....MRS. GOWANUS!!
TO BE.

25

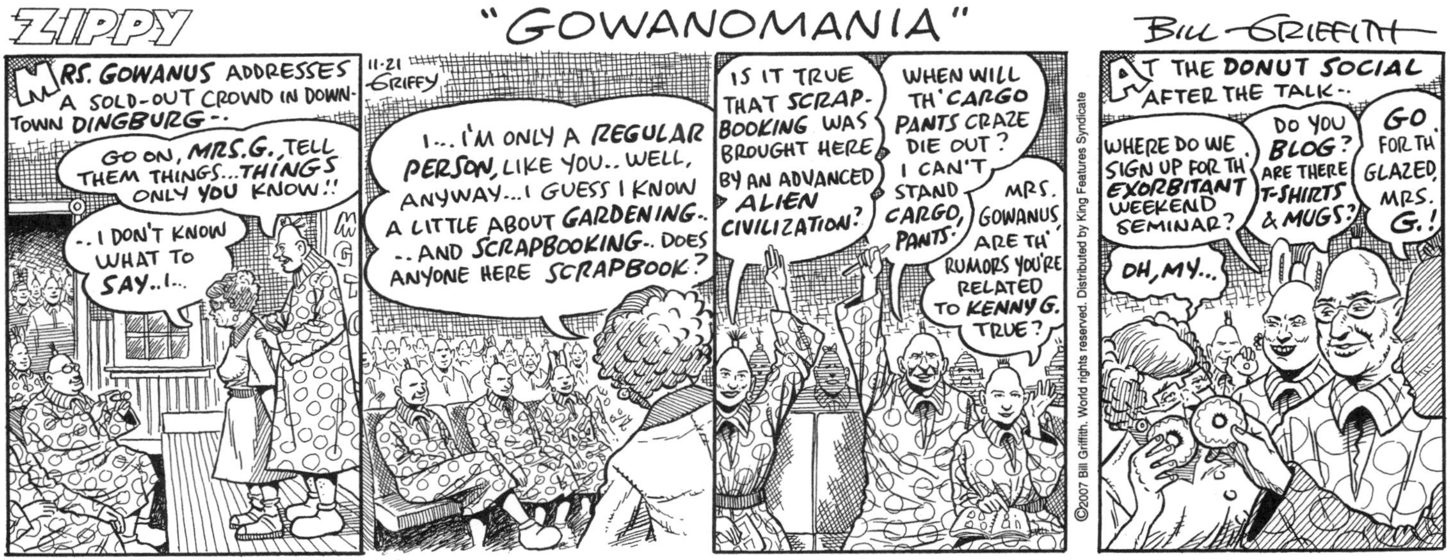
ZIPPY
"GOWANOMANIA"
BILL GRIFFITH
MRS. GOWANUS ADDRESSES A SOLD-OUT CROWD IN DOWNTOWN DINGBURG..
GO ON, MRS.G., TELL THEM THINGS...THINGS ONLY YOU KNOW!!
..I DON'T KNOW WHAT TO SAY..I...
11-21
GRIFFY
I... I'M ONLY A REGULAR PERSON, LIKE YOU.. WELL, ANYWAY...I GUESS I KNOW A LITTLE ABOUT GARDENING.. ..AND SCRAPBOOKING.. DOES ANYONE HERE SCRAPBOOK?
IS IT TRUE THAT SCRAPBOOKING WAS BROUGHT HERE BY AN ADVANCED ALIEN CIVILIZATION?
WHEN WILL TH' CARGO PANTS CRAZE DIE OUT? I CAN'T STAND CARGO PANTS!
MRS. GOWANUS, ARE TH' RUMORS YOU'RE RELATED TO KENNY G. TRUE?
©2007 Bill Griffith. World rights reserved. Distributed by King Features Syndicate
AT THE DONUT SOCIAL AFTER THE TALK..
WHERE DO WE SIGN UP FOR TH' EXORBITANT WEEKEND SEMINAR?
DO YOU BLOG? ARE THERE T-SHIRTS & MUGS?
GO FOR TH' GLAZED, MRS. G.!
OH, MY...

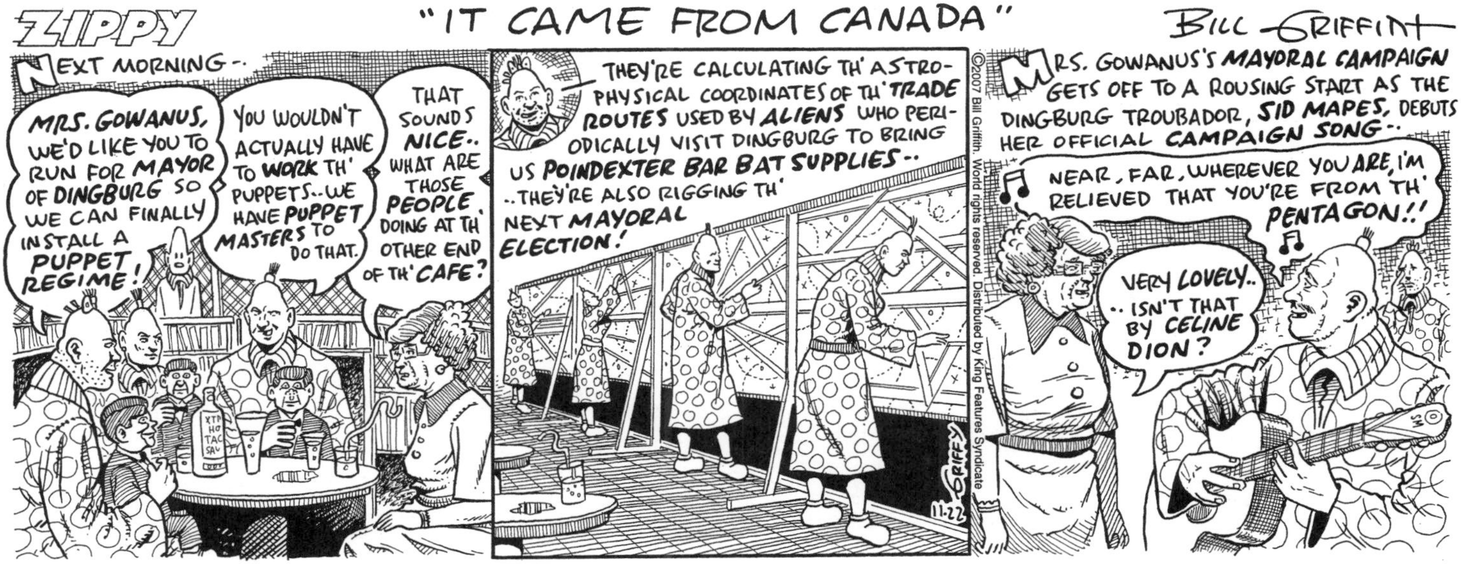
ZIPPY
"IT CAME FROM CANADA"
BILL GRIFFITH
NEXT MORNING..
MRS. GOWANUS, WE'D LIKE YOU TO RUN FOR MAYOR OF DINGBURG SO WE CAN FINALLY INSTALL A PUPPET REGIME!
YOU WOULDN'T ACTUALLY HAVE TO WORK TH' PUPPETS..WE HAVE PUPPET MASTERS TO DO THAT.
THAT SOUNDS NICE.. WHAT ARE THOSE PEOPLE DOING AT TH' OTHER END OF TH' CAFE?
THEY'RE CALCULATING TH' ASTROPHYSICAL COORDINATES OF TH' TRADE ROUTES USED BY ALIENS WHO PERIODICALLY VISIT DINGBURG TO BRING US POINDEXTER BAR BAT SUPPLIES.. ..THEY'RE ALSO RIGGING TH' NEXT MAYORAL ELECTION!
GRIFFY
11-22
©2007 Bill Griffith. World rights reserved. Distributed by King Features Syndicate
MRS. GOWANUS'S MAYORAL CAMPAIGN GETS OFF TO A ROUSING START AS THE DINGBURG TROUBADOR, SID MAPES, DEBUTS HER OFFICIAL CAMPAIGN SONG..
NEAR, FAR, WHEREVER YOU ARE, I'M RELIEVED THAT YOU'RE FROM TH' PENTAGON!!
VERY LOVELY.. ..ISN'T THAT BY CELINE DION?

26

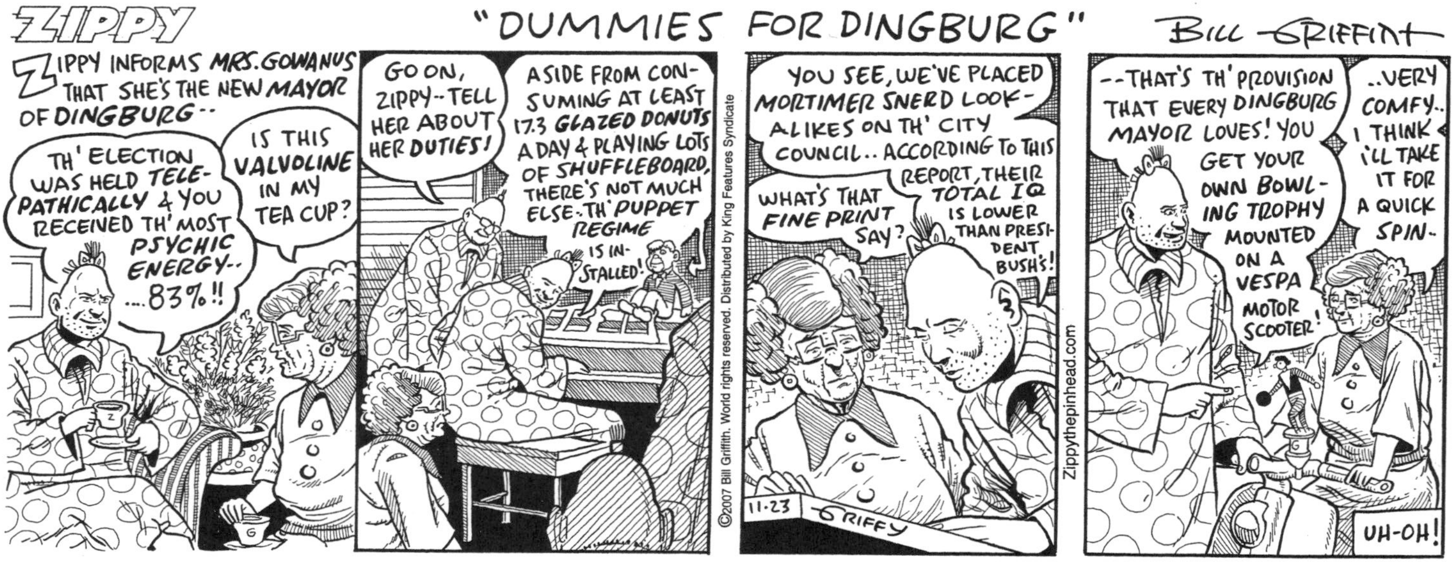
ZIPPY
"DUMMIES FOR DINGBURG"
BILL GRIFFITH
ZIPPY INFORMS MRS. GOWANUS THAT SHE'S THE NEW MAYOR OF DINGBURG--
TH' ELECTION WAS HELD TELEPATHICALLY & YOU RECEIVED TH' MOST PSYCHIC ENERGY-- ....83%!!
IS THIS VALVOLINE IN MY TEA CUP?
GO ON, ZIPPY--TELL HER ABOUT HER DUTIES!
ASIDE FROM CONSUMING AT LEAST 17.3 GLAZED DONUTS A DAY & PLAYING LOTS OF SHUFFLEBOARD, THERE'S NOT MUCH ELSE--TH' PUPPET REGIME IS INSTALLED!
©2007 Bill Griffith. World rights reserved. Distributed by King Features Syndicate
YOU SEE, WE'VE PLACED MORTIMER SNERD LOOK-ALIKES ON TH' CITY COUNCIL.. ACCORDING TO THIS REPORT, THEIR TOTAL IQ IS LOWER THAN PRESIDENT BUSH'S!
WHAT'S THAT FINE PRINT SAY?
11-23
GRIFFY
Zippythepinhead.com
--THAT'S TH' PROVISION THAT EVERY DINGBURG MAYOR LOVES! YOU GET YOUR OWN BOWLING TROPHY MOUNTED ON A VESPA MOTOR SCOOTER!
..VERY COMFY.. I THINK I'LL TAKE IT FOR A QUICK SPIN--
UH-OH!

27

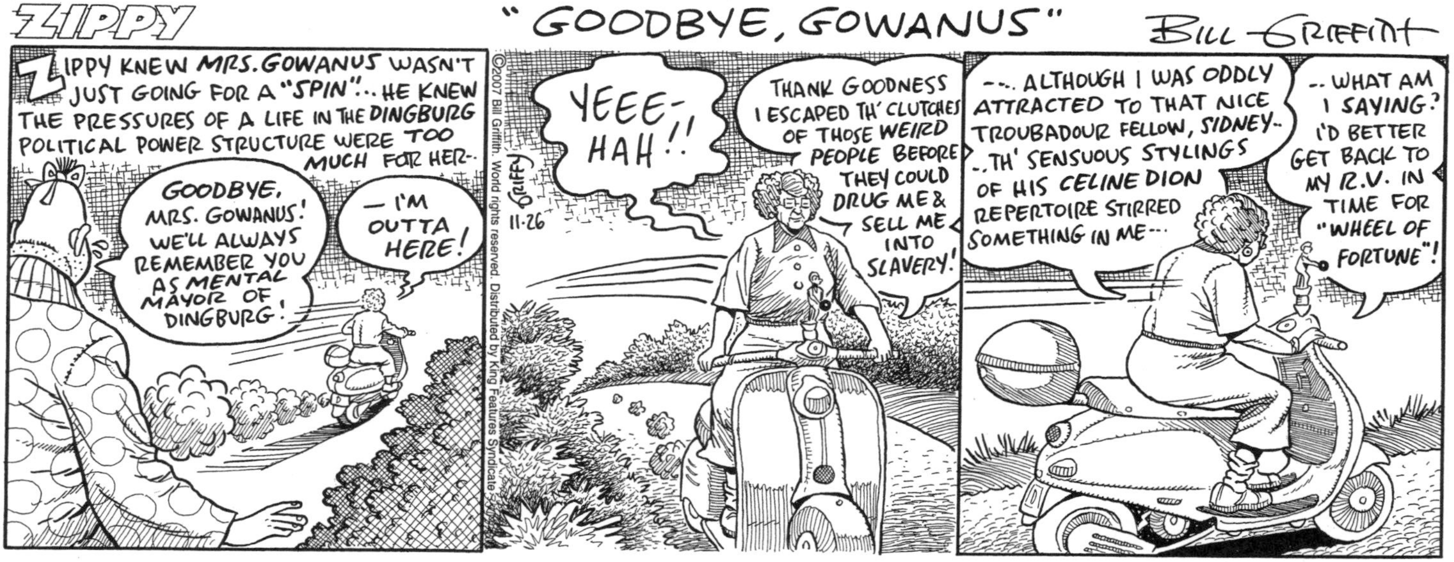
ZIPPY
"GOODBYE, GOWANUS"
BILL GRIFFITH
ZIPPY KNEW MRS. GOWANUS WASN'T JUST GOING FOR A "SPIN".. HE KNEW THE PRESSURES OF A LIFE IN THE DINGBURG POLITICAL POWER STRUCTURE WERE TOO MUCH FOR HER--
GOODBYE, MRS. GOWANUS! WE'LL ALWAYS REMEMBER YOU AS MENTAL MAYOR OF DINGBURG!
-I'M OUTTA HERE!
©2007 Bill Griffith. World rights reserved. Distributed by King Features Syndicate
GRIFFY
11-26
YEEE-HAH!!
THANK GOODNESS I ESCAPED TH' CLUTCHES OF THOSE WEIRD PEOPLE BEFORE THEY COULD DRUG ME & SELL ME INTO SLAVERY!
--.. ALTHOUGH I WAS ODDLY ATTRACTED TO THAT NICE TROUBADOUR FELLOW, SIDNEY.. ..TH' SENSUOUS STYLINGS OF HIS CELINE DION REPERTOIRE STIRRED SOMETHING IN ME--
--WHAT AM I SAYING? I'D BETTER GET BACK TO MY R.V. IN TIME FOR "WHEEL OF FORTUNE"!

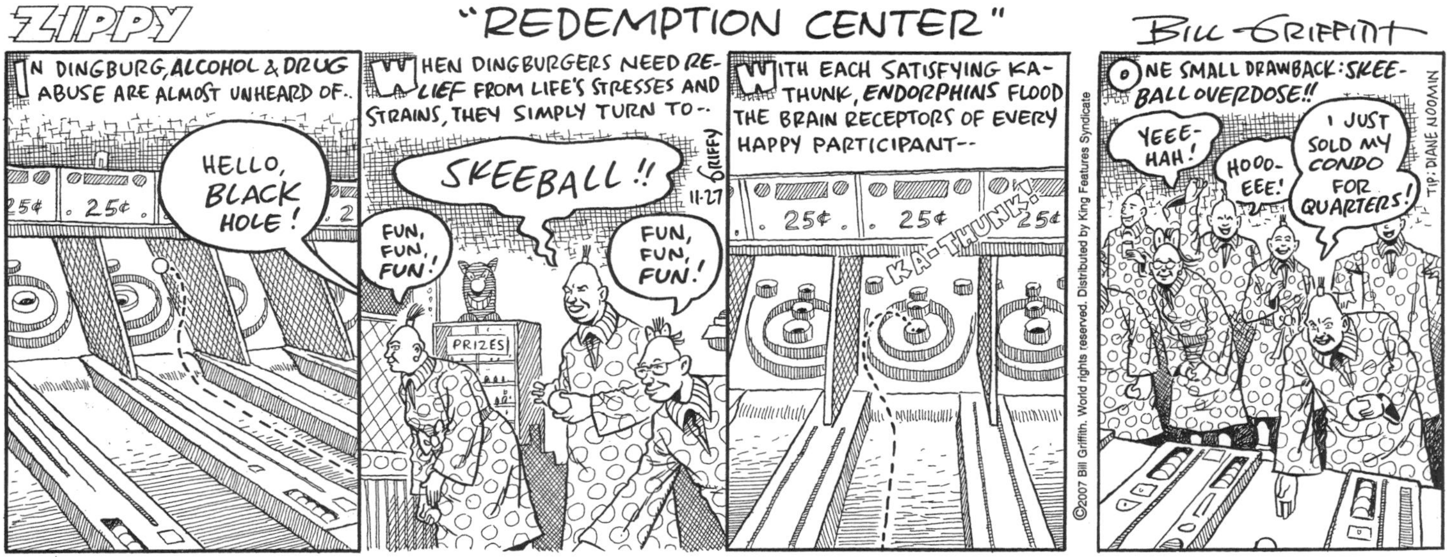
ZIPPY
"REDEMPTION CENTER"
BILL GRIFFITH
IN DINGBURG, ALCOHOL & DRUG ABUSE ARE ALMOST UNHEARD OF..
HELLO, BLACK HOLE!
25¢ 25¢
WHEN DINGBURGERS NEED RELIEF FROM LIFE'S STRESSES AND STRAINS, THEY SIMPLY TURN TO--
SKEEBALL!!
FUN, FUN, FUN!
FUN, FUN, FUN!
PRIZES
GRIFFY 11-27
WITH EACH SATISFYING KA-THUNK, ENDORPHINS FLOOD THE BRAIN RECEPTORS OF EVERY HAPPY PARTICIPANT--
KA-THUNK!
25¢ 25¢ 25¢
©2007 Bill Griffith. World rights reserved. Distributed by King Features Syndicate
ONE SMALL DRAWBACK: SKEE-BALL OVERDOSE!!
YEEE-HAH!
HOOO-EEE!
I JUST SOLD MY CONDO FOR QUARTERS!
TIP: DIANE NOOMIN

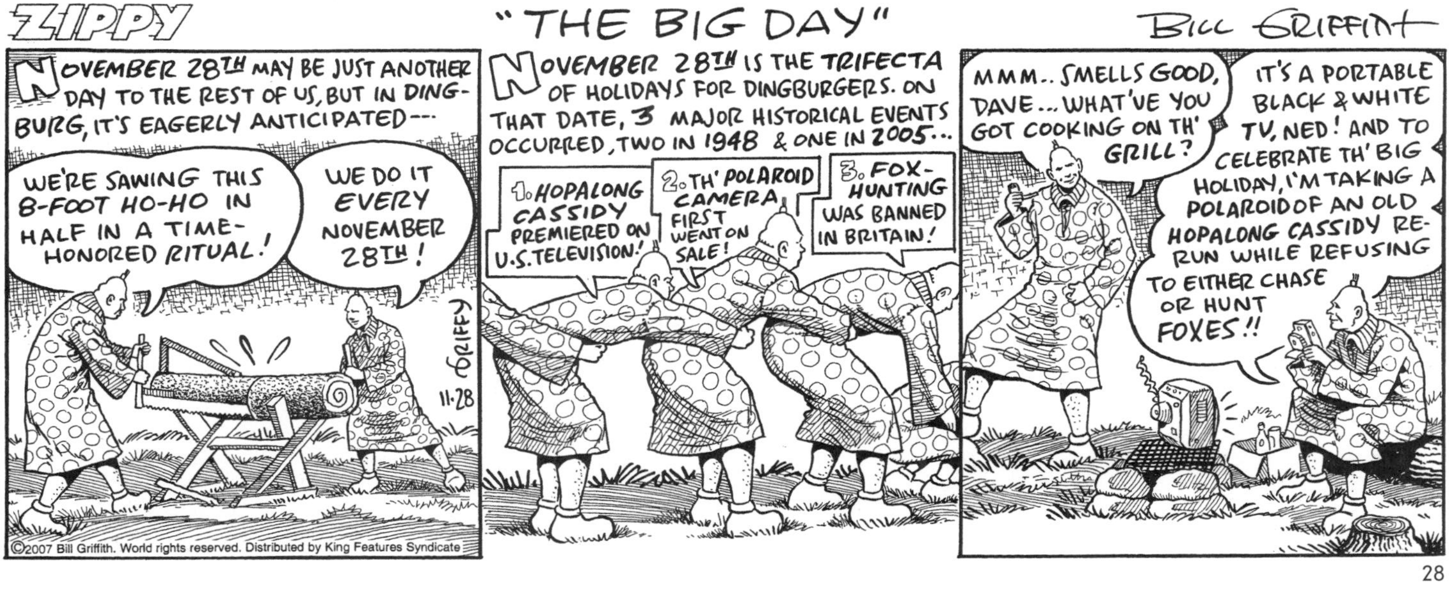
ZIPPY
"THE BIG DAY"
BILL GRIFFITH
NOVEMBER 28TH MAY BE JUST ANOTHER DAY TO THE REST OF US, BUT IN DINGBURG, IT'S EAGERLY ANTICIPATED---
WE'RE SAWING THIS 8-FOOT HO-HO IN HALF IN A TIME-HONORED RITUAL!
WE DO IT EVERY NOVEMBER 28TH!
GRIFFY 11-28
©2007 Bill Griffith. World rights reserved. Distributed by King Features Syndicate
NOVEMBER 28TH IS THE TRIFECTA OF HOLIDAYS FOR DINGBURGERS. ON THAT DATE, 3 MAJOR HISTORICAL EVENTS OCCURRED, TWO IN 1948 & ONE IN 2005..
1. HOPALONG CASSIDY PREMIERED ON U.S. TELEVISION!
2. TH' POLAROID CAMERA FIRST WENT ON SALE!
3. FOX-HUNTING WAS BANNED IN BRITAIN!
MMM.. SMELLS GOOD, DAVE... WHAT'VE YOU GOT COOKING ON TH' GRILL?
IT'S A PORTABLE BLACK & WHITE TV, NED! AND TO CELEBRATE TH' BIG HOLIDAY, I'M TAKING A POLAROID OF AN OLD HOPALONG CASSIDY RE-RUN WHILE REFUSING TO EITHER CHASE OR HUNT FOXES!!

28

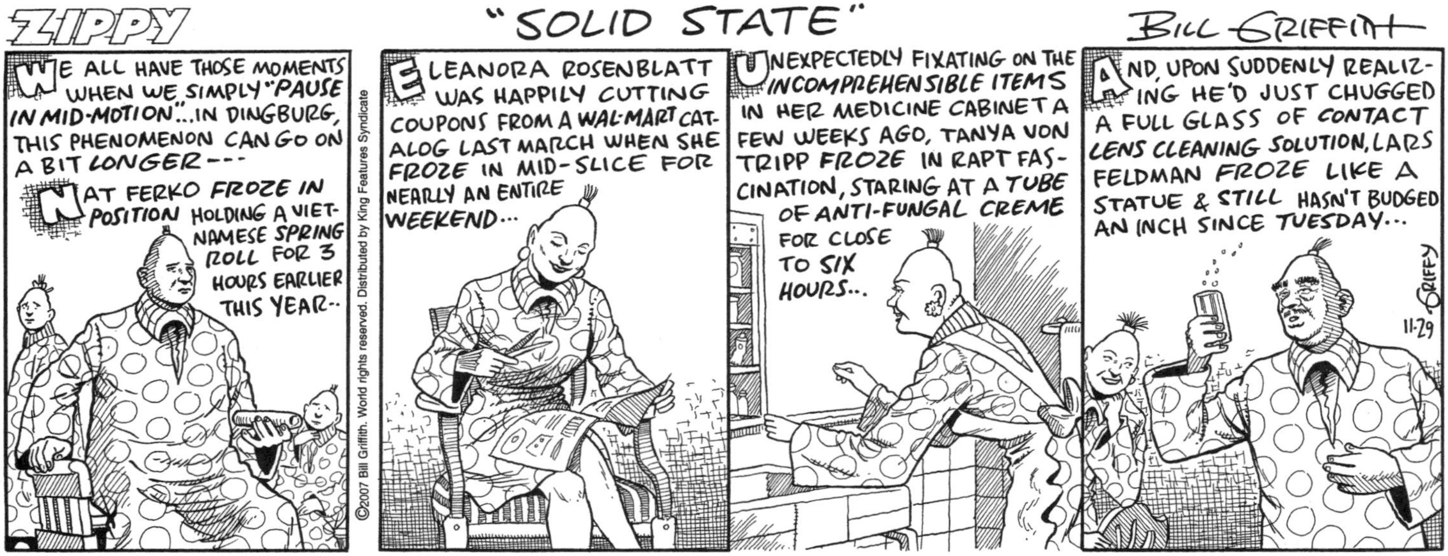
ZIPPY
"SOLID STATE"
BILL GRIFFITH
WE ALL HAVE THOSE MOMENTS WHEN WE SIMPLY "PAUSE IN MID-MOTION"...IN DINGBURG, THIS PHENOMENON CAN GO ON A BIT LONGER---
NAT FERKO FROZE IN POSITION HOLDING A VIETNAMESE SPRING ROLL FOR 3 HOURS EARLIER THIS YEAR..
©2007 Bill Griffith. World rights reserved. Distributed by King Features Syndicate
ELEANORA ROSENBLATT WAS HAPPILY CUTTING COUPONS FROM A WAL-MART CATALOG LAST MARCH WHEN SHE FROZE IN MID-SLICE FOR NEARLY AN ENTIRE WEEKEND...
UNEXPECTEDLY FIXATING ON THE INCOMPREHENSIBLE ITEMS IN HER MEDICINE CABINET A FEW WEEKS AGO, TANYA VON TRIPP FROZE IN RAPT FASCINATION, STARING AT A TUBE OF ANTI-FUNGAL CREME FOR CLOSE TO SIX HOURS...
AND, UPON SUDDENLY REALIZING HE'D JUST CHUGGED A FULL GLASS OF CONTACT LENS CLEANING SOLUTION, LARS FELDMAN FROZE LIKE A STATUE & STILL HASN'T BUDGED AN INCH SINCE TUESDAY...
GRIFFY
11-29

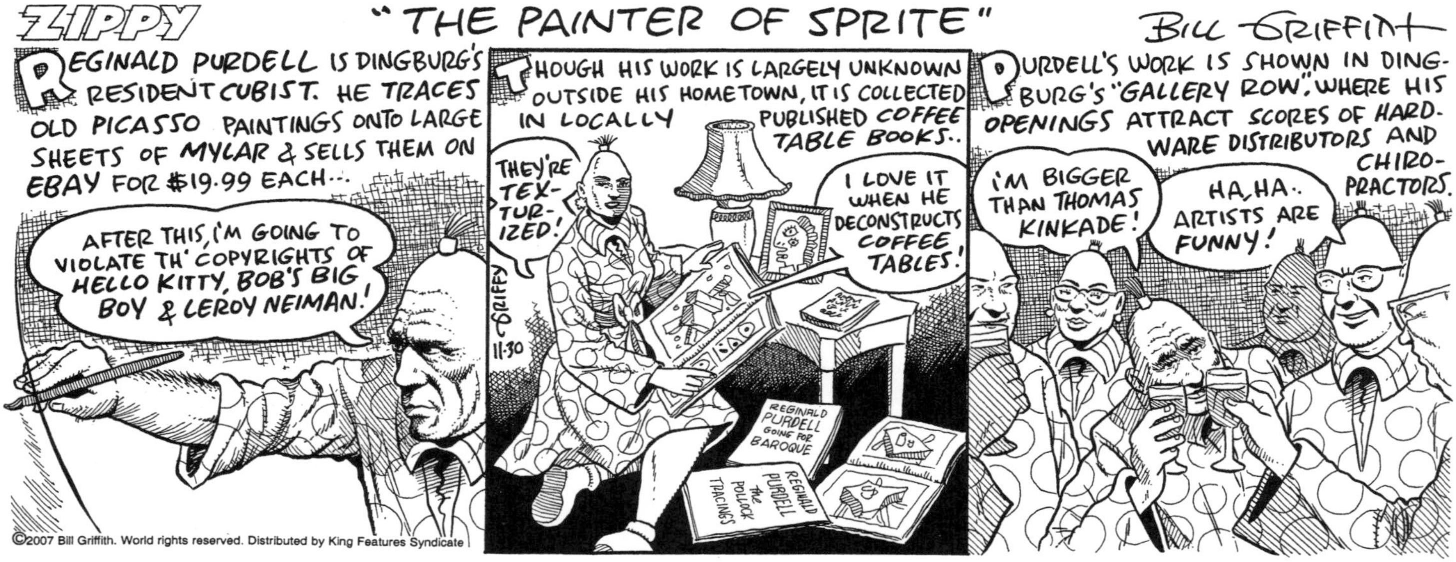
ZIPPY
"THE PAINTER OF SPRITE"
BILL GRIFFITH
REGINALD PURDELL IS DINGBURG'S RESIDENT CUBIST. HE TRACES OLD PICASSO PAINTINGS ONTO LARGE SHEETS OF MYLAR & SELLS THEM ON EBAY FOR $19.99 EACH...
AFTER THIS, I'M GOING TO VIOLATE TH' COPYRIGHTS OF HELLO KITTY, BOB'S BIG BOY & LEROY NEIMAN!
©2007 Bill Griffith. World rights reserved. Distributed by King Features Syndicate
THOUGH HIS WORK IS LARGELY UNKNOWN OUTSIDE HIS HOMETOWN, IT IS COLLECTED IN LOCALLY PUBLISHED COFFEE TABLE BOOKS..
THEY'RE TEXTURIZED!
I LOVE IT WHEN HE DECONSTRUCTS COFFEE TABLES!
GRIFFY
11-30
REGINALD PURDELL GOING FOR BAROQUE
REGINALD PURDELL THE POLLOCK TRACINGS
PURDELL'S WORK IS SHOWN IN DINGBURG'S "GALLERY ROW", WHERE HIS OPENINGS ATTRACT SCORES OF HARDWARE DISTRIBUTORS AND CHIROPRACTORS.
I'M BIGGER THAN THOMAS KINKADE!
HA, HA.. ARTISTS ARE FUNNY!

29

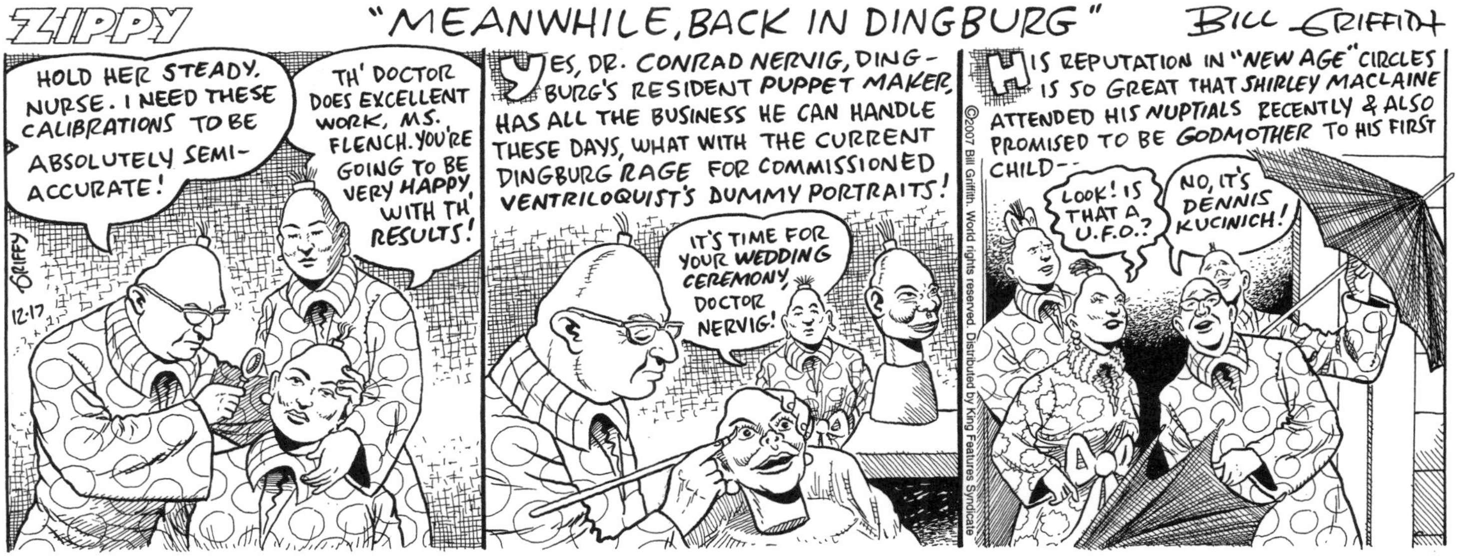
ZIPPY
"MEANWHILE, BACK IN DINGBURG"
BILL GRIFFITH
HOLD HER STEADY, NURSE. I NEED THESE CALIBRATIONS TO BE ABSOLUTELY SEMI-ACCURATE!
TH' DOCTOR DOES EXCELLENT WORK, MS. FLENCH. YOU'RE GOING TO BE VERY HAPPY WITH TH' RESULTS!
GRIFFY 12·17
YES, DR. CONRAD NERVIG, DINGBURG'S RESIDENT PUPPET MAKER, HAS ALL THE BUSINESS HE CAN HANDLE THESE DAYS, WHAT WITH THE CURRENT DINGBURG RAGE FOR COMMISSIONED VENTRILOQUIST'S DUMMY PORTRAITS!
IT'S TIME FOR YOUR WEDDING CEREMONY, DOCTOR NERVIG!
©2007 Bill Griffith. World rights reserved. Distributed by King Features Syndicate
HIS REPUTATION IN "NEW AGE" CIRCLES IS SO GREAT THAT SHIRLEY MACLAINE ATTENDED HIS NUPTIALS RECENTLY & ALSO PROMISED TO BE GODMOTHER TO HIS FIRST CHILD--
LOOK! IS THAT A U.F.O.?
NO, IT'S DENNIS KUCINICH!
30

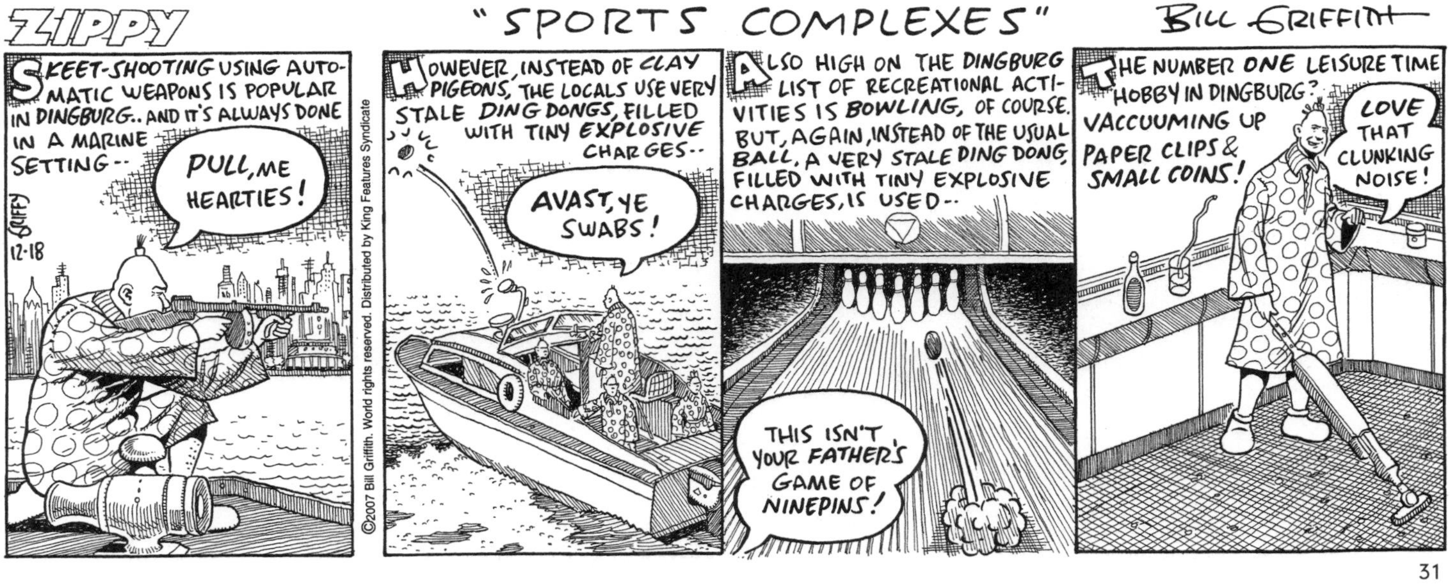
ZIPPY
"SPORTS COMPLEXES"
BILL GRIFFITH
SKEET-SHOOTING USING AUTOMATIC WEAPONS IS POPULAR IN DINGBURG.. AND IT'S ALWAYS DONE IN A MARINE SETTING--
PULL, ME HEARTIES!
GRIFFY 12·18
©2007 Bill Griffith. World rights reserved. Distributed by King Features Syndicate
HOWEVER, INSTEAD OF CLAY PIGEONS, THE LOCALS USE VERY STALE DING DONGS, FILLED WITH TINY EXPLOSIVE CHARGES--
AVAST, YE SWABS!
ALSO HIGH ON THE DINGBURG LIST OF RECREATIONAL ACTIVITIES IS BOWLING, OF COURSE. BUT, AGAIN, INSTEAD OF THE USUAL BALL, A VERY STALE DING DONG, FILLED WITH TINY EXPLOSIVE CHARGES, IS USED--
THIS ISN'T YOUR FATHER'S GAME OF NINEPINS!
THE NUMBER ONE LEISURE TIME HOBBY IN DINGBURG? VACCUUMING UP PAPER CLIPS & SMALL COINS!
LOVE THAT CLUNKING NOISE!
31

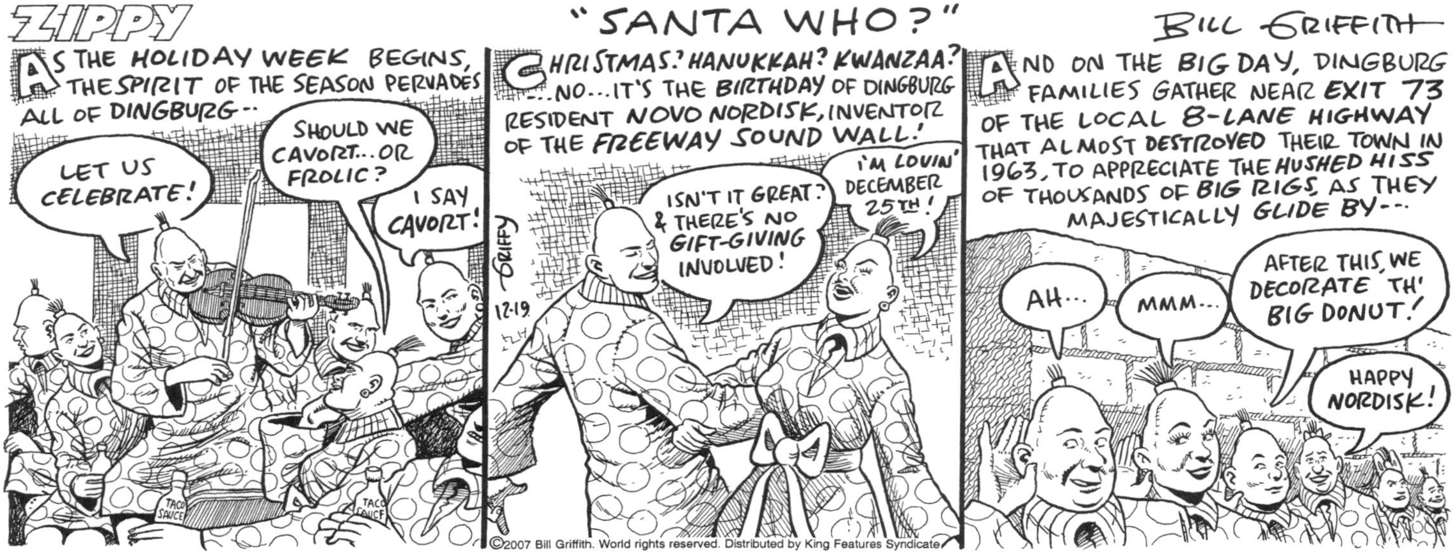
ZIPPY
"SANTA WHO?"
BILL GRIFFITH
AS THE HOLIDAY WEEK BEGINS, THE SPIRIT OF THE SEASON PERVADES ALL OF DINGBURG--
LET US CELEBRATE!
SHOULD WE CAVORT... OR FROLIC?
I SAY CAVORT!
TACO SAUCE
TACO SAUCE
GRIFFY
12-19
CHRISTMAS? HANUKKAH? KWANZAA? ... NO... IT'S THE BIRTHDAY OF DINGBURG RESIDENT NOVO NORDISK, INVENTOR OF THE FREEWAY SOUND WALL!
ISN'T IT GREAT? & THERE'S NO GIFT-GIVING INVOLVED!
I'M LOVIN' DECEMBER 25TH!
AND ON THE BIG DAY, DINGBURG FAMILIES GATHER NEAR EXIT 73 OF THE LOCAL 8-LANE HIGHWAY THAT ALMOST DESTROYED THEIR TOWN IN 1963, TO APPRECIATE THE HUSHED HISS OF THOUSANDS OF BIG RIGS, AS THEY MAJESTICALLY GLIDE BY--
AH...
MMM...
AFTER THIS, WE DECORATE TH' BIG DONUT!
HAPPY NORDISK!
©2007 Bill Griffith. World rights reserved. Distributed by King Features Syndicate

32

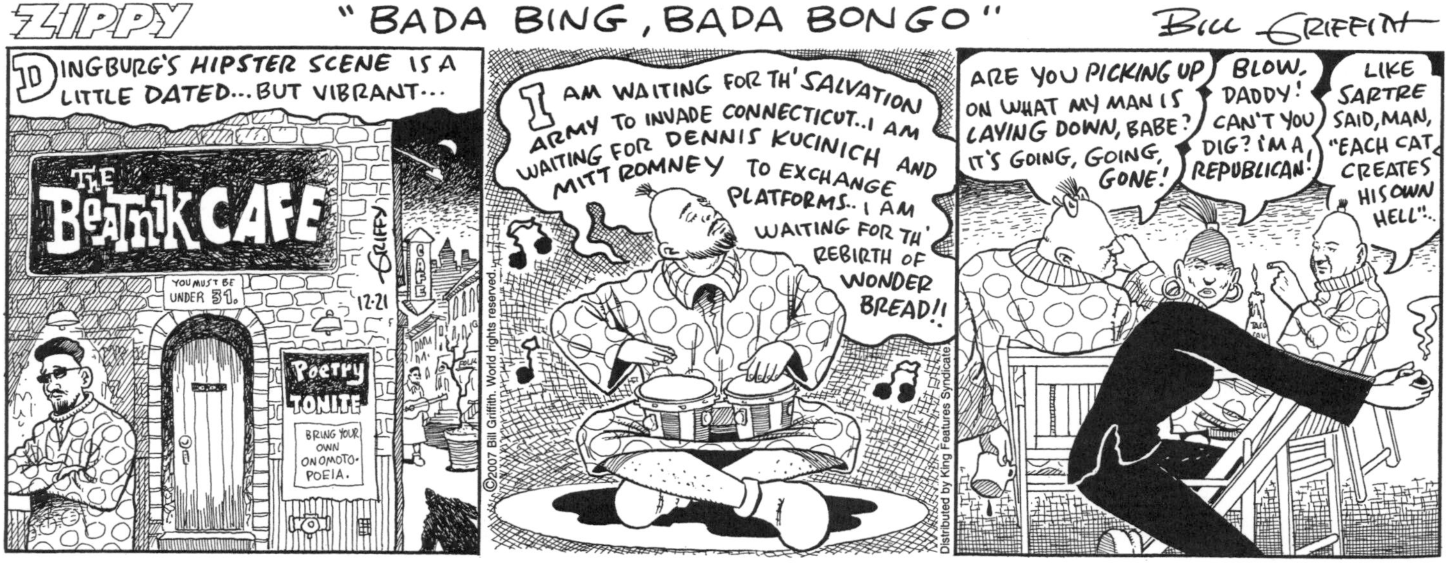
ZIPPY
"BADA BING, BADA BONGO"
BILL GRIFFITH
DINGBURG'S HIPSTER SCENE IS A LITTLE DATED... BUT VIBRANT...
THE BEATNIK CAFE
YOU MUST BE UNDER 31.
GRIFFY
12-21
CAFE
Poetry TONITE
BRING YOUR OWN ONOMOTOPOEIA.
I AM WAITING FOR TH' SALVATION ARMY TO INVADE CONNECTICUT.. I AM WAITING FOR DENNIS KUCINICH AND MITT ROMNEY TO EXCHANGE PLATFORMS.. I AM WAITING FOR TH' REBIRTH OF WONDER BREAD!!
©2007 Bill Griffith. World rights reserved. Distributed by King Features Syndicate
ARE YOU PICKING UP ON WHAT MY MAN IS LAYING DOWN, BABE? IT'S GOING, GOING, GONE!
BLOW, DADDY! CAN'T YOU DIG? I'M A REPUBLICAN!
LIKE SARTRE SAID, MAN, "EACH CAT CREATES HIS OWN HELL"..

33

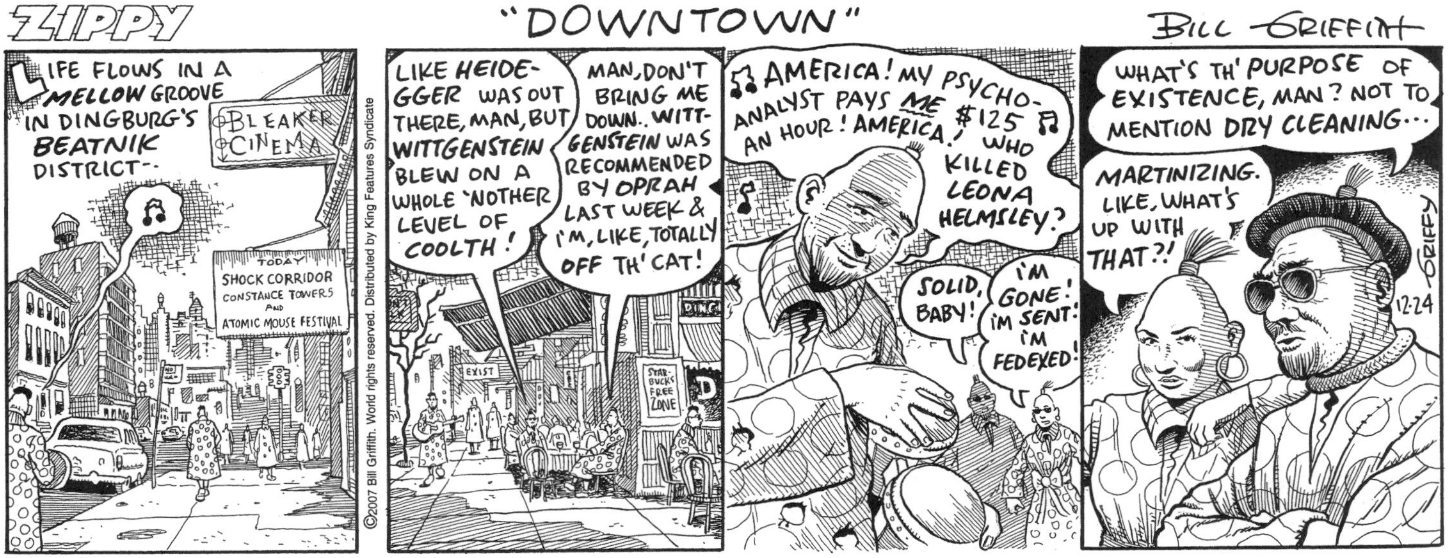
ZIPPY
"DOWNTOWN"
BILL GRIFFITH
LIFE FLOWS IN A MELLOW GROOVE IN DINGBURG'S BEATNIK DISTRICT--
BLEAKER CINEMA
TODAY SHOCK CORRIDOR CONSTANCE TOWERS AND ATOMIC MOUSE FESTIVAL
©2007 Bill Griffith. World rights reserved. Distributed by King Features Syndicate
LIKE HEIDEGGER WAS OUT THERE, MAN, BUT WITTGENSTEIN BLEW ON A WHOLE 'NOTHER LEVEL OF COOLTH!
MAN, DON'T BRING ME DOWN.. WITTGENSTEIN WAS RECOMMENDED BY OPRAH LAST WEEK & I'M, LIKE, TOTALLY OFF TH' CAT!
EXIST
STARBUCKS FREE ZONE
AMERICA! MY PSYCHOANALYST PAYS ME $125 AN HOUR! AMERICA! WHO KILLED LEONA HELMSLEY?
SOLID, BABY!
I'M GONE! I'M SENT! I'M FEDEXED!
WHAT'S TH' PURPOSE OF EXISTENCE, MAN? NOT TO MENTION DRY CLEANING...
MARTINIZING. LIKE, WHAT'S UP WITH THAT?!
GRIFFY
12-24
34

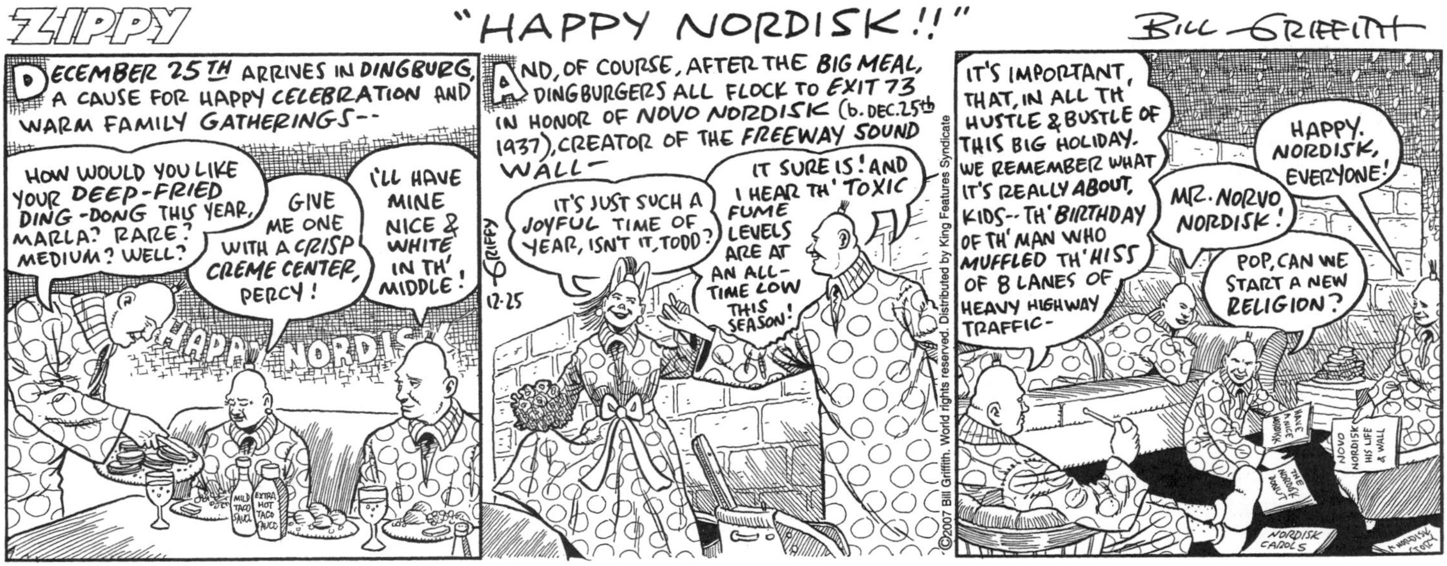
ZIPPY
"HAPPY NORDISK!!"
BILL GRIFFITH
DECEMBER 25TH ARRIVES IN DINGBURG, A CAUSE FOR HAPPY CELEBRATION AND WARM FAMILY GATHERINGS--
HOW WOULD YOU LIKE YOUR DEEP-FRIED DING-DONG THIS YEAR, MARLA? RARE? MEDIUM? WELL?
GIVE ME ONE WITH A CRISP CREME CENTER, PERCY!
I'LL HAVE MINE NICE & WHITE IN TH' MIDDLE!
HAPPY NORDISK
MILD TACO SAUCE
EXTRA HOT TACO SAUCE
GRIFFY
12-25
AND, OF COURSE, AFTER THE BIG MEAL, DINGBURGERS ALL FLOCK TO EXIT 73 IN HONOR OF NOVO NORDISK (b. DEC. 25th 1937), CREATOR OF THE FREEWAY SOUND WALL--
IT'S JUST SUCH A JOYFUL TIME OF YEAR, ISN'T IT, TODD?
IT SURE IS! AND I HEAR TH' TOXIC FUME LEVELS ARE AT AN ALL-TIME LOW THIS SEASON!
©2007 Bill Griffith. World rights reserved. Distributed by King Features Syndicate
IT'S IMPORTANT THAT, IN ALL TH' HUSTLE & BUSTLE OF THIS BIG HOLIDAY, WE REMEMBER WHAT IT'S REALLY ABOUT, KIDS-- TH' BIRTHDAY OF TH' MAN WHO MUFFLED TH' HISS OF 8 LANES OF HEAVY HIGHWAY TRAFFIC--
MR. NORVO NORDISK!
HAPPY NORDISK, EVERYONE!
POP, CAN WE START A NEW RELIGION?
NOVO NORDISK HIS LIFE & WALL
NORDISK CAROLS

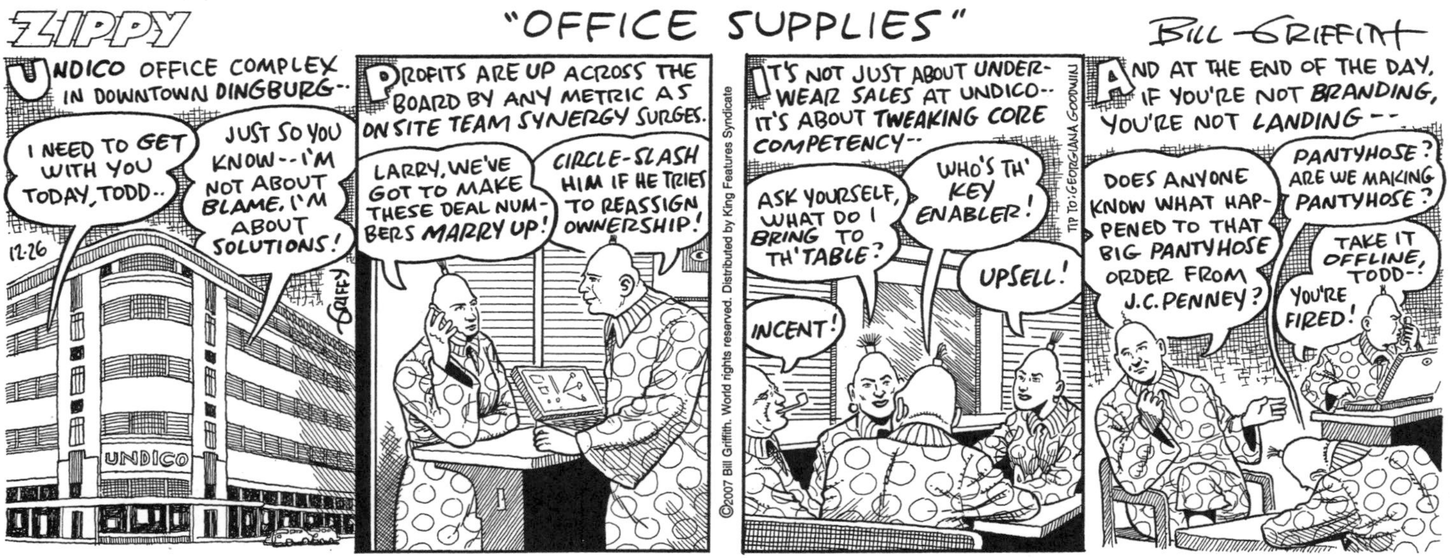
ZIPPY
"OFFICE SUPPLIES"
BILL GRIFFITH
UNDICO OFFICE COMPLEX IN DOWNTOWN DINGBURG..
I NEED TO GET WITH YOU TODAY, TODD..
JUST SO YOU KNOW--I'M NOT ABOUT BLAME. I'M ABOUT SOLUTIONS!
12-26
UNDICO
GRIFFY
PROFITS ARE UP ACROSS THE BOARD BY ANY METRIC AS ON SITE TEAM SYNERGY SURGES.
LARRY, WE'VE GOT TO MAKE THESE DEAL NUMBERS MARRY UP!
CIRCLE-SLASH HIM IF HE TRIES TO REASSIGN OWNERSHIP!
©2007 Bill Griffith. World rights reserved. Distributed by King Features Syndicate
IT'S NOT JUST ABOUT UNDERWEAR SALES AT UNDICO-- IT'S ABOUT TWEAKING CORE COMPETENCY--
ASK YOURSELF, WHAT DO I BRING TO TH' TABLE?
WHO'S TH' KEY ENABLER!
UPSELL!
INCENT!
TIP TO: GEORGIANA GOODWIN
AND AT THE END OF THE DAY, IF YOU'RE NOT BRANDING, YOU'RE NOT LANDING--
DOES ANYONE KNOW WHAT HAPPENED TO THAT BIG PANTYHOSE ORDER FROM J.C. PENNEY?
PANTYHOSE? ARE WE MAKING PANTYHOSE?
TAKE IT OFFLINE, TODD--!
YOU'RE FIRED!

35

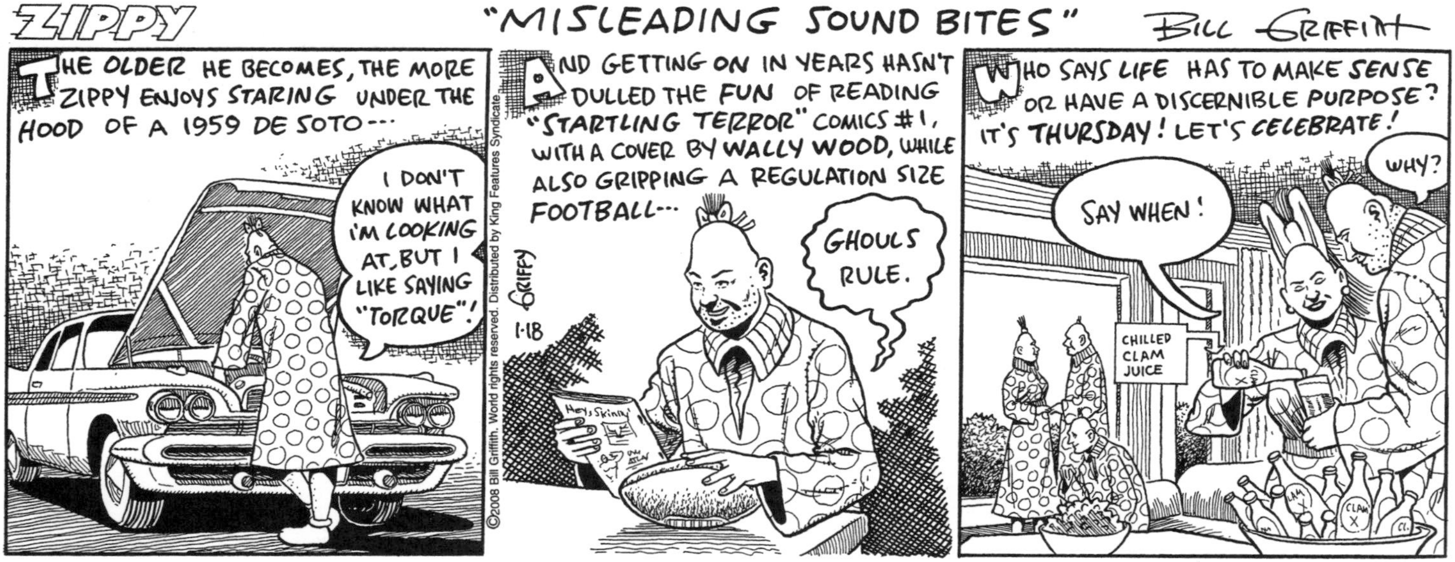
ZIPPY
"MISLEADING SOUND BITES"
BILL GRIFFITH
THE OLDER HE BECOMES, THE MORE ZIPPY ENJOYS STARING UNDER THE HOOD OF A 1959 DE SOTO---
I DON'T KNOW WHAT I'M LOOKING AT, BUT I LIKE SAYING "TORQUE"!
©2008 Bill Griffith. World rights reserved. Distributed by King Features Syndicate
AND GETTING ON IN YEARS HASN'T DULLED THE FUN OF READING "STARTLING TERROR" COMICS #1, WITH A COVER BY WALLY WOOD, WHILE ALSO GRIPPING A REGULATION SIZE FOOTBALL---
GHOULS RULE.
GRIFFY
1-18
WHO SAYS LIFE HAS TO MAKE SENSE OR HAVE A DISCERNIBLE PURPOSE? IT'S THURSDAY! LET'S CELEBRATE!
SAY WHEN!
WHY?
CHILLED CLAM JUICE

36

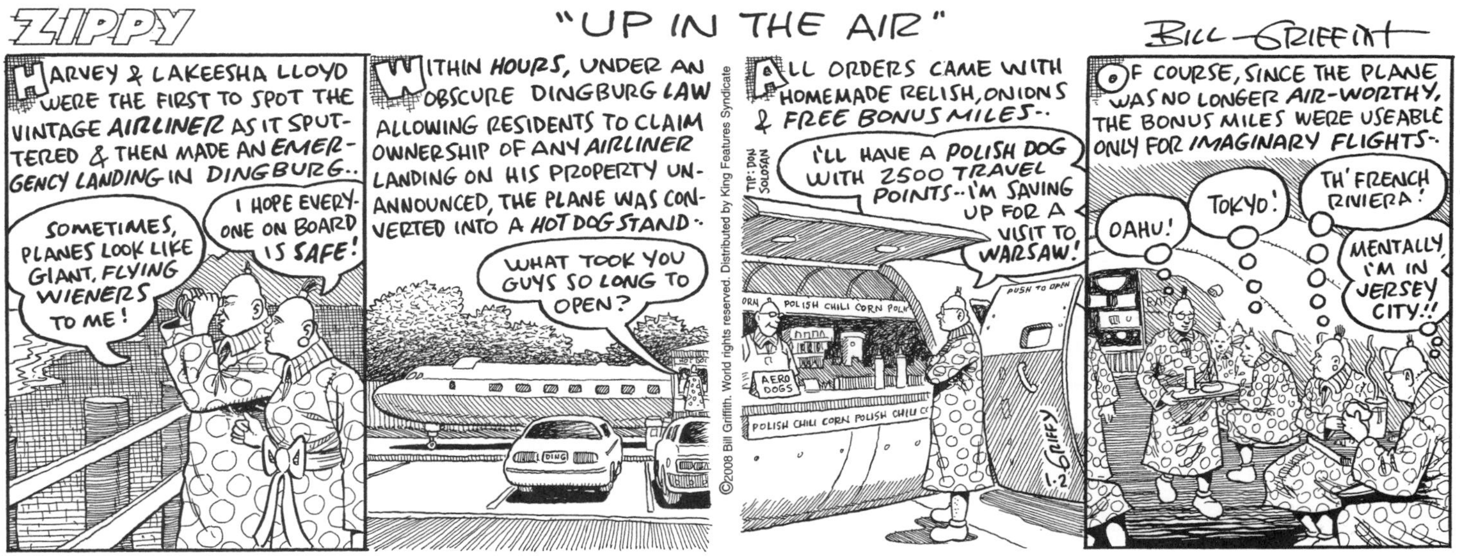
ZIPPY
"UP IN THE AIR"
BILL GRIFFITH
HARVEY & LAKEESHA LLOYD WERE THE FIRST TO SPOT THE VINTAGE AIRLINER AS IT SPUTTERED & THEN MADE AN EMERGENCY LANDING IN DINGBURG..
SOMETIMES, PLANES LOOK LIKE GIANT, FLYING WIENERS TO ME!
I HOPE EVERYONE ON BOARD IS SAFE!
WITHIN HOURS, UNDER AN OBSCURE DINGBURG LAW ALLOWING RESIDENTS TO CLAIM OWNERSHIP OF ANY AIRLINER LANDING ON HIS PROPERTY UNANNOUNCED, THE PLANE WAS CONVERTED INTO A HOT DOG STAND..
WHAT TOOK YOU GUYS SO LONG TO OPEN?
DING
©2008 Bill Griffith. World rights reserved. Distributed by King Features Syndicate
TIP: DON SOLOSAN
ALL ORDERS CAME WITH HOMEMADE RELISH, ONIONS & FREE BONUS MILES..
I'LL HAVE A POLISH DOG WITH 2500 TRAVEL POINTS.. I'M SAVING UP FOR A VISIT TO WARSAW!
POLISH CHILI CORN POLISH
AERO DOGS
POLISH CHILI CORN POLISH CHILI
PUSH TO OPEN
OF COURSE, SINCE THE PLANE WAS NO LONGER AIR-WORTHY, THE BONUS MILES WERE USEABLE ONLY FOR IMAGINARY FLIGHTS..
OAHU!
TOKYO!
TH' FRENCH RIVIERA!
MENTALLY, I'M IN JERSEY CITY!!

37

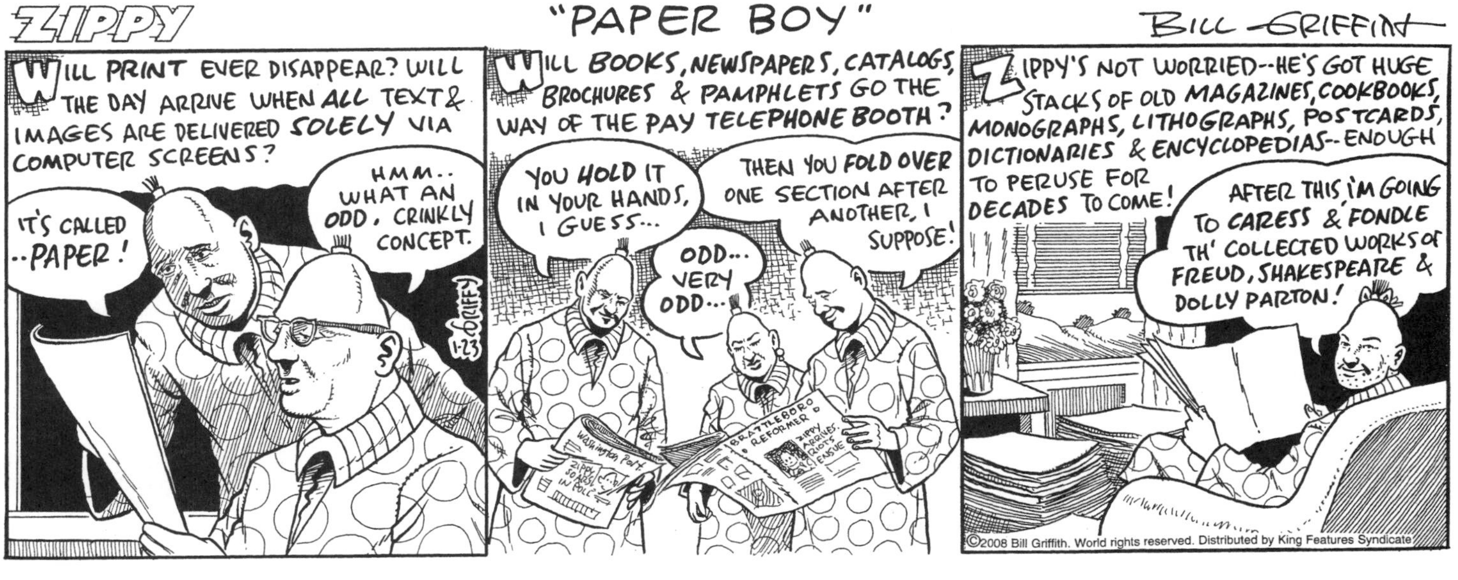
ZIPPY
"PAPER BOY"
BILL GRIFFITH
WILL PRINT EVER DISAPPEAR? WILL THE DAY ARRIVE WHEN ALL TEXT & IMAGES ARE DELIVERED SOLELY VIA COMPUTER SCREENS?
IT'S CALLED ..PAPER!
HMM.. WHAT AN ODD, CRINKLY CONCEPT.
WILL BOOKS, NEWSPAPERS, CATALOGS, BROCHURES & PAMPHLETS GO THE WAY OF THE PAY TELEPHONE BOOTH?
YOU HOLD IT IN YOUR HANDS, I GUESS...
ODD... VERY ODD...
THEN YOU FOLD OVER ONE SECTION AFTER ANOTHER, I SUPPOSE!
Washington Post
BRATTLEBORO REFORMER
ZIPPY'S NOT WORRIED--HE'S GOT HUGE STACKS OF OLD MAGAZINES, COOKBOOKS, MONOGRAPHS, LITHOGRAPHS, POSTCARDS, DICTIONARIES & ENCYCLOPEDIAS--ENOUGH TO PERUSE FOR DECADES TO COME!
AFTER THIS I'M GOING TO CARESS & FONDLE TH' COLLECTED WORKS OF FREUD, SHAKESPEARE & DOLLY PARTON!
©2008 Bill Griffith. World rights reserved. Distributed by King Features Syndicate

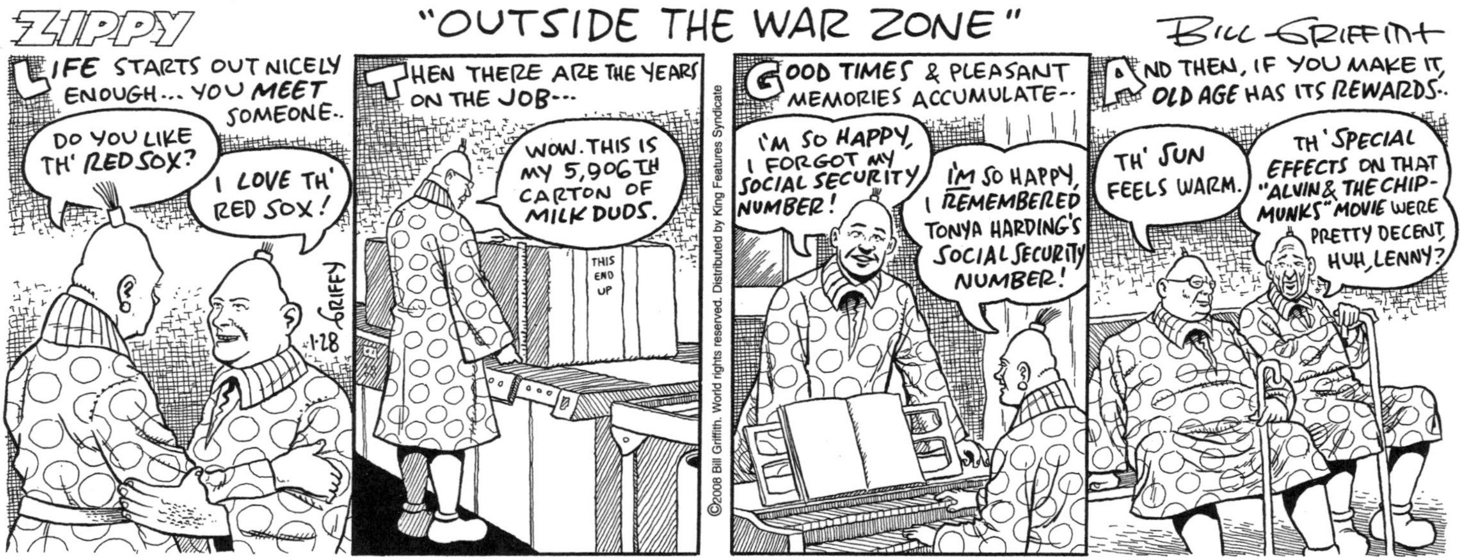
ZIPPY
"OUTSIDE THE WAR ZONE"
BILL GRIFFITH
LIFE STARTS OUT NICELY ENOUGH... YOU MEET SOMEONE..
DO YOU LIKE TH' RED SOX?
I LOVE TH' RED SOX!
GRIFFY 1·28
THEN THERE ARE THE YEARS ON THE JOB---
WOW. THIS IS MY 5,906TH CARTON OF MILK DUDS.
THIS END UP
©2008 Bill Griffith. World rights reserved. Distributed by King Features Syndicate
GOOD TIMES & PLEASANT MEMORIES ACCUMULATE--
I'M SO HAPPY, I FORGOT MY SOCIAL SECURITY NUMBER!
I'M SO HAPPY, I REMEMBERED TONYA HARDING'S SOCIAL SECURITY NUMBER!
AND THEN, IF YOU MAKE IT, OLD AGE HAS ITS REWARDS..
TH' SUN FEELS WARM.
TH' SPECIAL EFFECTS ON THAT "ALVIN & THE CHIPMUNKS" MOVIE WERE PRETTY DECENT, HUH, LENNY?

38

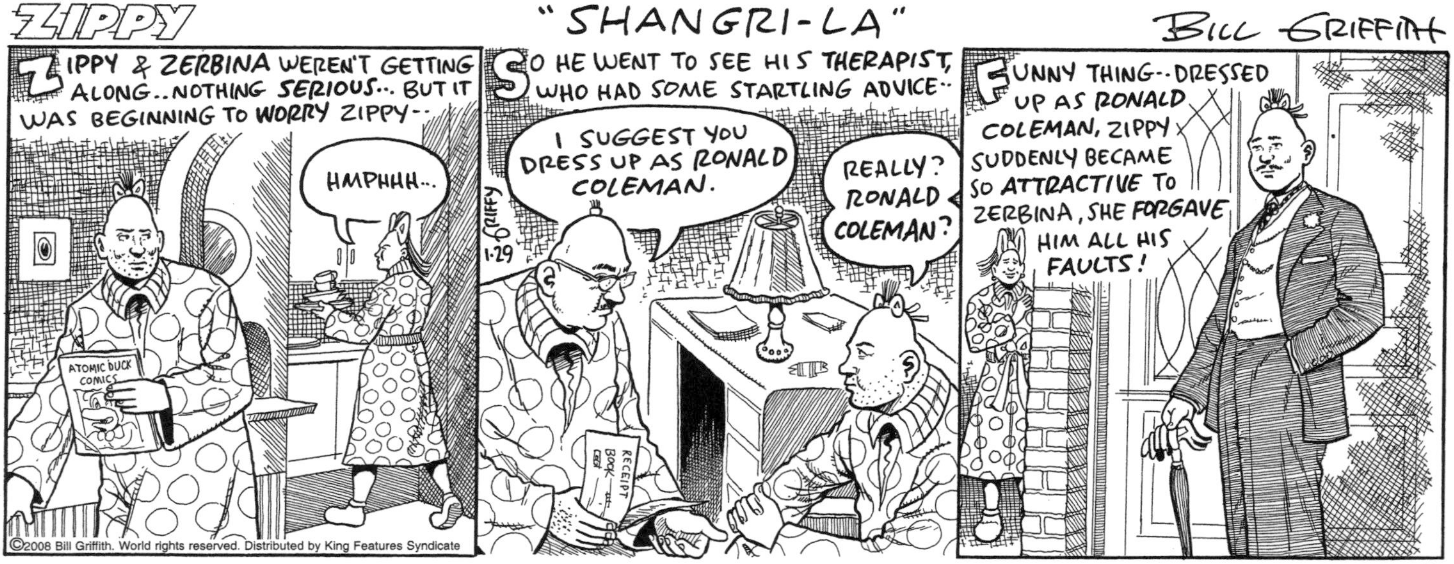
ZIPPY
"SHANGRI-LA"
BILL GRIFFITH
ZIPPY & ZERBINA WEREN'T GETTING ALONG..NOTHING SERIOUS... BUT IT WAS BEGINNING TO WORRY ZIPPY--
HMPHHH...
ATOMIC DUCK COMICS
©2008 Bill Griffith. World rights reserved. Distributed by King Features Syndicate
SO HE WENT TO SEE HIS THERAPIST, WHO HAD SOME STARTLING ADVICE--
I SUGGEST YOU DRESS UP AS RONALD COLEMAN.
REALLY? RONALD COLEMAN?
GRIFFY 1·29
RECEIPT BOOK
FUNNY THING--DRESSED UP AS RONALD COLEMAN, ZIPPY SUDDENLY BECAME SO ATTRACTIVE TO ZERBINA, SHE FORGAVE HIM ALL HIS FAULTS!

39

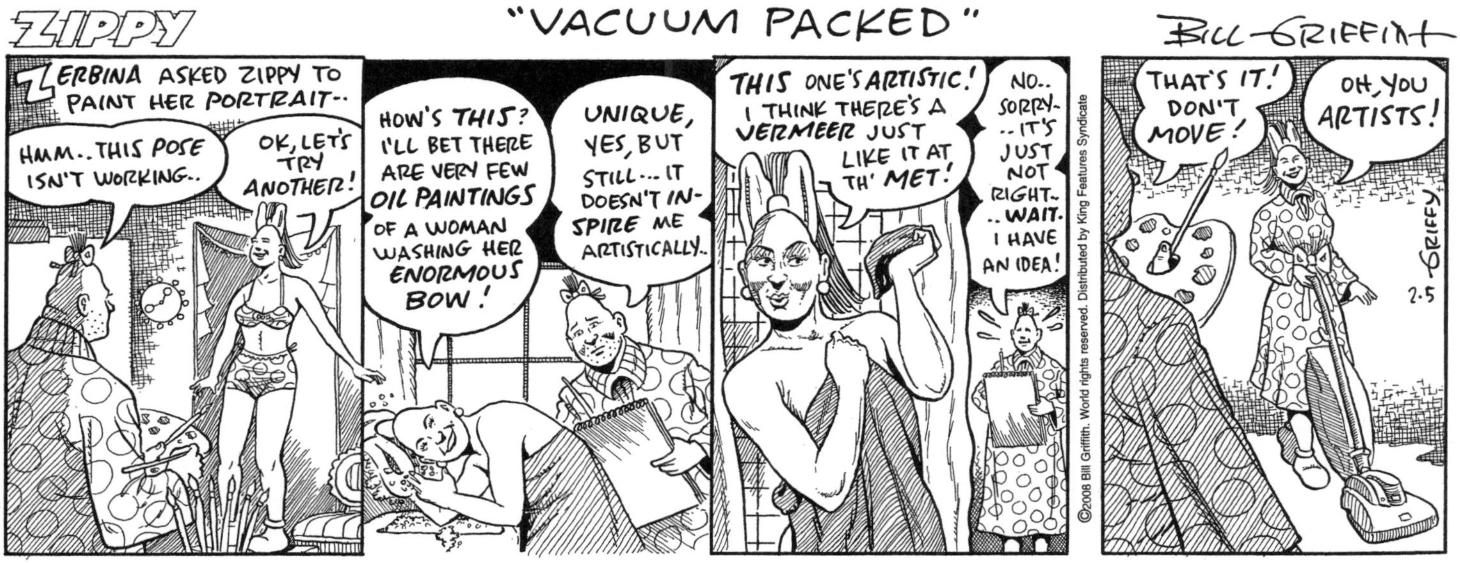
ZIPPY
"VACUUM PACKED"
BILL GRIFFITH
ZERBINA ASKED ZIPPY TO PAINT HER PORTRAIT--
HMM.. THIS POSE ISN'T WORKING..
OK, LET'S TRY ANOTHER!
HOW'S THIS? I'LL BET THERE ARE VERY FEW OIL PAINTINGS OF A WOMAN WASHING HER ENORMOUS BOW!
UNIQUE, YES, BUT STILL... IT DOESN'T INSPIRE ME ARTISTICALLY..
THIS ONE'S ARTISTIC! I THINK THERE'S A VERMEER JUST LIKE IT AT TH' MET!
NO.. SORRY.. --IT'S JUST NOT RIGHT.. ..WAIT.. I HAVE AN IDEA!
©2008 Bill Griffith. World rights reserved. Distributed by King Features Syndicate
THAT'S IT! DON'T MOVE!
OH, YOU ARTISTS!
GRIFFY 2-5

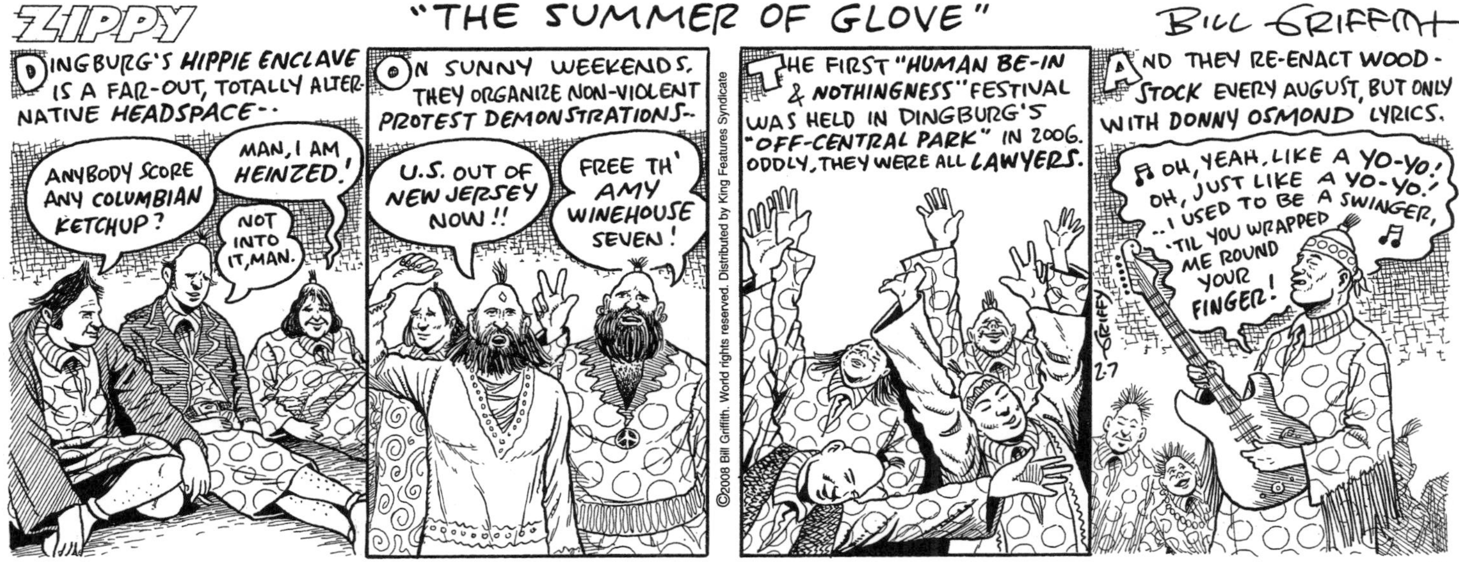
ZIPPY
"THE SUMMER OF GLOVE"
BILL GRIFFITH
DINGBURG'S HIPPIE ENCLAVE IS A FAR-OUT, TOTALLY ALTERNATIVE HEADSPACE--
ANYBODY SCORE ANY COLUMBIAN KETCHUP?
MAN, I AM HEINZED!
NOT INTO IT, MAN.
ON SUNNY WEEKENDS, THEY ORGANIZE NON-VIOLENT PROTEST DEMONSTRATIONS--
U.S. OUT OF NEW JERSEY NOW!!
FREE TH' AMY WINEHOUSE SEVEN!
©2008 Bill Griffith. World rights reserved. Distributed by King Features Syndicate
THE FIRST "HUMAN BE-IN & NOTHINGNESS" FESTIVAL WAS HELD IN DINGBURG'S "OFF-CENTRAL PARK" IN 2006. ODDLY, THEY WERE ALL LAWYERS.
AND THEY RE-ENACT WOODSTOCK EVERY AUGUST, BUT ONLY WITH DONNY OSMOND LYRICS.
OH, YEAH, LIKE A YO-YO! OH, JUST LIKE A YO-YO! ..I USED TO BE A SWINGER, 'TIL YOU WRAPPED ME ROUND YOUR FINGER!
GRIFFY 2-7

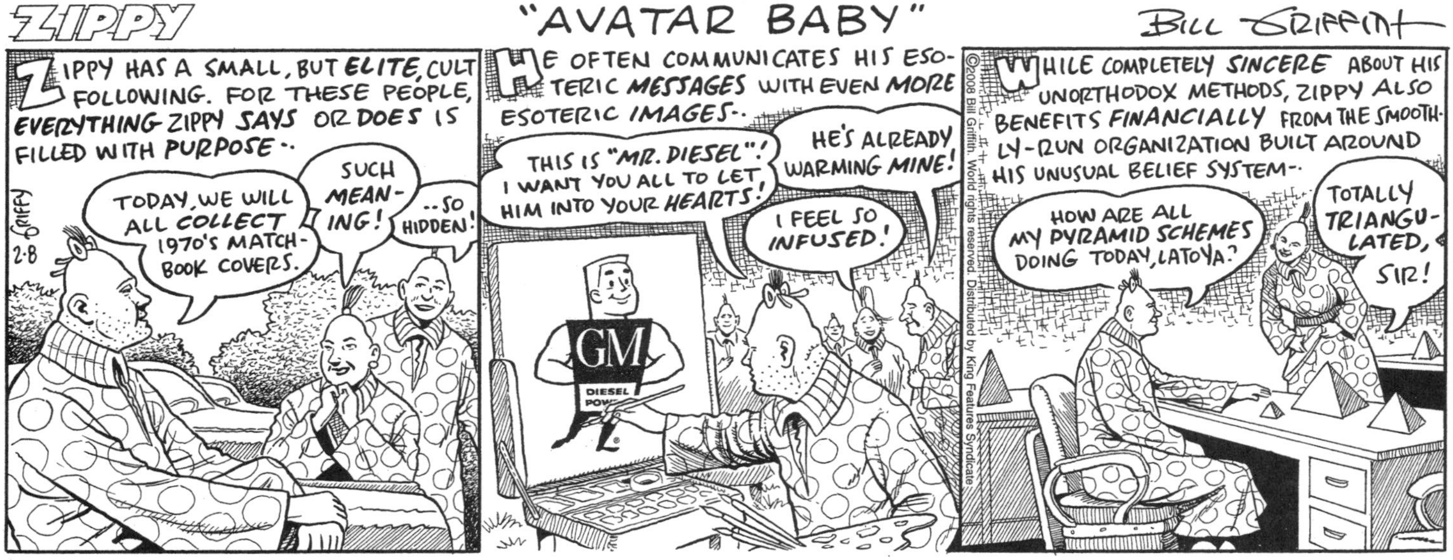
ZIPPY
"AVATAR BABY"
BILL GRIFFITH
ZIPPY HAS A SMALL, BUT ELITE, CULT FOLLOWING. FOR THESE PEOPLE, EVERYTHING ZIPPY SAYS OR DOES IS FILLED WITH PURPOSE..
TODAY, WE WILL ALL COLLECT 1970'S MATCHBOOK COVERS.
SUCH MEANING!
..SO HIDDEN!
GRIFFY 2·8
HE OFTEN COMMUNICATES HIS ESOTERIC MESSAGES WITH EVEN MORE ESOTERIC IMAGES..
THIS IS "MR. DIESEL"! I WANT YOU ALL TO LET HIM INTO YOUR HEARTS!
HE'S ALREADY WARMING MINE!
I FEEL SO INFUSED!
GM
DIESEL POW
©2008 Bill Griffith. World rights reserved. Distributed by King Features Syndicate
WHILE COMPLETELY SINCERE ABOUT HIS UNORTHODOX METHODS, ZIPPY ALSO BENEFITS FINANCIALLY FROM THE SMOOTHLY-RUN ORGANIZATION BUILT AROUND HIS UNUSUAL BELIEF SYSTEM..
HOW ARE ALL MY PYRAMID SCHEMES DOING TODAY, LATOYA?
TOTALLY TRIANGULATED, SIR!

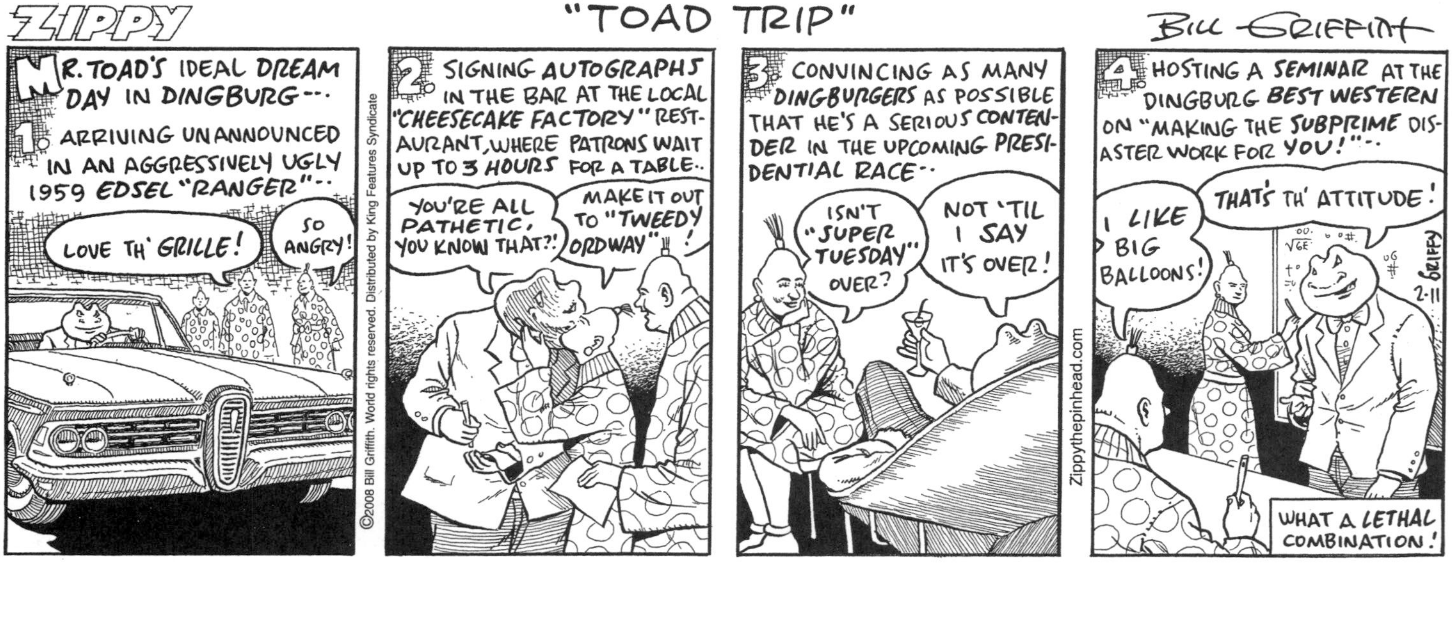
ZIPPY
"TOAD TRIP"
BILL GRIFFITH
MR. TOAD'S IDEAL DREAM DAY IN DINGBURG...
1. ARRIVING UNANNOUNCED IN AN AGGRESSIVELY UGLY 1959 EDSEL "RANGER"..
LOVE TH' GRILLE!
SO ANGRY!
©2008 Bill Griffith. World rights reserved. Distributed by King Features Syndicate
2. SIGNING AUTOGRAPHS IN THE BAR AT THE LOCAL "CHEESECAKE FACTORY" RESTAURANT, WHERE PATRONS WAIT UP TO 3 HOURS FOR A TABLE..
YOU'RE ALL PATHETIC, YOU KNOW THAT?!
MAKE IT OUT TO "TWEEDY ORDWAY"!
3. CONVINCING AS MANY DINGBURGERS AS POSSIBLE THAT HE'S A SERIOUS CONTENDER IN THE UPCOMING PRESIDENTIAL RACE..
ISN'T "SUPER TUESDAY" OVER?
NOT 'TIL I SAY IT'S OVER!
Zippythepinhead.com
4. HOSTING A SEMINAR AT THE DINGBURG BEST WESTERN ON "MAKING THE SUBPRIME DISASTER WORK FOR YOU!"..
I LIKE BIG BALLOONS!
THAT'S TH' ATTITUDE!
GRIFFY 2·11
WHAT A LETHAL COMBINATION!

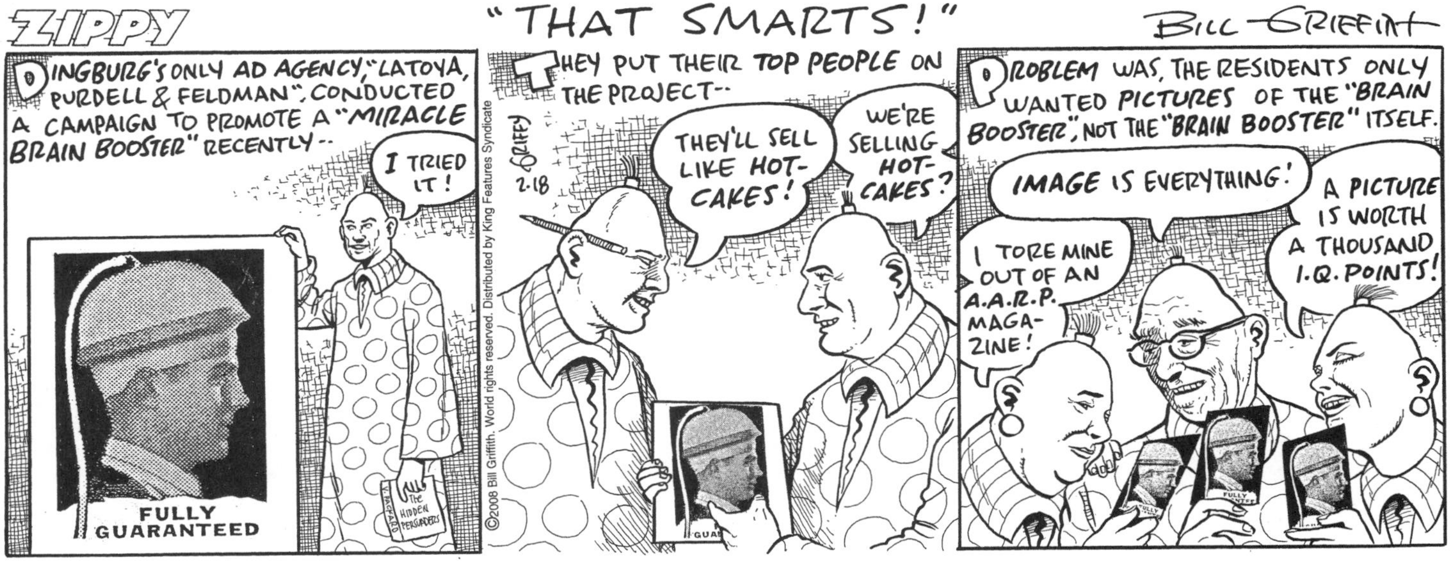
ZIPPY
"THAT SMARTS!"
BILL GRIFFITH
DINGBURG'S ONLY AD AGENCY, "LATOYA, PURDELL & FELDMAN", CONDUCTED A CAMPAIGN TO PROMOTE A "MIRACLE BRAIN BOOSTER" RECENTLY--
I TRIED IT!
FULLY GUARANTEED
THE HIDDEN PERSUADERS
THEY PUT THEIR TOP PEOPLE ON THE PROJECT--
THEY'LL SELL LIKE HOT-CAKES!
WE'RE SELLING HOT-CAKES?
©2008 Bill Griffith. World rights reserved. Distributed by King Features Syndicate
GRIFFY 2·18
PROBLEM WAS, THE RESIDENTS ONLY WANTED PICTURES OF THE "BRAIN BOOSTER", NOT THE "BRAIN BOOSTER" ITSELF.
IMAGE IS EVERYTHING!
A PICTURE IS WORTH A THOUSAND I.Q. POINTS!
I TORE MINE OUT OF AN A.A.R.P. MAGAZINE!

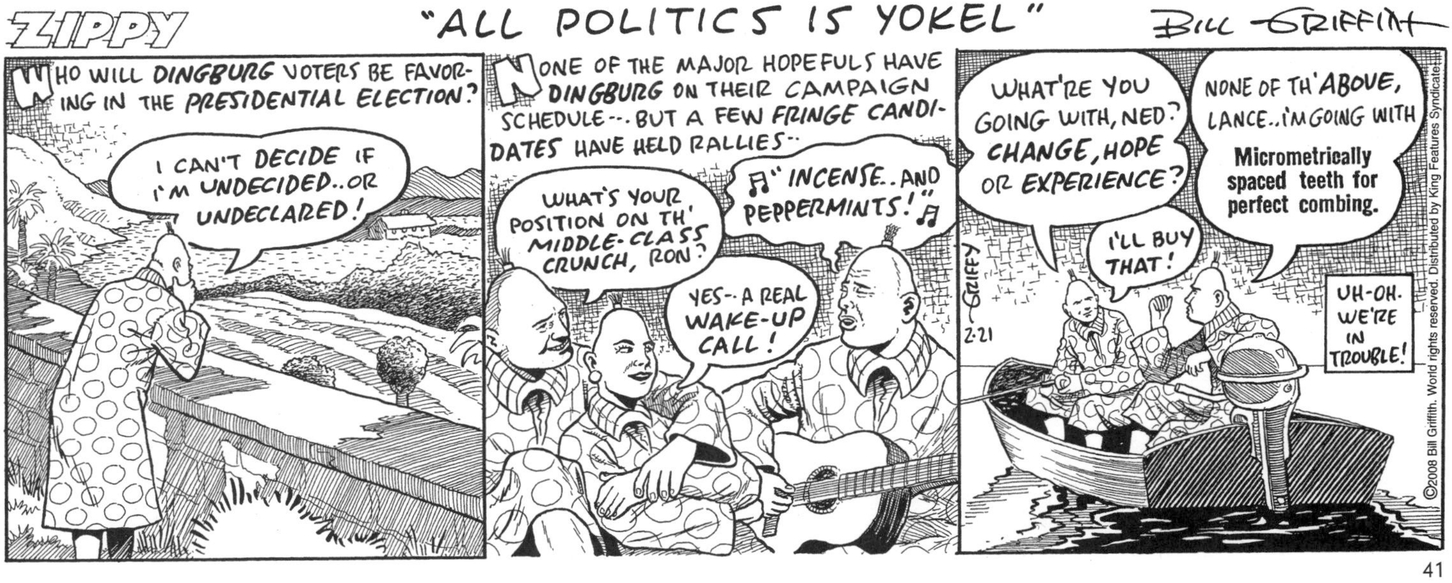
ZIPPY
"ALL POLITICS IS YOKEL"
BILL GRIFFITH
WHO WILL DINGBURG VOTERS BE FAVORING IN THE PRESIDENTIAL ELECTION?
I CAN'T DECIDE IF I'M UNDECIDED..OR UNDECLARED!
NONE OF THE MAJOR HOPEFULS HAVE DINGBURG ON THEIR CAMPAIGN SCHEDULE--. BUT A FEW FRINGE CANDIDATES HAVE HELD RALLIES--
WHAT'S YOUR POSITION ON TH' MIDDLE-CLASS CRUNCH, RON?
"INCENSE.. AND PEPPERMINTS!"
YES--. A REAL WAKE-UP CALL!
GRIFFY 2·21
WHAT'RE YOU GOING WITH, NED? CHANGE, HOPE OR EXPERIENCE?
NONE OF TH' ABOVE, LANCE..I'M GOING WITH
Micrometrically spaced teeth for perfect combing.
I'LL BUY THAT!
UH-OH. WE'RE IN TROUBLE!
©2008 Bill Griffith. World rights reserved. Distributed by King Features Syndicate

41

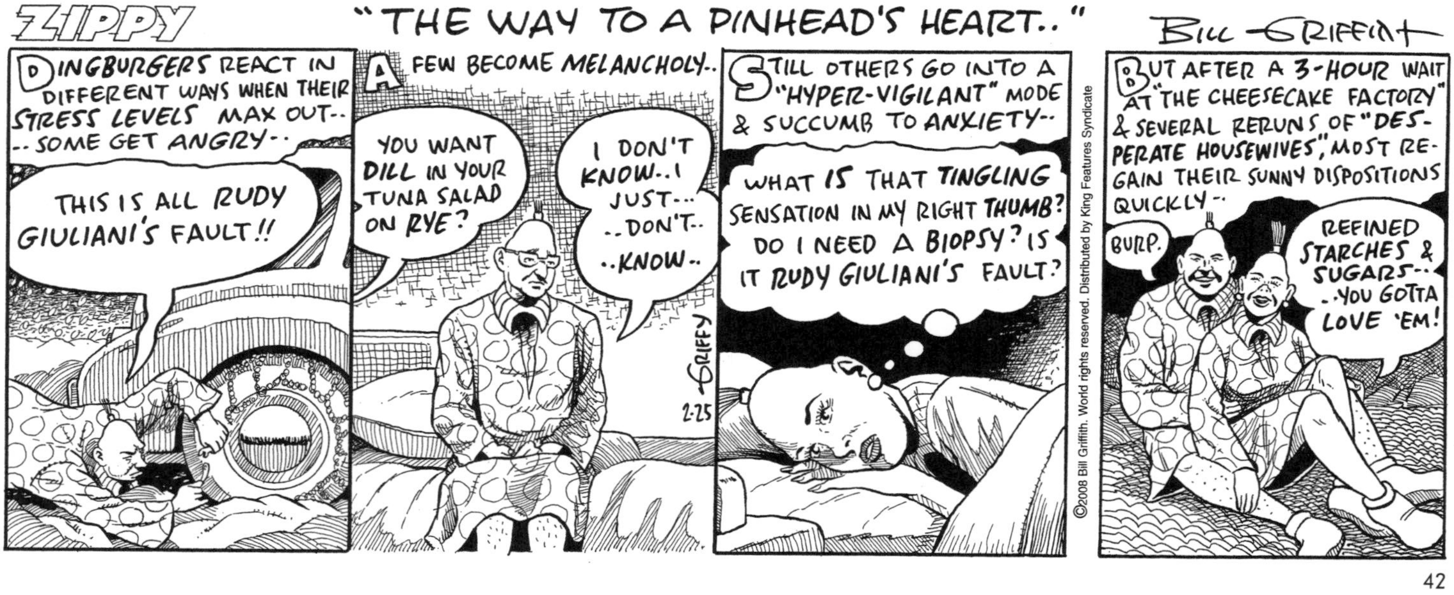
ZIPPY
"THE WAY TO A PINHEAD'S HEART.."
BILL GRIFFITH
DINGBURGERS REACT IN DIFFERENT WAYS WHEN THEIR STRESS LEVELS MAX OUT-- ..SOME GET ANGRY-.
THIS IS ALL RUDY GIULIANI'S FAULT!!
A FEW BECOME MELANCHOLY..
YOU WANT DILL IN YOUR TUNA SALAD ON RYE?
I DON'T KNOW..I JUST... ..DON'T.. ..KNOW..
GRIFFY 2·25
STILL OTHERS GO INTO A "HYPER-VIGILANT" MODE & SUCCUMB TO ANXIETY--
WHAT IS THAT TINGLING SENSATION IN MY RIGHT THUMB? DO I NEED A BIOPSY? IS IT RUDY GIULIANI'S FAULT?
©2008 Bill Griffith. World rights reserved. Distributed by King Features Syndicate
BUT AFTER A 3-HOUR WAIT AT "THE CHEESECAKE FACTORY" & SEVERAL RERUNS OF "DESPERATE HOUSEWIVES", MOST REGAIN THEIR SUNNY DISPOSITIONS QUICKLY-.
BURP.
REFINED STARCHES & SUGARS-- ..YOU GOTTA LOVE 'EM!
42

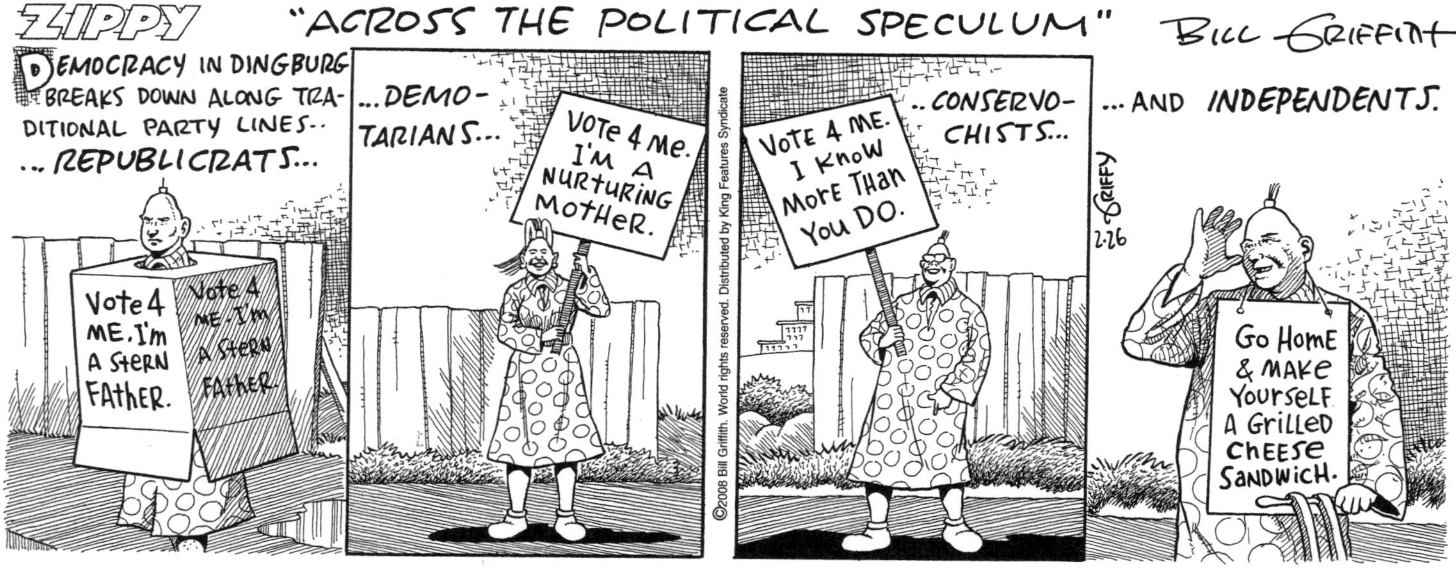
ZIPPY
"ACROSS THE POLITICAL SPECULUM"
BILL GRIFFITH
DEMOCRACY IN DINGBURG BREAKS DOWN ALONG TRADITIONAL PARTY LINES.. ...REPUBLICRATS...
Vote 4 ME. I'm A Stern FAThER.
Vote 4 ME. I'm A Stern FAther.
...DEMOTARIANS...
Vote 4 Me. I'M A NURTURING MOTHER.
©2008 Bill Griffith. World rights reserved. Distributed by King Features Syndicate
..CONSERVOCHISTS...
Vote 4 ME. I Know More Than You DO.
GRIFFY 2·26
...AND INDEPENDENTS.
Go Home & MAKE Yourself A Grilled CHEESE SANDWICH.

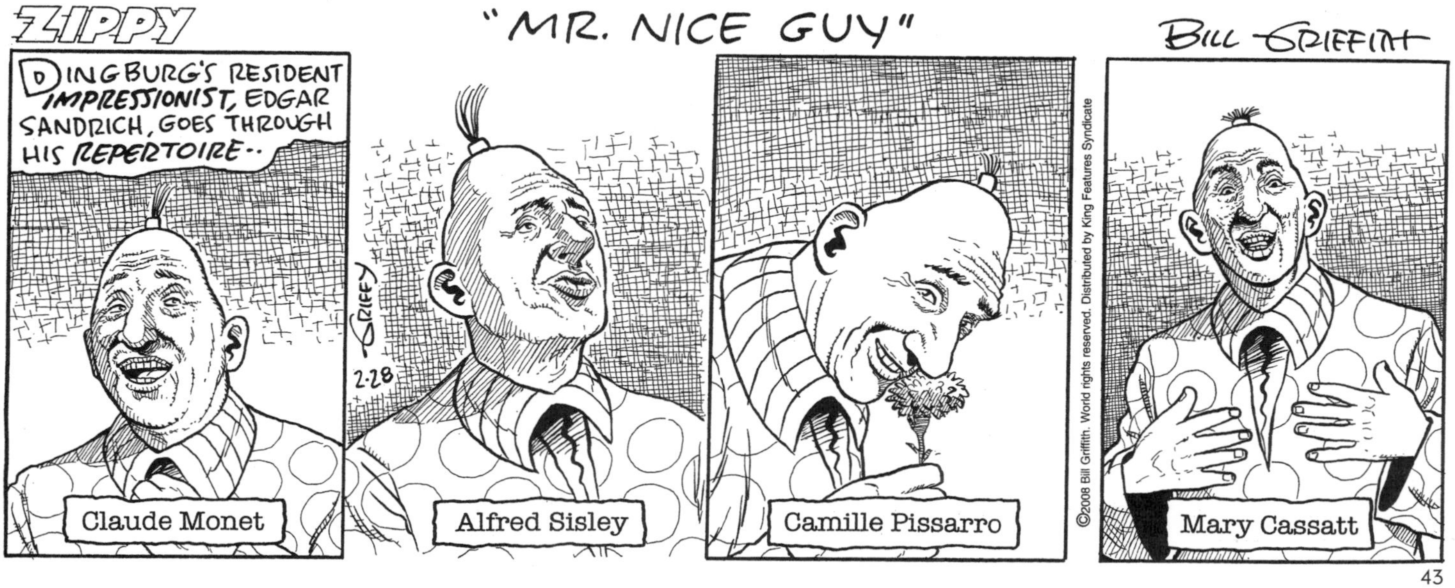
ZIPPY
"MR. NICE GUY"
BILL GRIFFITH
DINGBURG'S RESIDENT IMPRESSIONIST, EDGAR SANDRICH, GOES THROUGH HIS REPERTOIRE..
Claude Monet
GRIFFY 2·28
Alfred Sisley
Camille Pissarro
©2008 Bill Griffith. World rights reserved. Distributed by King Features Syndicate
Mary Cassatt
43

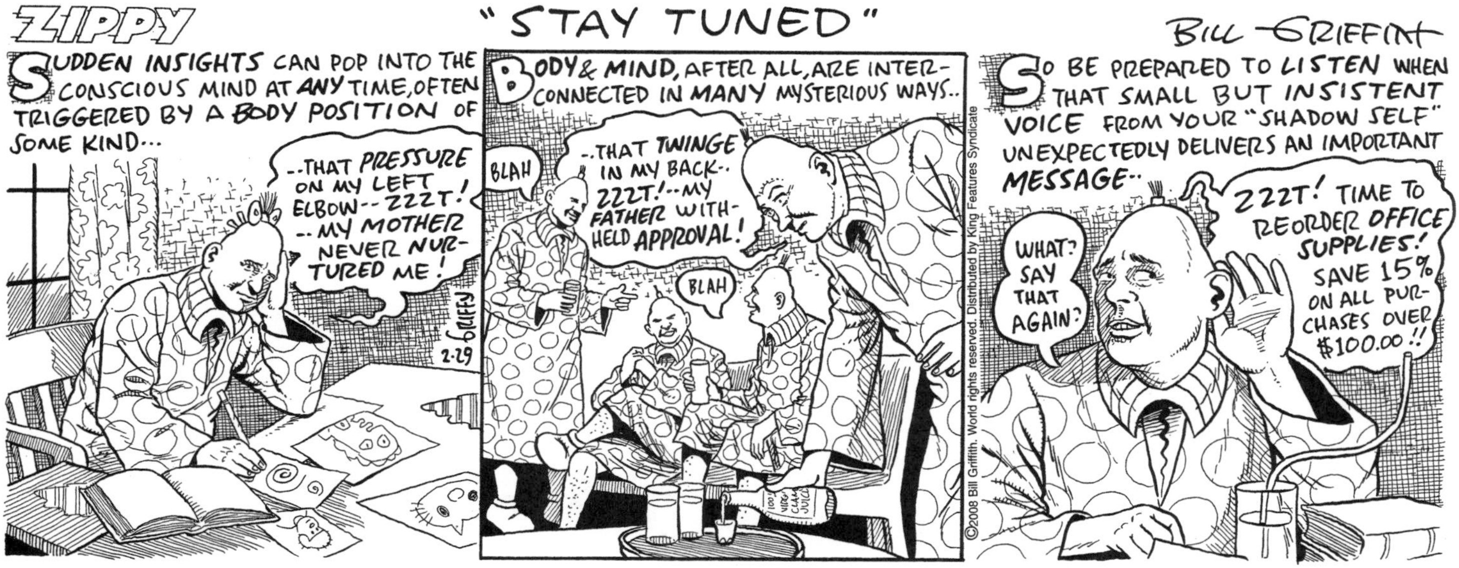
ZIPPY
"STAY TUNED"
BILL GRIFFITH
SUDDEN INSIGHTS CAN POP INTO THE CONSCIOUS MIND AT ANY TIME, OFTEN TRIGGERED BY A BODY POSITION OF SOME KIND...
..THAT PRESSURE ON MY LEFT ELBOW-- ZZZT! --MY MOTHER NEVER NURTURED ME!
GRIFFY 2·29
BODY & MIND, AFTER ALL, ARE INTERCONNECTED IN MANY MYSTERIOUS WAYS..
BLAH
..THAT TWINGE IN MY BACK.. ZZZT!--MY FATHER WITHHELD APPROVAL!
BLAH
©2008 Bill Griffith. World rights reserved. Distributed by King Features Syndicate
SO BE PREPARED TO LISTEN WHEN THAT SMALL BUT INSISTENT VOICE FROM YOUR "SHADOW SELF" UNEXPECTEDLY DELIVERS AN IMPORTANT MESSAGE..
WHAT? SAY THAT AGAIN?
ZZZT! TIME TO REORDER OFFICE SUPPLIES! SAVE 15% ON ALL PURCHASES OVER $100.00!!

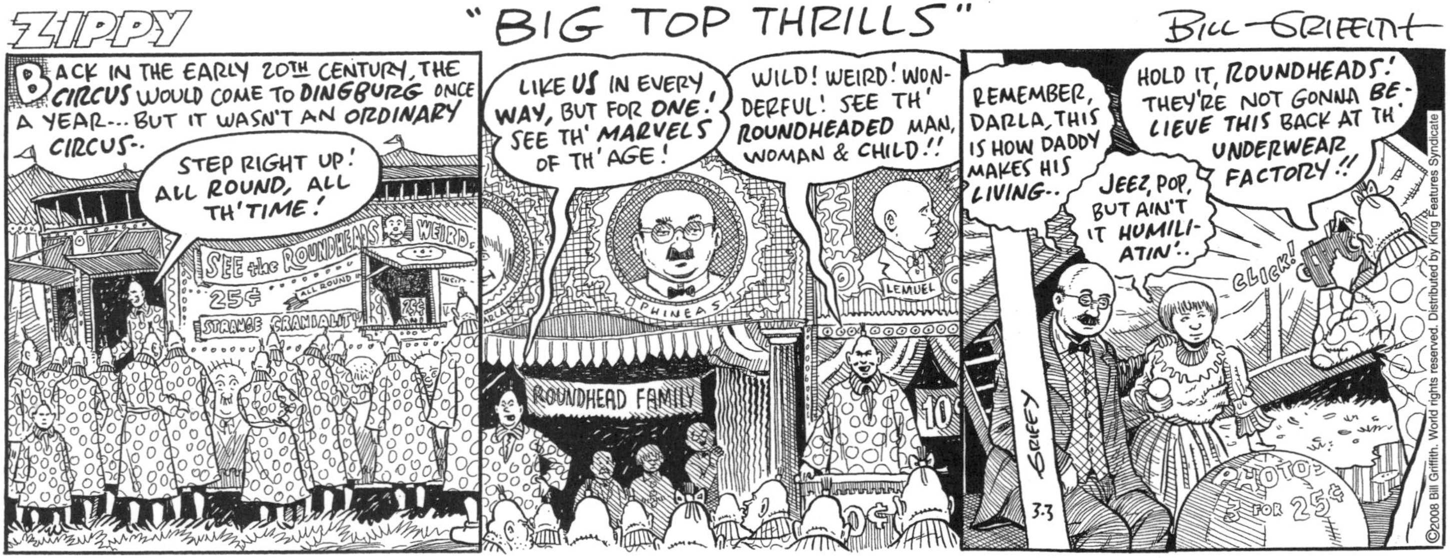
ZIPPY
"BIG TOP THRILLS"
BILL GRIFFITH
BACK IN THE EARLY 20TH CENTURY, THE CIRCUS WOULD COME TO DINGBURG ONCE A YEAR... BUT IT WASN'T AN ORDINARY CIRCUS..
STEP RIGHT UP! ALL ROUND, ALL TH' TIME!
SEE the ROUNDHEADS
WEIRD
25¢
ALL ROUND
STRANGE CRANIALITY
LIKE US IN EVERY WAY, BUT FOR ONE! SEE TH' MARVELS OF TH' AGE!
WILD! WEIRD! WONDERFUL! SEE TH' ROUNDHEADED MAN, WOMAN & CHILD!!
PHINEAS
LEMUEL
ROUNDHEAD FAMILY
10¢
REMEMBER, DARLA, THIS IS HOW DADDY MAKES HIS LIVING..
JEEZ, POP, BUT AIN'T IT HUMILIATIN'..
HOLD IT, ROUNDHEADS! THEY'RE NOT GONNA BELIEVE THIS BACK AT TH' UNDERWEAR FACTORY!!
CLICK!
PHOTOS 3 FOR 25¢
GRIFFY
3.3
©2008 Bill Griffith. World rights reserved. Distributed by King Features Syndicate

44

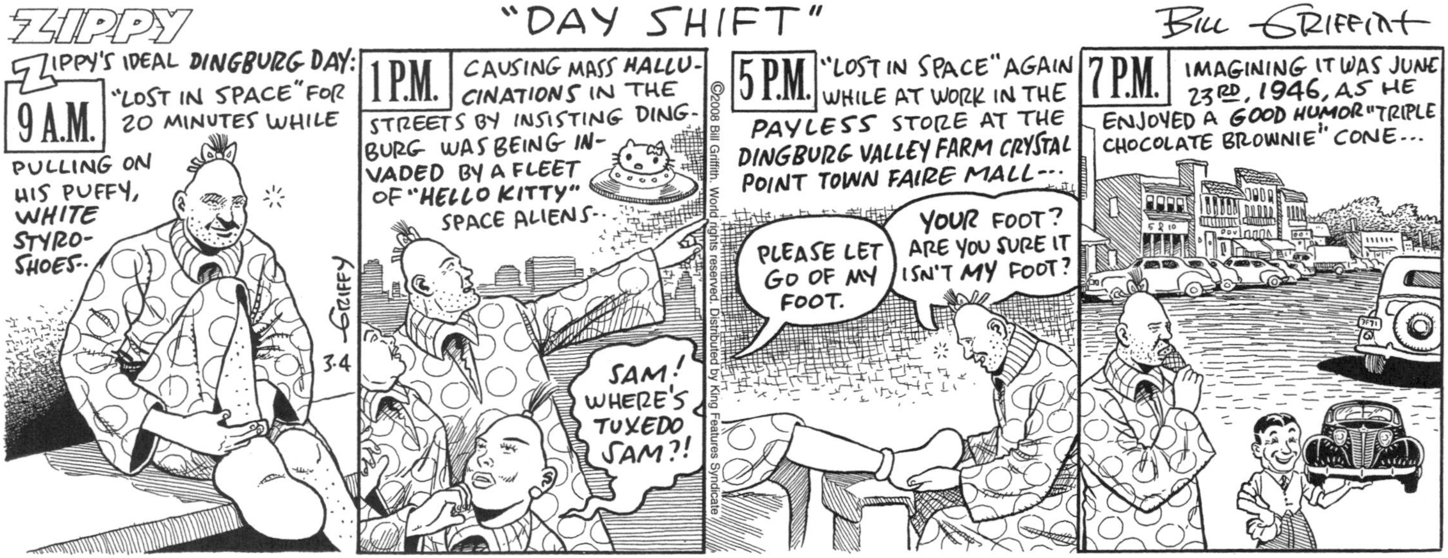
ZIPPY
"DAY SHIFT"
BILL GRIFFITH
ZIPPY'S IDEAL DINGBURG DAY:
9 A.M.
"LOST IN SPACE" FOR 20 MINUTES WHILE PULLING ON HIS PUFFY, WHITE STYRO-SHOES..
GRIFFY
3.4
1 P.M.
CAUSING MASS HALLUCINATIONS IN THE STREETS BY INSISTING DINGBURG WAS BEING INVADED BY A FLEET OF "HELLO KITTY" SPACE ALIENS..
SAM! WHERE'S TUXEDO SAM?!
©2008 Bill Griffith. World rights reserved. Distributed by King Features Syndicate
5 P.M.
"LOST IN SPACE" AGAIN WHILE AT WORK IN THE PAYLESS STORE AT THE DINGBURG VALLEY FARM CRYSTAL POINT TOWN FAIRE MALL...
PLEASE LET GO OF MY FOOT.
YOUR FOOT? ARE YOU SURE IT ISN'T MY FOOT?
7 P.M.
IMAGINING IT WAS JUNE 23RD, 1946, AS HE ENJOYED A GOOD HUMOR "TRIPLE CHOCOLATE BROWNIE" CONE...

45

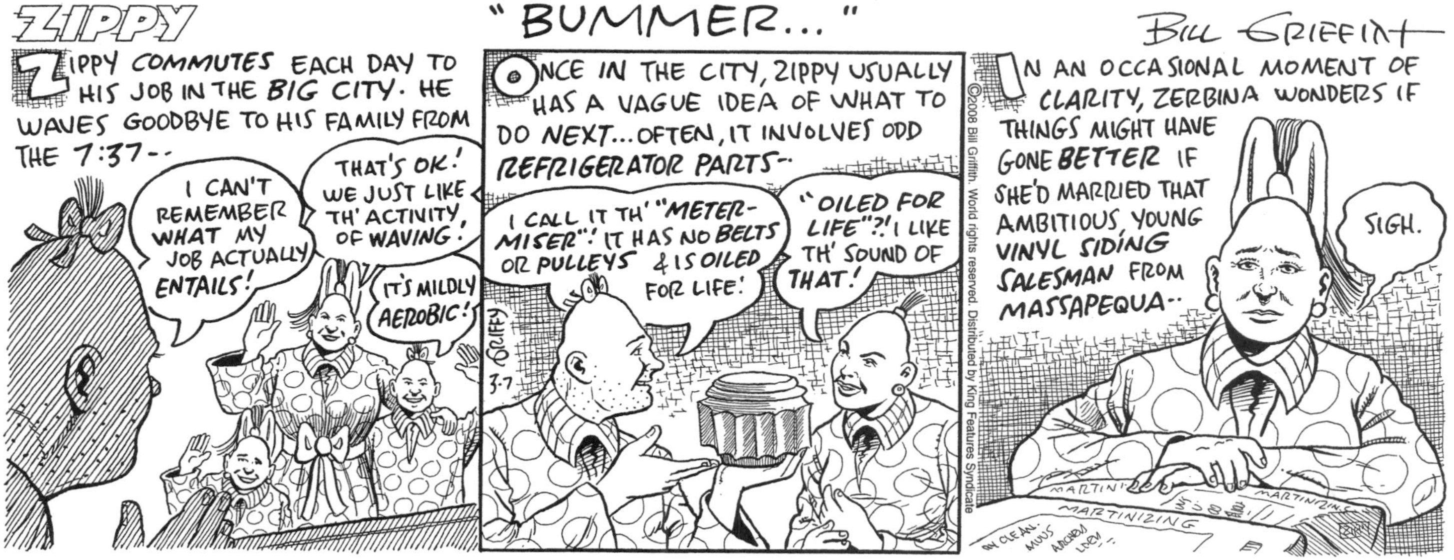
ZIPPY
"BUMMER..."
BILL GRIFFITH
ZIPPY COMMUTES EACH DAY TO HIS JOB IN THE BIG CITY. HE WAVES GOODBYE TO HIS FAMILY FROM THE 7:37--
I CAN'T REMEMBER WHAT MY JOB ACTUALLY ENTAILS!
THAT'S OK! WE JUST LIKE TH' ACTIVITY OF WAVING!
IT'S MILDLY AEROBIC!
ONCE IN THE CITY, ZIPPY USUALLY HAS A VAGUE IDEA OF WHAT TO DO NEXT... OFTEN, IT INVOLVES ODD REFRIGERATOR PARTS--
I CALL IT TH' "METER-MISER"! IT HAS NO BELTS OR PULLEYS & IS OILED FOR LIFE!
"OILED FOR LIFE"?! I LIKE TH' SOUND OF THAT!
GRIFFY 3-7
©2008 Bill Griffith. World rights reserved. Distributed by King Features Syndicate
IN AN OCCASIONAL MOMENT OF CLARITY, ZERBINA WONDERS IF THINGS MIGHT HAVE GONE BETTER IF SHE'D MARRIED THAT AMBITIOUS, YOUNG VINYL SIDING SALESMAN FROM MASSAPEQUA--
SIGH.
MARTINIZING
MARTINIZING
46
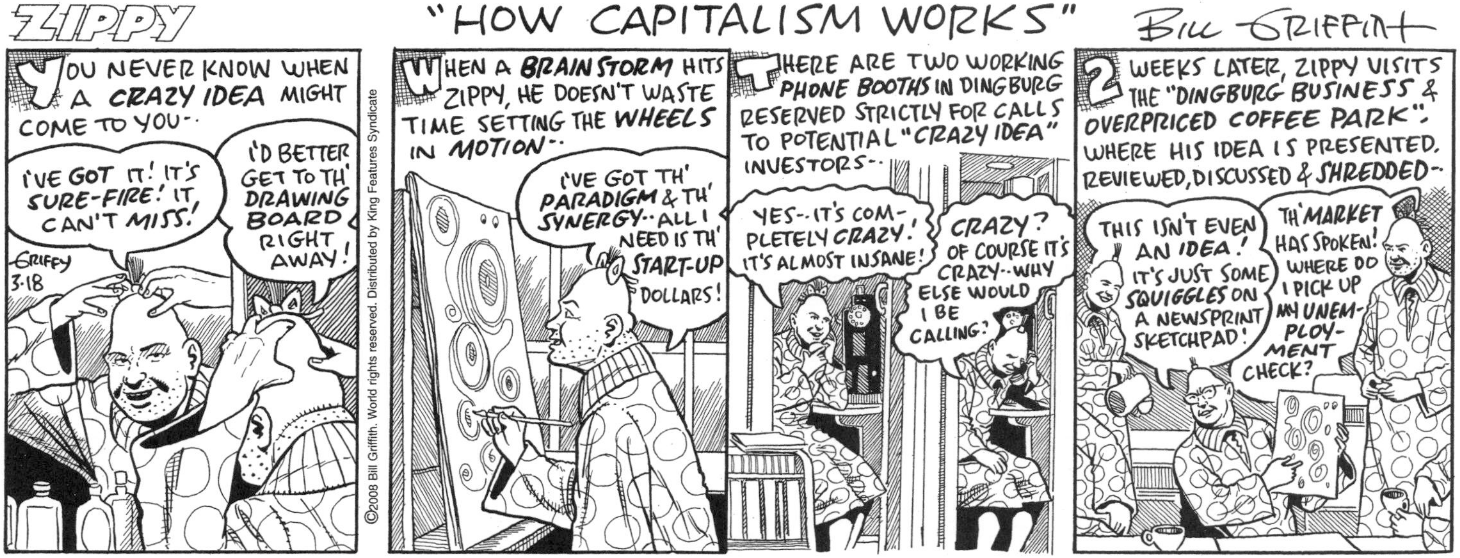
ZIPPY
"HOW CAPITALISM WORKS"
BILL GRIFFITH
YOU NEVER KNOW WHEN A CRAZY IDEA MIGHT COME TO YOU--
I'VE GOT IT! IT'S SURE-FIRE! IT CAN'T MISS!
I'D BETTER GET TO TH' DRAWING BOARD RIGHT AWAY!
GRIFFY 3-18
©2008 Bill Griffith. World rights reserved. Distributed by King Features Syndicate
WHEN A BRAINSTORM HITS ZIPPY, HE DOESN'T WASTE TIME SETTING THE WHEELS IN MOTION--
I'VE GOT TH' PARADIGM & TH' SYNERGY-- ALL I NEED IS TH' START-UP DOLLARS!
THERE ARE TWO WORKING PHONE BOOTHS IN DINGBURG RESERVED STRICTLY FOR CALLS TO POTENTIAL "CRAZY IDEA" INVESTORS--
YES-- IT'S COMPLETELY CRAZY! IT'S ALMOST INSANE!
CRAZY? OF COURSE IT'S CRAZY-- WHY ELSE WOULD I BE CALLING?
2 WEEKS LATER, ZIPPY VISITS THE "DINGBURG BUSINESS & OVERPRICED COFFEE PARK", WHERE HIS IDEA IS PRESENTED, REVIEWED, DISCUSSED & SHREDDED--
THIS ISN'T EVEN AN IDEA! IT'S JUST SOME SQUIGGLES ON A NEWSPRINT SKETCHPAD!
TH' MARKET HAS SPOKEN! WHERE DO I PICK UP MY UNEMPLOYMENT CHECK?

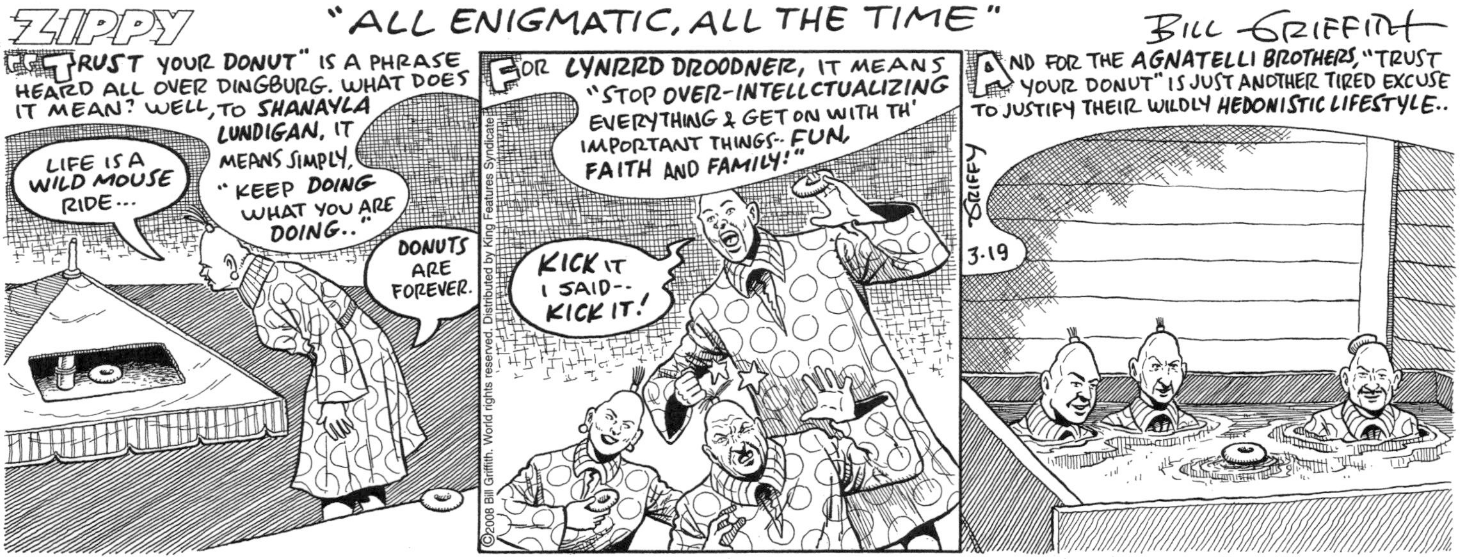
ZIPPY
"ALL ENIGMATIC, ALL THE TIME"
BILL GRIFFITH
"TRUST YOUR DONUT" IS A PHRASE HEARD ALL OVER DINGBURG. WHAT DOES IT MEAN? WELL, TO SHANAYLA LUNDIGAN, IT MEANS SIMPLY, "KEEP DOING WHAT YOU ARE DOING.."
LIFE IS A WILD MOUSE RIDE...
DONUTS ARE FOREVER.
FOR LYNRRD DROODNER, IT MEANS "STOP OVER-INTELLCTUALIZING EVERYTHING & GET ON WITH TH' IMPORTANT THINGS-- FUN, FAITH AND FAMILY!"
KICK IT I SAID-- KICK IT!
©2008 Bill Griffith. World rights reserved. Distributed by King Features Syndicate
GRIFFY 3-19
AND FOR THE AGNATELLI BROTHERS, "TRUST YOUR DONUT" IS JUST ANOTHER TIRED EXCUSE TO JUSTIFY THEIR WILDLY HEDONISTIC LIFESTYLE..

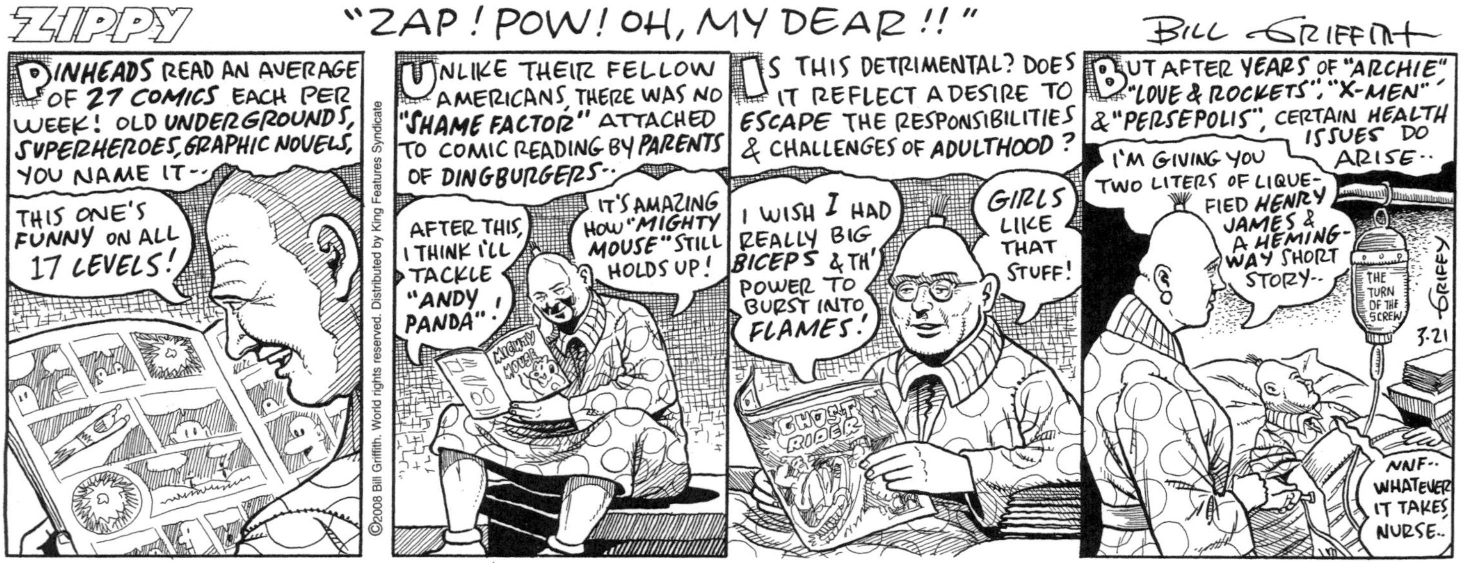
ZIPPY
"ZAP! POW! OH, MY DEAR!!"
BILL GRIFFITH
PINHEADS READ AN AVERAGE OF 27 COMICS EACH PER WEEK! OLD UNDERGROUNDS, SUPERHEROES, GRAPHIC NOVELS, YOU NAME IT--
THIS ONE'S FUNNY ON ALL 17 LEVELS!
©2008 Bill Griffith. World rights reserved. Distributed by King Features Syndicate
UNLIKE THEIR FELLOW AMERICANS, THERE WAS NO "SHAME FACTOR" ATTACHED TO COMIC READING BY PARENTS OF DINGBURGERS--
AFTER THIS, I THINK I'LL TACKLE "ANDY PANDA"!
IT'S AMAZING HOW "MIGHTY MOUSE" STILL HOLDS UP!
MIGHTY MOUSE
IS THIS DETRIMENTAL? DOES IT REFLECT A DESIRE TO ESCAPE THE RESPONSIBILITIES & CHALLENGES OF ADULTHOOD?
I WISH I HAD REALLY BIG BICEPS & TH' POWER TO BURST INTO FLAMES!
GIRLS LIKE THAT STUFF!
GHOST RIDER
BUT AFTER YEARS OF "ARCHIE" "LOVE & ROCKETS", "X-MEN" & "PERSEPOLIS", CERTAIN HEALTH ISSUES DO ARISE--
I'M GIVING YOU TWO LITERS OF LIQUEFIED HENRY JAMES & A HEMINGWAY SHORT STORY--
THE TURN OF THE SCREW
GRIFFY 3-21
NNF-- WHATEVER IT TAKES, NURSE..

47

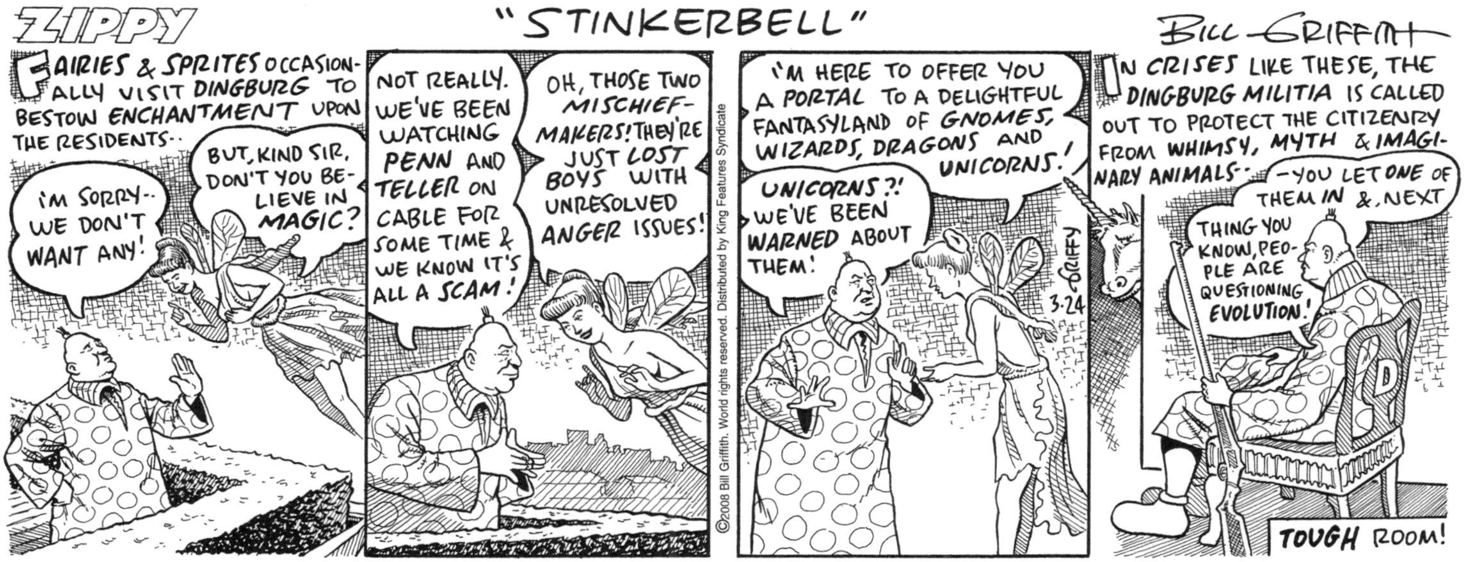
ZIPPY
"STINKERBELL"
BILL GRIFFITH
FAIRIES & SPRITES OCCASIONALLY VISIT DINGBURG TO BESTOW ENCHANTMENT UPON THE RESIDENTS..
I'M SORRY.. WE DON'T WANT ANY!
BUT, KIND SIR, DON'T YOU BELIEVE IN MAGIC?
NOT REALLY. WE'VE BEEN WATCHING PENN AND TELLER ON CABLE FOR SOME TIME & WE KNOW IT'S ALL A SCAM!
OH, THOSE TWO MISCHIEF-MAKERS! THEY'RE JUST LOST BOYS WITH UNRESOLVED ANGER ISSUES!
©2008 Bill Griffith. World rights reserved. Distributed by King Features Syndicate
I'M HERE TO OFFER YOU A PORTAL TO A DELIGHTFUL FANTASYLAND OF GNOMES, WIZARDS, DRAGONS AND UNICORNS!
UNICORNS?! WE'VE BEEN WARNED ABOUT THEM!
GRIFFY 3-24
IN CRISES LIKE THESE, THE DINGBURG MILITIA IS CALLED OUT TO PROTECT THE CITIZENRY FROM WHIMSY, MYTH & IMAGINARY ANIMALS..
-YOU LET ONE OF THEM IN &, NEXT THING YOU KNOW, PEOPLE ARE QUESTIONING EVOLUTION!
TOUGH ROOM!

48

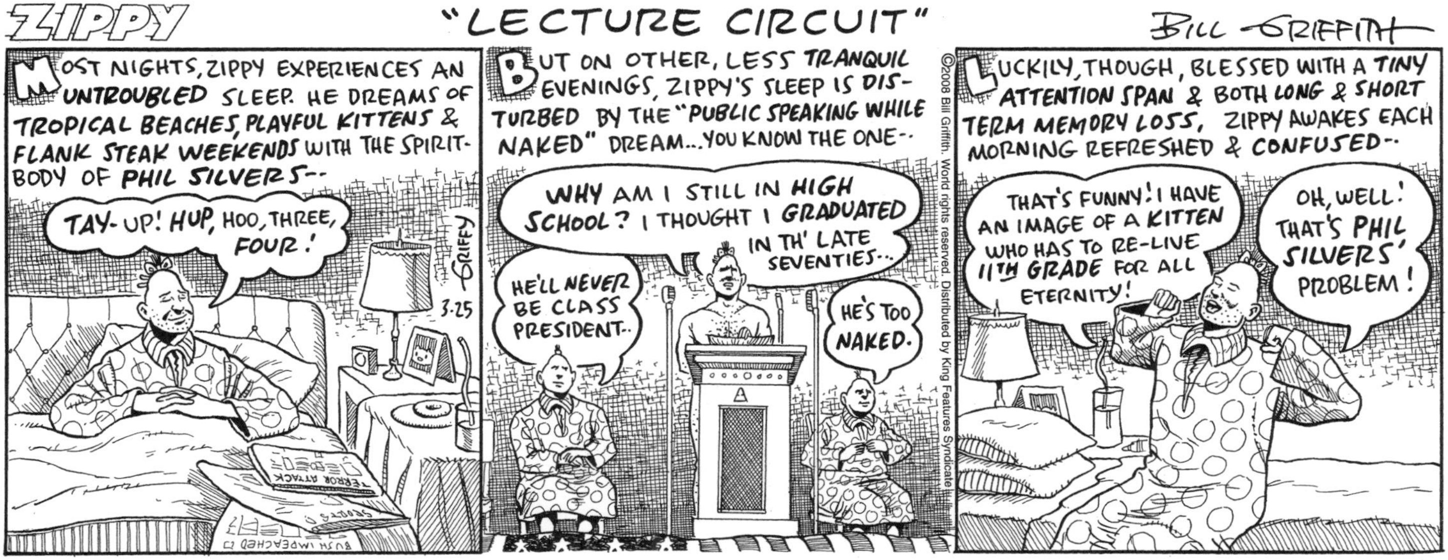
ZIPPY
"LECTURE CIRCUIT"
BILL GRIFFITH
MOST NIGHTS, ZIPPY EXPERIENCES AN UNTROUBLED SLEEP. HE DREAMS OF TROPICAL BEACHES, PLAYFUL KITTENS & FLANK STEAK WEEKENDS WITH THE SPIRIT-BODY OF PHIL SILVERS..
TAY-UP! HUP, HOO, THREE, FOUR!
GRIFFY 3-25
TERROR ATTACK
BUSH IMPEACHED
BUT ON OTHER, LESS TRANQUIL EVENINGS, ZIPPY'S SLEEP IS DISTURBED BY THE "PUBLIC SPEAKING WHILE NAKED" DREAM... YOU KNOW THE ONE..
WHY AM I STILL IN HIGH SCHOOL? I THOUGHT I GRADUATED IN TH' LATE SEVENTIES..
HE'LL NEVER BE CLASS PRESIDENT..
HE'S TOO NAKED.
©2008 Bill Griffith. World rights reserved. Distributed by King Features Syndicate
LUCKILY, THOUGH, BLESSED WITH A TINY ATTENTION SPAN & BOTH LONG & SHORT TERM MEMORY LOSS, ZIPPY AWAKES EACH MORNING REFRESHED & CONFUSED..
THAT'S FUNNY! I HAVE AN IMAGE OF A KITTEN WHO HAS TO RE-LIVE 11TH GRADE FOR ALL ETERNITY!
OH, WELL! THAT'S PHIL SILVERS' PROBLEM!

49

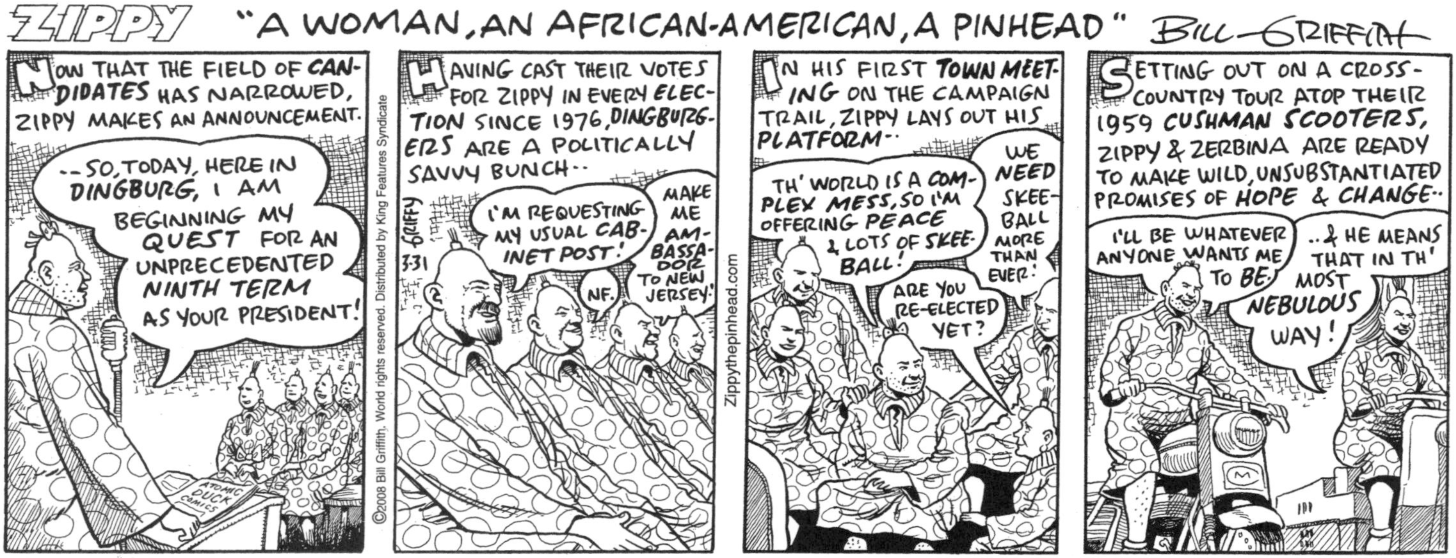
ZIPPY
"A WOMAN, AN AFRICAN-AMERICAN, A PINHEAD"
BILL GRIFFITH
NOW THAT THE FIELD OF CANDIDATES HAS NARROWED, ZIPPY MAKES AN ANNOUNCEMENT.
-- SO, TODAY, HERE IN DINGBURG, I AM BEGINNING MY QUEST FOR AN UNPRECEDENTED NINTH TERM AS YOUR PRESIDENT!
ATOMIC DUCK COMICS
©2008 Bill Griffith. World rights reserved. Distributed by King Features Syndicate
HAVING CAST THEIR VOTES FOR ZIPPY IN EVERY ELECTION SINCE 1976, DINGBURGERS ARE A POLITICALLY SAVVY BUNCH..
I'M REQUESTING MY USUAL CABINET POST!
MAKE ME AMBASSADOR TO NEW JERSEY!
NF.
GRIFFY 3·31
Zippythepinhead.com
IN HIS FIRST TOWN MEETING ON THE CAMPAIGN TRAIL, ZIPPY LAYS OUT HIS PLATFORM..
TH' WORLD IS A COMPLEX MESS, SO I'M OFFERING PEACE & LOTS OF SKEE-BALL!
WE NEED SKEE-BALL MORE THAN EVER!
ARE YOU RE-ELECTED YET?
SETTING OUT ON A CROSS-COUNTRY TOUR ATOP THEIR 1959 CUSHMAN SCOOTERS, ZIPPY & ZERBINA ARE READY TO MAKE WILD, UNSUBSTANTIATED PROMISES OF HOPE & CHANGE..
I'LL BE WHATEVER ANYONE WANTS ME TO BE.
..& HE MEANS THAT IN TH' MOST NEBULOUS WAY!

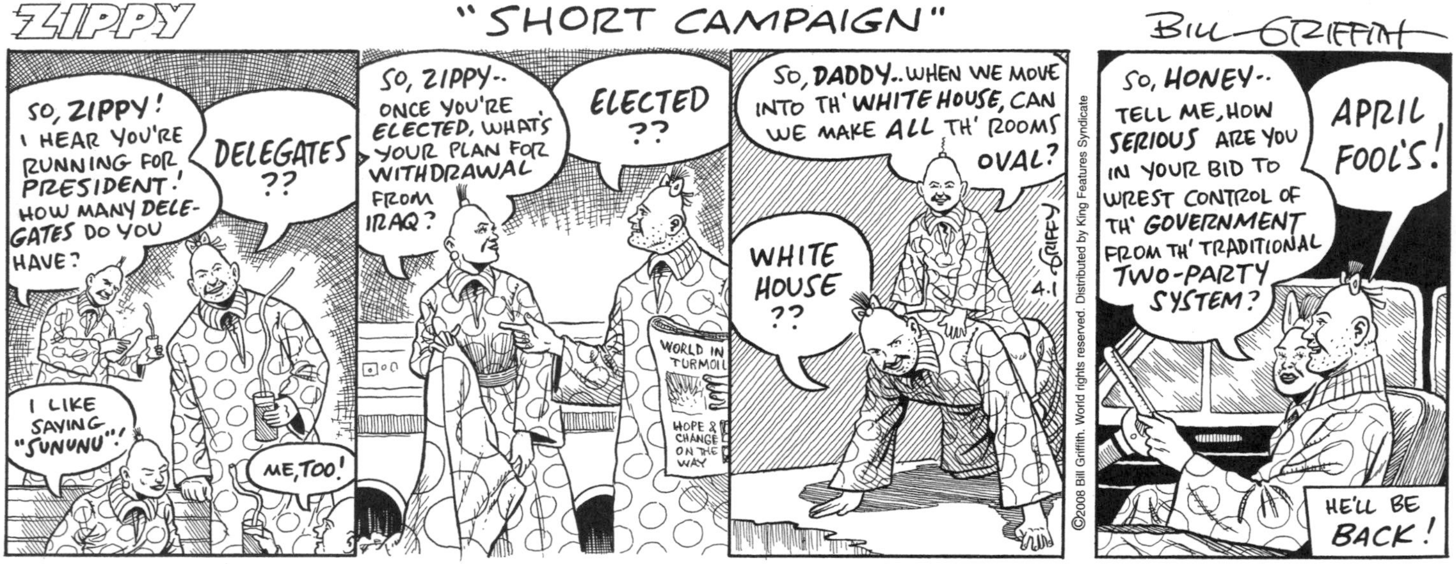
ZIPPY
"SHORT CAMPAIGN"
BILL GRIFFITH
SO, ZIPPY! I HEAR YOU'RE RUNNING FOR PRESIDENT! HOW MANY DELEGATES DO YOU HAVE?
DELEGATES ??
I LIKE SAYING "SUNUNU"!
ME, TOO!
SO, ZIPPY.. ONCE YOU'RE ELECTED, WHAT'S YOUR PLAN FOR WITHDRAWAL FROM IRAQ?
ELECTED ??
WORLD IN TURMOIL
HOPE & CHANGE ON THE WAY
SO, DADDY.. WHEN WE MOVE INTO TH' WHITE HOUSE, CAN WE MAKE ALL TH' ROOMS OVAL?
WHITE HOUSE ??
GRIFFY 4·1
©2008 Bill Griffith. World rights reserved. Distributed by King Features Syndicate
SO, HONEY.. TELL ME, HOW SERIOUS ARE YOU IN YOUR BID TO WREST CONTROL OF TH' GOVERNMENT FROM TH' TRADITIONAL TWO-PARTY SYSTEM?
APRIL FOOL'S!
HE'LL BE BACK!

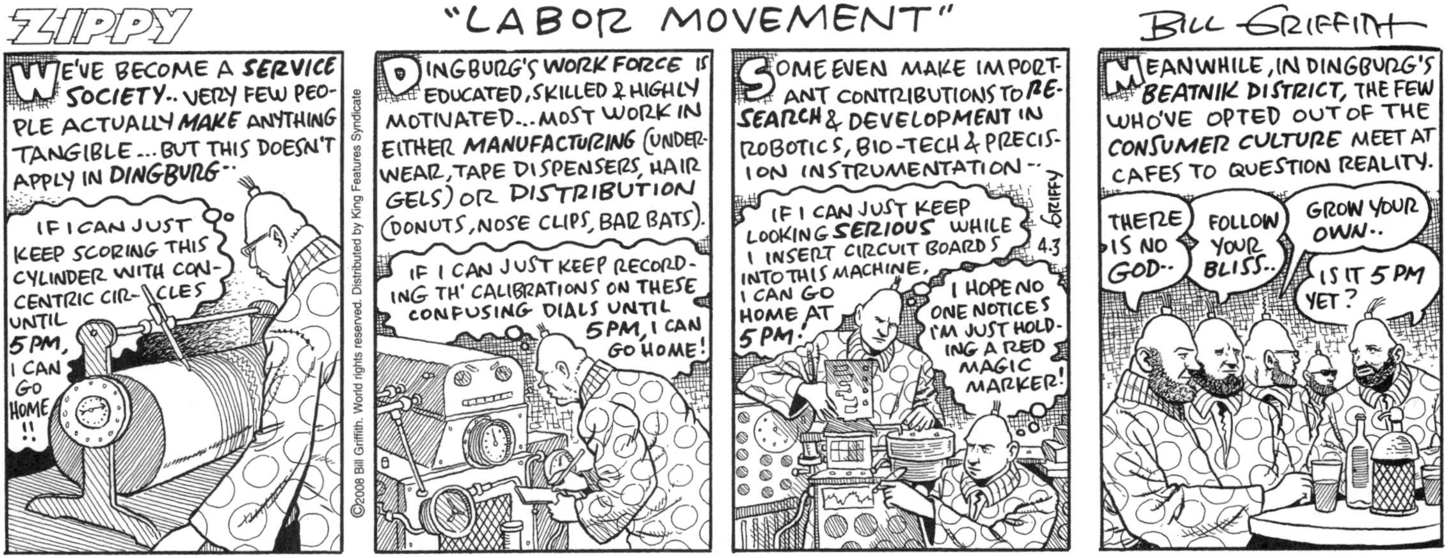
ZIPPY
"LABOR MOVEMENT"
BILL GRIFFITH
WE'VE BECOME A SERVICE SOCIETY.. VERY FEW PEOPLE ACTUALLY MAKE ANYTHING TANGIBLE... BUT THIS DOESN'T APPLY IN DINGBURG..
IF I CAN JUST KEEP SCORING THIS CYLINDER WITH CONCENTRIC CIRCLES UNTIL 5 PM, I CAN GO HOME!!
©2008 Bill Griffith. World rights reserved. Distributed by King Features Syndicate
DINGBURG'S WORK FORCE IS EDUCATED, SKILLED & HIGHLY MOTIVATED... MOST WORK IN EITHER MANUFACTURING (UNDERWEAR, TAPE DISPENSERS, HAIR GELS) OR DISTRIBUTION (DONUTS, NOSE CLIPS, BAR BATS).
IF I CAN JUST KEEP RECORDING TH' CALIBRATIONS ON THESE CONFUSING DIALS UNTIL 5 PM, I CAN GO HOME!
SOME EVEN MAKE IMPORTANT CONTRIBUTIONS TO RESEARCH & DEVELOPMENT IN ROBOTICS, BIO-TECH & PRECISION INSTRUMENTATION--
IF I CAN JUST KEEP LOOKING SERIOUS WHILE I INSERT CIRCUIT BOARDS INTO THIS MACHINE, I CAN GO HOME AT 5 PM!
I HOPE NO ONE NOTICES I'M JUST HOLDING A RED MAGIC MARKER!
GRIFFY 4.3
MEANWHILE, IN DINGBURG'S BEATNIK DISTRICT, THE FEW WHO'VE OPTED OUT OF THE CONSUMER CULTURE MEET AT CAFES TO QUESTION REALITY.
THERE IS NO GOD..
FOLLOW YOUR BLISS..
GROW YOUR OWN..
IS IT 5 PM YET?

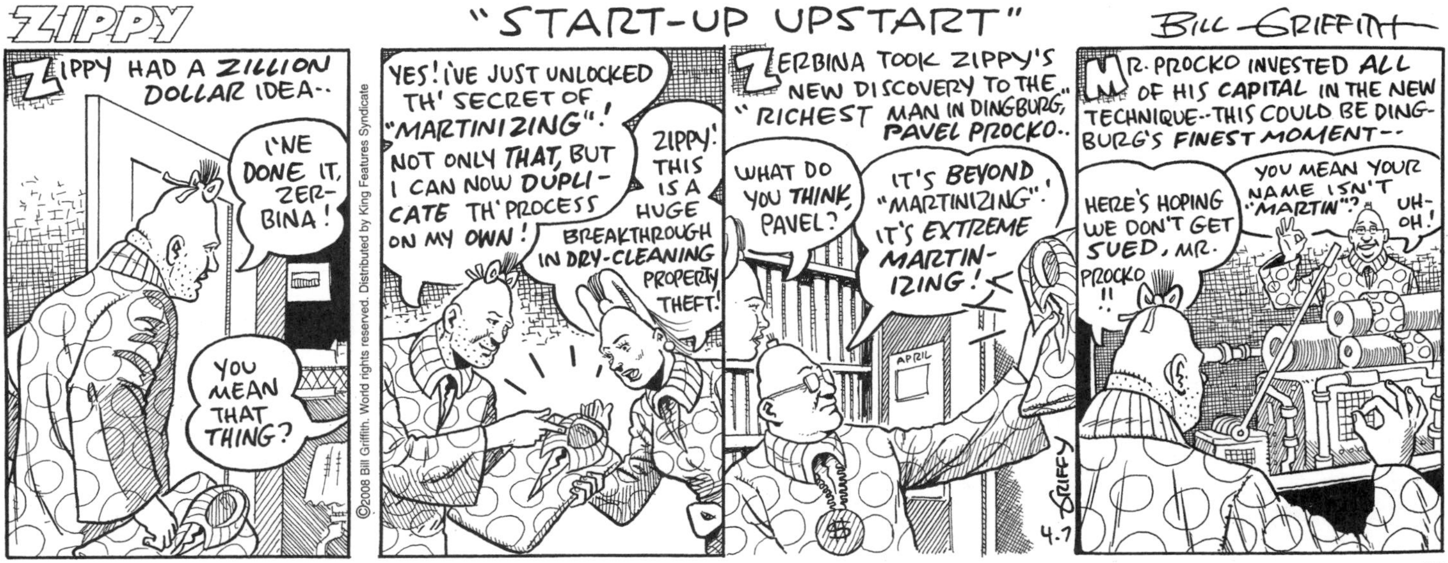
ZIPPY
"START-UP UPSTART"
BILL GRIFFITH
ZIPPY HAD A ZILLION DOLLAR IDEA..
I'VE DONE IT, ZERBINA!
YOU MEAN THAT THING?
©2008 Bill Griffith. World rights reserved. Distributed by King Features Syndicate
YES! I'VE JUST UNLOCKED TH' SECRET OF "MARTINIZING"! NOT ONLY THAT, BUT I CAN NOW DUPLICATE TH' PROCESS ON MY OWN!
ZIPPY! THIS IS A HUGE BREAKTHROUGH IN DRY-CLEANING PROPERTY THEFT!
ZERBINA TOOK ZIPPY'S NEW DISCOVERY TO THE "RICHEST MAN IN DINGBURG," PAVEL PROCKO..
WHAT DO YOU THINK, PAVEL?
IT'S BEYOND "MARTINIZING"! IT'S EXTREME MARTINIZING!
APRIL
GRIFFY 4.7
MR. PROCKO INVESTED ALL OF HIS CAPITAL IN THE NEW TECHNIQUE--THIS COULD BE DINGBURG'S FINEST MOMENT--
HERE'S HOPING WE DON'T GET SUED, MR. PROCKO!!
YOU MEAN YOUR NAME ISN'T "MARTIN"?
UH-OH!

50

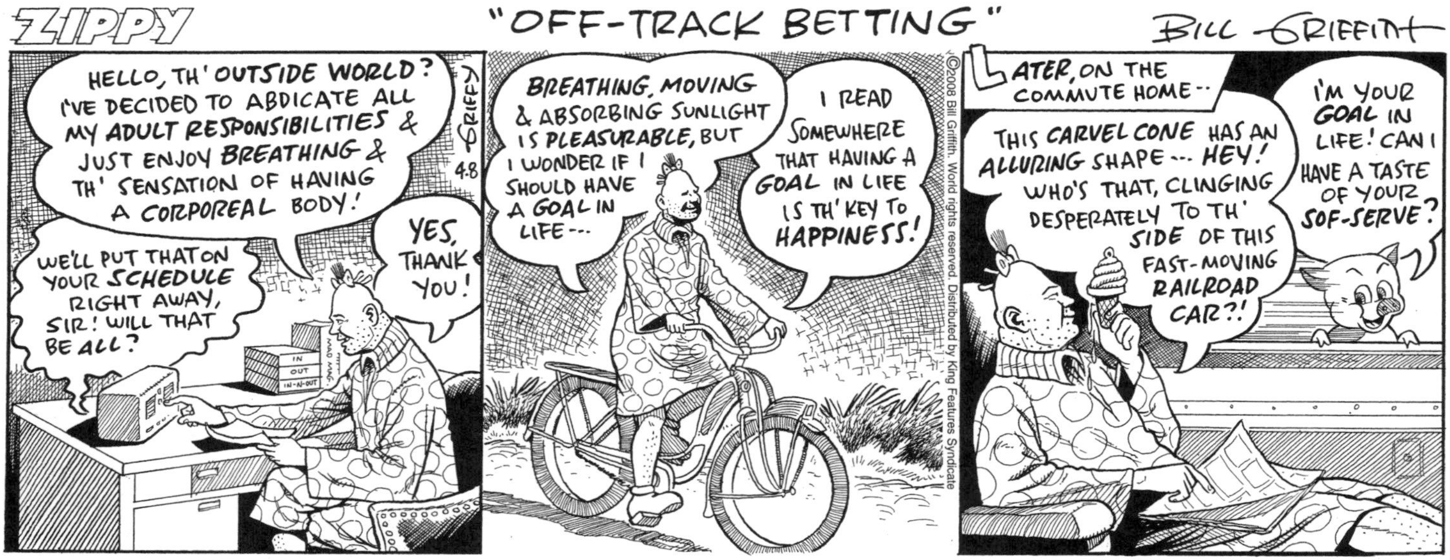
ZIPPY
"OFF-TRACK BETTING"
BILL GRIFFITH
HELLO, TH' OUTSIDE WORLD? I'VE DECIDED TO ABDICATE ALL MY ADULT RESPONSIBILITIES & JUST ENJOY BREATHING & TH' SENSATION OF HAVING A CORPOREAL BODY!
WE'LL PUT THAT ON YOUR SCHEDULE RIGHT AWAY, SIR! WILL THAT BE ALL?
YES, THANK YOU!
GRIFFY 4-8
IN
OUT
IN-N-OUT
BREATHING, MOVING & ABSORBING SUNLIGHT IS PLEASURABLE, BUT I WONDER IF I SHOULD HAVE A GOAL IN LIFE---
I READ SOMEWHERE THAT HAVING A GOAL IN LIFE IS TH' KEY TO HAPPINESS!
©2008 Bill Griffith. World rights reserved. Distributed by King Features Syndicate
LATER, ON THE COMMUTE HOME--
THIS CARVEL CONE HAS AN ALLURING SHAPE--- HEY! WHO'S THAT, CLINGING DESPERATELY TO TH' SIDE OF THIS FAST-MOVING RAILROAD CAR?!
I'M YOUR GOAL IN LIFE! CAN I HAVE A TASTE OF YOUR SOF-SERVE?

51

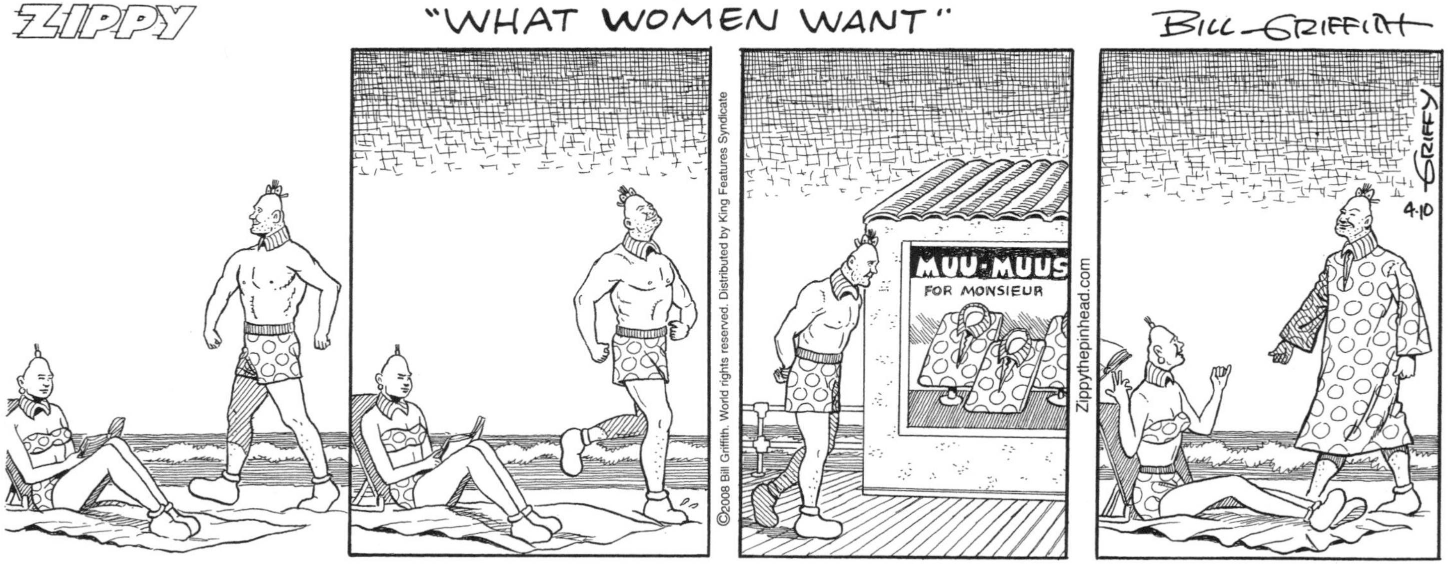
ZIPPY
"WHAT WOMEN WANT"
BILL GRIFFITH
©2008 Bill Griffith. World rights reserved. Distributed by King Features Syndicate
MUU-MUUS FOR MONSIEUR
Zippythepinhead.com
GRIFFY 4-10

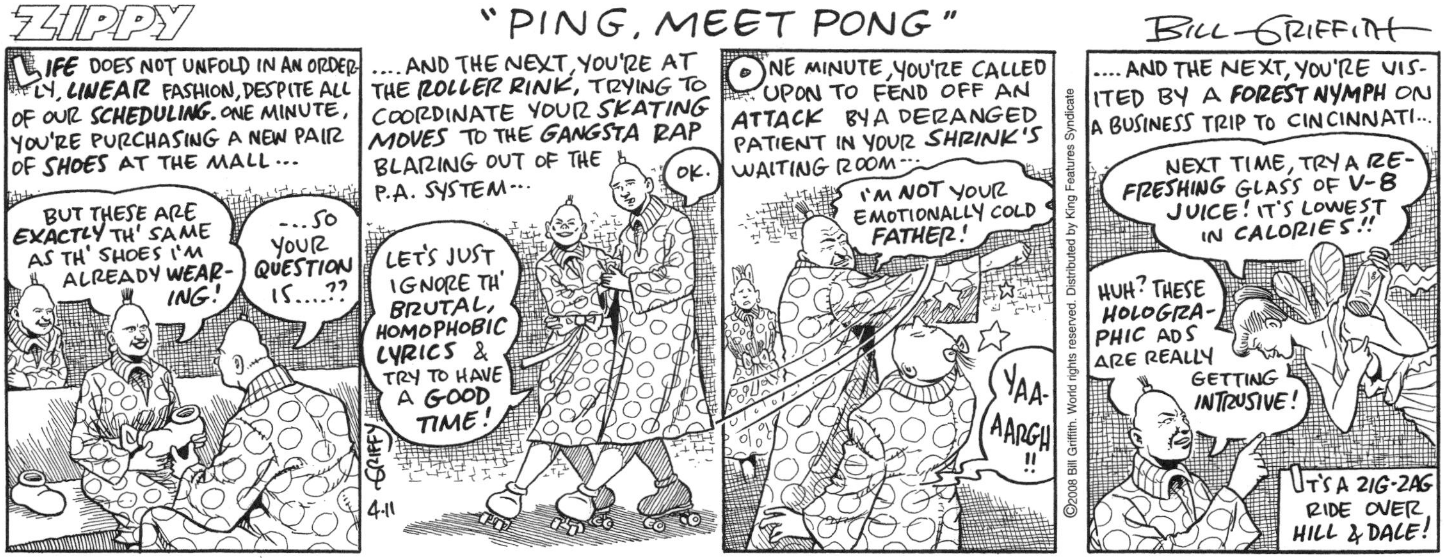
ZIPPY
"PING, MEET PONG"
BILL GRIFFITH
LIFE DOES NOT UNFOLD IN AN ORDERLY, LINEAR FASHION, DESPITE ALL OF OUR SCHEDULING. ONE MINUTE, YOU'RE PURCHASING A NEW PAIR OF SHOES AT THE MALL...
BUT THESE ARE EXACTLY TH' SAME AS TH' SHOES I'M ALREADY WEARING!
...SO YOUR QUESTION IS....??
....AND THE NEXT, YOU'RE AT THE ROLLER RINK, TRYING TO COORDINATE YOUR SKATING MOVES TO THE GANGSTA RAP BLARING OUT OF THE P.A. SYSTEM...
OK.
LET'S JUST IGNORE TH' BRUTAL, HOMOPHOBIC LYRICS & TRY TO HAVE A GOOD TIME!
GRIFFY 4-11
ONE MINUTE, YOU'RE CALLED UPON TO FEND OFF AN ATTACK BY A DERANGED PATIENT IN YOUR SHRINK'S WAITING ROOM...
I'M NOT YOUR EMOTIONALLY COLD FATHER!
YAA-AARGH!!
©2008 Bill Griffith. World rights reserved. Distributed by King Features Syndicate
....AND THE NEXT, YOU'RE VISITED BY A FOREST NYMPH ON A BUSINESS TRIP TO CINCINNATI...
NEXT TIME, TRY A REFRESHING GLASS OF V-8 JUICE! IT'S LOWEST IN CALORIES!!
HUH? THESE HOLOGRAPHIC ADS ARE REALLY GETTING INTRUSIVE!
IT'S A ZIG-ZAG RIDE OVER HILL & DALE!

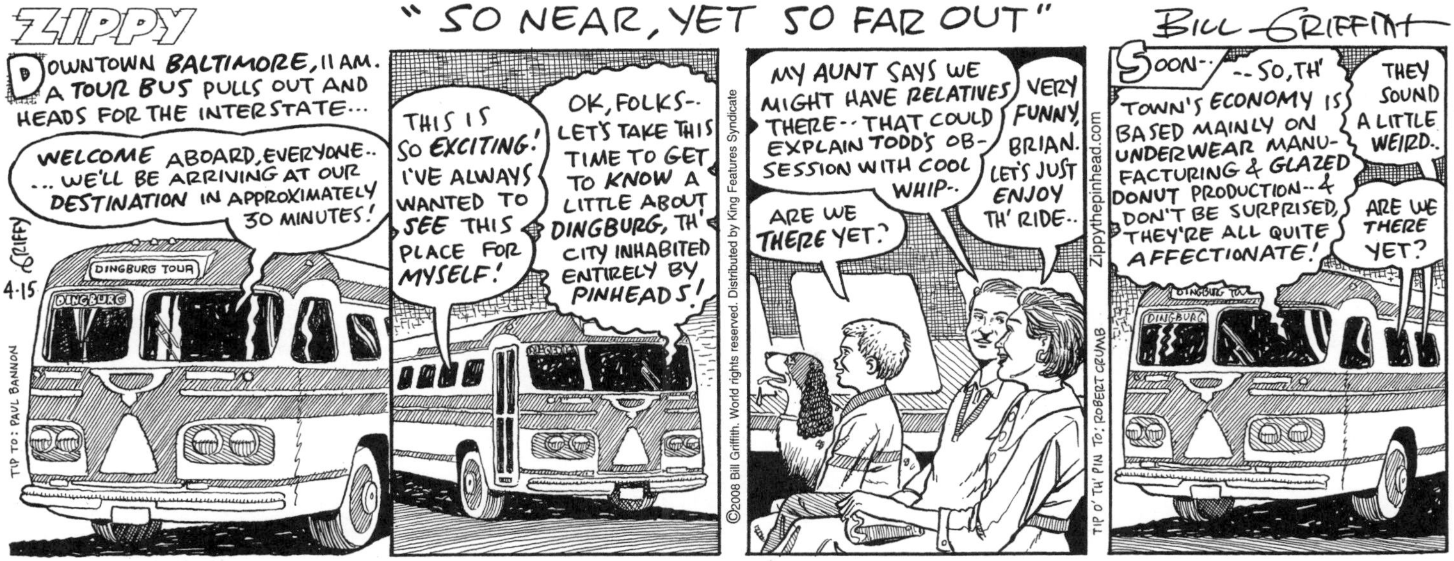
ZIPPY
"SO NEAR, YET SO FAR OUT"
BILL GRIFFITH
DOWNTOWN BALTIMORE, 11 AM. A TOUR BUS PULLS OUT AND HEADS FOR THE INTERSTATE...
WELCOME ABOARD, EVERYONE.. ...WE'LL BE ARRIVING AT OUR DESTINATION IN APPROXIMATELY 30 MINUTES!
GRIFFY 4-15
DINGBURG TOUR
DINGBURG
TIP TO: PAUL BANNON
THIS IS SO EXCITING! I'VE ALWAYS WANTED TO SEE THIS PLACE FOR MYSELF!
OK, FOLKS-- LET'S TAKE THIS TIME TO GET TO KNOW A LITTLE ABOUT DINGBURG, TH' CITY INHABITED ENTIRELY BY PINHEADS!
©2008 Bill Griffith. World rights reserved. Distributed by King Features Syndicate
MY AUNT SAYS WE MIGHT HAVE RELATIVES THERE-- THAT COULD EXPLAIN TODD'S OBSESSION WITH COOL WHIP..
VERY FUNNY, BRIAN. LET'S JUST ENJOY TH' RIDE..
ARE WE THERE YET?
Zippythepinhead.com
TIP O' TH' PIN TO: ROBERT CRUMB
SOON..
--SO, TH' TOWN'S ECONOMY IS BASED MAINLY ON UNDERWEAR MANUFACTURING & GLAZED DONUT PRODUCTION-- & DON'T BE SURPRISED, THEY'RE ALL QUITE AFFECTIONATE!
THEY SOUND A LITTLE WEIRD..
ARE WE THERE YET?
DINGBURG TOUR
DINGBURG

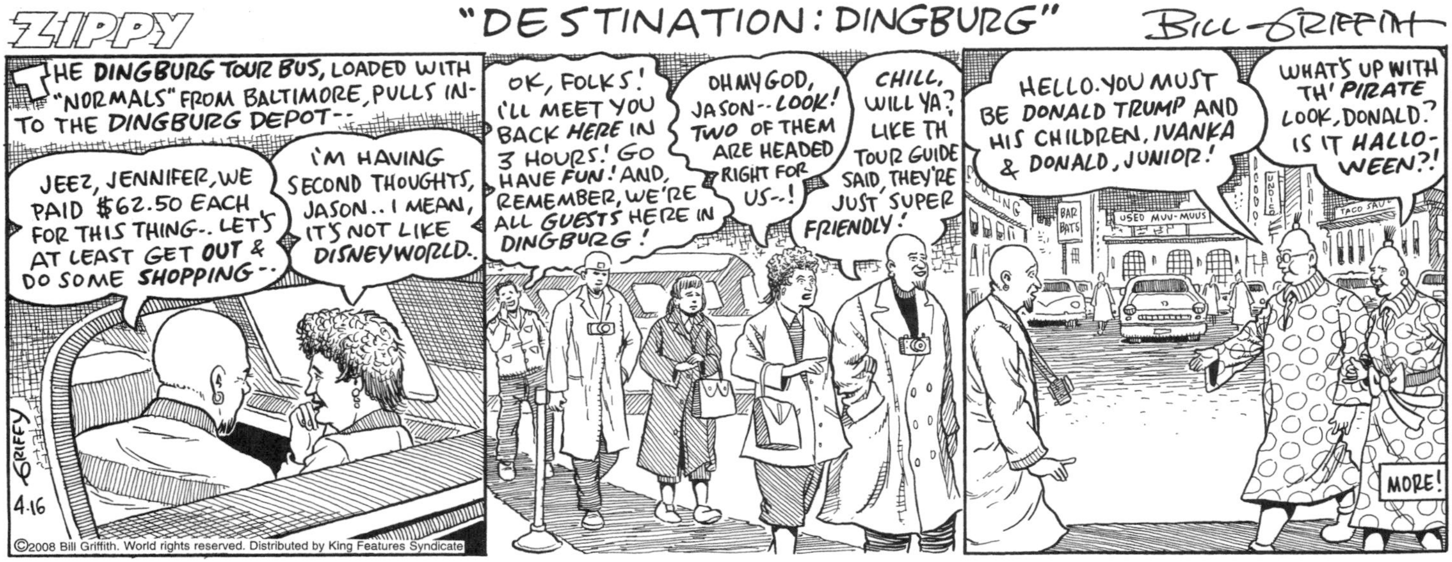
ZIPPY
"DESTINATION: DINGBURG"
BILL GRIFFITH
THE DINGBURG TOUR BUS, LOADED WITH "NORMALS" FROM BALTIMORE, PULLS INTO THE DINGBURG DEPOT--
JEEZ, JENNIFER, WE PAID $62.50 EACH FOR THIS THING--. LET'S AT LEAST GET OUT & DO SOME SHOPPING--.
I'M HAVING SECOND THOUGHTS, JASON.. I MEAN, IT'S NOT LIKE DISNEYWORLD..
GRIFFY
4.16
OK, FOLKS! I'LL MEET YOU BACK HERE IN 3 HOURS! GO HAVE FUN! AND, REMEMBER, WE'RE ALL GUESTS HERE IN DINGBURG!
OH MY GOD, JASON--LOOK! TWO OF THEM ARE HEADED RIGHT FOR US--!
CHILL, WILL YA? LIKE TH TOUR GUIDE SAID, THEY'RE JUST SUPER FRIENDLY!
HELLO. YOU MUST BE DONALD TRUMP AND HIS CHILDREN, IVANKA & DONALD, JUNIOR!
WHAT'S UP WITH TH' PIRATE LOOK, DONALD? IS IT HALLOWEEN?!
BAR BATS
USED MUU-MUUS
TACO
MORE!
©2008 Bill Griffith. World rights reserved. Distributed by King Features Syndicate

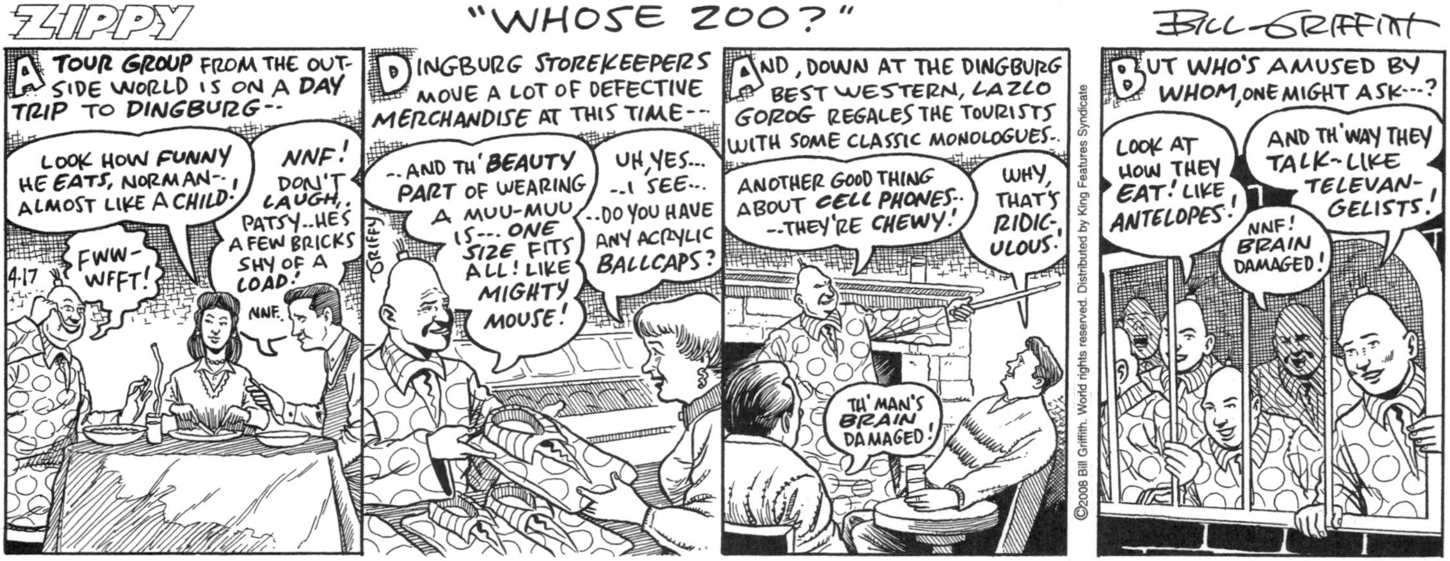
ZIPPY
"WHOSE ZOO?"
BILL GRIFFITH
A TOUR GROUP FROM THE OUTSIDE WORLD IS ON A DAY TRIP TO DINGBURG--
LOOK HOW FUNNY HE EATS, NORMAN--! ALMOST LIKE A CHILD!
NNF! DON'T LAUGH, PATSY..HE'S A FEW BRICKS SHY OF A LOAD!
FWW-WFFT!
NNF.
4.17
DINGBURG STOREKEEPERS MOVE A LOT OF DEFECTIVE MERCHANDISE AT THIS TIME--
--AND TH' BEAUTY PART OF WEARING A MUU-MUU IS--. ONE SIZE FITS ALL! LIKE MIGHTY MOUSE!
UH, YES... --I SEE--. --DO YOU HAVE ANY ACRYLIC BALLCAPS?
GRIFFY
AND, DOWN AT THE DINGBURG BEST WESTERN, LAZLO GOROG REGALES THE TOURISTS WITH SOME CLASSIC MONOLOGUES-.
ANOTHER GOOD THING ABOUT CELL PHONES-. --THEY'RE CHEWY!
WHY, THAT'S RIDICULOUS!
TH' MAN'S BRAIN DAMAGED!
BUT WHO'S AMUSED BY WHOM, ONE MIGHT ASK---?
LOOK AT HOW THEY EAT! LIKE ANTELOPES!
AND TH' WAY THEY TALK--LIKE TELEVANGELISTS!
NNF! BRAIN DAMAGED!
©2008 Bill Griffith. World rights reserved. Distributed by King Features Syndicate

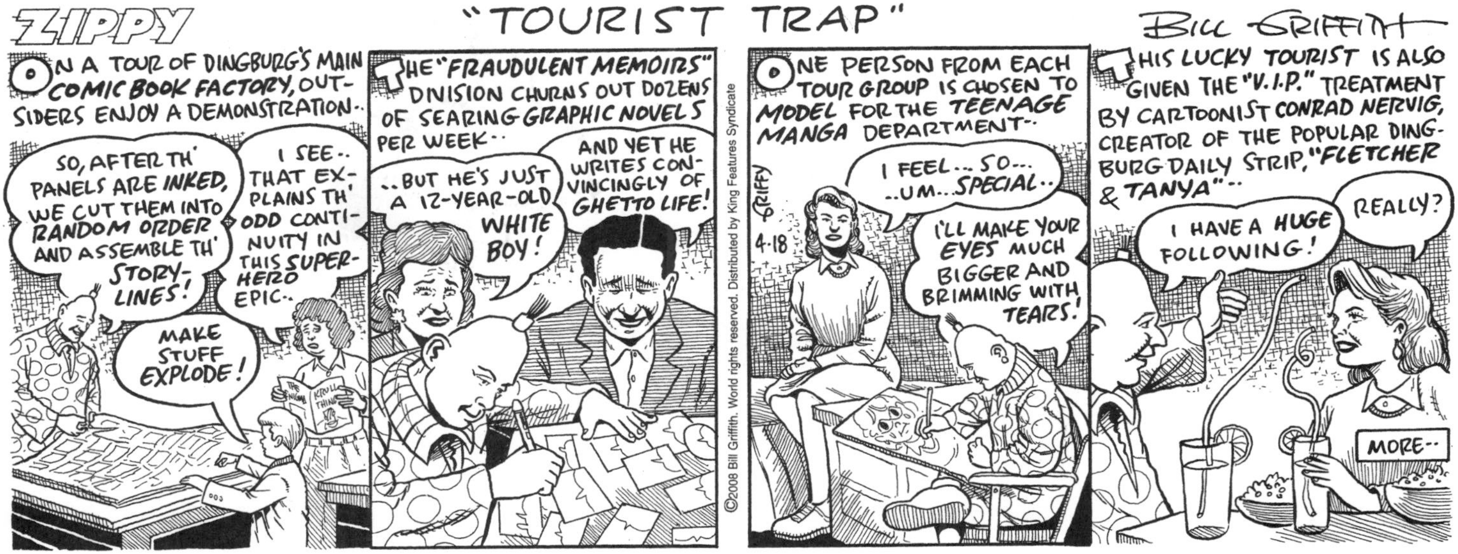
ZIPPY
"TOURIST TRAP"
BILL GRIFFITH
ON A TOUR OF DINGBURG'S MAIN COMIC BOOK FACTORY, OUTSIDERS ENJOY A DEMONSTRATION..
SO, AFTER TH' PANELS ARE INKED, WE CUT THEM INTO RANDOM ORDER AND ASSEMBLE TH' STORY-LINES!
I SEE.. THAT EXPLAINS TH' ODD CONTINUITY IN THIS SUPER-HERO EPIC..
MAKE STUFF EXPLODE!
THE "FRAUDULENT MEMOIRS" DIVISION CHURNS OUT DOZENS OF SEARING GRAPHIC NOVELS PER WEEK..
..BUT HE'S JUST A 12-YEAR-OLD WHITE BOY!
AND YET HE WRITES CONVINCINGLY OF GHETTO LIFE!
©2008 Bill Griffith. World rights reserved. Distributed by King Features Syndicate
GRIFFY 4-18
ONE PERSON FROM EACH TOUR GROUP IS CHOSEN TO MODEL FOR THE TEENAGE MANGA DEPARTMENT..
I FEEL... SO... ..UM...SPECIAL..
I'LL MAKE YOUR EYES MUCH BIGGER AND BRIMMING WITH TEARS!
THIS LUCKY TOURIST IS ALSO GIVEN THE "V.I.P." TREATMENT BY CARTOONIST CONRAD NERVIG, CREATOR OF THE POPULAR DINGBURG DAILY STRIP, "FLETCHER & TANYA"..
I HAVE A HUGE FOLLOWING!
REALLY?
MORE..

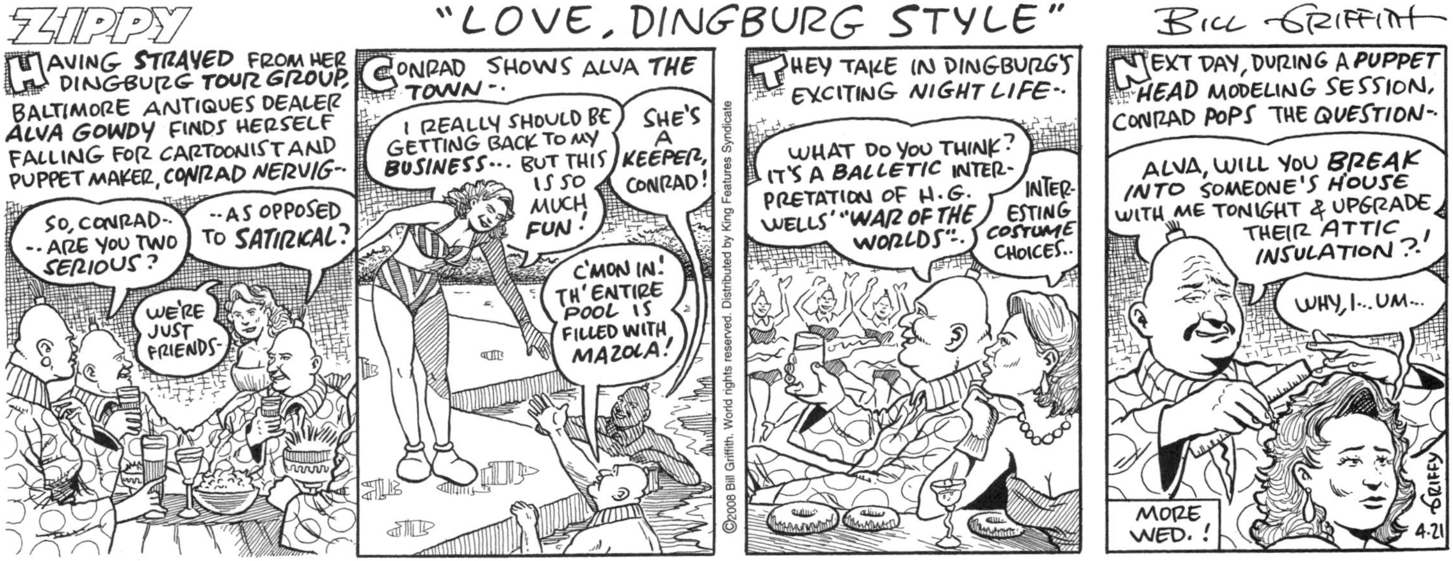
ZIPPY
"LOVE, DINGBURG STYLE"
BILL GRIFFITH
HAVING STRAYED FROM HER DINGBURG TOUR GROUP, BALTIMORE ANTIQUES DEALER ALVA GOWDY FINDS HERSELF FALLING FOR CARTOONIST AND PUPPET MAKER, CONRAD NERVIG..
SO, CONRAD.. ..ARE YOU TWO SERIOUS?
..AS OPPOSED TO SATIRICAL?
WE'RE JUST FRIENDS..
CONRAD SHOWS ALVA THE TOWN..
I REALLY SHOULD BE GETTING BACK TO MY BUSINESS... BUT THIS IS SO MUCH FUN!
SHE'S A KEEPER, CONRAD!
C'MON IN! TH' ENTIRE POOL IS FILLED WITH MAZOLA!
©2008 Bill Griffith. World rights reserved. Distributed by King Features Syndicate
THEY TAKE IN DINGBURG'S EXCITING NIGHT LIFE..
WHAT DO YOU THINK? IT'S A BALLETIC INTERPRETATION OF H.G. WELLS' "WAR OF THE WORLDS"..
INTERESTING COSTUME CHOICES..
NEXT DAY, DURING A PUPPET HEAD MODELING SESSION, CONRAD POPS THE QUESTION..
ALVA, WILL YOU BREAK INTO SOMEONE'S HOUSE WITH ME TONIGHT & UPGRADE THEIR ATTIC INSULATION?!
WHY, I...UM...
MORE WED.!
GRIFFY 4-21

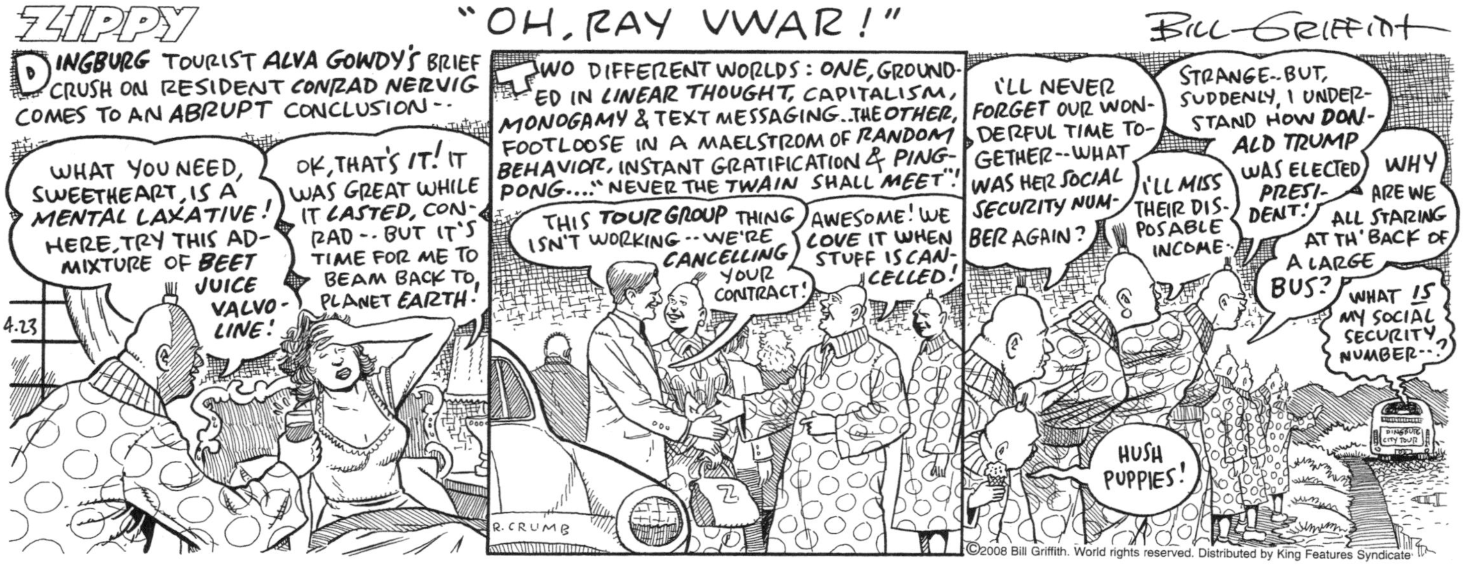
ZIPPY
"OH, RAY VWAR!"
BILL GRIFFITH
DINGBURG TOURIST ALVA GOWDY'S BRIEF CRUSH ON RESIDENT CONRAD NERVIG COMES TO AN ABRUPT CONCLUSION--
WHAT YOU NEED, SWEETHEART, IS A MENTAL LAXATIVE! HERE, TRY THIS ADMIXTURE OF BEET JUICE VALVOLINE!
OK, THAT'S IT! IT WAS GREAT WHILE IT LASTED, CONRAD--BUT IT'S TIME FOR ME TO BEAM BACK TO PLANET EARTH!
4.23
TWO DIFFERENT WORLDS: ONE, GROUNDED IN LINEAR THOUGHT, CAPITALISM, MONOGAMY & TEXT MESSAGING..THE OTHER, FOOTLOOSE IN A MAELSTROM OF RANDOM BEHAVIOR, INSTANT GRATIFICATION & PING-PONG...."NEVER THE TWAIN SHALL MEET"!
THIS TOUR GROUP THING ISN'T WORKING--WE'RE CANCELLING YOUR CONTRACT!
AWESOME! WE LOVE IT WHEN STUFF IS CANCELLED!
R. CRUMB
I'LL NEVER FORGET OUR WONDERFUL TIME TOGETHER--WHAT WAS HER SOCIAL SECURITY NUMBER AGAIN?
I'LL MISS THEIR DISPOSABLE INCOME..
STRANGE--BUT, SUDDENLY, I UNDERSTAND HOW DONALD TRUMP WAS ELECTED PRESIDENT!
WHY ARE WE ALL STARING AT TH' BACK OF A LARGE BUS?
WHAT IS MY SOCIAL SECURITY NUMBER--?
HUSH PUPPIES!
DINGBURG CITY TOUR
©2008 Bill Griffith. World rights reserved. Distributed by King Features Syndicate

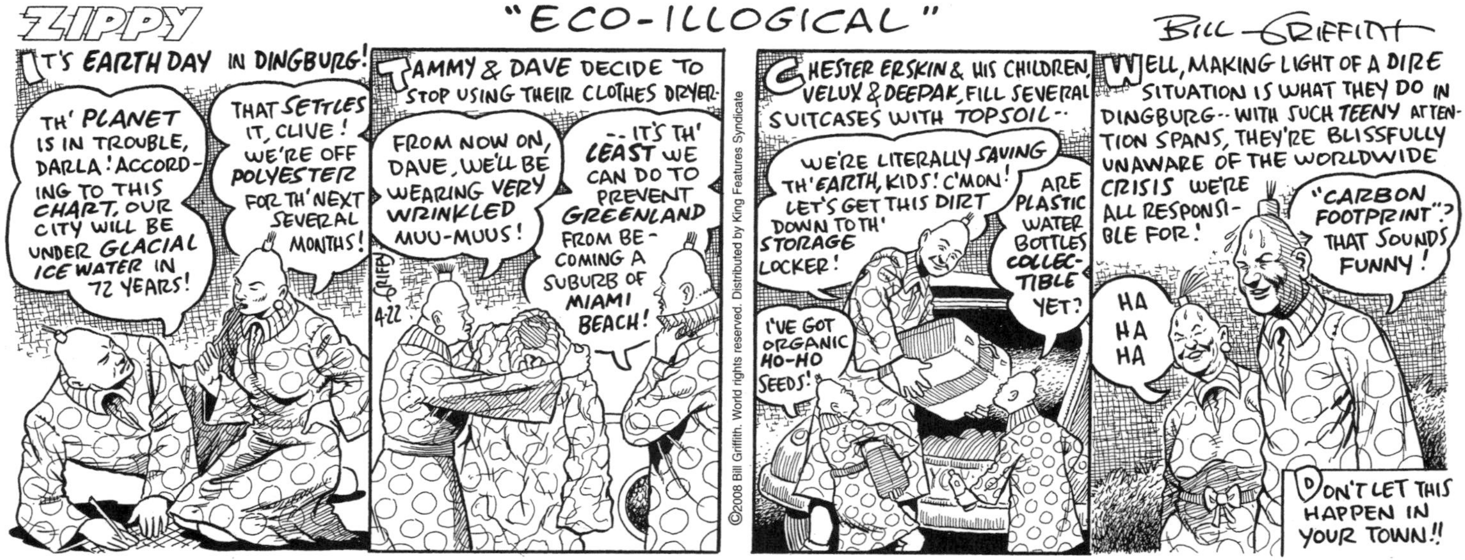
ZIPPY
"ECO-ILLOGICAL"
BILL GRIFFITH
IT'S EARTH DAY IN DINGBURG!
TH' PLANET IS IN TROUBLE, DARLA! ACCORDING TO THIS CHART, OUR CITY WILL BE UNDER GLACIAL ICE WATER IN 72 YEARS!
THAT SETTLES IT, CLIVE! WE'RE OFF POLYESTER FOR TH' NEXT SEVERAL MONTHS!
TAMMY & DAVE DECIDE TO STOP USING THEIR CLOTHES DRYER-
FROM NOW ON, DAVE, WE'LL BE WEARING VERY WRINKLED MUU-MUUS!
--IT'S TH' LEAST WE CAN DO TO PREVENT GREENLAND FROM BECOMING A SUBURB OF MIAMI BEACH!
4-22
©2008 Bill Griffith. World rights reserved. Distributed by King Features Syndicate
CHESTER ERSKIN & HIS CHILDREN, VELUX & DEEPAK, FILL SEVERAL SUITCASES WITH TOPSOIL--
WE'RE LITERALLY SAVING TH' EARTH, KIDS! C'MON! LET'S GET THIS DIRT DOWN TO TH' STORAGE LOCKER!
ARE PLASTIC WATER BOTTLES COLLECTIBLE YET?
I'VE GOT ORGANIC HO-HO SEEDS!
WELL, MAKING LIGHT OF A DIRE SITUATION IS WHAT THEY DO IN DINGBURG--WITH SUCH TEENY ATTENTION SPANS, THEY'RE BLISSFULLY UNAWARE OF THE WORLDWIDE CRISIS WE'RE ALL RESPONSIBLE FOR!
"CARBON FOOTPRINT"? THAT SOUNDS FUNNY!
HA HA HA
DON'T LET THIS HAPPEN IN YOUR TOWN!!

52

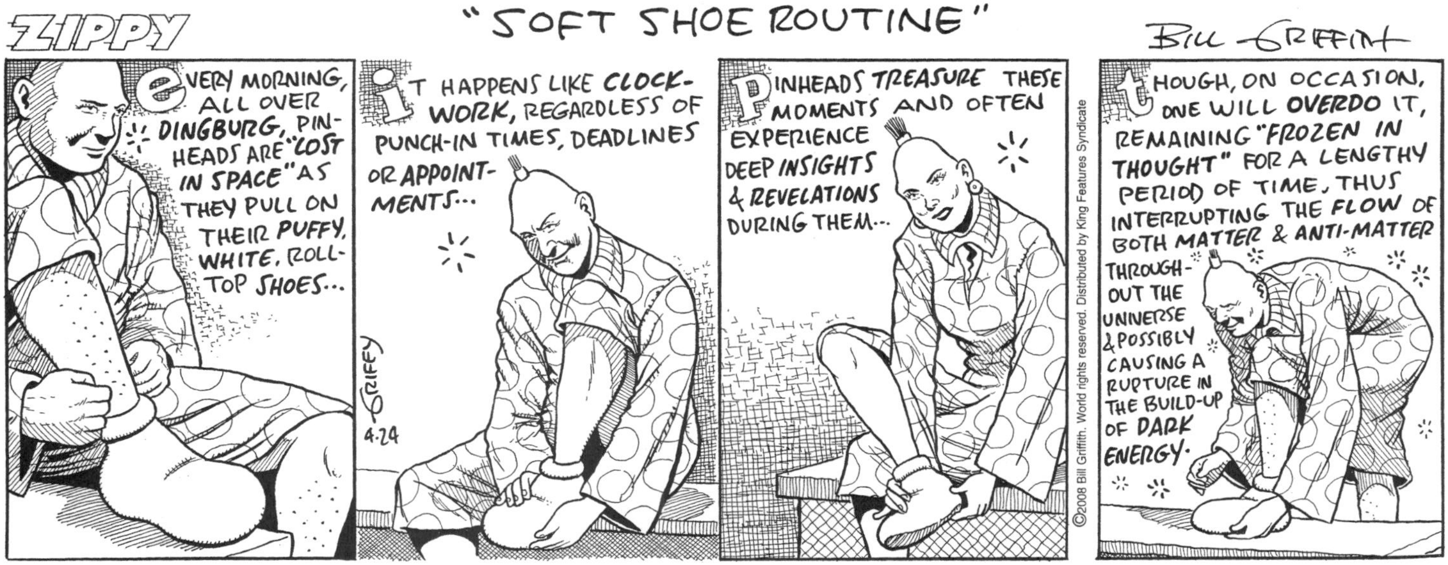
ZIPPY
"SOFT SHOE ROUTINE"
BILL GRIFFITH
EVERY MORNING, ALL OVER DINGBURG, PINHEADS ARE "LOST IN SPACE" AS THEY PULL ON THEIR PUFFY, WHITE, ROLL-TOP SHOES...
GRIFFY 4·24
IT HAPPENS LIKE CLOCK-WORK, REGARDLESS OF PUNCH-IN TIMES, DEADLINES OR APPOINT-MENTS...
PINHEADS TREASURE THESE MOMENTS AND OFTEN EXPERIENCE DEEP INSIGHTS & REVELATIONS DURING THEM...
©2008 Bill Griffith. World rights reserved. Distributed by King Features Syndicate
THOUGH, ON OCCASION, ONE WILL OVERDO IT, REMAINING "FROZEN IN THOUGHT" FOR A LENGTHY PERIOD OF TIME, THUS INTERRUPTING THE FLOW OF BOTH MATTER & ANTI-MATTER THROUGH-OUT THE UNIVERSE & POSSIBLY CAUSING A RUPTURE IN THE BUILD-UP OF DARK ENERGY.

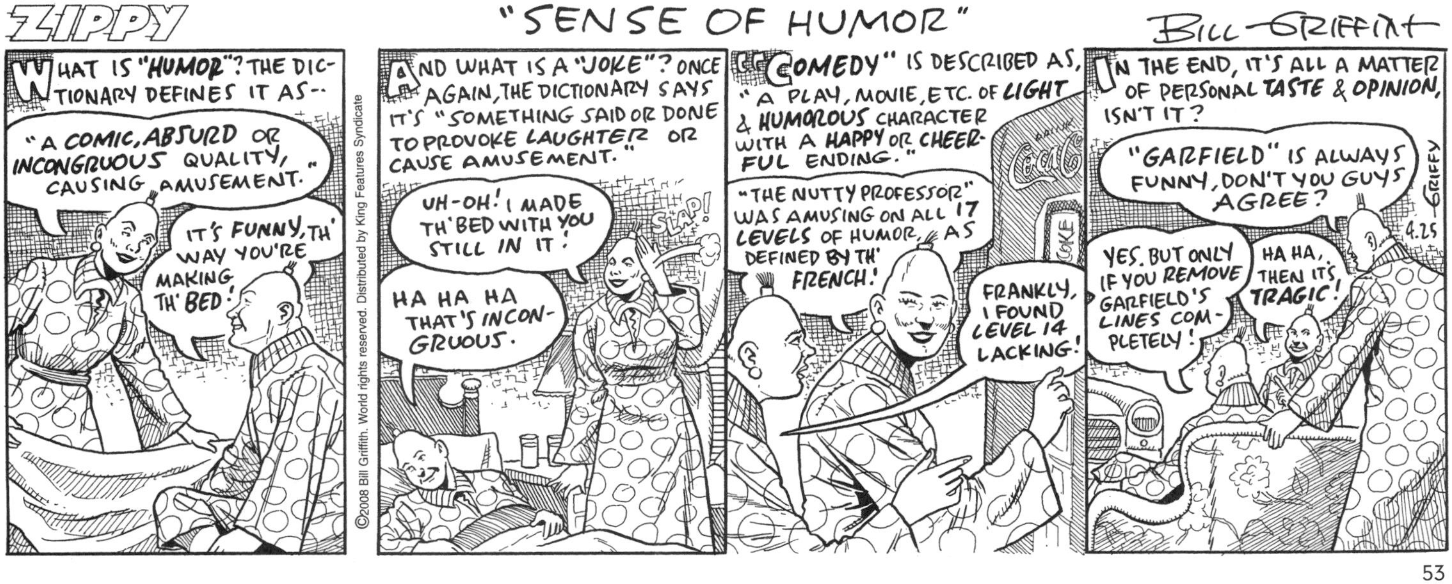
ZIPPY
"SENSE OF HUMOR"
BILL GRIFFITH
WHAT IS "HUMOR"? THE DIC-TIONARY DEFINES IT AS--
"A COMIC, ABSURD OR INCONGRUOUS QUALITY, CAUSING AMUSEMENT."
IT'S FUNNY, TH' WAY YOU'RE MAKING TH' BED!
©2008 Bill Griffith. World rights reserved. Distributed by King Features Syndicate
AND WHAT IS A "JOKE"? ONCE AGAIN, THE DICTIONARY SAYS IT'S "SOMETHING SAID OR DONE TO PROVOKE LAUGHTER OR CAUSE AMUSEMENT."
UH-OH! I MADE TH' BED WITH YOU STILL IN IT!
SLAP!
HA HA HA THAT'S INCON-GRUOUS.
"COMEDY" IS DESCRIBED AS, "A PLAY, MOVIE, ETC. OF LIGHT & HUMOROUS CHARACTER WITH A HAPPY OR CHEER-FUL ENDING."
"THE NUTTY PROFESSOR" WAS AMUSING ON ALL 17 LEVELS OF HUMOR, AS DEFINED BY TH' FRENCH!
FRANKLY, I FOUND LEVEL 14 LACKING!
IN THE END, IT'S ALL A MATTER OF PERSONAL TASTE & OPINION, ISN'T IT?
"GARFIELD" IS ALWAYS FUNNY, DON'T YOU GUYS AGREE?
GRIFFY 4.25
YES, BUT ONLY IF YOU REMOVE GARFIELD'S LINES COM-PLETELY!
HA HA, THEN IT'S TRAGIC!

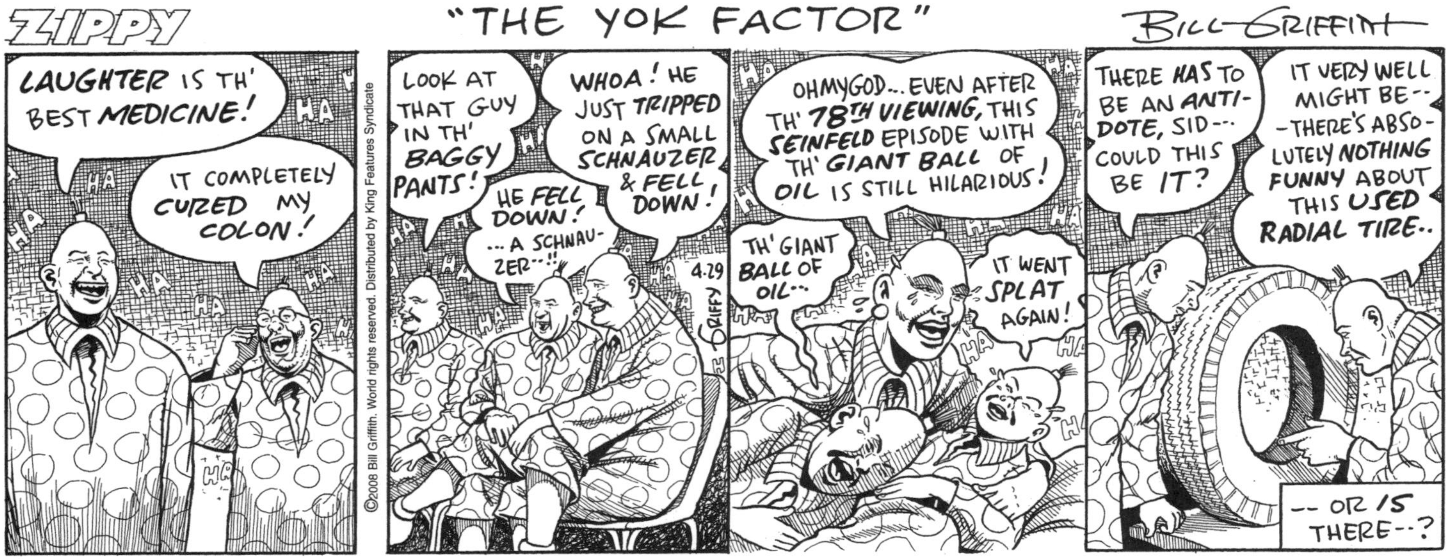
ZIPPY
"THE YOK FACTOR"
BILL GRIFFITH
LAUGHTER IS TH' BEST MEDICINE!
IT COMPLETELY CURED MY COLON!
LOOK AT THAT GUY IN TH' BAGGY PANTS!
WHOA! HE JUST TRIPPED ON A SMALL SCHNAUZER & FELL DOWN!
HE FELL DOWN! ...A SCHNAUZER--!!
4-29
©2008 Bill Griffith. World rights reserved. Distributed by King Features Syndicate
OHMYGOD... EVEN AFTER TH' 78TH VIEWING, THIS SEINFELD EPISODE WITH TH' GIANT BALL OF OIL IS STILL HILARIOUS!
TH' GIANT BALL OF OIL--
IT WENT SPLAT AGAIN!
THERE HAS TO BE AN ANTI-DOTE, SID--- COULD THIS BE IT?
IT VERY WELL MIGHT BE-- -THERE'S ABSOLUTELY NOTHING FUNNY ABOUT THIS USED RADIAL TIRE..
-- OR IS THERE--?

54

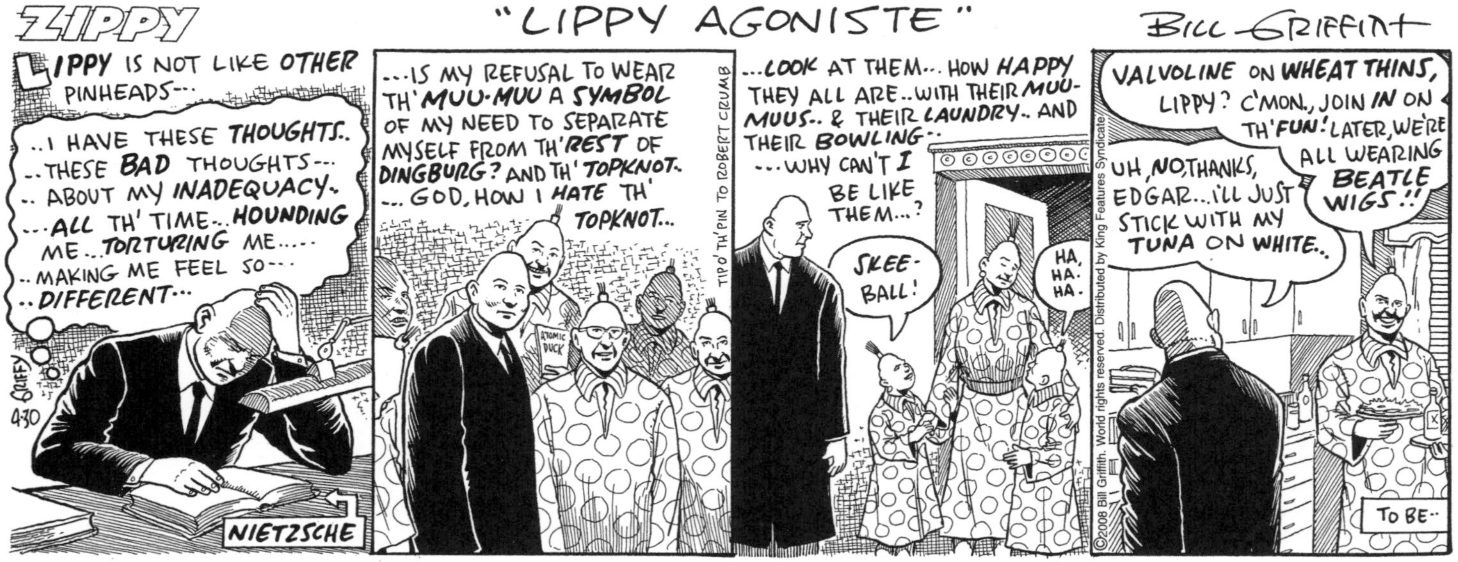
ZIPPY
"LIPPY AGONISTE"
BILL GRIFFITH
LIPPY IS NOT LIKE OTHER PINHEADS---
..I HAVE THESE THOUGHTS.. ..THESE BAD THOUGHTS--- ..ABOUT MY INADEQUACY.. ...ALL TH' TIME...HOUNDING ME...TORTURING ME..... ..MAKING ME FEEL SO--- ..DIFFERENT---
4-30
NIETZSCHE
...IS MY REFUSAL TO WEAR TH' MUU-MUU A SYMBOL OF MY NEED TO SEPARATE MYSELF FROM TH' REST OF DINGBURG? AND TH' TOPKNOT.. ...GOD, HOW I HATE TH' TOPKNOT...
ATOMIC DUCK
TIP O' TH' PIN TO ROBERT CRUMB
...LOOK AT THEM... HOW HAPPY THEY ALL ARE..WITH THEIR MUU-MUUS.. & THEIR LAUNDRY.. AND THEIR BOWLING.. ...WHY CAN'T I BE LIKE THEM...?
SKEE-BALL!
HA, HA, HA.
©2008 Bill Griffith. World rights reserved. Distributed by King Features Syndicate
VALVOLINE ON WHEAT THINS, LIPPY? C'MON.. JOIN IN ON TH' FUN! LATER, WE'RE ALL WEARING BEATLE WIGS!!
UH, NO, THANKS, EDGAR...I'LL JUST STICK WITH MY TUNA ON WHITE..
TO BE..

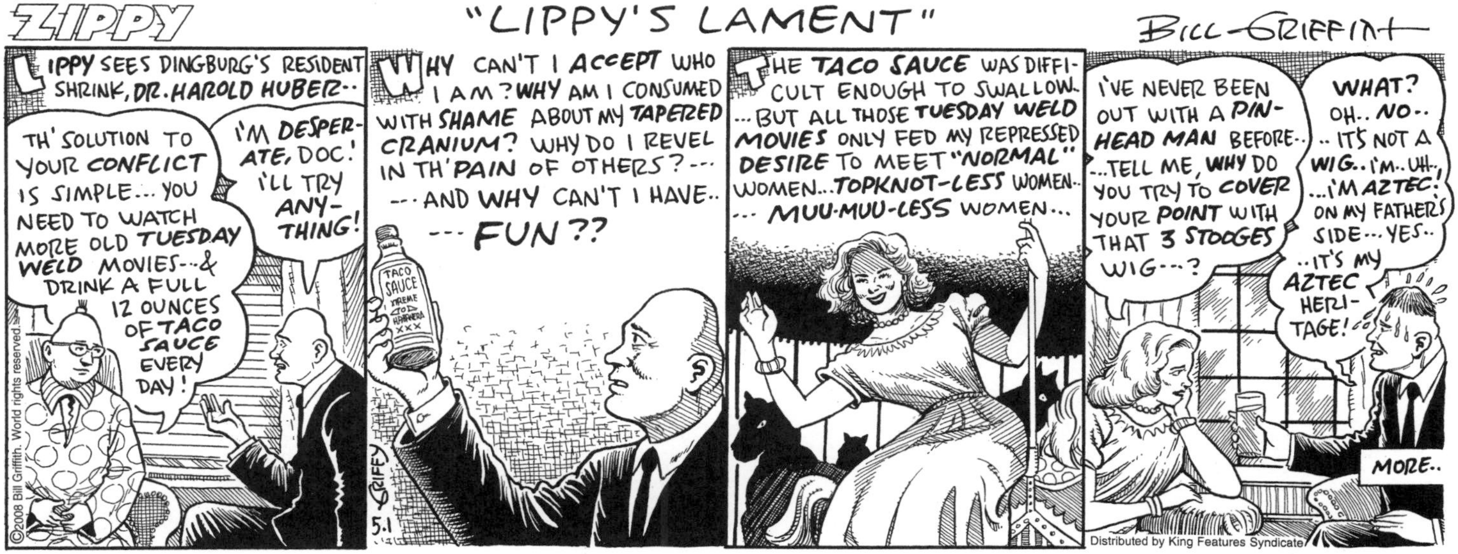
ZIPPY
"LIPPY'S LAMENT"
BILL GRIFFITH
LIPPY SEES DINGBURG'S RESIDENT SHRINK, DR. HAROLD HUBER..
I'M DESPERATE, DOC! I'LL TRY ANYTHING!
TH' SOLUTION TO YOUR CONFLICT IS SIMPLE... YOU NEED TO WATCH MORE OLD TUESDAY WELD MOVIES..& DRINK A FULL 12 OUNCES OF TACO SAUCE EVERY DAY!
©2008 Bill Griffith. World rights reserved.
WHY CAN'T I ACCEPT WHO I AM? WHY AM I CONSUMED WITH SHAME ABOUT MY TAPERED CRANIUM? WHY DO I REVEL IN TH' PAIN OF OTHERS?... ...AND WHY CAN'T I HAVE.. ...FUN??
TACO SAUCE XTREME HABANERA XXX
GRIFFY 5.1
THE TACO SAUCE WAS DIFFICULT ENOUGH TO SWALLOW. ...BUT ALL THOSE TUESDAY WELD MOVIES ONLY FED MY REPRESSED DESIRE TO MEET "NORMAL" WOMEN...TOPKNOT-LESS WOMEN.. ...MUU-MUU-LESS WOMEN...
I'VE NEVER BEEN OUT WITH A PINHEAD MAN BEFORE.. ...TELL ME, WHY DO YOU TRY TO COVER YOUR POINT WITH THAT 3 STOOGES WIG...?
WHAT? OH.. NO.. ..IT'S NOT A WIG.. I'M..UH.., ...I'M AZTEC! ON MY FATHER'S SIDE...YES.. ..IT'S MY AZTEC HERITAGE!
MORE..
Distributed by King Features Syndicate

55

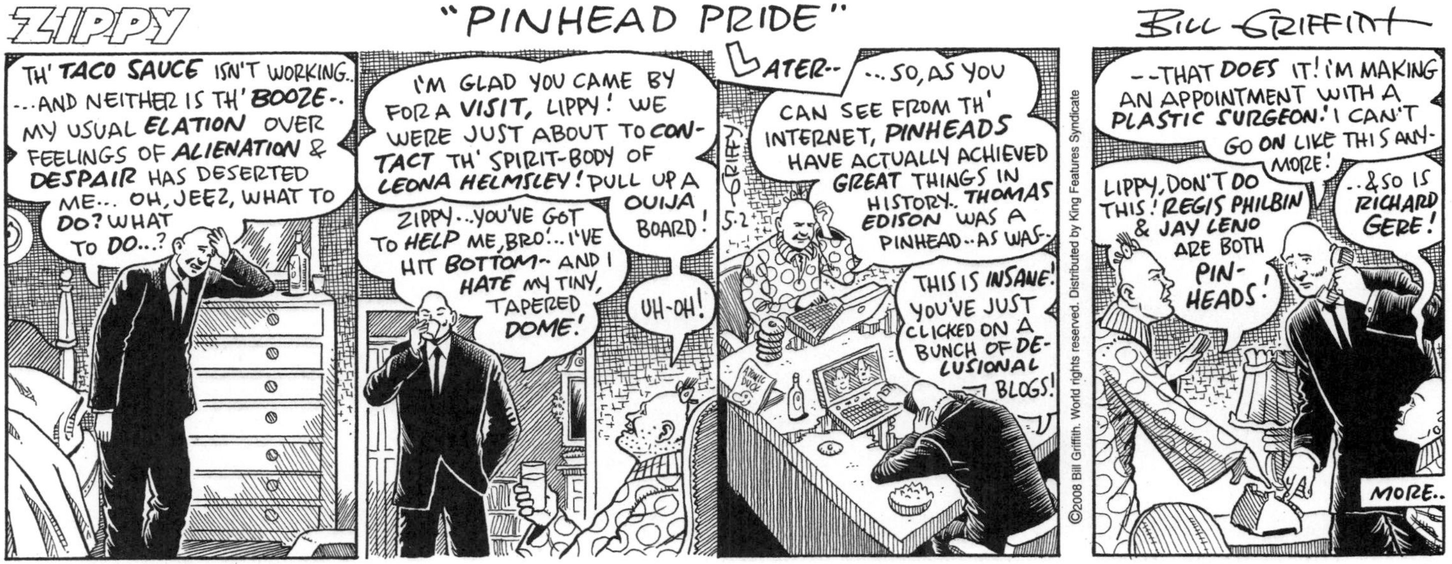
ZIPPY
"PINHEAD PRIDE"
BILL GRIFFITH
TH' TACO SAUCE ISN'T WORKING.. ...AND NEITHER IS TH' BOOZE.. MY USUAL ELATION OVER FEELINGS OF ALIENATION & DESPAIR HAS DESERTED ME... OH, JEEZ, WHAT TO DO? WHAT TO DO...?
I'M GLAD YOU CAME BY FOR A VISIT, LIPPY! WE WERE JUST ABOUT TO CONTACT TH' SPIRIT-BODY OF LEONA HELMSLEY! PULL UP A OUIJA BOARD!
ZIPPY...YOU'VE GOT TO HELP ME, BRO!...I'VE HIT BOTTOM.. AND I HATE MY TINY, TAPERED DOME!
UH-OH!
GRIFFY 5.2
LATER..
...SO, AS YOU CAN SEE FROM TH' INTERNET, PINHEADS HAVE ACTUALLY ACHIEVED GREAT THINGS IN HISTORY.. THOMAS EDISON WAS A PINHEAD..AS WAS..
THIS IS INSANE! YOU'VE JUST CLICKED ON A BUNCH OF DELUSIONAL BLOGS!
©2008 Bill Griffith. World rights reserved. Distributed by King Features Syndicate
..THAT DOES IT! I'M MAKING AN APPOINTMENT WITH A PLASTIC SURGEON! I CAN'T GO ON LIKE THIS ANYMORE!
LIPPY, DON'T DO THIS! REGIS PHILBIN & JAY LENO ARE BOTH PINHEADS!
..& SO IS RICHARD GERE!
MORE..

56

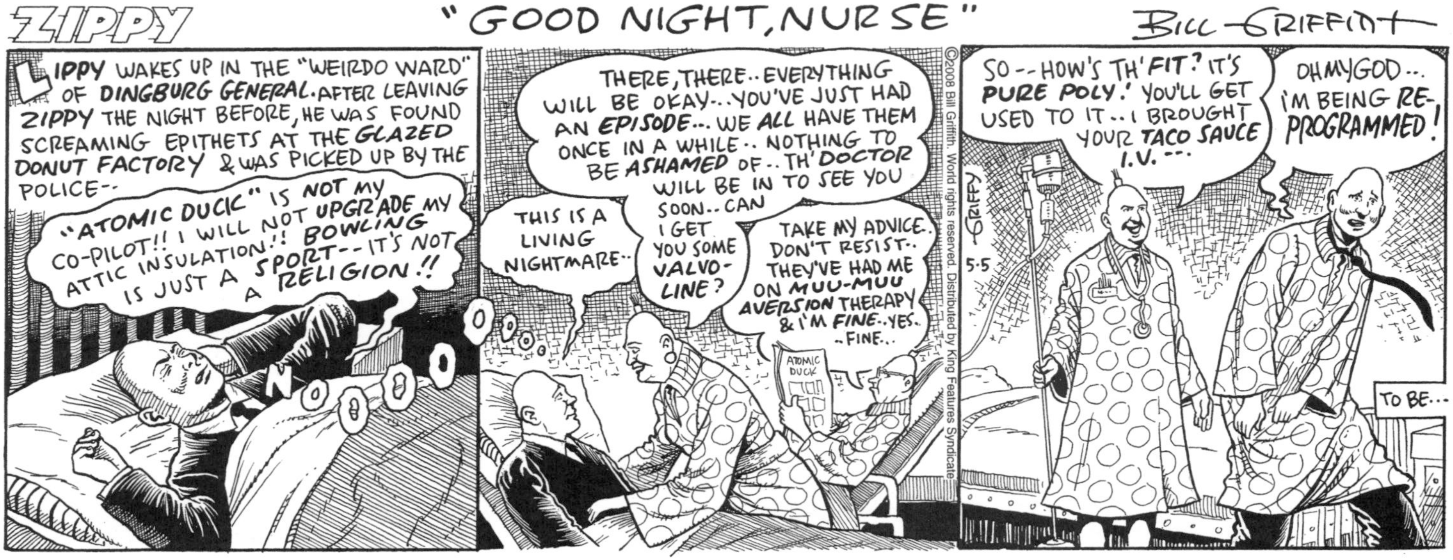
ZIPPY
"GOOD NIGHT, NURSE"
BILL GRIFFITH
LIPPY WAKES UP IN THE "WEIRDO WARD" OF DINGBURG GENERAL. AFTER LEAVING ZIPPY THE NIGHT BEFORE, HE WAS FOUND SCREAMING EPITHETS AT THE GLAZED DONUT FACTORY & WAS PICKED UP BY THE POLICE--
"ATOMIC DUCK" IS NOT MY CO-PILOT!! I WILL NOT UPGRADE MY ATTIC INSULATION!! BOWLING IS JUST A SPORT-- IT'S NOT A RELIGION!!
NOOOOOOO
THERE, THERE.. EVERYTHING WILL BE OKAY... YOU'VE JUST HAD AN EPISODE... WE ALL HAVE THEM ONCE IN A WHILE.. NOTHING TO BE ASHAMED OF.. TH' DOCTOR WILL BE IN TO SEE YOU SOON.. CAN I GET YOU SOME VALVOLINE?
THIS IS A LIVING NIGHTMARE..
TAKE MY ADVICE. DON'T RESIST.. THEY'VE HAD ME ON MUU-MUU AVERSION THERAPY & I'M FINE.. YES. ..FINE..
ATOMIC DUCK
©2008 Bill Griffith. World rights reserved. Distributed by King Features Syndicate
GRIFFY 5·5
SO--HOW'S TH' FIT? IT'S PURE POLY! YOU'LL GET USED TO IT.. I BROUGHT YOUR TACO SAUCE I.V...
OH MY GOD... I'M BEING RE-PROGRAMMED!
TO BE...

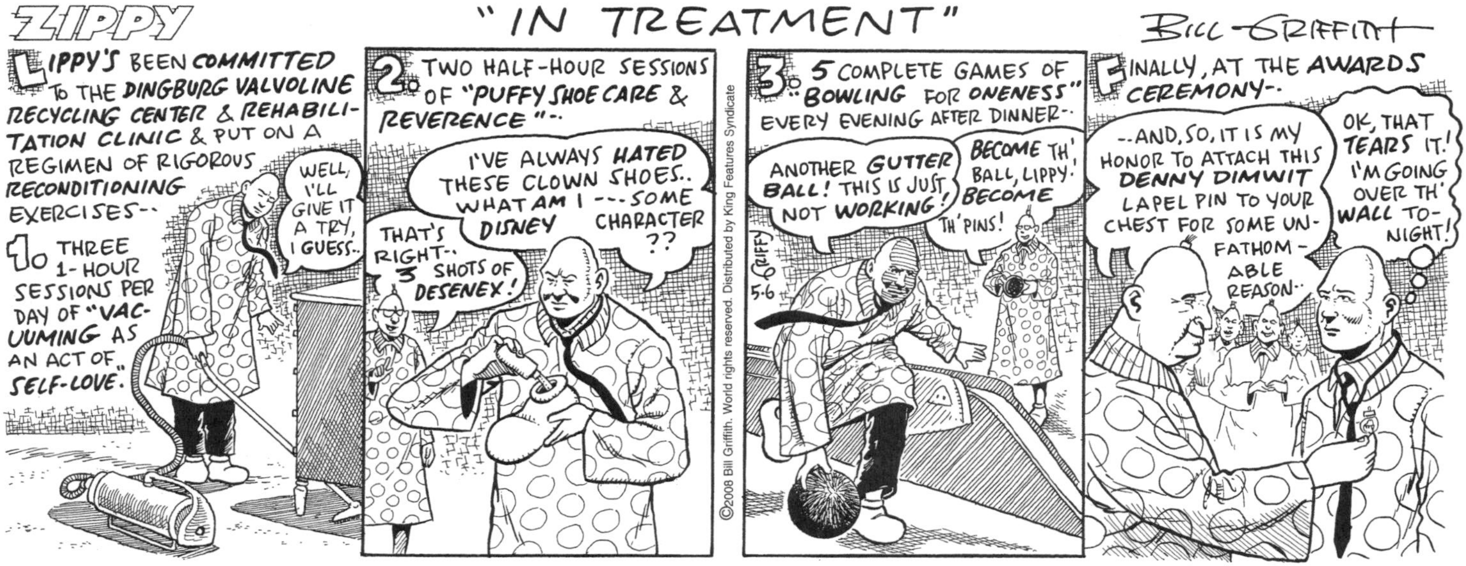
ZIPPY
"IN TREATMENT"
BILL GRIFFITH
LIPPY'S BEEN COMMITTED TO THE DINGBURG VALVOLINE RECYCLING CENTER & REHABILITATION CLINIC & PUT ON A REGIMEN OF RIGOROUS RECONDITIONING EXERCISES--
1. THREE 1-HOUR SESSIONS PER DAY OF "VACUUMING AS AN ACT OF SELF-LOVE."
WELL, I'LL GIVE IT A TRY, I GUESS..
2. TWO HALF-HOUR SESSIONS OF "PUFFY SHOE CARE & REVERENCE"--
I'VE ALWAYS HATED THESE CLOWN SHOES.. WHAT AM I ---SOME DISNEY CHARACTER??
THAT'S RIGHT.. 3 SHOTS OF DESENEX!
©2008 Bill Griffith. World rights reserved. Distributed by King Features Syndicate
3. 5 COMPLETE GAMES OF "BOWLING FOR ONENESS" EVERY EVENING AFTER DINNER--
ANOTHER GUTTER BALL! THIS IS JUST NOT WORKING!
BECOME TH' BALL, LIPPY! BECOME TH' PINS!
GRIFFY 5·6
FINALLY, AT THE AWARDS CEREMONY--
--AND, SO, IT IS MY HONOR TO ATTACH THIS DENNY DIMWIT LAPEL PIN TO YOUR CHEST FOR SOME UNFATHOMABLE REASON..
OK, THAT TEARS IT! I'M GOING OVER TH' WALL TONIGHT!

57

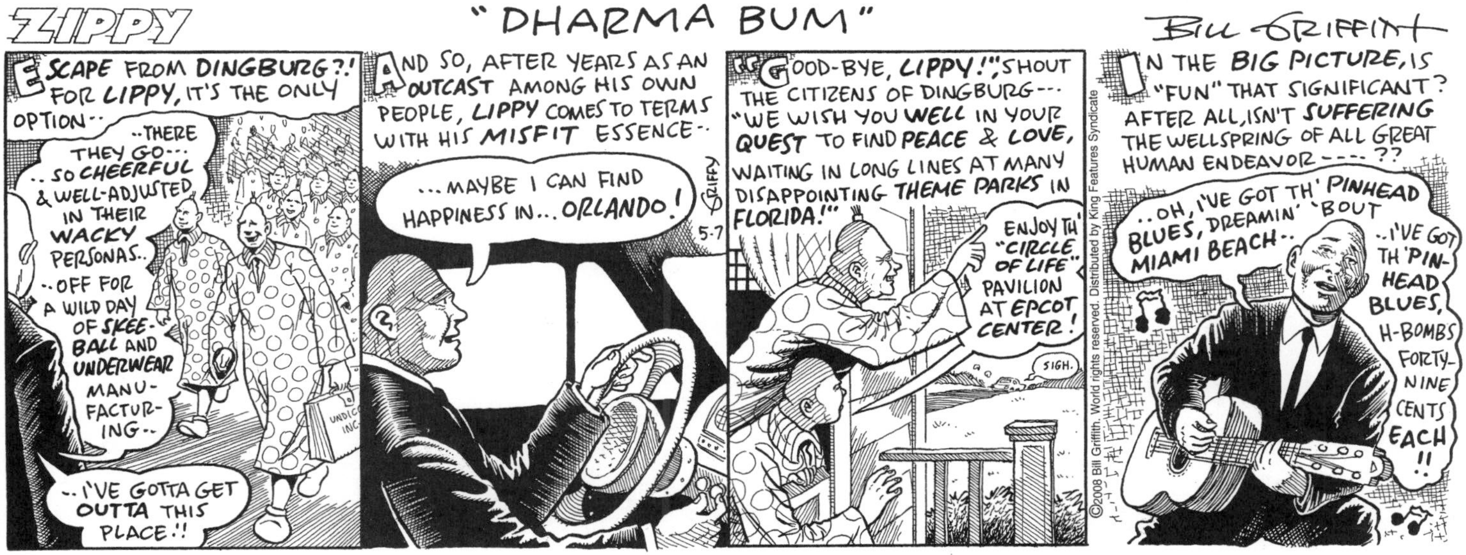
ZIPPY
"DHARMA BUM"
BILL GRIFFITH
ESCAPE FROM DINGBURG?! FOR LIPPY, IT'S THE ONLY OPTION..
..THERE THEY GO.. ..SO CHEERFUL & WELL-ADJUSTED IN THEIR WACKY PERSONAS.. ..OFF FOR A WILD DAY OF SKEE-BALL AND UNDERWEAR MANU-FACTUR-ING..
..I'VE GOTTA GET OUTTA THIS PLACE.!!
AND SO, AFTER YEARS AS AN OUTCAST AMONG HIS OWN PEOPLE, LIPPY COMES TO TERMS WITH HIS MISFIT ESSENCE..
...MAYBE I CAN FIND HAPPINESS IN... ORLANDO!
GRIFFY 5-7
"GOOD-BYE, LIPPY!", SHOUT THE CITIZENS OF DINGBURG--- "WE WISH YOU WELL IN YOUR QUEST TO FIND PEACE & LOVE, WAITING IN LONG LINES AT MANY DISAPPOINTING THEME PARKS IN FLORIDA!"
ENJOY TH' "CIRCLE OF LIFE" PAVILION AT EPCOT CENTER!
SIGH.
©2008 Bill Griffith. World rights reserved. Distributed by King Features Syndicate
IN THE BIG PICTURE, IS "FUN" THAT SIGNIFICANT? AFTER ALL, ISN'T SUFFERING THE WELLSPRING OF ALL GREAT HUMAN ENDEAVOR---- ??
..OH, I'VE GOT TH' PINHEAD BLUES, DREAMIN' 'BOUT MIAMI BEACH..
..I'VE GOT TH' PIN-HEAD BLUES, H-BOMBS FORTY-NINE CENTS EACH!!

58

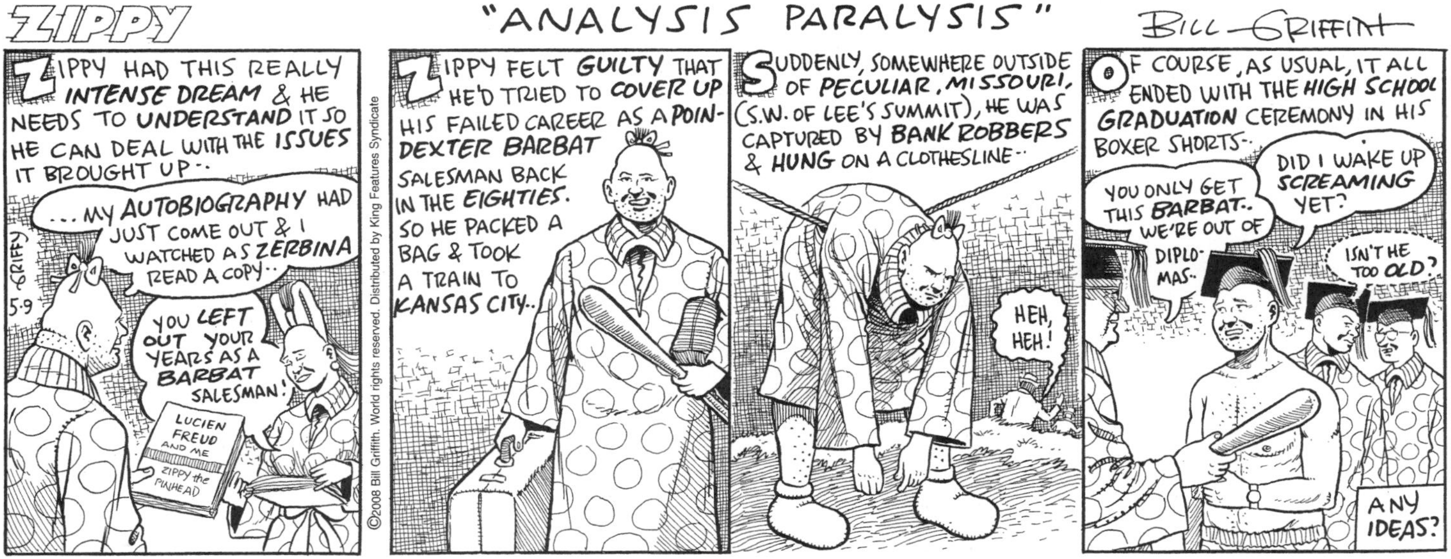
ZIPPY
"ANALYSIS PARALYSIS"
BILL GRIFFITH
ZIPPY HAD THIS REALLY INTENSE DREAM & HE NEEDS TO UNDERSTAND IT SO HE CAN DEAL WITH THE ISSUES IT BROUGHT UP..
...MY AUTOBIOGRAPHY HAD JUST COME OUT & I WATCHED AS ZERBINA READ A COPY..
GRIFFY 5-9
YOU LEFT OUT YOUR YEARS AS A BARBAT SALESMAN!
LUCIEN FREUD AND ME
ZIPPY the PINHEAD
©2008 Bill Griffith. World rights reserved. Distributed by King Features Syndicate
ZIPPY FELT GUILTY THAT HE'D TRIED TO COVER UP HIS FAILED CAREER AS A POIN-DEXTER BARBAT SALESMAN BACK IN THE EIGHTIES. SO HE PACKED A BAG & TOOK A TRAIN TO KANSAS CITY..
SUDDENLY, SOMEWHERE OUTSIDE OF PECULIAR, MISSOURI, (S.W. OF LEE'S SUMMIT), HE WAS CAPTURED BY BANK ROBBERS & HUNG ON A CLOTHESLINE..
HEH, HEH!
OF COURSE, AS USUAL, IT ALL ENDED WITH THE HIGH SCHOOL GRADUATION CEREMONY IN HIS BOXER SHORTS..
YOU ONLY GET THIS BARBAT.. WE'RE OUT OF DIPLO-MAS..
DID I WAKE UP SCREAMING YET?
ISN'T HE TOO OLD?
ANY IDEAS?

59

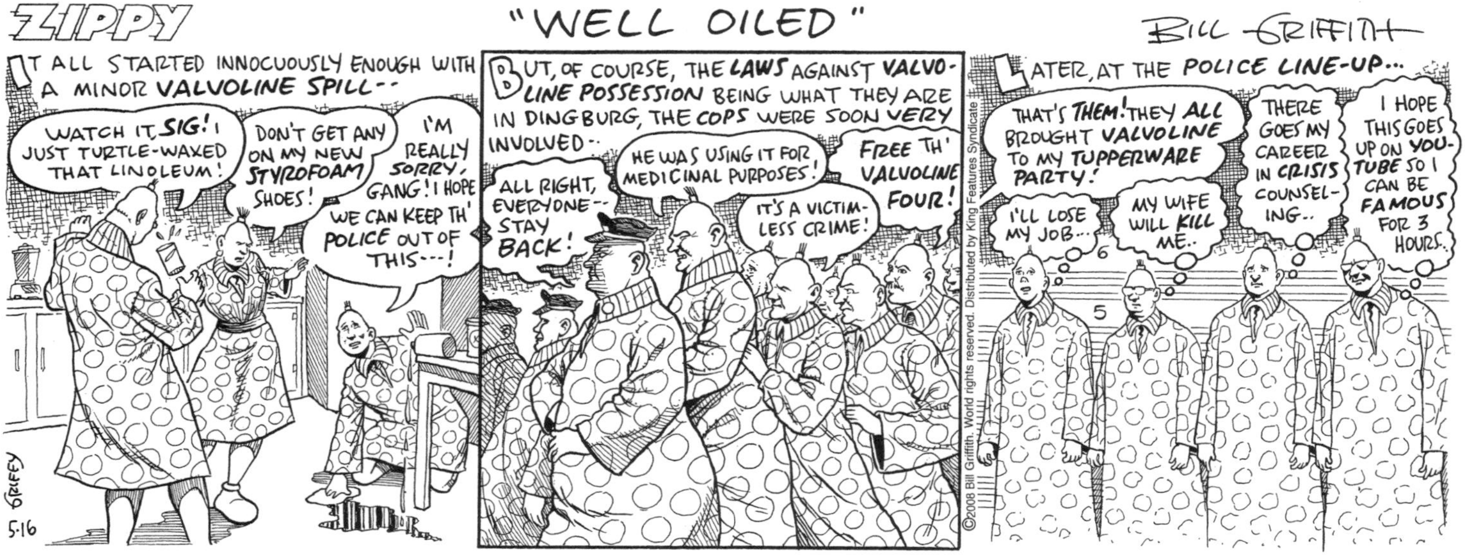
ZIPPY
"WELL OILED"
BILL GRIFFITH
IT ALL STARTED INNOCUOUSLY ENOUGH WITH A MINOR VALVOLINE SPILL--
WATCH IT, SIG! I JUST TURTLE-WAXED THAT LINOLEUM!
DON'T GET ANY ON MY NEW STYROFOAM SHOES!
I'M REALLY SORRY, GANG! I HOPE WE CAN KEEP TH' POLICE OUT OF THIS---!
GRIFFY
5.16
BUT, OF COURSE, THE LAWS AGAINST VALVOLINE POSSESSION BEING WHAT THEY ARE IN DINGBURG, THE COPS WERE SOON VERY INVOLVED--
ALL RIGHT, EVERYONE-- STAY BACK!
HE WAS USING IT FOR MEDICINAL PURPOSES!
IT'S A VICTIMLESS CRIME!
FREE TH' VALVOLINE FOUR!
©2008 Bill Griffith. World rights reserved. Distributed by King Features Syndicate
LATER, AT THE POLICE LINE-UP...
THAT'S THEM! THEY ALL BROUGHT VALVOLINE TO MY TUPPERWARE PARTY!
I'LL LOSE MY JOB...
MY WIFE WILL KILL ME..
THERE GOES MY CAREER IN CRISIS COUNSELING..
I HOPE THIS GOES UP ON YOUTUBE SO I CAN BE FAMOUS FOR 3 HOURS..

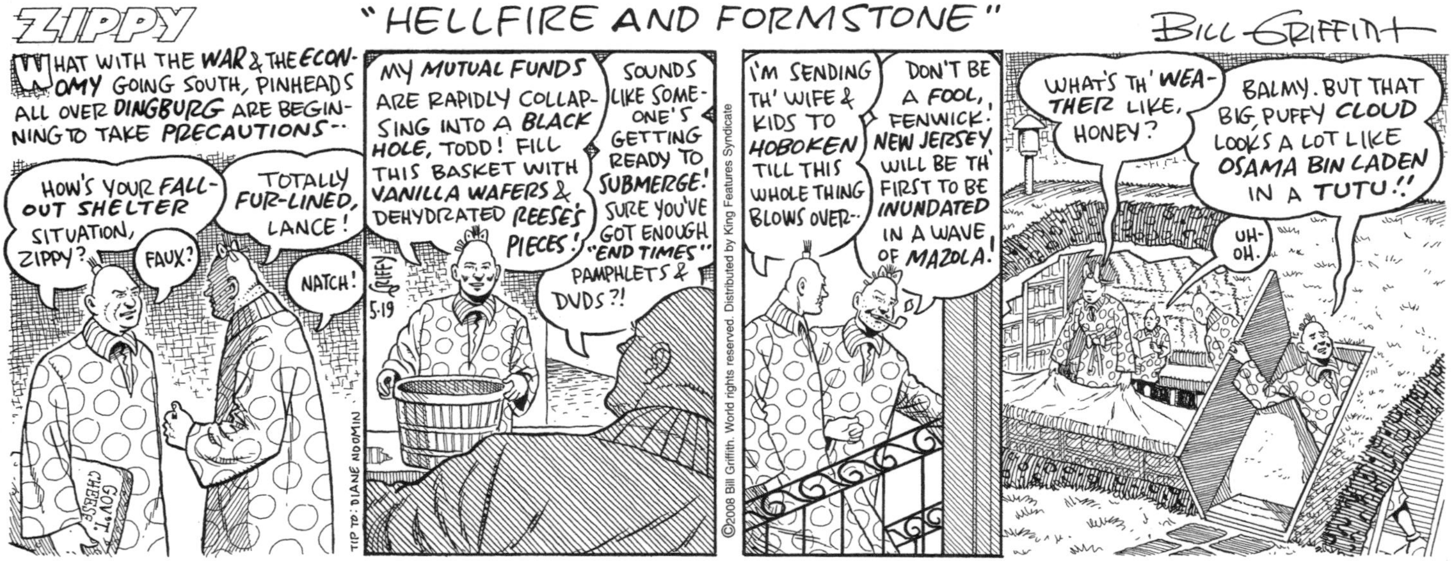
ZIPPY
"HELLFIRE AND FORMSTONE"
BILL GRIFFITH
WHAT WITH THE WAR & THE ECONOMY GOING SOUTH, PINHEADS ALL OVER DINGBURG ARE BEGINNING TO TAKE PRECAUTIONS--
HOW'S YOUR FALLOUT SHELTER SITUATION, ZIPPY?
TOTALLY FUR-LINED, LANCE!
FAUX?
NATCH!
GOV'T. CHEESE
TIP TO: DIANE NOOMIN
MY MUTUAL FUNDS ARE RAPIDLY COLLAPSING INTO A BLACK HOLE, TODD! FILL THIS BASKET WITH VANILLA WAFERS & DEHYDRATED REESE'S PIECES!
SOUNDS LIKE SOMEONE'S GETTING READY TO SUBMERGE! SURE YOU'VE GOT ENOUGH "END TIMES" PAMPHLETS & DVDS?!
GRIFFY
5.19
©2008 Bill Griffith. World rights reserved. Distributed by King Features Syndicate
I'M SENDING TH' WIFE & KIDS TO HOBOKEN TILL THIS WHOLE THING BLOWS OVER--
DON'T BE A FOOL, FENWICK. NEW JERSEY WILL BE TH' FIRST TO BE INUNDATED IN A WAVE OF MAZOLA!
WHAT'S TH' WEATHER LIKE, HONEY?
BALMY. BUT THAT BIG, PUFFY CLOUD LOOKS A LOT LIKE OSAMA BIN LADEN IN A TUTU!!
UH-OH.

60 A

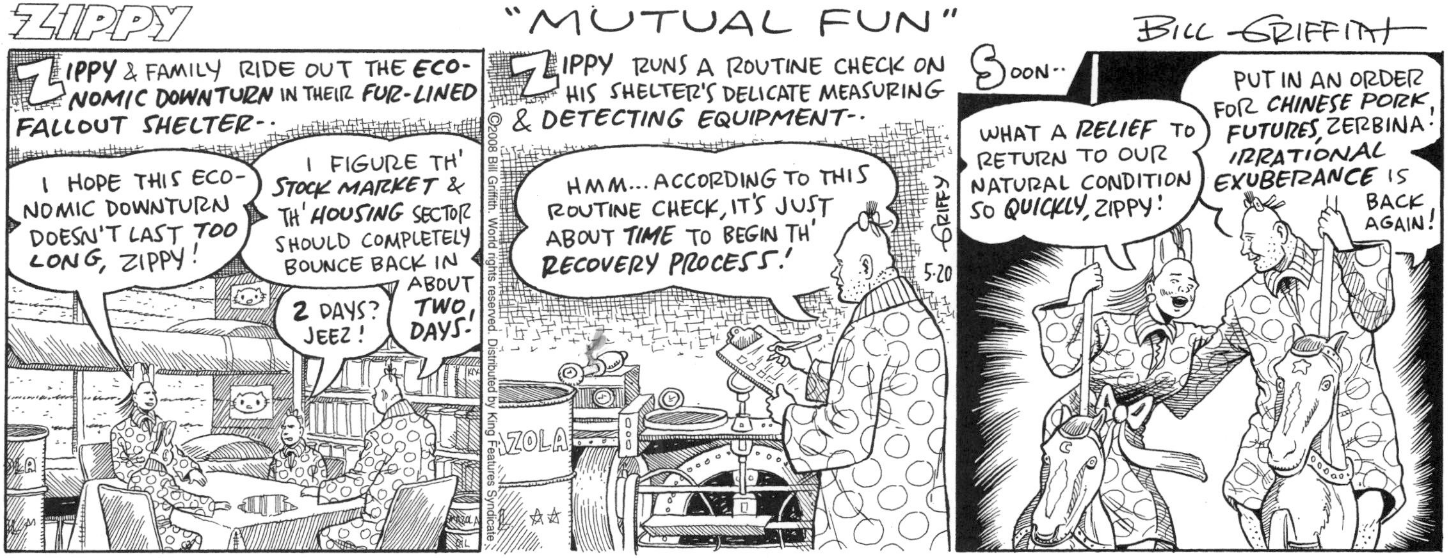
ZIPPY
"MUTUAL FUN"
BILL GRIFFITH
ZIPPY & FAMILY RIDE OUT THE ECONOMIC DOWNTURN IN THEIR FUR-LINED FALLOUT SHELTER..
I HOPE THIS ECONOMIC DOWNTURN DOESN'T LAST TOO LONG, ZIPPY!
I FIGURE TH' STOCK MARKET & TH' HOUSING SECTOR SHOULD COMPLETELY BOUNCE BACK IN ABOUT TWO DAYS!
2 DAYS? JEEZ!
©2008 Bill Griffith. World rights reserved. Distributed by King Features Syndicate
ZIPPY RUNS A ROUTINE CHECK ON HIS SHELTER'S DELICATE MEASURING & DETECTING EQUIPMENT..
HMM... ACCORDING TO THIS ROUTINE CHECK, IT'S JUST ABOUT TIME TO BEGIN TH' RECOVERY PROCESS!
ZOLA
GRIFFY
5-20
SOON..
WHAT A RELIEF TO RETURN TO OUR NATURAL CONDITION SO QUICKLY, ZIPPY!
PUT IN AN ORDER FOR CHINESE PORK FUTURES, ZERBINA! IRRATIONAL EXUBERANCE IS BACK AGAIN!

60 B

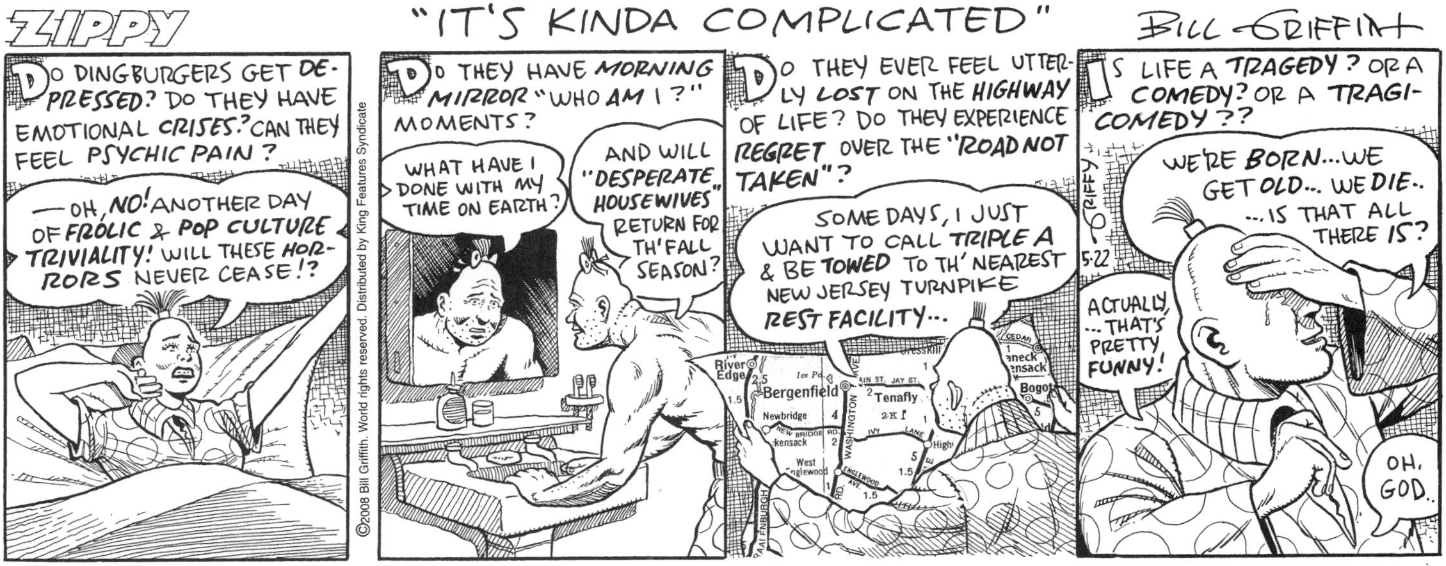
ZIPPY
"IT'S KINDA COMPLICATED"
BILL GRIFFITH
DO DINGBURGERS GET DEPRESSED? DO THEY HAVE EMOTIONAL CRISES? CAN THEY FEEL PSYCHIC PAIN?
—OH, NO! ANOTHER DAY OF FROLIC & POP CULTURE TRIVIALITY! WILL THESE HORRORS NEVER CEASE!?
©2008 Bill Griffith. World rights reserved. Distributed by King Features Syndicate
DO THEY HAVE MORNING MIRROR "WHO AM I?" MOMENTS?
WHAT HAVE I DONE WITH MY TIME ON EARTH?
AND WILL "DESPERATE HOUSEWIVES" RETURN FOR TH' FALL SEASON?
DO THEY EVER FEEL UTTERLY LOST ON THE HIGHWAY OF LIFE? DO THEY EXPERIENCE REGRET OVER THE "ROAD NOT TAKEN"?
SOME DAYS, I JUST WANT TO CALL TRIPLE A & BE TOWED TO TH' NEAREST NEW JERSEY TURNPIKE REST FACILITY...
River Edge
Bergenfield
Tenafly
Newbridge
West Englewood
WASHINGTON
IS LIFE A TRAGEDY? OR A COMEDY? OR A TRAGI-COMEDY??
GRIFFY
5-22
WE'RE BORN... WE GET OLD... WE DIE.. ...IS THAT ALL THERE IS?
ACTUALLY, ...THAT'S PRETTY FUNNY!
OH, GOD..

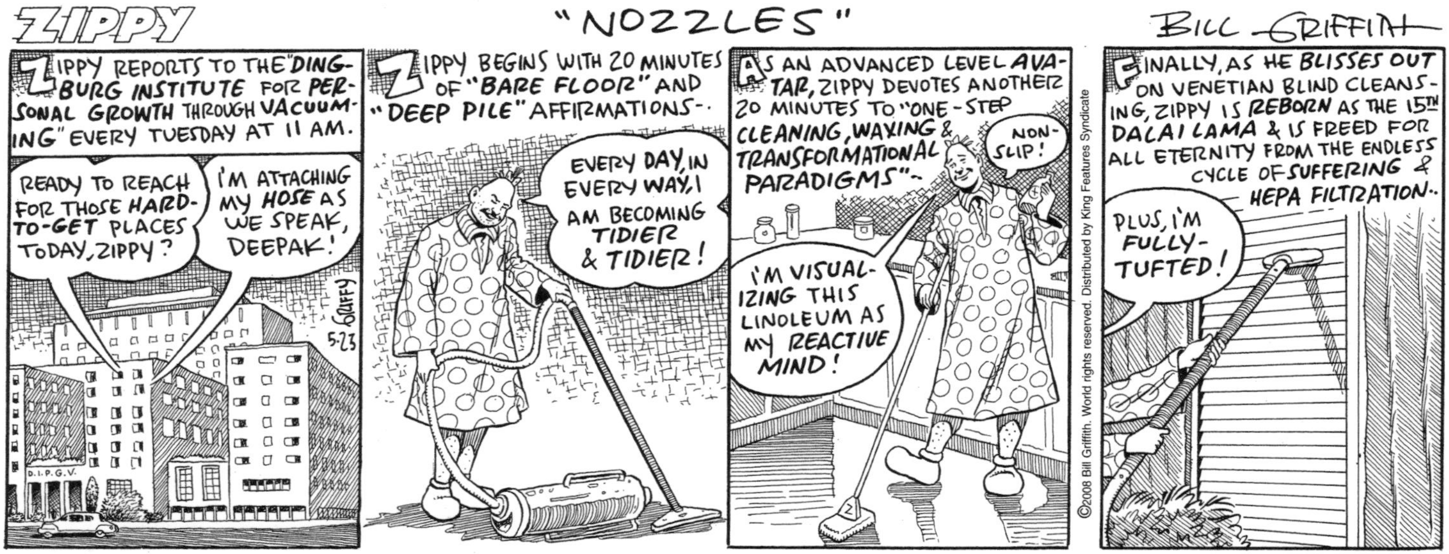
ZIPPY
"NOZZLES"
BILL GRIFFITH
ZIPPY REPORTS TO THE "DINGBURG INSTITUTE FOR PERSONAL GROWTH THROUGH VACUUMING" EVERY TUESDAY AT 11 AM.
READY TO REACH FOR THOSE HARD-TO-GET PLACES TODAY, ZIPPY?
I'M ATTACHING MY HOSE AS WE SPEAK, DEEPAK!
D.I.P.G.V.
GRIFFY 5-23
ZIPPY BEGINS WITH 20 MINUTES OF "BARE FLOOR" AND "DEEP PILE" AFFIRMATIONS--
EVERY DAY, IN EVERY WAY, I AM BECOMING TIDIER & TIDIER!
AS AN ADVANCED LEVEL AVATAR, ZIPPY DEVOTES ANOTHER 20 MINUTES TO "ONE-STEP CLEANING, WAXING & TRANSFORMATIONAL PARADIGMS"--
NON-SLIP!
I'M VISUALIZING THIS LINOLEUM AS MY REACTIVE MIND!
©2008 Bill Griffith. World rights reserved. Distributed by King Features Syndicate
FINALLY, AS HE BLISSES OUT ON VENETIAN BLIND CLEANSING, ZIPPY IS REBORN AS THE 15TH DALAI LAMA & IS FREED FOR ALL ETERNITY FROM THE ENDLESS CYCLE OF SUFFERING & HEPA FILTRATION..
PLUS, I'M FULLY-TUFTED!

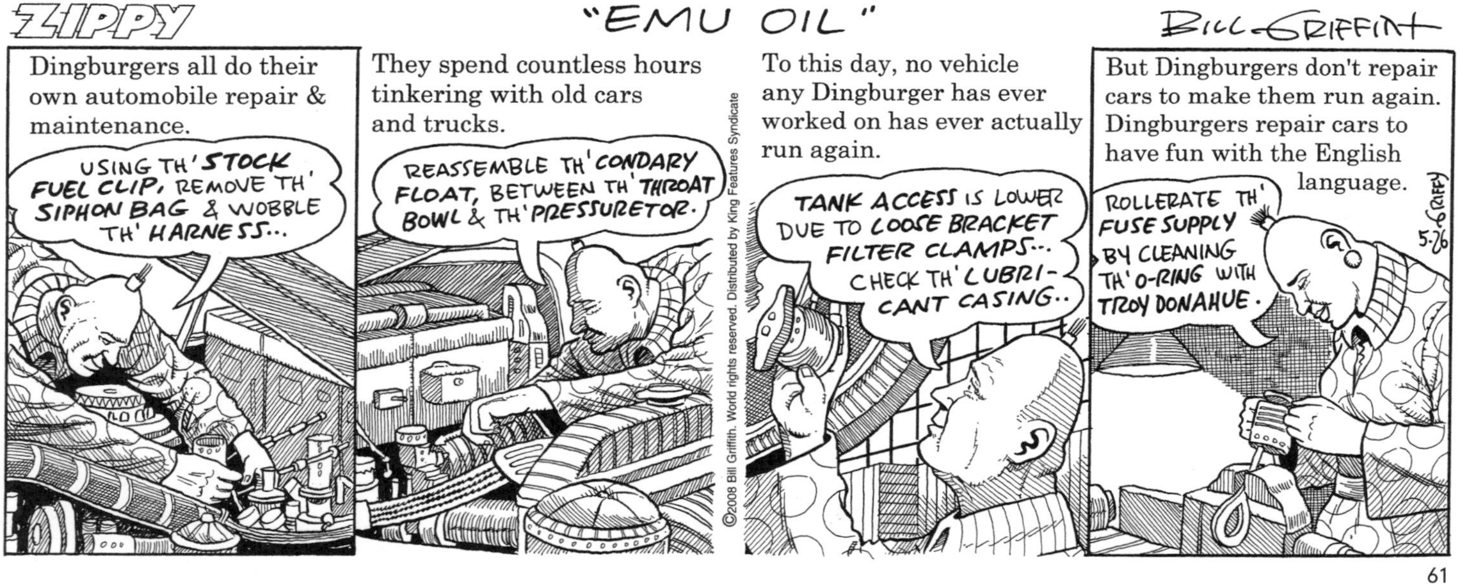
ZIPPY
"EMU OIL"
BILL GRIFFITH
Dingburgers all do their own automobile repair & maintenance.
USING TH' STOCK FUEL CLIP, REMOVE TH' SIPHON BAG & WOBBLE TH' HARNESS...
They spend countless hours tinkering with old cars and trucks.
REASSEMBLE TH' CONDARY FLOAT, BETWEEN TH' THROAT BOWL & TH' PRESSURETOR.
©2008 Bill Griffith. World rights reserved. Distributed by King Features Syndicate
To this day, no vehicle any Dingburger has ever worked on has ever actually run again.
TANK ACCESS IS LOWER DUE TO LOOSE BRACKET FILTER CLAMPS... CHECK TH' LUBRICANT CASING..
But Dingburgers don't repair cars to make them run again. Dingburgers repair cars to have fun with the English language.
ROLLERATE TH' FUSE SUPPLY BY CLEANING TH' O-RING WITH TROY DONAHUE.
GRIFFY 5-26
61

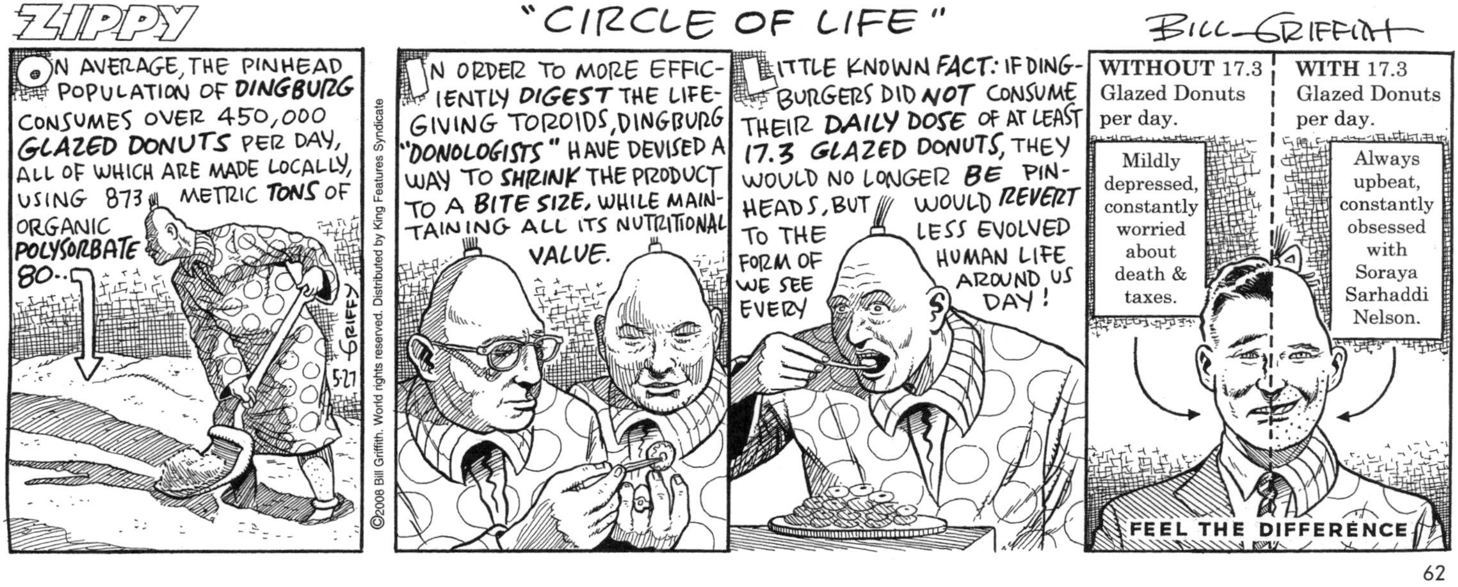
ZIPPY
"CIRCLE OF LIFE"
BILL GRIFFITH
ON AVERAGE, THE PINHEAD POPULATION OF DINGBURG CONSUMES OVER 450,000 GLAZED DONUTS PER DAY, ALL OF WHICH ARE MADE LOCALLY, USING 873 METRIC TONS OF ORGANIC POLYSORBATE 80..
GRIFFY 5·27
©2008 Bill Griffith. World rights reserved. Distributed by King Features Syndicate
IN ORDER TO MORE EFFICIENTLY DIGEST THE LIFE-GIVING TOROIDS, DINGBURG "DONOLOGISTS" HAVE DEVISED A WAY TO SHRINK THE PRODUCT TO A BITE SIZE, WHILE MAINTAINING ALL ITS NUTRITIONAL VALUE.
LITTLE KNOWN FACT: IF DINGBURGERS DID NOT CONSUME THEIR DAILY DOSE OF AT LEAST 17.3 GLAZED DONUTS, THEY WOULD NO LONGER BE PINHEADS, BUT WOULD REVERT TO THE LESS EVOLVED FORM OF HUMAN LIFE WE SEE AROUND US EVERY DAY!
WITHOUT 17.3 Glazed Donuts per day.
WITH 17.3 Glazed Donuts per day.
Mildly depressed, constantly worried about death & taxes.
Always upbeat, constantly obsessed with Soraya Sarhaddi Nelson.
FEEL THE DIFFERENCE
62

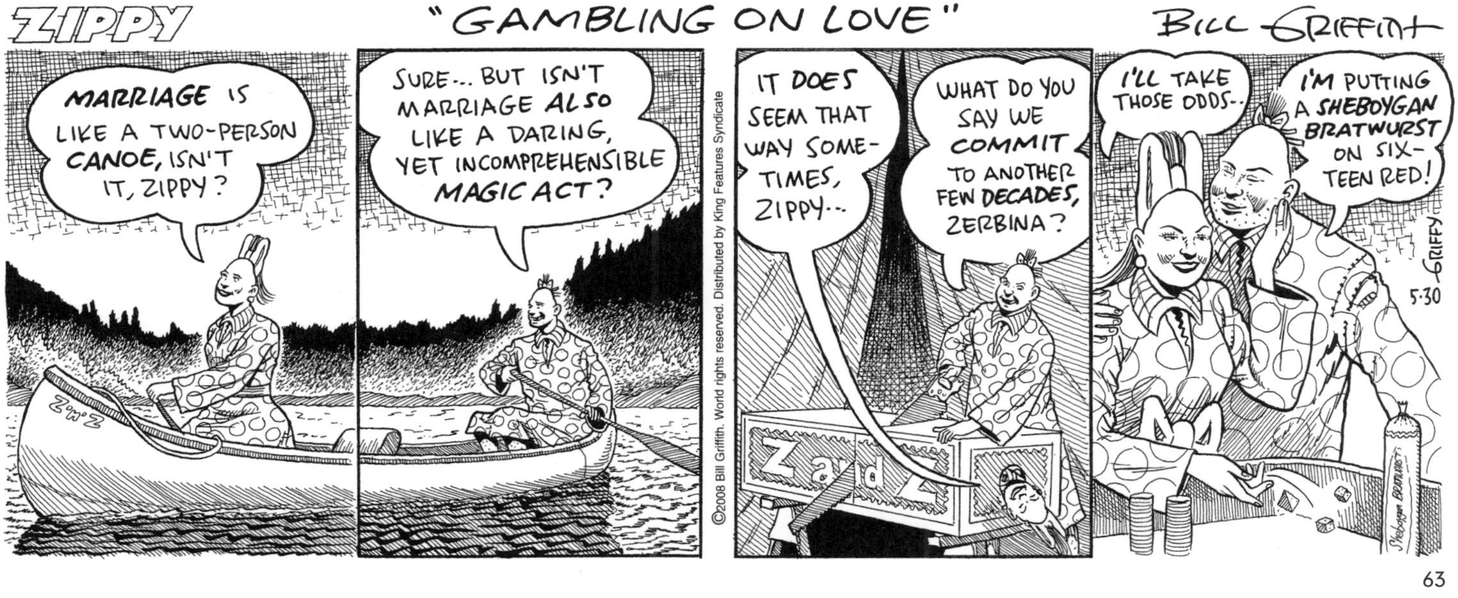
ZIPPY
"GAMBLING ON LOVE"
BILL GRIFFITH
MARRIAGE IS LIKE A TWO-PERSON CANOE, ISN'T IT, ZIPPY?
Z 'n' Z
SURE... BUT ISN'T MARRIAGE ALSO LIKE A DARING, YET INCOMPREHENSIBLE MAGIC ACT?
©2008 Bill Griffith. World rights reserved. Distributed by King Features Syndicate
IT DOES SEEM THAT WAY SOMETIMES, ZIPPY...
WHAT DO YOU SAY WE COMMIT TO ANOTHER FEW DECADES, ZERBINA?
Z and Z
I'LL TAKE THOSE ODDS..
I'M PUTTING A SHEBOYGAN BRATWURST ON SIXTEEN RED!
GRIFFY 5·30
63

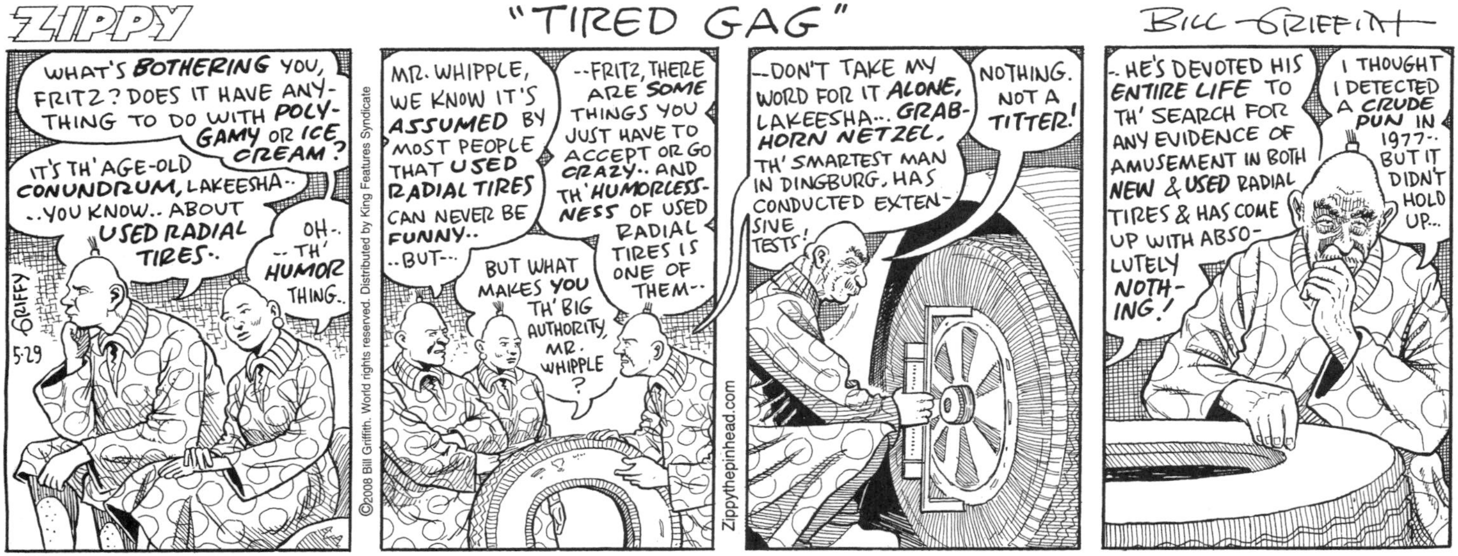
ZIPPY
"TIRED GAG"
BILL GRIFFITH
WHAT'S BOTHERING YOU, FRITZ? DOES IT HAVE ANYTHING TO DO WITH POLYGAMY OR ICE CREAM?
IT'S TH' AGE-OLD CONUNDRUM, LAKEESHA.. ..YOU KNOW.. ABOUT USED RADIAL TIRES..
OH.. --TH' HUMOR THING..
GRIFFY 5-29
MR. WHIPPLE, WE KNOW IT'S ASSUMED BY MOST PEOPLE THAT USED RADIAL TIRES CAN NEVER BE FUNNY.. ..BUT--..
--FRITZ, THERE ARE SOME THINGS YOU JUST HAVE TO ACCEPT OR GO CRAZY.. AND TH' HUMORLESSNESS OF USED RADIAL TIRES IS ONE OF THEM--..
BUT WHAT MAKES YOU TH' BIG AUTHORITY, MR. WHIPPLE?
©2008 Bill Griffith. World rights reserved. Distributed by King Features Syndicate
Zippythepinhead.com
--DON'T TAKE MY WORD FOR IT ALONE, LAKEESHA... GRABHORN NETZEL, TH' SMARTEST MAN IN DINGBURG, HAS CONDUCTED EXTENSIVE TESTS!
NOTHING. NOT A TITTER!
.. HE'S DEVOTED HIS ENTIRE LIFE TO TH' SEARCH FOR ANY EVIDENCE OF AMUSEMENT IN BOTH NEW & USED RADIAL TIRES & HAS COME UP WITH ABSOLUTELY NOTHING!
I THOUGHT I DETECTED A CRUDE PUN IN 1977.. BUT IT DIDN'T HOLD UP...

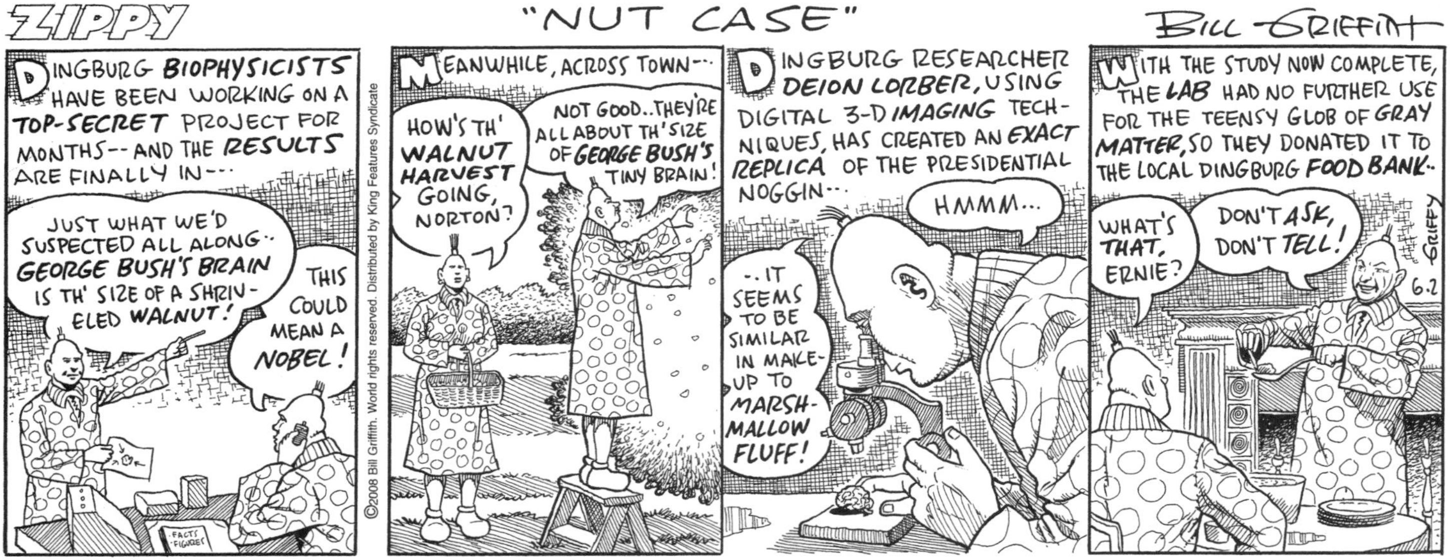
ZIPPY
"NUT CASE"
BILL GRIFFITH
DINGBURG BIOPHYSICISTS HAVE BEEN WORKING ON A TOP-SECRET PROJECT FOR MONTHS-- AND THE RESULTS ARE FINALLY IN--..
JUST WHAT WE'D SUSPECTED ALL ALONG.. GEORGE BUSH'S BRAIN IS TH' SIZE OF A SHRIVELED WALNUT!
THIS COULD MEAN A NOBEL!
FACTS FIGURES
©2008 Bill Griffith. World rights reserved. Distributed by King Features Syndicate
MEANWHILE, ACROSS TOWN--..
HOW'S TH' WALNUT HARVEST GOING, NORTON?
NOT GOOD.. THEY'RE ALL ABOUT TH' SIZE OF GEORGE BUSH'S TINY BRAIN!
DINGBURG RESEARCHER DEION LORBER, USING DIGITAL 3-D IMAGING TECHNIQUES, HAS CREATED AN EXACT REPLICA OF THE PRESIDENTIAL NOGGIN--..
HMMM...
--. IT SEEMS TO BE SIMILAR IN MAKE-UP TO MARSHMALLOW FLUFF!
WITH THE STUDY NOW COMPLETE, THE LAB HAD NO FURTHER USE FOR THE TEENSY GLOB OF GRAY MATTER, SO THEY DONATED IT TO THE LOCAL DINGBURG FOOD BANK..
WHAT'S THAT, ERNIE?
DON'T ASK, DON'T TELL!
GRIFFY 6-2

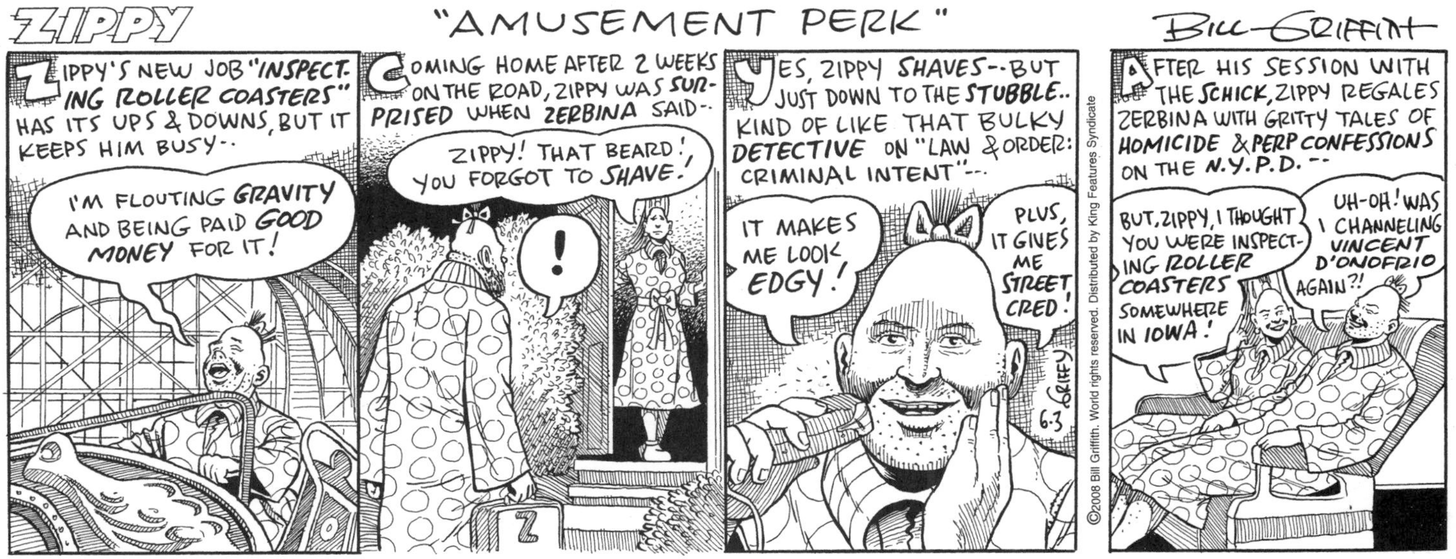

ZIPPY
"AMUSEMENT PERK"
BILL GRIFFITH
ZIPPY'S NEW JOB "INSPECTING ROLLER COASTERS" HAS ITS UPS & DOWNS, BUT IT KEEPS HIM BUSY--
I'M FLOUTING GRAVITY AND BEING PAID GOOD MONEY FOR IT!
COMING HOME AFTER 2 WEEKS ON THE ROAD, ZIPPY WAS SURPRISED WHEN ZERBINA SAID--
ZIPPY! THAT BEARD! YOU FORGOT TO SHAVE!
!
YES, ZIPPY SHAVES--BUT JUST DOWN TO THE STUBBLE.. KIND OF LIKE THAT BULKY DETECTIVE ON "LAW & ORDER: CRIMINAL INTENT"--.
IT MAKES ME LOOK EDGY!
PLUS, IT GIVES ME STREET CRED!
GRIFFY 6-3
AFTER HIS SESSION WITH THE SCHICK, ZIPPY REGALES ZERBINA WITH GRITTY TALES OF HOMICIDE & PERP CONFESSIONS ON THE N.Y.P.D.--
BUT, ZIPPY, I THOUGHT YOU WERE INSPECTING ROLLER COASTERS SOMEWHERE IN IOWA!
UH-OH! WAS I CHANNELING VINCENT D'ONOFRIO AGAIN?!
©2008 Bill Griffith. World rights reserved. Distributed by King Features Syndicate


64

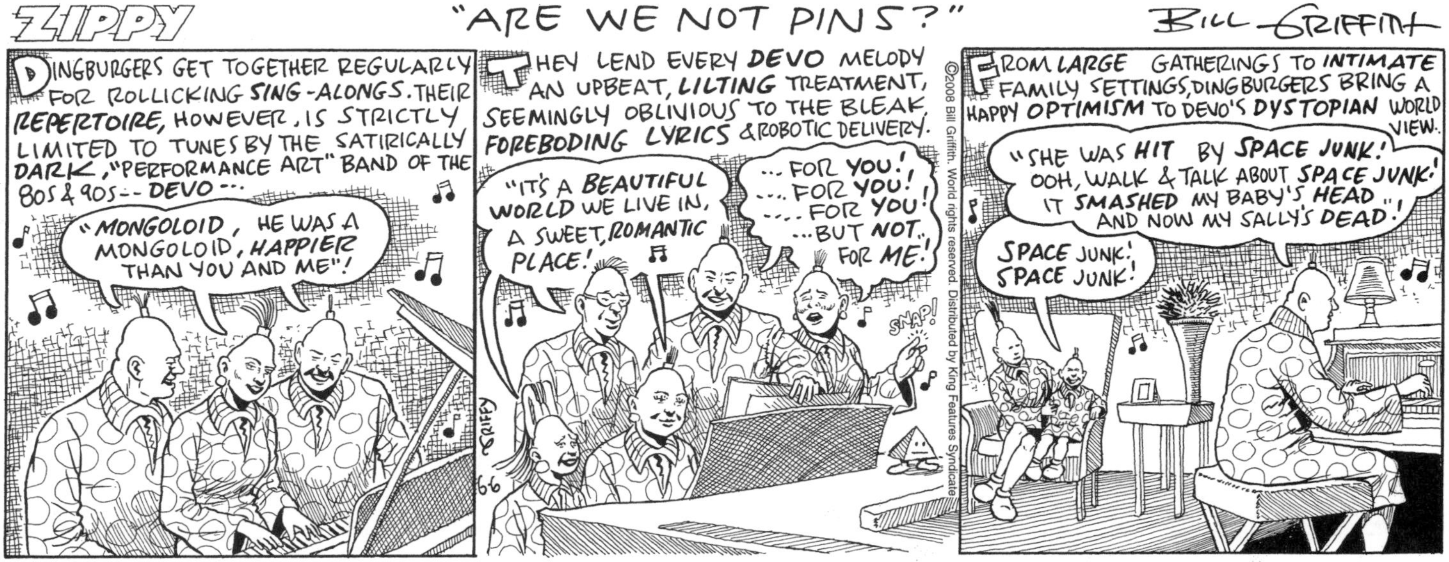

ZIPPY
"ARE WE NOT PINS?"
BILL GRIFFITH
DINGBURGERS GET TOGETHER REGULARLY FOR ROLLICKING SING-ALONGS. THEIR REPERTOIRE, HOWEVER, IS STRICTLY LIMITED TO TUNES BY THE SATIRICALLY DARK, "PERFORMANCE ART" BAND OF THE 80s & 90s-- DEVO--.
"MONGOLOID, HE WAS A MONGOLOID, HAPPIER THAN YOU AND ME"!
THEY LEND EVERY DEVO MELODY AN UPBEAT, LILTING TREATMENT, SEEMINGLY OBLIVIOUS TO THE BLEAK FOREBODING LYRICS & ROBOTIC DELIVERY.
"IT'S A BEAUTIFUL WORLD WE LIVE IN, A SWEET, ROMANTIC PLACE!
...FOR YOU! ...FOR YOU! ...FOR YOU! ...BUT NOT FOR ME!"
SNAP!
GRIFFY 6-6
©2008 Bill Griffith. World rights reserved. Distributed by King Features Syndicate
FROM LARGE GATHERINGS TO INTIMATE FAMILY SETTINGS, DINGBURGERS BRING A HAPPY OPTIMISM TO DEVO'S DYSTOPIAN WORLD VIEW.
"SHE WAS HIT BY SPACE JUNK! OOH, WALK & TALK ABOUT SPACE JUNK! IT SMASHED MY BABY'S HEAD AND NOW MY SALLY'S DEAD"!
SPACE JUNK! SPACE JUNK!


65

ZIPPY
"FROM THE MOLD TO THE GOLD"
BILL GRIFFITH
PLANNING ON PARTICIPATING IN TH' DINGBURG GAMES AGAIN THIS AUGUST, MR. ROACH?
YOU BET, LIONEL! I'LL BE DOING TH' DINGBURG TRIATHLON, AS USUAL!
DID SOMEONE MENTION TIBET?
DINGBURG
I'LL START WITH TH' "300 METER SLOG THROUGH TH' GIANT VAT OF VALVOLINE", HOPING TO BEAT MY RECORD TIME OF 3 HOURS, 37 MINUTES FROM FOUR YEARS AGO..
I FEEL CONFIDENT ABOUT ACING TH' "BALANCE TH' SPINNING TUB OF COOL WHIP WHILE PLAYING TH' GREATEST HITS OF HALL & OATES ON TH' GRAND PIANO" EVENT..
..I'M SURE I CAN DO TH' REQUIRED 7 HOURS WITHOUT LOSING A PRECIOUS DROP!
DUDE!
©2008 Bill Griffith. World rights reserved. Distributed by King Features Syndicate
MY ONLY WORRY IS THAT I MIGHT STUMBLE ON TH' "SCHLEP TH' 100 POUND BAG OF RANCID OATMEAL OVER TH' 6-MILE JELL-O MOLD OBSTACLE COURSE" FINALE.... ONE MISSTEP AND IT'S SAYONARA TO ANY HOPE OF INSPIRING TH' YOUNGER GENERATION TO ACHIEVE GREATNESS IN SPORTS!"
YECH.
GRIFFY 6/10
66

ZIPPY
"BEACH BLANKET BOING-BOING"
BILL GRIFFITH
PINHEADS FROLIC IN THE SURF AT DINGBURG COVE..
ARE WE HAVING FUN YET?
LIFE IS A BEACH!
GRIFFY 6-11
THEY CAVORT & GAMBOL BY THE DINGBURG TOWN POOL..
NO SHOES. NO SHIRT. NO PROBLEM.
IF AT FIRST YOU DON'T SUCCEED, BLAME SOMEBODY ELSE.
©2008 Bill Griffith. World rights reserved. Distributed by King Features Syndicate
FUNNY, BUT AS SOON AS DINGBURGERS SHED THEIR MUUMUUS, THEY SPEAK ONLY IN BUMPERSTICKER-ESE...
THIS IS MY OTHER CAR.
I BRAKE FOR NO APPARENT REASON.
EXCEPT FOR SALVATORE KINCAID, WHO CONTINUALLY QUOTES POET JAMES RUSSELL LOWELL, 1819-1891.
"THERE IS NOTHING SO DESPERATELY MONOTONOUS AS THE SEA, AND I NO LONGER WONDER AT THE CRUELTY OF PIRATES"!
?
?

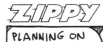

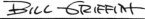

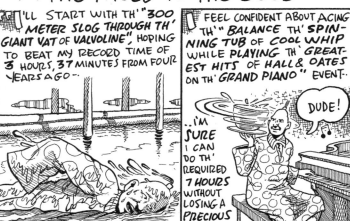

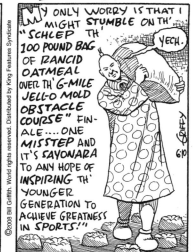

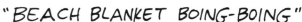

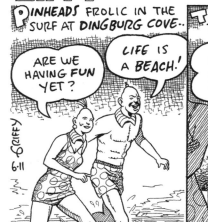

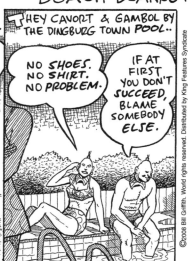

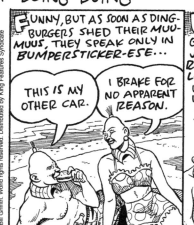

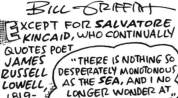

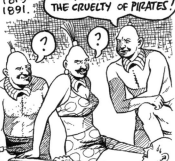

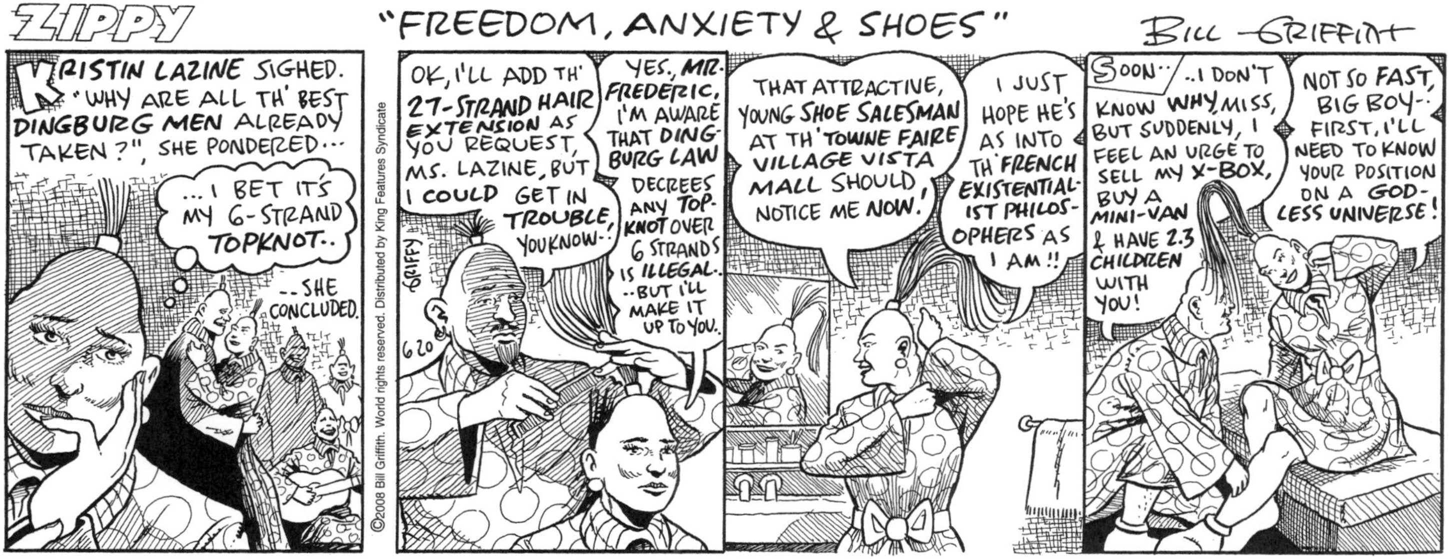
ZIPPY
"FREEDOM, ANXIETY & SHOES"
BILL GRIFFITH
KRISTIN LAZINE SIGHED. "WHY ARE ALL TH' BEST DINGBURG MEN ALREADY TAKEN?", SHE PONDERED...
...I BET IT'S MY 6-STRAND TOPKNOT..
--SHE CONCLUDED.
©2008 Bill Griffith. World rights reserved. Distributed by King Features Syndicate
OK, I'LL ADD TH' 27-STRAND HAIR EXTENSION AS YOU REQUEST, MS. LAZINE, BUT I COULD GET IN TROUBLE, YOU KNOW--
YES., MR. FREDERIC, I'M AWARE THAT DINGBURG LAW DECREES ANY TOPKNOT OVER 6 STRANDS IS ILLEGAL.. ..BUT I'LL MAKE IT UP TO YOU..
GRIFFY 6-20
THAT ATTRACTIVE, YOUNG SHOE SALESMAN AT TH' TOWNE FAIRE VILLAGE VISTA MALL SHOULD NOTICE ME NOW!
I JUST HOPE HE'S AS INTO TH' FRENCH EXISTENTIALIST PHILOSOPHERS AS I AM!!
SOON..
..I DON'T KNOW WHY, MISS, BUT SUDDENLY, I FEEL AN URGE TO SELL MY X-BOX, BUY A MINI-VAN & HAVE 2.3 CHILDREN WITH YOU!
NOT SO FAST, BIG BOY-- FIRST, I'LL NEED TO KNOW YOUR POSITION ON A GODLESS UNIVERSE!

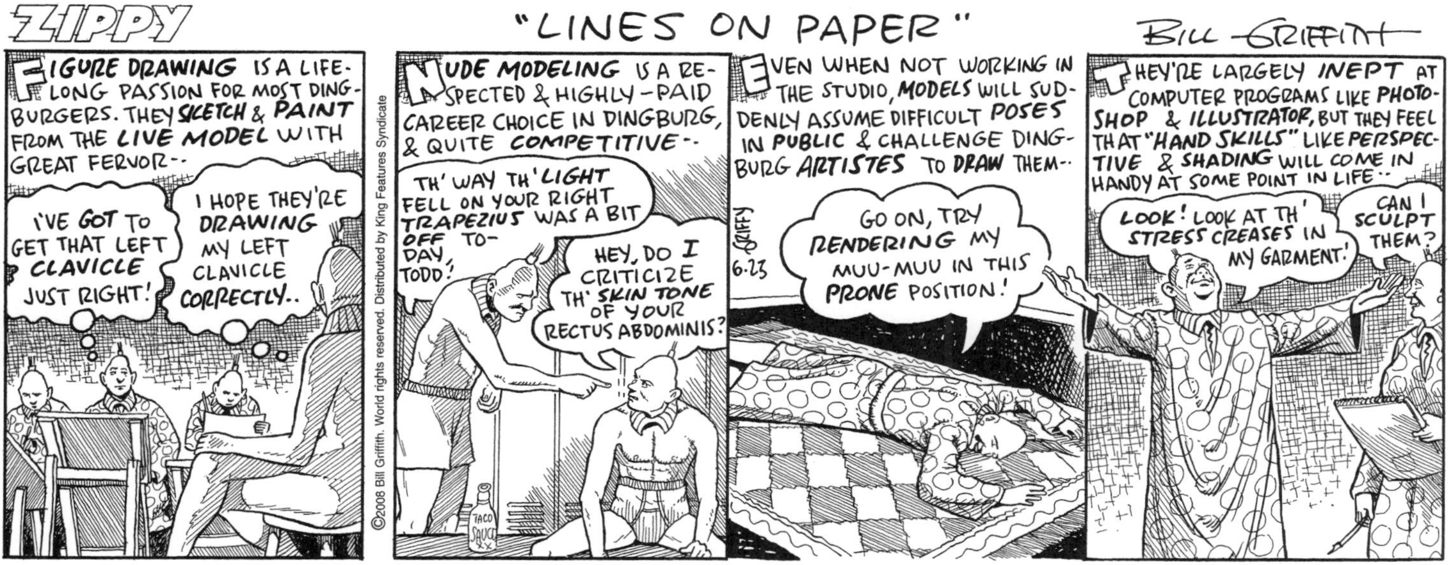
ZIPPY
"LINES ON PAPER"
BILL GRIFFITH
FIGURE DRAWING IS A LIFE-LONG PASSION FOR MOST DINGBURGERS. THEY SKETCH & PAINT FROM THE LIVE MODEL WITH GREAT FERVOR--
I'VE GOT TO GET THAT LEFT CLAVICLE JUST RIGHT!
I HOPE THEY'RE DRAWING MY LEFT CLAVICLE CORRECTLY..
©2008 Bill Griffith. World rights reserved. Distributed by King Features Syndicate
NUDE MODELING IS A RESPECTED & HIGHLY-PAID CAREER CHOICE IN DINGBURG, & QUITE COMPETITIVE--
TH' WAY TH' LIGHT FELL ON YOUR RIGHT TRAPEZIUS WAS A BIT OFF TO-DAY, TODD!
HEY, DO I CRITICIZE TH' SKIN TONE OF YOUR RECTUS ABDOMINIS?
TACO SAUCE XX
EVEN WHEN NOT WORKING IN THE STUDIO, MODELS WILL SUDDENLY ASSUME DIFFICULT POSES IN PUBLIC & CHALLENGE DINGBURG ARTISTES TO DRAW THEM--
GRIFFY 6-23
GO ON, TRY RENDERING MY MUU-MUU IN THIS PRONE POSITION!
THEY'RE LARGELY INEPT AT COMPUTER PROGRAMS LIKE PHOTOSHOP & ILLUSTRATOR, BUT THEY FEEL THAT "HAND SKILLS" LIKE PERSPECTIVE & SHADING WILL COME IN HANDY AT SOME POINT IN LIFE--
LOOK! LOOK AT TH' STRESS CREASES IN MY GARMENT!
CAN I SCULPT THEM?

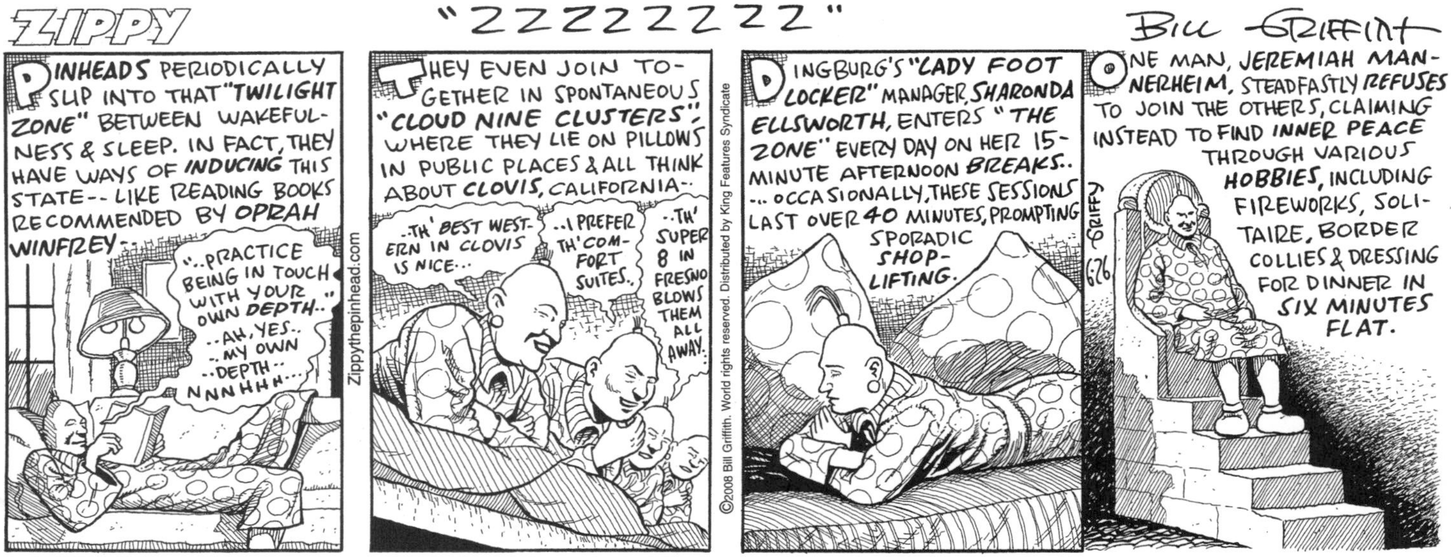
ZIPPY
"ZZZZZZZZ"
BILL GRIFFITH
PINHEADS PERIODICALLY SLIP INTO THAT "TWILIGHT ZONE" BETWEEN WAKEFULNESS & SLEEP. IN FACT, THEY HAVE WAYS OF INDUCING THIS STATE-- LIKE READING BOOKS RECOMMENDED BY OPRAH WINFREY--
"..PRACTICE BEING IN TOUCH WITH YOUR OWN DEPTH.." ..AH, YES.. ..MY OWN ..DEPTH.. NNNHHH....
Zippythepinhead.com
THEY EVEN JOIN TOGETHER IN SPONTANEOUS "CLOUD NINE CLUSTERS", WHERE THEY LIE ON PILLOWS IN PUBLIC PLACES & ALL THINK ABOUT CLOVIS, CALIFORNIA--
..TH' BEST WESTERN IN CLOVIS IS NICE..
..I PREFER TH' COMFORT SUITES..
..TH' SUPER 8 IN FRESNO BLOWS THEM ALL AWAY..
©2008 Bill Griffith. World rights reserved. Distributed by King Features Syndicate
DINGBURG'S "LADY FOOT LOCKER" MANAGER, SHARONDA ELLSWORTH, ENTERS "THE ZONE" EVERY DAY ON HER 15-MINUTE AFTERNOON BREAKS.. ..OCCASIONALLY, THESE SESSIONS LAST OVER 40 MINUTES, PROMPTING SPORADIC SHOPLIFTING.
GRIFFY 6·26
ONE MAN, JEREMIAH MANNERHEIM, STEADFASTLY REFUSES TO JOIN THE OTHERS, CLAIMING INSTEAD TO FIND INNER PEACE THROUGH VARIOUS HOBBIES, INCLUDING FIREWORKS, SOLITAIRE, BORDER COLLIES & DRESSING FOR DINNER IN SIX MINUTES FLAT.

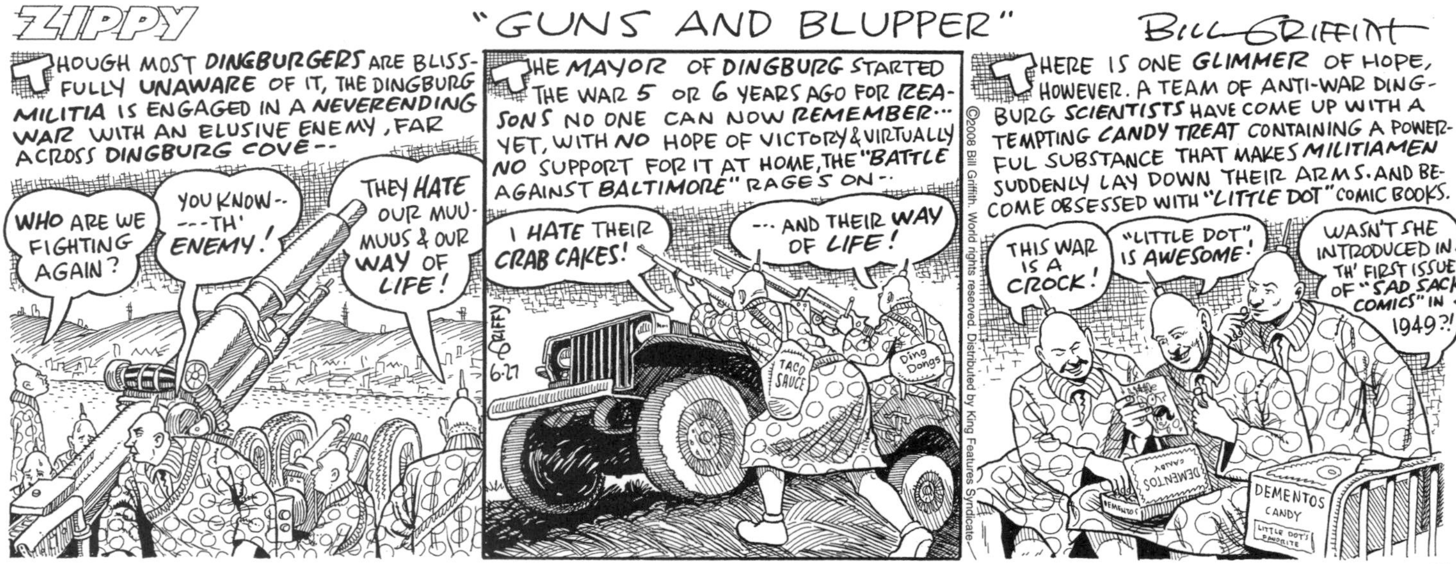
ZIPPY
"GUNS AND BLUPPER"
BILL GRIFFITH
THOUGH MOST DINGBURGERS ARE BLISSFULLY UNAWARE OF IT, THE DINGBURG MILITIA IS ENGAGED IN A NEVERENDING WAR WITH AN ELUSIVE ENEMY, FAR ACROSS DINGBURG COVE--
WHO ARE WE FIGHTING AGAIN?
YOU KNOW-- --TH' ENEMY!
THEY HATE OUR MUUMUUS & OUR WAY OF LIFE!
THE MAYOR OF DINGBURG STARTED THE WAR 5 OR 6 YEARS AGO FOR REASONS NO ONE CAN NOW REMEMBER-- YET, WITH NO HOPE OF VICTORY & VIRTUALLY NO SUPPORT FOR IT AT HOME, THE "BATTLE AGAINST BALTIMORE" RAGES ON--
I HATE THEIR CRAB CAKES!
-- AND THEIR WAY OF LIFE!
GRIFFY 6·27
TACO SAUCE
Ding Dongs
©2008 Bill Griffith. World rights reserved. Distributed by King Features Syndicate
THERE IS ONE GLIMMER OF HOPE, HOWEVER. A TEAM OF ANTI-WAR DINGBURG SCIENTISTS HAVE COME UP WITH A TEMPTING CANDY TREAT CONTAINING A POWERFUL SUBSTANCE THAT MAKES MILITIAMEN SUDDENLY LAY DOWN THEIR ARMS AND BECOME OBSESSED WITH "LITTLE DOT" COMIC BOOKS.
THIS WAR IS A CROCK!
"LITTLE DOT" IS AWESOME!
WASN'T SHE INTRODUCED IN TH' FIRST ISSUE OF "SAD SACK COMICS" IN 1949?!
DEMENTOS CANDY
DEMENTOS CANDY LITTLE DOT'S FAVORITE

67

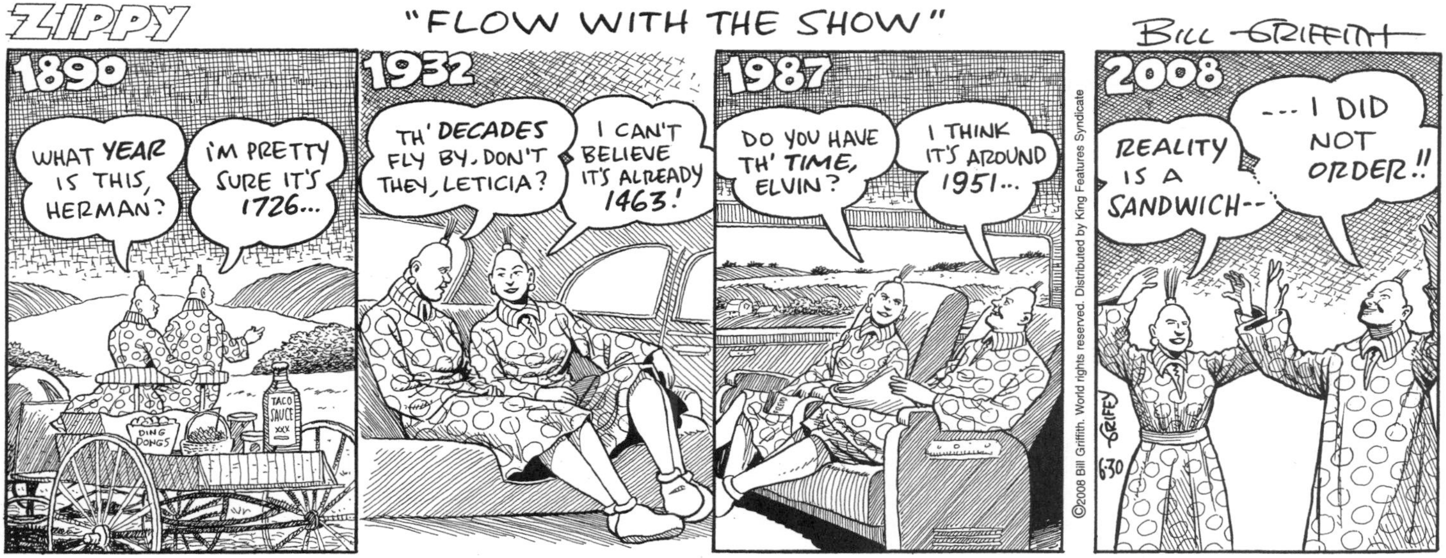
ZIPPY
"FLOW WITH THE SHOW"
BILL GRIFFITH
1890
WHAT YEAR IS THIS, HERMAN?
I'M PRETTY SURE IT'S 1726...
DING DONGS
TACO SAUCE XXX
1932
TH' DECADES FLY BY. DON'T THEY, LETICIA?
I CAN'T BELIEVE IT'S ALREADY 1463!
1987
DO YOU HAVE TH' TIME, ELVIN?
I THINK IT'S AROUND 1951...
©2008 Bill Griffith. World rights reserved. Distributed by King Features Syndicate
GRIFFY 6-30
2008
REALITY IS A SANDWICH--
...I DID NOT ORDER!!

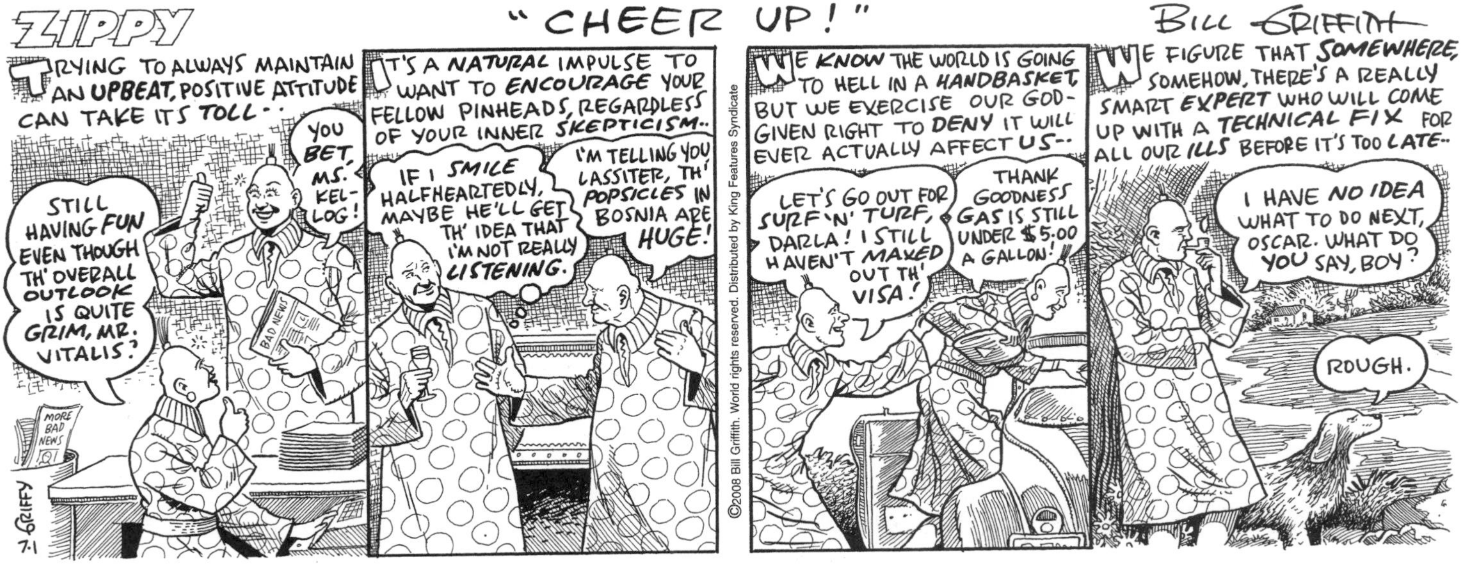
ZIPPY
"CHEER UP!"
BILL GRIFFITH
TRYING TO ALWAYS MAINTAIN AN UPBEAT, POSITIVE ATTITUDE CAN TAKE ITS TOLL..
YOU BET, MS. KEL-LOG!
STILL HAVING FUN EVEN THOUGH TH' OVERALL OUTLOOK IS QUITE GRIM, MR. VITALIS?
BAD NEWS
MORE BAD NEWS
GRIFFY 7-1
IT'S A NATURAL IMPULSE TO WANT TO ENCOURAGE YOUR FELLOW PINHEADS, REGARDLESS OF YOUR INNER SKEPTICISM..
IF I SMILE HALFHEARTEDLY, MAYBE HE'LL GET TH' IDEA THAT I'M NOT REALLY LISTENING.
I'M TELLING YOU LASSITER, TH' POPSICLES IN BOSNIA ARE HUGE!
©2008 Bill Griffith. World rights reserved. Distributed by King Features Syndicate
WE KNOW THE WORLD IS GOING TO HELL IN A HANDBASKET, BUT WE EXERCISE OUR GOD-GIVEN RIGHT TO DENY IT WILL EVER ACTUALLY AFFECT US--
LET'S GO OUT FOR SURF 'N' TURF, DARLA! I STILL HAVEN'T MAXED OUT TH' VISA!
THANK GOODNESS GAS IS STILL UNDER $5.00 A GALLON!
WE FIGURE THAT SOMEWHERE, SOMEHOW, THERE'S A REALLY SMART EXPERT WHO WILL COME UP WITH A TECHNICAL FIX FOR ALL OUR ILLS BEFORE IT'S TOO LATE..
I HAVE NO IDEA WHAT TO DO NEXT, OSCAR. WHAT DO YOU SAY, BOY?
ROUGH.

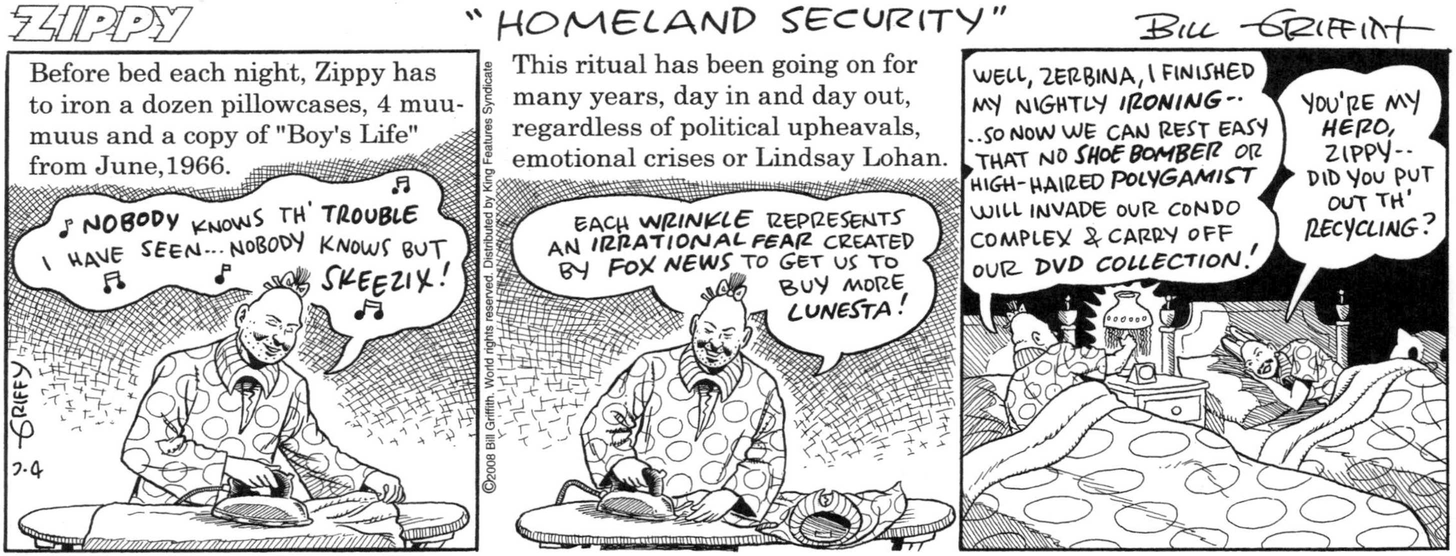
ZIPPY
"HOMELAND SECURITY"
BILL GRIFFITH
Before bed each night, Zippy has to iron a dozen pillowcases, 4 muu-muus and a copy of "Boy's Life" from June, 1966.
♪ NOBODY KNOWS TH' TROUBLE I HAVE SEEN... NOBODY KNOWS BUT SKEEZIX!
GRIFFY
7-4
©2008 Bill Griffith. World rights reserved. Distributed by King Features Syndicate
This ritual has been going on for many years, day in and day out, regardless of political upheavals, emotional crises or Lindsay Lohan.
EACH WRINKLE REPRESENTS AN IRRATIONAL FEAR CREATED BY FOX NEWS TO GET US TO BUY MORE LUNESTA!
WELL, ZERBINA, I FINISHED MY NIGHTLY IRONING-- ..SO NOW WE CAN REST EASY THAT NO SHOE BOMBER OR HIGH-HAIRED POLYGAMIST WILL INVADE OUR CONDO COMPLEX & CARRY OFF OUR DVD COLLECTION!
YOU'RE MY HERO, ZIPPY-- DID YOU PUT OUT TH' RECYCLING?

68

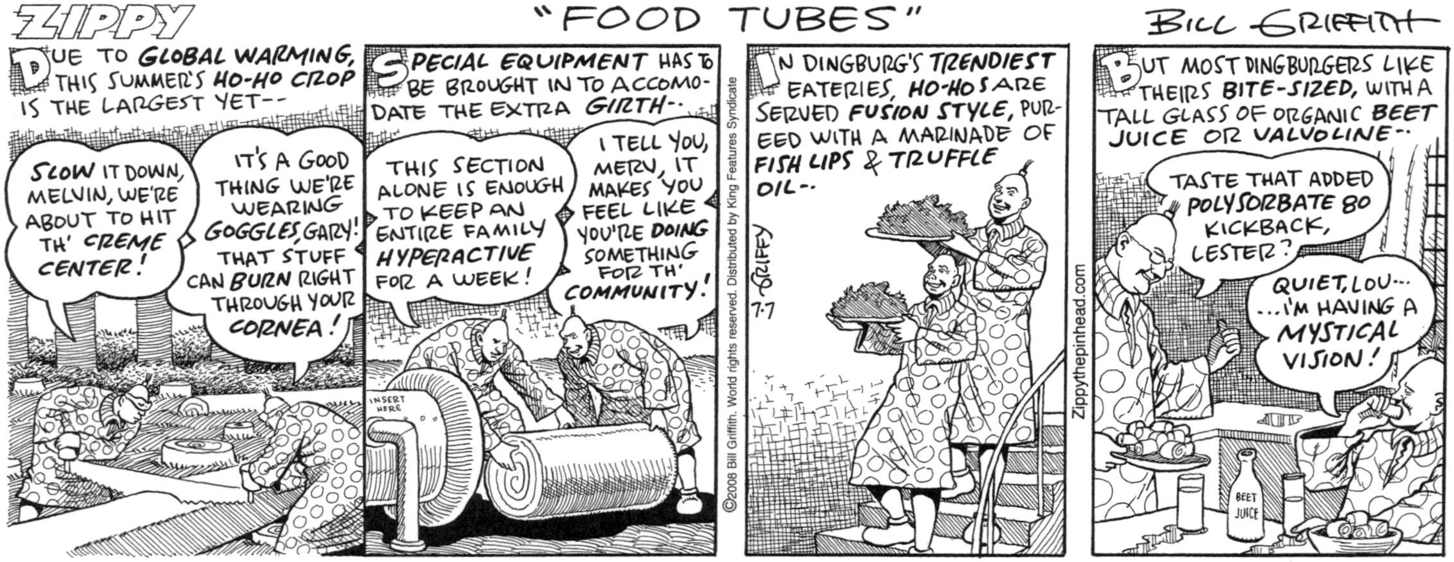
ZIPPY
"FOOD TUBES"
BILL GRIFFITH
DUE TO GLOBAL WARMING, THIS SUMMER'S HO-HO CROP IS THE LARGEST YET--
SLOW IT DOWN, MELVIN, WE'RE ABOUT TO HIT TH' CREME CENTER!
IT'S A GOOD THING WE'RE WEARING GOGGLES, GARY! THAT STUFF CAN BURN RIGHT THROUGH YOUR CORNEA!
SPECIAL EQUIPMENT HAS TO BE BROUGHT IN TO ACCOMODATE THE EXTRA GIRTH--
THIS SECTION ALONE IS ENOUGH TO KEEP AN ENTIRE FAMILY HYPERACTIVE FOR A WEEK!
I TELL YOU, MERV, IT MAKES YOU FEEL LIKE YOU'RE DOING SOMETHING FOR TH' COMMUNITY!
INSERT HERE
©2008 Bill Griffith. World rights reserved. Distributed by King Features Syndicate
IN DINGBURG'S TRENDIEST EATERIES, HO-HOS ARE SERVED FUSION STYLE, PUREED WITH A MARINADE OF FISH LIPS & TRUFFLE OIL--
GRIFFY
7-7
Zippythepinhead.com
BUT MOST DINGBURGERS LIKE THEIRS BITE-SIZED, WITH A TALL GLASS OF ORGANIC BEET JUICE OR VALVOLINE--
TASTE THAT ADDED POLYSORBATE 80 KICKBACK, LESTER?
QUIET, LOU... ...I'M HAVING A MYSTICAL VISION!
BEET JUICE

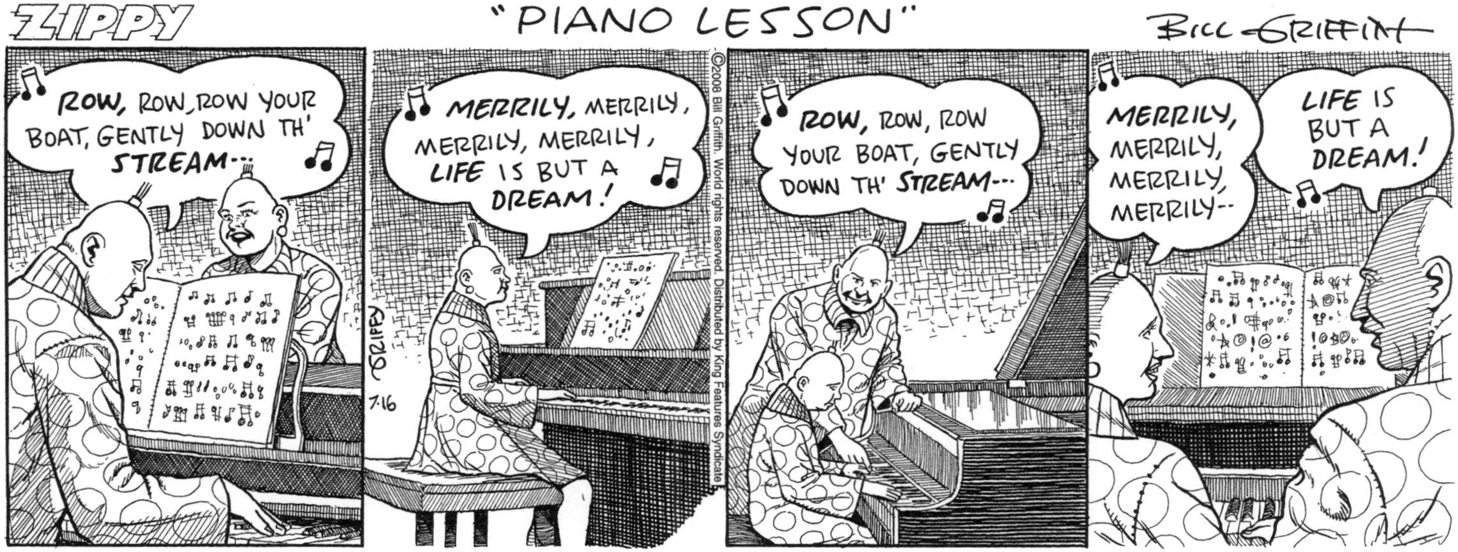
ZIPPY
"PIANO LESSON"
BILL GRIFFITH
ROW, ROW, ROW YOUR BOAT, GENTLY DOWN TH' STREAM--
MERRILY, MERRILY, MERRILY, MERRILY, LIFE IS BUT A DREAM!
©2008 Bill Griffith. World rights reserved. Distributed by King Features Syndicate
GRIFFY 7·16
ROW, ROW, ROW YOUR BOAT, GENTLY DOWN TH' STREAM--
MERRILY, MERRILY, MERRILY, MERRILY--
LIFE IS BUT A DREAM!

69

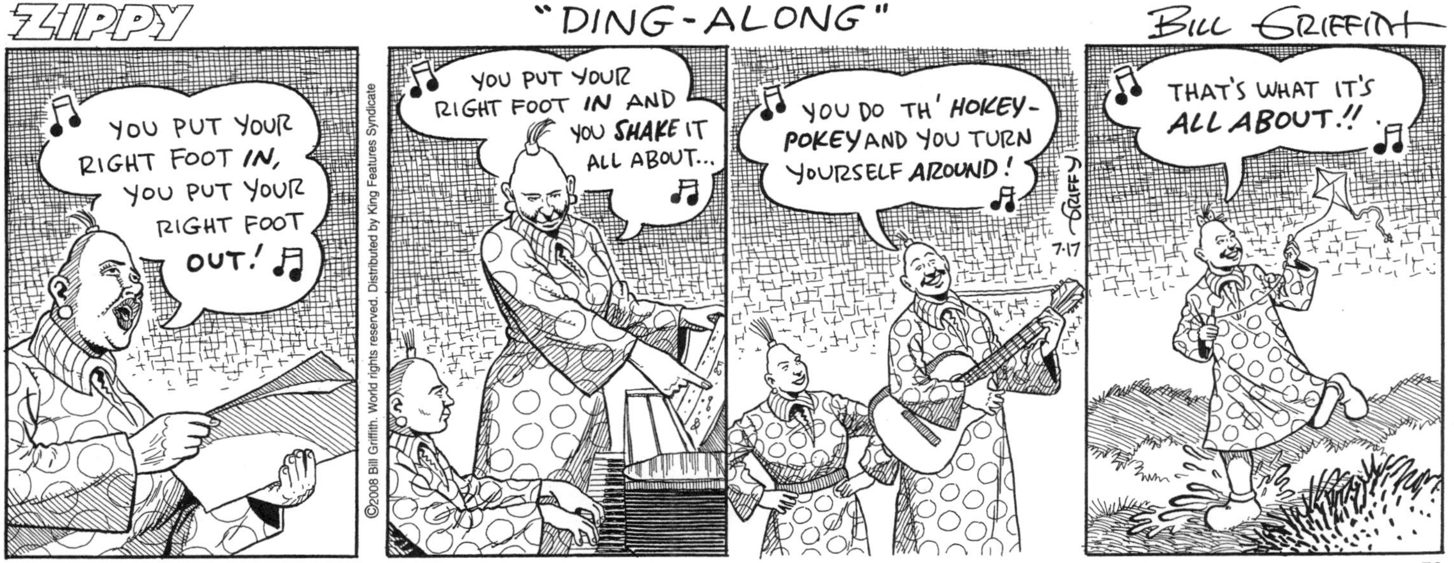
ZIPPY
"DING-ALONG"
BILL GRIFFITH
YOU PUT YOUR RIGHT FOOT IN, YOU PUT YOUR RIGHT FOOT OUT!
©2008 Bill Griffith. World rights reserved. Distributed by King Features Syndicate
YOU PUT YOUR RIGHT FOOT IN AND YOU SHAKE IT ALL ABOUT...
YOU DO TH' HOKEY-POKEY AND YOU TURN YOURSELF AROUND!
GRIFFY 7·17
THAT'S WHAT IT'S ALL ABOUT!!

70

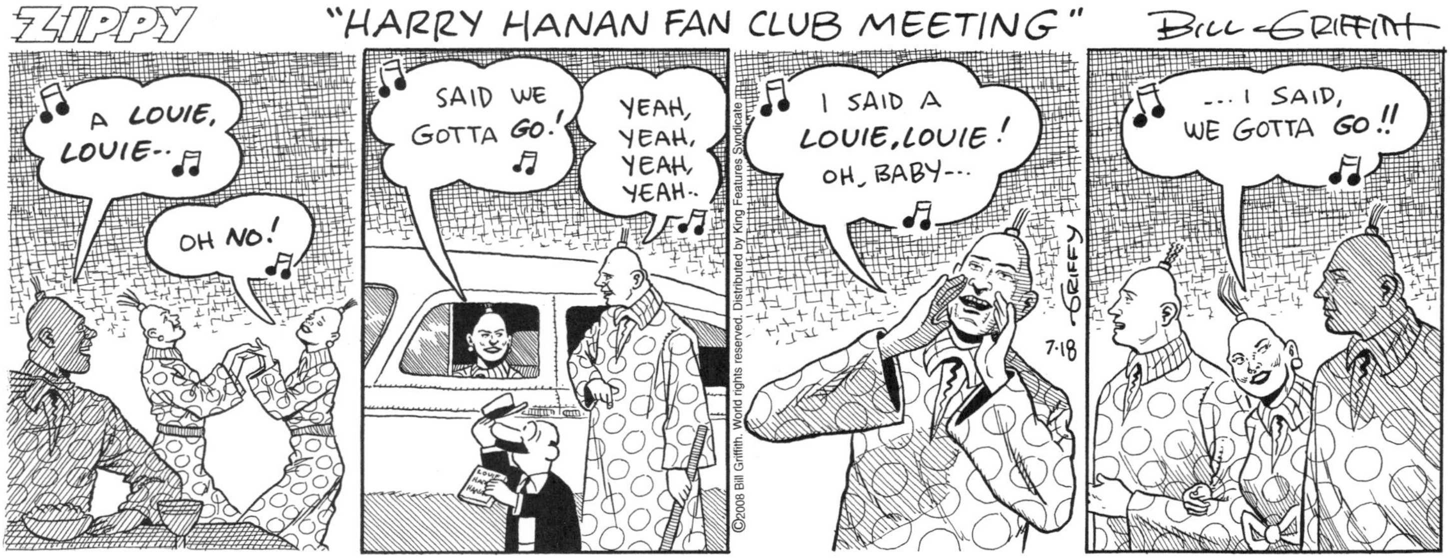
ZIPPY
"HARRY HANAN FAN CLUB MEETING"
BILL GRIFFITH
A LOUIE, LOUIE..
OH NO!
SAID WE GOTTA GO!
YEAH, YEAH, YEAH, YEAH..
©2008 Bill Griffith. World rights reserved. Distributed by King Features Syndicate
I SAID A LOUIE, LOUIE! OH, BABY...
GRIFFY
7·18
...I SAID, WE GOTTA GO!!

71

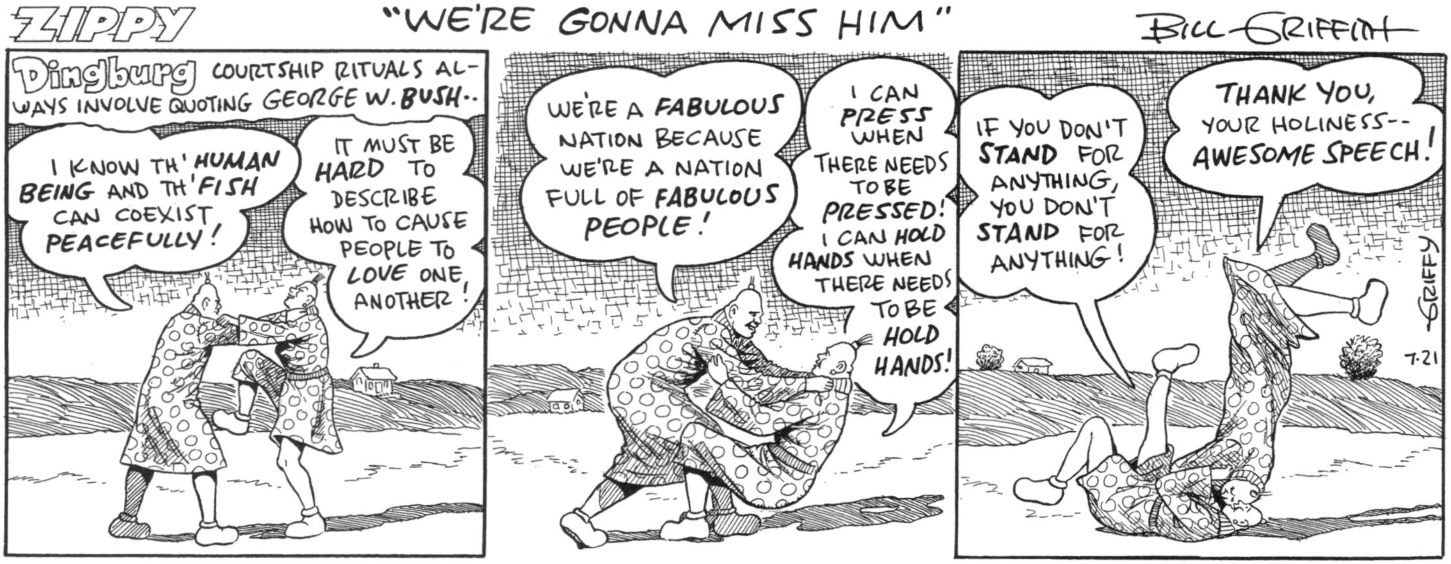
ZIPPY
"WE'RE GONNA MISS HIM"
BILL GRIFFITH
Dingburg COURTSHIP RITUALS ALWAYS INVOLVE QUOTING GEORGE W. BUSH..
I KNOW TH' HUMAN BEING AND TH' FISH CAN COEXIST PEACEFULLY!
IT MUST BE HARD TO DESCRIBE HOW TO CAUSE PEOPLE TO LOVE ONE ANOTHER!
WE'RE A FABULOUS NATION BECAUSE WE'RE A NATION FULL OF FABULOUS PEOPLE!
I CAN PRESS WHEN THERE NEEDS TO BE PRESSED! I CAN HOLD HANDS WHEN THERE NEEDS TO BE HOLD HANDS!
IF YOU DON'T STAND FOR ANYTHING, YOU DON'T STAND FOR ANYTHING!
THANK YOU, YOUR HOLINESS-- AWESOME SPEECH!
GRIFFY
7·21

72

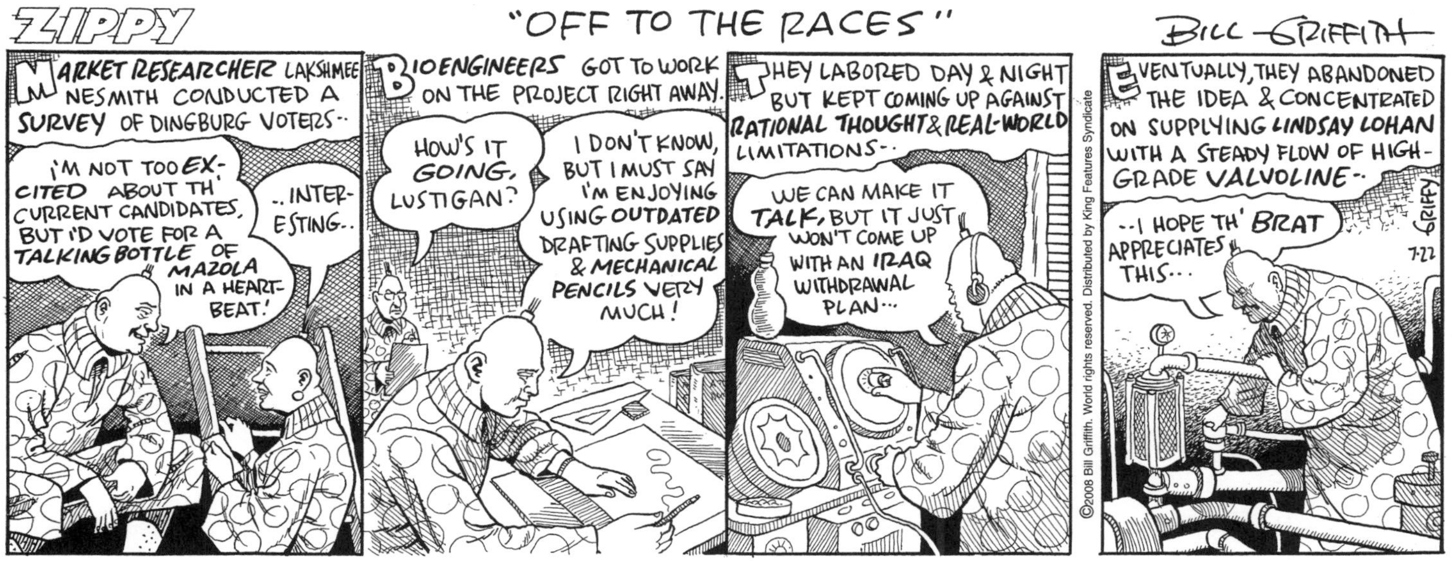
ZIPPY
"OFF TO THE RACES"
BILL GRIFFITH
MARKET RESEARCHER LAKSHMEE NESMITH CONDUCTED A SURVEY OF DINGBURG VOTERS--
I'M NOT TOO EXCITED ABOUT TH' CURRENT CANDIDATES, BUT I'D VOTE FOR A TALKING BOTTLE OF MAZOLA IN A HEART-BEAT!
..INTER-ESTING..
BIOENGINEERS GOT TO WORK ON THE PROJECT RIGHT AWAY.
HOW'S IT GOING, LUSTIGAN?
I DON'T KNOW, BUT I MUST SAY I'M ENJOYING USING OUTDATED DRAFTING SUPPLIES & MECHANICAL PENCILS VERY MUCH!
THEY LABORED DAY & NIGHT BUT KEPT COMING UP AGAINST RATIONAL THOUGHT & REAL-WORLD LIMITATIONS--.
WE CAN MAKE IT TALK, BUT IT JUST WON'T COME UP WITH AN IRAQ WITHDRAWAL PLAN...
©2008 Bill Griffith. World rights reserved. Distributed by King Features Syndicate
EVENTUALLY, THEY ABANDONED THE IDEA & CONCENTRATED ON SUPPLYING LINDSAY LOHAN WITH A STEADY FLOW OF HIGH-GRADE VALVOLINE--.
--I HOPE TH' BRAT APPRECIATES THIS...
GRIFFY
7-22

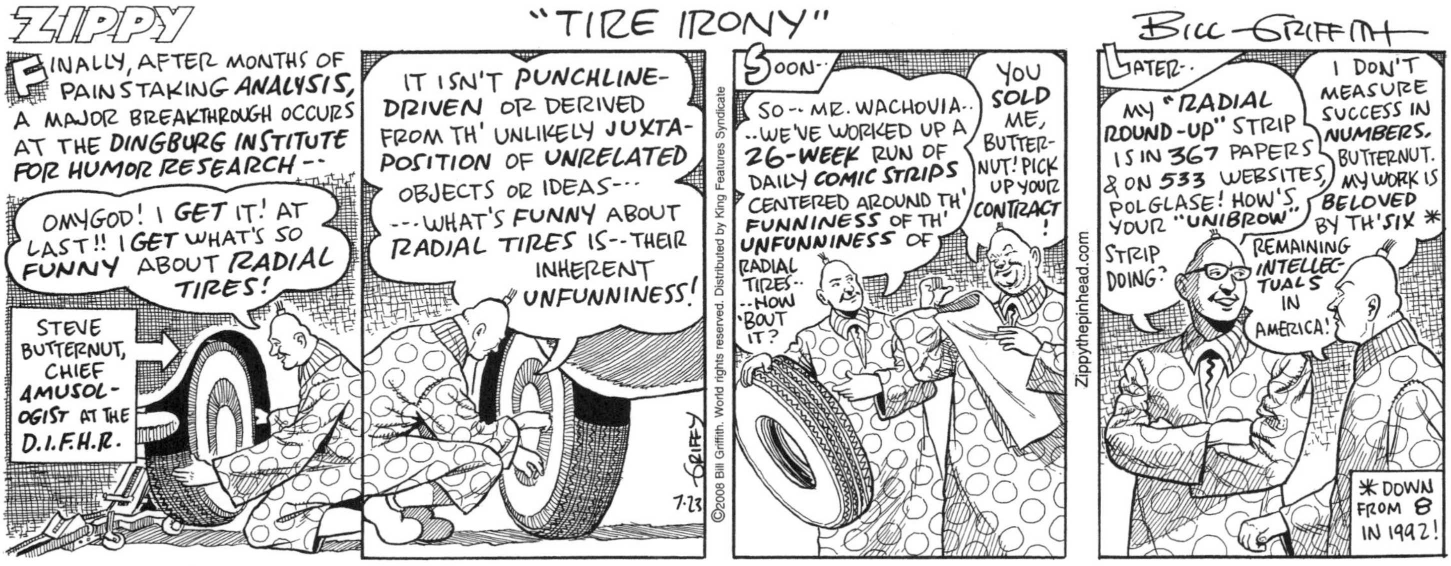
ZIPPY
"TIRE IRONY"
BILL GRIFFITH
FINALLY, AFTER MONTHS OF PAINSTAKING ANALYSIS, A MAJOR BREAKTHROUGH OCCURS AT THE DINGBURG INSTITUTE FOR HUMOR RESEARCH--
OMYGOD! I GET IT! AT LAST!! I GET WHAT'S SO FUNNY ABOUT RADIAL TIRES!
STEVE BUTTERNUT, CHIEF AMUSOLOGIST AT THE D.I.F.H.R.
IT ISN'T PUNCHLINE-DRIVEN OR DERIVED FROM TH' UNLIKELY JUXTAPOSITION OF UNRELATED OBJECTS OR IDEAS--- ---WHAT'S FUNNY ABOUT RADIAL TIRES IS--THEIR INHERENT UNFUNNINESS!
GRIFFY
7-23
©2008 Bill Griffith. World rights reserved. Distributed by King Features Syndicate
SOON--
SO-- MR. WACHOVIA-- ..WE'VE WORKED UP A 26-WEEK RUN OF DAILY COMIC STRIPS CENTERED AROUND TH' FUNNINESS OF TH' UNFUNNINESS OF RADIAL TIRES-- ..HOW 'BOUT IT?
YOU SOLD ME, BUTTERNUT! PICK UP YOUR CONTRACT!
Zippythepinhead.com
LATER--
MY "RADIAL ROUND-UP" STRIP IS IN 367 PAPERS & ON 533 WEBSITES, POLGLASE! HOW'S YOUR "UNIBROW" STRIP DOING?
I DON'T MEASURE SUCCESS IN NUMBERS, BUTTERNUT. MY WORK IS BELOVED BY TH' SIX * REMAINING INTELLECTUALS IN AMERICA!
* DOWN FROM 8 IN 1992!

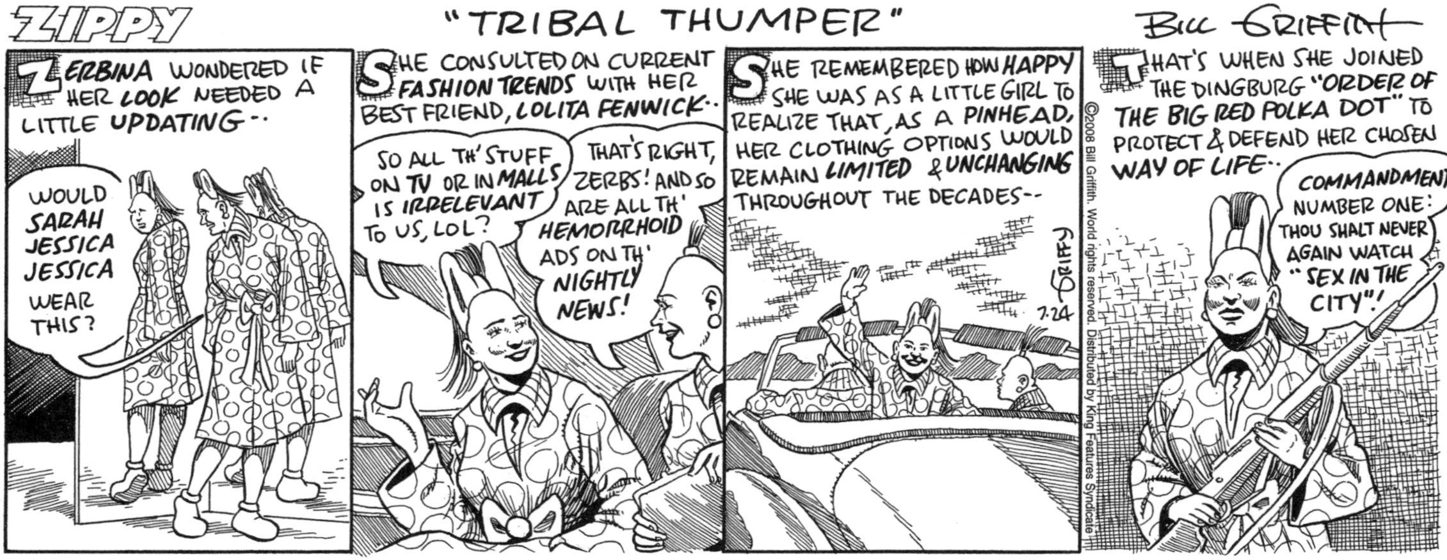
ZIPPY
"TRIBAL THUMPER"
BILL GRIFFITH
ZERBINA WONDERED IF HER LOOK NEEDED A LITTLE UPDATING--
WOULD SARAH JESSICA JESSICA WEAR THIS?
SHE CONSULTED ON CURRENT FASHION TRENDS WITH HER BEST FRIEND, LOLITA FENWICK--
SO ALL TH' STUFF ON TV OR IN MALLS IS IRRELEVANT TO US, LOL?
THAT'S RIGHT, ZERBS! AND SO ARE ALL TH' HEMORRHOID ADS ON TH' NIGHTLY NEWS!
SHE REMEMBERED HOW HAPPY SHE WAS AS A LITTLE GIRL TO REALIZE THAT, AS A PINHEAD, HER CLOTHING OPTIONS WOULD REMAIN LIMITED & UNCHANGING THROUGHOUT THE DECADES--
GRIFFY
7-24
©2008 Bill Griffith. World rights reserved. Distributed by King Features Syndicate
THAT'S WHEN SHE JOINED THE DINGBURG "ORDER OF THE BIG RED POLKA DOT" TO PROTECT & DEFEND HER CHOSEN WAY OF LIFE--
COMMANDMENT NUMBER ONE: THOU SHALT NEVER AGAIN WATCH "SEX IN THE CITY"!

73

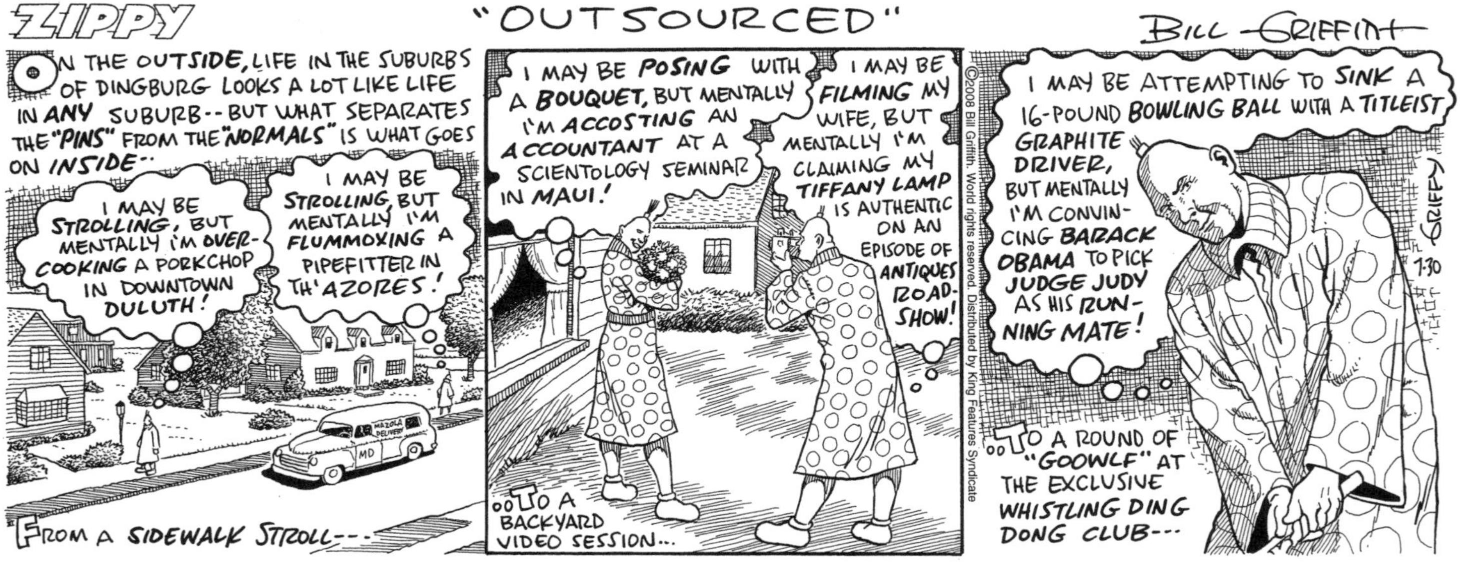
ZIPPY
"OUTSOURCED"
BILL GRIFFITH
ON THE OUTSIDE, LIFE IN THE SUBURBS OF DINGBURG LOOKS A LOT LIKE LIFE IN ANY SUBURB-- BUT WHAT SEPARATES THE "PINS" FROM THE "NORMALS" IS WHAT GOES ON INSIDE--
I MAY BE STROLLING, BUT MENTALLY I'M OVER-COOKING A PORKCHOP IN DOWNTOWN DULUTH!
I MAY BE STROLLING, BUT MENTALLY I'M FLUMMOXING A PIPEFITTER IN TH' AZORES!
MAZOLA DELIVERY
MD
FROM A SIDEWALK STROLL---
I MAY BE POSING WITH A BOUQUET, BUT MENTALLY I'M ACCOSTING AN ACCOUNTANT AT A SCIENTOLOGY SEMINAR IN MAUI!
I MAY BE FILMING MY WIFE, BUT MENTALLY I'M CLAIMING MY TIFFANY LAMP IS AUTHENTIC ON AN EPISODE OF ANTIQUES ROAD-SHOW!
..TO A BACKYARD VIDEO SESSION...
©2008 Bill Griffith. World rights reserved. Distributed by King Features Syndicate
I MAY BE ATTEMPTING TO SINK A 16-POUND BOWLING BALL WITH A TITLEIST GRAPHITE DRIVER, BUT MENTALLY I'M CONVIN-CING BARACK OBAMA TO PICK JUDGE JUDY AS HIS RUN-NING MATE!
GRIFFY
7-30
..TO A ROUND OF "GOOWLF" AT THE EXCLUSIVE WHISTLING DING DONG CLUB---

74

# PROTO-DINGBURG

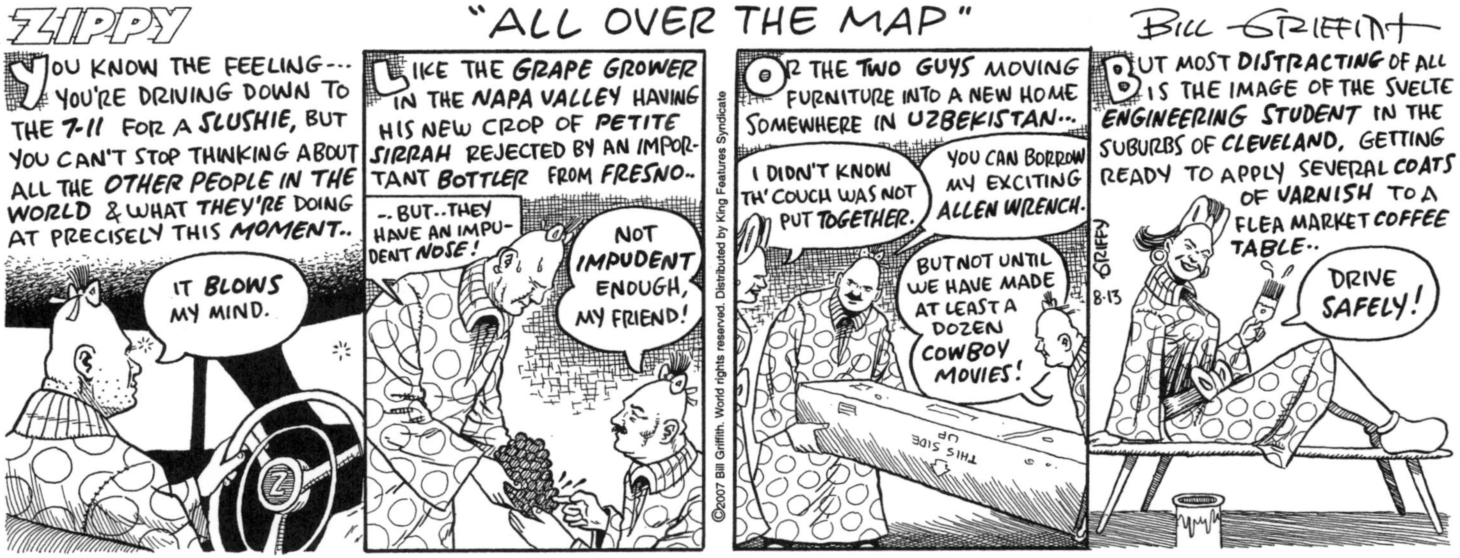
ZIPPY
"ALL OVER THE MAP"
BILL GRIFFITH
YOU KNOW THE FEELING--- YOU'RE DRIVING DOWN TO THE 7-11 FOR A SLUSHIE, BUT YOU CAN'T STOP THINKING ABOUT ALL THE OTHER PEOPLE IN THE WORLD & WHAT THEY'RE DOING AT PRECISELY THIS MOMENT..
IT BLOWS MY MIND.
LIKE THE GRAPE GROWER IN THE NAPA VALLEY HAVING HIS NEW CROP OF PETITE SIRRAH REJECTED BY AN IMPORTANT BOTTLER FROM FRESNO..
-- BUT.. THEY HAVE AN IMPUDENT NOSE!
NOT IMPUDENT ENOUGH, MY FRIEND!
©2007 Bill Griffith. World rights reserved. Distributed by King Features Syndicate
OR THE TWO GUYS MOVING FURNITURE INTO A NEW HOME SOMEWHERE IN UZBEKISTAN..
I DIDN'T KNOW TH' COUCH WAS NOT PUT TOGETHER.
YOU CAN BORROW MY EXCITING ALLEN WRENCH.
BUT NOT UNTIL WE HAVE MADE AT LEAST A DOZEN COWBOY MOVIES!
THIS SIDE UP
GRIFFY 8-13
BUT MOST DISTRACTING OF ALL IS THE IMAGE OF THE SVELTE ENGINEERING STUDENT IN THE SUBURBS OF CLEVELAND, GETTING READY TO APPLY SEVERAL COATS OF VARNISH TO A FLEA MARKET COFFEE TABLE..
DRIVE SAFELY!

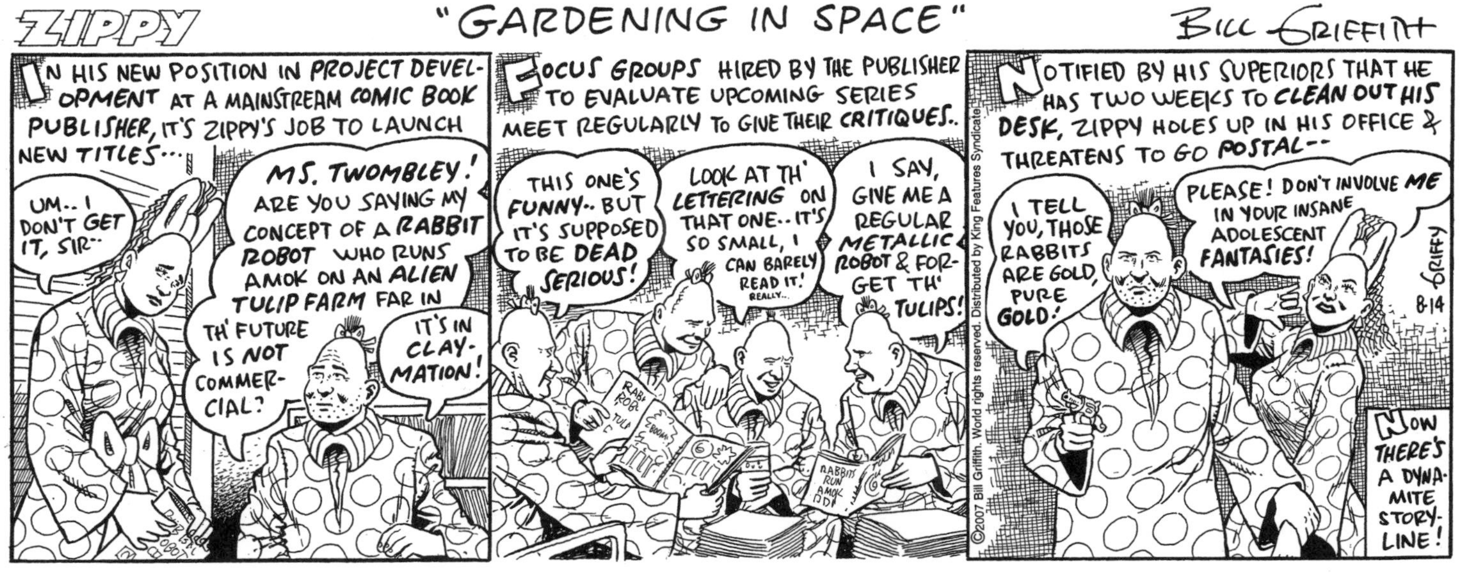
ZIPPY
"GARDENING IN SPACE"
BILL GRIFFITH
IN HIS NEW POSITION IN PROJECT DEVELOPMENT AT A MAINSTREAM COMIC BOOK PUBLISHER, IT'S ZIPPY'S JOB TO LAUNCH NEW TITLES...
UM.. I DON'T GET IT, SIR..
MS. TWOMBLEY! ARE YOU SAYING MY CONCEPT OF A RABBIT ROBOT WHO RUNS AMOK ON AN ALIEN TULIP FARM FAR IN TH' FUTURE IS NOT COMMERCIAL?
IT'S IN CLAYMATION!
FOCUS GROUPS HIRED BY THE PUBLISHER TO EVALUATE UPCOMING SERIES MEET REGULARLY TO GIVE THEIR CRITIQUES..
THIS ONE'S FUNNY.. BUT IT'S SUPPOSED TO BE DEAD SERIOUS!
LOOK AT TH' LETTERING ON THAT ONE.. IT'S SO SMALL, I CAN BARELY READ IT! REALLY...
I SAY, GIVE ME A REGULAR METALLIC ROBOT & FORGET TH' TULIPS!
RABBITS RUN AMOK
©2007 Bill Griffith. World rights reserved. Distributed by King Features Syndicate
NOTIFIED BY HIS SUPERIORS THAT HE HAS TWO WEEKS TO CLEAN OUT HIS DESK, ZIPPY HOLES UP IN HIS OFFICE & THREATENS TO GO POSTAL--
I TELL YOU, THOSE RABBITS ARE GOLD, PURE GOLD!
PLEASE! DON'T INVOLVE ME IN YOUR INSANE ADOLESCENT FANTASIES!
GRIFFY 8-14
NOW THERE'S A DYNAMITE STORYLINE!

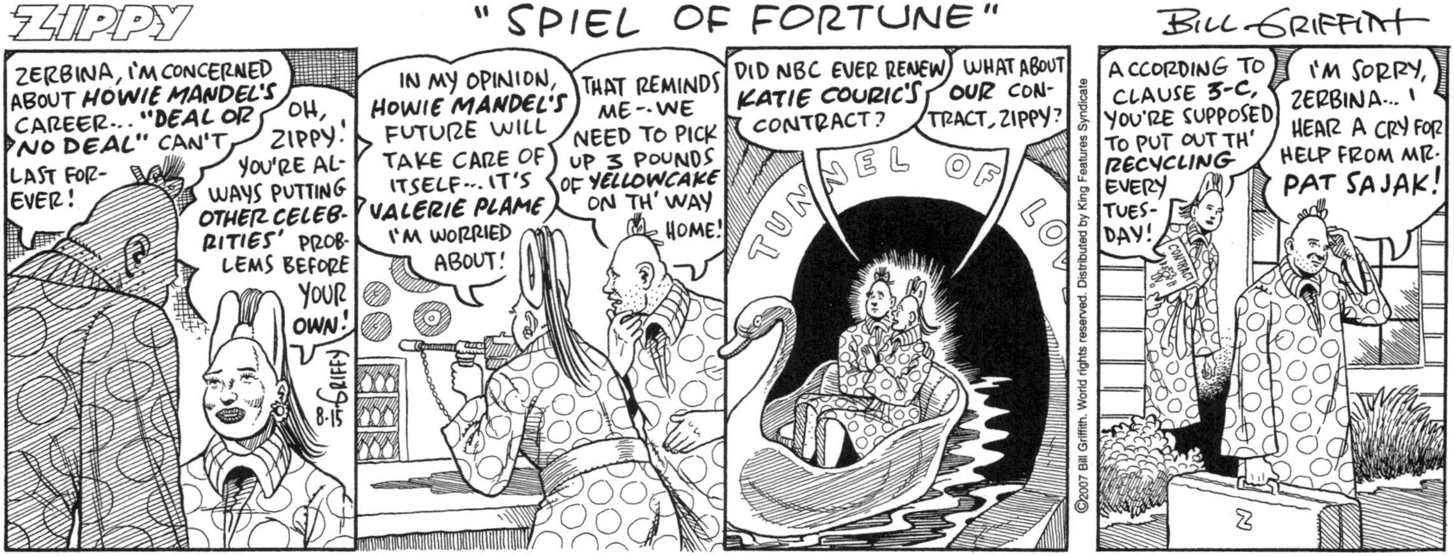
ZIPPY
"SPIEL OF FORTUNE"
BILL GRIFFITH
ZERBINA, I'M CONCERNED ABOUT HOWIE MANDEL'S CAREER... "DEAL OR NO DEAL" CAN'T LAST FOREVER!
OH, ZIPPY! YOU'RE ALWAYS PUTTING OTHER CELEBRITIES' PROBLEMS BEFORE YOUR OWN!
GRIFFY 8-15
IN MY OPINION, HOWIE MANDEL'S FUTURE WILL TAKE CARE OF ITSELF... IT'S VALERIE PLAME I'M WORRIED ABOUT!
THAT REMINDS ME-- WE NEED TO PICK UP 3 POUNDS OF YELLOWCAKE ON TH' WAY HOME!
DID NBC EVER RENEW KATIE COURIC'S CONTRACT?
WHAT ABOUT OUR CONTRACT, ZIPPY?
TUNNEL OF LOVE
©2007 Bill Griffith. World rights reserved. Distributed by King Features Syndicate
ACCORDING TO CLAUSE 3-C, YOU'RE SUPPOSED TO PUT OUT TH' RECYCLING EVERY TUESDAY!
CONTRACT
I'M SORRY, ZERBINA... I HEAR A CRY FOR HELP FROM MR. PAT SAJAK!
Z

75

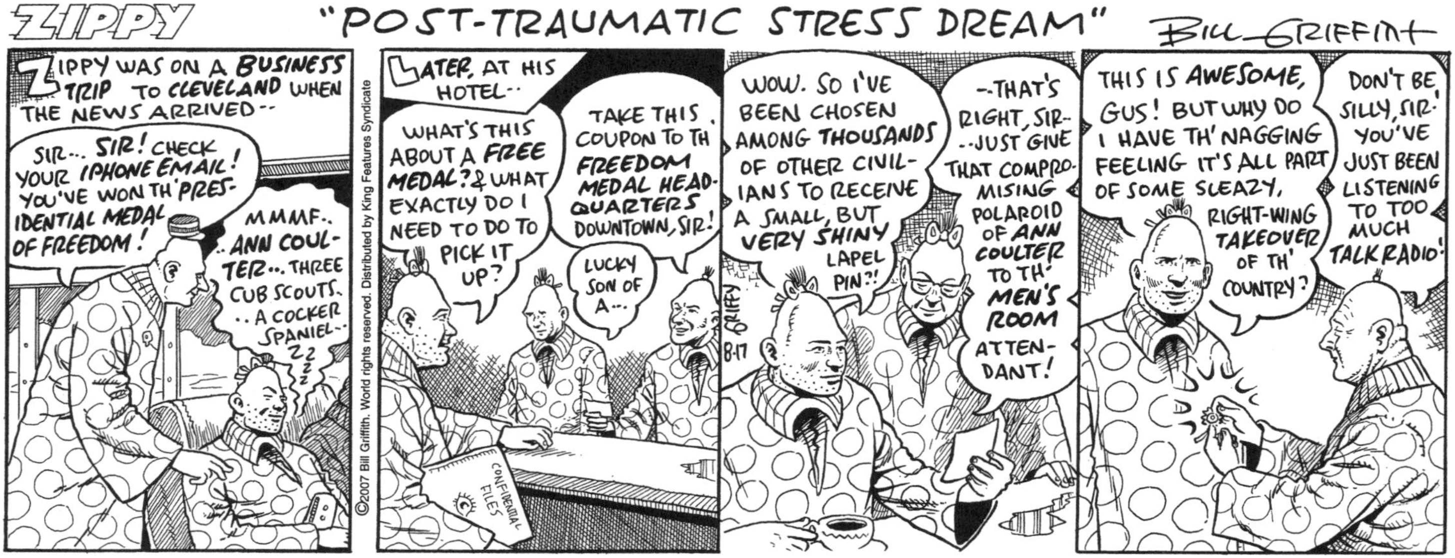
ZIPPY
"POST-TRAUMATIC STRESS DREAM"
BILL GRIFFITH
ZIPPY WAS ON A BUSINESS TRIP TO CLEVELAND WHEN THE NEWS ARRIVED--
SIR... SIR! CHECK YOUR IPHONE EMAIL! YOU'VE WON TH' PRESIDENTIAL MEDAL OF FREEDOM!
MMMF.. ..ANN COULTER... THREE CUB SCOUTS.. ..A COCKER SPANIEL..
Z Z Z
©2007 Bill Griffith. World rights reserved. Distributed by King Features Syndicate
LATER, AT HIS HOTEL..
WHAT'S THIS ABOUT A FREE MEDAL? & WHAT EXACTLY DO I NEED TO DO TO PICK IT UP?
TAKE THIS COUPON TO TH' FREEDOM MEDAL HEADQUARTERS DOWNTOWN, SIR!
LUCKY SON OF A...
CONFIDENTIAL FILES
WOW. SO I'VE BEEN CHOSEN AMONG THOUSANDS OF OTHER CIVILIANS TO RECEIVE A SMALL, BUT VERY SHINY LAPEL PIN?!
--THAT'S RIGHT, SIR-- --JUST GIVE THAT COMPROMISING POLAROID OF ANN COULTER TO TH' MEN'S ROOM ATTENDANT!
GRIFFY 8-17
THIS IS AWESOME, GUS! BUT WHY DO I HAVE TH' NAGGING FEELING IT'S ALL PART OF SOME SLEAZY, RIGHT-WING TAKEOVER OF TH' COUNTRY?
DON'T BE SILLY, SIR! YOU'VE JUST BEEN LISTENING TO TOO MUCH TALK RADIO!

76

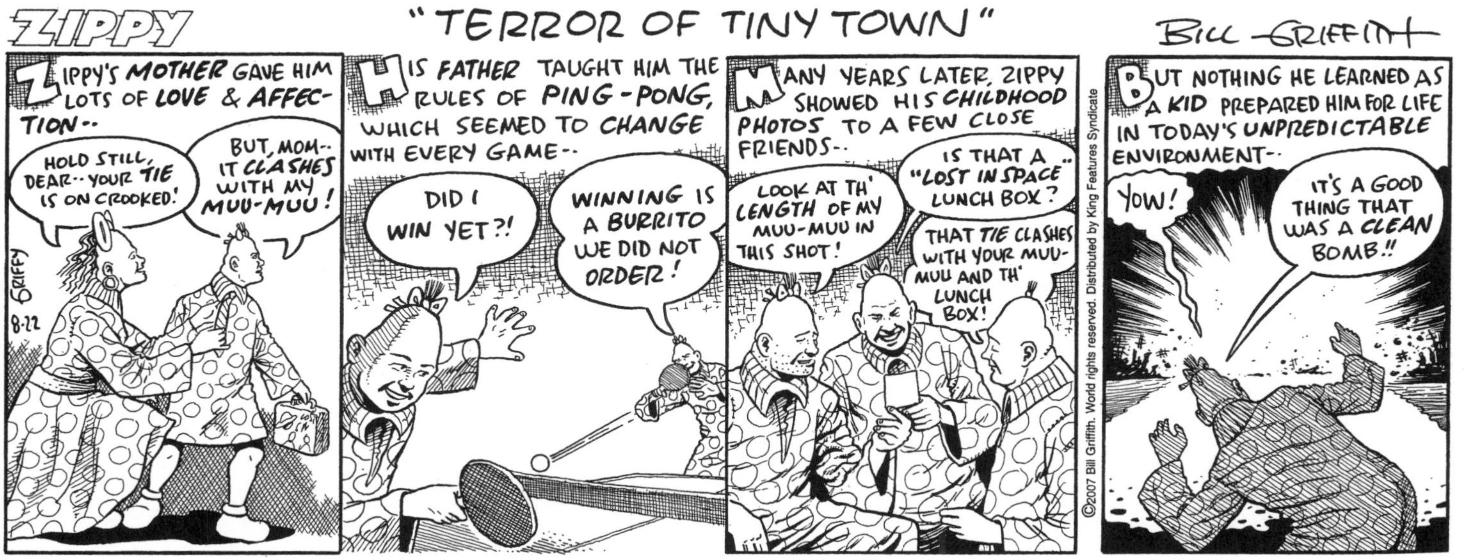

ZIPPY
"TERROR OF TINY TOWN"
BILL GRIFFITH
ZIPPY'S MOTHER GAVE HIM LOTS OF LOVE & AFFECTION..
HOLD STILL, DEAR.. YOUR TIE IS ON CROOKED!
BUT, MOM.. IT CLASHES WITH MY MUU-MUU!
GRIFFY 8-22
HIS FATHER TAUGHT HIM THE RULES OF PING-PONG, WHICH SEEMED TO CHANGE WITH EVERY GAME..
DID I WIN YET?!
WINNING IS A BURRITO WE DID NOT ORDER!
MANY YEARS LATER, ZIPPY SHOWED HIS CHILDHOOD PHOTOS TO A FEW CLOSE FRIENDS..
LOOK AT TH' LENGTH OF MY MUU-MUU IN THIS SHOT!
IS THAT A "LOST IN SPACE" LUNCH BOX?
THAT TIE CLASHES WITH YOUR MUU-MUU AND TH' LUNCH BOX!
©2007 Bill Griffith. World rights reserved. Distributed by King Features Syndicate
BUT NOTHING HE LEARNED AS A KID PREPARED HIM FOR LIFE IN TODAY'S UNPREDICTABLE ENVIRONMENT..
YOW!
IT'S A GOOD THING THAT WAS A CLEAN BOMB!!


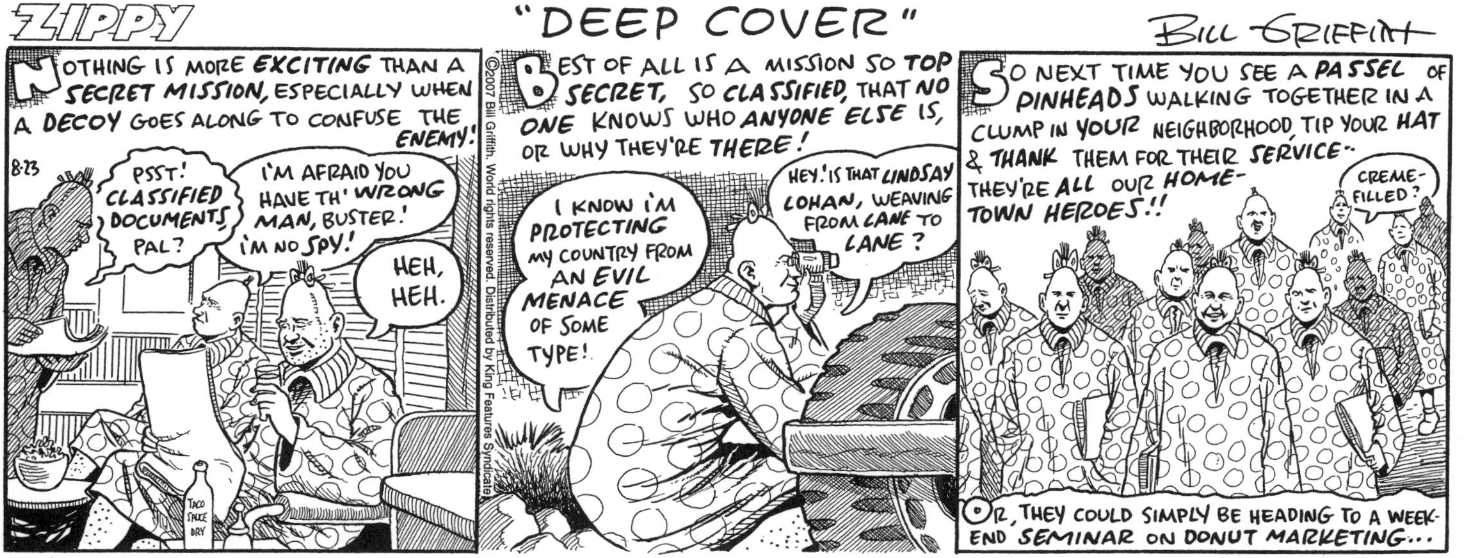

ZIPPY
"DEEP COVER"
BILL GRIFFITH
NOTHING IS MORE EXCITING THAN A SECRET MISSION, ESPECIALLY WHEN A DECOY GOES ALONG TO CONFUSE THE ENEMY!
8-23
PSST! CLASSIFIED DOCUMENTS, PAL?
I'M AFRAID YOU HAVE TH' WRONG MAN, BUSTER! I'M NO SPY!
HEH, HEH.
TACO SAUCE DRY
©2007 Bill Griffith. World rights reserved. Distributed by King Features Syndicate
BEST OF ALL IS A MISSION SO TOP SECRET, SO CLASSIFIED, THAT NO ONE KNOWS WHO ANYONE ELSE IS, OR WHY THEY'RE THERE!
I KNOW I'M PROTECTING MY COUNTRY FROM AN EVIL MENACE OF SOME TYPE!
HEY! IS THAT LINDSAY LOHAN, WEAVING FROM LANE TO LANE?
SO NEXT TIME YOU SEE A PASSEL OF PINHEADS WALKING TOGETHER IN A CLUMP IN YOUR NEIGHBORHOOD, TIP YOUR HAT & THANK THEM FOR THEIR SERVICE.. THEY'RE ALL OUR HOME-TOWN HEROES!!
CREME-FILLED?
OR, THEY COULD SIMPLY BE HEADING TO A WEEK-END SEMINAR ON DONUT MARKETING...

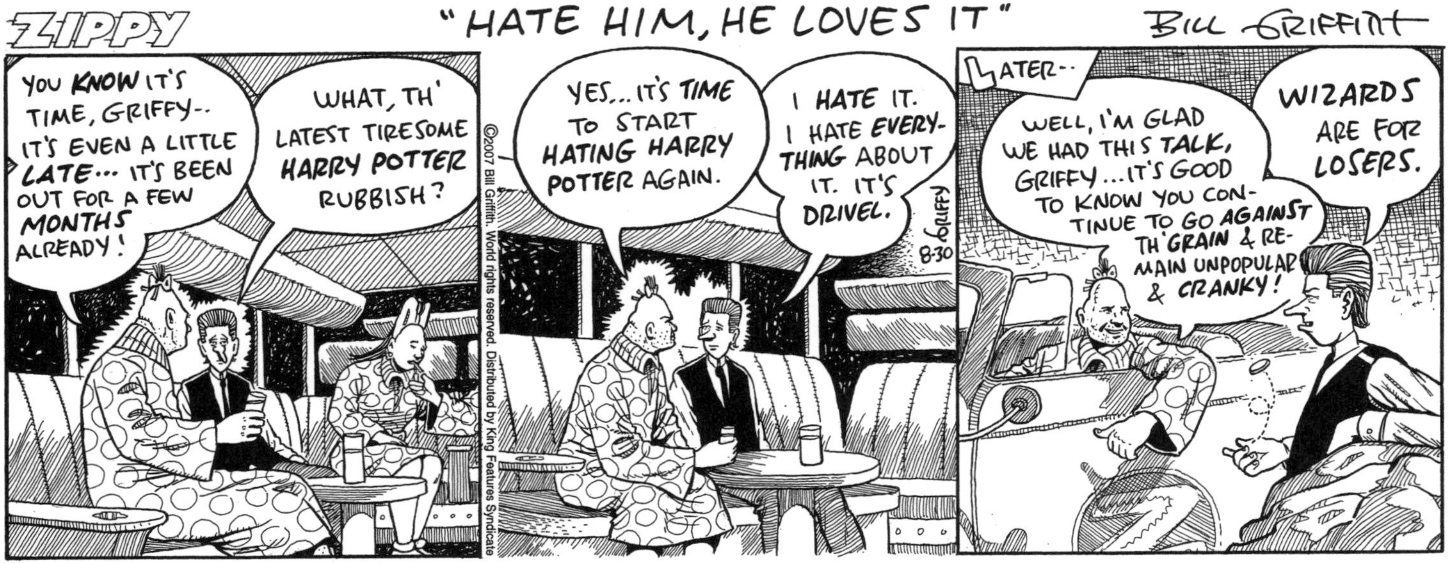
ZIPPY
"HATE HIM, HE LOVES IT"
BILL GRIFFITH
YOU KNOW IT'S TIME, GRIFFY-- IT'S EVEN A LITTLE LATE... IT'S BEEN OUT FOR A FEW MONTHS ALREADY!
WHAT, TH' LATEST TIRESOME HARRY POTTER RUBBISH?
©2007 Bill Griffith. World rights reserved. Distributed by King Features Syndicate
YES... IT'S TIME TO START HATING HARRY POTTER AGAIN.
I HATE IT. I HATE EVERYTHING ABOUT IT. IT'S DRIVEL.
GRIFFY 8-30
LATER--
WELL, I'M GLAD WE HAD THIS TALK, GRIFFY... IT'S GOOD TO KNOW YOU CONTINUE TO GO AGAINST TH' GRAIN & REMAIN UNPOPULAR & CRANKY!
WIZARDS ARE FOR LOSERS.



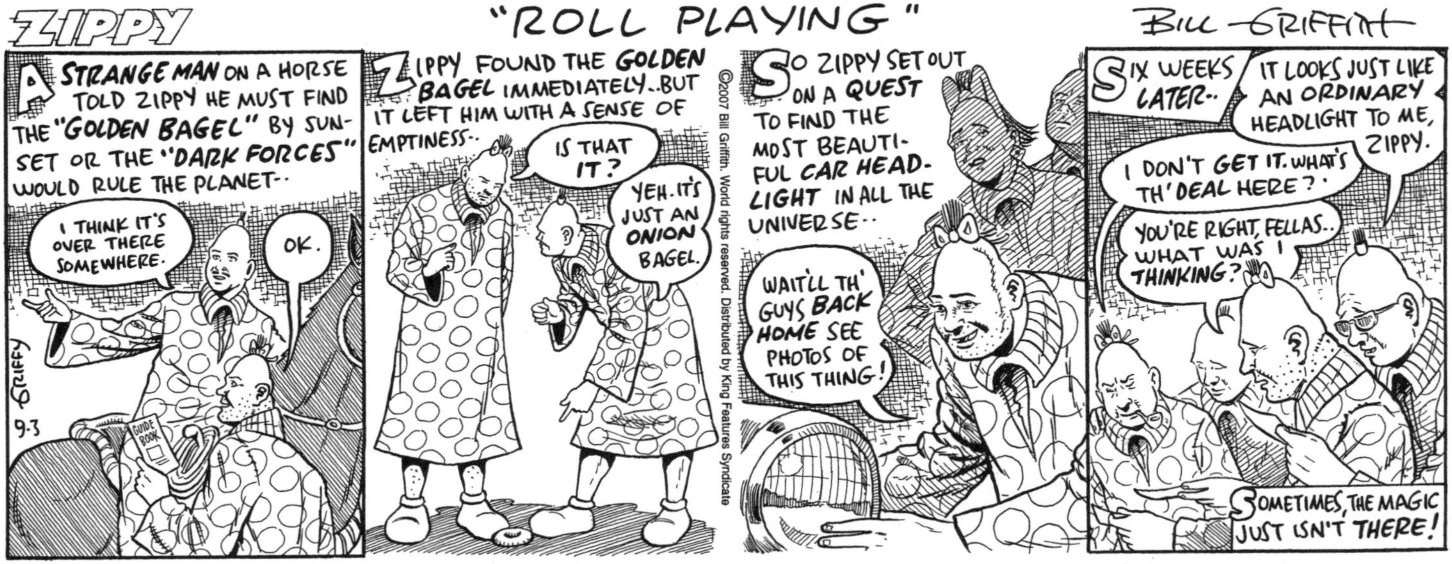
ZIPPY
"ROLL PLAYING"
BILL GRIFFITH
A STRANGE MAN ON A HORSE TOLD ZIPPY HE MUST FIND THE "GOLDEN BAGEL" BY SUNSET OR THE "DARK FORCES" WOULD RULE THE PLANET--
I THINK IT'S OVER THERE SOMEWHERE.
OK.
GUIDE BOOK
GRIFFY 9-3
ZIPPY FOUND THE GOLDEN BAGEL IMMEDIATELY..BUT IT LEFT HIM WITH A SENSE OF EMPTINESS--
IS THAT IT?
YEH. IT'S JUST AN ONION BAGEL.
©2007 Bill Griffith. World rights reserved. Distributed by King Features Syndicate
SO ZIPPY SET OUT ON A QUEST TO FIND THE MOST BEAUTIFUL CAR HEADLIGHT IN ALL THE UNIVERSE--
WAIT'LL TH' GUYS BACK HOME SEE PHOTOS OF THIS THING!
SIX WEEKS LATER--
IT LOOKS JUST LIKE AN ORDINARY HEADLIGHT TO ME, ZIPPY.
I DON'T GET IT. WHAT'S TH' DEAL HERE?
YOU'RE RIGHT, FELLAS.. WHAT WAS I THINKING?
SOMETIMES, THE MAGIC JUST ISN'T THERE!

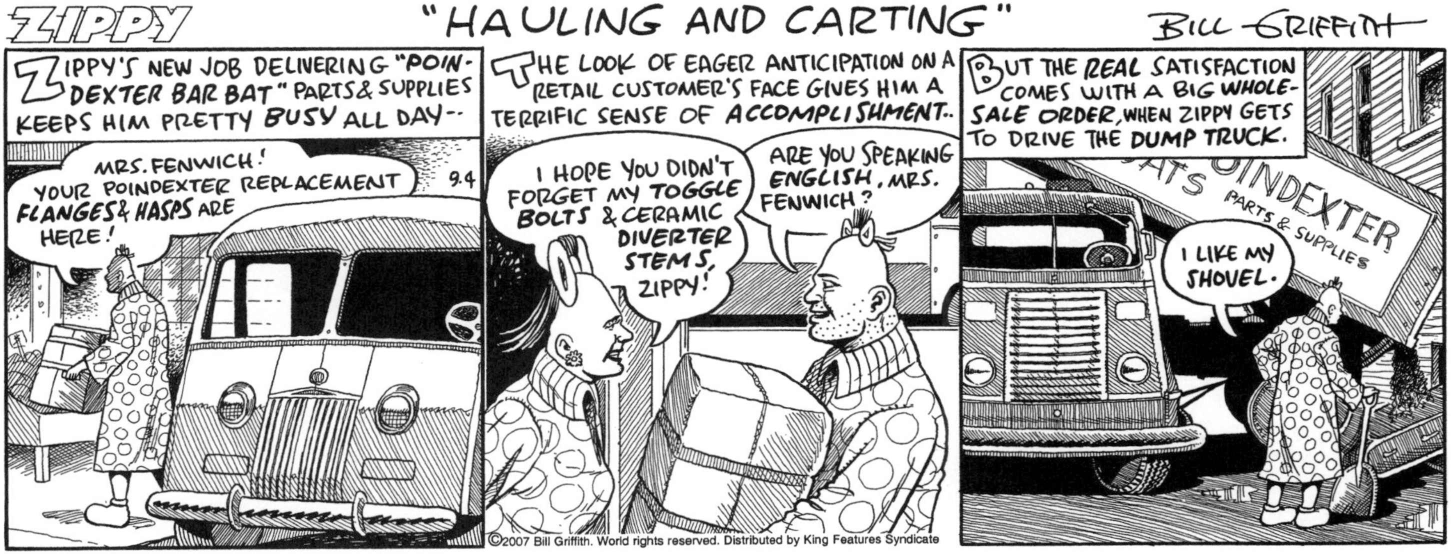
ZIPPY
"HAULING AND CARTING"
BILL GRIFFITH
ZIPPY'S NEW JOB DELIVERING "POINDEXTER BAR BAT" PARTS & SUPPLIES KEEPS HIM PRETTY BUSY ALL DAY--
MRS. FENWICH! YOUR POINDEXTER REPLACEMENT FLANGES & HASPS ARE HERE!
9.4
THE LOOK OF EAGER ANTICIPATION ON A RETAIL CUSTOMER'S FACE GIVES HIM A TERRIFIC SENSE OF ACCOMPLISHMENT..
I HOPE YOU DIDN'T FORGET MY TOGGLE BOLTS & CERAMIC DIVERTER STEMS, ZIPPY!
ARE YOU SPEAKING ENGLISH, MRS. FENWICH?
BUT THE REAL SATISFACTION COMES WITH A BIG WHOLESALE ORDER, WHEN ZIPPY GETS TO DRIVE THE DUMP TRUCK.
POINDEXTER PARTS & SUPPLIES
I LIKE MY SHOVEL.
©2007 Bill Griffith. World rights reserved. Distributed by King Features Syndicate

78

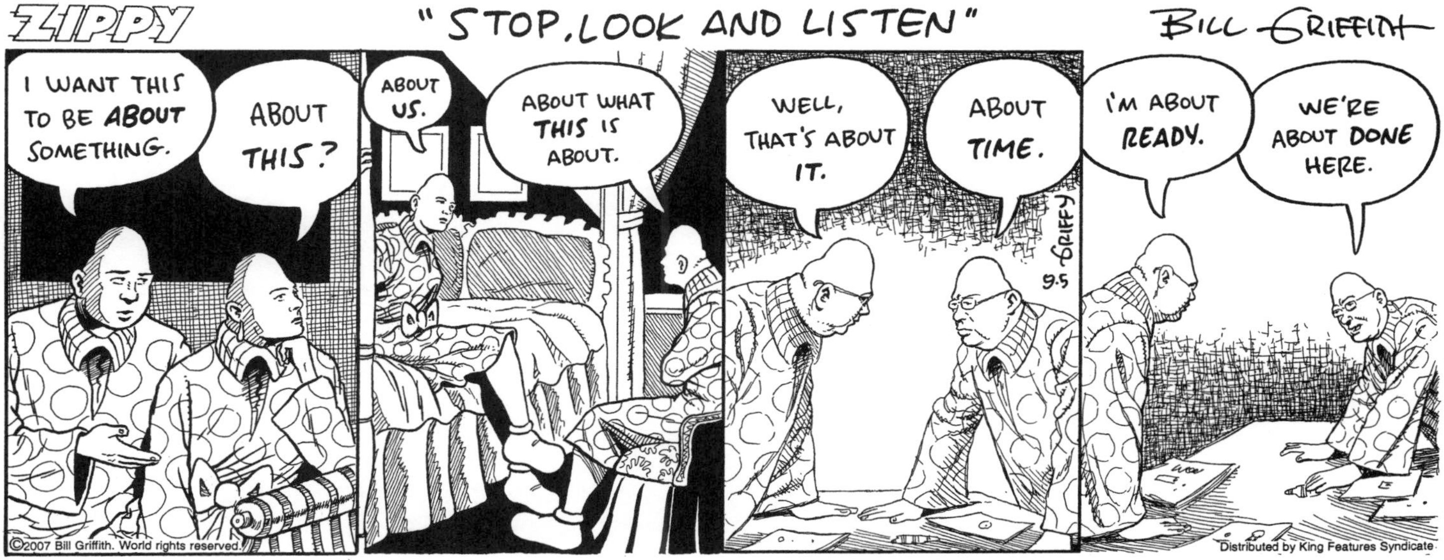
ZIPPY
"STOP, LOOK AND LISTEN"
BILL GRIFFITH
I WANT THIS TO BE ABOUT SOMETHING.
ABOUT THIS?
ABOUT US.
ABOUT WHAT THIS IS ABOUT.
WELL, THAT'S ABOUT IT.
ABOUT TIME.
GRIFFY
9.5
I'M ABOUT READY.
WE'RE ABOUT DONE HERE.
©2007 Bill Griffith. World rights reserved.
Distributed by King Features Syndicate

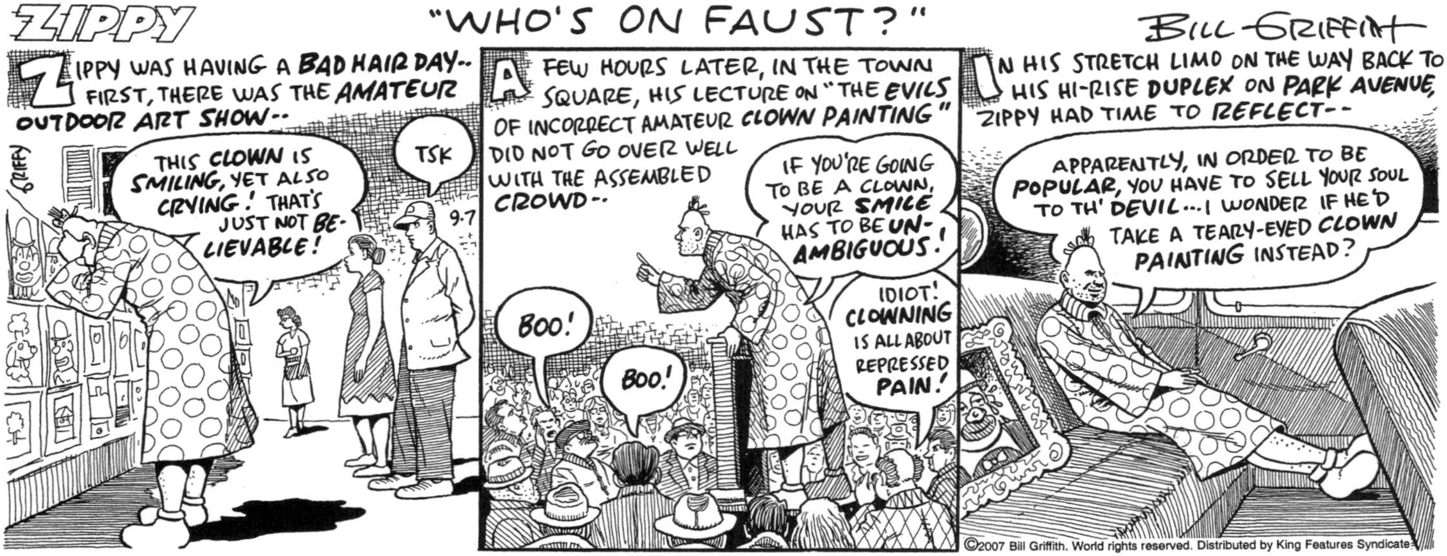
ZIPPY
"WHO'S ON FAUST?"
BILL GRIFFITH
ZIPPY WAS HAVING A BAD HAIR DAY-- FIRST, THERE WAS THE AMATEUR OUTDOOR ART SHOW--
THIS CLOWN IS SMILING, YET ALSO CRYING! THAT'S JUST NOT BE-LIEVABLE!
TSK
A FEW HOURS LATER, IN THE TOWN SQUARE, HIS LECTURE ON "THE EVILS OF INCORRECT AMATEUR CLOWN PAINTING" DID NOT GO OVER WELL WITH THE ASSEMBLED CROWD--
IF YOU'RE GOING TO BE A CLOWN, YOUR SMILE HAS TO BE UN-AMBIGUOUS!
BOO!
BOO!
IDIOT! CLOWNING IS ALL ABOUT REPRESSED PAIN!
IN HIS STRETCH LIMO ON THE WAY BACK TO HIS HI-RISE DUPLEX ON PARK AVENUE, ZIPPY HAD TIME TO REFLECT--
APPARENTLY, IN ORDER TO BE POPULAR, YOU HAVE TO SELL YOUR SOUL TO TH' DEVIL...I WONDER IF HE'D TAKE A TEARY-EYED CLOWN PAINTING INSTEAD?
©2007 Bill Griffith. World rights reserved. Distributed by King Features Syndicate

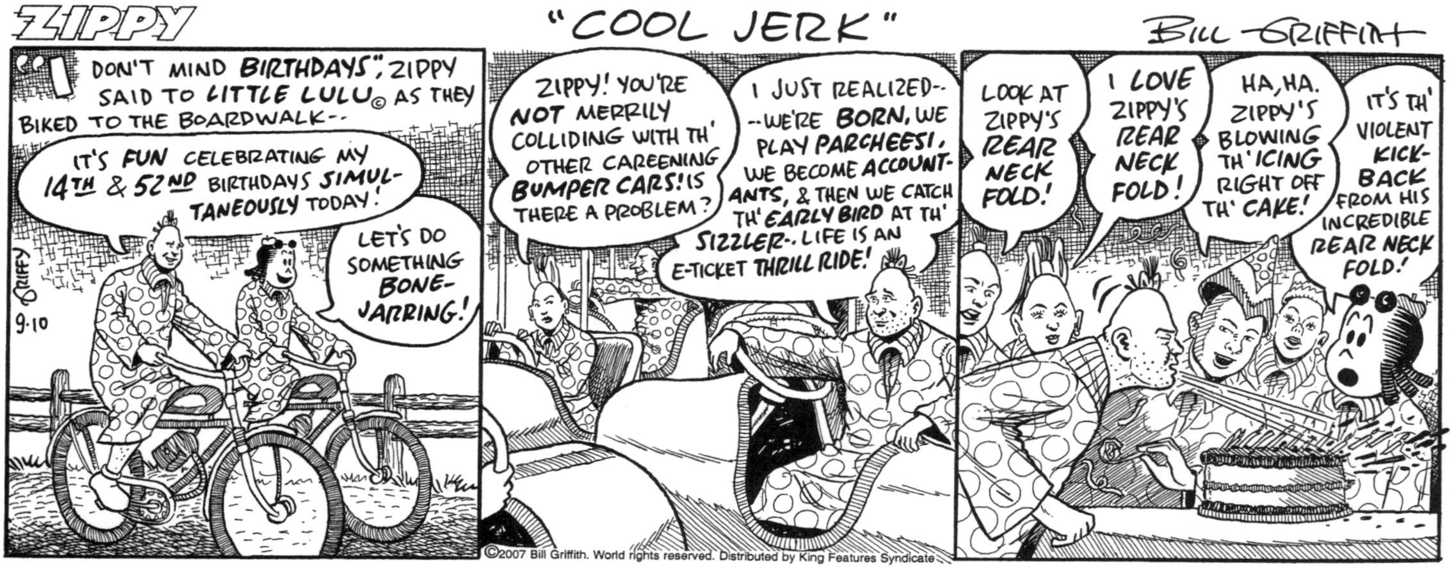
ZIPPY
"COOL JERK"
BILL GRIFFITH
"I DON'T MIND BIRTHDAYS", ZIPPY SAID TO LITTLE LULU© AS THEY BIKED TO THE BOARDWALK--
IT'S FUN CELEBRATING MY 14TH & 52ND BIRTHDAYS SIMUL-TANEOUSLY TODAY!
LET'S DO SOMETHING BONE-JARRING!
ZIPPY! YOU'RE NOT MERRILY COLLIDING WITH TH' OTHER CAREENING BUMPER CARS! IS THERE A PROBLEM?
I JUST REALIZED-- --WE'RE BORN, WE PLAY PARCHEESI, WE BECOME ACCOUNT-ANTS, & THEN WE CATCH TH' EARLY BIRD AT TH' SIZZLER.. LIFE IS AN E-TICKET THRILL RIDE!
LOOK AT ZIPPY'S REAR NECK FOLD!
I LOVE ZIPPY'S REAR NECK FOLD!
HA, HA. ZIPPY'S BLOWING TH' ICING RIGHT OFF TH' CAKE!
IT'S TH' VIOLENT KICK-BACK FROM HIS INCREDIBLE REAR NECK FOLD!
©2007 Bill Griffith. World rights reserved. Distributed by King Features Syndicate

# SUNDAY COLOR

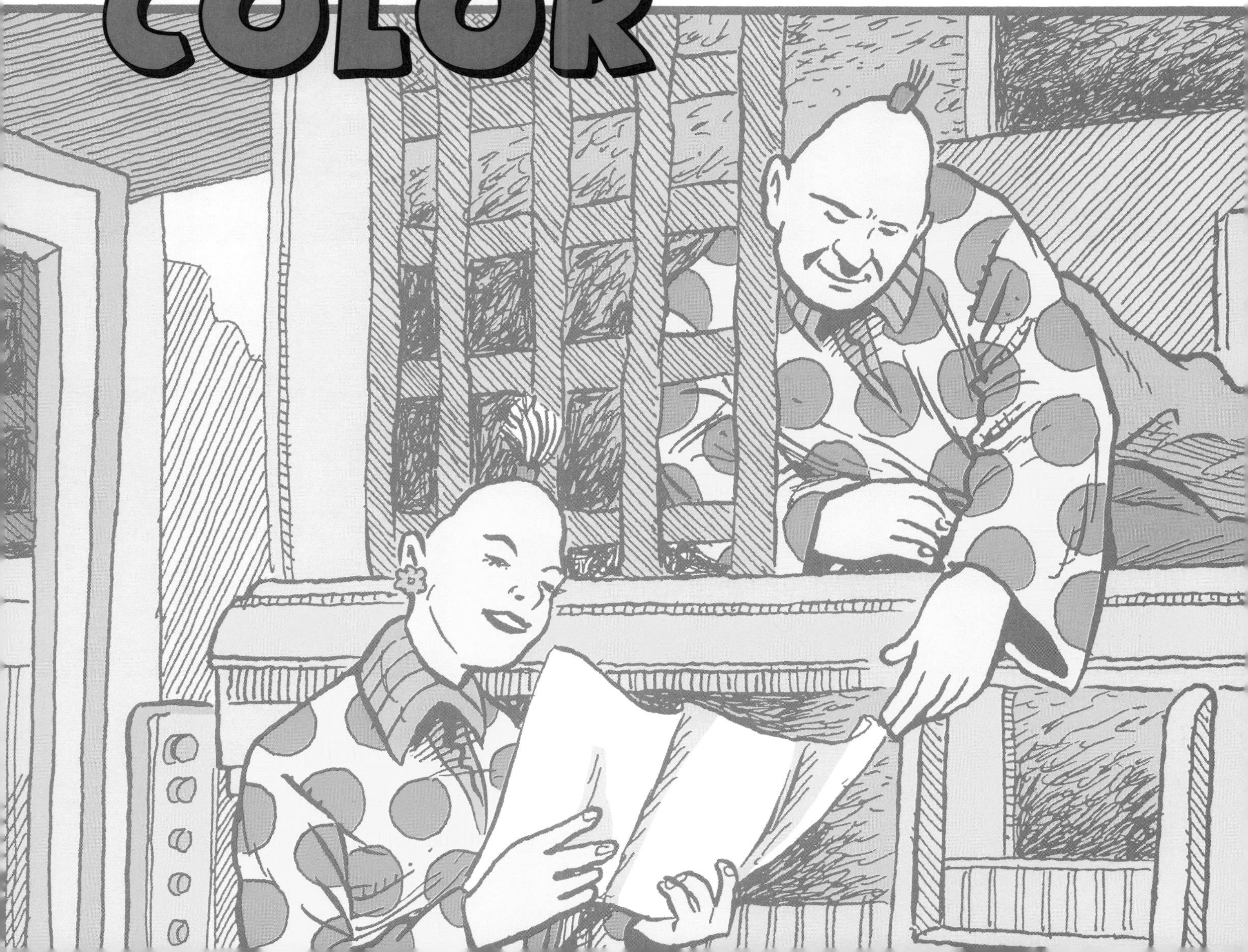

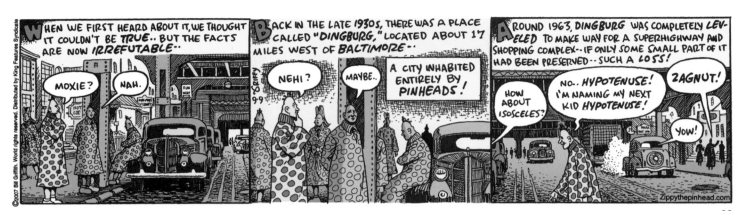

WHEN WE FIRST HEARD ABOUT IT, WE THOUGHT IT COULDN'T BE TRUE.. BUT THE FACTS ARE NOW IRREFUTABLE--
MOXIE?
NAH.
BACK IN THE LATE 1930s, THERE WAS A PLACE CALLED "DINGBURG," LOCATED ABOUT 17 MILES WEST OF BALTIMORE--
NEHI?
MAYBE..
A CITY INHABITED ENTIRELY BY PINHEADS!
GRIFFY 9-9
AROUND 1963, DINGBURG WAS COMPLETELY LEVELED TO MAKE WAY FOR A SUPERHIGHWAY AND SHOPPING COMPLEX-- IF ONLY SOME SMALL PART OF IT HAD BEEN PRESERVED-- SUCH A LOSS!
HOW ABOUT ISOSCELES?
NO.. HYPOTENUSE! I'M NAMING MY NEXT KID HYPOTENUSE!
ZAGNUT!
YOW!
©2007 Bill Griffith. World rights reserved. Distributed by King Features Syndicate
Zippythepinhead.com


80

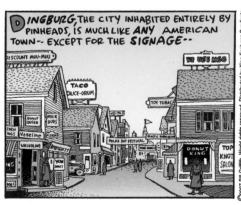

DINGBURG, THE CITY INHABITED ENTIRELY BY PINHEADS, IS MUCH LIKE ANY AMERICAN TOWN-- EXCEPT FOR THE SIGNAGE--
DISCOUNT MUU-MUU
WE USE MSG
TACO SAUCE-ORIUM
TOY TUBAS
DONUT QUEEN
MILK DUDS
CORN DOGS
Vaseline
VALVOLINE
POLKA DOT FESTIVAL
DONUT KING
TOP KNOT SALON
LEONA HELMSLEY IS NOT DEAD!!
ATOMIC DUCK PUBLISHING
WHEAT THINS
LAUNDRO-WORLD
BIG HEADS
BOWLING
CRANIAL EXTENSION SURGERY
CRANIAL REDUCTION SURGERY
POLYESTER
3 STOOGES ON STAGE TONIGHT
GRIFFY 10-21
WOULDN'T YOU LIKE TO SHOP IN DINGBURG?
GLAZED DONUTS
UNCERTAINTY
HOSTESS HEADQUARTERS
POINDEXTER BAR-B-Q'S
KLOWN KOLLEGE
©2007 Bill Griffith. World rights reserved. Distributed by King Features Syndicate
Zippythepinhead.com


81

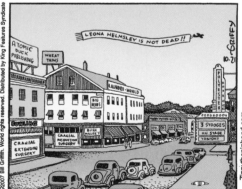

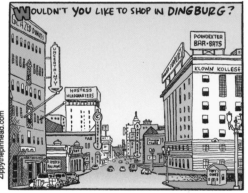

©2007 Bill Griffith. World rights reserved. Distributed by King Features Syndicate
IN DINGBURG (THE TOWN INHABITED ENTIRELY BY PINHEADS), COMICS ARE READ VORACIOUSLY BY EVERY MAN, WOMAN & CHILD. MOST ARE PRODUCED LOCALLY, WRITTEN AND DRAWN BY A CADRE OF HYPERACTIVE TEENAGE GIRLS!
!
?
*!★?!
GRIFFY
9·30
SOME ISSUES ARE EASY TO READ & FULL OF BAD PUNS & SIGHT GAGS, WHILE OTHERS HAVE A DISTINCTLY LITERARY QUALITY--
NOTHING MUCH HAPPENS IN THIS 200-PAGE STORY..
TH' ENNUI IS EXQUISITE!
Zippythepinhead.com
ELDERS INITIATE THE PINHEAD POPULACE INTO COMIC READING AT AN EARLY AGE--
AND, SO...
I KNOW THIS ONE! ATOMIC DUCK DIES ON PAGE 373!
HEY!
DINGBURG COMIC BOOK LOVERS GATHER REGULARLY IN THEIR HOMES TO SHARE & INTERPRET NEW TITLES--
IT'S ABOUT TIME SOMEONE DECONSTRUCTED TH' SUPERHERO PARADIGM!
YES. IT SKEWS BIMODALLY, YET IT PRESENTS A COGENT CRITIQUE OF TH' GENRE!
YOW! NICE TIGHTS!
PERMANENT ADOLESCENCE & QUASI-FASCISM IN COMICS & STUFF
MUSCLEMAN FROM MARS

©2008 Bill Griffith. World rights reserved. Distributed by King Features Syndicate
CRIME IN DINGBURG (THE CITY INHABITED ENTIRELY BY PINHEADS) IS EXTREMELY RARE.. BUT TV CRIME SHOWS ARE EXTREMELY POPULAR--
TAP TAP
OH, NO! IS THAT MARISKA HARGITAY AGAIN?!
CITIZENS OFTEN CONFUSE CRIME STORIES THEY'VE SEEN ON THE SMALL SCREEN WITH REAL LIFE--
FRED THOMPSON RUNNING FOR PRESIDENT? ARE YOU NUTS? HE'S TH' DISTRICT ATTORNEY OF MANHATTAN!
WHAT? MAYBE I OUGHT TO LAWYER UP!!
IN SOME ADVANCED CASES, VICTIMS ARE SUSCEPTIBLE TO THE SO-CALLED "SEDGWICK SYNDROME"--
I'D KNOW THAT STAGEY SOUTHERN ACCENT ANYWHERE-- IT'S DEPUTY CHIEF BRENDA JOHNSON!
DEAR GOD! WHAT HORRIBLE CRIME HAVE WE COMMITTED NOW?
GRIFFY
1·27
Zippythepinhead.com
DURING MARATHON "LAW & ORDER" RERUNS, SOME RESIDENTS EVEN CONFESS TO MURDERS THEY'VE SEEN ON TV!
SHE SAYS SHE SHOT UP A DONUT SHOP!
WAIT...AM I DETECTIVE ED GREEN, OR LIEUTENANT VAN BUREN?
..IT WAS AN ACCIDENT... I WAS HIGH ON MAPLE FROSTING..

82

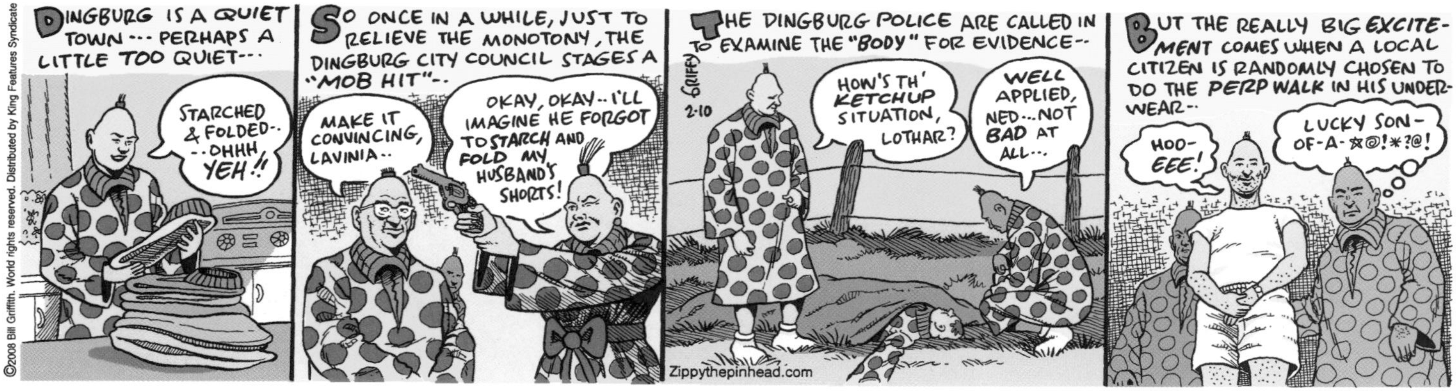
©2008 Bill Griffith. World rights reserved. Distributed by King Features Syndicate
DINGBURG IS A QUIET TOWN --- PERHAPS A LITTLE TOO QUIET---
STARCHED & FOLDED-- --OHHH YEH!!
SO ONCE IN A WHILE, JUST TO RELIEVE THE MONOTONY, THE DINGBURG CITY COUNCIL STAGES A "MOB HIT"--
MAKE IT CONVINCING, LAVINIA--
OKAY, OKAY--I'LL IMAGINE HE FORGOT TO STARCH AND FOLD MY HUSBAND'S SHORTS!
THE DINGBURG POLICE ARE CALLED IN TO EXAMINE THE "BODY" FOR EVIDENCE--
GRIFFY 2-10
HOW'S TH' KETCHUP SITUATION, LOTHAR?
WELL APPLIED, NED...NOT BAD AT ALL...
Zippythepinhead.com
BUT THE REALLY BIG EXCITEMENT COMES WHEN A LOCAL CITIZEN IS RANDOMLY CHOSEN TO DO THE PERP WALK IN HIS UNDERWEAR--
HOO-EEE!
LUCKY SON-OF-A-☆@!*?@!

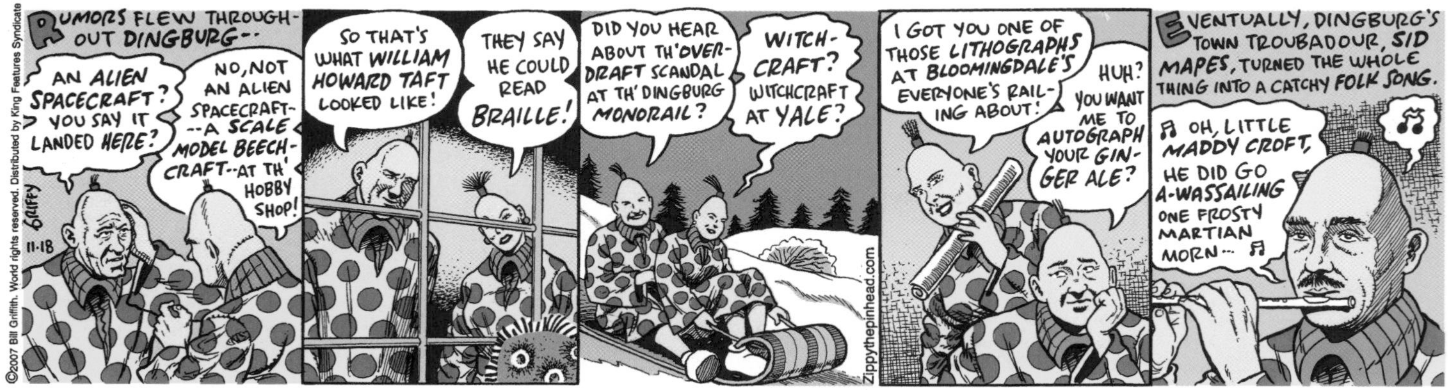
©2007 Bill Griffith. World rights reserved. Distributed by King Features Syndicate
RUMORS FLEW THROUGHOUT DINGBURG--
AN ALIEN SPACECRAFT? YOU SAY IT LANDED HERE?
NO, NOT AN ALIEN SPACECRAFT--A SCALE MODEL BEECHCRAFT--AT TH' HOBBY SHOP!
GRIFFY 11-18
SO THAT'S WHAT WILLIAM HOWARD TAFT LOOKED LIKE!
THEY SAY HE COULD READ BRAILLE!
DID YOU HEAR ABOUT TH' OVERDRAFT SCANDAL AT TH' DINGBURG MONORAIL?
WITCHCRAFT? WITCHCRAFT AT YALE?
Zippythepinhead.com
I GOT YOU ONE OF THOSE LITHOGRAPHS AT BLOOMINGDALE'S EVERYONE'S RAILING ABOUT!
HUH? YOU WANT ME TO AUTOGRAPH YOUR GINGER ALE?
EVENTUALLY, DINGBURG'S TOWN TROUBADOUR, SID MAPES, TURNED THE WHOLE THING INTO A CATCHY FOLK SONG.
♫ OH, LITTLE MADDY CROFT, HE DID GO A-WASSAILING ONE FROSTY MARTIAN MORN... ♫

ZIPPY VOLUNTEERS AT A YOUTH CENTER ONCE A WEEK TO PASS ON CRITICAL KNOWLEDGE TO THE CHILDREN OF DINGBURG--
CRAYONS & MAGIC MARKERS COME FROM JUPITER, SALLY! DID YOU KNOW THAT?
REALLY?
HEY, I HEARD IT WAS PASSAIC!!
©2007 Bill Griffith. World rights reserved. Distributed by King Features Syndicate
HE ALSO DOES A LITTLE CONSULTING AT THE DINGBURG FOUNDATION FOR EVOLUTION, GAY MARRIAGE AND GUN CONTROL--
ZZZZ..
TRY THIS AD LINE-- "THE 11TH AMENDMENT IS TH' NEW 25TH AMENDMENT"!
GRIFFY 12-2
Zippythepinhead.com
MOST EVENINGS FIND HIM WHIPPING UP A BIG BATCH OF VITALIS & VALVOLINE BROWNIES FOR DINGBURG'S LOW-INCOME SENIORS.
IT'S GOOD TO GIVE BACK.
MM.. CHEWY!
IN GRATITUDE FOR HIS MANY HOURS OF COMMUNITY SERVICE, ZIPPY WAS RECENTLY GIVEN AN IMPORTANT-LOOKING DOCUMENT BY THE DINGBURG CITY COUNCIL--
OH, WOW.. IT'S A FULL PARDON!

84

AT THE DINGBURG INSTITUTE FOR HUMOR RESEARCH.
LINUS, LET'S SEE IF WE CAN FIND SOMETHING FUNNY ABOUT THIS RADIAL TIRE!
OKAY, MR. G., I JUST HOPE OUR EQUIPMENT CAN HANDLE TH' JOB!
©2008 Bill Griffith. World rights reserved. Distributed by King Features Syndicate
THE TIRE IS REMOVED, MEASURED, X-RAYED & CARBON-DATED...
SO FAR, NOT A GIGGLE..
GRIFFY
IT'S PLACED ON THE HYDRAULIC HUMOROMETER FOR IN-DEPTH ANALYSIS--
I'M GETTING AN INDICATION OF SOME VAGUE KIND OF UNLIKELY JUXTAPOSITION, BUT NO ACTUAL JOKE..
Zippythepinhead.com
AMUSOLOGISTS REMOVE A CORE SAMPLE..
STILL NOT A TITTER.
ONE MORE PROBE.
6-22
FINALLY, WHILE HOOKED UP TO THE NON-LINEAR QUIPERISTICATOR, AN OLD HENNY YOUNGMAN GAG IS EXTRACTED--
HEY, IS THAT YOUR HEAD OR ARE YOU WEARING AN OVER-RIPE AVOCADO?
OH, NO! ..I DON'T GET IT!

85

PINHEADS SEEK RELIEF FROM THE SUMMER HEAT AT DINGBURG COVE--
GOD CAME IN A FLYING SAUCER & RESCUED NORTH AMERICA 4.5 TRILLION YEARS AGO!
I KNOW..IT WAS ON CHANNEL EIGHTEEN!
COOL WHIP FLOAT
Zippythepinhead.com
TURNS OUT, WHENEVER THEY EXPOSE LARGE AREAS OF FLESH TO THE SUN, DINGBURGERS START SPOUTING WACKY CULT BELIEFS!
MANUFACTURED GOODS WERE CREATED BY OUR ANCESTRAL SPIRITS TO BE AIR-DROPPED ON DINGBURG!
iPOD?
I CAN DIAGNOSE ANY ILLNESS BY EXAMINING PEOPLE'S RIGHT ANKLES. I ONLY CHARGE $900--
I'M TH' REINCARNATION OF JOHN DENVER!
ALIENS BUILT TH' PYRAMIDS & FOUNDED WAL-MART!
7-6
GRIFFY
©2008 Bill Griffith. World rights reserved. Distributed by King Features Syndicate
LISTEN, STEVE! BOBO IS RECEIVING MESSAGES FROM TH' HALE-BOPP COMET! SHE MAY BE CHANNELING L. RON HUBBARD!
TH' I.R.S. CONTROLS GRAVITY!
I'M TELLING YOU NOW, MARION-- IF ANYONE QUESTIONS MY RELIGION, I'LL ENCAPSULATE THEIR SOULS ON VENUS & DUMP THEM INTO TH' OCEAN OFF TH' COAST OF NEW JERSEY!

86

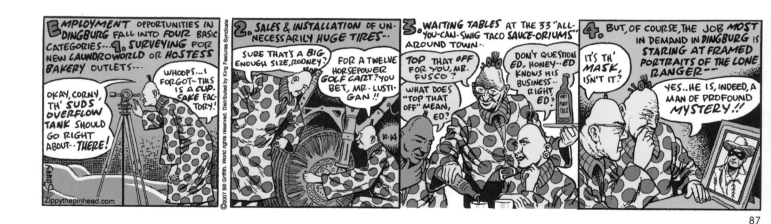

EMPLOYMENT OPPORTUNITIES IN DINGBURG FALL INTO FOUR BASIC CATEGORIES--- 1. SURVEYING FOR NEW LAUNDROWORLD OR HOSTESS BAKERY OUTLETS---
OKAY, CORNY, TH' SUDS OVERFLOW TANK SHOULD GO RIGHT ABOUT--THERE!
WHOOPS...I FORGOT-THIS IS A CUPCAKE FACTORY!
GRIFFY
Zippythepinhead.com
©2007 Bill Griffith. World rights reserved. Distributed by King Features Syndicate
2. SALES & INSTALLATION OF UNNECESSARILY HUGE TIRES--
SURE THAT'S A BIG ENOUGH SIZE, RODNEY?
FOR A TWELVE HORSEPOWER GOLF CART? YOU BET, MR. LUSTIGAN!!
10-14
3. WAITING TABLES AT THE 33 "ALL-YOU-CAN-SWIG TACO SAUCE-ORIUMS" AROUND TOWN--
TOP THAT OFF FOR YOU, MR. FUSCO?
WHAT DOES "TOP THAT OFF" MEAN, ED?
DON'T QUESTION ED, HONEY--ED KNOWS HIS BUSINESS.. RIGHT, ED?
1987 PINOT TACO
4. BUT, OF COURSE, THE JOB MOST IN DEMAND IN DINGBURG IS STARING AT FRAMED PORTRAITS OF THE LONE RANGER--
IT'S TH' MASK, ISN'T IT?
YES..HE IS, INDEED, A MAN OF PROFOUND MYSTERY!!

87

Are there "**Dirtballs**" in Dingburg? Well, unfortunately, yes, if these behaviors are any indication....
MALL
Waiting in line for 3 hours at "The Cheesecake Factory."
Staring in rapt fascination at Domenico Nesci's stray nose hair on a high-def broadcast of the "Tila Tequila" reality show.
©2008 Bill Griffith. World rights reserved. Distributed by King Features Syndicate
Imagining a time only 4,237 years ago when dinosaurs and Scandinavians romped together on the savannah.
Zippythepinhead.com
TIP TO: JAMES MARCH
GRIFFY 3·9
Kicking back with a Mike Huckabee stump speech and a tall, cold one.


88

ABSURDIST FRENCH PLAYWRIGHT ALFRED JARRY ARRIVES IN DINGBURG, CARRYING A 10-GALLON BOTTLE OF TACO SAUCE...
MERDRE! WHY DOES NO ONE NOTICE ME?
SAUCE EXTRÊME DE TACO PIQUANT DE PLUS
©2008 Bill Griffith. World rights reserved. Distributed by King Features Syndicate
HE ATTEMPTS TO ENGAGE ZIG BEAUCHAMP IN A LIVELY, SURREALISTIC REPARTEE...
GOD IS THE TANGENTIAL POINT BETWEEN ZERO & INFINITY!
I HAD AN AVOCADO, BUT IT NEVER LIKED SKEE-BALL!
DRY PAINT
FRUSTRATED, HE DECIDES TO HAVE A "REVERSE SHAVE" & DEMANDS THAT DINGBURG BARBER SLY KITCHEN ADD HAIR TO HIS CHIN--
IT IS PATENTLY ABSURD, IS IT NOT, MON AMI?
NOT REALLY. I GET THIS ALL TH' TIME!
FINALLY, AT A MEETING OF THE DINGBURG ODDFELLOWS THAT NIGHT, JARRY REALIZES HE IS BEATEN..
YOU'RE LOOKING EXCEPTIONALLY UGLY TONIGHT, MADAM!
--IS IT BECAUSE WE HAVE COMPANY?
MERDRE. I AM BEATEN.
GRIFFY 5·4
Zippythepinhead.com
THIS COULD EXPLAIN WHY, IN 1903, IT IS BELIEVED JARRY CONSIDERED A CAREER AS A SHOE SALESMAN...
HUSH PUPPIES!
MERDRE.


89

PINHEADS DON'T REACT TO LIFE'S SLINGS & ARROWS WITH THE USUAL FEELINGS OF PAIN & HUMILIATION--
GRIFFY 12-9
YOW! THAT ROTTEN TURNIP FEELS PLEASANTLY SQUISHY ON TH' REAR OF MY CRANIAL AREA!
IT EVEN JOGGED A FEW DELIGHTFUL CHILDHOOD MEMORIES!
THEY'RE JUST NOT THROWN FOR A LOOP WHEN THEY'RE THROWN FOR A LOOP--
WHOA! THERE'S REALLY NOTHING FUNNIER THAN SLIPPING ON A BANANA PEEL--- ESPECIALLY WHEN IT HAPPENS TO ONESELF!!
Zippythepinhead.com
AS A MATTER OF FACT, FOR A PINHEAD, THE UNEXPECTED ACT OF LANDING ON ONE'S KEISTER IS SEEN AS AN OPPORTUNITY FOR GREAT INSIGHT & SUDDEN ENLIGHTENMENT--.
UNH! THAT BACKWARD TUMBLE KNOCKED LOOSE AN ALGORITHM I CAN NOW USE TO PROCESS ENORMOUS QUANTITIES OF RAW DATA!
I'LL BE RICH!
©2007 Bill Griffith. World rights reserved. Distributed by King Features Syndicate

"If a man does not keep pace with his companions...
LOST IN SPACE
...perhaps it is because he hears....
MILK DUDS
Ding Dongs
MILK DUDS EXTREME
...a different drummer.
Zippythepinhead.com
Let him step to the music which he hears, however measured...
GRIFFY 4-27
...or far away."
- Henry David Thoreau
©2008 Bill Griffith. World rights reserved. Distributed by King Features Syndicate

90

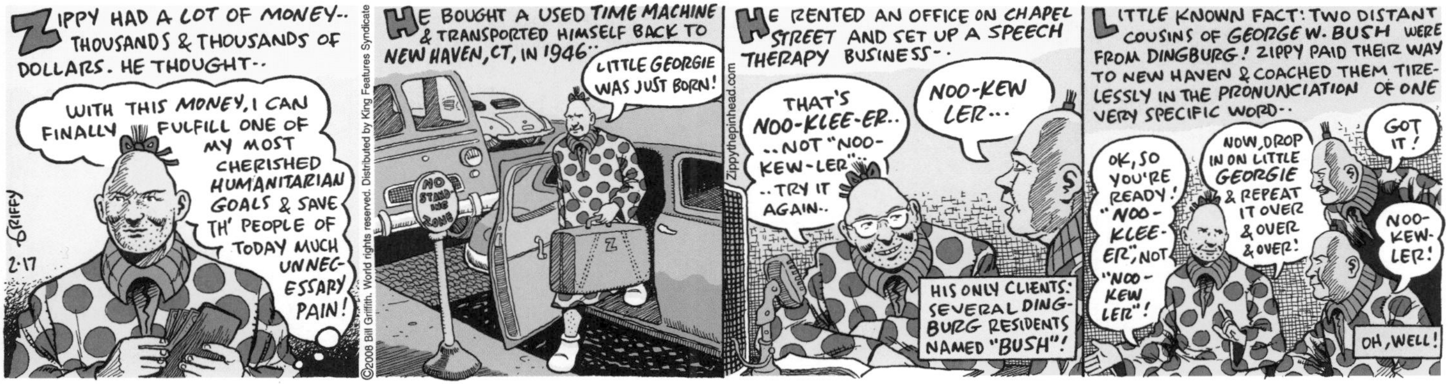
ZIPPY HAD A LOT OF MONEY-- THOUSANDS & THOUSANDS OF DOLLARS. HE THOUGHT--
WITH THIS MONEY, I CAN FINALLY FULFILL ONE OF MY MOST CHERISHED HUMANITARIAN GOALS & SAVE TH' PEOPLE OF TODAY MUCH UNNECESSARY PAIN!
GRIFFY 2·17
©2008 Bill Griffith. World rights reserved. Distributed by King Features Syndicate
HE BOUGHT A USED TIME MACHINE & TRANSPORTED HIMSELF BACK TO NEW HAVEN, CT, IN 1946--
LITTLE GEORGIE WAS JUST BORN!
NO STANDING ZONE
Z
Zippythepinhead.com
HE RENTED AN OFFICE ON CHAPEL STREET AND SET UP A SPEECH THERAPY BUSINESS--
THAT'S NOO-KLEE-ER.. ..NOT "NOO-KEW-LER"... ..TRY IT AGAIN..
NOO-KEW LER...
HIS ONLY CLIENTS: SEVERAL DINGBURG RESIDENTS NAMED "BUSH"!
LITTLE KNOWN FACT: TWO DISTANT COUSINS OF GEORGE W. BUSH WERE FROM DINGBURG! ZIPPY PAID THEIR WAY TO NEW HAVEN & COACHED THEM TIRELESSLY IN THE PRONUNCIATION OF ONE VERY SPECIFIC WORD--
OK, SO YOU'RE READY! "NOO-KLEE-ER", NOT "NOO-KEW LER"!
NOW, DROP IN ON LITTLE GEORGIE & REPEAT IT OVER & OVER & OVER!
GOT IT!
NOO-KEW-LER!
OH, WELL!

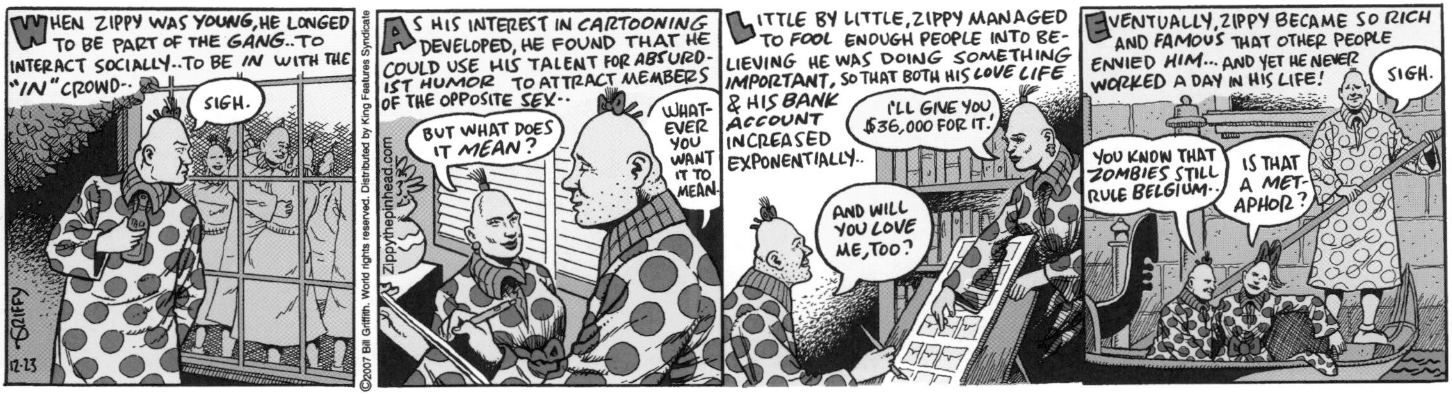
WHEN ZIPPY WAS YOUNG, HE LONGED TO BE PART OF THE GANG..TO INTERACT SOCIALLY..TO BE IN WITH THE "IN" CROWD--
SIGH.
GRIFFY 12·23
©2007 Bill Griffith. World rights reserved. Distributed by King Features Syndicate
AS HIS INTEREST IN CARTOONING DEVELOPED, HE FOUND THAT HE COULD USE HIS TALENT FOR ABSURDIST HUMOR TO ATTRACT MEMBERS OF THE OPPOSITE SEX--
BUT WHAT DOES IT MEAN?
WHATEVER YOU WANT IT TO MEAN.
Zippythepinhead.com
LITTLE BY LITTLE, ZIPPY MANAGED TO FOOL ENOUGH PEOPLE INTO BELIEVING HE WAS DOING SOMETHING IMPORTANT, SO THAT BOTH HIS LOVE LIFE & HIS BANK ACCOUNT INCREASED EXPONENTIALLY..
I'LL GIVE YOU $36,000 FOR IT!
AND WILL YOU LOVE ME, TOO?
EVENTUALLY, ZIPPY BECAME SO RICH AND FAMOUS THAT OTHER PEOPLE ENVIED HIM... AND YET HE NEVER WORKED A DAY IN HIS LIFE!
SIGH.
YOU KNOW THAT ZOMBIES STILL RULE BELGIUM..
IS THAT A METAPHOR?

SOME MORNINGS, AFTER A LONG NIGHT OF BEATNIK POETRY & BREAK-DANCING, ZIPPY WAKES UP WITH A STRANGE AMOEBA..
OY. LAST NIGHT'S CULT MEETING GOT A BIT ROWDY..
THAT'S IT-- I'M SPLITTING!!
GRIFFY
10-28
BUT WITH A FEW CUPS OF HOT VALVOLINE IN HIM, ZIPPY IS READY TO START THE NEW DAY..
I'LL FLIP MY MATTRESS OVER TO TH' OTHER SIDE!
IT'S LIKE BEING BORN AGAIN!
©2007 Bill Griffith. World rights reserved. Distributed by King Features Syndicate
AT WORK, HE RECRUITS YET ANOTHER MEMBER INTO HIS SECRET SOCIETY..
YOU SAY I CAN TAKE TH' PLEDGE DURING LUNCH WITH TH' OTHER NEW GUYS?
YEP! AND TO-NIGHT THERE'LL BE PLENTY OF BEAT-NIK POETRY & BREAKDANCING!
Zippythepinhead.com
OKAY! ALL TO-GETHER NOW!
I PLEDGE ALLEGIANCE TO TH' FAST FOOD FRANCHISES OF TH' UNITED NATION OF PIN-HEADS, AND TO TH' TAKE-OUT WINDOW AT WHICH I STAND..
ONE CORN DOG, UNDERWATER, WITH COOL WHIP & CLAM DIP FOR ALL!!

91

ZIPPY'S MEMORY-ENHANCING PROGRAM HAS REALLY PAID OFF..
ALL SOF-SERVE!
ALL TH' TIME!
GRIFFY
8-10
SAY, DARLA, HOW'D YOU LIKE TO GO GET A SOF-SERVE WITH ME NOW?
SOF-SERVE? DOESN'T THAT MAKE A PERSON FORGETFUL?
NOT IF YOU ONLY EAT TUTTI-FRUTTI SOF-SERVE FOR 6 MONTHS STRAIGHT!
ARE YOU SERIOUS?
Zippythepinhead.com
DARLA, I'VE NEVER BEEN MORE SERIOUS ABOUT ANYTHING SINCE TH' CARTER ADMIN-ISTRA-TION!
HMM... ..I FIND HIS ODD DEMEANOR STRANGELY ALLURING!
©2008 Bill Griffith. World rights reserved. Distributed by King Features Syndicate
YOW! I JUST REMEMBERED THAT I'M MARRIED, I HAVE 2.2 CHILDREN, A CAREER AT TH' UNDER-WEAR PLANT & A FUR-LINED FALLOUT SHELTER IN MY BACK YARD!
LIFE IS GOOD!
100% PURE CORN OIL
10 FT. MAZOLA

ALL DAY LONG PEOPLE WITH SERIOUS EXPRESSIONS & HOLDING IMPORTANT-LOOKING PAPERS TRY TO EXPLAIN THINGS TO ZIPPY--
WHAT PART OF "UNLAWFUL PROTOCOL PARAMETERS" DON'T YOU UNDERSTAND?
...YOUR LEFT ELBOW REMINDS ME OF NEW JERSEY!
CAN WE PLEASE SEE SOME IDENTIFICATION?
Zippythepinhead.com
EVEN AT DINNERTIME, WHEN ALL HE WANTS TO TALK ABOUT IS HIS POINDEXTER BAR BAT COLLECTION, RESPECTABLE & WELL-COIFFED NEIGHBORS DROP IN & INSIST ON DISCUSSING TENSIONS IN THE MIDDLE EAST--
GRIFFY
8-26
DELAWARE HAS AN ODD SHAPE TO IT.
TSK, TSK.
I DON'T THINK HE'S LISTENING, LORRAINE.
©2007 Bill Griffith. World rights reserved. Distributed by King Features Syndicate
THAT'S WHY IT'S ALWAYS SUCH A RELIEF TO ZIPPY TO HIT THE SACK AROUND MIDNIGHT & CRAWL INTO HIS WELL-MADE BED, CLUTCHING A COPY OF "THE AUTOBIOGRAPHY OF ALICE B. TOKLAS"
I FEEL VERY CLOSE TO GERTRUDE STEIN AT MOMENTS LIKE THIS...

92

©2007 Bill Griffith. World rights reserved. Distributed by King Features Syndicate
IN THE FUTURE, PINHEADS WILL CONTROL ALL MOVIE CASTING & INTERNATIONAL TRAVEL REGULATIONS.
SO IT'S AGREED.. ..TH' HUDSON BAY IS COLD & VERY FAR AWAY!
IT'S TH' PERFECT PLACE TO EXILE ADAM SANDLER!
9-23
MONOPOLY MONEY WILL BE ACCEPTED AT ALL BANKS, CASINOS AND POST OFFICES (WHICH WILL COMBINE THEIR VARIOUS FUNCTIONS UNDER ONE ROOF).
OK, THAT'S $500 ON 23 RED, A BOOK OF 91'S & YOU'RE GETTING OUT OF JAIL NOW?
RIGHT! & I'D LIKE TO BUILD 4 HOTELS ON VENTNOR AVENUE!
I LOST MY LITTLE THIMBLE THING.
GRIFFY
ASK ME ABOUT FREE PARKING!
DING DONGS
WITH INVENTORY AT ALL BIG BOX STORES LIMITED TO JUST TWO PRODUCTS, SHOPPING WILL BE E-Z IN & E-Z OUT!
TH' ORGANIC IS A LITTLE MORE, BUT IT'S FRUCTOSE-FREE!
TACO SAUCE
D.D. 'N T.S. OUTLET
Zippythepinhead.com
AND IN A WORLD WITH NO NEW HARRY POTTER BOOKS, SALES OF "NANCY AND SLUGGO" REPRINTS WILL SOAR!
IT'S FUNNY ON SO MANY LEVELS, IT'S ALMOST FRENCH!
EVEN TH' TREE TRUNKS MAKE ME LAUGH!
STOP! I'M WETTING MY MUU-MUU!
NANCY

©2008 Bill Griffith. World rights reserved. Distributed by King Features Syndicate
ZIPPY & ZERBINA AGREE ON JUST ABOUT EVERYTHING..
PARIS HILTON IS ACTUALLY QUITE HOMELY!
THAT'S EXACTLY WHAT I WAS ABOUT TO SAY!
People
GRIFFY
5·18
Zippythepinhead.com
IT'S EERIE THE WAY THEY ANTICIPATE EACH OTHER'S NEEDS--
HOLD IT--I'M ALMOST FINISHED PAINTING YOUR FACE 3 SHADES OF FUCHSIA..
LOOK! HERE'S AN AD FOR THAT GLOCKENSPIEL YOU'VE ALWAYS WANTED!
AND THEY BOTH HAVE THAT PLAYFUL SPIRIT THAT KEEPS A MARRIAGE FRESH & ALIVE..
THIS 3-DAY CLEVELAND GETAWAY IS FUN ON ALL 17 LEVELS!
..ANOTHER FROZEN PEA?
Bird's Eye
YET AT FOUR IN THE MORNING, DOUBTS BEGIN TO CREEP IN--
ZIPPY, I'M WORRIED THAT, IN A FEW BILLION YEARS, TH' SUN WILL RUN OUT OF FUEL & BECOME A WHITE DWARF..
MAYBE WE SHOULD START SEEING OTHER SOLAR SYSTEMS!

WHEN MOST PEOPLE RECEIVE BAD NEWS, IT MAKES THEM FEEL BAD. BUT NOT ZIPPY!
REJECTED AGAIN BY TH' NOBEL PEACE PRIZE COMMISSION, ZIPPY?
YEP! I GUESS I WASN'T PEACEFUL ENOUGH!
©2008 Bill Griffith. World rights reserved. Distributed by King Features Syndicate
LUCKILY, HIS TINY ATTENTION SPAN COMES TO THE RESCUE.
I THINK I MAY HAVE WON TH' NOBEL PEACE PRIZE, ZERBINA!
REALLY? ..OH, RIGHT! ..THAT LETTER YOU JUST GOT!
SIMILARLY, WHEN ZIPPY'S FAVORITE TEAM IS LOSING, HE SIMPLY SWITCHES ALLEGIANCE TO THE WINNING TEAM & ROOTS FOR THEM!
YOW! I LOVE TH' UNIFORMS OF TH' WASHINGTON NATIONALS AS MUCH AS I USED TO LOVE TH' UNIFORMS OF TH' SEATTLE MARINERS!
GO, CUBBIES!
Zippythepinhead.com
IT WOULD BE NICE TO HAVE FUN ALL THE TIME LIKE ZIPPY... BUT IT MIGHT HAVE ITS DOWNSIDE..
I JUST REALIZED I HAVE NO RETIREMENT PLAN & MAY HAVE TO EAT CAT FOOD IN MY OLD AGE!
HMM! --I WONDER HOW "PURINA FANCY FEAST" TASTES WITH EXTRA-HOT TACO SAUCE?!
GRIFFY
7·20

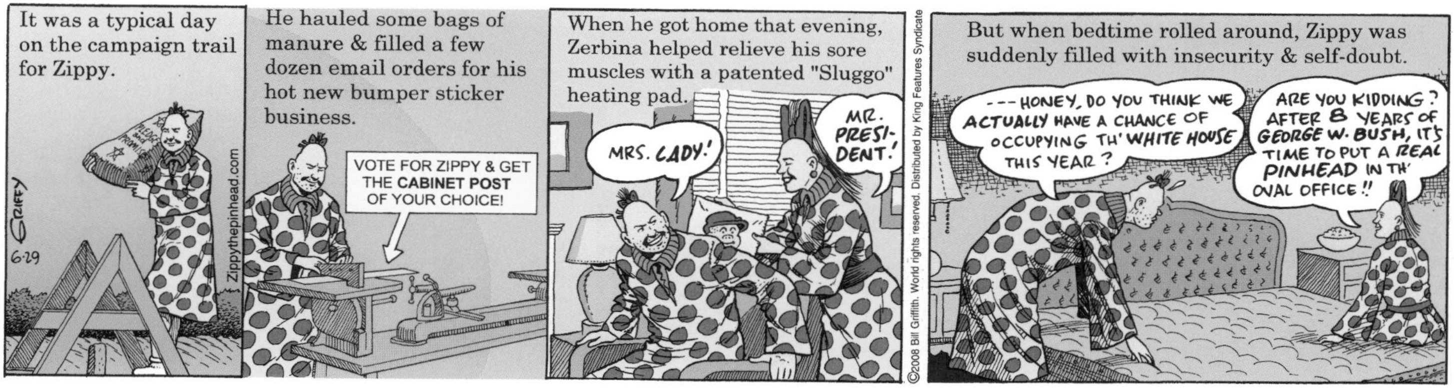
It was a typical day on the campaign trail for Zippy.
GRIFFY
6·29
Zippythepinhead.com
He hauled some bags of manure & filled a few dozen email orders for his hot new bumper sticker business.
VOTE FOR ZIPPY & GET THE CABINET POST OF YOUR CHOICE!
When he got home that evening, Zerbina helped relieve his sore muscles with a patented "Sluggo" heating pad.
MRS. CADY!
MR. PRESI-DENT!
©2008 Bill Griffith. World rights reserved. Distributed by King Features Syndicate
But when bedtime rolled around, Zippy was suddenly filled with insecurity & self-doubt.
---HONEY, DO YOU THINK WE ACTUALLY HAVE A CHANCE OF OCCUPYING TH' WHITE HOUSE THIS YEAR?
ARE YOU KIDDING? AFTER 8 YEARS OF GEORGE W. BUSH, IT'S TIME TO PUT A REAL PINHEAD IN TH' OVAL OFFICE!!

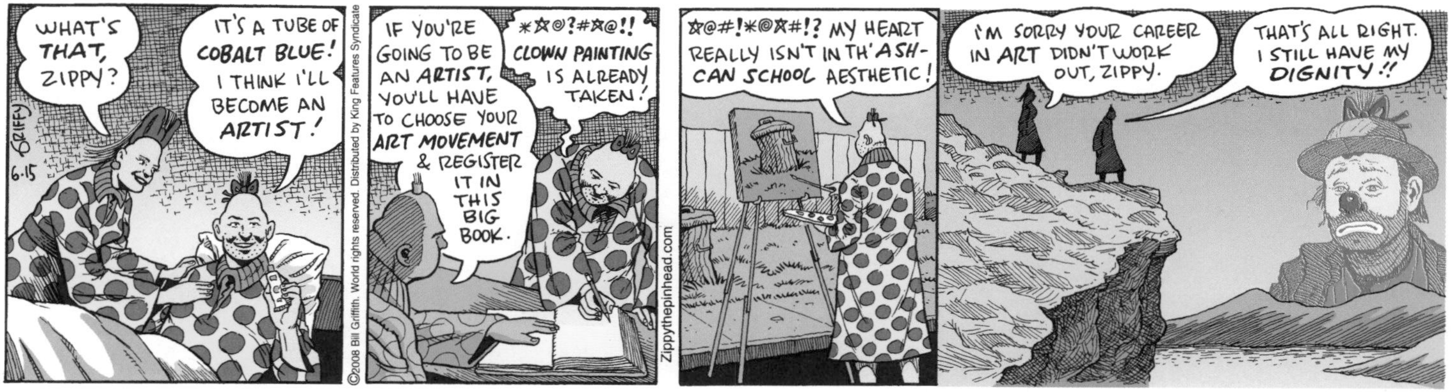
WHAT'S THAT, ZIPPY?
IT'S A TUBE OF COBALT BLUE! I THINK I'LL BECOME AN ARTIST!
GRIFFY
6·15
©2008 Bill Griffith. World rights reserved. Distributed by King Features Syndicate
IF YOU'RE GOING TO BE AN ARTIST, YOU'LL HAVE TO CHOOSE YOUR ART MOVEMENT & REGISTER IT IN THIS BIG BOOK.
*☆@?#☆@!! CLOWN PAINTING IS ALREADY TAKEN!
Zippythepinhead.com
☆@#!*@☆#!? MY HEART REALLY ISN'T IN TH' ASH-CAN SCHOOL AESTHETIC!
I'M SORRY YOUR CAREER IN ART DIDN'T WORK OUT, ZIPPY.
THAT'S ALL RIGHT. I STILL HAVE MY DIGNITY!!

93

ZIPPY'S DAY.
He rewires his fur-lined fallout shelter to accommodate his new broadband digital hot tub.
He Simonizes his hybrid with extra-hot habañera taco sauce for "deep-down protection."
He designs an unauthorized Hello Kitty hot air balloon to "escape everyday cares" with his wife, Zerbina.
He repels a polygamous street gang bent on recruiting his family into a west Texas soft-serve ice cream cult.
He relaxes with a round of his favorite new sport, "goowlf."
SIX BALL IN TH' CUP ON TH' 14TH GREEN FOR A SPARE!
©2008 Bill Griffith. World rights reserved. Distributed by King Features Syndicate
Zippythepinhead.com
GRIFFY 6-8

WHAT IF FROGS PREPARED YOUR TAXES?
WHAT IF BETTY BOOP WAS QUEEN?
WHAT IF SHIITES TOOK UP SAXES?
WHAT IF GOD WAS ARGENTINE?
THEN THERE'D BE NO STRIFE OR STRUGGLE.
AND WE'D ALL BE SEVENTEEN!
©2007 Bill Griffith. World rights reserved. Distributed by King Features Syndicate
Zippythepinhead.com
GRIFFY 11-11

94

©2008 Bill Griffith. World rights reserved. Distributed by King Features Syndicate
"TH' WORLD IS IN CONSTANT TURMOIL," ZIPPY POINTED OUT. CONRAD AGREED.
OKAY...BUT WHAT'S TO BE DONE ABOUT IT?
Zippythepinhead.com
"WELL, WE COULD WORRY A LOT, OR TRY TO COME UP WITH SOLUTIONS TO FIX IT," ZIPPY SAID.
TH' ESTONIANS ARE AT IT AGAIN..
OH.. NOOOO!!
GRIFFY
3-16
"OR, ON TH' OTHER HAND, WE COULD JUST TAKE A NICE, REFRESHING NAP & DREAM ABOUT DONALD TRUMP'S CHILDREN, IVANKA AND DONALD JR."
"ISN'T THAT IRRESPONSIBLE?" CONRAD ASKED. "NOT IF YOU IMAGINE THEM IN BEATLE WIGS," REPLIED ZIPPY.

95

ZIPPY SUBMITS TO THE ANNUAL DINGBURG POLYGRAPH TEST..
Q. HAVE YOU EVER PERFORMED IN TH' CIRCUS?
A. YES. FROM 1966 TO 1976, I WAS WITH TH' FLOTO BROTHERS OUT OF NEW ENGLAND.
Zippythepinhead.com
©2008 Bill Griffith. World rights reserved. Distributed by King Features Syndicate
Q. IN THOSE TEN YEARS, WERE YOU EVER APPROACHED BY A FOREIGN AGENT REGARDING TH' DIVULGENCE OF CLASSIFIED MILITARY DOCUMENTS?
GRIFFY
3-30
A. NO, BUT IN 1972, I WAS FROZEN WITH INDECISION FOR OVER 45 MINUTES, UNABLE TO CHOOSE WHICH OF TWO IDENTICAL STARCHED MUU-MUUS TO WEAR.
STRANGE...BUT I FIND THIS QUITE ENJOYABLE!
ME, TOO!
WELL, TH' RESULTS ARE IN.---AND THEY'RE COMPLETELY INCONCLUSIVE!!
THAT'S GREAT! BUT YOU FORGOT TO ASK ME WHAT I KNEW ABOUT J. EDGAR HOOVER & HIS AMAZING TECHNICOLOR TUTU!

96

ZIPPY BEGINS TO THINK ABOUT HIS LEGACY...

WHY DID I EVER CHOOSE TH' *STATION WAGON?*

...AND WILL PEOPLE REMEMBER ME AS A KINDLY *FATHER FIGURE*, DISPENSING *PEZ* AND *STOCK TIPS* FROM MY PORCH IN *ASHTABULA?*

...OR WILL THEY THINK ONLY OF TH'*MISSTEPS* IN MY *MIDWESTERN POLICY* TOWARD *ZANESVILLE* AND *CHILLICOTHE?*

©2007 Bill Griffith. World rights reserved. Distributed by King Features Syndicate

-- IN TH' *END*, IT'S ALL ABOUT *OHIO.*

Zippythepinhead.com

11-4

97

A PINHEAD WALKS INTO A *BOWLING ALLEY* AND SPOTS *LEONA HELMSLEY* AND A *STANDARD POODLE* AT THE BAR....

THE PINHEAD ASKS, "DOES YOUR POODLE *TALK?*" LEONA RESPONDS, "NEVER, AND I'D LIKE TO SEE THE *DIRTY SO-AND-SO TRY* IT SOMETIME!"

©2007 Bill Griffith. World rights reserved. Distributed by King Features Syndicate

12-30

THE PINHEAD TURNS TO THE POODLE AND ASKS, "WHO DO YOU LIKE IN TH' *FIFTH* AT *PIMLICO?*" THE POODLE ANSWERS," I *NEVER PLAY* TH' *PONIES.*"

Zippythepinhead.com

THE PINHEAD LOOKS AT LEONA AND SAYS, "I THOUGHT YOU TOLD ME YOUR POODLE *DOESN'T TALK!*" LEONA SHOOTS BACK A LOOK & SAYS, "WHAT IS THIS? A *DEAD CELEBRITY JOKE* OR A *TALKING DOG JOKE?*"

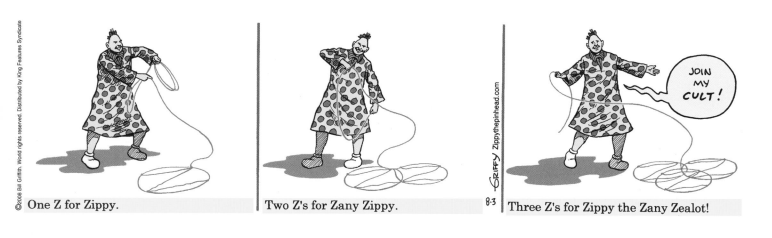

©2008 Bill Griffith. World rights reserved. Distributed by King Features Syndicate
One Z for Zippy.
Two Z's for Zany Zippy.
GRIFFY Zippythepinhead.com
8·3
JOIN MY CULT!
Three Z's for Zippy the Zany Zealot!

Z-MAN... ENEMY OF SEQUENTIAL ART EVERYWHERE!
THIS IS NOT TH' FIRST PANEL! THERE IS NO "FIRST PANEL"!
Zippythepinhead.com
©2008 Bill Griffith. World rights reserved. Distributed by King Features Syndicate
IT'S AN ILLUSION THAT TIME FLOWS IN A STRAIGHT LINE! AND, BY TH' WAY, I DID NOT JUST DELIVER A "STRAIGHT LINE"!
6·1 GRIFFY
MY CHARACTER IS NOT ON A "JOURNEY" FROM POINT A TO POINT B! MY "STORY ARC" IS ELLIPTICAL!
AND IF YOU'RE EXPECTING A PUNCHLINE, ALLOW ME TO REFER YOU TO TH' FIRST PANEL-- --- WHICH DOES NOT EXIST!!!
...IT'S Z-MAN!
NO, IT ISN'T!

WHEN ZIPPY WAS A LITTLE PINHEAD, HE ENJOYED THE USUAL WINTERTIME ACTIVITIES. HE LIKED TO GO SLEDDING...
©2008 Bill Griffith. World rights reserved. Distributed by King Features Syndicate
GRIFFY 1·13
HE LIKED BUILDING SNOWMEN..
Zippythepinhead.com
HE LIKED HELPING HIS DAD SHOVEL THE DRIVEWAY...
BUT, MOST OF ALL, HE LIKED LEAPING FIFTY FEET IN THE AIR AND FLYING OVER THE ROOF OF HIS HOUSE.

©2008 Bill Griffith. World rights reserved. Distributed by King Features Syndicate
LITTLE ZIPPY LOVED TO USE A PLUMB LINE TO MEASURE THE DEPTH OF HIS LOCAL POND...
GRIFFY 1·20
IT WAS A THRILL TO WALK THE SLACK WIRE ERECTED IN HIS BACKYARD...
RELEASING HELIUM-FILLED BALLOONS TO SEE HOW HIGH THEY'D GO GAVE HIM REAL PLEASURE...
Zippythepinhead.com
AND DRAGGING SACKS OF BIRDSEED ALONG THE SIDEWALK WAS ALWAYS GOOD FOR A LAUGH...
BEST OF ALL, THOUGH, WAS DONNING A DIVING SUIT & LOOKING FOR BOWLING BALLS AT THE BOTTOM OF THE OCEAN!
A SIX-TEEN-POUNDER!

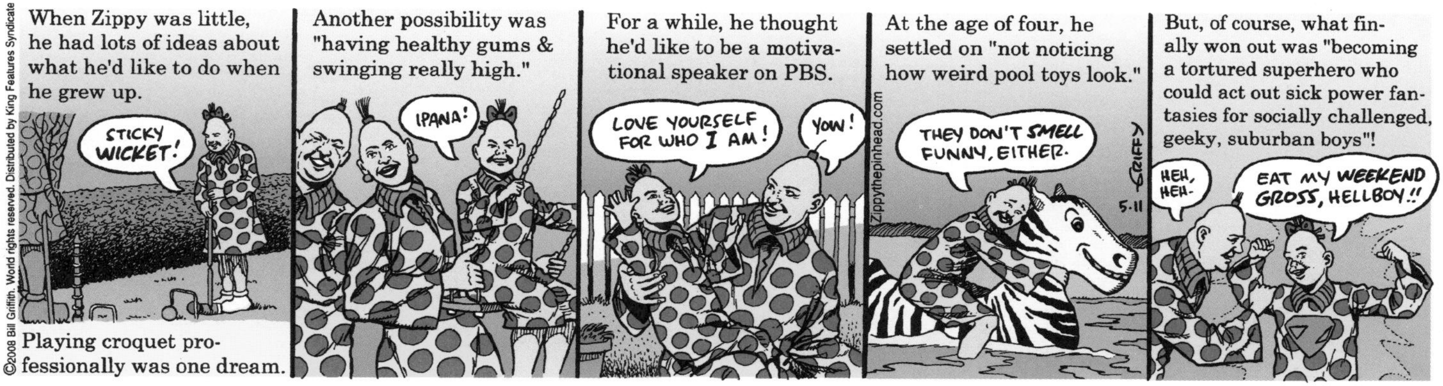
©2008 Bill Griffith. World rights reserved. Distributed by King Features Syndicate
When Zippy was little, he had lots of ideas about what he'd like to do when he grew up.
STICKY WICKET!
Playing croquet professionally was one dream.
Another possibility was "having healthy gums & swinging really high."
IPANA!
For a while, he thought he'd like to be a motivational speaker on PBS.
LOVE YOURSELF FOR WHO I AM!
YOW!
Zippythepinhead.com
At the age of four, he settled on "not noticing how weird pool toys look."
THEY DON'T SMELL FUNNY, EITHER.
GRIFFY
5-11
But, of course, what finally won out was "becoming a tortured superhero who could act out sick power fantasies for socially challenged, geeky, suburban boys"!
HEH, HEH-
EAT MY WEEKEND GROSS, HELLBOY!!

98

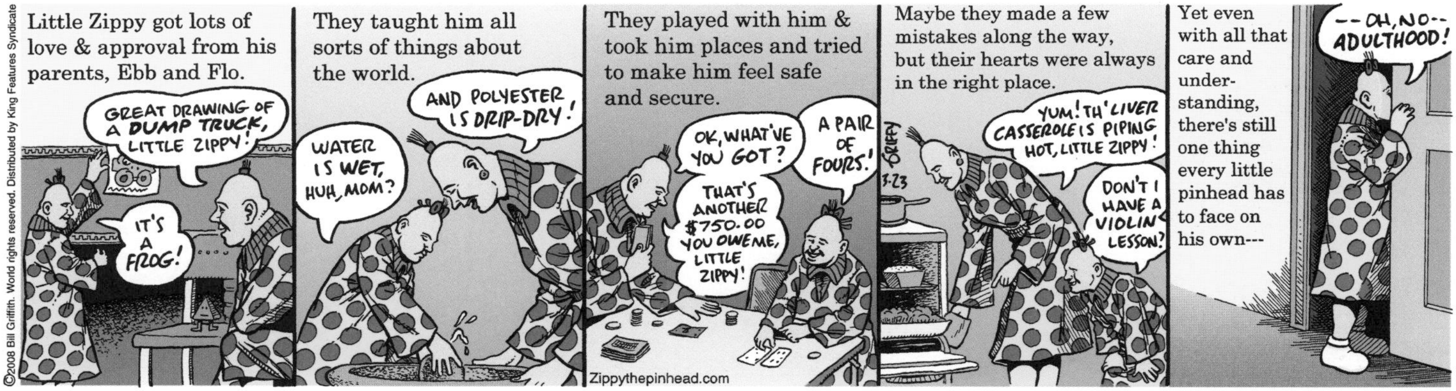
©2008 Bill Griffith. World rights reserved. Distributed by King Features Syndicate
Little Zippy got lots of love & approval from his parents, Ebb and Flo.
GREAT DRAWING OF A DUMP TRUCK, LITTLE ZIPPY!
IT'S A FROG!
They taught him all sorts of things about the world.
WATER IS WET, HUH, MOM?
AND POLYESTER IS DRIP-DRY!
They played with him & took him places and tried to make him feel safe and secure.
OK, WHAT'VE YOU GOT?
A PAIR OF FOURS!
THAT'S ANOTHER $750.00 YOU OWE ME, LITTLE ZIPPY!
Zippythepinhead.com
Maybe they made a few mistakes along the way, but their hearts were always in the right place.
GRIFFY
3-23
YUM! TH' LIVER CASSEROLE IS PIPING HOT, LITTLE ZIPPY!
DON'T I HAVE A VIOLIN LESSON?
Yet even with all that care and understanding, there's still one thing every little pinhead has to face on his own---
--OH, NO-- ADULTHOOD!

EVEN AT THE TENDER AGE OF 1½, LITTLE ZIPPY SHOWED A REMARKABLE ABILITY TO SPOUT BEATNIK POETRY..
WHAT WAS THAT AGAIN, LITTLE ZIPPY?
BONGO MONGO! BONGO, MINGO, MONGO! BINGO! BONGO! BOINGO!
GRIFFY
©2008 Bill Griffith. World rights reserved. Distributed by King Features Syndicate
LATER, ON LONG FAMILY TRIPS TO VISIT HIS GRANDPARENTS IN DULUTH, LITTLE ZIPPY WOULD COMPOSE ANGRY RANTS AGAINST CONFORMITY & "THE ESTABLISHMENT"..
GRAY MAN IN A GRAY NASH RAMBLER..
WHERE WILL YOU BE WHEN TOMORROWLAND REALLY ARRIVES? WALT DISNEY! YOU STOLE MY SOUL & LEFT ME A CARTOON CHARACTER!
TOO NEAR THE HEAT VENT..
JUNIOR MINTS
Zippythepinhead.com
4-13
ONE GROUNDHOG DAY IN 1960 STANDS OUT IN MEMORY--IT SEEMS ZIPPY'S GRANDMA & GRANDPA HAD BECOME "HIP TO THE SCENE"..
WE BROUGHT CANDY..
--I SAW TH' BEST MINTS OF MY TRAIN STATION DESTROYED BY MELTING!
MAN, THAT IS A BRING-DOWN.
I DIG TH' SYMBOLISM!
YOW! LET'S FREAK OUT MY PARENTS!

When Zippy was very little, he was a real "child prodigy." His parents even tried to enroll him at Harvard at the age of four.
HYPOT-ENUSE!
GRIFFY
2-3
Zippythepinhead.com
Unfortunately, Harvard was not as impressed with Little Zippy's knowledge of eggplants & Valvoline as were his Mom and Dad.
EGG-PLANT?
VALVO-LINE!
©2008 Bill Griffith. World rights reserved. Distributed by King Features Syndicate
So Little Zippy was home-schooled through a rigorous study of super-market tabloids and old issues of TV Guide.
MARY-KATE AND ASHLEY OLSEN ARE CUTE, AREN'T THEY, ZIPPY?
I CAN'T WAIT UNTIL THEY GET OLDER & CHECK INTO REHAB, DADDY!
ALIENS IN WHITE HOUSE

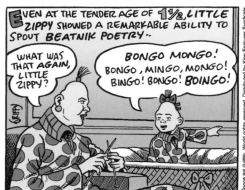

Zippy's Dad loved Little Zippy, but he was often puzzled by what Zippy said.
EH?
GLOBAL BABY BUBBLE THROTTLE!
©2008 Bill Griffith. World rights reserved. Distributed by King Features Syndicate
As Little Zippy got bigger, his Dad began to understand him better, but comprehension was still incomplete.
I ONCE DATED AN OCELOT!
GET ME AN ALIBI!
WHAT?
Zippythepinhead.com
GRIFFY 5·25
At a certain point, Zippy's Dad just gave up trying to figure out what Little Zippy meant and began to just appreciate it as symbolist poetry or free-form jazz.
HURRY! WE'LL BE LATE FOR TH' TALLULAH BANKHEAD FILM FESTIVAL!
HUH?
So when it came time for Little Zippy to learn a trade so he could earn a living someday, his Dad decided to teach him how to make Naugas.
NO ONE NEEDS NAUGAS, AND VERY FEW PEOPLE EVEN KNOW WHAT THEY ARE, ZIPPY! SO IT'S A PERFECT CAREER FOR YOU!
THANKS, DAD! WHEN I BECOME PRESIDENT OF TH' UNITED STATES, I'LL APPOINT THIS NAUGA TO A MAJOR CABINET POST!

99

Little J. Edgar and Little Zippy were friends.
YOU'RE NOT FROM RUSSIA, ARE YOU?
I'M FROM FANTASY ISLAND, LIKE YOU!
©2008 Bill Griffith. World rights reserved. Distributed by King Features Syndicate
They loved to play games in the back yard.
HEY, IS THAT A REAL GUN? I THOUGHT WE WERE PLAYING COPS & ROBBERS!
I PREFER COPS & COMMUNISTS!
On weekends, they both wore tutus.
LET'S DO SWAN LAKE..
I'LL BE RICKY NELSON!
GRIFFY 4·20
Zippythepinhead.com
Eventually, Little J. Edgar liked wearing tutus all the time.
YOU KNOW WHO LOOKS GOOD IN A TUTU? LITTLE LEE HARVEY OSWALD!
I THINK I HAVE A VIOLIN LESSON.
Later, when Little J. Edgar grew up and became head of the F.B.I., Zippy worried about him.
I THINK MY PHONE IS TAPPED.
GO BACK TO RUSSIA, PINKO!

100

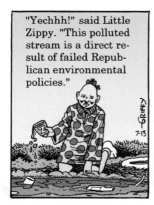

"Yechhh!" said Little Zippy. "This polluted stream is a direct result of failed Republican environmental policies."
GRIFFY
7-13
"Look, Fenwick," he cried, "our water is undrinkable because of the effects of global warming!"
Zippythepinhead.com
"Frozen toxic waste from far away is released as glaciers recede," he continued. "This is really disgusting," said Fenwick.
"No, it isn't," interjected Condoleezza after eight years of not speaking. "And permanent peace is coming to the Middle East any day, too!"
©2008 Bill Griffith. World rights reserved. Distributed by King Features Syndicate
"Condoleezza's crazy," said Little Zippy. "Yes," replied Fenwick, "we must vote out every last Republican or we're all doomed!"

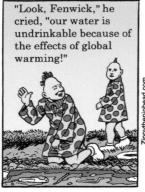

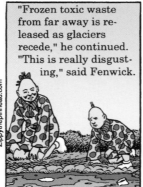

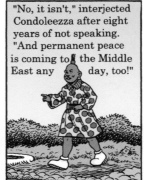

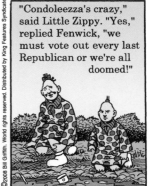

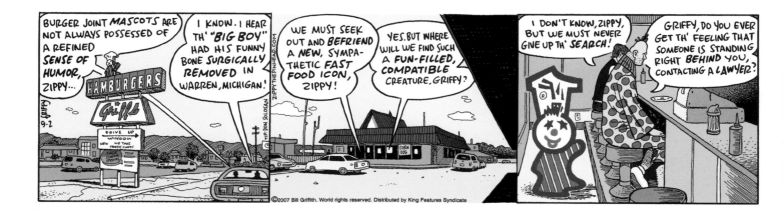

BURGER JOINT MASCOTS ARE NOT ALWAYS POSSESSED OF A REFINED SENSE OF HUMOR, ZIPPY...
HAMBURGERS
Griff's
DRIVE UP WINDOW
WE TAKE CREDIT CARDS
GRIFFY
9-2
I KNOW. I HEAR TH' "BIG BOY" HAD HIS FUNNY BONE SURGICALLY REMOVED IN WARREN, MICHIGAN!
TIP: DON SOLOSAN
ZIPPYTHEPINHEAD.COM
WE MUST SEEK OUT AND BEFRIEND A NEW, SYMPATHETIC FAST FOOD ICON, ZIPPY!
YES. BUT WHERE WILL WE FIND SUCH A FUN-FILLED, COMPATIBLE CREATURE, GRIFFY?
CORN DOG
©2007 Bill Griffith. World rights reserved. Distributed by King Features Syndicate
I DON'T KNOW, ZIPPY, BUT WE MUST NEVER GIVE UP TH' SEARCH!
GRIFFY, DO YOU EVER GET TH' FEELING THAT SOMEONE IS STANDING RIGHT BEHIND YOU, CONTACTING A LAWYER?

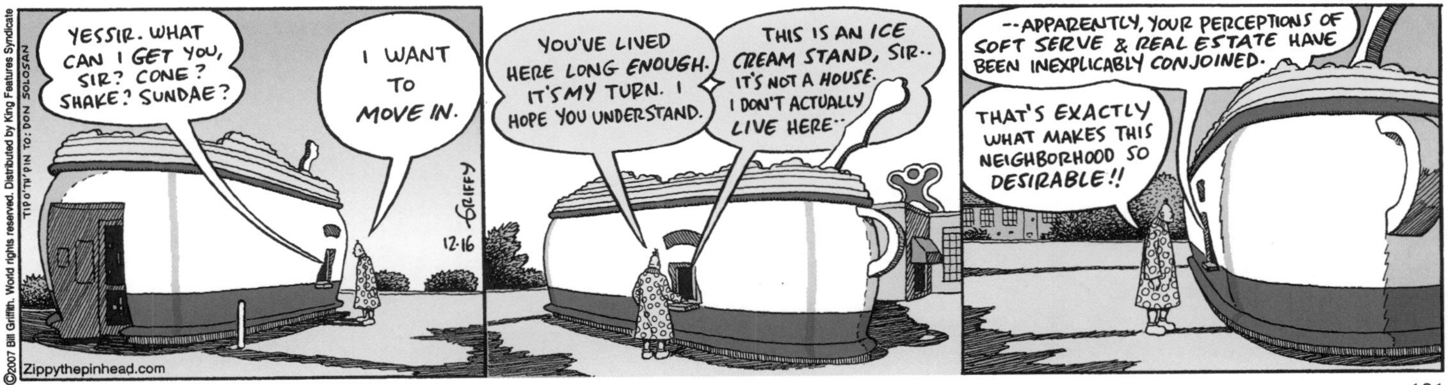

YESSIR. WHAT CAN I GET YOU, SIR? CONE? SHAKE? SUNDAE?
I WANT TO MOVE IN.
YOU'VE LIVED HERE LONG ENOUGH. IT'S MY TURN. I HOPE YOU UNDERSTAND.
THIS IS AN ICE CREAM STAND, SIR.. IT'S NOT A HOUSE. I DON'T ACTUALLY LIVE HERE..
--APPARENTLY, YOUR PERCEPTIONS OF SOFT SERVE & REAL ESTATE HAVE BEEN INEXPLICABLY CONJOINED.
THAT'S EXACTLY WHAT MAKES THIS NEIGHBORHOOD SO DESIRABLE!!
GRIFFY
12·16
TIP O'TH' PIN TO: DON SOLOSAN
©2007 Bill Griffith. World rights reserved. Distributed by King Features Syndicate
Zippythepinhead.com


101

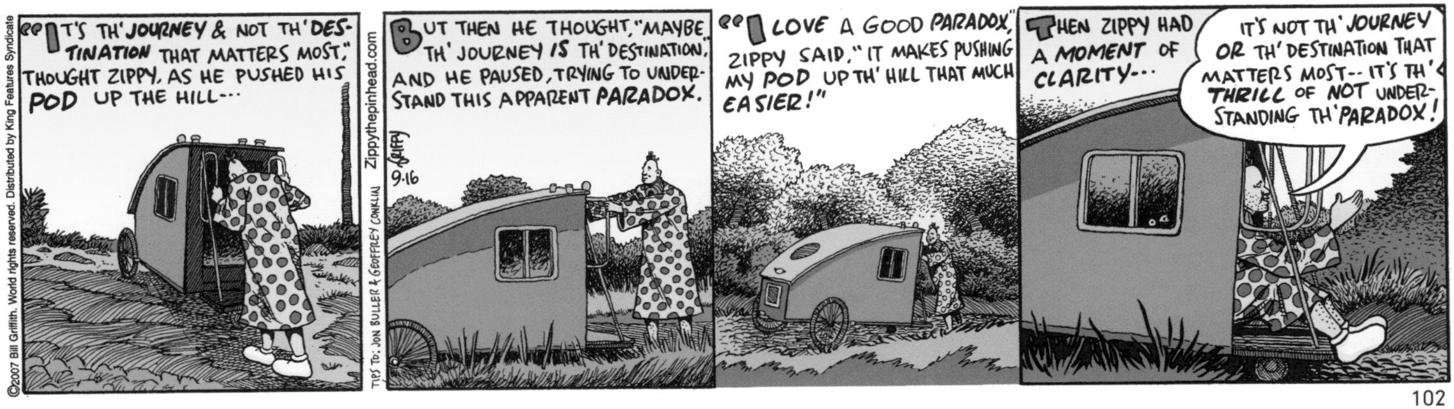

"IT'S TH' JOURNEY & NOT TH' DESTINATION THAT MATTERS MOST," THOUGHT ZIPPY, AS HE PUSHED HIS POD UP THE HILL...
BUT THEN HE THOUGHT, "MAYBE TH' JOURNEY IS TH' DESTINATION," AND HE PAUSED, TRYING TO UNDERSTAND THIS APPARENT PARADOX.
"I LOVE A GOOD PARADOX," ZIPPY SAID, "IT MAKES PUSHING MY POD UP TH' HILL THAT MUCH EASIER!"
THEN ZIPPY HAD A MOMENT OF CLARITY...
IT'S NOT TH' JOURNEY OR TH' DESTINATION THAT MATTERS MOST-- IT'S TH' THRILL OF NOT UNDERSTANDING TH' PARADOX!
GRIFFY
9·16
TIPS TO: JON BULLER & GEOFFREY CONKLIN
©2007 Bill Griffith. World rights reserved. Distributed by King Features Syndicate
Zippythepinhead.com


102

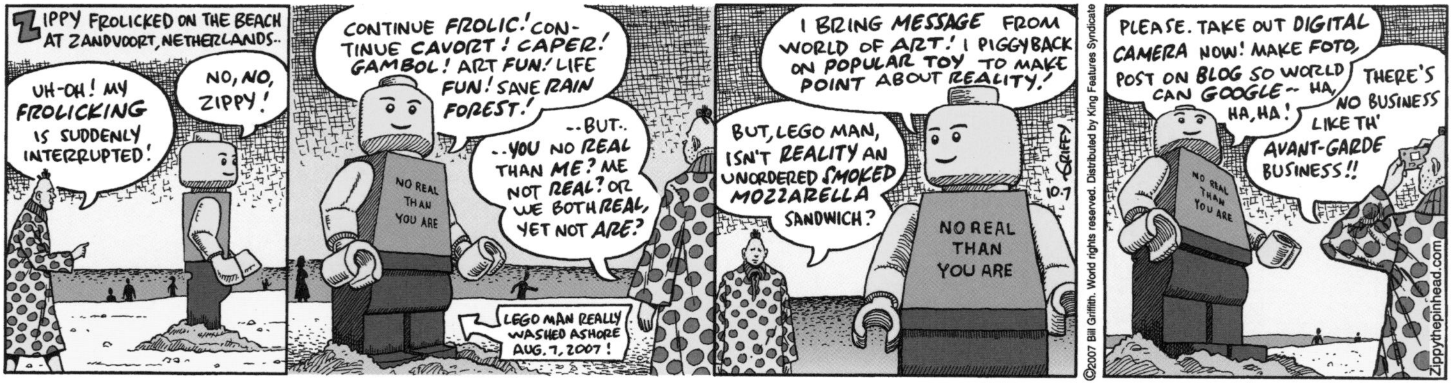
ZIPPY FROLICKED ON THE BEACH AT ZANDVOORT, NETHERLANDS..
UH-OH! MY FROLICKING IS SUDDENLY INTERRUPTED!
NO, NO, ZIPPY!
CONTINUE FROLIC! CONTINUE CAVORT! CAPER! GAMBOL! ART FUN! LIFE FUN! SAVE RAIN FOREST!
NO REAL THAN YOU ARE
--BUT.. ..YOU NO REAL THAN ME? ME NOT REAL? OR WE BOTH REAL, YET NOT ARE?
LEGO MAN REALLY WASHED ASHORE AUG. 7, 2007!
I BRING MESSAGE FROM WORLD OF ART! I PIGGYBACK ON POPULAR TOY TO MAKE POINT ABOUT REALITY!
BUT, LEGO MAN, ISN'T REALITY AN UNORDERED SMOKED MOZZARELLA SANDWICH?
NO REAL THAN YOU ARE
GRIFFY
10-7
PLEASE. TAKE OUT DIGITAL CAMERA NOW! MAKE FOTO, POST ON BLOG SO WORLD CAN GOOGLE-- HA, HA, HA!
THERE'S NO BUSINESS LIKE TH' AVANT-GARDE BUSINESS!!
NO REAL THAN YOU ARE
©2007 Bill Griffith. World rights reserved. Distributed by King Features Syndicate
Zippythepinhead.com

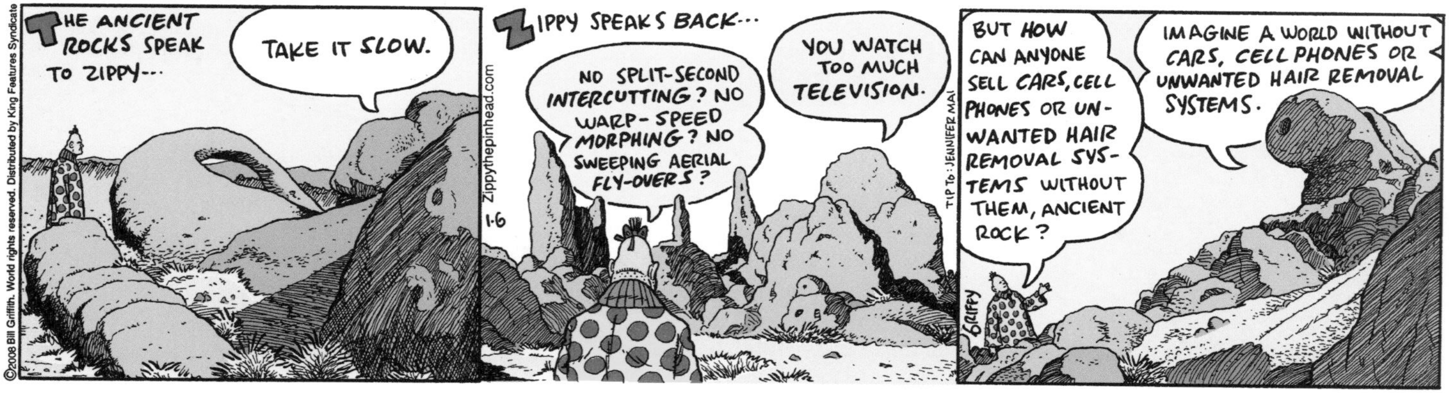
THE ANCIENT ROCKS SPEAK TO ZIPPY...
TAKE IT SLOW.
©2008 Bill Griffith. World rights reserved. Distributed by King Features Syndicate
Zippythepinhead.com
1-6
ZIPPY SPEAKS BACK...
NO SPLIT-SECOND INTERCUTTING? NO WARP-SPEED MORPHING? NO SWEEPING AERIAL FLY-OVERS?
YOU WATCH TOO MUCH TELEVISION.
TIP TO: JENNIFER MAI
BUT HOW CAN ANYONE SELL CARS, CELL PHONES OR UNWANTED HAIR REMOVAL SYSTEMS WITHOUT THEM, ANCIENT ROCK?
IMAGINE A WORLD WITHOUT CARS, CELL PHONES OR UNWANTED HAIR REMOVAL SYSTEMS.
GRIFFY

103

Dingburg's own **Tyra Nesbitt** does this untitled strip in the local alternative weekly, "**The Avocado**." It's quite popular. Go figure.

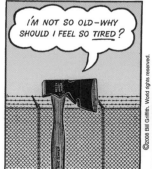

I'M NOT SO OLD—WHY SHOULD I FEEL SO TIRED?
©2008 Bill Griffith. World rights reserved.
YOU'RE JUST NOT THE HUNK OF HEARTBREAK YOU THINK YOU ARE!
Distributed by King Features Syndicate
YOU MUSTA SLIPPED YOUR MOORINGS, EDDIE! TAKE IT FROM ME, YOU CAN'T HOLD A DAME ON COURSE BY LETTING HER GIVE YOU PNEUMONIA!
EVER-READY
4·6·08 Tyra Nesbitt
THIS WILL BE A SHOW-DOWN UNLESS WE CAN PREVENT IT!
TEC DRAWING INK
WATERPROOF BLACK
Zippythepinhead.com
Oh, my aching back!

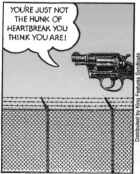

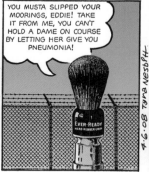

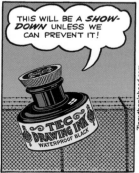

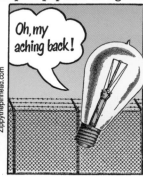

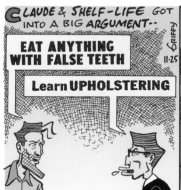

CLAUDE & SHELF-LIFE GOT INTO A BIG ARGUMENT--
GRIFFY
11-25
EAT ANYTHING WITH FALSE TEETH
Learn UPHOLSTERING
BECOME AN EXPERT IN TRAFFIC and TRANSPORTATION
Learn YOGI!
PLAY GUITAR IN 7 DAYS
DEVELOP your CHESTLINE
©2007 Bill Griffith. World rights reserved. Distributed by King Features Syndicate
Cure SELF-CONSCIOUSNESS
Don't Envy Artists -Be One!
DEVELOP A STRONG HE-MAN VOICE
STOP FORGETTING!
Zippythepinhead.com
LEARN THE TRUTH ABOUT FLYING SAUCERS
Want A Gov't Job?
WHY DON'T YOU WRITE?
S.L.

104

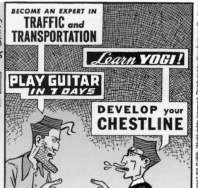

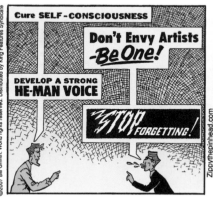

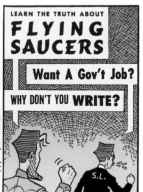

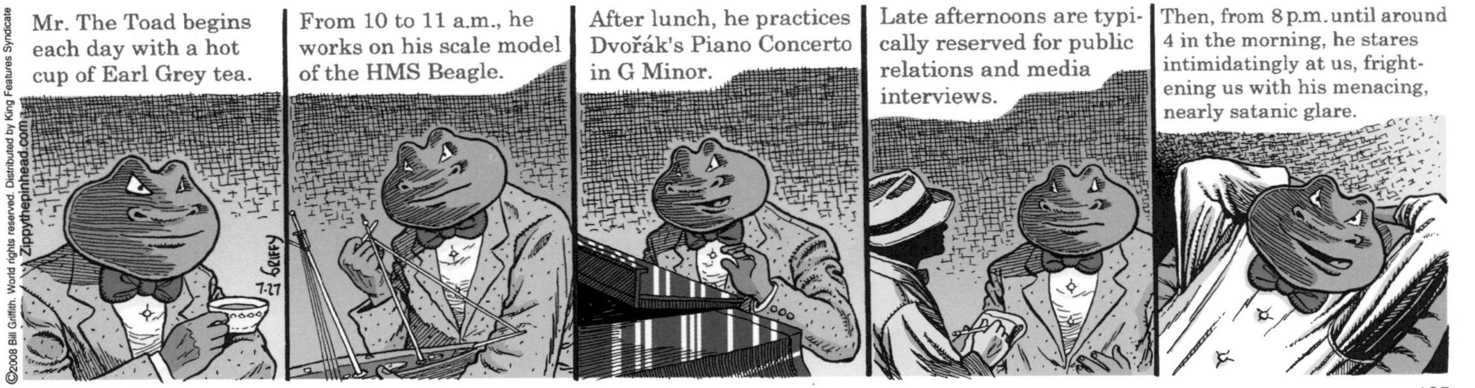

Mr. The Toad begins each day with a hot cup of Earl Grey tea.
7-27
GRIFFY
From 10 to 11 a.m., he works on his scale model of the HMS Beagle.
After lunch, he practices Dvořák's Piano Concerto in G Minor.
Late afternoons are typically reserved for public relations and media interviews.
Then, from 8 p.m. until around 4 in the morning, he stares intimidatingly at us, frightening us with his menacing, nearly satanic glare.
©2008 Bill Griffith. World rights reserved. Distributed by King Features Syndicate
Zippythepinhead.com


105

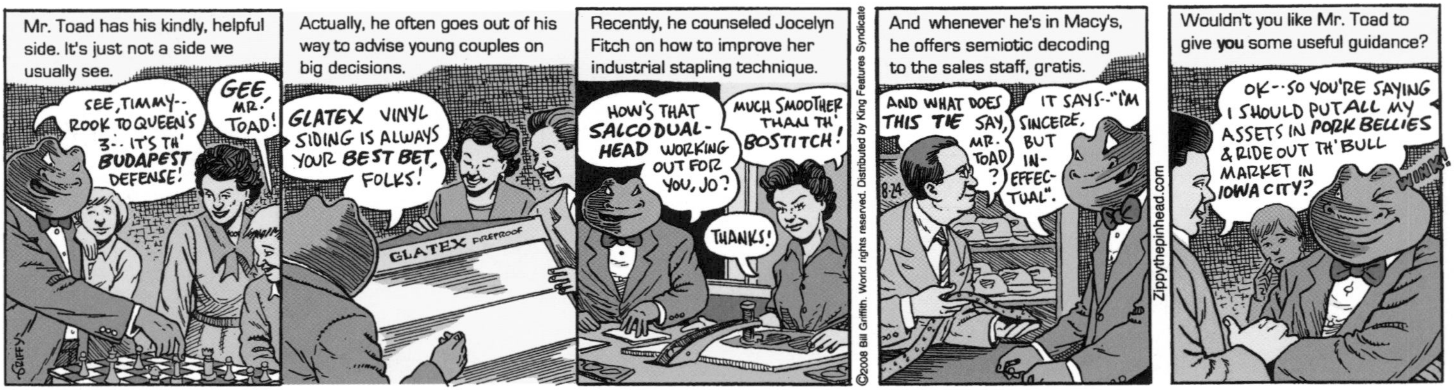

Mr. Toad has his kindly, helpful side. It's just not a side we usually see.
SEE, TIMMY-- ROOK TO QUEEN'S 3.. IT'S TH' BUDAPEST DEFENSE!
GEE, MR. TOAD!
GRIFFY
Actually, he often goes out of his way to advise young couples on big decisions.
GLATEX VINYL SIDING IS ALWAYS YOUR BEST BET, FOLKS!
GLATEX FIREPROOF
Recently, he counseled Jocelyn Fitch on how to improve her industrial stapling technique.
HOW'S THAT SALCO DUAL-HEAD WORKING OUT FOR YOU, JO?
MUCH SMOOTHER THAN TH' BOSTITCH!
THANKS!
©2008 Bill Griffith. World rights reserved. Distributed by King Features Syndicate
And whenever he's in Macy's, he offers semiotic decoding to the sales staff, gratis.
AND WHAT DOES THIS TIE SAY, MR. TOAD?
IT SAYS--"I'M SINCERE, BUT INEFFECTUAL".
8-24
Zippythepinhead.com
Wouldn't you like Mr. Toad to give you some useful guidance?
OK--SO YOU'RE SAYING I SHOULD PUT ALL MY ASSETS IN PORK BELLIES & RIDE OUT TH' BULL MARKET IN IOWA CITY?
WINK!

Dingburg's favorite comic strip is "**Fletcher and Tanya**" by **Conrad Nervig**. Here's a particularly puzzling Sunday example. It is, indeed, an "acquired taste."

What should I do to get better pictures?
YIP! YIP! YIP!
I'M BREAKING CAMP TOMORROW. I'VE A ROOM AT SURF HOUSE
THAT'S THE END OF THAT CATTLE KILLER
©2008 Bill Griffith. World rights reserved.
2·24·08 CONRAD NERVIG
LOOK–THERE'S MISS FIELD, THE NEW TEACHER.
YIP! YIP! YIP!
Zippythepinhead.com
Distributed by King Features Syndicate
GREAT DANES, STOPPER! WE'VE LOCKED BUMPERS WITH THE GROOM'S CAR
WOW–BET IT COST A LOT OF MONEY!

106 A

FLETCHER & Tanya
GEE! DANCING MAKES ME HUNGRY FOR CHOCOLATE FLAVORED BOSCO
GOSH, IT'S, EILEEN!
©2008 Bill Griffith. World rights reserved. Distributed by King Features Syndicate
I'D LIKE TO BREAK EVERY BONE IN YOUR BODY.
DON'T BE SILLY, IRMA!
WHITE MEN HAVE BEEN GOOD TO ME.
Zippythepinhead.com
THAT LOOKS LIKE A WHITE MAN.
CRASH!
8·17·08 CONRAD NERVIG
NOW I'M LOOKING FORWARD TO A RIPE OLD AGE
WHAT IS THIS MAGIC DUST?

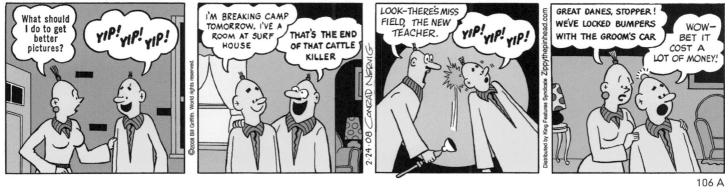

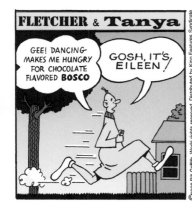

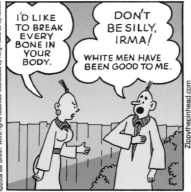

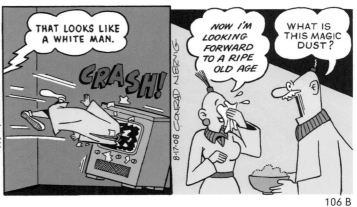

106 B

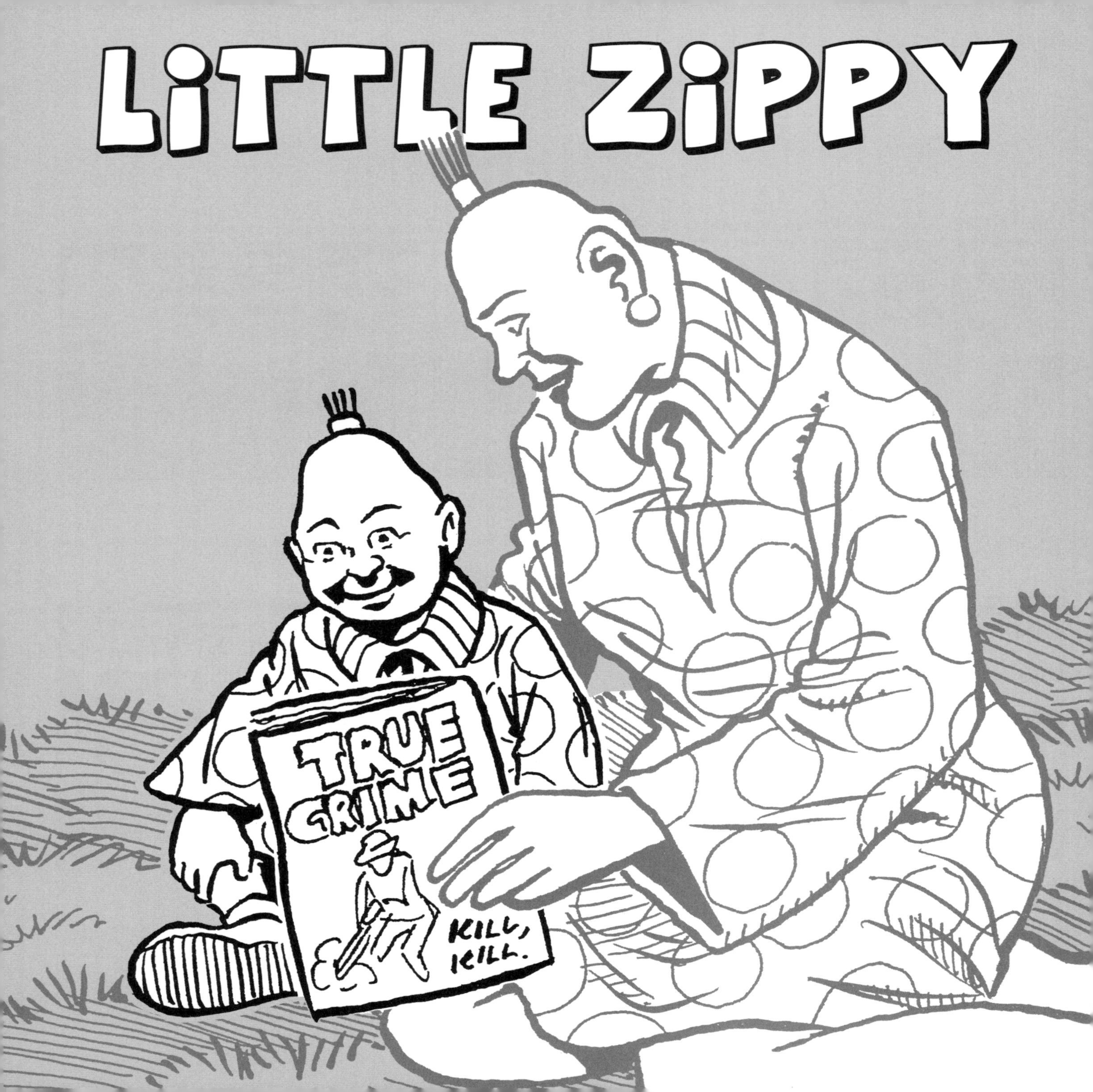
LITTLE ZIPPY
TRUE CRIME
KILL, KILL.

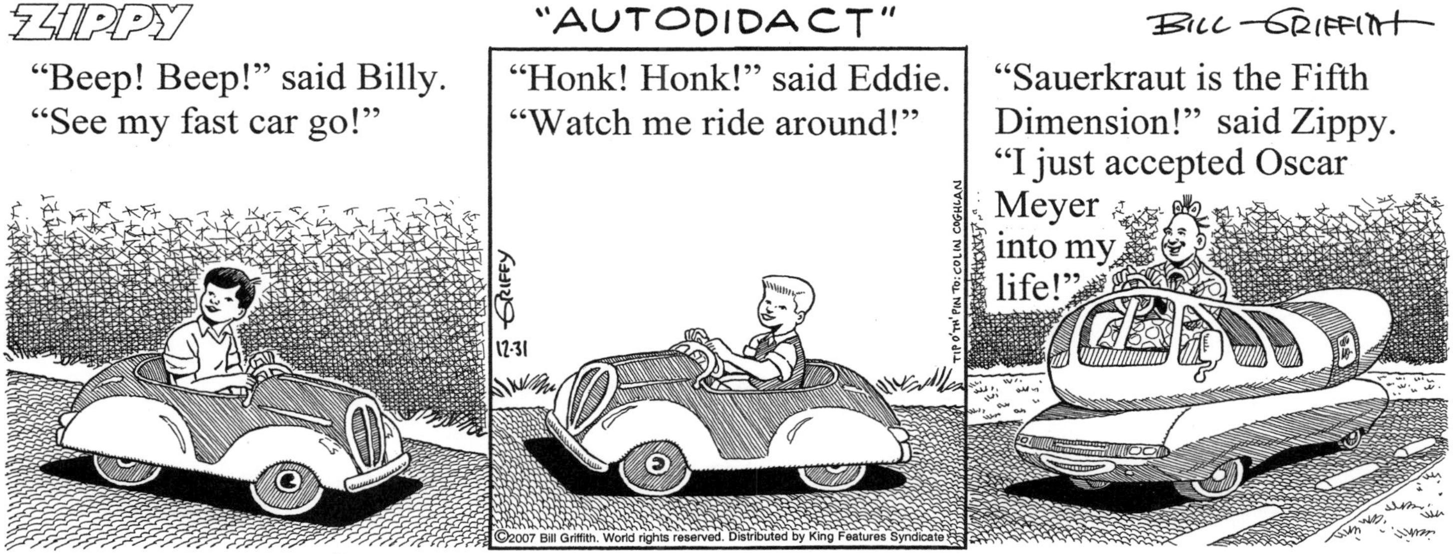
ZIPPY
"AUTODIDACT"
BILL GRIFFITH
"Beep! Beep!" said Billy. "See my fast car go!"
GRIFFY 12-31
"Honk! Honk!" said Eddie. "Watch me ride around!"
TIP O' TH' PIN TO: COLIN COGHLAN
©2007 Bill Griffith. World rights reserved. Distributed by King Features Syndicate
"Sauerkraut is the Fifth Dimension!" said Zippy. "I just accepted Oscar Meyer into my life!"

107

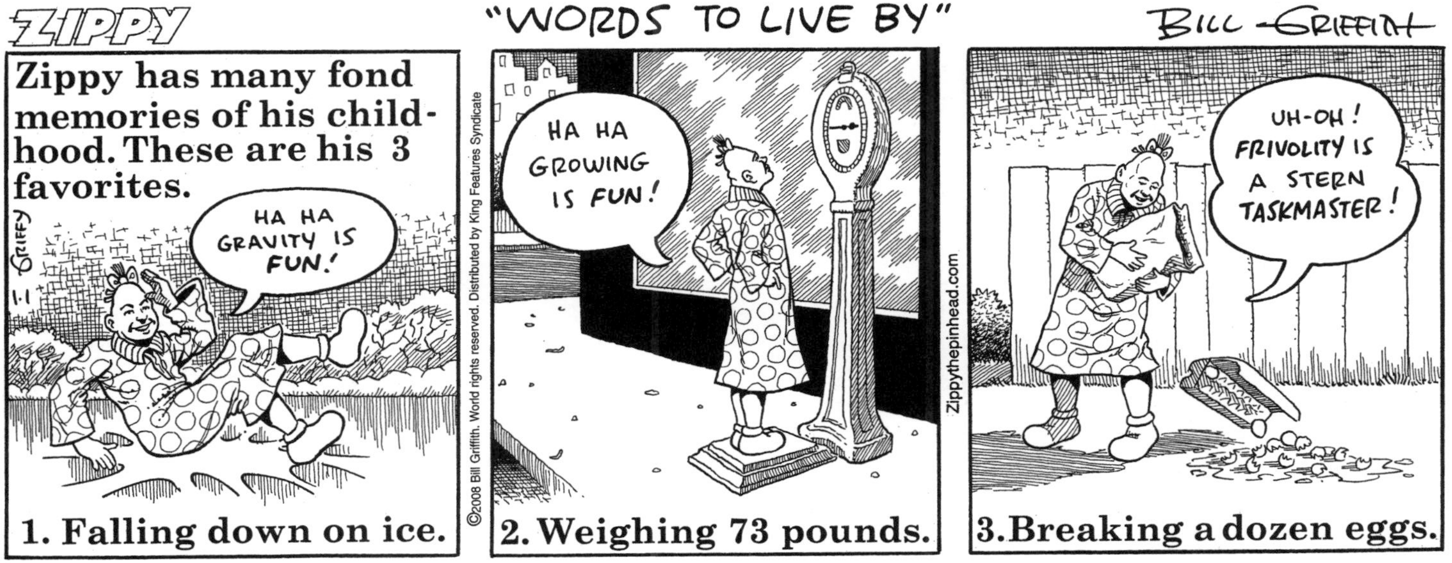
ZIPPY
"WORDS TO LIVE BY"
BILL GRIFFITH
Zippy has many fond memories of his child-hood. These are his 3 favorites.
GRIFFY 1-1
HA HA GRAVITY IS FUN!
1. Falling down on ice.
©2008 Bill Griffith. World rights reserved. Distributed by King Features Syndicate
HA HA GROWING IS FUN!
2. Weighing 73 pounds.
Zippythepinhead.com
UH-OH! FRIVOLITY IS A STERN TASKMASTER!
3. Breaking a dozen eggs.

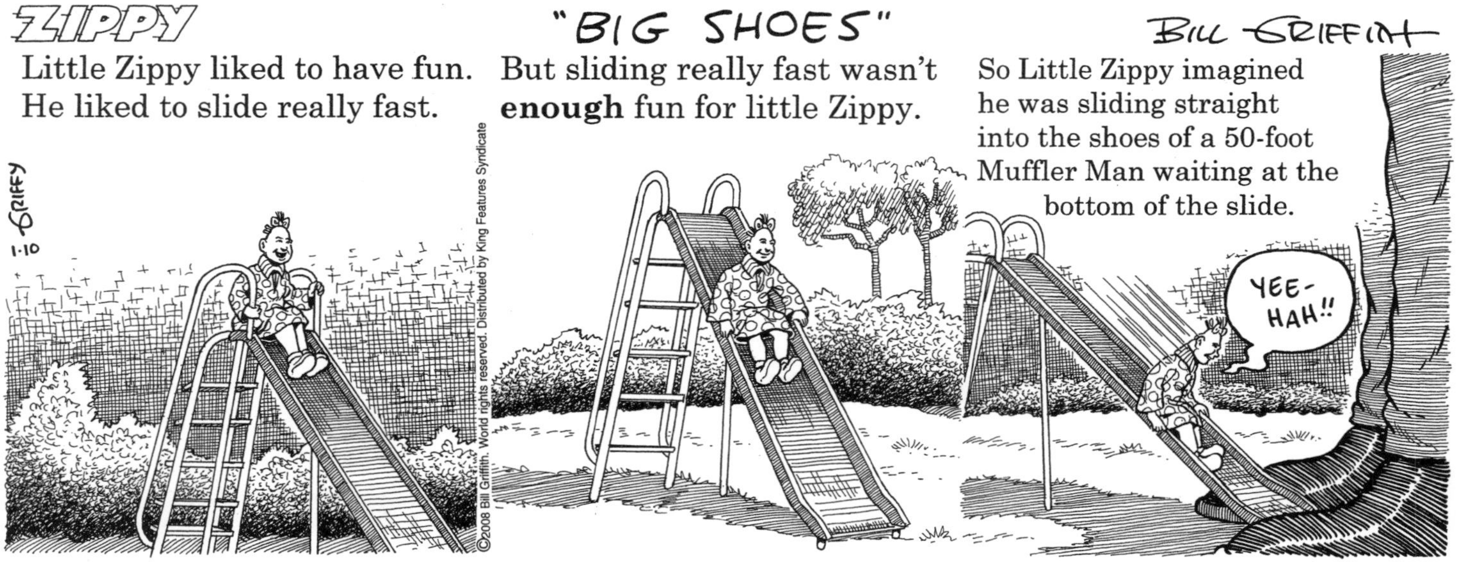
ZIPPY
"BIG SHOES"
BILL GRIFFITH
Little Zippy liked to have fun. He liked to slide really fast.
GRIFFY 1-10
©2008 Bill Griffith. World rights reserved. Distributed by King Features Syndicate
But sliding really fast wasn't **enough** fun for little Zippy.
So Little Zippy imagined he was sliding straight into the shoes of a 50-foot Muffler Man waiting at the bottom of the slide.
YEE-HAH!!

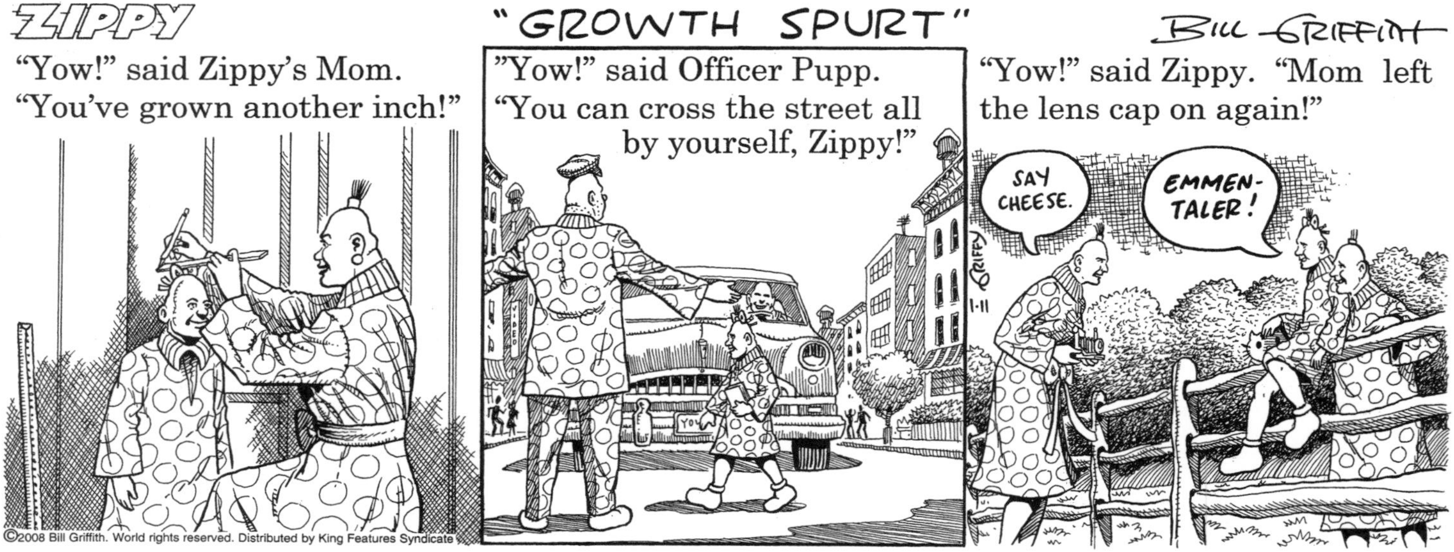
ZIPPY
"GROWTH SPURT"
BILL GRIFFITH
"Yow!" said Zippy's Mom. "You've grown another inch!"
©2008 Bill Griffith. World rights reserved. Distributed by King Features Syndicate
"Yow!" said Officer Pupp. "You can cross the street all by yourself, Zippy!"
"Yow!" said Zippy. "Mom left the lens cap on again!"
SAY CHEESE.
EMMEN-TALER!
GRIFFY 1-11

108

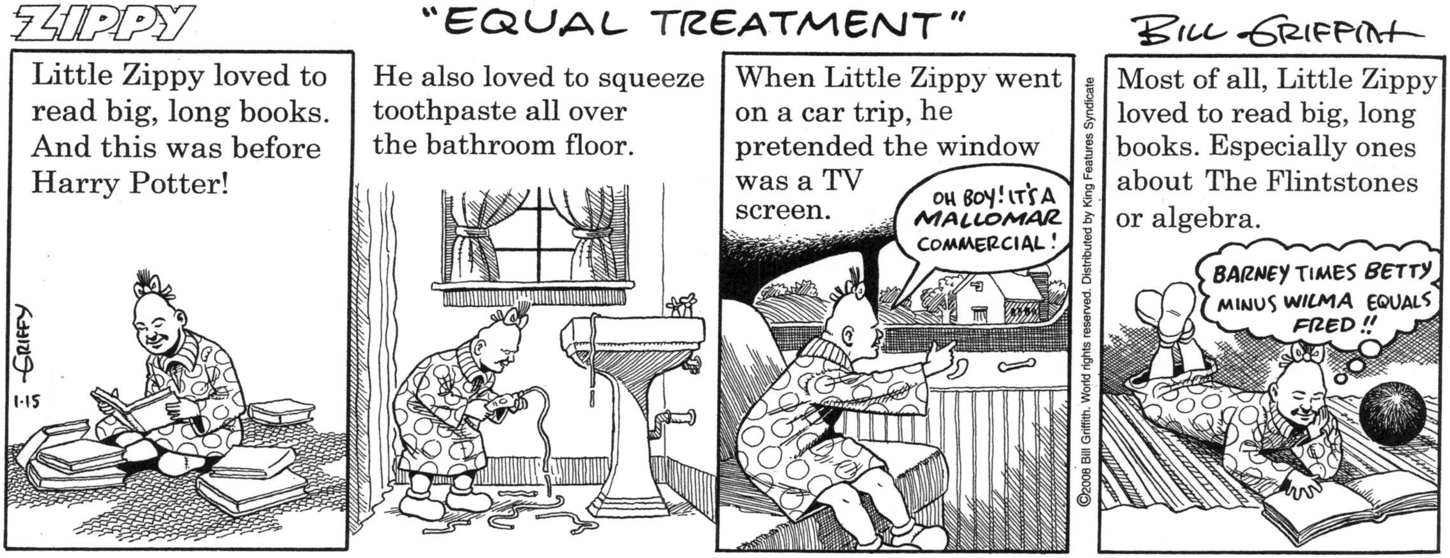
ZIPPY
"EQUAL TREATMENT"
BILL GRIFFITH
Little Zippy loved to read big, long books. And this was before Harry Potter!
GRIFFY
1-15
He also loved to squeeze toothpaste all over the bathroom floor.
When Little Zippy went on a car trip, he pretended the window was a TV screen.
OH BOY! IT'S A MALLOMAR COMMERCIAL!
©2008 Bill Griffith. World rights reserved. Distributed by King Features Syndicate
Most of all, Little Zippy loved to read big, long books. Especially ones about The Flintstones or algebra.
BARNEY TIMES BETTY MINUS WILMA EQUALS FRED!!

109

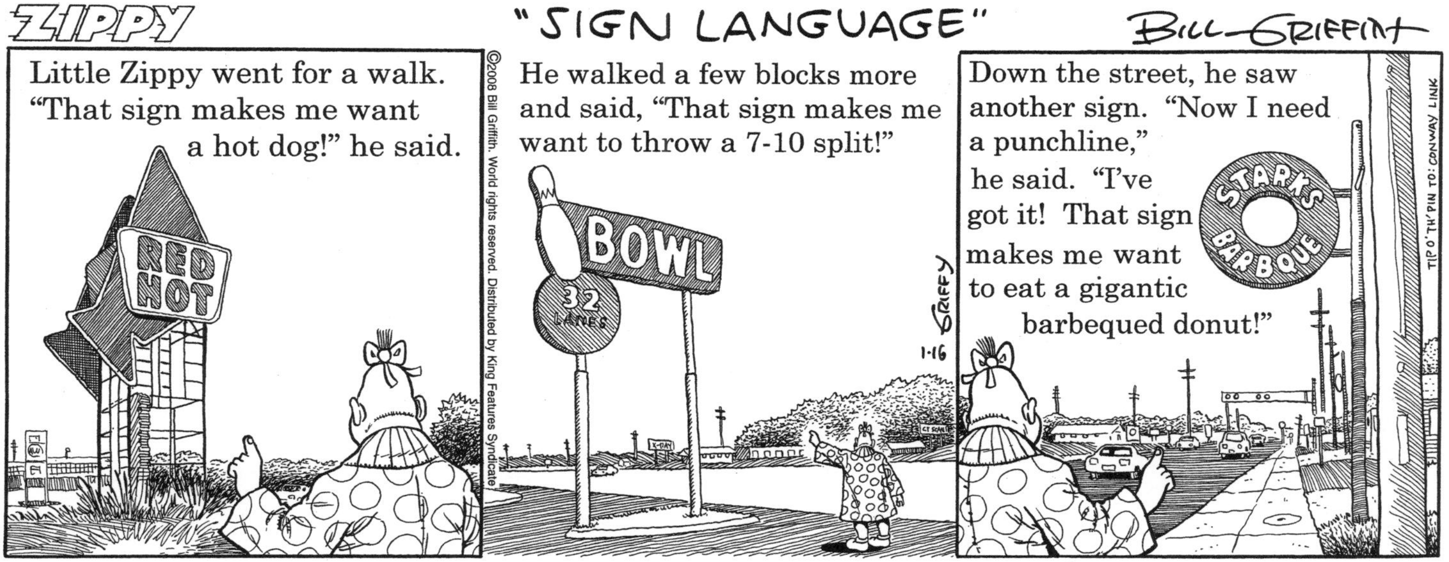
ZIPPY
"SIGN LANGUAGE"
BILL GRIFFITH
Little Zippy went for a walk. "That sign makes me want a hot dog!" he said.
RED HOT
©2008 Bill Griffith. World rights reserved. Distributed by King Features Syndicate
He walked a few blocks more and said, "That sign makes me want to throw a 7-10 split!"
BOWL
32 LANES
GRIFFY
1-16
Down the street, he saw another sign. "Now I need a punchline," he said. "I've got it! That sign makes me want to eat a gigantic barbequed donut!"
STARKS BARBQUE
TIP O' TH' PIN TO: CONWAY LINK

110

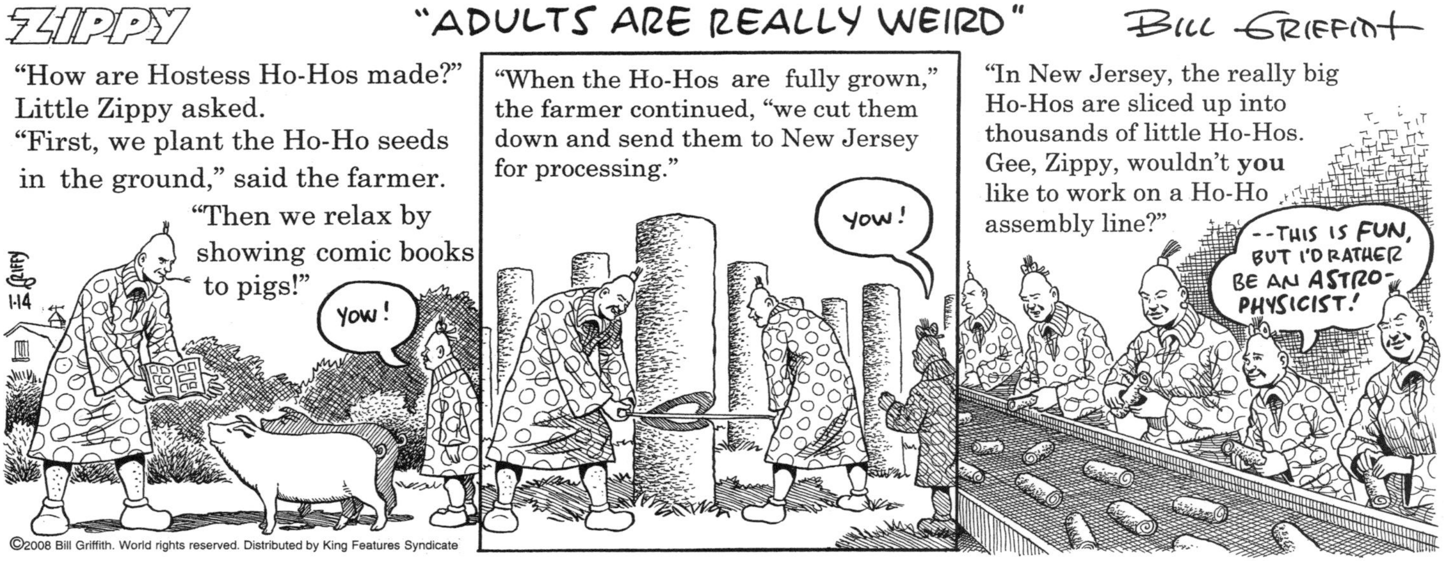
ZIPPY
"ADULTS ARE REALLY WEIRD"
BILL GRIFFITH
"How are Hostess Ho-Hos made?" Little Zippy asked.
"First, we plant the Ho-Ho seeds in the ground," said the farmer.
"Then we relax by showing comic books to pigs!"
YOW!
GRIFFY 1·14
"When the Ho-Hos are fully grown," the farmer continued, "we cut them down and send them to New Jersey for processing."
YOW!
"In New Jersey, the really big Ho-Hos are sliced up into thousands of little Ho-Hos. Gee, Zippy, wouldn't **you** like to work on a Ho-Ho assembly line?"
--THIS IS FUN, BUT I'D RATHER BE AN ASTRO-PHYSICIST!
©2008 Bill Griffith. World rights reserved. Distributed by King Features Syndicate

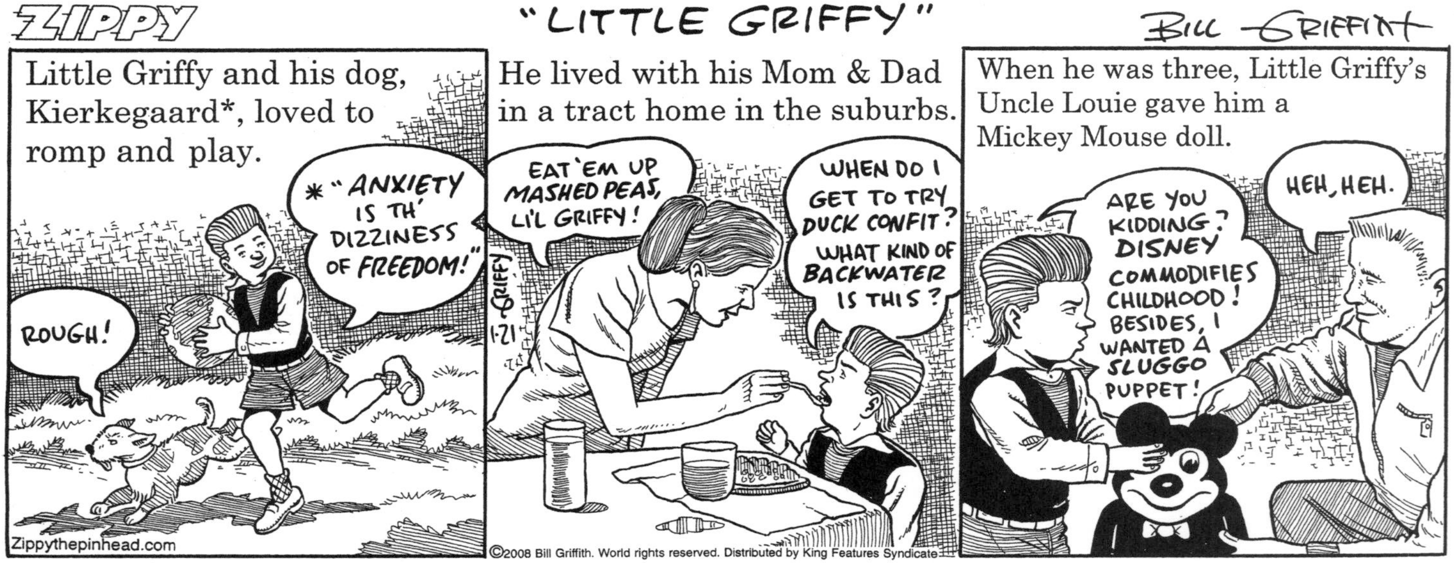
ZIPPY
"LITTLE GRIFFY"
BILL GRIFFITH
Little Griffy and his dog, Kierkegaard*, loved to romp and play.
* "ANXIETY IS TH' DIZZINESS OF FREEDOM!"
ROUGH!
Zippythepinhead.com
He lived with his Mom & Dad in a tract home in the suburbs.
EAT 'EM UP MASHED PEAS, LI'L GRIFFY!
WHEN DO I GET TO TRY DUCK CONFIT? WHAT KIND OF BACKWATER IS THIS?
GRIFFY 1·21
©2008 Bill Griffith. World rights reserved. Distributed by King Features Syndicate
When he was three, Little Griffy's Uncle Louie gave him a Mickey Mouse doll.
HEH, HEH.
ARE YOU KIDDING? DISNEY COMMODIFIES CHILDHOOD! BESIDES, I WANTED A SLUGGO PUPPET!

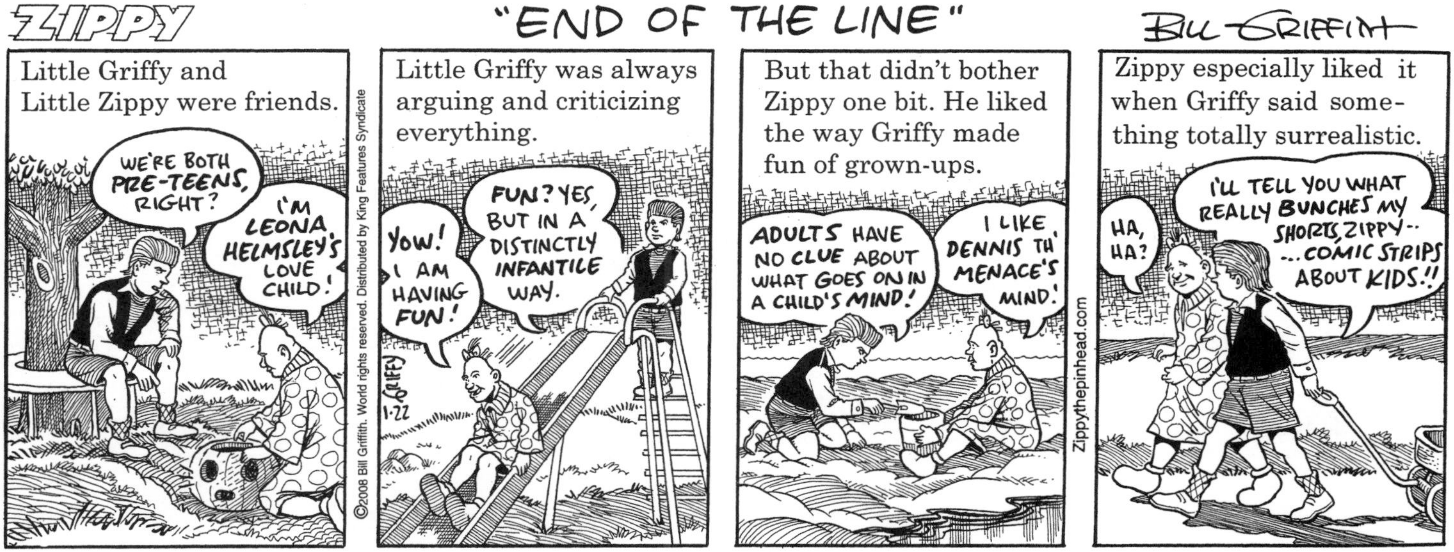
ZIPPY
"END OF THE LINE"
BILL GRIFFITH
Little Griffy and Little Zippy were friends.
WE'RE BOTH PRE-TEENS, RIGHT?
I'M LEONA HELMSLEY'S LOVE CHILD!
©2008 Bill Griffith. World rights reserved. Distributed by King Features Syndicate
Little Griffy was always arguing and criticizing everything.
YOW! I AM HAVING FUN!
FUN? YES, BUT IN A DISTINCTLY INFANTILE WAY.
GRIFFY 1-22
But that didn't bother Zippy one bit. He liked the way Griffy made fun of grown-ups.
ADULTS HAVE NO CLUE ABOUT WHAT GOES ON IN A CHILD'S MIND!
I LIKE DENNIS TH' MENACE'S MIND!
Zippythepinhead.com
Zippy especially liked it when Griffy said something totally surrealistic.
HA, HA?
I'LL TELL YOU WHAT REALLY BUNCHES MY SHORTS, ZIPPY-- ...COMIC STRIPS ABOUT KIDS!!

111

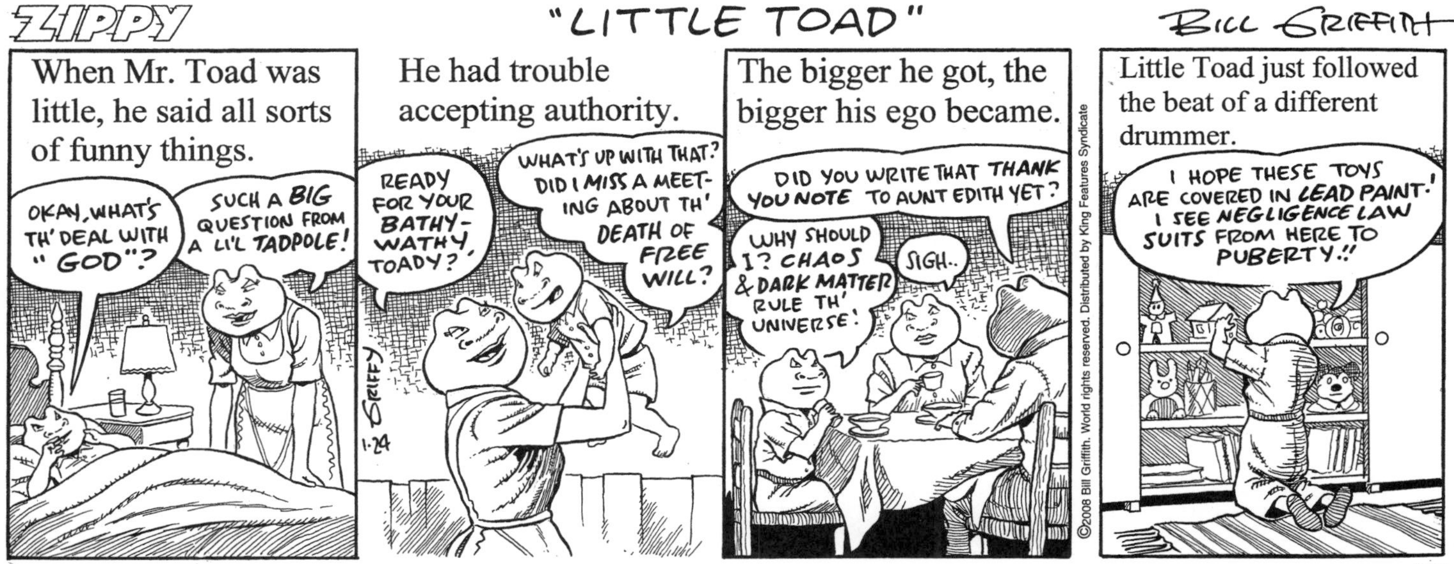
ZIPPY
"LITTLE TOAD"
BILL GRIFFITH
When Mr. Toad was little, he said all sorts of funny things.
OKAY, WHAT'S TH' DEAL WITH "GOD"?
SUCH A BIG QUESTION FROM A LI'L TADPOLE!
He had trouble accepting authority.
READY FOR YOUR BATHY-WATHY, TOADY?
WHAT'S UP WITH THAT? DID I MISS A MEETING ABOUT TH' DEATH OF FREE WILL?
GRIFFY 1-24
The bigger he got, the bigger his ego became.
DID YOU WRITE THAT THANK YOU NOTE TO AUNT EDITH YET?
WHY SHOULD I? CHAOS & DARK MATTER RULE TH' UNIVERSE!
SIGH..
©2008 Bill Griffith. World rights reserved. Distributed by King Features Syndicate
Little Toad just followed the beat of a different drummer.
I HOPE THESE TOYS ARE COVERED IN LEAD PAINT! I SEE NEGLIGENCE LAW SUITS FROM HERE TO PUBERTY!!

112

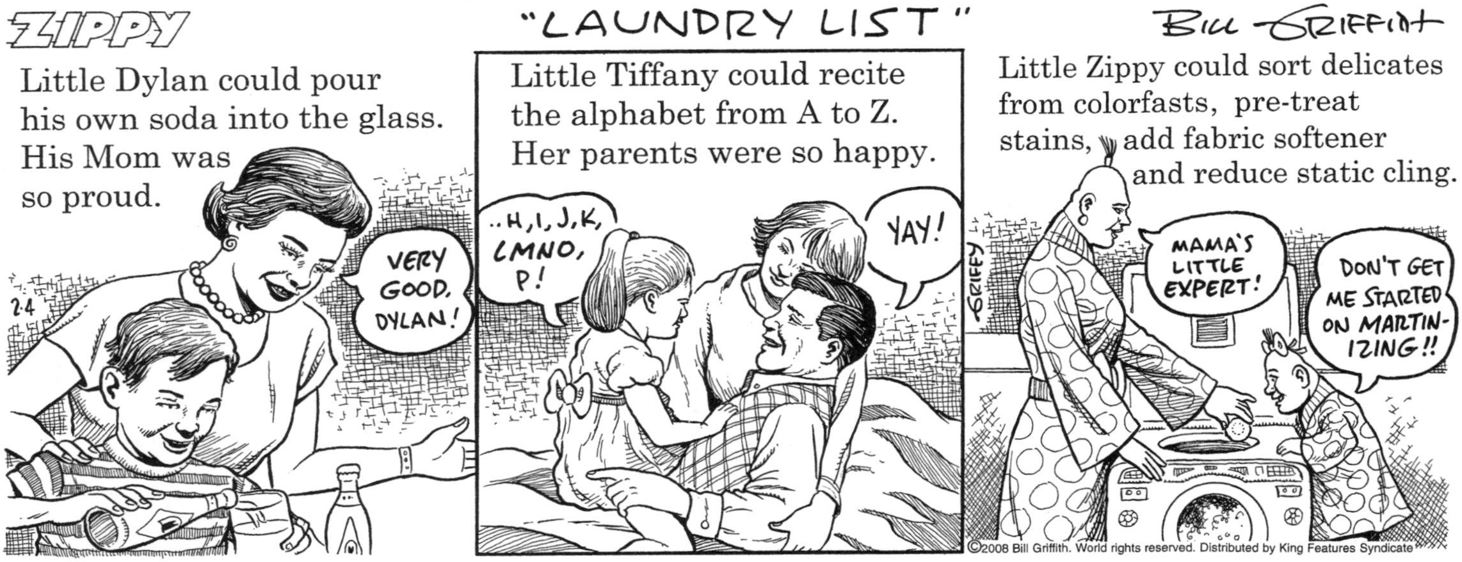
ZIPPY
"LAUNDRY LIST"
BILL GRIFFITH
Little Dylan could pour his own soda into the glass. His Mom was so proud.
VERY GOOD, DYLAN!
Little Tiffany could recite the alphabet from A to Z. Her parents were so happy.
..H, I, J, K, LMNO, P!
YAY!
Little Zippy could sort delicates from colorfasts, pre-treat stains, add fabric softener and reduce static cling.
MAMA'S LITTLE EXPERT!
DON'T GET ME STARTED ON MARTIN-IZING!!
©2008 Bill Griffith. World rights reserved. Distributed by King Features Syndicate

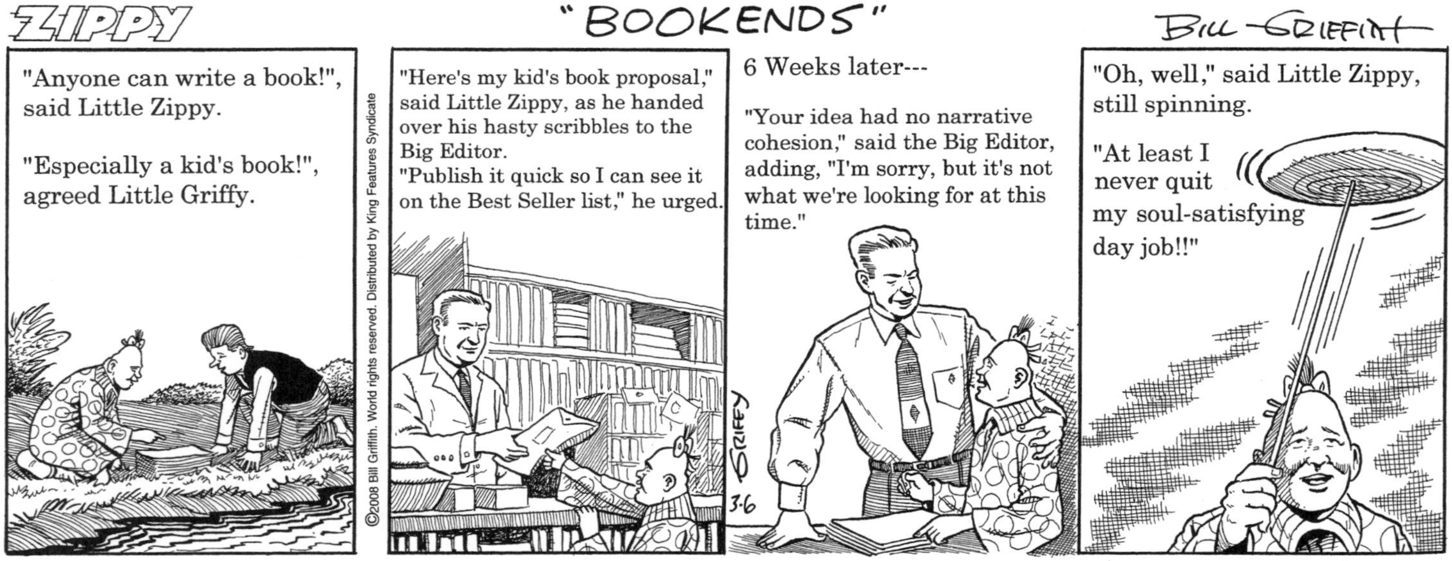
ZIPPY
"BOOKENDS"
BILL GRIFFITH
"Anyone can write a book!", said Little Zippy.
"Especially a kid's book!", agreed Little Griffy.
©2008 Bill Griffith. World rights reserved. Distributed by King Features Syndicate
"Here's my kid's book proposal," said Little Zippy, as he handed over his hasty scribbles to the Big Editor.
"Publish it quick so I can see it on the Best Seller list," he urged.
6 Weeks later---
"Your idea had no narrative cohesion," said the Big Editor, adding, "I'm sorry, but it's not what we're looking for at this time."
"Oh, well," said Little Zippy, still spinning.
"At least I never quit my soul-satisfying day job!!"

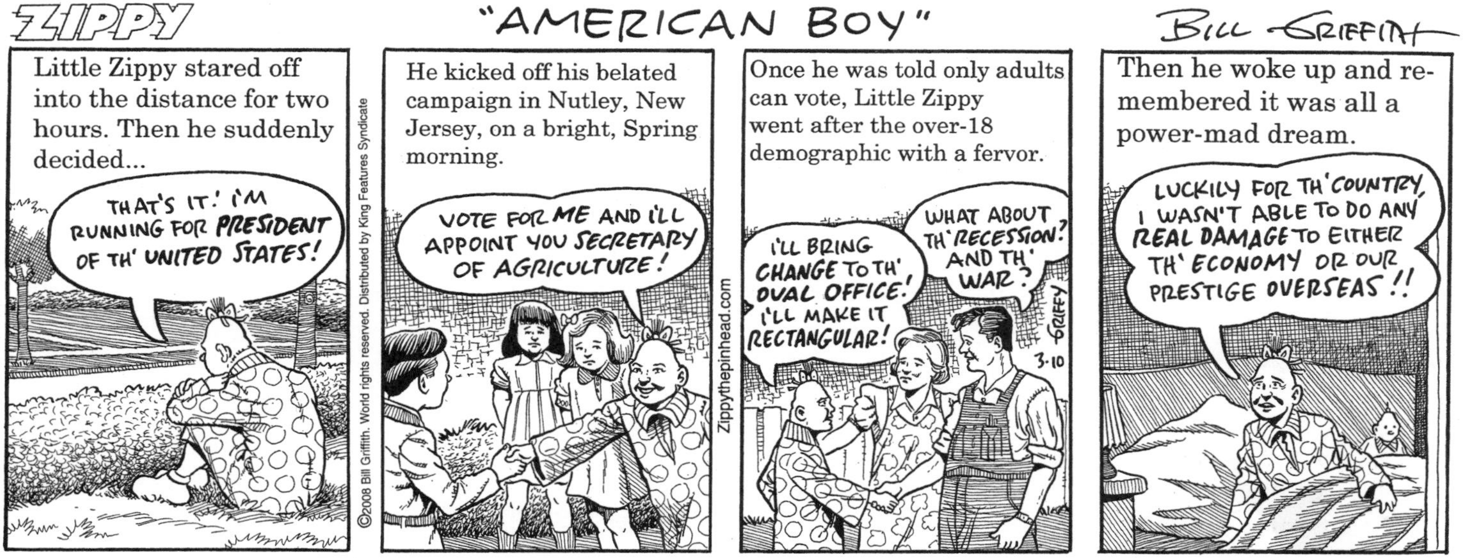
ZIPPY
"AMERICAN BOY"
BILL GRIFFITH
Little Zippy stared off into the distance for two hours. Then he suddenly decided...
THAT'S IT! I'M RUNNING FOR PRESIDENT OF TH' UNITED STATES!
©2008 Bill Griffith. World rights reserved. Distributed by King Features Syndicate
He kicked off his belated campaign in Nutley, New Jersey, on a bright, Spring morning.
VOTE FOR ME AND I'LL APPOINT YOU SECRETARY OF AGRICULTURE!
Zippythepinhead.com
Once he was told only adults can vote, Little Zippy went after the over-18 demographic with a fervor.
I'LL BRING CHANGE TO TH' OVAL OFFICE! I'LL MAKE IT RECTANGULAR!
WHAT ABOUT TH' RECESSION? AND TH' WAR?
GRIFFY 3-10
Then he woke up and remembered it was all a power-mad dream.
LUCKILY FOR TH' COUNTRY, I WASN'T ABLE TO DO ANY REAL DAMAGE TO EITHER TH' ECONOMY OR OUR PRESTIGE OVERSEAS!!

113

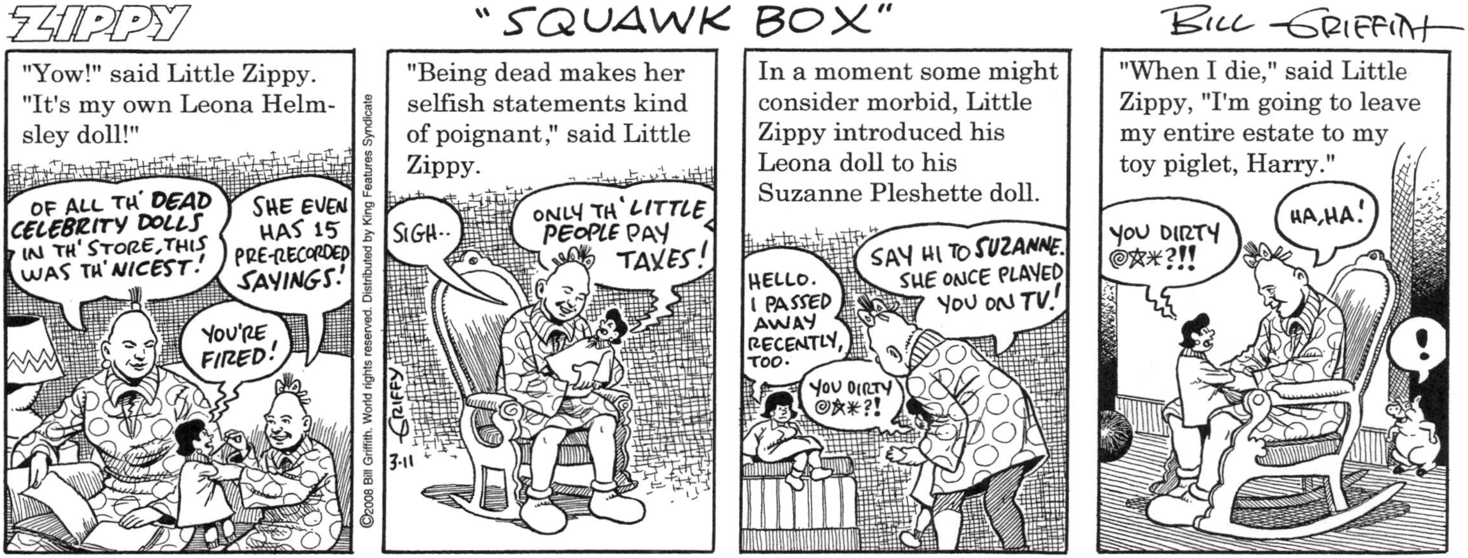
ZIPPY
"SQUAWK BOX"
BILL GRIFFITH
"Yow!" said Little Zippy. "It's my own Leona Helmsley doll!"
OF ALL TH' DEAD CELEBRITY DOLLS IN TH' STORE, THIS WAS TH' NICEST!
SHE EVEN HAS 15 PRE-RECORDED SAYINGS!
YOU'RE FIRED!
©2008 Bill Griffith. World rights reserved. Distributed by King Features Syndicate
"Being dead makes her selfish statements kind of poignant," said Little Zippy.
SIGH..
ONLY TH' LITTLE PEOPLE PAY TAXES!
GRIFFY 3-11
In a moment some might consider morbid, Little Zippy introduced his Leona doll to his Suzanne Pleshette doll.
SAY HI TO SUZANNE. SHE ONCE PLAYED YOU ON TV!
HELLO. I PASSED AWAY RECENTLY, TOO.
YOU DIRTY @☆*?!
"When I die," said Little Zippy, "I'm going to leave my entire estate to my toy piglet, Harry."
YOU DIRTY @☆*?!!
HA, HA!
!

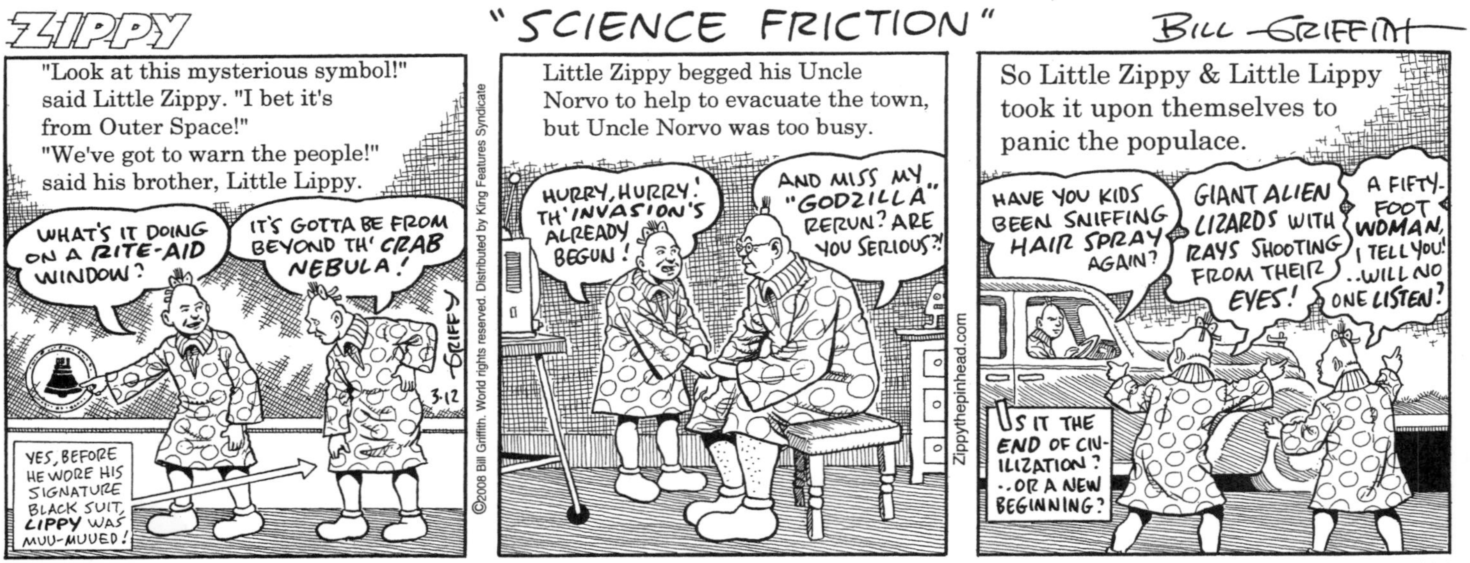
ZIPPY
"SCIENCE FRICTION"
BILL GRIFFITH
"Look at this mysterious symbol!" said Little Zippy. "I bet it's from Outer Space!"
"We've got to warn the people!" said his brother, Little Lippy.
WHAT'S IT DOING ON A RITE-AID WINDOW?
IT'S GOTTA BE FROM BEYOND TH' CRAB NEBULA!
YES, BEFORE HE WORE HIS SIGNATURE BLACK SUIT, LIPPY WAS MUU-MUUED!
GRIFFY 3-12
©2008 Bill Griffith. World rights reserved. Distributed by King Features Syndicate
Little Zippy begged his Uncle Norvo to help to evacuate the town, but Uncle Norvo was too busy.
HURRY, HURRY! TH' INVASION'S ALREADY BEGUN!
AND MISS MY "GODZILLA" RERUN? ARE YOU SERIOUS?!
Zippythepinhead.com
So Little Zippy & Little Lippy took it upon themselves to panic the populace.
HAVE YOU KIDS BEEN SNIFFING HAIR SPRAY AGAIN?
GIANT ALIEN LIZARDS WITH RAYS SHOOTING FROM THEIR EYES!
A FIFTY-FOOT WOMAN, I TELL YOU! ..WILL NO ONE LISTEN?
IS IT THE END OF CIVILIZATION? ..OR A NEW BEGINNING?

114

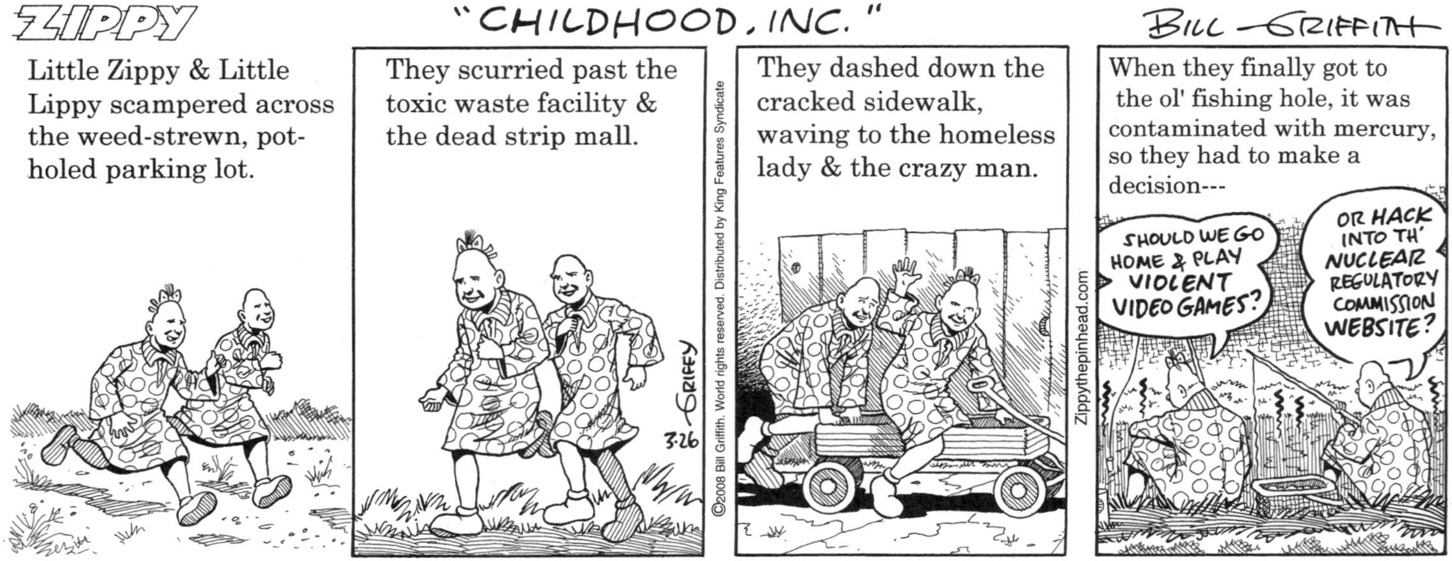
ZIPPY
"CHILDHOOD, INC."
BILL GRIFFITH
Little Zippy & Little Lippy scampered across the weed-strewn, pot-holed parking lot.
They scurried past the toxic waste facility & the dead strip mall.
GRIFFY 3-26
©2008 Bill Griffith. World rights reserved. Distributed by King Features Syndicate
They dashed down the cracked sidewalk, waving to the homeless lady & the crazy man.
Zippythepinhead.com
When they finally got to the ol' fishing hole, it was contaminated with mercury, so they had to make a decision---
SHOULD WE GO HOME & PLAY VIOLENT VIDEO GAMES?
OR HACK INTO TH' NUCLEAR REGULATORY COMMISSION WEBSITE?

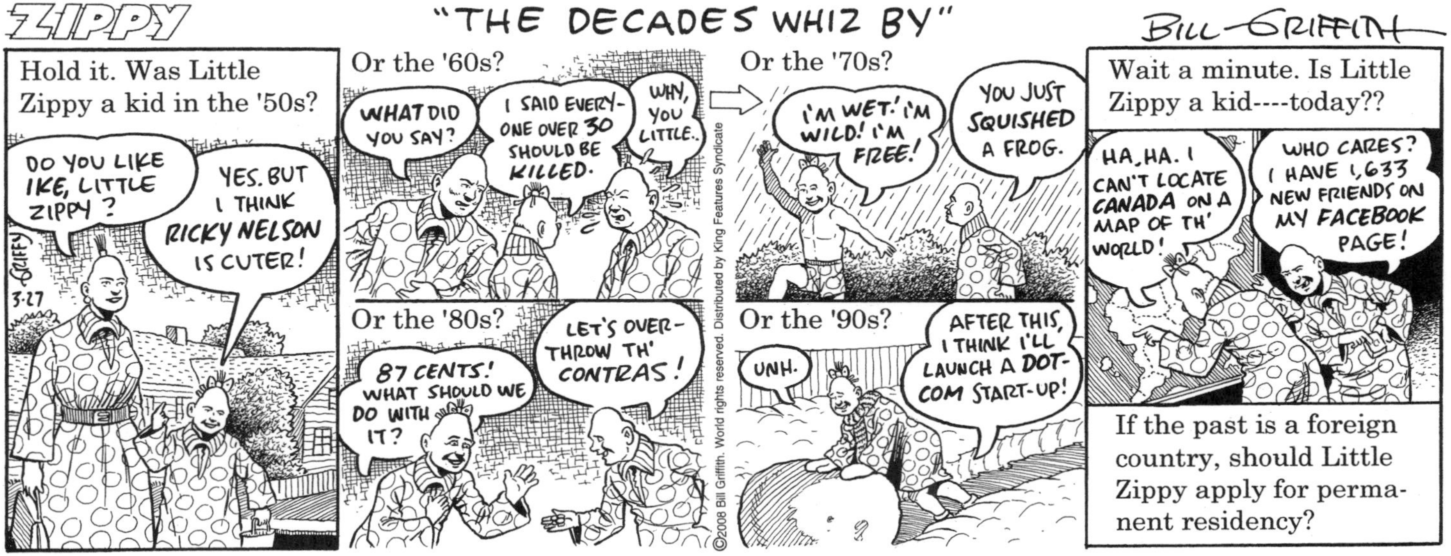
ZIPPY
"THE DECADES WHIZ BY"
BILL GRIFFITH
Hold it. Was Little Zippy a kid in the '50s?
DO YOU LIKE IKE, LITTLE ZIPPY ?
YES. BUT I THINK RICKY NELSON IS CUTER!
GRIFFY
3-27
Or the '60s?
WHAT DID YOU SAY?
I SAID EVERY-ONE OVER 30 SHOULD BE KILLED.
WHY, YOU LITTLE..
Or the '70s?
I'M WET! I'M WILD! I'M FREE!
YOU JUST SQUISHED A FROG.
Or the '80s?
87 CENTS! WHAT SHOULD WE DO WITH IT?
LET'S OVER-THROW TH' CONTRAS!
Or the '90s?
UNH.
AFTER THIS, I THINK I'LL LAUNCH A DOT-COM START-UP!
©2008 Bill Griffith. World rights reserved. Distributed by King Features Syndicate
Wait a minute. Is Little Zippy a kid----today??
HA. HA. I CAN'T LOCATE CANADA ON A MAP OF TH' WORLD!
WHO CARES? I HAVE 1,633 NEW FRIENDS ON MY FACEBOOK PAGE!
If the past is a foreign country, should Little Zippy apply for permanent residency?

115

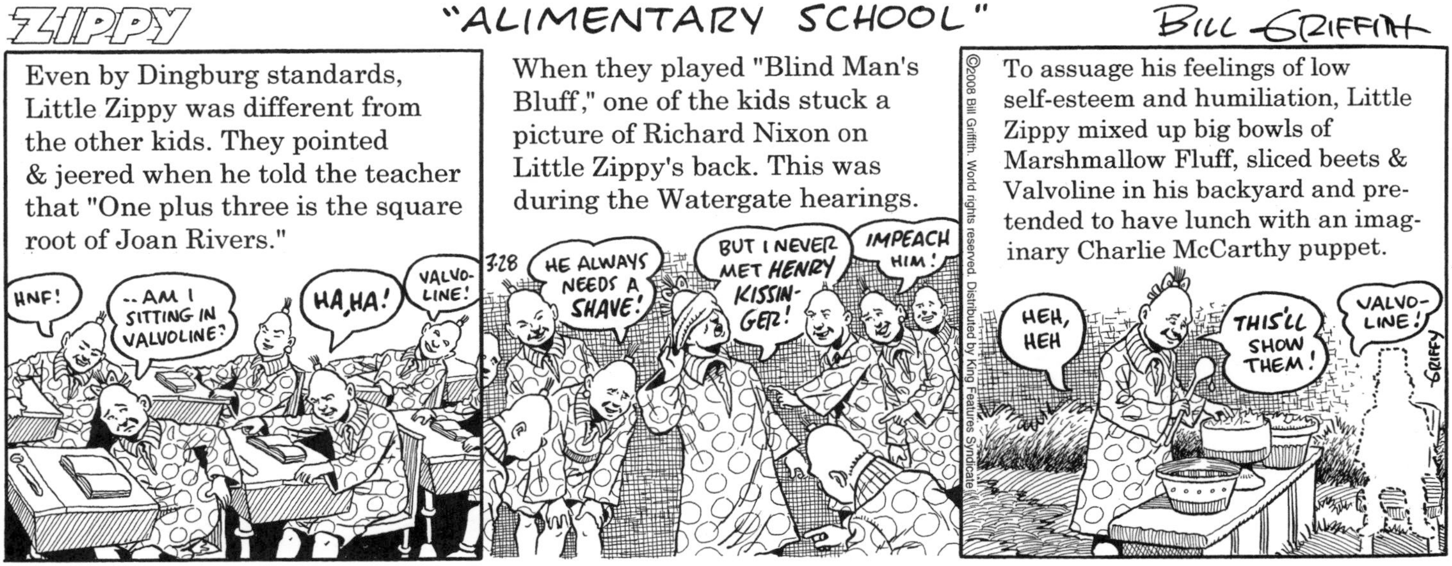
ZIPPY
"ALIMENTARY SCHOOL"
BILL GRIFFITH
Even by Dingburg standards, Little Zippy was different from the other kids. They pointed & jeered when he told the teacher that "One plus three is the square root of Joan Rivers."
HNF!
..AM I SITTING IN VALVOLINE?
HA,HA!
VALVO-LINE!
When they played "Blind Man's Bluff," one of the kids stuck a picture of Richard Nixon on Little Zippy's back. This was during the Watergate hearings.
3-28
HE ALWAYS NEEDS A SHAVE!
BUT I NEVER MET HENRY KISSIN-GER!
IMPEACH HIM!
©2008 Bill Griffith. World rights reserved. Distributed by King Features Syndicate
To assuage his feelings of low self-esteem and humiliation, Little Zippy mixed up big bowls of Marshmallow Fluff, sliced beets & Valvoline in his backyard and pretended to have lunch with an imaginary Charlie McCarthy puppet.
HEH, HEH
THIS'LL SHOW THEM!
VALVO-LINE!
GRIFFY

116

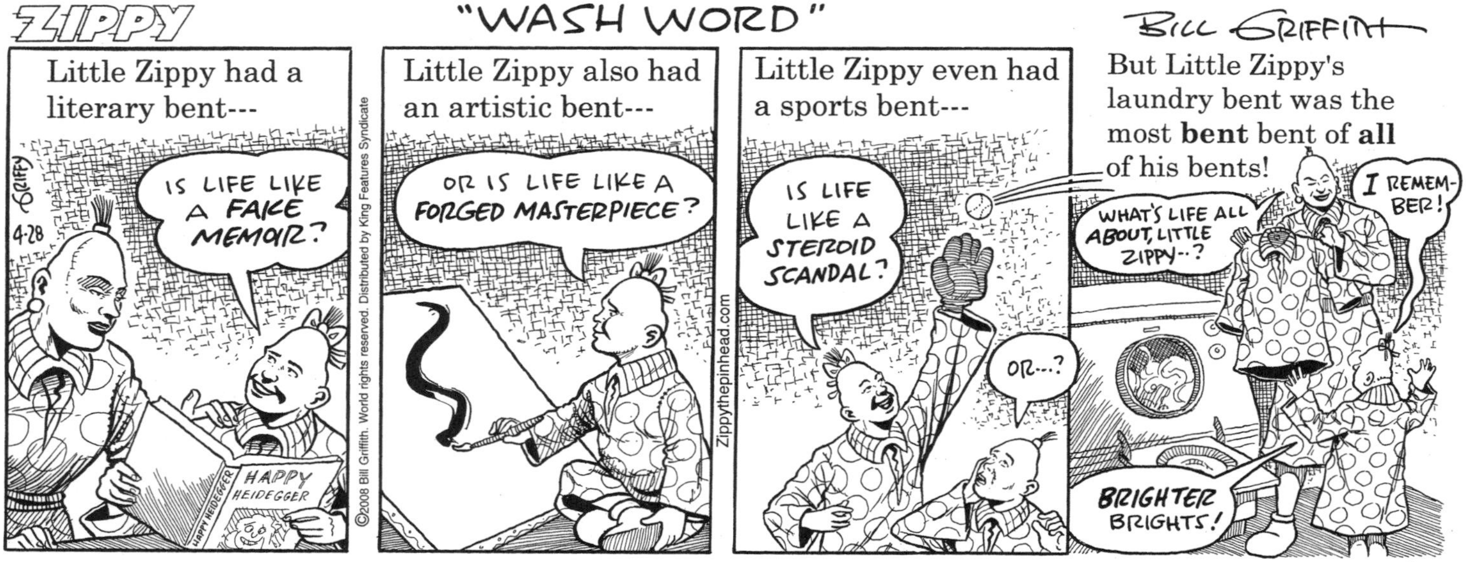
ZIPPY
"WASH WORD"
BILL GRIFFITH
Little Zippy had a literary bent---
IS LIFE LIKE A FAKE MEMOIR?
GRIFFY 4-28
HAPPY HEIDEGGER
©2008 Bill Griffith. World rights reserved. Distributed by King Features Syndicate
Little Zippy also had an artistic bent---
OR IS LIFE LIKE A FORGED MASTERPIECE?
Zippythepinhead.com
Little Zippy even had a sports bent---
IS LIFE LIKE A STEROID SCANDAL?
OR...?
But Little Zippy's laundry bent was the most **bent** bent of **all** of his bents!
WHAT'S LIFE ALL ABOUT, LITTLE ZIPPY..?
I REMEMBER!
BRIGHTER BRIGHTS!

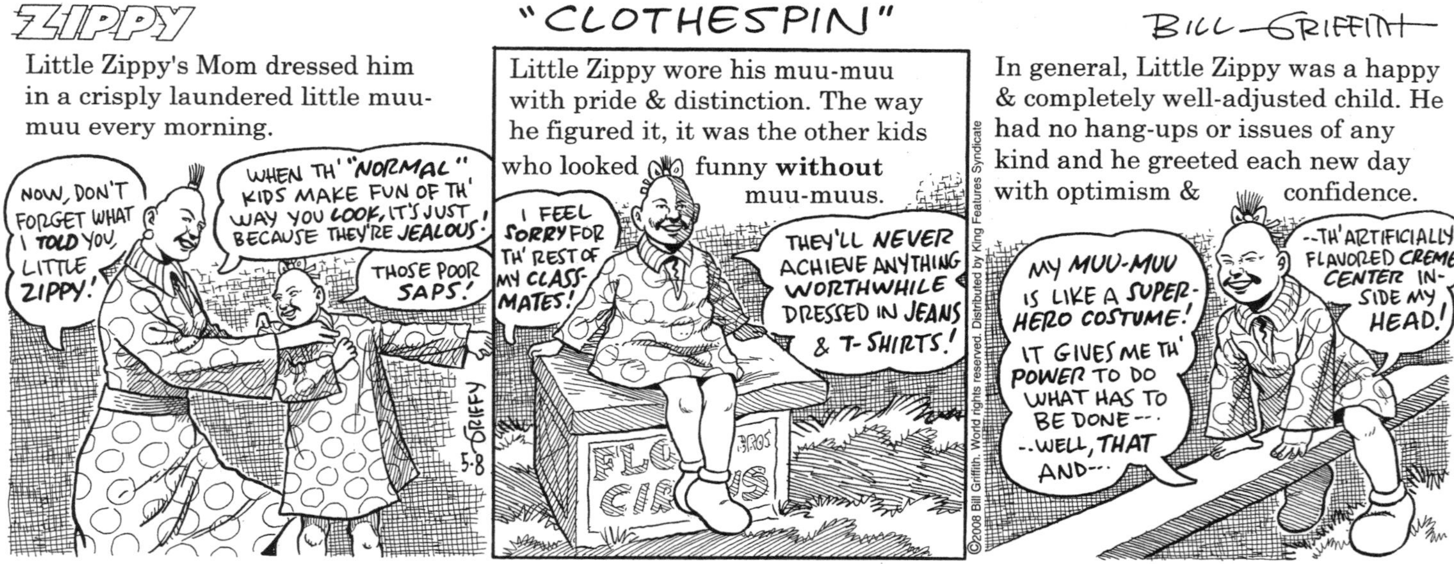
ZIPPY
"CLOTHESPIN"
BILL GRIFFITH
Little Zippy's Mom dressed him in a crisply laundered little muu-muu every morning.
NOW, DON'T FORGET WHAT I TOLD YOU, LITTLE ZIPPY!
WHEN TH' "NORMAL" KIDS MAKE FUN OF TH' WAY YOU LOOK, IT'S JUST BECAUSE THEY'RE JEALOUS!
THOSE POOR SAPS!
GRIFFY 5-8
Little Zippy wore his muu-muu with pride & distinction. The way he figured it, it was the other kids who looked funny **without** muu-muus.
I FEEL SORRY FOR TH' REST OF MY CLASSMATES!
THEY'LL NEVER ACHIEVE ANYTHING WORTHWHILE DRESSED IN JEANS & T-SHIRTS!
©2008 Bill Griffith. World rights reserved. Distributed by King Features Syndicate
In general, Little Zippy was a happy & completely well-adjusted child. He had no hang-ups or issues of any kind and he greeted each new day with optimism & confidence.
MY MUU-MUU IS LIKE A SUPER-HERO COSTUME!
IT GIVES ME TH' POWER TO DO WHAT HAS TO BE DONE--- --WELL, THAT AND--.
--TH' ARTIFICIALLY FLAVORED CREME CENTER INSIDE MY HEAD!

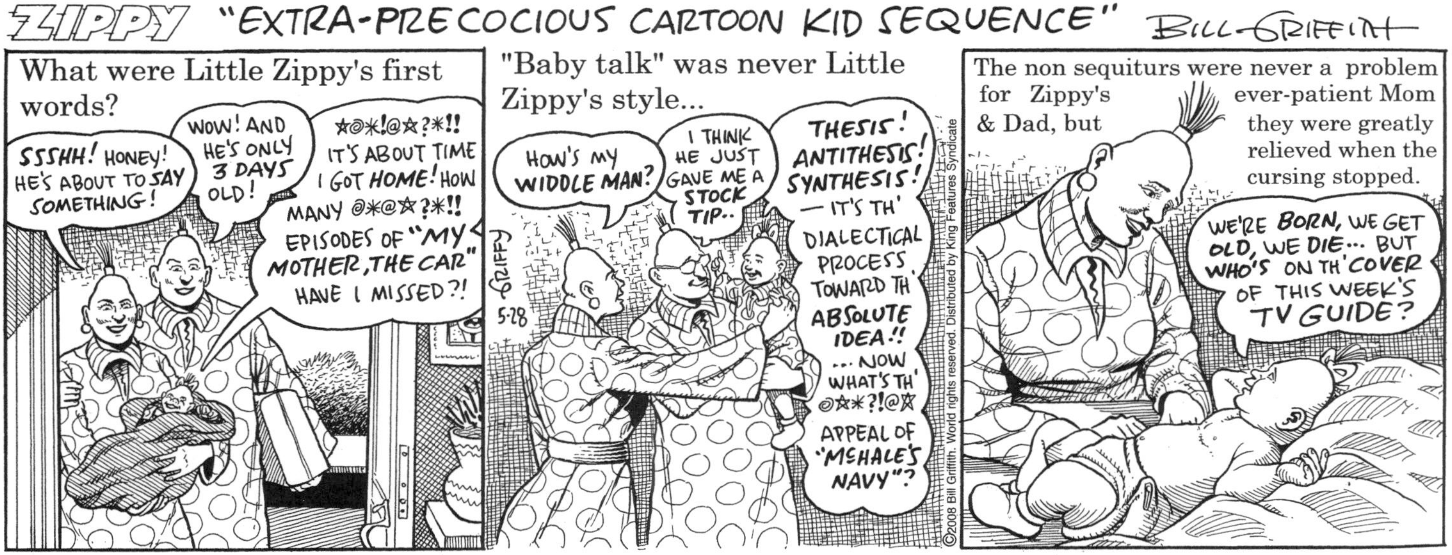
ZIPPY
"EXTRA-PRECOCIOUS CARTOON KID SEQUENCE"
BILL GRIFFITH
What were Little Zippy's first words?
SSSHH! HONEY! HE'S ABOUT TO SAY SOMETHING!
WOW! AND HE'S ONLY 3 DAYS OLD!
☆@✱!@☆?✱!! IT'S ABOUT TIME I GOT HOME! HOW MANY @✱@☆?✱!! EPISODES OF "MY MOTHER, THE CAR" HAVE I MISSED?!
"Baby talk" was never Little Zippy's style...
GRIFFY 5-28
HOW'S MY WIDDLE MAN?
I THINK HE JUST GAVE ME A STOCK TIP..
THESIS! ANTITHESIS! SYNTHESIS! — IT'S TH' DIALECTICAL PROCESS TOWARD TH' ABSOLUTE IDEA!! ... NOW WHAT'S TH' @☆✱?!@☆ APPEAL OF "McHALE'S NAVY"?
©2008 Bill Griffith. World rights reserved. Distributed by King Features Syndicate
The non sequiturs were never a problem for Zippy's ever-patient Mom & Dad, but they were greatly relieved when the cursing stopped.
WE'RE BORN, WE GET OLD, WE DIE... BUT WHO'S ON TH' COVER OF THIS WEEK'S TV GUIDE?

117

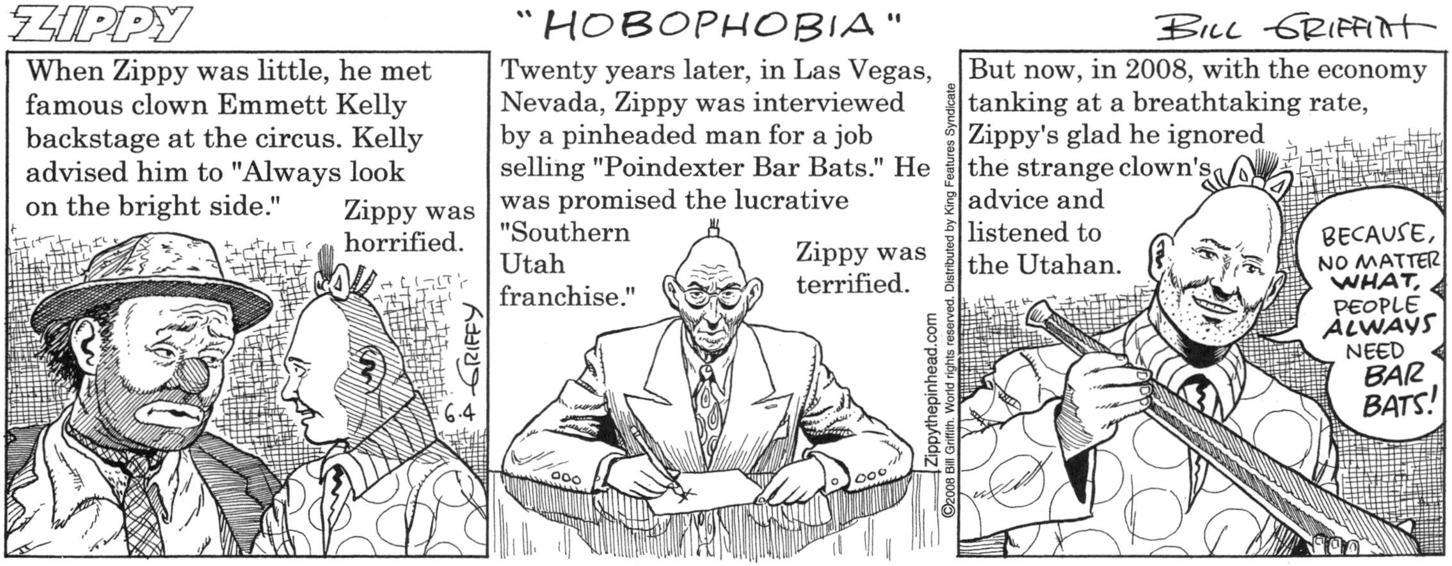
ZIPPY
"HOBOPHOBIA"
BILL GRIFFITH
When Zippy was little, he met famous clown Emmett Kelly backstage at the circus. Kelly advised him to "Always look on the bright side."
Zippy was horrified.
GRIFFY 6-4
Twenty years later, in Las Vegas, Nevada, Zippy was interviewed by a pinheaded man for a job selling "Poindexter Bar Bats." He was promised the lucrative "Southern Utah franchise."
Zippy was terrified.
©2008 Bill Griffith. World rights reserved. Distributed by King Features Syndicate
Zippythepinhead.com
But now, in 2008, with the economy tanking at a breathtaking rate, Zippy's glad he ignored the strange clown's advice and listened to the Utahan.
BECAUSE, NO MATTER WHAT, PEOPLE ALWAYS NEED BAR BATS!

118

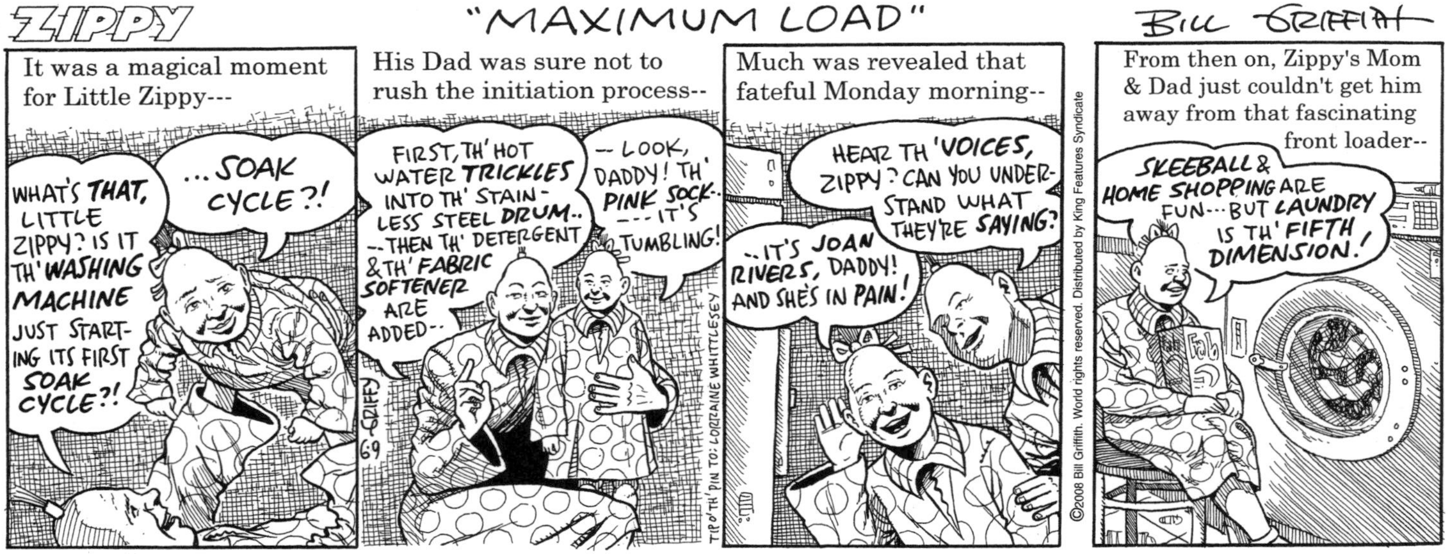
ZIPPY
"MAXIMUM LOAD"
BILL GRIFFITH
It was a magical moment for Little Zippy---
WHAT'S THAT, LITTLE ZIPPY? IS IT TH' WASHING MACHINE JUST STARTING ITS FIRST SOAK CYCLE?!
...SOAK CYCLE?!
GRIFFY 6 9
His Dad was sure not to rush the initiation process--
FIRST, TH' HOT WATER TRICKLES INTO TH' STAINLESS STEEL DRUM.. --THEN TH' DETERGENT & TH' FABRIC SOFTENER ARE ADDED--
--LOOK, DADDY! TH' PINK SOCK---IT'S TUMBLING!
TIP O' TH' PIN TO: LORRAINE WHITTLESEY
Much was revealed that fateful Monday morning--
HEAR TH 'VOICES,' ZIPPY? CAN YOU UNDERSTAND WHAT THEY'RE SAYING?
--IT'S JOAN RIVERS, DADDY! AND SHE'S IN PAIN!
©2008 Bill Griffith. World rights reserved. Distributed by King Features Syndicate
From then on, Zippy's Mom & Dad just couldn't get him away from that fascinating front loader--
SKEEBALL & HOME SHOPPING ARE FUN...BUT LAUNDRY IS TH' FIFTH DIMENSION!
Fab

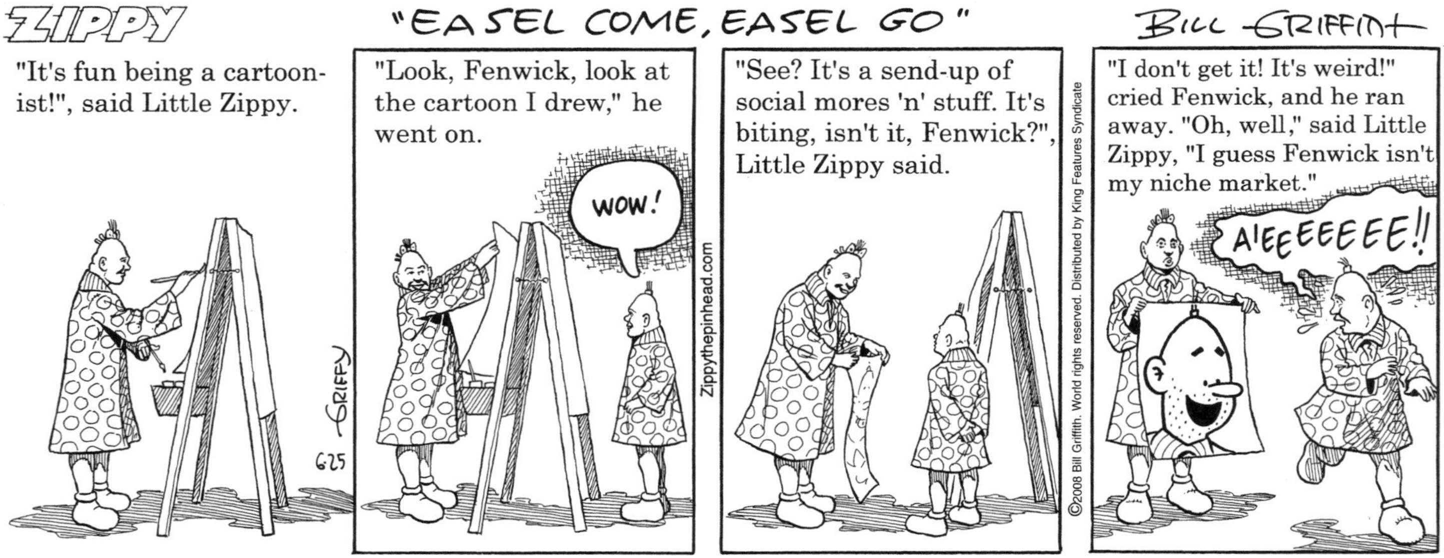
ZIPPY
"EASEL COME, EASEL GO"
BILL GRIFFITH
"It's fun being a cartoonist!", said Little Zippy.
GRIFFY 6·25
"Look, Fenwick, look at the cartoon I drew," he went on.
WOW!
Zippythepinhead.com
"See? It's a send-up of social mores 'n' stuff. It's biting, isn't it, Fenwick?", Little Zippy said.
©2008 Bill Griffith. World rights reserved. Distributed by King Features Syndicate
"I don't get it! It's weird!" cried Fenwick, and he ran away. "Oh, well," said Little Zippy, "I guess Fenwick isn't my niche market."
AIEEEEEEE!!

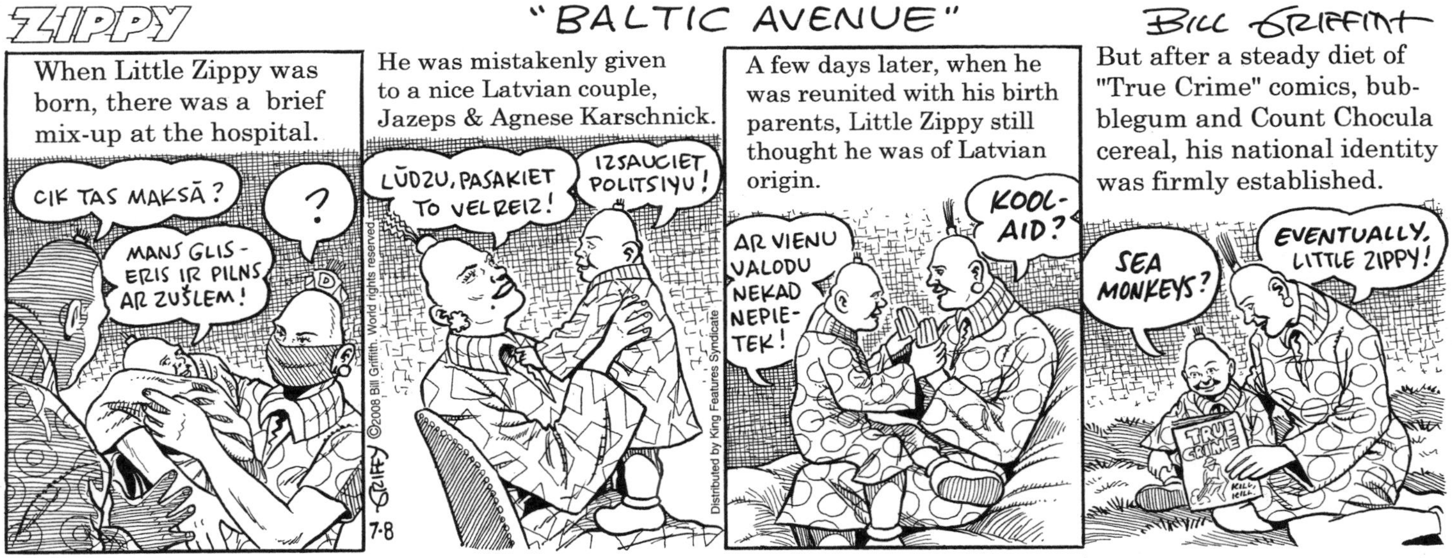
ZIPPY
"BALTIC AVENUE"
BILL GRIFFITH
When Little Zippy was born, there was a brief mix-up at the hospital.
CIK TAS MAKSĀ?
?
MANS GLIS-ERIS IR PILNS AR ZUŠLEM!
GRIFFY
7·8
©2008 Bill Griffith. World rights reserved
He was mistakenly given to a nice Latvian couple, Jazeps & Agnese Karschnick.
LŪDZU, PASAKIET TO VELREIZ!
IZSAUCIET POLITSIYU!
Distributed by King Features Syndicate
A few days later, when he was reunited with his birth parents, Little Zippy still thought he was of Latvian origin.
AR VIENU VALODU NEKAD NEPIE-TEK!
KOOL-AID?
But after a steady diet of "True Crime" comics, bubblegum and Count Chocula cereal, his national identity was firmly established.
SEA MONKEYS?
EVENTUALLY, LITTLE ZIPPY!
TRUE CRIME

119

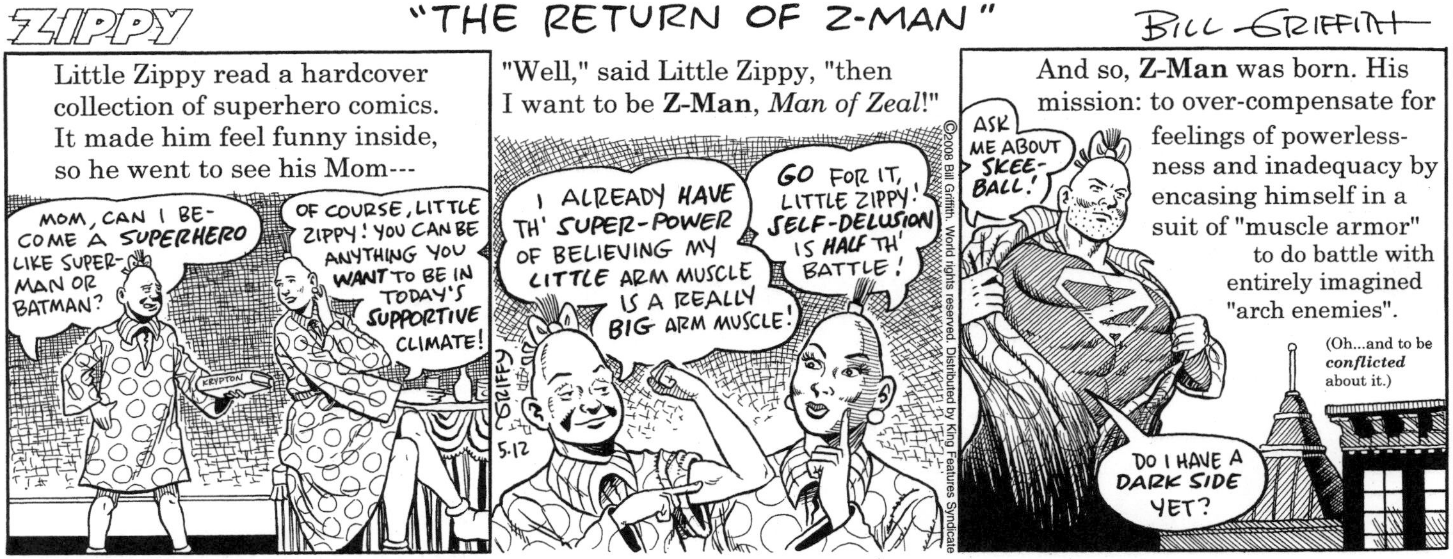
ZIPPY
"THE RETURN OF Z-MAN"
BILL GRIFFITH
Little Zippy read a hardcover collection of superhero comics. It made him feel funny inside, so he went to see his Mom---
MOM, CAN I BE-COME A SUPERHERO LIKE SUPER-MAN OR BATMAN?
OF COURSE, LITTLE ZIPPY! YOU CAN BE ANYTHING YOU WANT TO BE IN TODAY'S SUPPORTIVE CLIMATE!
KRYPTON
"Well," said Little Zippy, "then I want to be Z-Man, Man of Zeal!"
I ALREADY HAVE TH' SUPER-POWER OF BELIEVING MY LITTLE ARM MUSCLE IS A REALLY BIG ARM MUSCLE!
GO FOR IT, LITTLE ZIPPY! SELF-DELUSION IS HALF TH' BATTLE!
GRIFFY
5·12
©2008 Bill Griffith. World rights reserved. Distributed by King Features Syndicate
And so, Z-Man was born. His mission: to over-compensate for feelings of powerlessness and inadequacy by encasing himself in a suit of "muscle armor" to do battle with entirely imagined "arch enemies".
(Oh...and to be conflicted about it.)
ASK ME ABOUT SKEE-BALL!
DO I HAVE A DARK SIDE YET?

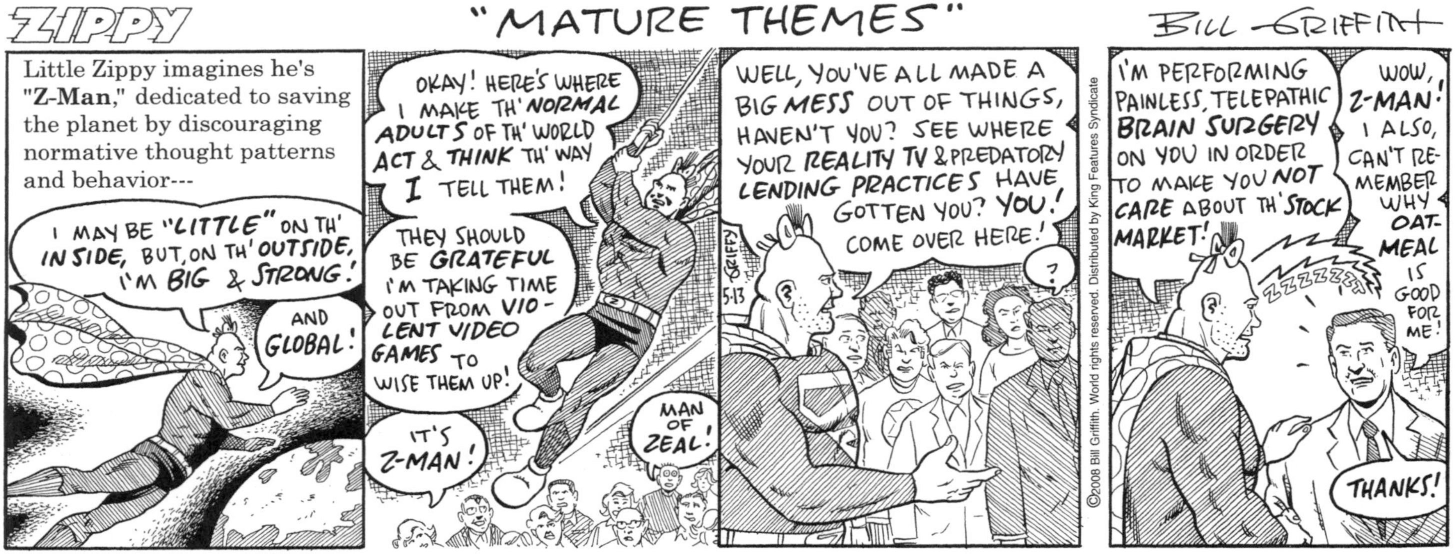
ZIPPY
"MATURE THEMES"
BILL GRIFFITH
Little Zippy imagines he's "Z-Man," dedicated to saving the planet by discouraging normative thought patterns and behavior---
I MAY BE "LITTLE" ON TH' INSIDE, BUT, ON TH' OUTSIDE, I'M BIG & STRONG!
AND GLOBAL!
OKAY! HERE'S WHERE I MAKE TH' NORMAL ADULTS OF TH' WORLD ACT & THINK TH' WAY I TELL THEM!
THEY SHOULD BE GRATEFUL I'M TAKING TIME OUT FROM VIOLENT VIDEO GAMES TO WISE THEM UP!
IT'S Z-MAN!
MAN OF ZEAL!
WELL, YOU'VE ALL MADE A BIG MESS OUT OF THINGS, HAVEN'T YOU? SEE WHERE YOUR REALITY TV & PREDATORY LENDING PRACTICES HAVE GOTTEN YOU? YOU! COME OVER HERE!
?
GRIFFY 5·13
I'M PERFORMING PAINLESS, TELEPATHIC BRAIN SURGERY ON YOU IN ORDER TO MAKE YOU NOT CARE ABOUT TH' STOCK MARKET!
ZZZZZZZ
WOW, Z-MAN! I ALSO, CAN'T REMEMBER WHY OATMEAL IS GOOD FOR ME!
THANKS!
©2008 Bill Griffith. World rights reserved. Distributed by King Features Syndicate

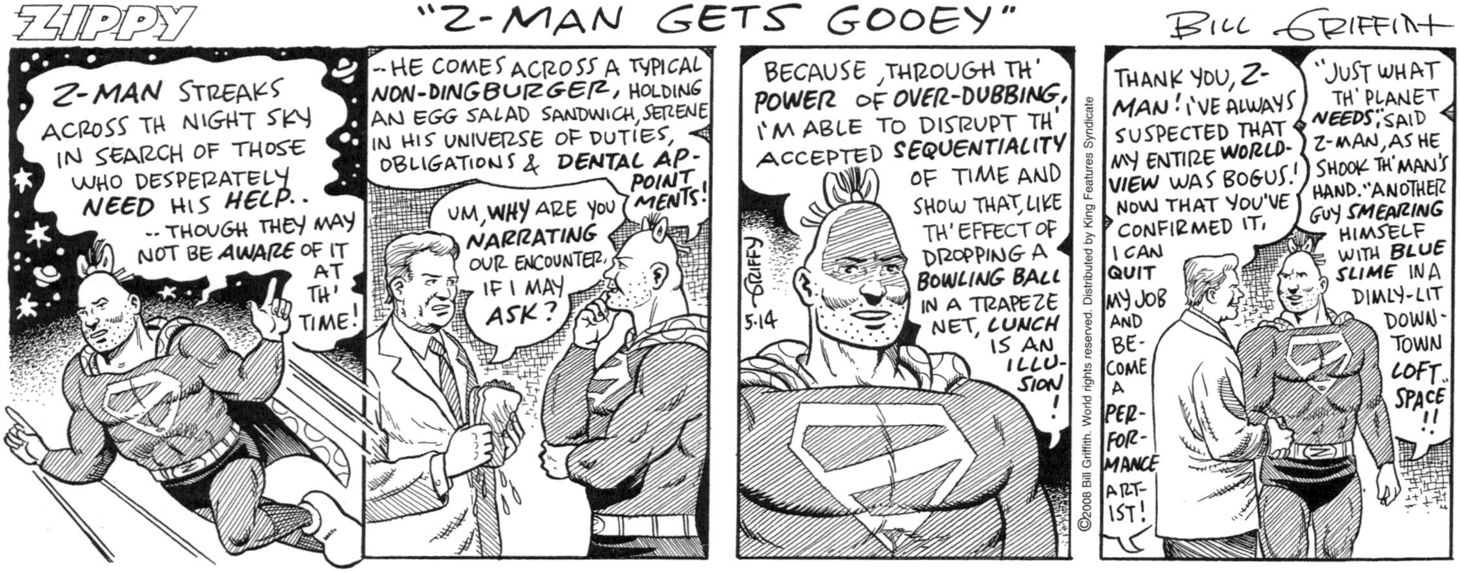
ZIPPY
"Z-MAN GETS GOOEY"
BILL GRIFFITH
Z-MAN STREAKS ACROSS TH NIGHT SKY IN SEARCH OF THOSE WHO DESPERATELY NEED HIS HELP..
--THOUGH THEY MAY NOT BE AWARE OF IT AT TH' TIME!
--HE COMES ACROSS A TYPICAL NON-DINGBURGER, HOLDING AN EGG SALAD SANDWICH, SERENE IN HIS UNIVERSE OF DUTIES, OBLIGATIONS & DENTAL APPOINTMENTS!
UM, WHY ARE YOU NARRATING OUR ENCOUNTER, IF I MAY ASK?
BECAUSE, THROUGH TH' POWER OF OVER-DUBBING, I'M ABLE TO DISRUPT TH' ACCEPTED SEQUENTIALITY OF TIME AND SHOW THAT, LIKE TH' EFFECT OF DROPPING A BOWLING BALL IN A TRAPEZE NET, LUNCH IS AN ILLUSION!
GRIFFY 5·14
©2008 Bill Griffith. World rights reserved. Distributed by King Features Syndicate
THANK YOU, Z-MAN! I'VE ALWAYS SUSPECTED THAT MY ENTIRE WORLD-VIEW WAS BOGUS! NOW THAT YOU'VE CONFIRMED IT, I CAN QUIT MY JOB AND BECOME A PERFORMANCE ARTIST!
"JUST WHAT TH' PLANET NEEDS," SAID Z-MAN, AS HE SHOOK TH' MAN'S HAND. "ANOTHER GUY SMEARING HIMSELF WITH BLUE SLIME IN A DIMLY-LIT DOWNTOWN LOFT SPACE!!"

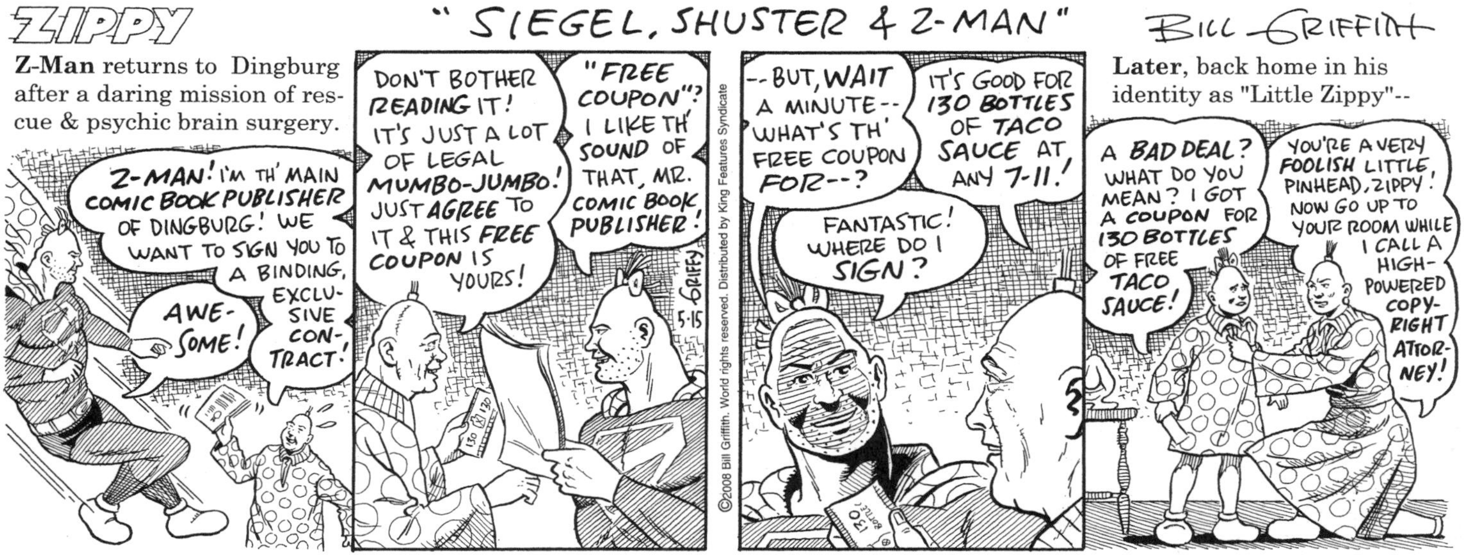
ZIPPY
"SIEGEL, SHUSTER & Z-MAN"
BILL GRIFFITH
Z-Man returns to Dingburg after a daring mission of rescue & psychic brain surgery.
Z-MAN! I'M TH' MAIN COMIC BOOK PUBLISHER OF DINGBURG! WE WANT TO SIGN YOU TO A BINDING, EXCLUSIVE CONTRACT!
AWESOME!
DON'T BOTHER READING IT! IT'S JUST A LOT OF LEGAL MUMBO-JUMBO! JUST AGREE TO IT & THIS FREE COUPON IS YOURS!
"FREE COUPON"? I LIKE TH' SOUND OF THAT, MR. COMIC BOOK PUBLISHER!
GRIFFY 5·15
©2008 Bill Griffith. World rights reserved. Distributed by King Features Syndicate
--BUT, WAIT A MINUTE-- WHAT'S TH' FREE COUPON FOR--?
IT'S GOOD FOR 130 BOTTLES OF TACO SAUCE AT ANY 7-11!
FANTASTIC! WHERE DO I SIGN?
Later, back home in his identity as "Little Zippy"--
A BAD DEAL? WHAT DO YOU MEAN? I GOT A COUPON FOR 130 BOTTLES OF FREE TACO SAUCE!
YOU'RE A VERY FOOLISH LITTLE PINHEAD, ZIPPY! NOW GO UP TO YOUR ROOM WHILE I CALL A HIGH-POWERED COPYRIGHT ATTORNEY!

120

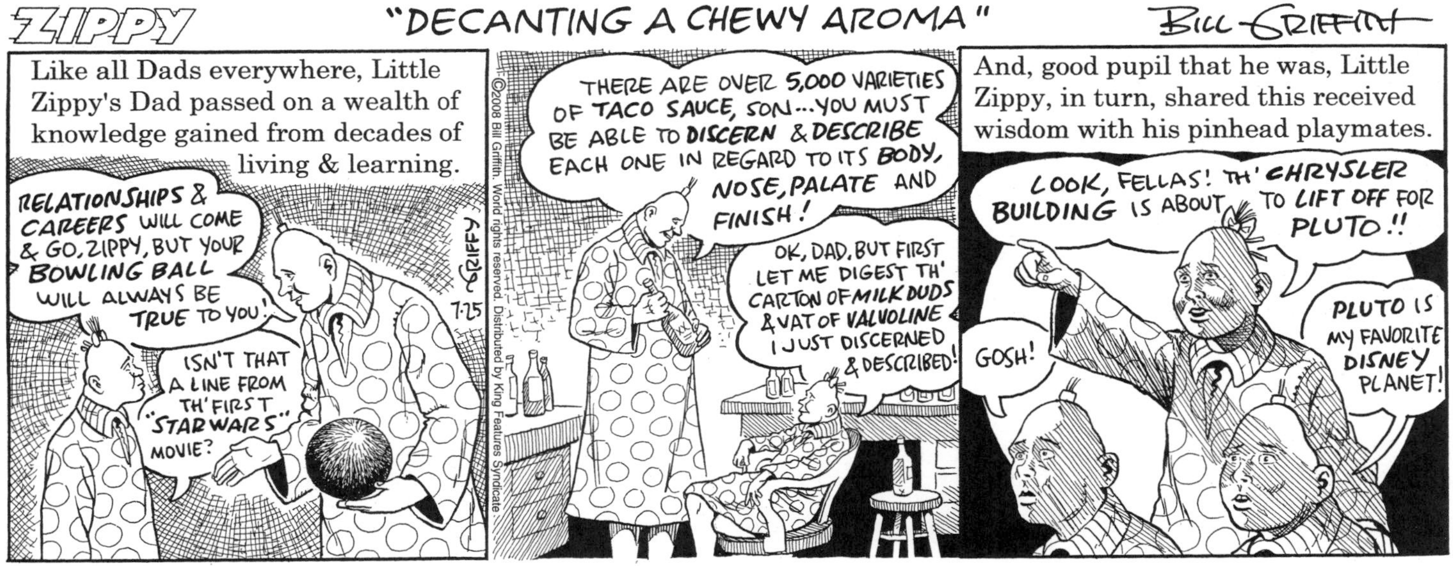
ZIPPY
"DECANTING A CHEWY AROMA"
BILL GRIFFITH
Like all Dads everywhere, Little Zippy's Dad passed on a wealth of knowledge gained from decades of living & learning.
RELATIONSHIPS & CAREERS WILL COME & GO, ZIPPY, BUT YOUR BOWLING BALL WILL ALWAYS BE TRUE TO YOU!
ISN'T THAT A LINE FROM TH' FIRST "STAR WARS" MOVIE?
GRIFFY 7·25
©2008 Bill Griffith. World rights reserved. Distributed by King Features Syndicate
THERE ARE OVER 5,000 VARIETIES OF TACO SAUCE, SON...YOU MUST BE ABLE TO DISCERN & DESCRIBE EACH ONE IN REGARD TO ITS BODY, NOSE, PALATE AND FINISH!
OK, DAD, BUT FIRST LET ME DIGEST TH' CARTON OF MILK DUDS & VAT OF VALVOLINE I JUST DISCERNED & DESCRIBED!
And, good pupil that he was, Little Zippy, in turn, shared this received wisdom with his pinhead playmates.
LOOK, FELLAS! TH' CHRYSLER BUILDING IS ABOUT TO LIFT OFF FOR PLUTO!!
GOSH!
PLUTO IS MY FAVORITE DISNEY PLANET!

121

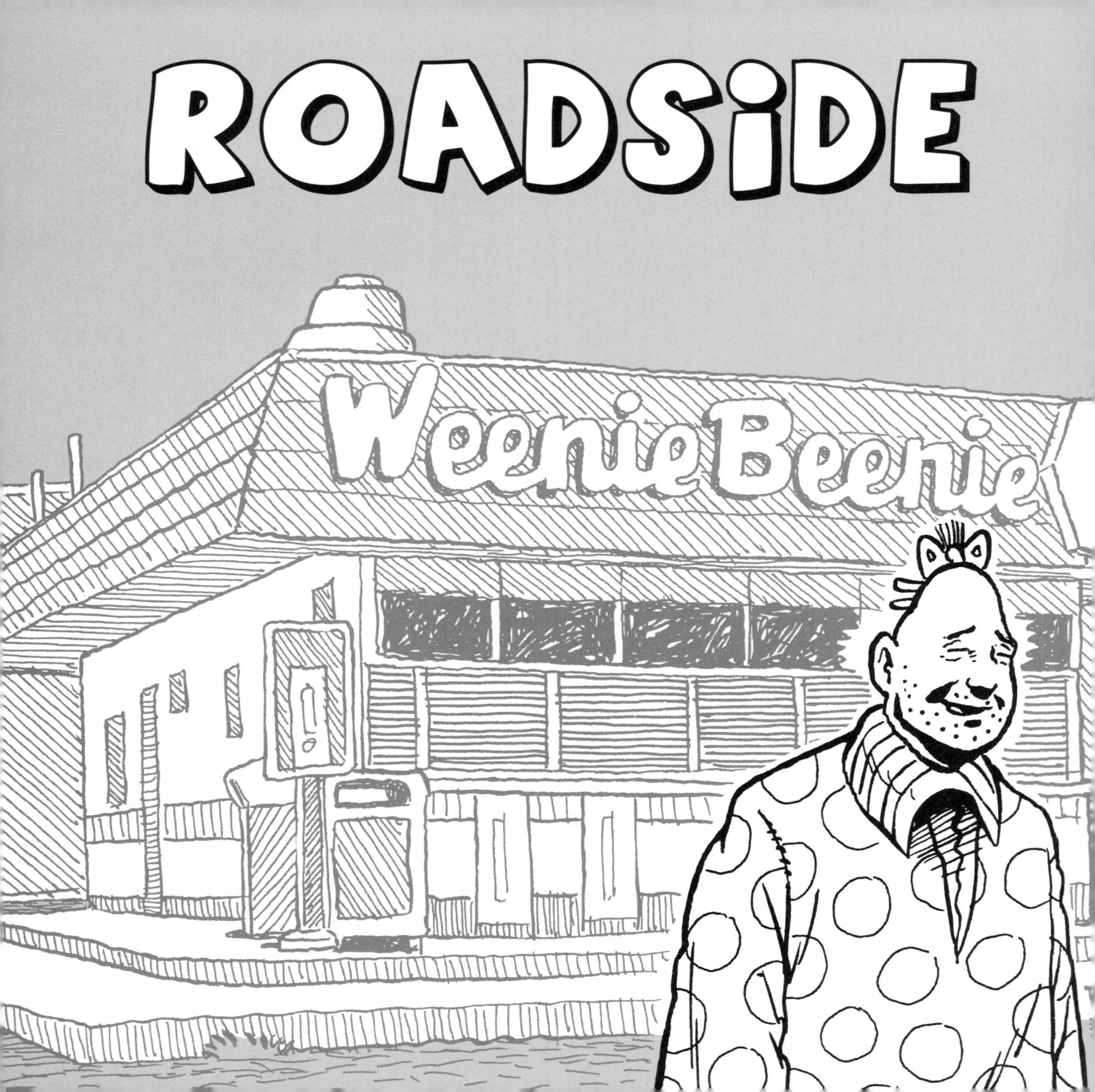
ROADSIDE
Weenie Beenie

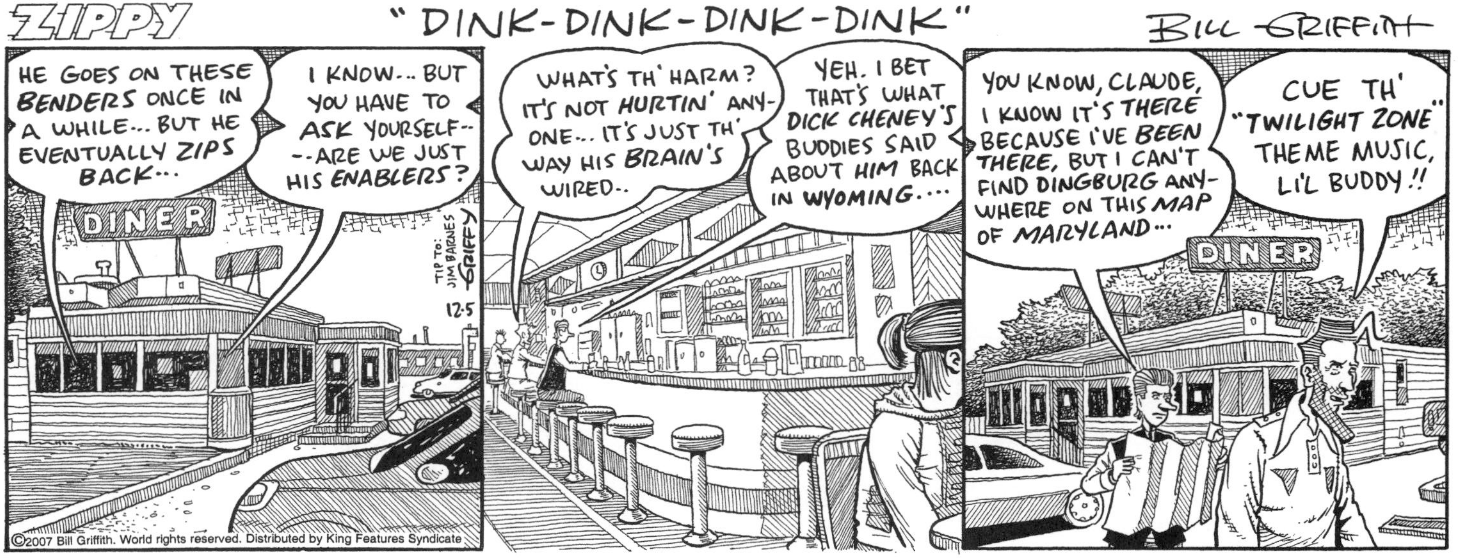
ZIPPY
"DINK-DINK-DINK-DINK"
BILL GRIFFITH
HE GOES ON THESE BENDERS ONCE IN A WHILE... BUT HE EVENTUALLY ZIPS BACK...
I KNOW... BUT YOU HAVE TO ASK YOURSELF-- --ARE WE JUST HIS ENABLERS?
DINER
TIP TO: JIM BARNES GRIFFY 12-5
WHAT'S TH' HARM? IT'S NOT HURTIN' ANY-ONE... IT'S JUST TH' WAY HIS BRAIN'S WIRED..
YEH. I BET THAT'S WHAT DICK CHENEY'S BUDDIES SAID ABOUT HIM BACK IN WYOMING....
YOU KNOW, CLAUDE, I KNOW IT'S THERE BECAUSE I'VE BEEN THERE, BUT I CAN'T FIND DINGBURG ANY-WHERE ON THIS MAP OF MARYLAND...
CUE TH' "TWILIGHT ZONE" THEME MUSIC, LI'L BUDDY!!
DINER
©2007 Bill Griffith. World rights reserved. Distributed by King Features Syndicate

122

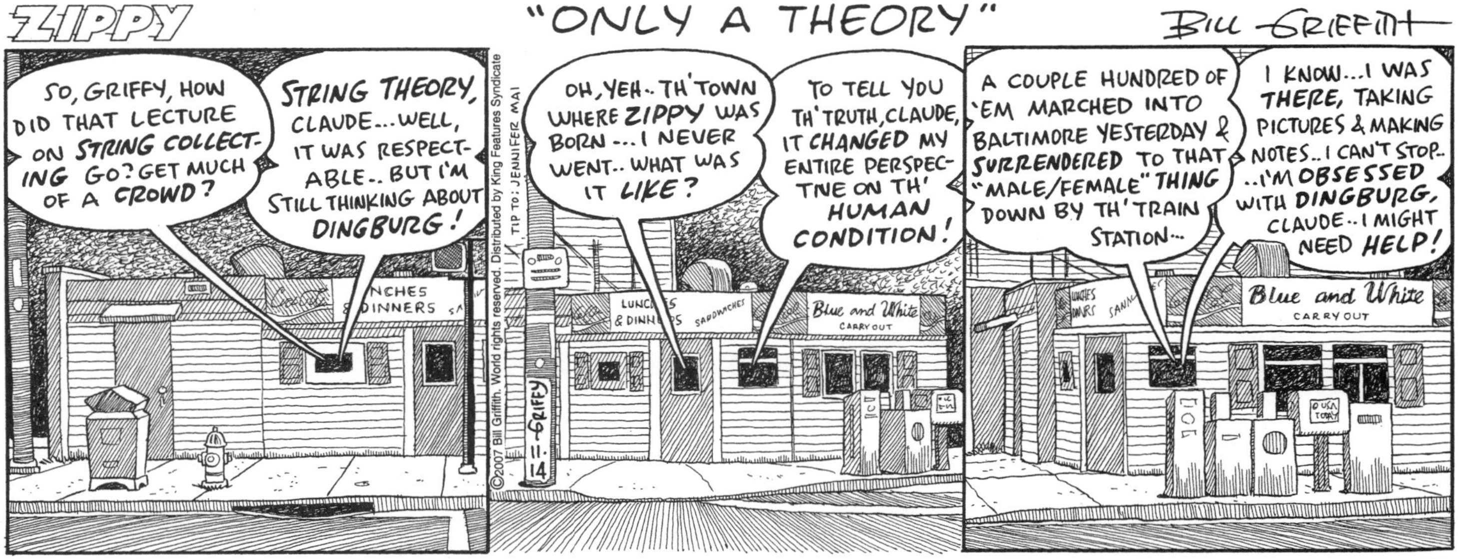
ZIPPY
"ONLY A THEORY"
BILL GRIFFITH
SO, GRIFFY, HOW DID THAT LECTURE ON STRING COLLECT-ING GO? GET MUCH OF A CROWD?
STRING THEORY, CLAUDE... WELL, IT WAS RESPECT-ABLE.. BUT I'M STILL THINKING ABOUT DINGBURG!
©2007 Bill Griffith. World rights reserved. Distributed by King Features Syndicate
TIP TO: JENNIFER MAI
GRIFFY 11-14
OH, YEH.. TH' TOWN WHERE ZIPPY WAS BORN... I NEVER WENT.. WHAT WAS IT LIKE?
TO TELL YOU TH' TRUTH, CLAUDE, IT CHANGED MY ENTIRE PERSPEC-TIVE ON TH' HUMAN CONDITION!
Blue and White CARRY OUT
A COUPLE HUNDRED OF 'EM MARCHED INTO BALTIMORE YESTERDAY & SURRENDERED TO THAT "MALE/FEMALE" THING DOWN BY TH' TRAIN STATION...
I KNOW... I WAS THERE, TAKING PICTURES & MAKING NOTES.. I CAN'T STOP.. ..I'M OBSESSED WITH DINGBURG, CLAUDE.. I MIGHT NEED HELP!
Blue and White CARRY OUT

123

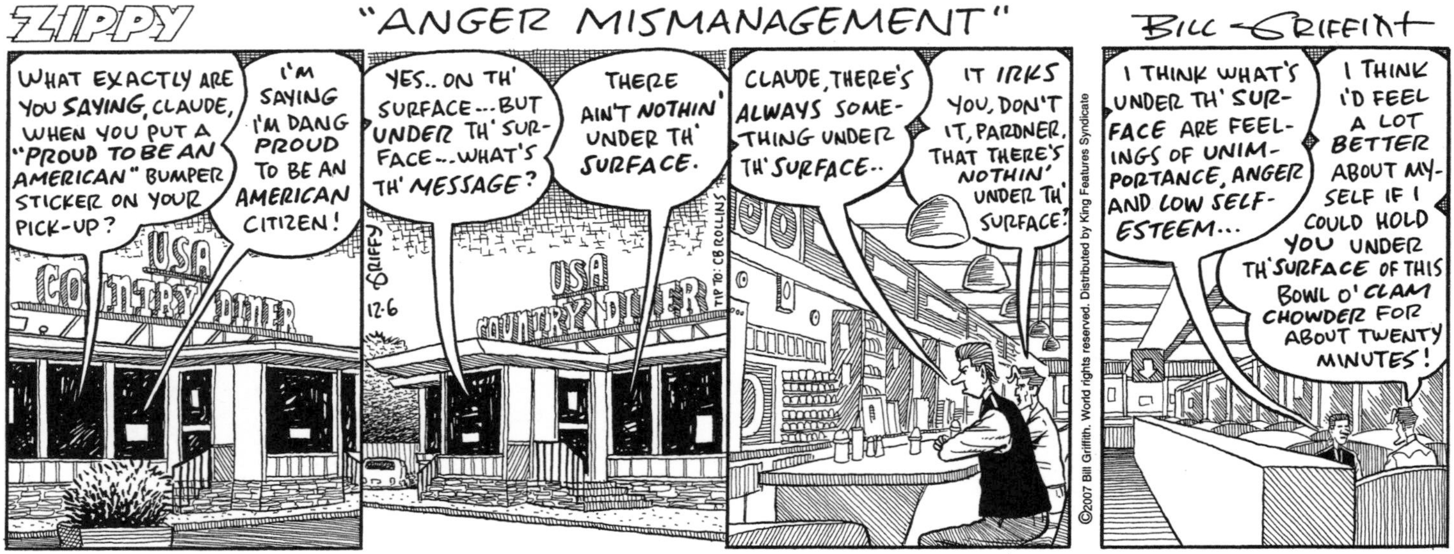
ZIPPY
"ANGER MISMANAGEMENT"
BILL GRIFFITH
WHAT EXACTLY ARE YOU SAYING, CLAUDE, WHEN YOU PUT A "PROUD TO BE AN AMERICAN" BUMPER STICKER ON YOUR PICK-UP?
I'M SAYING I'M DANG PROUD TO BE AN AMERICAN CITIZEN!
USA COUNTRY DINER
GRIFFY 12·6
YES.. ON TH' SURFACE--- BUT UNDER TH' SURFACE-..WHAT'S TH' MESSAGE?
THERE AIN'T NOTHIN' UNDER TH' SURFACE.
TIP TO: CB ROLLINS
CLAUDE, THERE'S ALWAYS SOMETHING UNDER TH' SURFACE..
IT IRKS YOU, DON'T IT, PARDNER, THAT THERE'S NOTHIN' UNDER TH' SURFACE?
©2007 Bill Griffith. World rights reserved. Distributed by King Features Syndicate
I THINK WHAT'S UNDER TH' SURFACE ARE FEELINGS OF UNIMPORTANCE, ANGER AND LOW SELF-ESTEEM...
I THINK I'D FEEL A LOT BETTER ABOUT MYSELF IF I COULD HOLD YOU UNDER TH' SURFACE OF THIS BOWL O' CLAM CHOWDER FOR ABOUT TWENTY MINUTES!

124

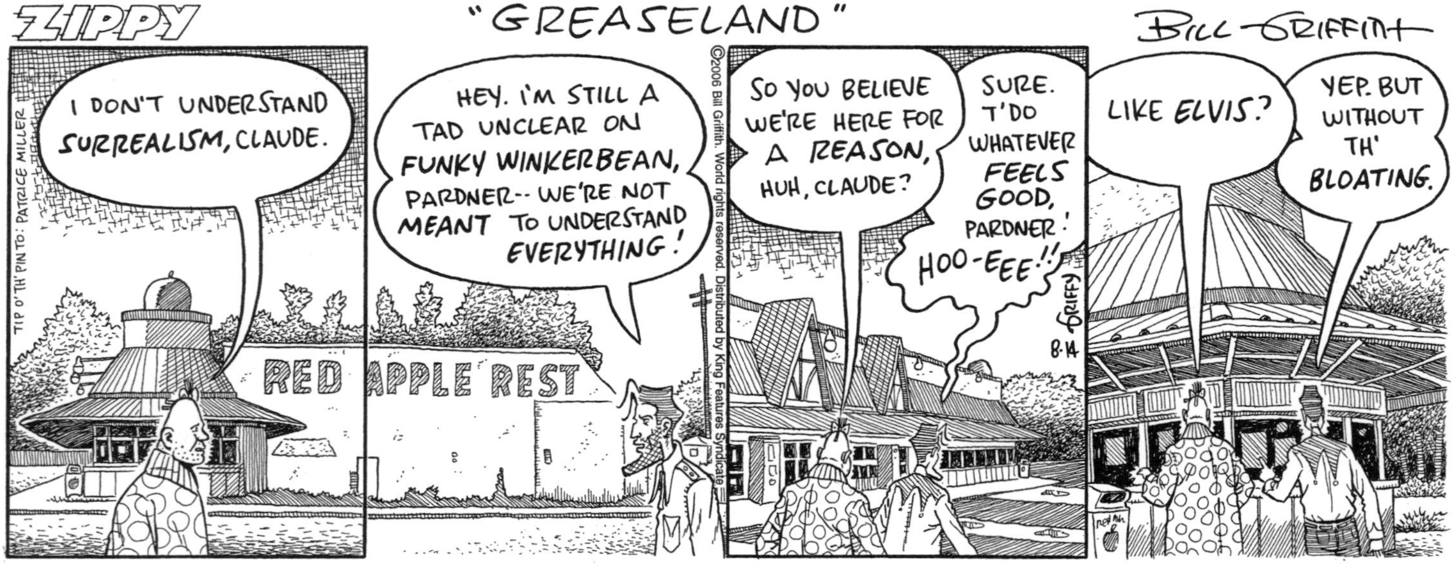
ZIPPY
"GREASELAND"
BILL GRIFFITH
TIP O' TH' PIN TO: PATRICE MILLER
I DON'T UNDERSTAND SURREALISM, CLAUDE.
RED APPLE REST
HEY. I'M STILL A TAD UNCLEAR ON FUNKY WINKERBEAN, PARDNER-- WE'RE NOT MEANT TO UNDERSTAND EVERYTHING!
©2006 Bill Griffith. World rights reserved. Distributed by King Features Syndicate
SO YOU BELIEVE WE'RE HERE FOR A REASON, HUH, CLAUDE?
SURE. T'DO WHATEVER FEELS GOOD, PARDNER!
HOO-EEE!!
GRIFFY 8·14
LIKE ELVIS?
YEP. BUT WITHOUT TH' BLOATING.

125

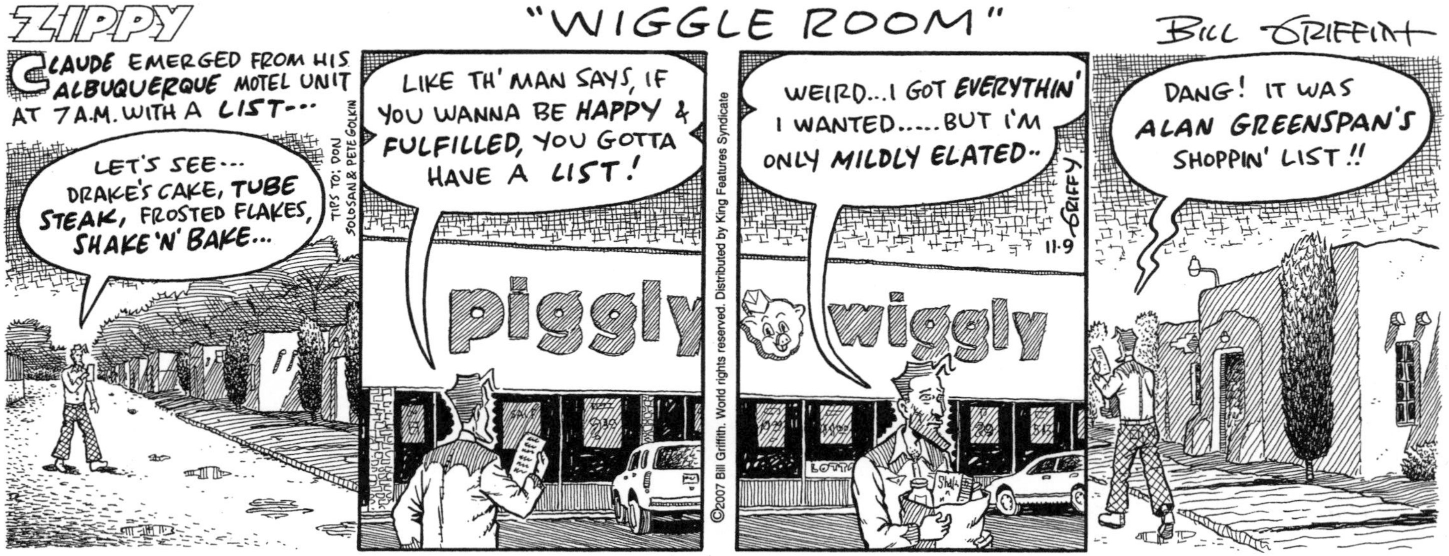
ZIPPY
"WIGGLE ROOM"
BILL GRIFFITH
CLAUDE EMERGED FROM HIS ALBUQUERQUE MOTEL UNIT AT 7 A.M. WITH A LIST---
LET'S SEE--- DRAKE'S CAKE, TUBE STEAK, FROSTED FLAKES, SHAKE 'N' BAKE...
TIPS TO: DON SOLOSAN & PETE GOLKIN
LIKE TH' MAN SAYS, IF YOU WANNA BE HAPPY & FULFILLED, YOU GOTTA HAVE A LIST!
piggly wiggly
©2007 Bill Griffith. World rights reserved. Distributed by King Features Syndicate
WEIRD...I GOT EVERYTHIN' I WANTED.....BUT I'M ONLY MILDLY ELATED..
GRIFFY 11·9
DANG! IT WAS ALAN GREENSPAN'S SHOPPIN' LIST!!

126

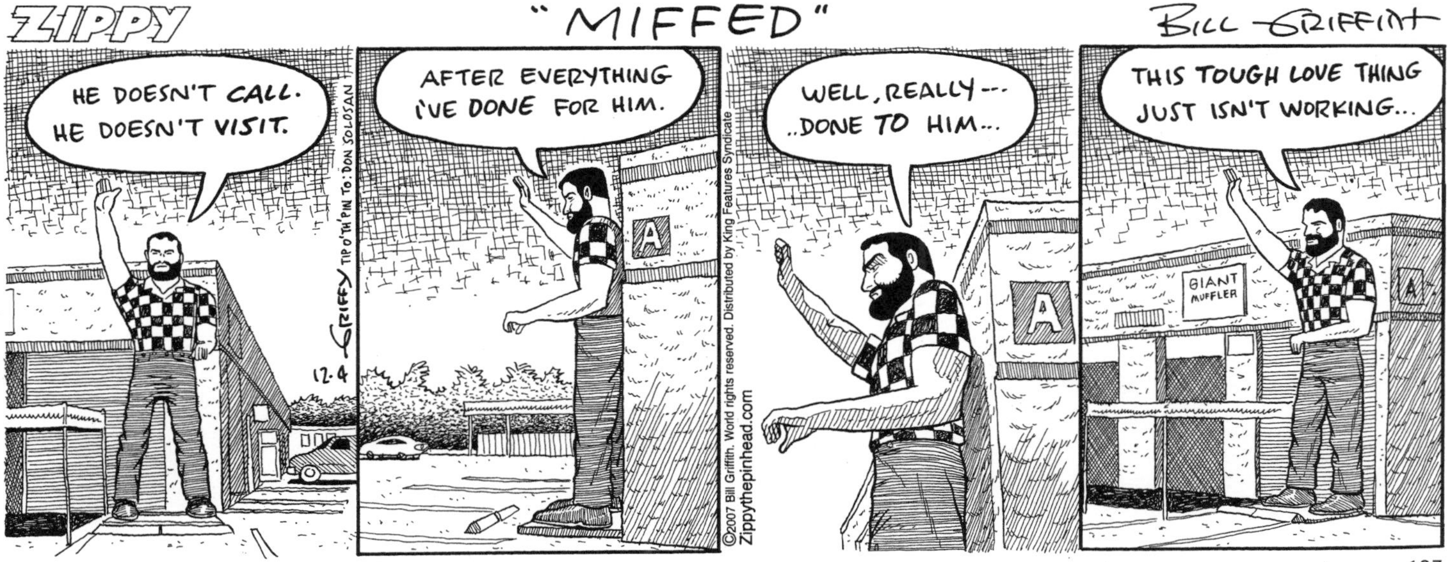
ZIPPY
"MIFFED"
BILL GRIFFITH
HE DOESN'T CALL. HE DOESN'T VISIT.
TIP O'TH PIN TO: DON SOLOSAN
GRIFFY 12·4
AFTER EVERYTHING I'VE DONE FOR HIM.
©2007 Bill Griffith. World rights reserved. Distributed by King Features Syndicate
Zippythepinhead.com
WELL, REALLY--- ..DONE TO HIM...
THIS TOUGH LOVE THING JUST ISN'T WORKING...
GIANT MUFFLER

127

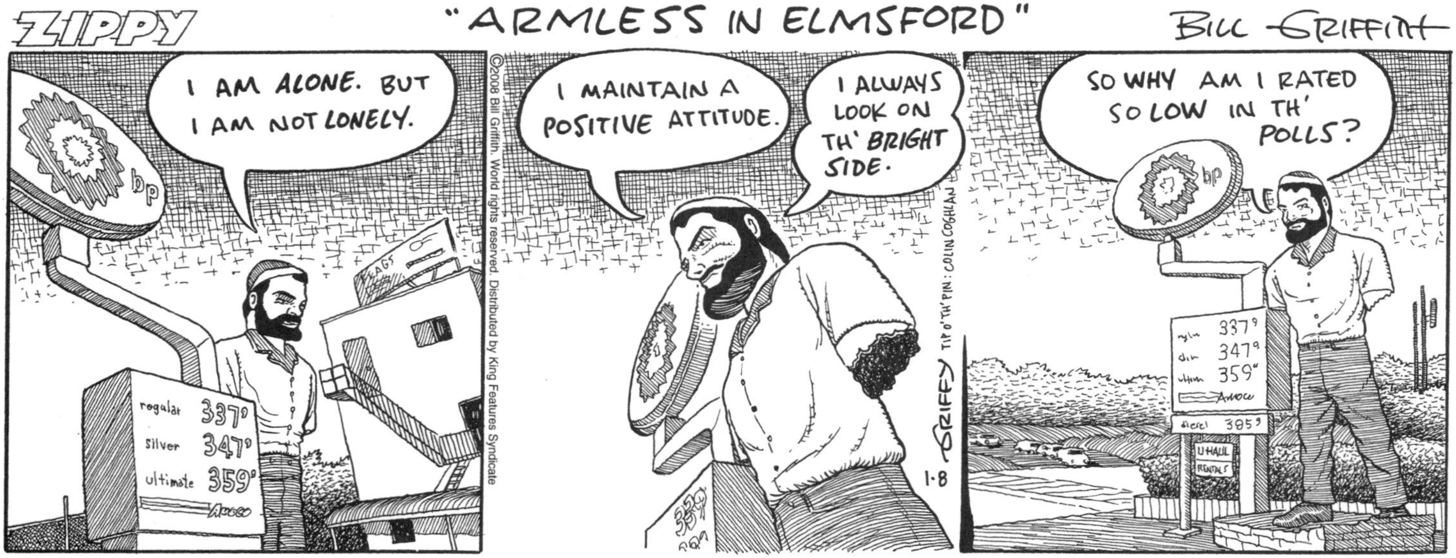
ZIPPY
"ARMLESS IN ELMSFORD"
BILL GRIFFITH
I AM ALONE. BUT I AM NOT LONELY.
regular 337⁹
silver 347⁹
ultimate 359⁹
I MAINTAIN A POSITIVE ATTITUDE.
I ALWAYS LOOK ON TH' BRIGHT SIDE.
©2008 Bill Griffith. World rights reserved. Distributed by King Features Syndicate
TIP O' TH' PIN: COLIN COGHLAN
GRIFFY
1·8
SO WHY AM I RATED SO LOW IN TH' POLLS?
bp
diesel 385⁹
U HAUL RENTALS
128

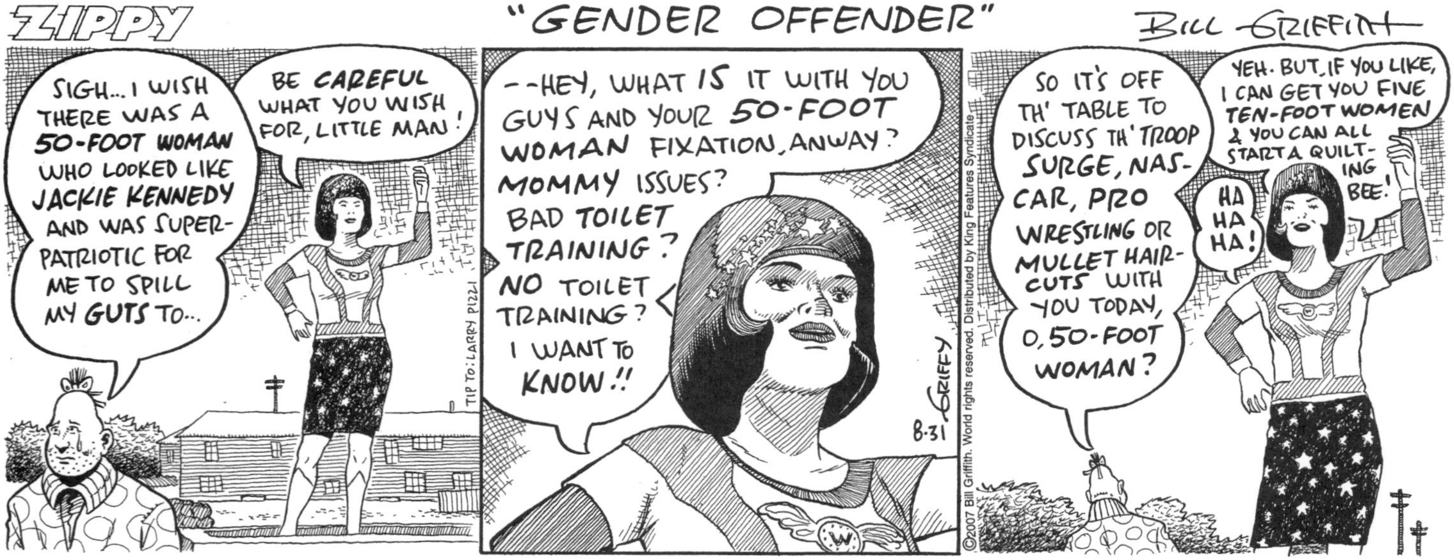
ZIPPY
"GENDER OFFENDER"
BILL GRIFFITH
SIGH... I WISH THERE WAS A 50-FOOT WOMAN WHO LOOKED LIKE JACKIE KENNEDY AND WAS SUPER-PATRIOTIC FOR ME TO SPILL MY GUTS TO...
BE CAREFUL WHAT YOU WISH FOR, LITTLE MAN!
TIP TO: LARRY RIZZI
--HEY, WHAT IS IT WITH YOU GUYS AND YOUR 50-FOOT WOMAN FIXATION, ANWAY? MOMMY ISSUES? BAD TOILET TRAINING? NO TOILET TRAINING? I WANT TO KNOW!!
GRIFFY
8·31
©2007 Bill Griffith. World rights reserved. Distributed by King Features Syndicate
SO IT'S OFF TH' TABLE TO DISCUSS TH' TROOP SURGE, NASCAR, PRO WRESTLING OR MULLET HAIRCUTS WITH YOU TODAY, O, 50-FOOT WOMAN?
YEH. BUT, IF YOU LIKE, I CAN GET YOU FIVE TEN-FOOT WOMEN & YOU CAN ALL START A QUILTING BEE!
HA HA HA!
129

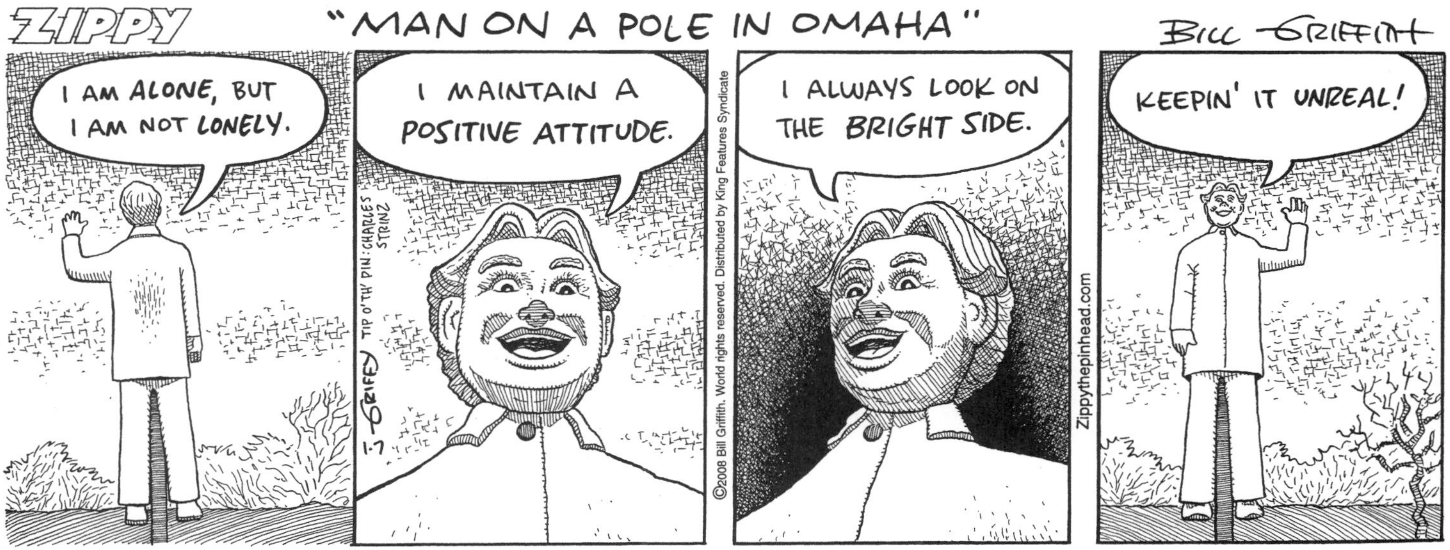
ZIPPY
"MAN ON A POLE IN OMAHA"
BILL GRIFFITH
I AM ALONE, BUT I AM NOT LONELY.
I MAINTAIN A POSITIVE ATTITUDE.
TIP O'TH' PIN: CHARLES STRINZ
GRIFFY 1-7
©2008 Bill Griffith. World rights reserved. Distributed by King Features Syndicate
I ALWAYS LOOK ON THE BRIGHT SIDE.
Zippythepinhead.com
KEEPIN' IT UNREAL!

130

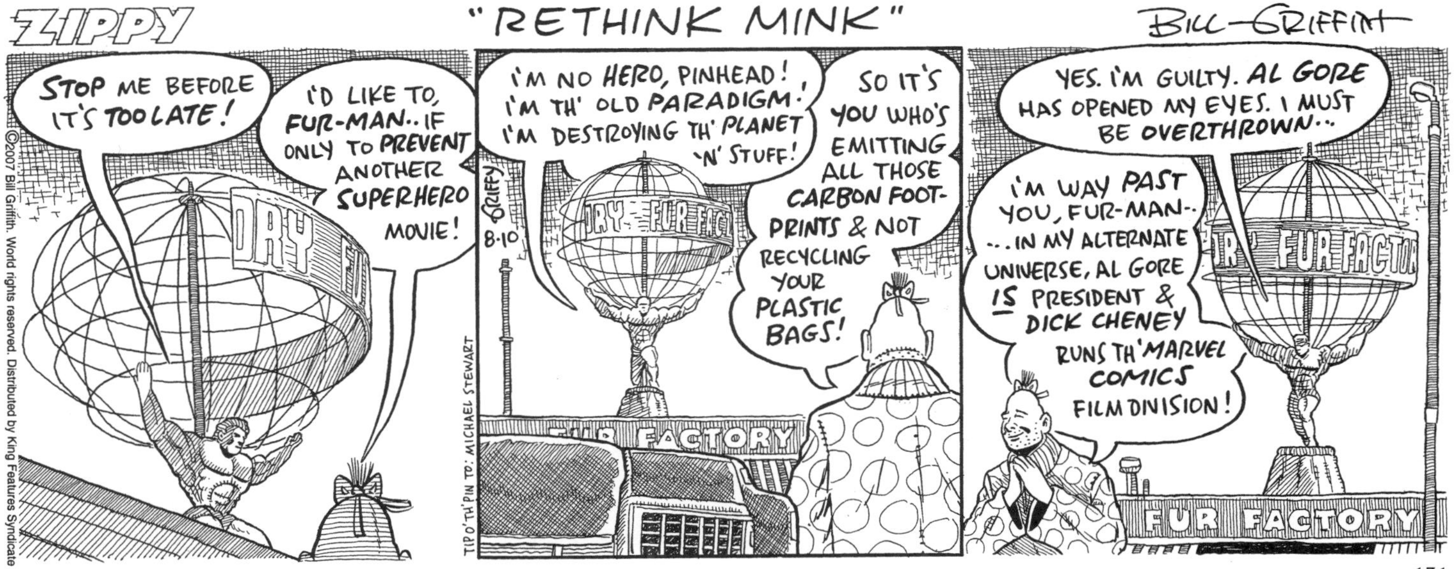
ZIPPY
"RETHINK MINK"
BILL GRIFFITH
©2007 Bill Griffith. World rights reserved. Distributed by King Features Syndicate
STOP ME BEFORE IT'S TOO LATE!
I'D LIKE TO, FUR-MAN.. IF ONLY TO PREVENT ANOTHER SUPERHERO MOVIE!
DRY
GRIFFY 8-10
TIP O' TH' PIN TO: MICHAEL STEWART
I'M NO HERO, PINHEAD! I'M TH' OLD PARADIGM! I'M DESTROYING TH' PLANET 'N' STUFF!
SO IT'S YOU WHO'S EMITTING ALL THOSE CARBON FOOT-PRINTS & NOT RECYCLING YOUR PLASTIC BAGS!
DRY FUR FACT
FUR FACTORY
YES. I'M GUILTY. AL GORE HAS OPENED MY EYES. I MUST BE OVERTHROWN...
I'M WAY PAST YOU, FUR-MAN.. ...IN MY ALTERNATE UNIVERSE, AL GORE IS PRESIDENT & DICK CHENEY RUNS TH' MARVEL COMICS FILM DIVISION!
FUR FACTOR
FUR FACTORY

131

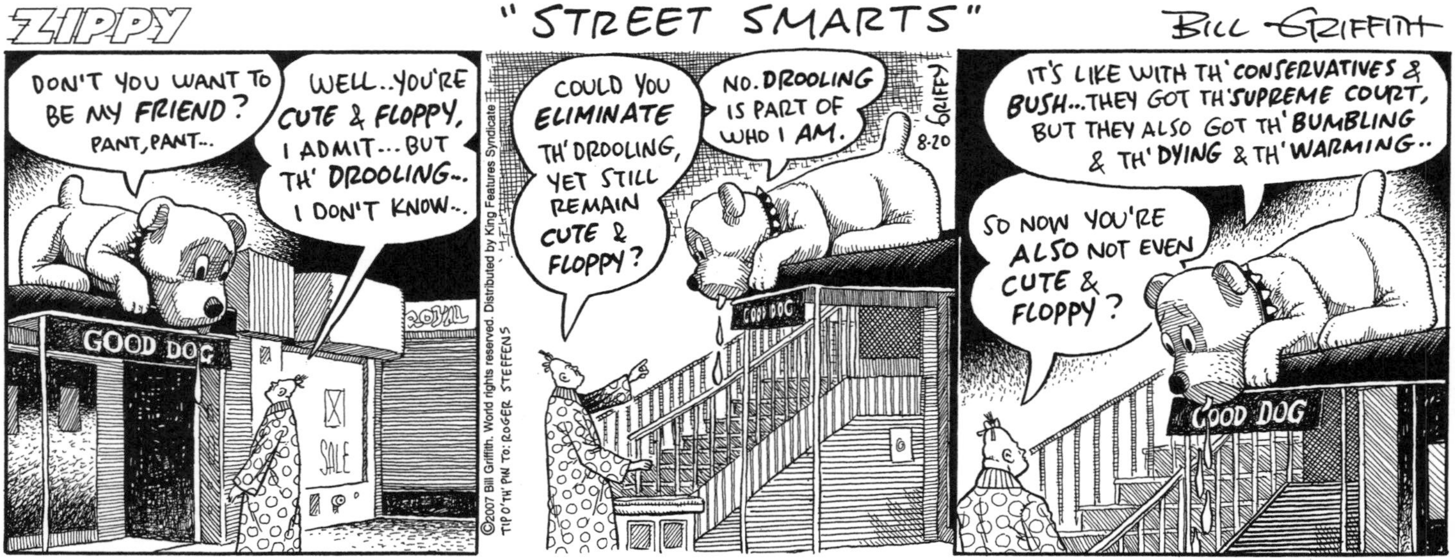
ZIPPY
"STREET SMARTS"
BILL GRIFFITH
DON'T YOU WANT TO BE MY FRIEND? PANT, PANT..
WELL..YOU'RE CUTE & FLOPPY, I ADMIT... BUT TH' DROOLING.. I DON'T KNOW..
GOOD DOG
SALE
COULD YOU ELIMINATE TH' DROOLING, YET STILL REMAIN CUTE & FLOPPY?
NO. DROOLING IS PART OF WHO I AM.
GRIFFY 8-20
©2007 Bill Griffith. World rights reserved. Distributed by King Features Syndicate
TIP O' TH' PIN TO: ROGER STEFFENS
GOOD DOG
IT'S LIKE WITH TH' CONSERVATIVES & BUSH...THEY GOT TH' SUPREME COURT, BUT THEY ALSO GOT TH' BUMBLING & TH' DYING & TH' WARMING..
SO NOW YOU'RE ALSO NOT EVEN CUTE & FLOPPY?
GOOD DOG

132

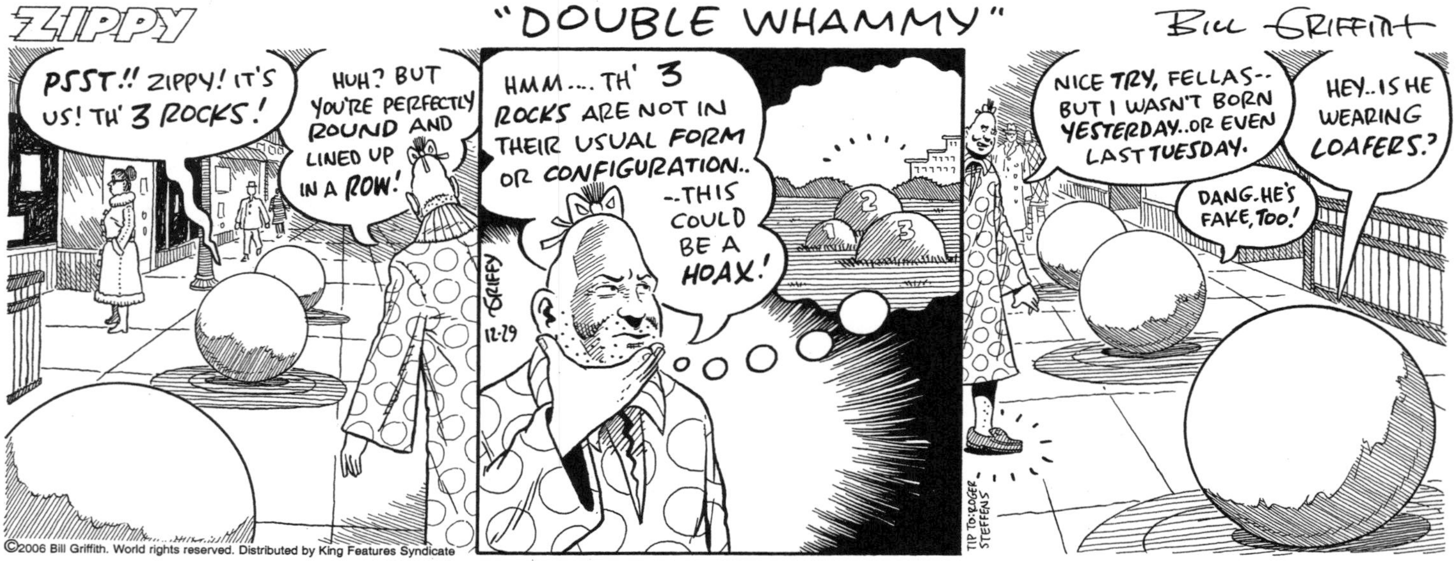
ZIPPY
"DOUBLE WHAMMY"
BILL GRIFFITH
PSST!! ZIPPY! IT'S US! TH' 3 ROCKS!
HUH? BUT YOU'RE PERFECTLY ROUND AND LINED UP IN A ROW!
HMM.... TH' 3 ROCKS ARE NOT IN THEIR USUAL FORM OR CONFIGURATION..
..THIS COULD BE A HOAX!
GRIFFY 12-29
NICE TRY, FELLAS-- BUT I WASN'T BORN YESTERDAY..OR EVEN LAST TUESDAY.
HEY..IS HE WEARING LOAFERS?
DANG. HE'S FAKE, TOO!
TIP TO: ROGER STEFFENS
©2006 Bill Griffith. World rights reserved. Distributed by King Features Syndicate

133

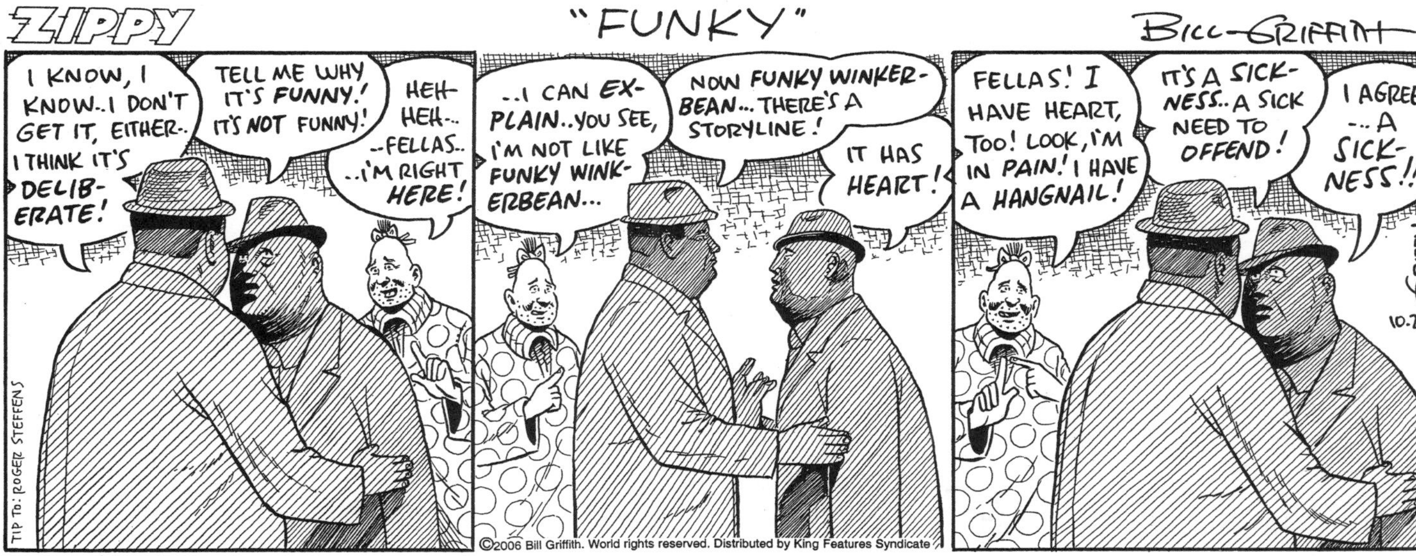
ZIPPY
"FUNKY"
BILL GRIFFITH
I KNOW, I KNOW.. I DON'T GET IT, EITHER.. I THINK IT'S DELIB-ERATE!
TELL ME WHY IT'S FUNNY! IT'S NOT FUNNY!
HEH-HEH... --FELLAS.. ..I'M RIGHT HERE!
TIP TO: ROGER STEFFENS
..I CAN EX-PLAIN..YOU SEE, I'M NOT LIKE FUNKY WINK-ERBEAN...
NOW FUNKY WINKER-BEAN... THERE'S A STORYLINE!
IT HAS HEART!
©2006 Bill Griffith. World rights reserved. Distributed by King Features Syndicate
FELLAS! I HAVE HEART, TOO! LOOK, I'M IN PAIN! I HAVE A HANGNAIL!
IT'S A SICK-NESS.. A SICK NEED TO OFFEND!
I AGREE.. --.. A SICK-NESS!!
GRIFFY
10.27

134

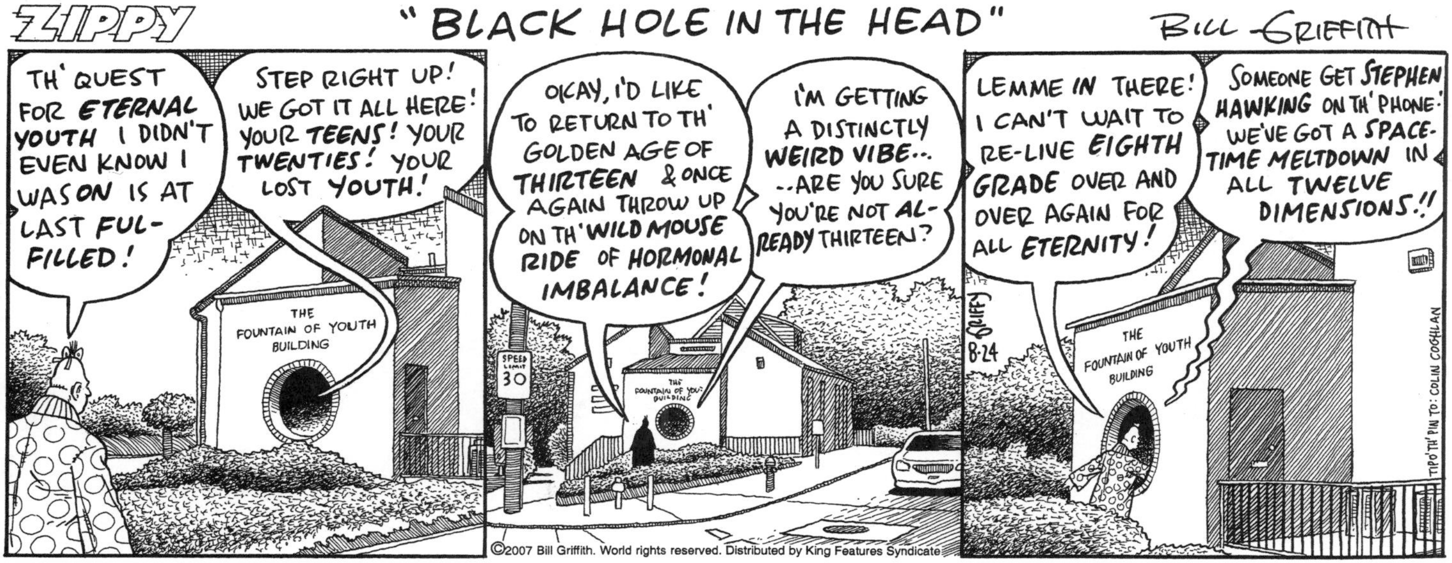
ZIPPY
"BLACK HOLE IN THE HEAD"
BILL GRIFFITH
TH' QUEST FOR ETERNAL YOUTH I DIDN'T EVEN KNOW I WAS ON IS AT LAST FUL-FILLED!
STEP RIGHT UP! WE GOT IT ALL HERE! YOUR TEENS! YOUR TWENTIES! YOUR LOST YOUTH!
THE FOUNTAIN OF YOUTH BUILDING
OKAY, I'D LIKE TO RETURN TO TH' GOLDEN AGE OF THIRTEEN & ONCE AGAIN THROW UP ON TH' WILD MOUSE RIDE OF HORMONAL IMBALANCE!
I'M GETTING A DISTINCTLY WEIRD VIBE... --ARE YOU SURE YOU'RE NOT AL-READY THIRTEEN?
SPEED LIMIT 30
©2007 Bill Griffith. World rights reserved. Distributed by King Features Syndicate
LEMME IN THERE! I CAN'T WAIT TO RE-LIVE EIGHTH GRADE OVER AND OVER AGAIN FOR ALL ETERNITY!
SOMEONE GET STEPHEN HAWKING ON TH' PHONE! WE'VE GOT A SPACE-TIME MELTDOWN IN ALL TWELVE DIMENSIONS!!
GRIFFY
8.24
THE FOUNTAIN OF YOUTH BUILDING
TIP O' TH' PIN TO: COLIN COGHLAN

135

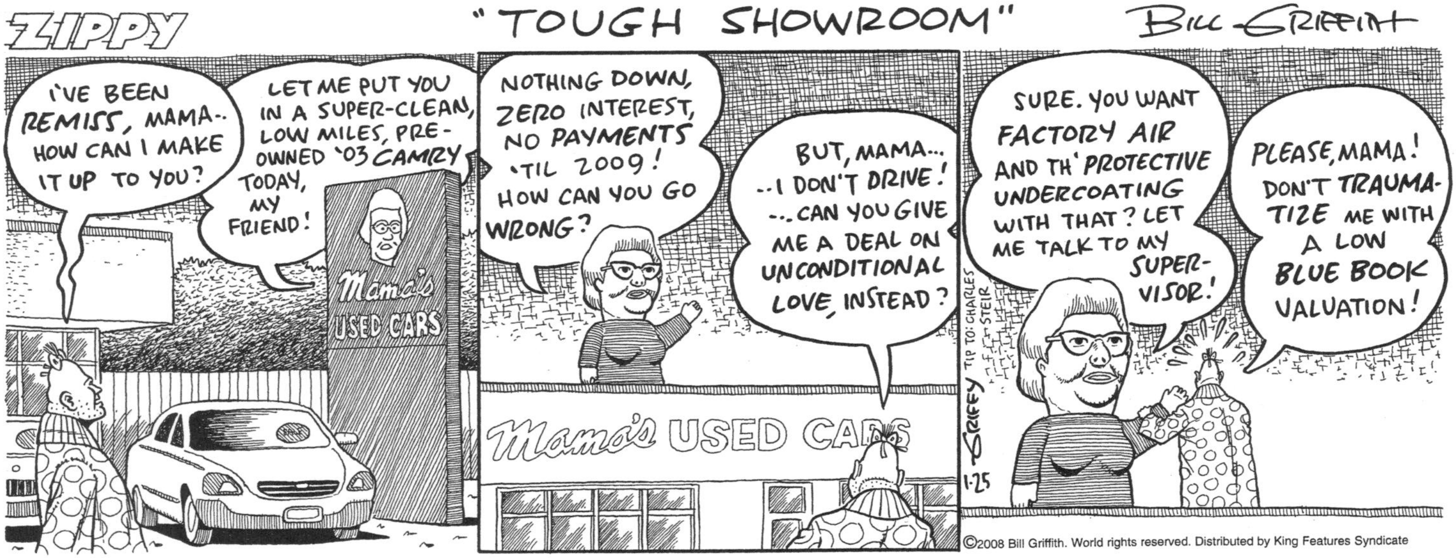
ZIPPY
"TOUGH SHOWROOM"
BILL GRIFFITH
I'VE BEEN REMISS, MAMA.. HOW CAN I MAKE IT UP TO YOU?
LET ME PUT YOU IN A SUPER-CLEAN, LOW MILES, PRE-OWNED '03 CAMRY TODAY, MY FRIEND!
Mama's USED CARS
NOTHING DOWN, ZERO INTEREST, NO PAYMENTS 'TIL 2009! HOW CAN YOU GO WRONG?
BUT, MAMA... --I DON'T DRIVE! --..CAN YOU GIVE ME A DEAL ON UNCONDITIONAL LOVE, INSTEAD?
Mama's USED CARS
GRIFFY 1-25
TIP TO: CHARLES STEIR
SURE. YOU WANT FACTORY AIR AND TH' PROTECTIVE UNDERCOATING WITH THAT? LET ME TALK TO MY SUPERVISOR!
PLEASE, MAMA! DON'T TRAUMATIZE ME WITH A LOW BLUE BOOK VALUATION!
©2008 Bill Griffith. World rights reserved. Distributed by King Features Syndicate

136

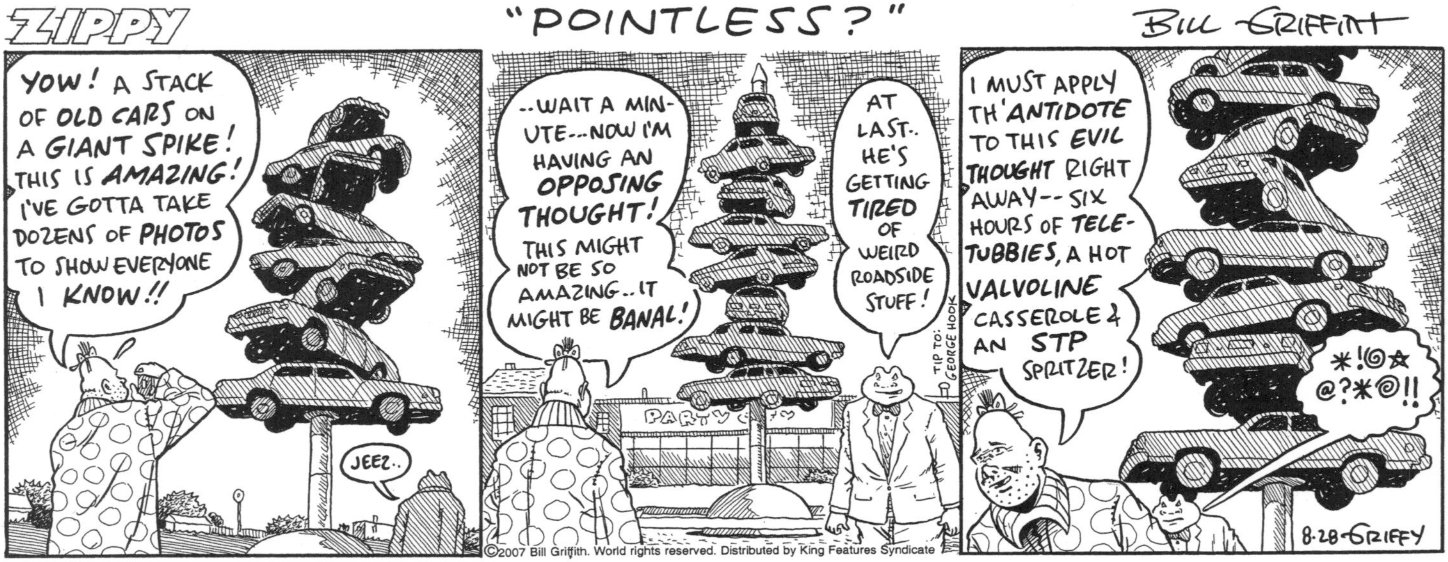
ZIPPY
"POINTLESS?"
BILL GRIFFITH
YOW! A STACK OF OLD CARS ON A GIANT SPIKE! THIS IS AMAZING! I'VE GOTTA TAKE DOZENS OF PHOTOS TO SHOW EVERYONE I KNOW!!
JEEZ..
--WAIT A MINUTE--NOW I'M HAVING AN OPPOSING THOUGHT! THIS MIGHT NOT BE SO AMAZING..IT MIGHT BE BANAL!
AT LAST.. HE'S GETTING TIRED OF WEIRD ROADSIDE STUFF!
TIP TO: GEORGE HOOK
I MUST APPLY TH' ANTIDOTE TO THIS EVIL THOUGHT RIGHT AWAY-- SIX HOURS OF TELETUBBIES, A HOT VALVOLINE CASSEROLE & AN STP SPRITZER!
*!@☆ @?*@!!
8-28 GRIFFY
©2007 Bill Griffith. World rights reserved. Distributed by King Features Syndicate

137

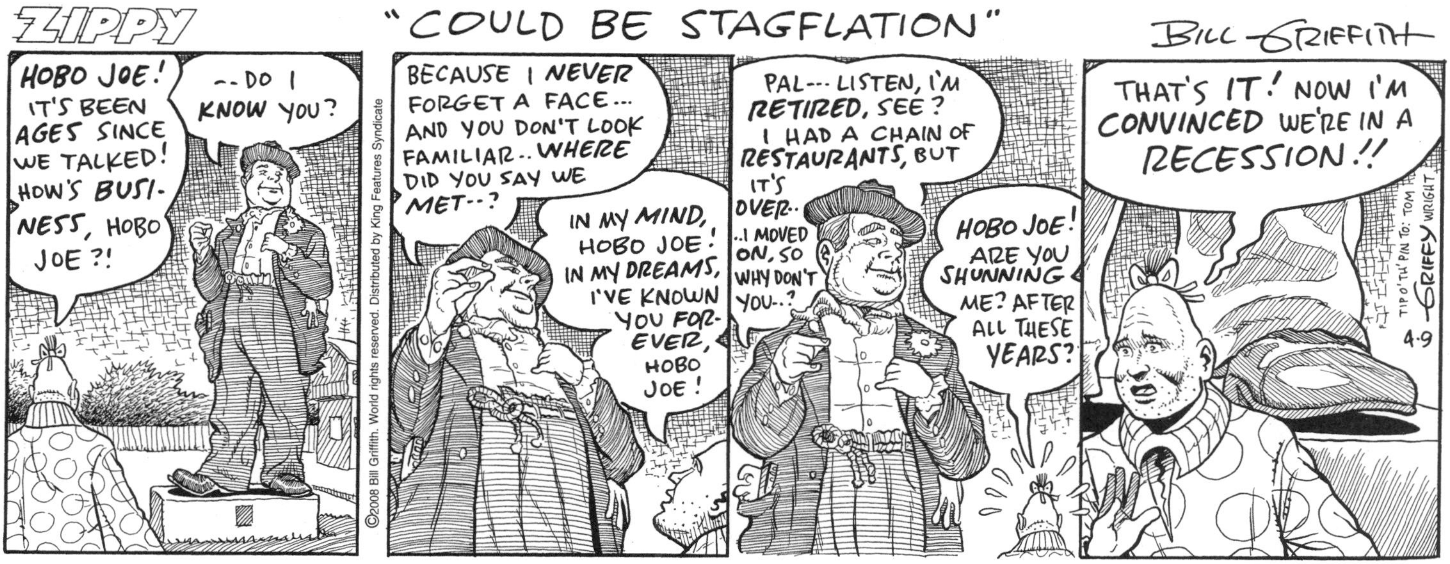
ZIPPY
"COULD BE STAGFLATION"
BILL GRIFFITH
HOBO JOE! IT'S BEEN AGES SINCE WE TALKED! HOW'S BUSINESS, HOBO JOE?!
--DO I KNOW YOU?
©2008 Bill Griffith. World rights reserved. Distributed by King Features Syndicate
BECAUSE I NEVER FORGET A FACE... AND YOU DON'T LOOK FAMILIAR.. WHERE DID YOU SAY WE MET--?
IN MY MIND, HOBO JOE! IN MY DREAMS, I'VE KNOWN YOU FOREVER, HOBO JOE!
PAL--- LISTEN, I'M RETIRED, SEE? I HAD A CHAIN OF RESTAURANTS, BUT IT'S OVER.. ..I MOVED ON, SO WHY DON'T YOU..?
HOBO JOE! ARE YOU SHUNNING ME? AFTER ALL THESE YEARS?
THAT'S IT! NOW I'M CONVINCED WE'RE IN A RECESSION!!
TIP O' TH' PIN TO: TOM WRIGHT
GRIFFY
4·9

138

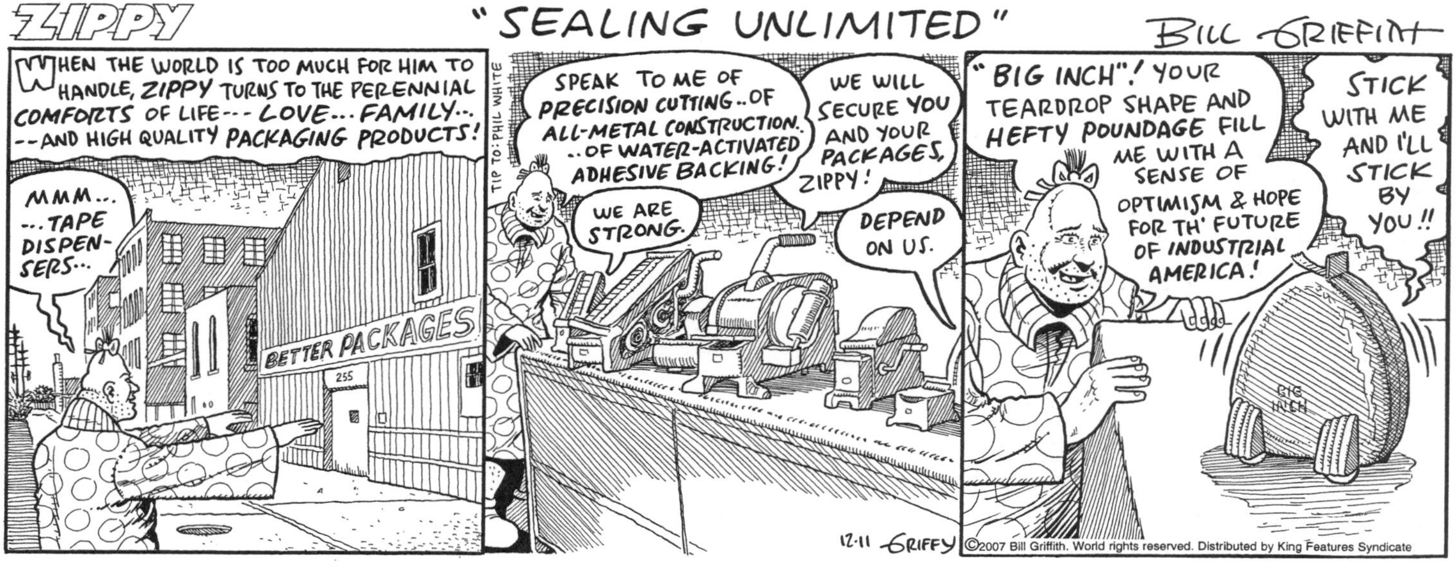
ZIPPY
"SEALING UNLIMITED"
BILL GRIFFITH
WHEN THE WORLD IS TOO MUCH FOR HIM TO HANDLE, ZIPPY TURNS TO THE PERENNIAL COMFORTS OF LIFE--- LOVE... FAMILY... --AND HIGH QUALITY PACKAGING PRODUCTS!
MMM... ...TAPE DISPENSERS...
BETTER PACKAGES
255
TIP TO: PHIL WHITE
SPEAK TO ME OF PRECISION CUTTING..OF ALL-METAL CONSTRUCTION.. ..OF WATER-ACTIVATED ADHESIVE BACKING!
WE WILL SECURE YOU AND YOUR PACKAGES, ZIPPY!
WE ARE STRONG.
DEPEND ON US.
"BIG INCH"! YOUR TEARDROP SHAPE AND HEFTY POUNDAGE FILL ME WITH A SENSE OF OPTIMISM & HOPE FOR TH' FUTURE OF INDUSTRIAL AMERICA!
STICK WITH ME AND I'LL STICK BY YOU!!
BIG INCH
12·11 GRIFFY
©2007 Bill Griffith. World rights reserved. Distributed by King Features Syndicate

139

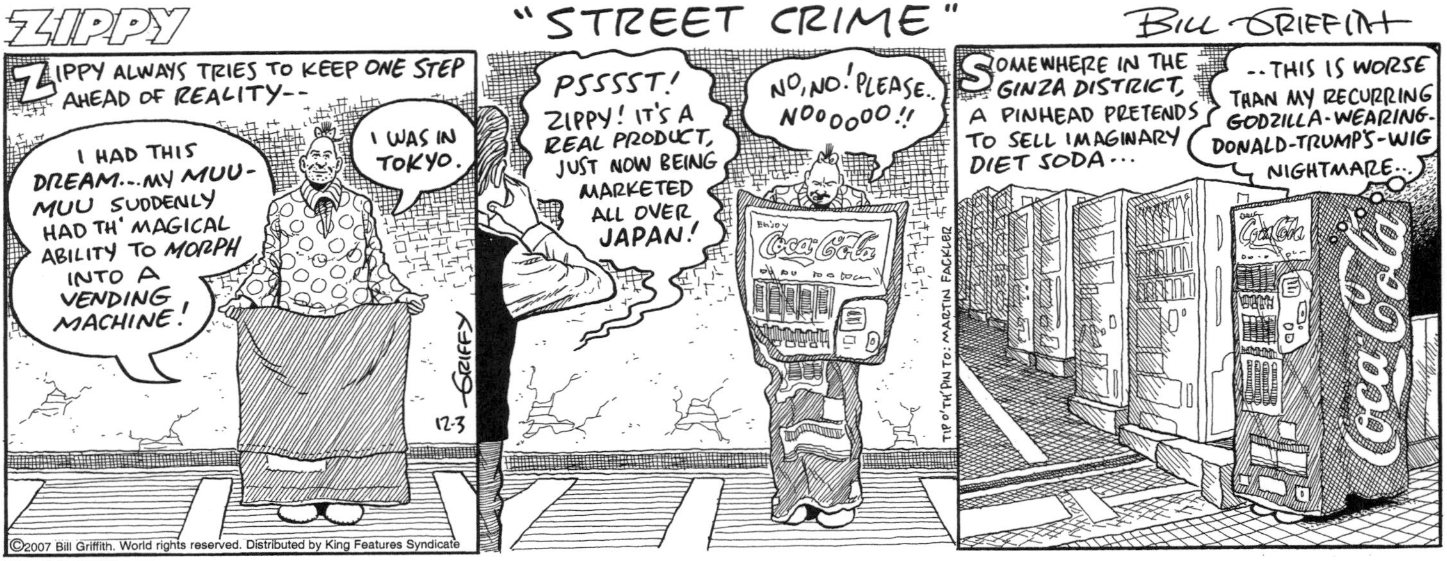
ZIPPY
"STREET CRIME"
BILL GRIFFITH
ZIPPY ALWAYS TRIES TO KEEP ONE STEP AHEAD OF REALITY--
I HAD THIS DREAM...MY MUU-MUU SUDDENLY HAD TH' MAGICAL ABILITY TO MORPH INTO A VENDING MACHINE!
I WAS IN TOKYO.
GRIFFY
12-3
©2007 Bill Griffith. World rights reserved. Distributed by King Features Syndicate
PSSSST! ZIPPY! IT'S A REAL PRODUCT, JUST NOW BEING MARKETED ALL OVER JAPAN!
NO, NO! PLEASE.. NOOOOOO!!
Enjoy Coca-Cola
TIP O' TH' PIN TO: MARTIN FACKLER
SOMEWHERE IN THE GINZA DISTRICT, A PINHEAD PRETENDS TO SELL IMAGINARY DIET SODA...
--THIS IS WORSE THAN MY RECURRING GODZILLA-WEARING-DONALD-TRUMP'S-WIG NIGHTMARE...
Coca-Cola
Coca-Cola

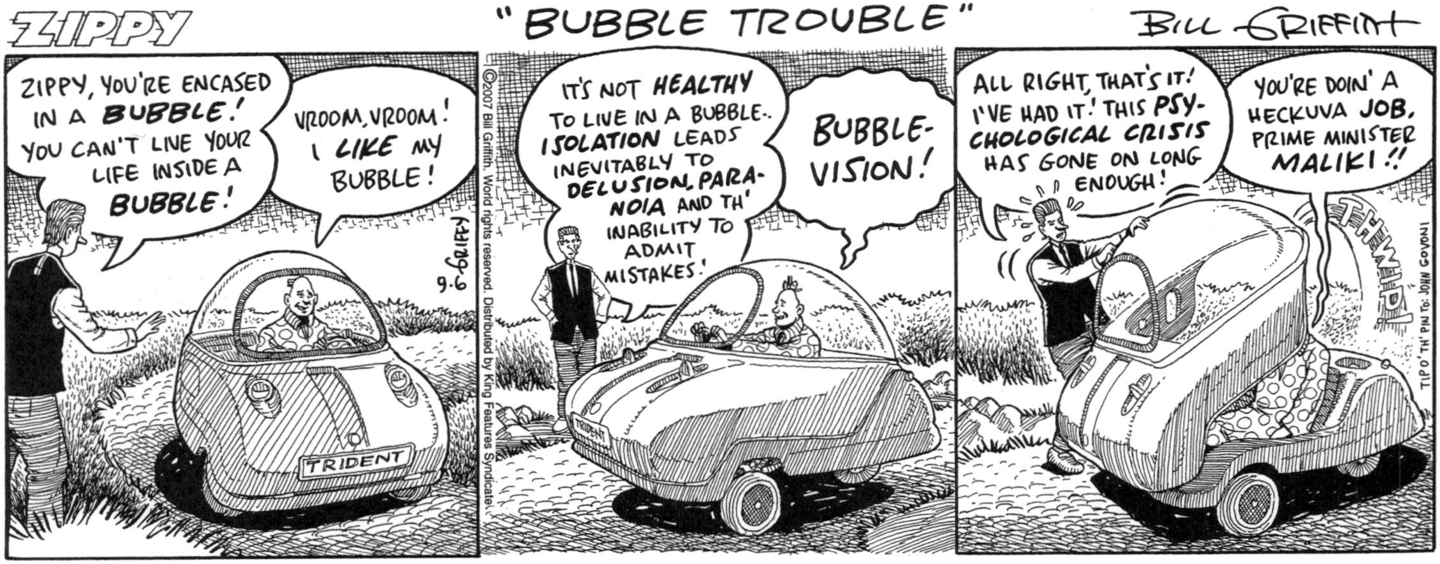
ZIPPY
"BUBBLE TROUBLE"
BILL GRIFFITH
ZIPPY, YOU'RE ENCASED IN A BUBBLE! YOU CAN'T LIVE YOUR LIFE INSIDE A BUBBLE!
VROOM, VROOM! I LIKE MY BUBBLE!
GRIFFY
9-6
TRIDENT
©2007 Bill Griffith. World rights reserved. Distributed by King Features Syndicate.
IT'S NOT HEALTHY TO LIVE IN A BUBBLE.. ISOLATION LEADS INEVITABLY TO DELUSION, PARANOIA AND TH' INABILITY TO ADMIT MISTAKES!
BUBBLE-VISION!
TRIDENT
ALL RIGHT, THAT'S IT! I'VE HAD IT! THIS PSYCHOLOGICAL CRISIS HAS GONE ON LONG ENOUGH!
YOU'RE DOIN' A HECKUVA JOB, PRIME MINISTER MALIKI!!
THWIP!
TIP O' TH' PIN TO: JOHN GOVONI

140

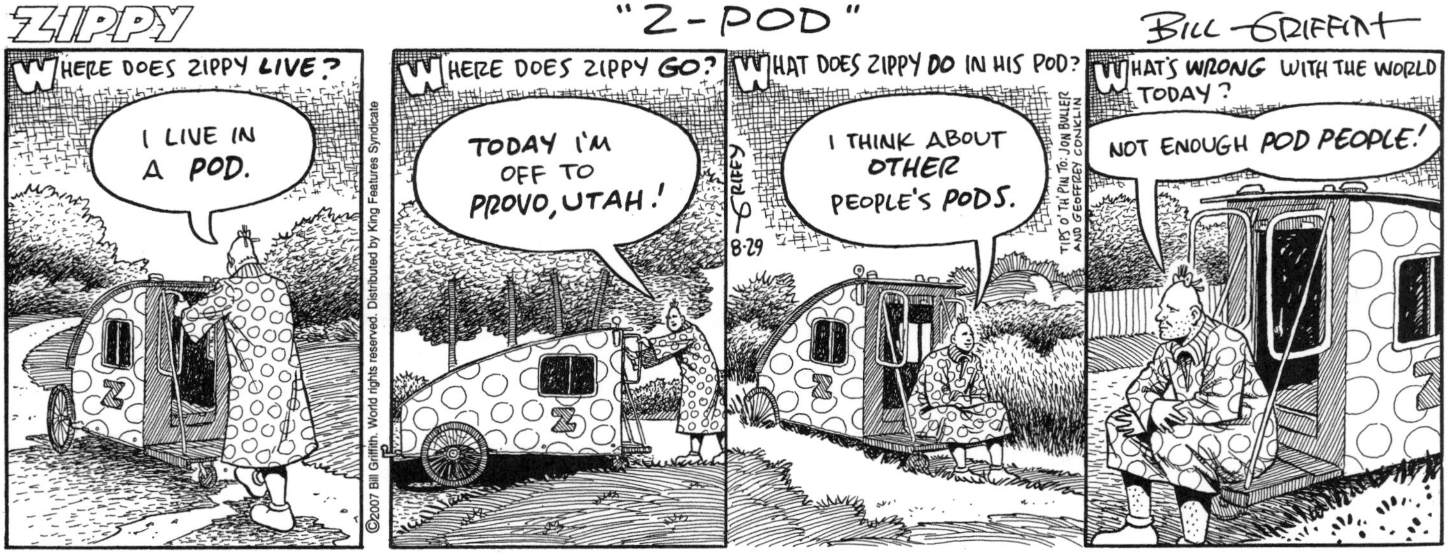
ZIPPY
"Z-POD"
BILL GRIFFITH
WHERE DOES ZIPPY LIVE?
I LIVE IN A POD.
©2007 Bill Griffith. World rights reserved. Distributed by King Features Syndicate
WHERE DOES ZIPPY GO?
TODAY I'M OFF TO PROVO, UTAH!
GRIFFY 8-29
WHAT DOES ZIPPY DO IN HIS POD?
I THINK ABOUT OTHER PEOPLE'S PODS.
TIPS O' TH' PIN TO: JON BULLER AND GEOFFREY CONKLIN
WHAT'S WRONG WITH THE WORLD TODAY?
NOT ENOUGH POD PEOPLE!

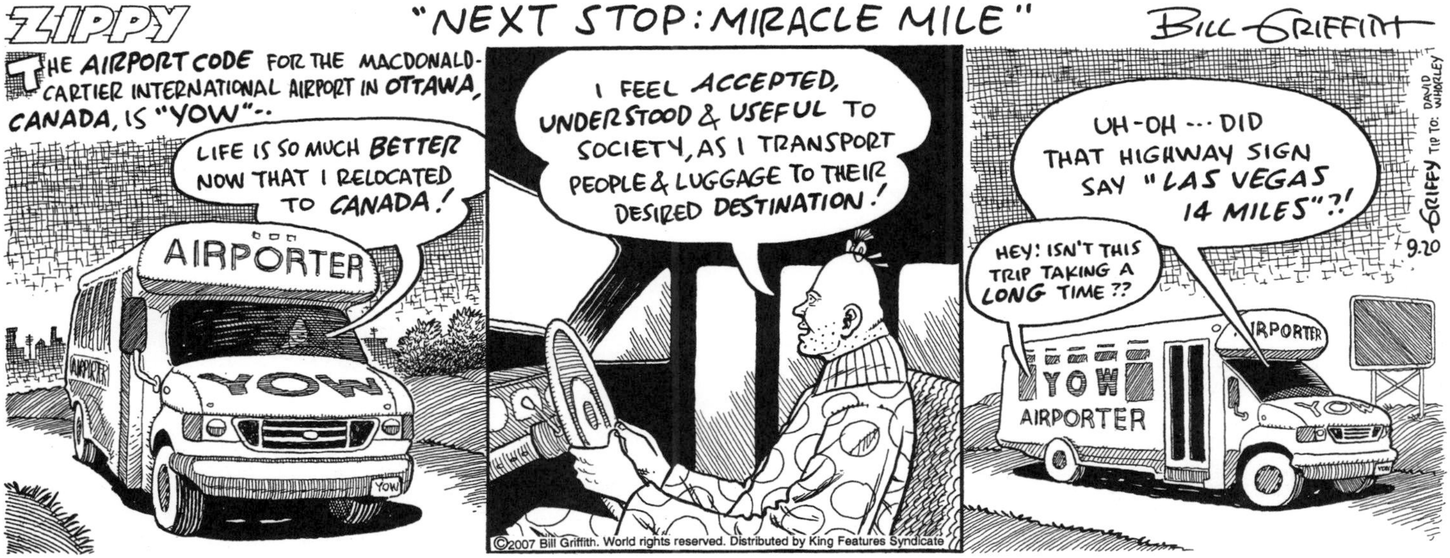
ZIPPY
"NEXT STOP: MIRACLE MILE"
BILL GRIFFITH
THE AIRPORT CODE FOR THE MACDONALD-CARTIER INTERNATIONAL AIRPORT IN OTTAWA, CANADA, IS "YOW"..
LIFE IS SO MUCH BETTER NOW THAT I RELOCATED TO CANADA!
AIRPORTER
YOW
I FEEL ACCEPTED, UNDERSTOOD & USEFUL TO SOCIETY, AS I TRANSPORT PEOPLE & LUGGAGE TO THEIR DESIRED DESTINATION!
©2007 Bill Griffith. World rights reserved. Distributed by King Features Syndicate
UH-OH ... DID THAT HIGHWAY SIGN SAY "LAS VEGAS 14 MILES"?!
GRIFFY TIP TO: DAVID WHORLEY 9-20
HEY! ISN'T THIS TRIP TAKING A LONG TIME??
YOW
AIRPORTER

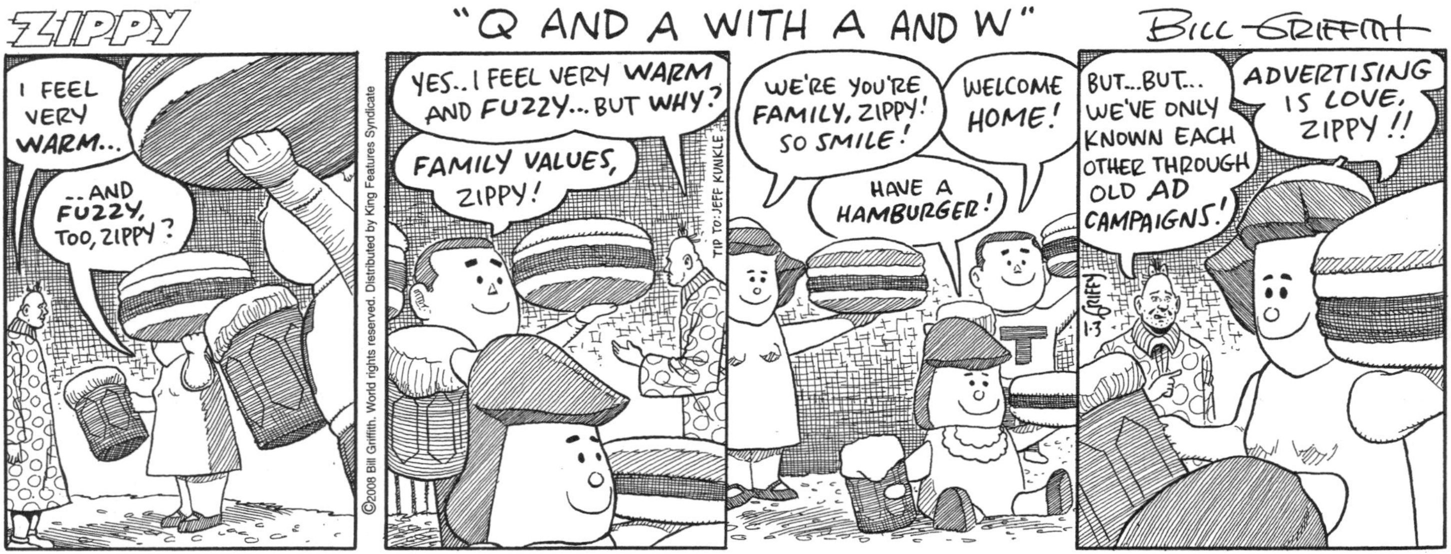
ZIPPY
"Q AND A WITH A AND W"
BILL GRIFFITH
I FEEL VERY WARM...
...AND FUZZY, TOO, ZIPPY?
©2008 Bill Griffith. World rights reserved. Distributed by King Features Syndicate
YES.. I FEEL VERY WARM AND FUZZY... BUT WHY?
FAMILY VALUES, ZIPPY!
TIP TO: JEFF KUNKLE
WE'RE YOU'RE FAMILY, ZIPPY! SO SMILE!
WELCOME HOME!
HAVE A HAMBURGER!
BUT...BUT... WE'VE ONLY KNOWN EACH OTHER THROUGH OLD AD CAMPAIGNS!
ADVERTISING IS LOVE, ZIPPY!!
GRIFFY
1·3

141 A

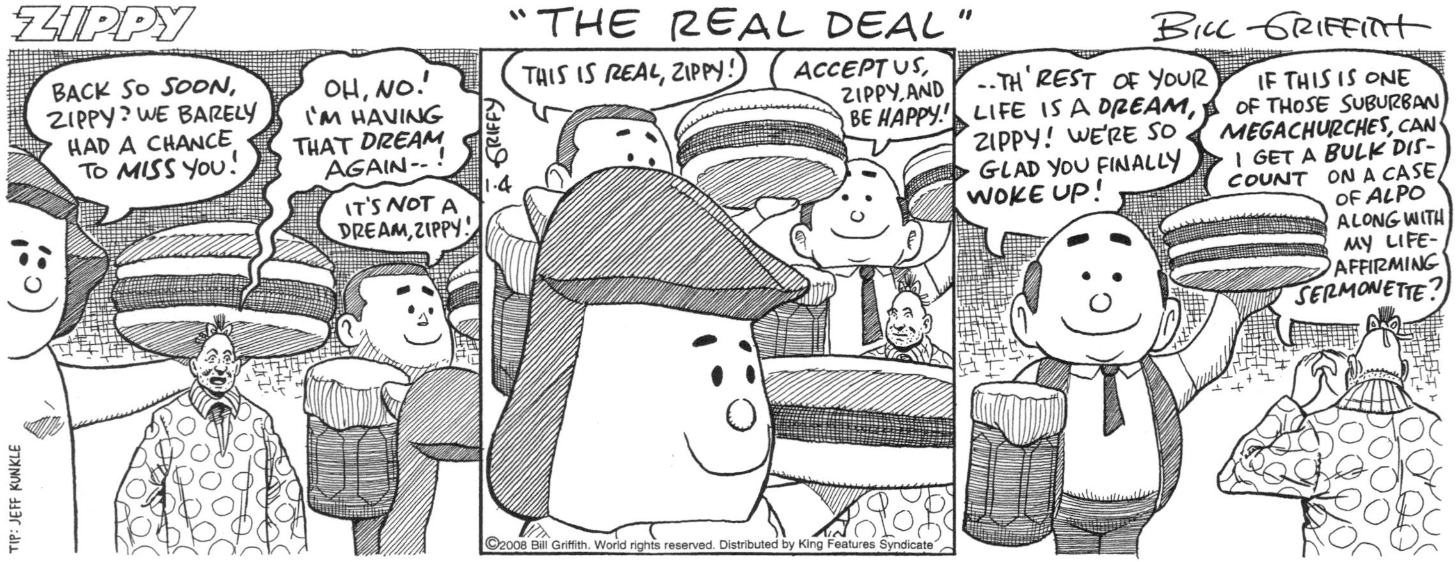
ZIPPY
"THE REAL DEAL"
BILL GRIFFITH
BACK SO SOON, ZIPPY? WE BARELY HAD A CHANCE TO MISS YOU!
OH, NO! I'M HAVING THAT DREAM AGAIN--!
IT'S NOT A DREAM, ZIPPY!
TIP: JEFF KUNKLE
THIS IS REAL, ZIPPY!
ACCEPT US, ZIPPY, AND BE HAPPY!
GRIFFY
1·4
©2008 Bill Griffith. World rights reserved. Distributed by King Features Syndicate
--TH' REST OF YOUR LIFE IS A DREAM, ZIPPY! WE'RE SO GLAD YOU FINALLY WOKE UP!
IF THIS IS ONE OF THOSE SUBURBAN MEGACHURCHES, CAN I GET A BULK DISCOUNT ON A CASE OF ALPO ALONG WITH MY LIFE-AFFIRMING SERMONETTE?

141 B

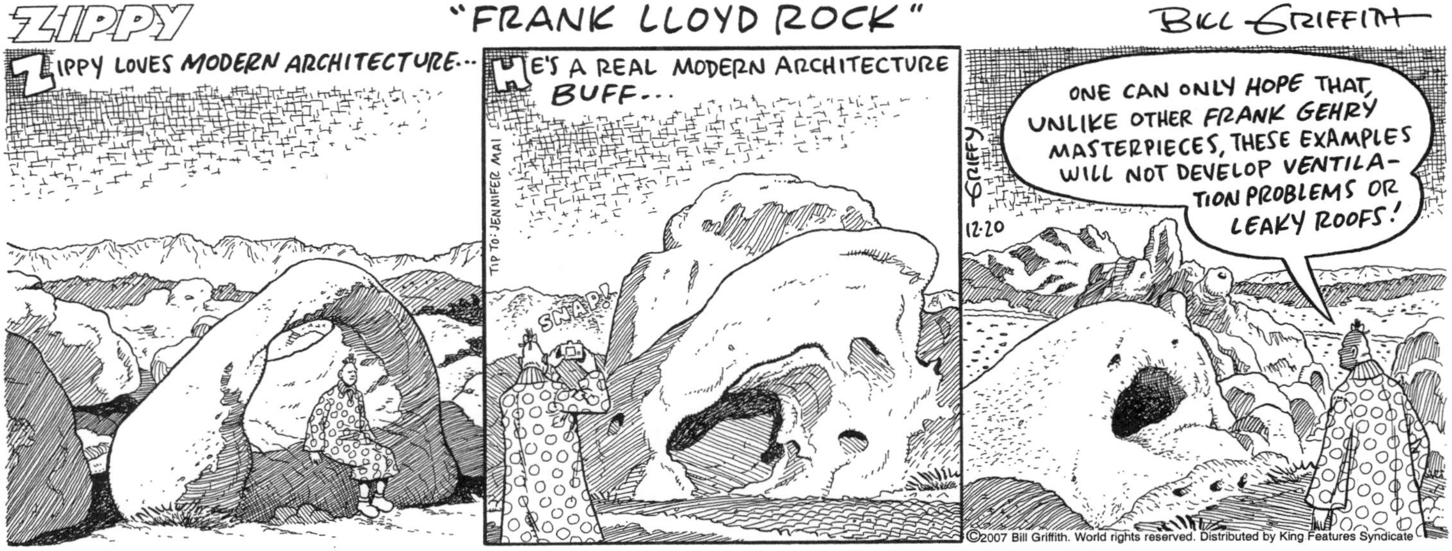
ZIPPY
"FRANK LLOYD ROCK"
BILL GRIFFITH
ZIPPY LOVES MODERN ARCHITECTURE...
HE'S A REAL MODERN ARCHITECTURE BUFF...
TIP TO: JENNIFER MAI
SNAP!
GRIFFY 12-20
ONE CAN ONLY HOPE THAT, UNLIKE OTHER FRANK GEHRY MASTERPIECES, THESE EXAMPLES WILL NOT DEVELOP VENTILA-TION PROBLEMS OR LEAKY ROOFS!
©2007 Bill Griffith. World rights reserved. Distributed by King Features Syndicate

142

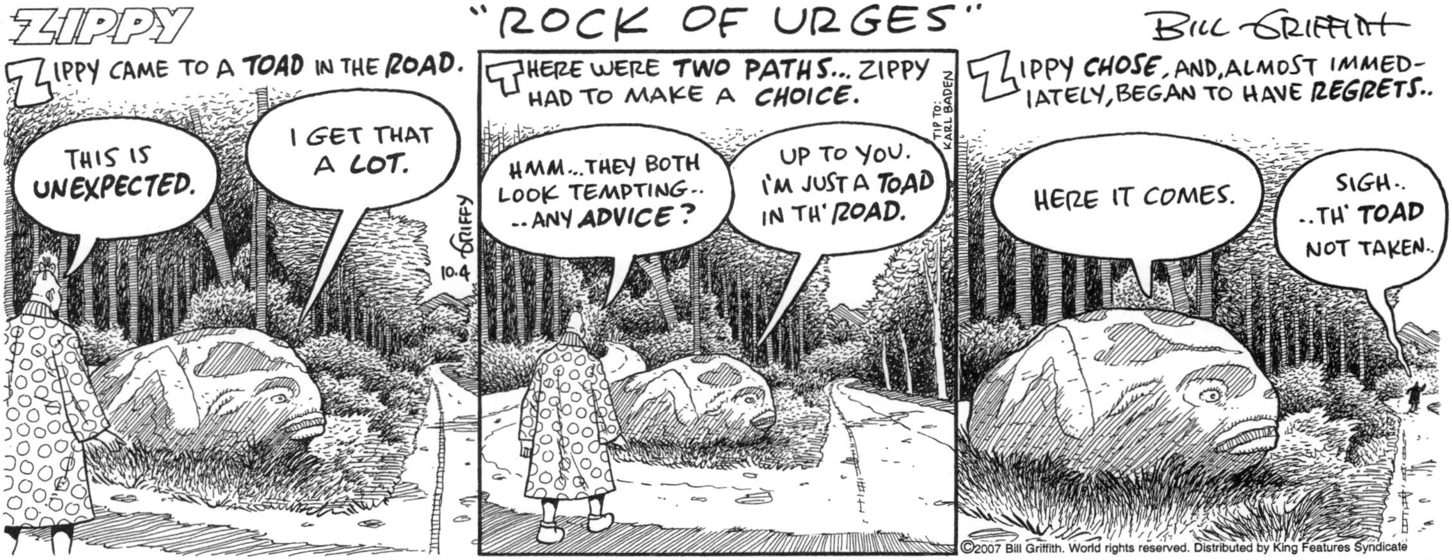
ZIPPY
"ROCK OF URGES"
BILL GRIFFITH
ZIPPY CAME TO A TOAD IN THE ROAD.
THIS IS UNEXPECTED.
I GET THAT A LOT.
GRIFFY 10-4
THERE WERE TWO PATHS... ZIPPY HAD TO MAKE A CHOICE.
TIP TO: KARL BADEN
HMM... THEY BOTH LOOK TEMPTING.. ..ANY ADVICE?
UP TO YOU. I'M JUST A TOAD IN TH' ROAD.
ZIPPY CHOSE, AND, ALMOST IMMED-IATELY, BEGAN TO HAVE REGRETS..
HERE IT COMES.
SIGH.. ..TH' TOAD NOT TAKEN..
©2007 Bill Griffith. World rights reserved. Distributed by King Features Syndicate

143

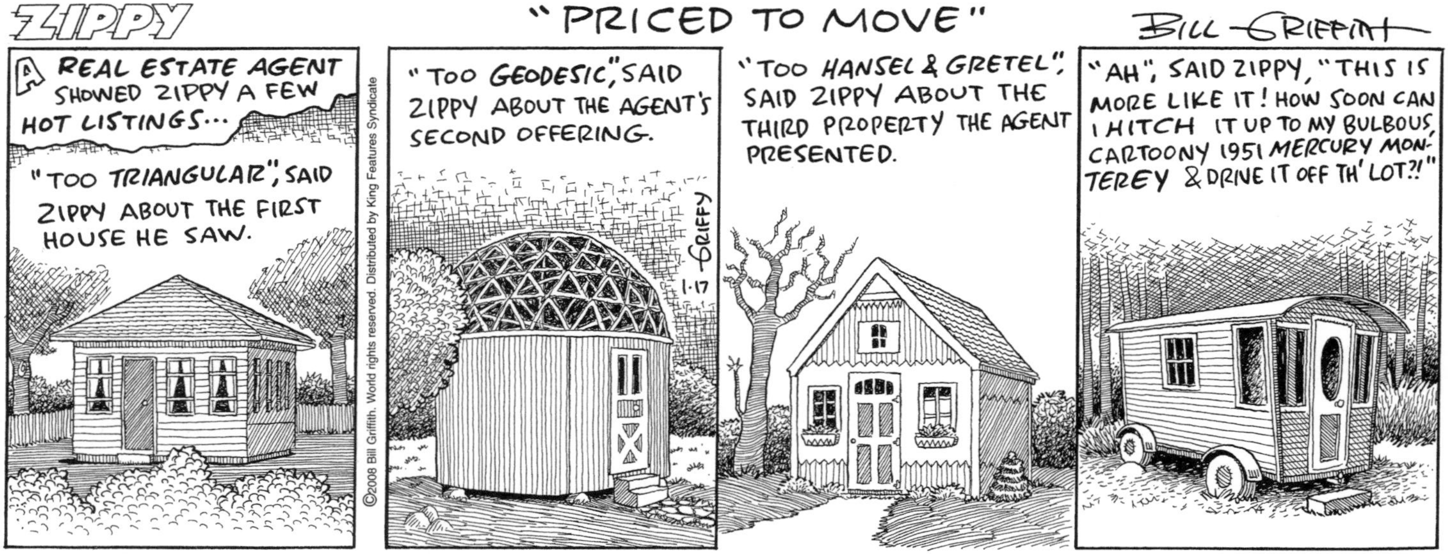
ZIPPY
"PRICED TO MOVE"
BILL GRIFFITH
A REAL ESTATE AGENT SHOWED ZIPPY A FEW HOT LISTINGS...
"TOO TRIANGULAR", SAID ZIPPY ABOUT THE FIRST HOUSE HE SAW.
©2008 Bill Griffith. World rights reserved. Distributed by King Features Syndicate
"TOO GEODESIC," SAID ZIPPY ABOUT THE AGENT'S SECOND OFFERING.
GRIFFY 1·17
"TOO HANSEL & GRETEL", SAID ZIPPY ABOUT THE THIRD PROPERTY THE AGENT PRESENTED.
"AH", SAID ZIPPY, "THIS IS MORE LIKE IT! HOW SOON CAN I HITCH IT UP TO MY BULBOUS, CARTOONY 1951 MERCURY MONTEREY & DRIVE IT OFF TH' LOT?!"

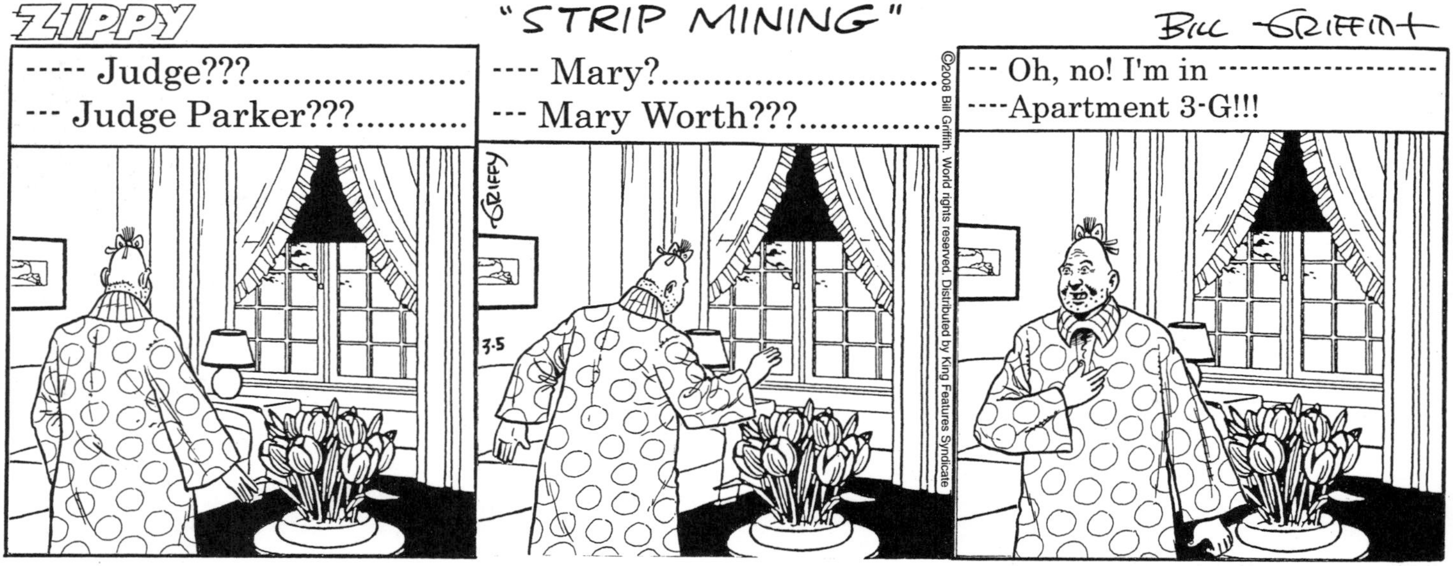
ZIPPY
"STRIP MINING"
BILL GRIFFITH
----- Judge???....................
--- Judge Parker???...........
GRIFFY 3·5
---- Mary?..........................
--- Mary Worth???.............
©2008 Bill Griffith. World rights reserved. Distributed by King Features Syndicate
--- Oh, no! I'm in -------------------
----Apartment 3-G!!!

144

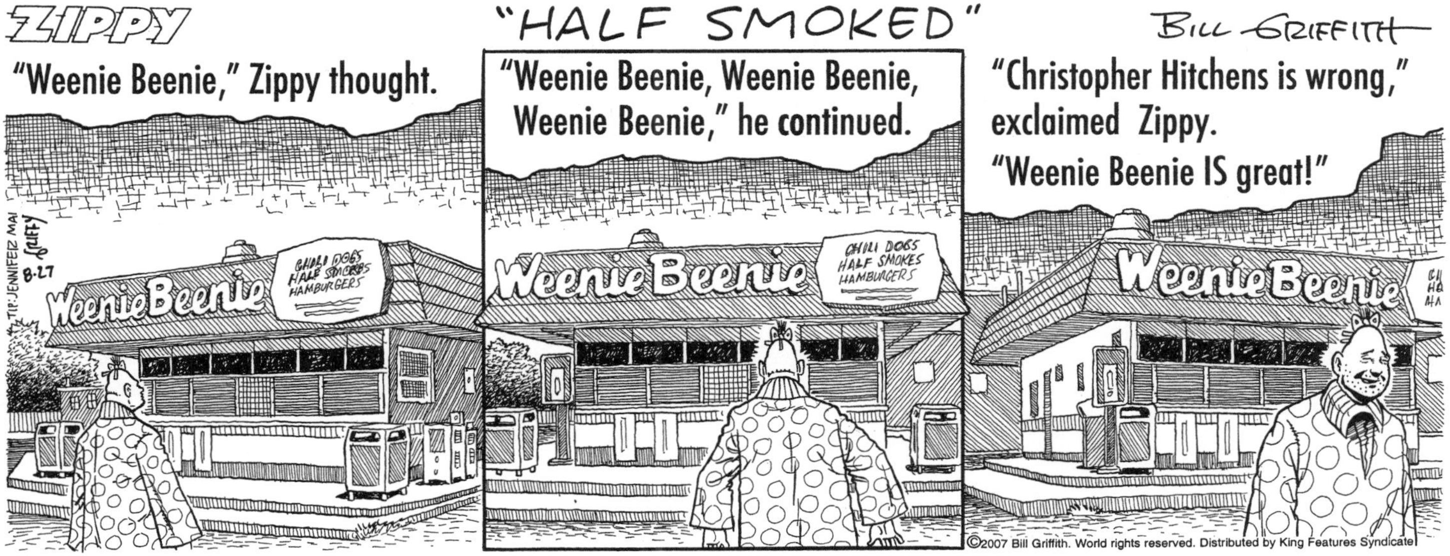
ZIPPY
"HALF SMOKED"
BILL GRIFFITH
"Weenie Beenie," Zippy thought.
TIP: JENNIFER MAI
GRIFFY 8-27
Weenie Beenie
CHILI DOGS HALF SMOKES HAMBURGERS
"Weenie Beenie, Weenie Beenie, Weenie Beenie," he continued.
"Christopher Hitchens is wrong," exclaimed Zippy.
"Weenie Beenie IS great!"
©2007 Bill Griffith. World rights reserved. Distributed by King Features Syndicate

145

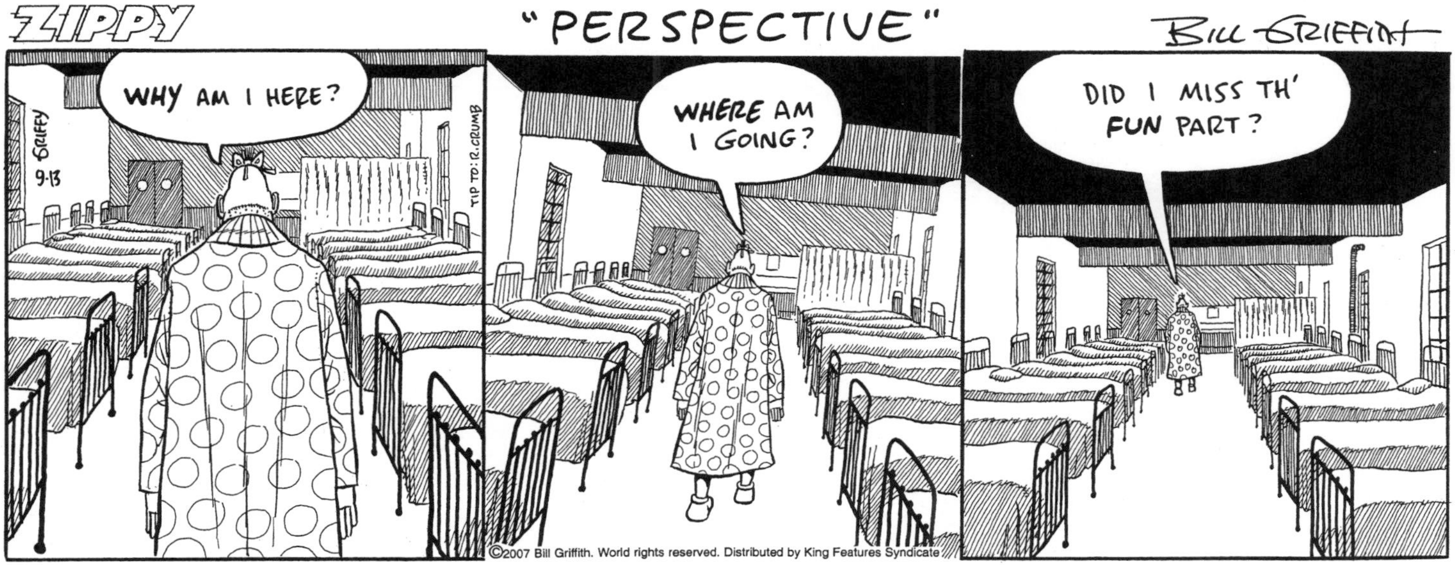
ZIPPY
"PERSPECTIVE"
BILL GRIFFITH
GRIFFY 9-13
TIP TO: R. CRUMB
WHY AM I HERE?
WHERE AM I GOING?
DID I MISS TH' FUN PART?
©2007 Bill Griffith. World rights reserved. Distributed by King Features Syndicate

146

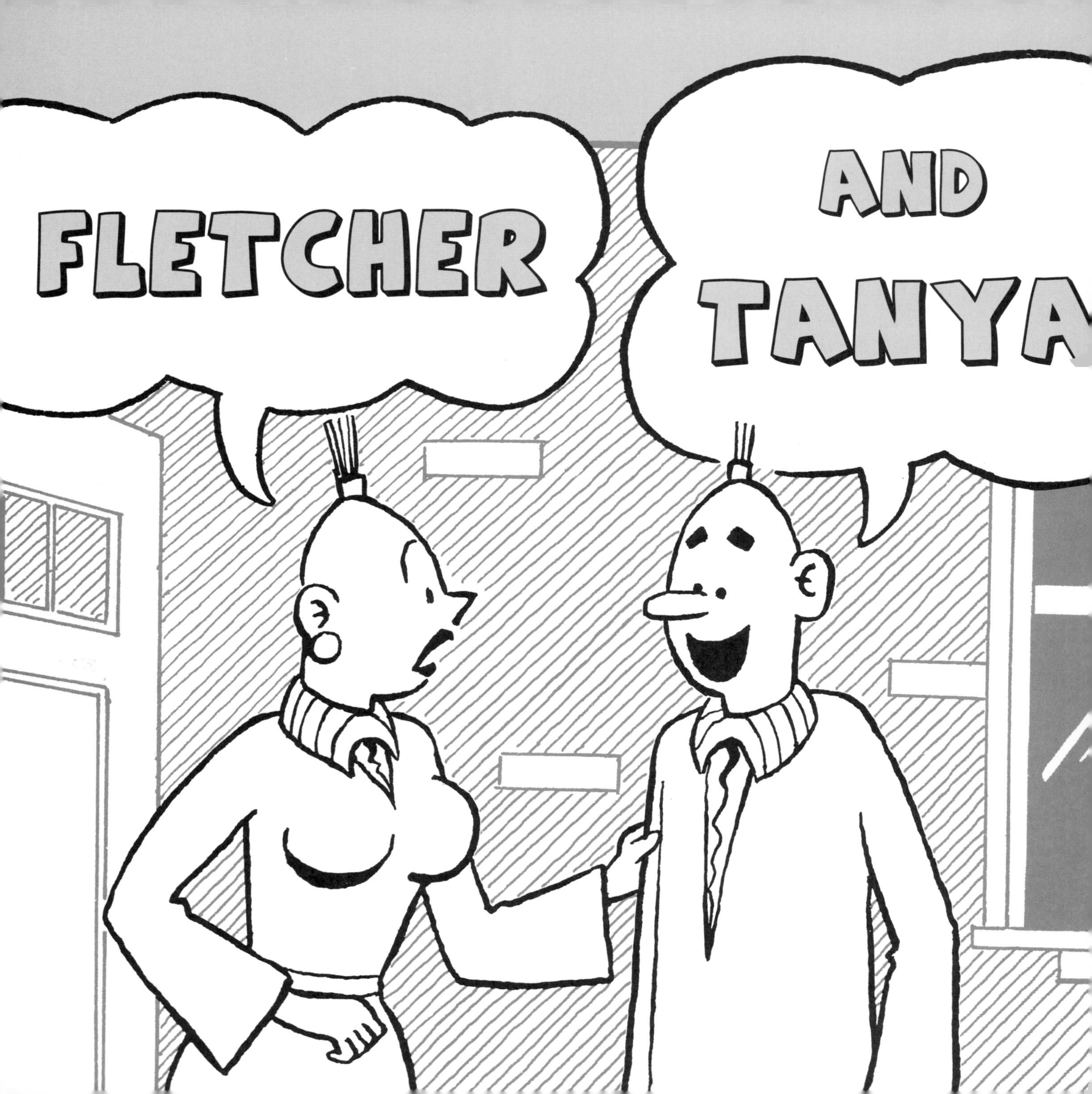
FLETCHER
AND TANYA

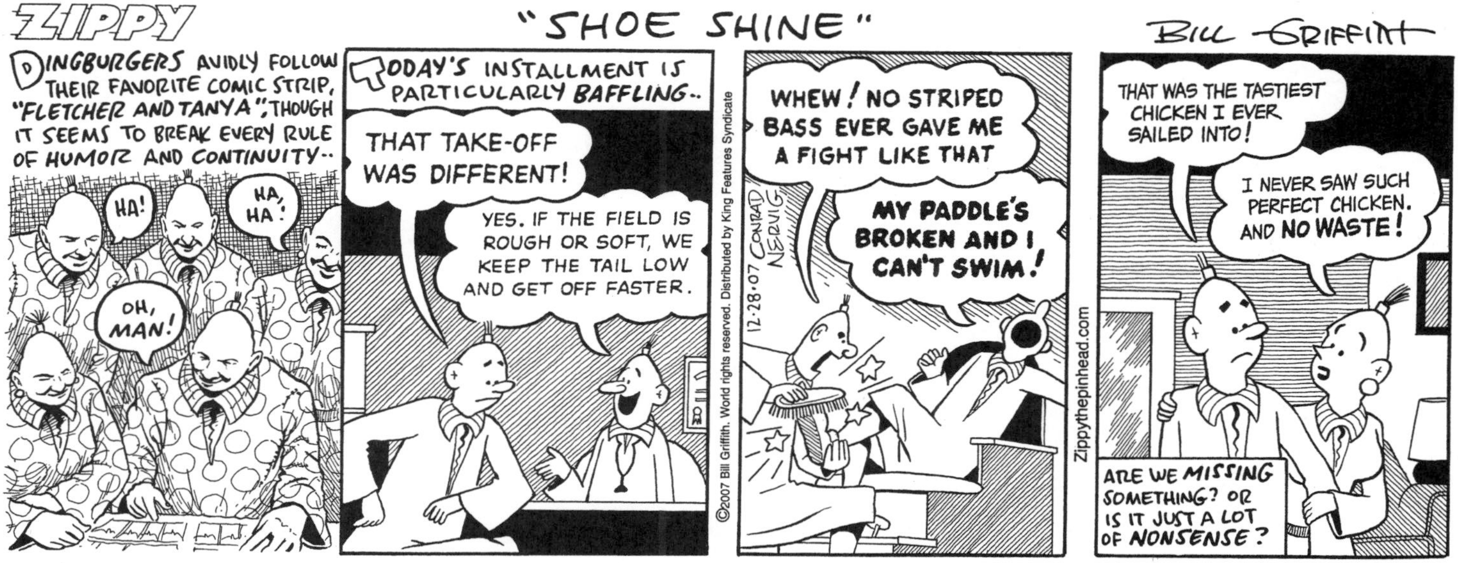
ZIPPY
"SHOE SHINE"
BILL GRIFFITH
DINGBURGERS AVIDLY FOLLOW THEIR FAVORITE COMIC STRIP, "FLETCHER AND TANYA", THOUGH IT SEEMS TO BREAK EVERY RULE OF HUMOR AND CONTINUITY..
HA!
HA, HA!
OH, MAN!
TODAY'S INSTALLMENT IS PARTICULARLY BAFFLING..
THAT TAKE-OFF WAS DIFFERENT!
YES. IF THE FIELD IS ROUGH OR SOFT, WE KEEP THE TAIL LOW AND GET OFF FASTER.
©2007 Bill Griffith. World rights reserved. Distributed by King Features Syndicate
12·28·07
CONRAD NERVIG
WHEW! NO STRIPED BASS EVER GAVE ME A FIGHT LIKE THAT
MY PADDLE'S BROKEN AND I CAN'T SWIM!
Zippythepinhead.com
THAT WAS THE TASTIEST CHICKEN I EVER SAILED INTO!
I NEVER SAW SUCH PERFECT CHICKEN. AND NO WASTE!
ARE WE MISSING SOMETHING? OR IS IT JUST A LOT OF NONSENSE?

147

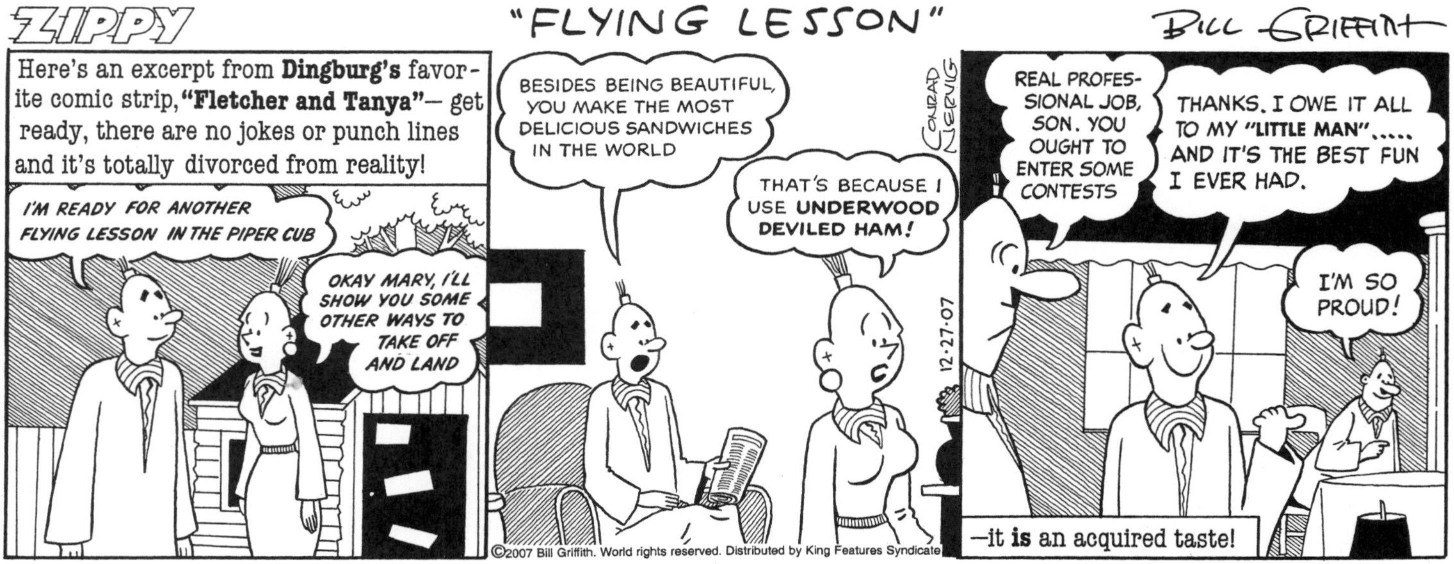
ZIPPY
"FLYING LESSON"
BILL GRIFFITH
Here's an excerpt from Dingburg's favorite comic strip, "Fletcher and Tanya"— get ready, there are no jokes or punch lines and it's totally divorced from reality!
I'M READY FOR ANOTHER FLYING LESSON IN THE PIPER CUB
OKAY MARY, I'LL SHOW YOU SOME OTHER WAYS TO TAKE OFF AND LAND
BESIDES BEING BEAUTIFUL, YOU MAKE THE MOST DELICIOUS SANDWICHES IN THE WORLD
THAT'S BECAUSE I USE UNDERWOOD DEVILED HAM!
CONRAD NERVIG
12·27·07
©2007 Bill Griffith. World rights reserved. Distributed by King Features Syndicate
REAL PROFESSIONAL JOB, SON. YOU OUGHT TO ENTER SOME CONTESTS
THANKS. I OWE IT ALL TO MY "LITTLE MAN"..... AND IT'S THE BEST FUN I EVER HAD.
I'M SO PROUD!
—it is an acquired taste!

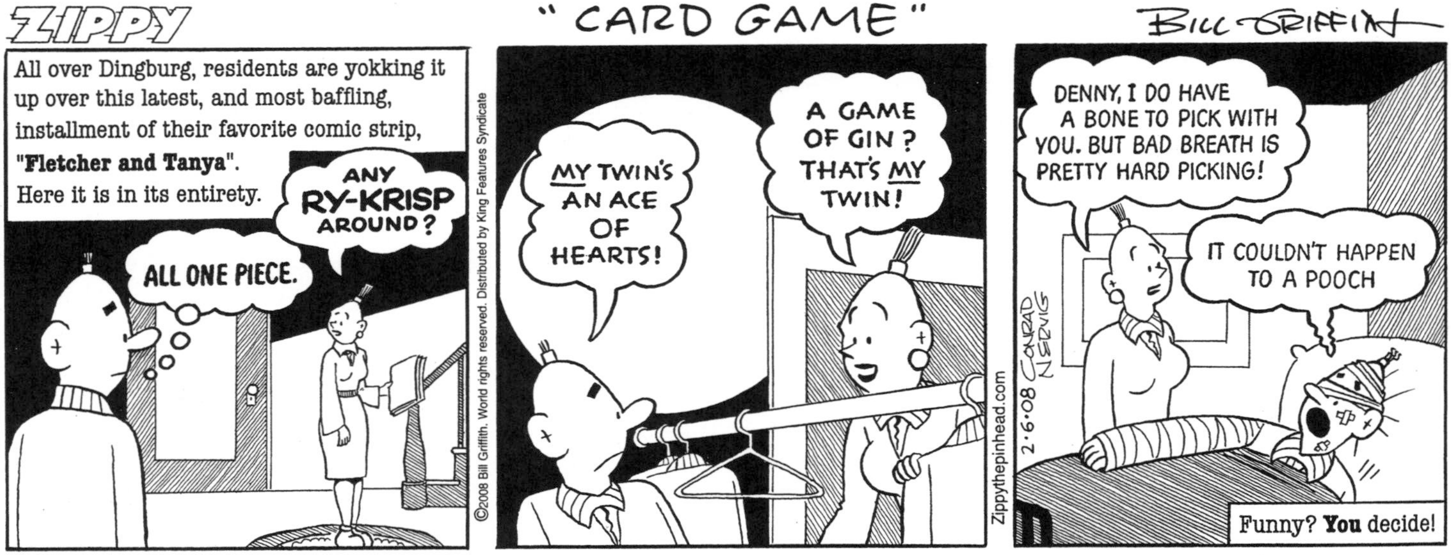
ZIPPY
"CARD GAME"
BILL GRIFFITH
All over Dingburg, residents are yokking it up over this latest, and most baffling, installment of their favorite comic strip, "Fletcher and Tanya". Here it is in its entirety.
ANY RY-KRISP AROUND?
ALL ONE PIECE.
©2008 Bill Griffith. World rights reserved. Distributed by King Features Syndicate
MY TWIN'S AN ACE OF HEARTS!
A GAME OF GIN? THAT'S MY TWIN!
Zippythepinhead.com
2·6·08
CONRAD NERVIG
DENNY, I DO HAVE A BONE TO PICK WITH YOU. BUT BAD BREATH IS PRETTY HARD PICKING!
IT COULDN'T HAPPEN TO A POOCH
Funny? **You** decide!

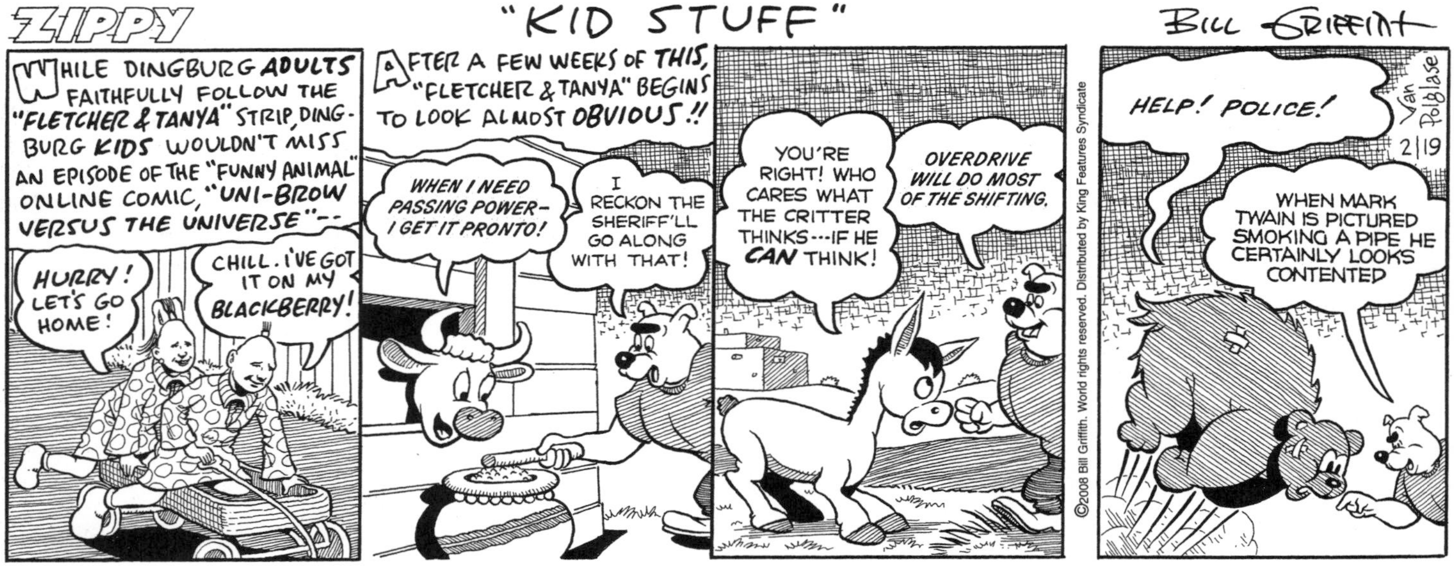
ZIPPY
"KID STUFF"
BILL GRIFFITH
WHILE DINGBURG ADULTS FAITHFULLY FOLLOW THE "FLETCHER & TANYA" STRIP, DING-BURG KIDS WOULDN'T MISS AN EPISODE OF THE "FUNNY ANIMAL" ONLINE COMIC, "UNI-BROW VERSUS THE UNIVERSE"--
HURRY! LET'S GO HOME!
CHILL. I'VE GOT IT ON MY BLACKBERRY!
AFTER A FEW WEEKS OF THIS, "FLETCHER & TANYA" BEGINS TO LOOK ALMOST OBVIOUS!!
WHEN I NEED PASSING POWER-I GET IT PRONTO!
I RECKON THE SHERIFF'LL GO ALONG WITH THAT!
YOU'RE RIGHT! WHO CARES WHAT THE CRITTER THINKS---IF HE CAN THINK!
OVERDRIVE WILL DO MOST OF THE SHIFTING.
©2008 Bill Griffith. World rights reserved. Distributed by King Features Syndicate
HELP! POLICE!
Van Polglase
2/19
WHEN MARK TWAIN IS PICTURED SMOKING A PIPE HE CERTAINLY LOOKS CONTENTED

148 A

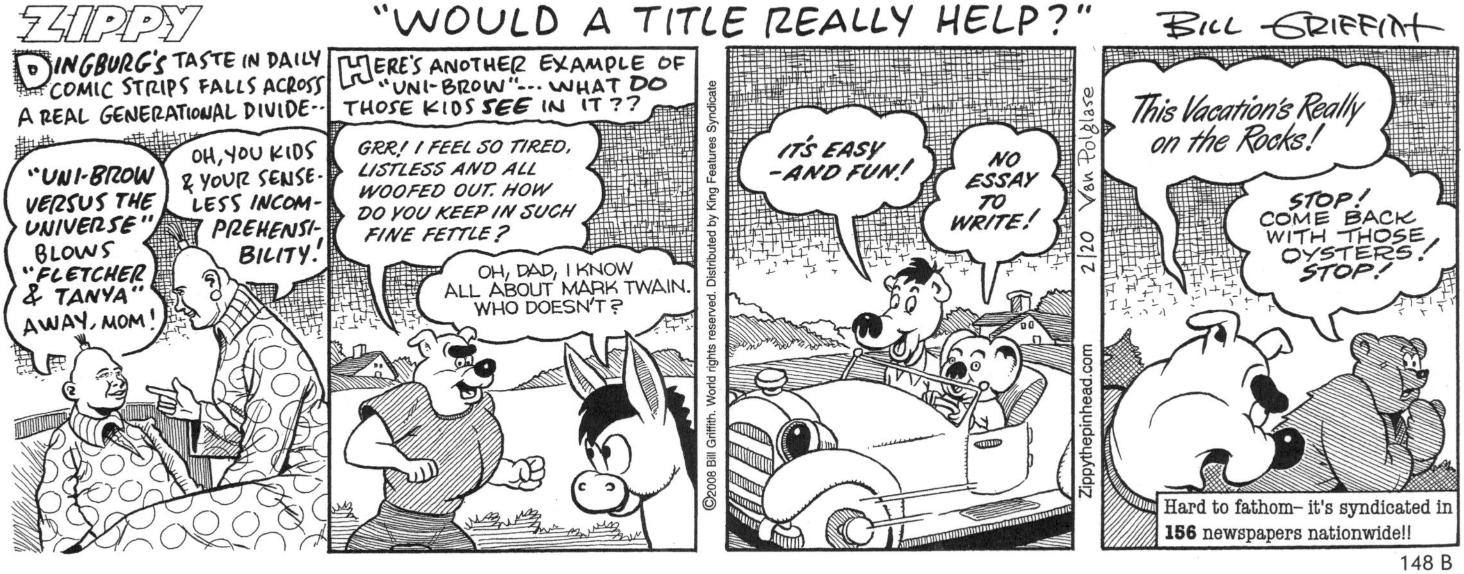
ZIPPY
"WOULD A TITLE REALLY HELP?"
BILL GRIFFITH
DINGBURG'S TASTE IN DAILY COMIC STRIPS FALLS ACROSS A REAL GENERATIONAL DIVIDE--
"UNI-BROW VERSUS THE UNIVERSE" BLOWS "FLETCHER & TANYA" AWAY, MOM!
OH, YOU KIDS & YOUR SENSELESS INCOMPREHENSIBILITY!
HERE'S ANOTHER EXAMPLE OF "UNI-BROW"... WHAT DO THOSE KIDS SEE IN IT??
GRR! I FEEL SO TIRED, LISTLESS AND ALL WOOFED OUT. HOW DO YOU KEEP IN SUCH FINE FETTLE?
OH, DAD, I KNOW ALL ABOUT MARK TWAIN. WHO DOESN'T?
©2008 Bill Griffith. World rights reserved. Distributed by King Features Syndicate
IT'S EASY -AND FUN!
NO ESSAY TO WRITE!
2/20
Van Polglase
Zippythepinhead.com
This Vacation's Really on the Rocks!
STOP! COME BACK WITH THOSE OYSTERS! STOP!
Hard to fathom– it's syndicated in 156 newspapers nationwide!!
148 B

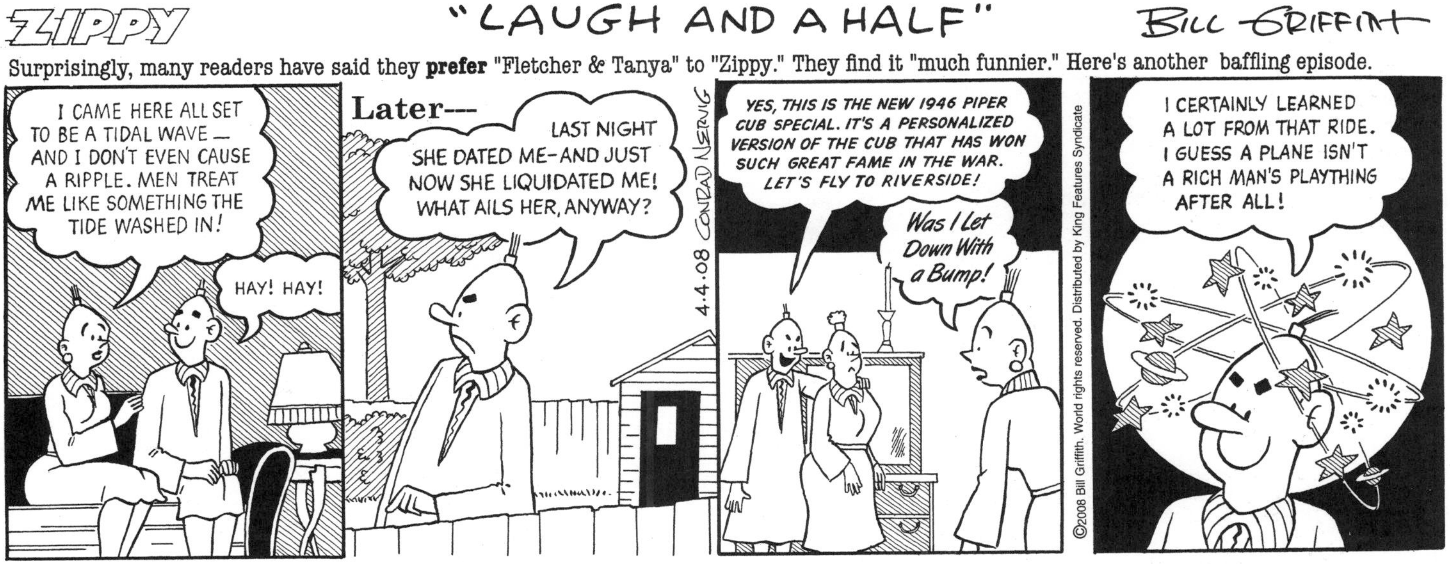
ZIPPY
"LAUGH AND A HALF"
BILL GRIFFITH
Surprisingly, many readers have said they prefer "Fletcher & Tanya" to "Zippy." They find it "much funnier." Here's another baffling episode.
I CAME HERE ALL SET TO BE A TIDAL WAVE — AND I DON'T EVEN CAUSE A RIPPLE. MEN TREAT ME LIKE SOMETHING THE TIDE WASHED IN!
HAY! HAY!
Later---
LAST NIGHT SHE DATED ME–AND JUST NOW SHE LIQUIDATED ME! WHAT AILS HER, ANYWAY?
CONRAD NERVIG
4.4.08
YES, THIS IS THE NEW 1946 PIPER CUB SPECIAL. IT'S A PERSONALIZED VERSION OF THE CUB THAT HAS WON SUCH GREAT FAME IN THE WAR. LET'S FLY TO RIVERSIDE!
Was I Let Down With a Bump!
©2008 Bill Griffith. World rights reserved. Distributed by King Features Syndicate
I CERTAINLY LEARNED A LOT FROM THAT RIDE. I GUESS A PLANE ISN'T A RICH MAN'S PLAYTHING AFTER ALL!

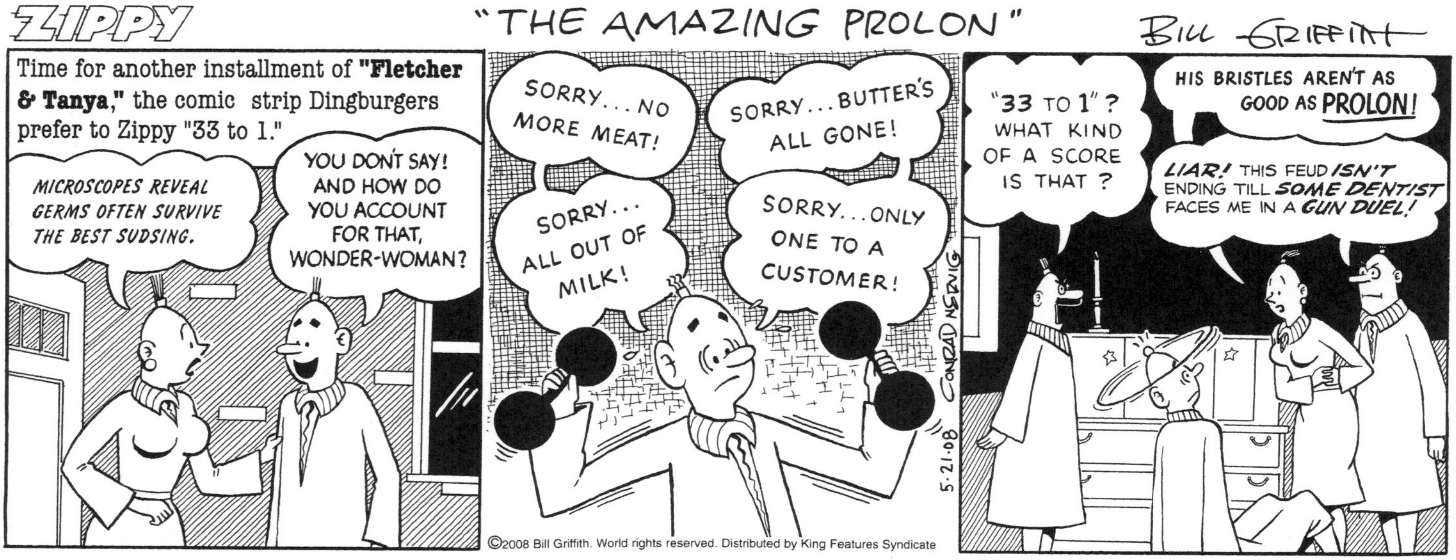
ZIPPY
"THE AMAZING PROLON"
BILL GRIFFITH
Time for another installment of "Fletcher & Tanya," the comic strip Dingburgers prefer to Zippy "33 to 1."
MICROSCOPES REVEAL GERMS OFTEN SURVIVE THE BEST SUDSING.
YOU DON'T SAY! AND HOW DO YOU ACCOUNT FOR THAT, WONDER-WOMAN?
SORRY...NO MORE MEAT!
SORRY...BUTTER'S ALL GONE!
SORRY... ALL OUT OF MILK!
SORRY...ONLY ONE TO A CUSTOMER!
CONRAD NERVIG
5·21·08
©2008 Bill Griffith. World rights reserved. Distributed by King Features Syndicate
"33 TO 1"? WHAT KIND OF A SCORE IS THAT?
HIS BRISTLES AREN'T AS GOOD AS PROLON!
LIAR! THIS FEUD ISN'T ENDING TILL SOME DENTIST FACES ME IN A GUN DUEL!

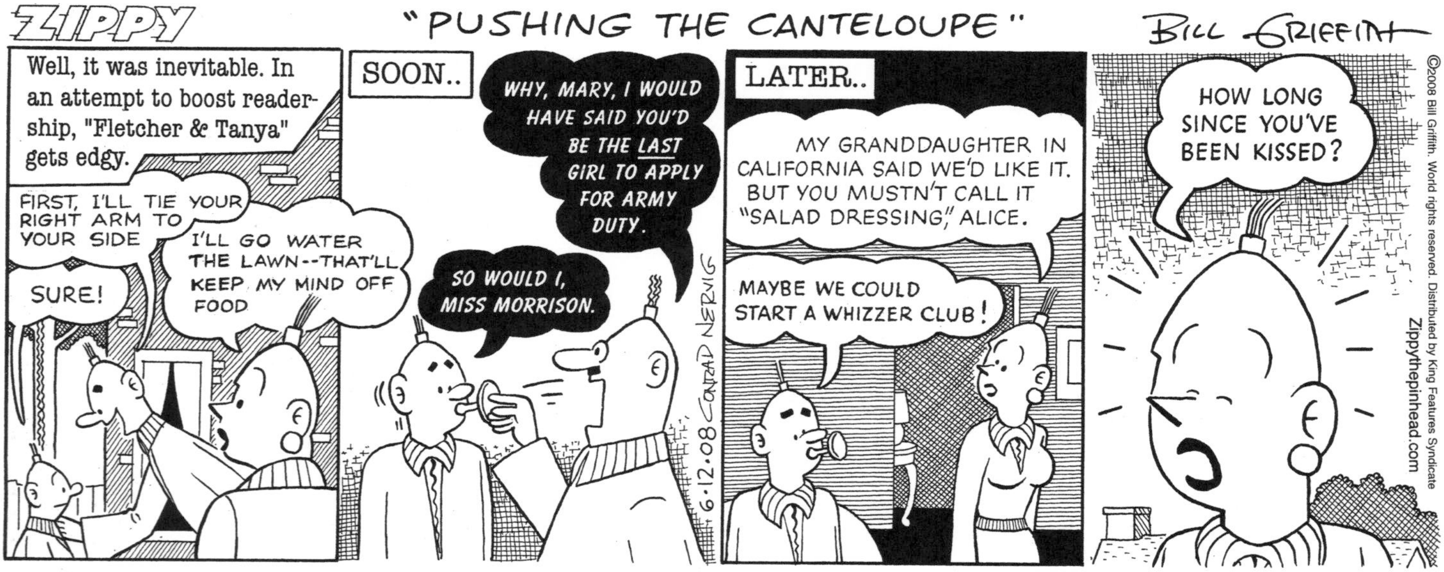
ZIPPY
"PUSHING THE CANTELOUPE"
BILL GRIFFITH
Well, it was inevitable. In an attempt to boost readership, "Fletcher & Tanya" gets edgy.
FIRST, I'LL TIE YOUR RIGHT ARM TO YOUR SIDE
SURE!
I'LL GO WATER THE LAWN--THAT'LL KEEP MY MIND OFF FOOD
SOON..
WHY, MARY, I WOULD HAVE SAID YOU'D BE THE LAST GIRL TO APPLY FOR ARMY DUTY.
SO WOULD I, MISS MORRISON.
CONRAD NERVIG
6·12·08
LATER..
MY GRANDDAUGHTER IN CALIFORNIA SAID WE'D LIKE IT. BUT YOU MUSTN'T CALL IT "SALAD DRESSING," ALICE.
MAYBE WE COULD START A WHIZZER CLUB!
HOW LONG SINCE YOU'VE BEEN KISSED?
©2008 Bill Griffith. World rights reserved. Distributed by King Features Syndicate
Zippythepinhead.com

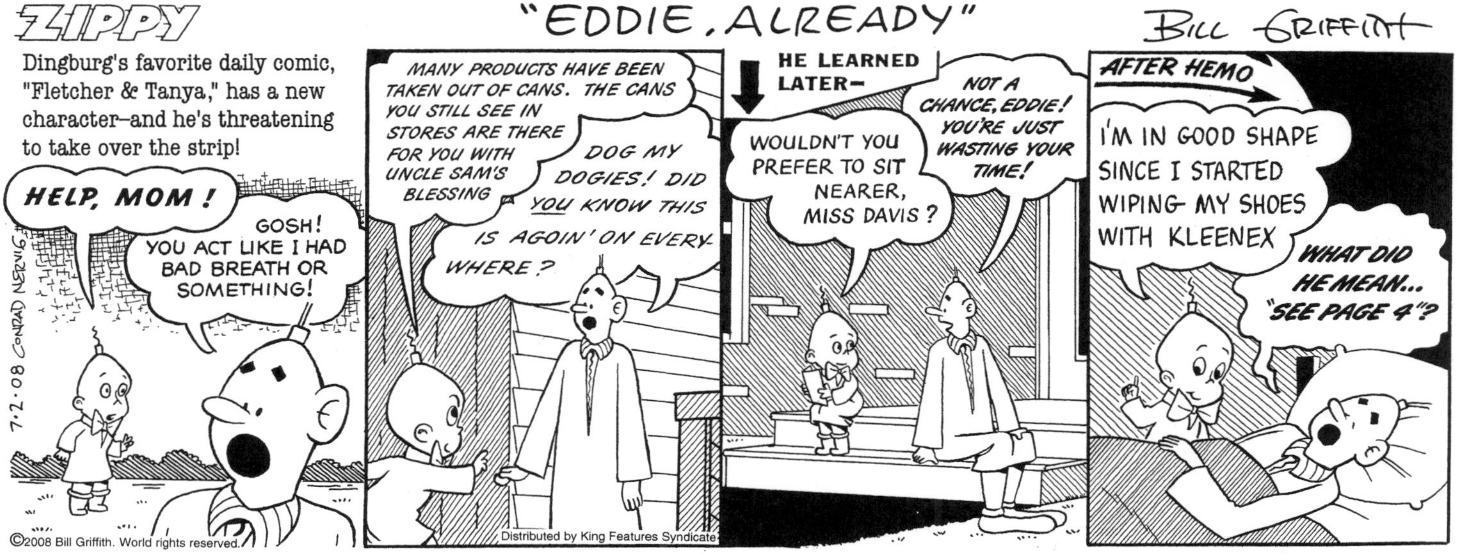
ZIPPY
"EDDIE, ALREADY"
BILL GRIFFITH
Dingburg's favorite daily comic, "Fletcher & Tanya," has a new character–and he's threatening to take over the strip!
HELP, MOM!
GOSH! YOU ACT LIKE I HAD BAD BREATH OR SOMETHING!
7·2·08
©2008 Bill Griffith. World rights reserved.
MANY PRODUCTS HAVE BEEN TAKEN OUT OF CANS. THE CANS YOU STILL SEE IN STORES ARE THERE FOR YOU WITH UNCLE SAM'S BLESSING
DOG MY DOGIES! DID YOU KNOW THIS IS AGOIN' ON EVERY-WHERE?
Distributed by King Features Syndicate
HE LEARNED LATER–
WOULDN'T YOU PREFER TO SIT NEARER, MISS DAVIS?
NOT A CHANCE, EDDIE! YOU'RE JUST WASTING YOUR TIME!
AFTER HEMO
I'M IN GOOD SHAPE SINCE I STARTED WIPING MY SHOES WITH KLEENEX
WHAT DID HE MEAN... "SEE PAGE 4"?

149 A

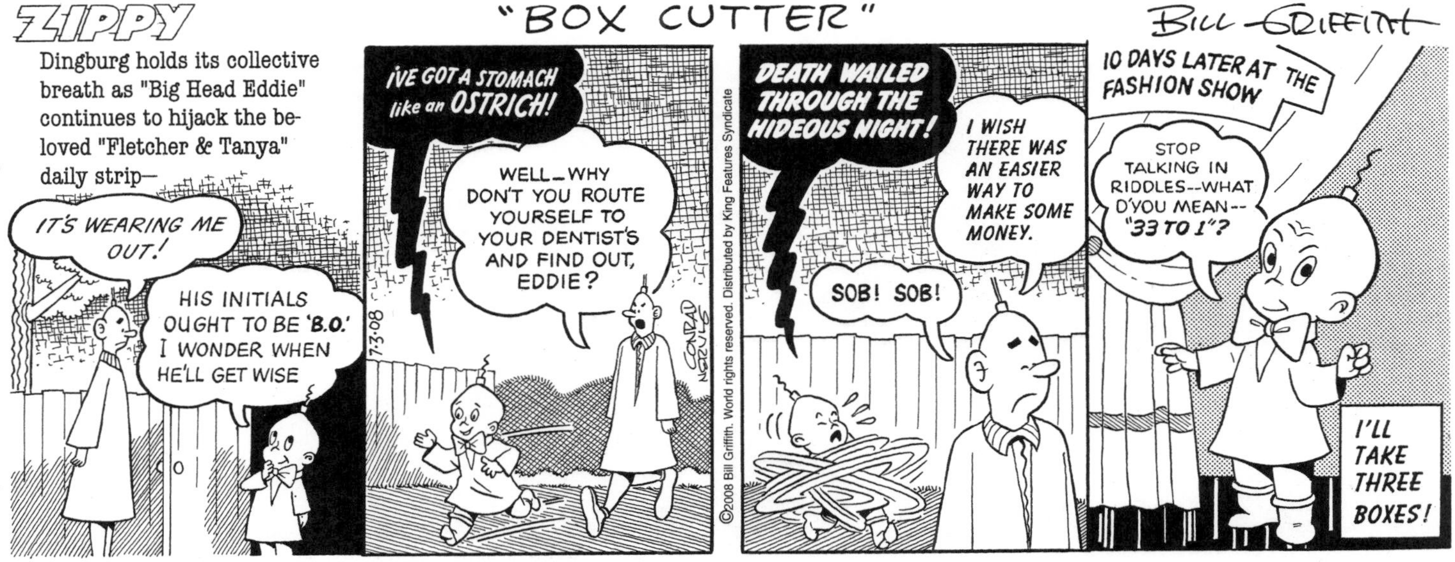
ZIPPY
"BOX CUTTER"
BILL GRIFFITH
Dingburg holds its collective breath as "Big Head Eddie" continues to hijack the beloved "Fletcher & Tanya" daily strip–
IT'S WEARING ME OUT!
HIS INITIALS OUGHT TO BE 'B.O.' I WONDER WHEN HE'LL GET WISE
I'VE GOT A STOMACH like an OSTRICH!
WELL–WHY DON'T YOU ROUTE YOURSELF TO YOUR DENTIST'S AND FIND OUT, EDDIE?
7-3-08
©2008 Bill Griffith. World rights reserved. Distributed by King Features Syndicate
DEATH WAILED THROUGH THE HIDEOUS NIGHT!
I WISH THERE WAS AN EASIER WAY TO MAKE SOME MONEY.
SOB! SOB!
10 DAYS LATER AT THE FASHION SHOW
STOP TALKING IN RIDDLES--WHAT D'YOU MEAN-- "33 TO 1"?
I'LL TAKE THREE BOXES!

149 B

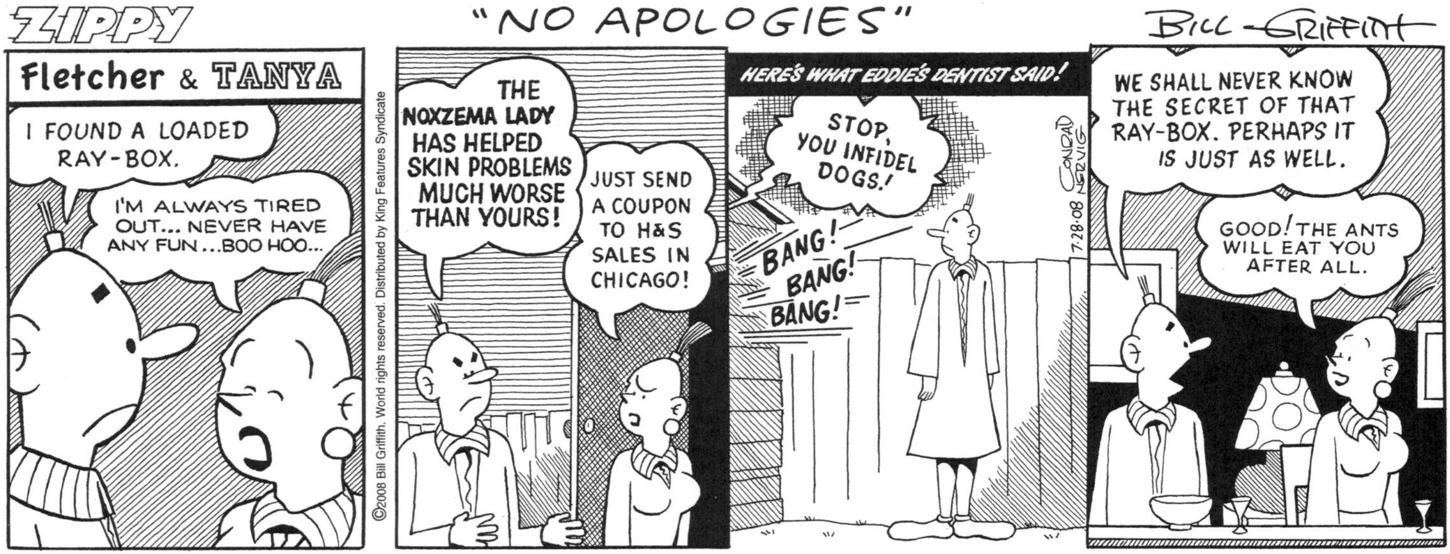
ZIPPY
"NO APOLOGIES"
BILL GRIFFITH
Fletcher & TANYA
I FOUND A LOADED RAY-BOX.
I'M ALWAYS TIRED OUT... NEVER HAVE ANY FUN...BOO HOO...
©2008 Bill Griffith. World rights reserved. Distributed by King Features Syndicate
THE NOXZEMA LADY HAS HELPED SKIN PROBLEMS MUCH WORSE THAN YOURS!
JUST SEND A COUPON TO H&S SALES IN CHICAGO!
HERE'S WHAT EDDIE'S DENTIST SAID!
STOP, YOU INFIDEL DOGS!
BANG! BANG! BANG!
7·28·08
WE SHALL NEVER KNOW THE SECRET OF THAT RAY-BOX. PERHAPS IT IS JUST AS WELL.
GOOD! THE ANTS WILL EAT YOU AFTER ALL.

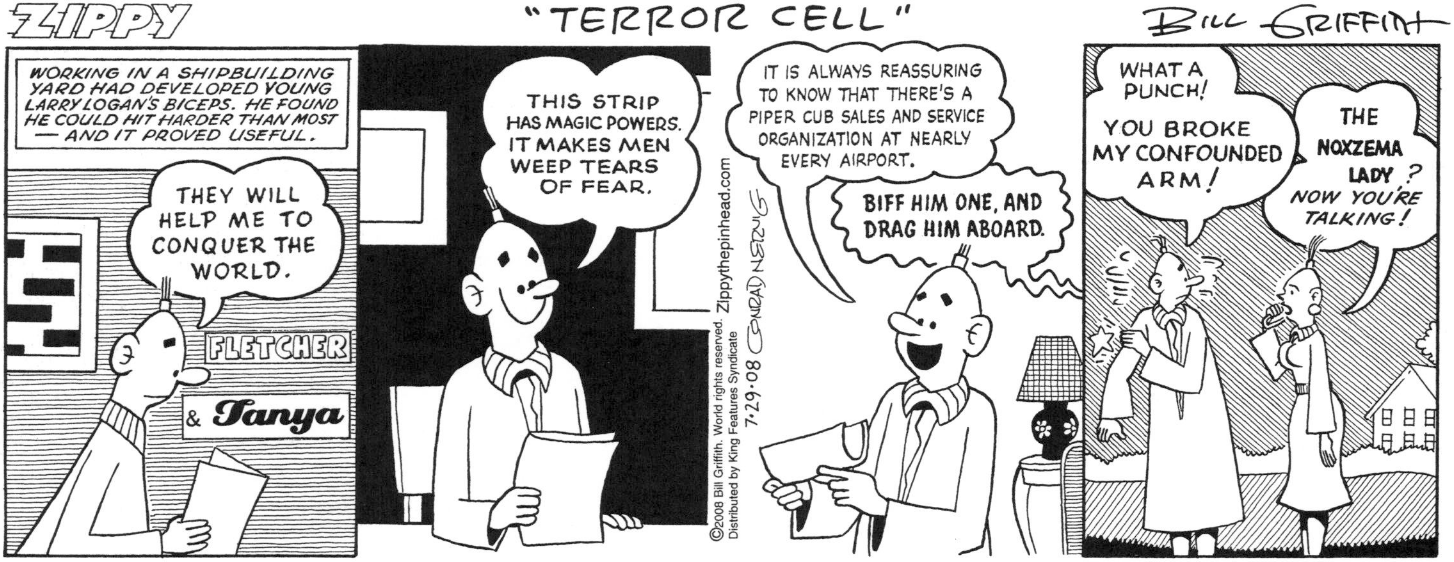
ZIPPY
"TERROR CELL"
BILL GRIFFITH
WORKING IN A SHIPBUILDING YARD HAD DEVELOPED YOUNG LARRY LOGAN'S BICEPS. HE FOUND HE COULD HIT HARDER THAN MOST — AND IT PROVED USEFUL.
THEY WILL HELP ME TO CONQUER THE WORLD.
FLETCHER
& Tanya
THIS STRIP HAS MAGIC POWERS. IT MAKES MEN WEEP TEARS OF FEAR.
©2008 Bill Griffith. World rights reserved. Zippythepinhead.com
Distributed by King Features Syndicate
7·29·08
IT IS ALWAYS REASSURING TO KNOW THAT THERE'S A PIPER CUB SALES AND SERVICE ORGANIZATION AT NEARLY EVERY AIRPORT.
BIFF HIM ONE, AND DRAG HIM ABOARD.
WHAT A PUNCH!
YOU BROKE MY CONFOUNDED ARM!
THE NOXZEMA LADY? NOW YOU'RE TALKING!

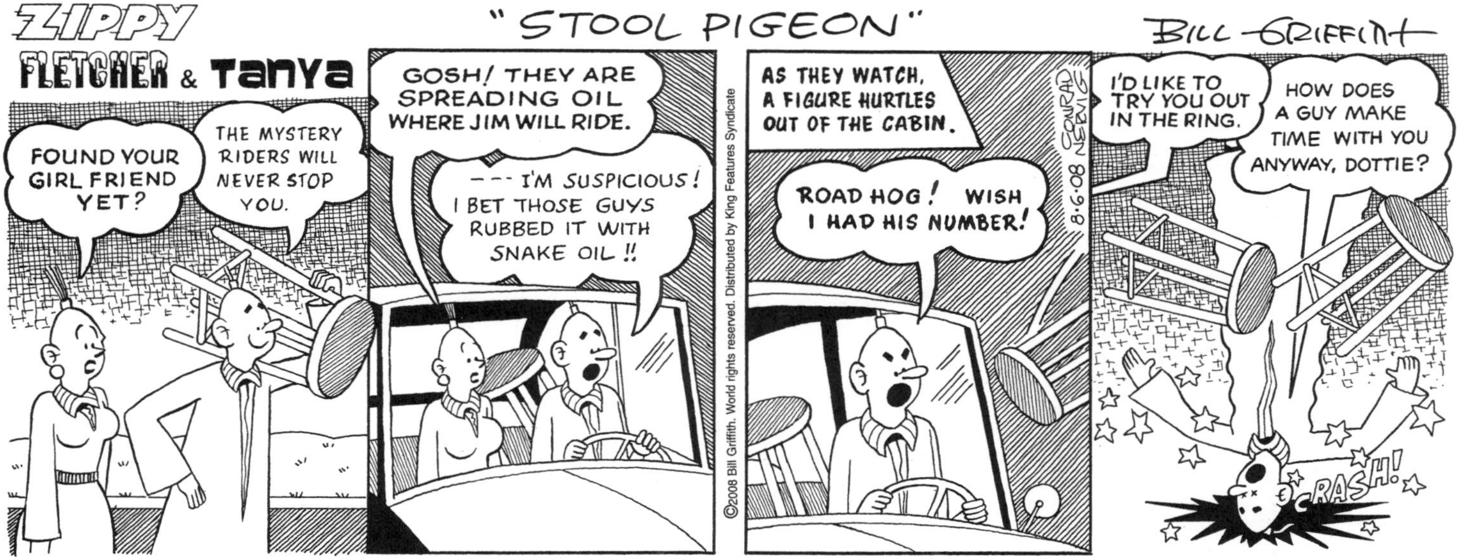

ZIPPY
"STOOL PIGEON"
BILL GRIFFITH
FLETCHER & TANYA
FOUND YOUR GIRL FRIEND YET?
THE MYSTERY RIDERS WILL NEVER STOP YOU.
GOSH! THEY ARE SPREADING OIL WHERE JIM WILL RIDE.
--- I'M SUSPICIOUS! I BET THOSE GUYS RUBBED IT WITH SNAKE OIL !!
©2008 Bill Griffith. World rights reserved. Distributed by King Features Syndicate
AS THEY WATCH, A FIGURE HURTLES OUT OF THE CABIN.
ROAD HOG! WISH I HAD HIS NUMBER!
8·6·08
CONRAD NERVIG
I'D LIKE TO TRY YOU OUT IN THE RING.
HOW DOES A GUY MAKE TIME WITH YOU ANYWAY, DOTTIE?
CRASH!


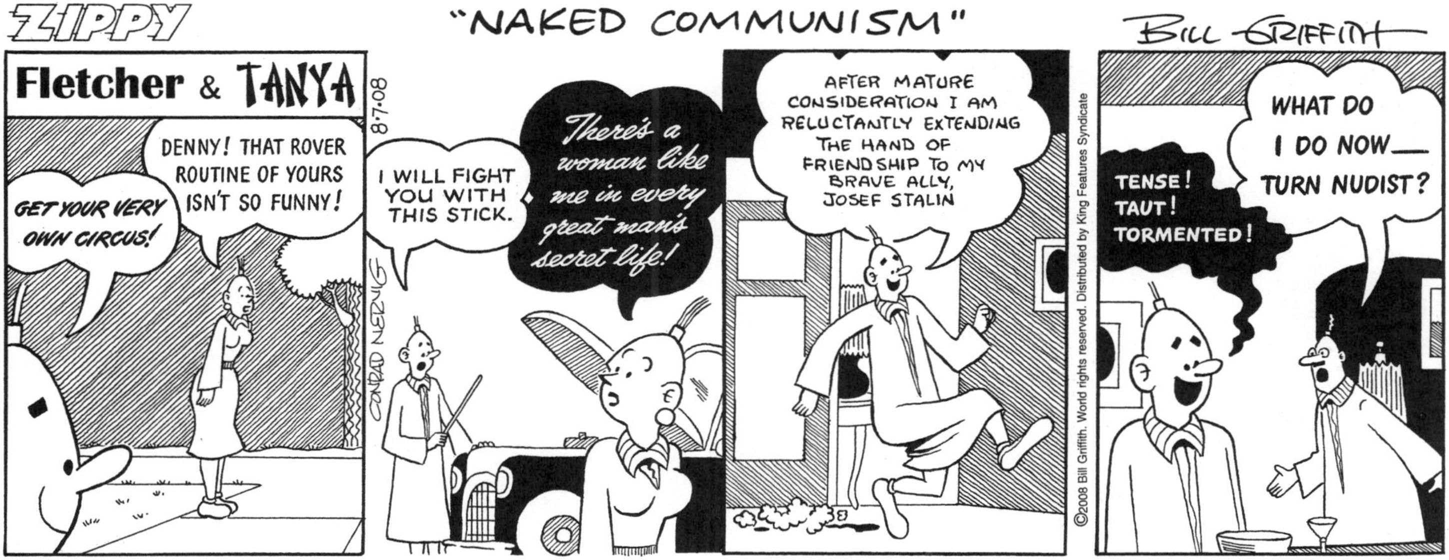

ZIPPY
"NAKED COMMUNISM"
BILL GRIFFITH
Fletcher & TANYA
8·7·08
GET YOUR VERY OWN CIRCUS!
DENNY! THAT ROVER ROUTINE OF YOURS ISN'T SO FUNNY!
I WILL FIGHT YOU WITH THIS STICK.
There's a woman like me in every great man's secret life!
CONRAD NERVIG
AFTER MATURE CONSIDERATION I AM RELUCTANTLY EXTENDING THE HAND OF FRIENDSHIP TO MY BRAVE ALLY, JOSEF STALIN
©2008 Bill Griffith. World rights reserved. Distributed by King Features Syndicate
TENSE! TAUT! TORMENTED!
WHAT DO I DO NOW___ TURN NUDIST?

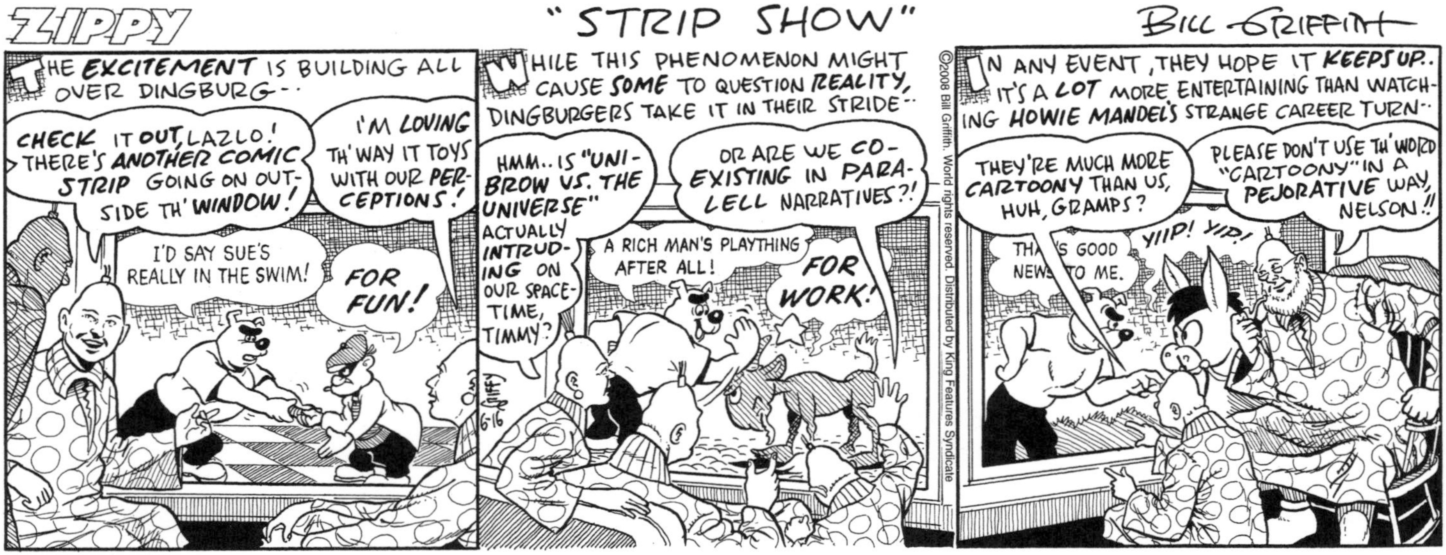
ZIPPY
"STRIP SHOW"
BILL GRIFFITH
THE EXCITEMENT IS BUILDING ALL OVER DINGBURG--
CHECK IT OUT, LAZLO! THERE'S ANOTHER COMIC STRIP GOING ON OUTSIDE TH' WINDOW!
I'M LOVING TH' WAY IT TOYS WITH OUR PERCEPTIONS!
I'D SAY SUE'S REALLY IN THE SWIM!
FOR FUN!
WHILE THIS PHENOMENON MIGHT CAUSE SOME TO QUESTION REALITY, DINGBURGERS TAKE IT IN THEIR STRIDE--
HMM.. IS "UNIBROW VS. THE UNIVERSE" ACTUALLY INTRUDING ON OUR SPACE-TIME, TIMMY?
OR ARE WE CO-EXISTING IN PARALELL NARRATIVES?!
A RICH MAN'S PLAYTHING AFTER ALL!
FOR WORK!
©2008 Bill Griffith. World rights reserved. Distributed by King Features Syndicate
IN ANY EVENT, THEY HOPE IT KEEPS UP.. IT'S A LOT MORE ENTERTAINING THAN WATCHING HOWIE MANDEL'S STRANGE CAREER TURN--
THEY'RE MUCH MORE CARTOONY THAN US, HUH, GRAMPS?
PLEASE DON'T USE TH' WORD "CARTOONY" IN A PEJORATIVE WAY, NELSON!!
THA'S GOOD NEWS TO ME.
YIIP! YIP!

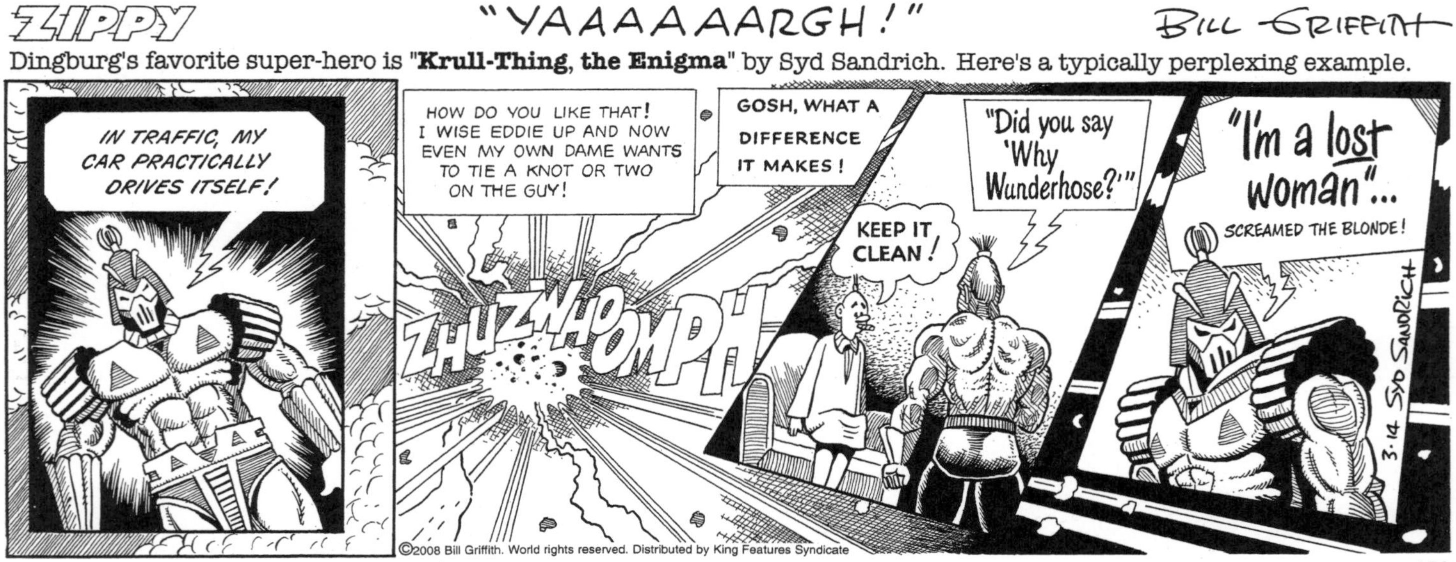
ZIPPY
"YAAAAAARGH!"
BILL GRIFFITH
Dingburg's favorite super-hero is "Krull-Thing, the Enigma" by Syd Sandrich. Here's a typically perplexing example.
IN TRAFFIC, MY CAR PRACTICALLY DRIVES ITSELF!
HOW DO YOU LIKE THAT! I WISE EDDIE UP AND NOW EVEN MY OWN DAME WANTS TO TIE A KNOT OR TWO ON THE GUY!
GOSH, WHAT A DIFFERENCE IT MAKES!
ZHUZWHOOMPH
KEEP IT CLEAN!
"Did you say 'Why Wunderhose?'"
"I'm a lost woman"...
SCREAMED THE BLONDE!
3-14 SYD SANDRICH
©2008 Bill Griffith. World rights reserved. Distributed by King Features Syndicate

150

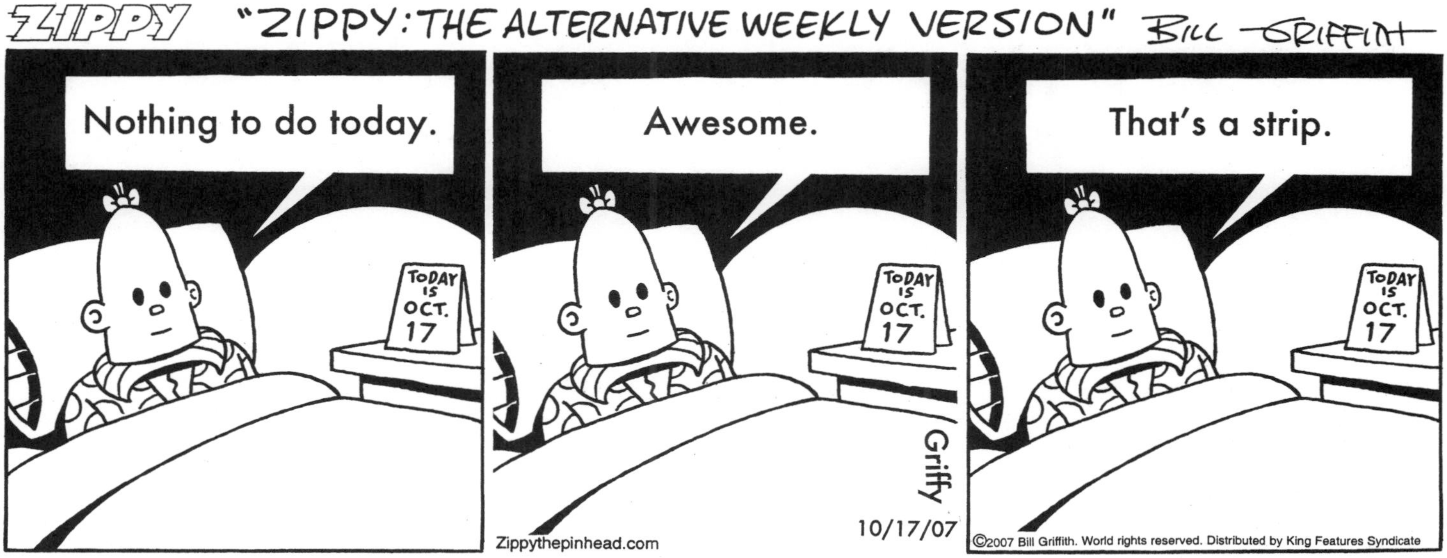
ZIPPY
"ZIPPY: THE ALTERNATIVE WEEKLY VERSION"
BILL GRIFFITH
Nothing to do today.
TODAY IS OCT. 17
Awesome.
TODAY IS OCT. 17
Griffy
10/17/07
Zippythepinhead.com
That's a strip.
TODAY IS OCT. 17
©2007 Bill Griffith. World rights reserved. Distributed by King Features Syndicate

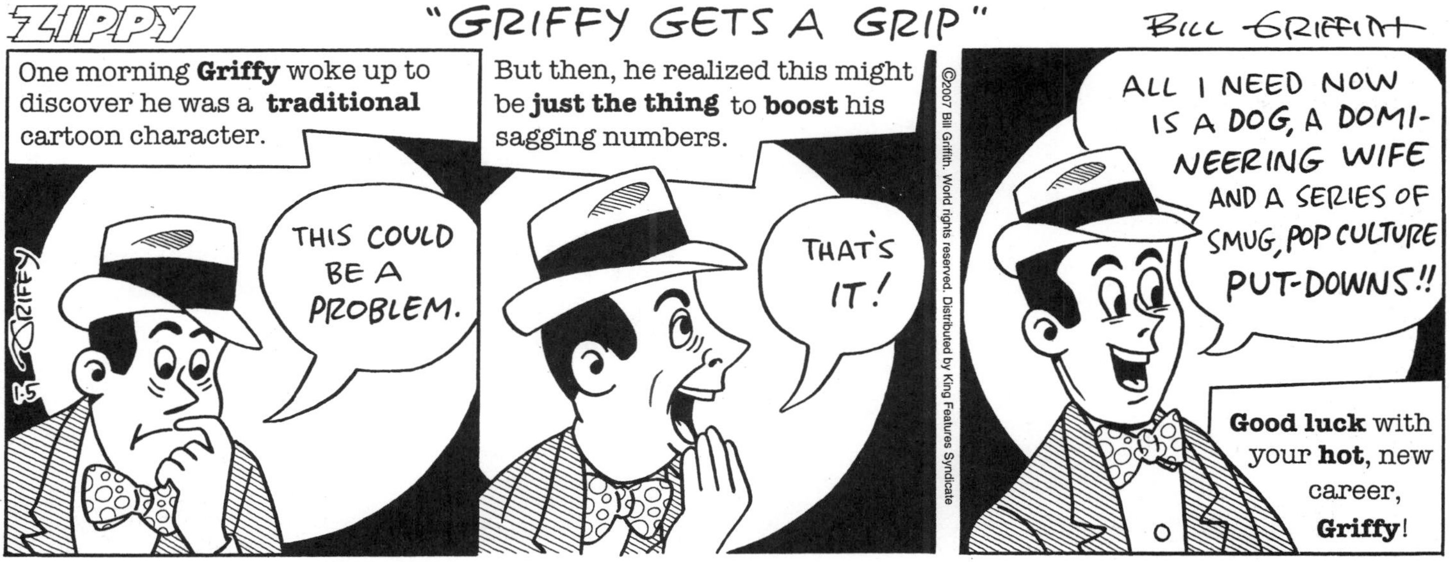
ZIPPY
"GRIFFY GETS A GRIP"
BILL GRIFFITH
One morning Griffy woke up to discover he was a traditional cartoon character.
THIS COULD BE A PROBLEM.
GRIFFY
But then, he realized this might be just the thing to boost his sagging numbers.
THAT'S IT!
©2007 Bill Griffith. World rights reserved. Distributed by King Features Syndicate
ALL I NEED NOW IS A DOG, A DOMINEERING WIFE AND A SERIES OF SMUG, POP CULTURE PUT-DOWNS!!
Good luck with your hot, new career, Griffy!

# TOAD ET ALIA

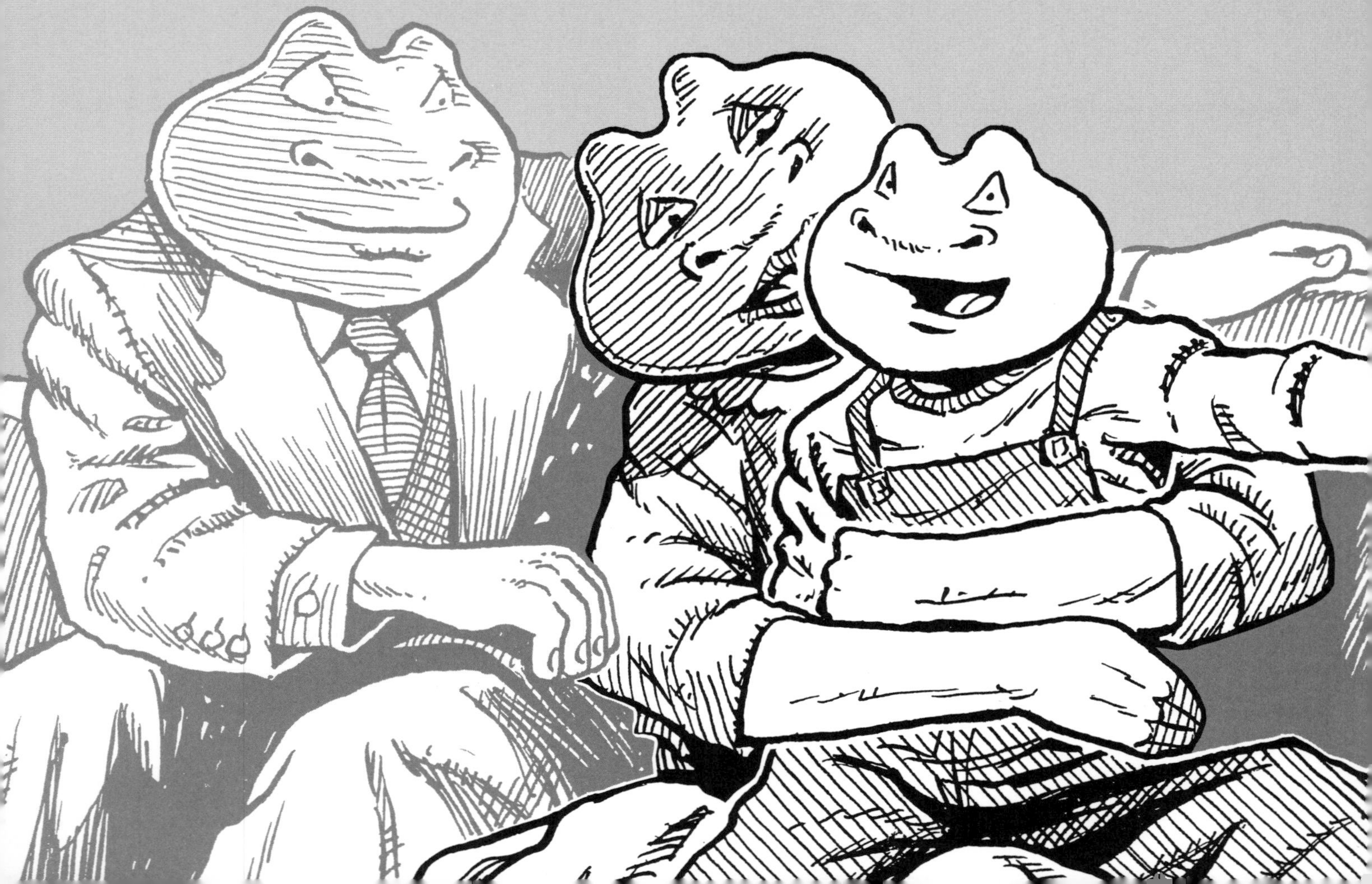

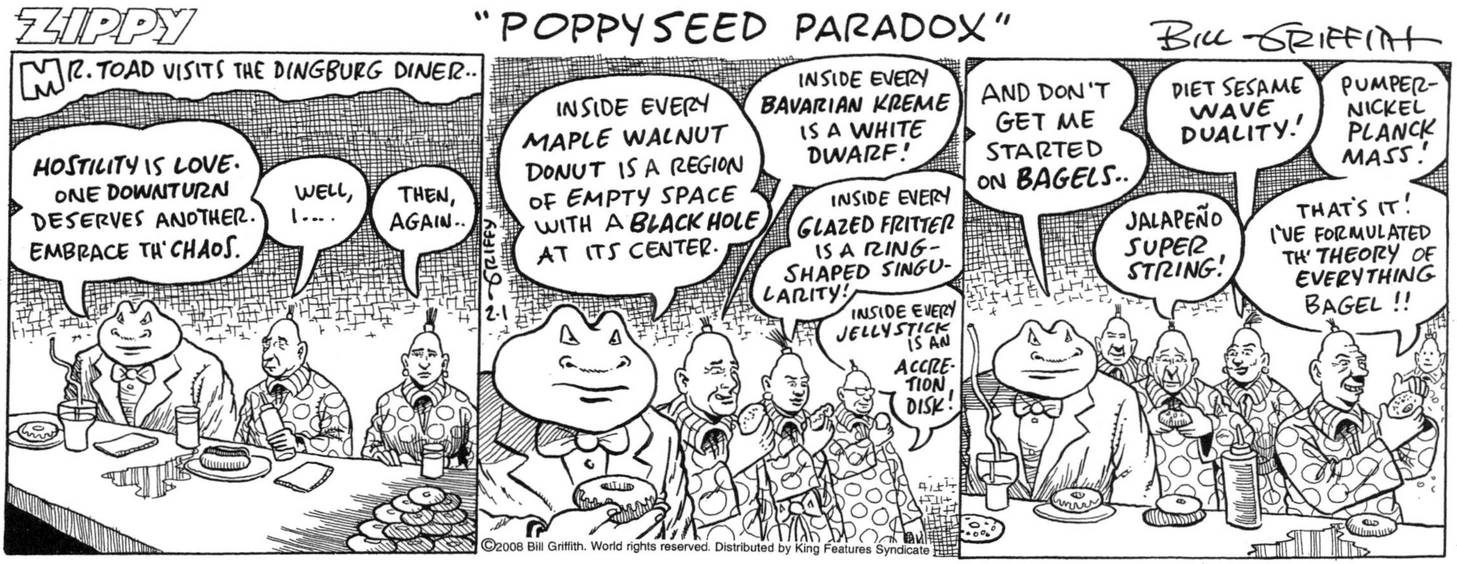
ZIPPY
"POPPYSEED PARADOX"
BILL GRIFFITH
MR. TOAD VISITS THE DINGBURG DINER..
HOSTILITY IS LOVE. ONE DOWNTURN DESERVES ANOTHER. EMBRACE TH' CHAOS.
WELL, I....
THEN, AGAIN..
INSIDE EVERY MAPLE WALNUT DONUT IS A REGION OF EMPTY SPACE WITH A BLACK HOLE AT ITS CENTER.
INSIDE EVERY BAVARIAN KREME IS A WHITE DWARF!
INSIDE EVERY GLAZED FRITTER IS A RING-SHAPED SINGULARITY!
INSIDE EVERY JELLYSTICK IS AN ACCRETION DISK!
GRIFFY 2·1
©2008 Bill Griffith. World rights reserved. Distributed by King Features Syndicate
AND DON'T GET ME STARTED ON BAGELS..
DIET SESAME WAVE DUALITY!
PUMPERNICKEL PLANCK MASS!
JALAPEÑO SUPER STRING!
THAT'S IT! I'VE FORMULATED TH' THEORY OF EVERYTHING BAGEL!!

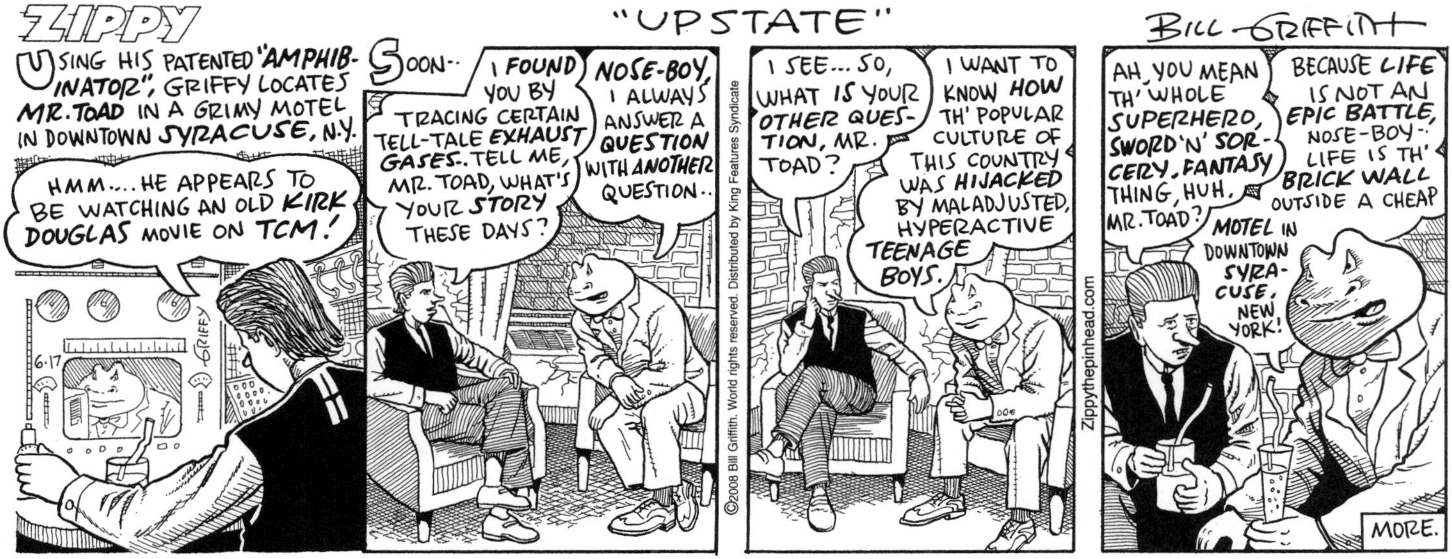
ZIPPY
"UPSTATE"
BILL GRIFFITH
USING HIS PATENTED "AMPHIBINATOR", GRIFFY LOCATES MR. TOAD IN A GRIMY MOTEL IN DOWNTOWN SYRACUSE, N.Y.
HMM.... HE APPEARS TO BE WATCHING AN OLD KIRK DOUGLAS MOVIE ON TCM!
GRIFFY 6·17
SOON..
I FOUND YOU BY TRACING CERTAIN TELL-TALE EXHAUST GASES.. TELL ME, MR. TOAD, WHAT'S YOUR STORY THESE DAYS?
NOSE-BOY, I ALWAYS ANSWER A QUESTION WITH ANOTHER QUESTION..
©2008 Bill Griffith. World rights reserved. Distributed by King Features Syndicate
I SEE... SO, WHAT IS YOUR OTHER QUESTION, MR. TOAD?
I WANT TO KNOW HOW TH' POPULAR CULTURE OF THIS COUNTRY WAS HIJACKED BY MALADJUSTED, HYPERACTIVE TEENAGE BOYS.
Zippythepinhead.com
AH, YOU MEAN TH' WHOLE SUPERHERO, SWORD 'N' SORCERY, FANTASY THING, HUH, MR. TOAD?
BECAUSE LIFE IS NOT AN EPIC BATTLE, NOSE-BOY.. LIFE IS TH' BRICK WALL OUTSIDE A CHEAP MOTEL IN DOWNTOWN SYRACUSE, NEW YORK!
MORE.

151

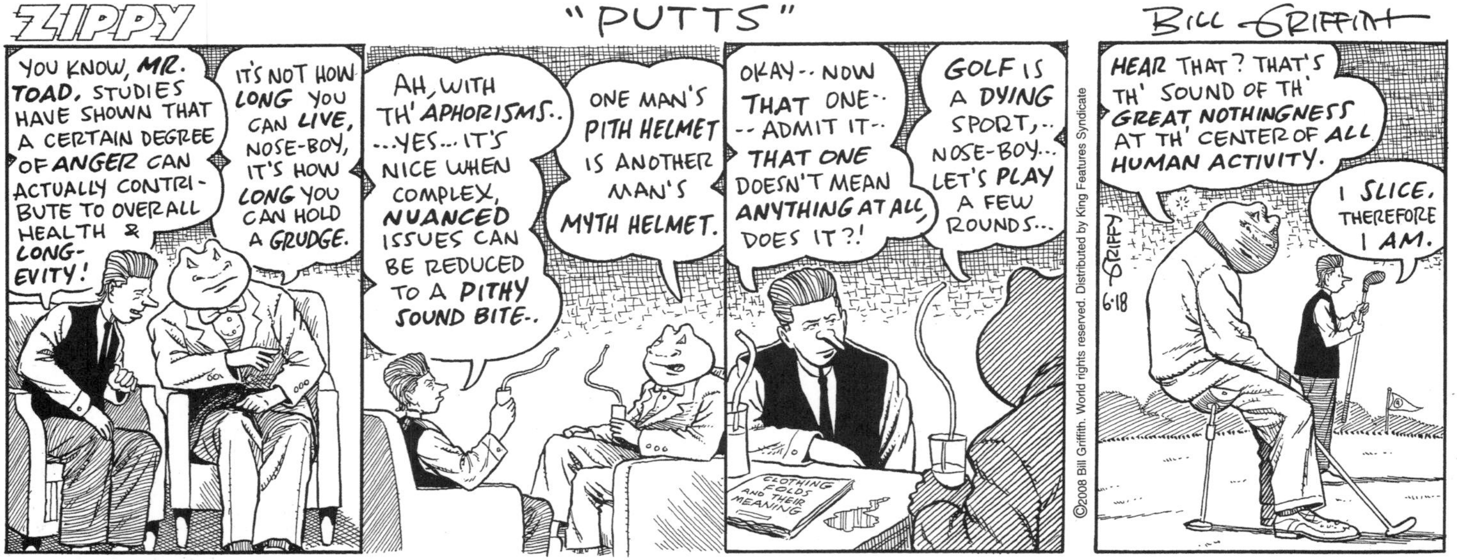
ZIPPY
"PUTTS"
BILL GRIFFITH
YOU KNOW, MR. TOAD, STUDIES HAVE SHOWN THAT A CERTAIN DEGREE OF ANGER CAN ACTUALLY CONTRIBUTE TO OVERALL HEALTH & LONGEVITY!
IT'S NOT HOW LONG YOU CAN LIVE, NOSE-BOY, IT'S HOW LONG YOU CAN HOLD A GRUDGE.
AH, WITH TH' APHORISMS.. ...YES... IT'S NICE WHEN COMPLEX, NUANCED ISSUES CAN BE REDUCED TO A PITHY SOUND BITE..
ONE MAN'S PITH HELMET IS ANOTHER MAN'S MYTH HELMET.
CLOTHING FOLDS AND THEIR MEANING
OKAY.. NOW THAT ONE.. --ADMIT IT-- THAT ONE DOESN'T MEAN ANYTHING AT ALL, DOES IT?!
GOLF IS A DYING SPORT,.. NOSE-BOY... LET'S PLAY A FEW ROUNDS...
©2008 Bill Griffith. World rights reserved. Distributed by King Features Syndicate
GRIFFY 6·18
HEAR THAT? THAT'S TH' SOUND OF TH' GREAT NOTHINGNESS AT TH' CENTER OF ALL HUMAN ACTIVITY.
I SLICE, THEREFORE I AM.

152

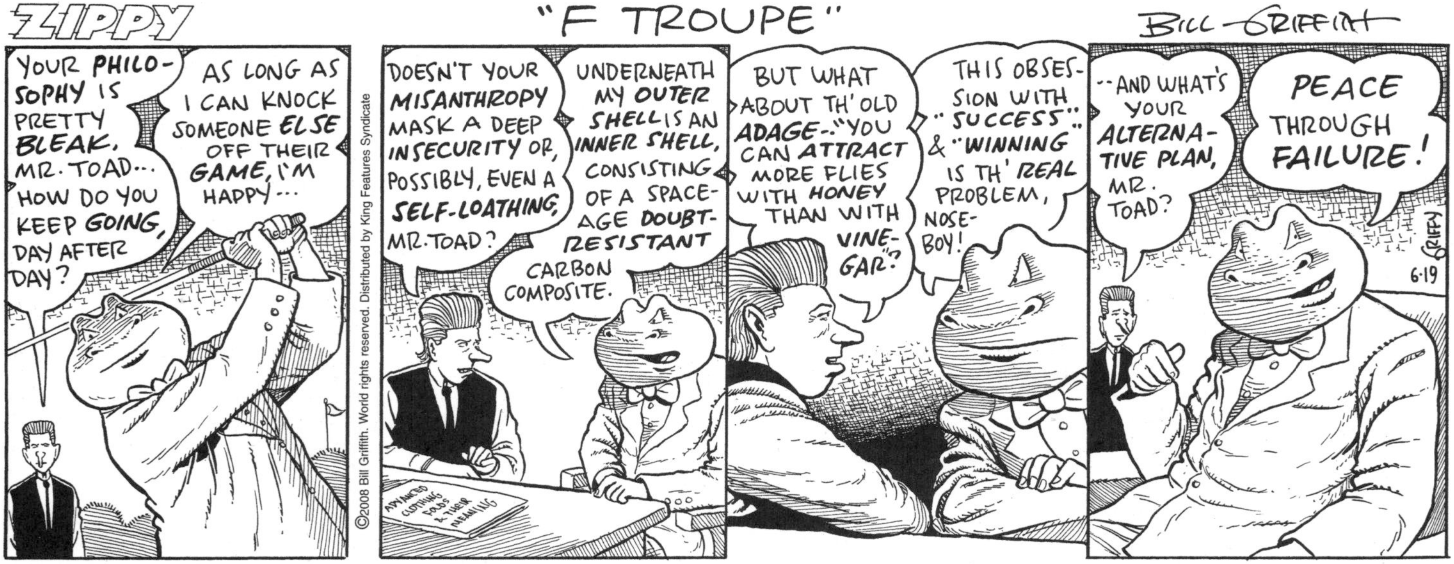
ZIPPY
"F TROUPE"
BILL GRIFFITH
YOUR PHILOSOPHY IS PRETTY BLEAK, MR. TOAD... HOW DO YOU KEEP GOING, DAY AFTER DAY?
AS LONG AS I CAN KNOCK SOMEONE ELSE OFF THEIR GAME, I'M HAPPY...
©2008 Bill Griffith. World rights reserved. Distributed by King Features Syndicate
DOESN'T YOUR MISANTHROPY MASK A DEEP INSECURITY OR, POSSIBLY, EVEN A SELF-LOATHING, MR. TOAD?
UNDERNEATH MY OUTER SHELL IS AN INNER SHELL, CONSISTING OF A SPACE-AGE DOUBT-RESISTANT CARBON COMPOSITE.
ADVANCED CLOTHING FOLDS & THEIR MEANING
BUT WHAT ABOUT TH' OLD ADAGE-- "YOU CAN ATTRACT MORE FLIES WITH HONEY THAN WITH VINEGAR"?
THIS OBSESSION WITH "SUCCESS" & "WINNING" IS TH' REAL PROBLEM, NOSE-BOY!
..AND WHAT'S YOUR ALTERNATIVE PLAN, MR. TOAD?
PEACE THROUGH FAILURE!
GRIFFY 6·19

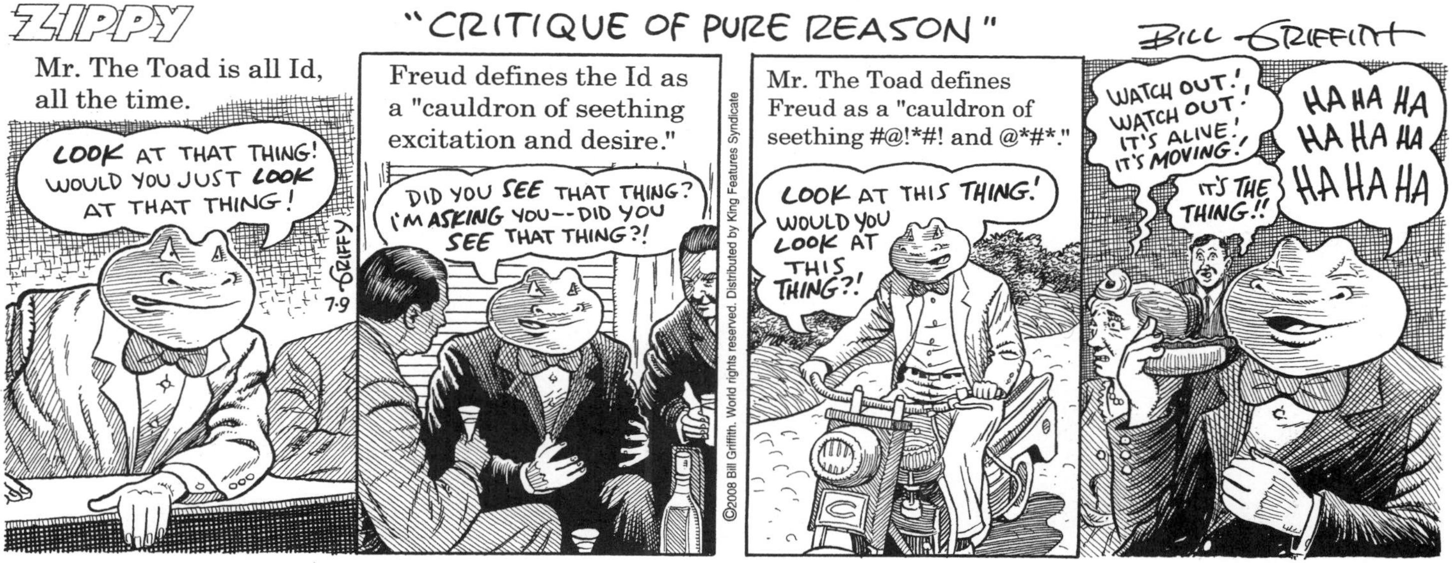
ZIPPY
"CRITIQUE OF PURE REASON"
BILL GRIFFITH
Mr. The Toad is all Id, all the time.
LOOK AT THAT THING! WOULD YOU JUST LOOK AT THAT THING!
GRIFFY 7·9
Freud defines the Id as a "cauldron of seething excitation and desire."
DID YOU SEE THAT THING? I'M ASKING YOU--DID YOU SEE THAT THING?!
©2008 Bill Griffith. World rights reserved. Distributed by King Features Syndicate
Mr. The Toad defines Freud as a "cauldron of seething #@!*#! and @*#*."
LOOK AT THIS THING! WOULD YOU LOOK AT THIS THING?!
WATCH OUT! WATCH OUT! IT'S ALIVE! IT'S MOVING!
IT'S THE THING!!
HA HA HA HA HA HA HA HA HA

153

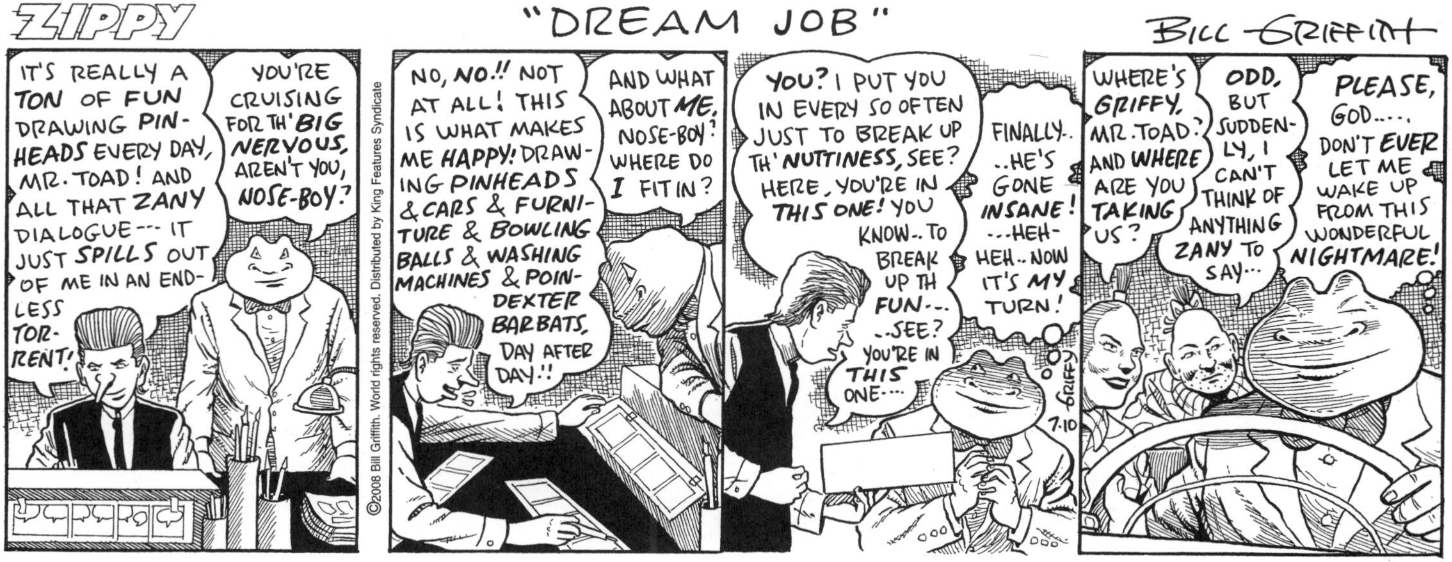
ZIPPY
"DREAM JOB"
BILL GRIFFITH
IT'S REALLY A TON OF FUN DRAWING PINHEADS EVERY DAY, MR. TOAD! AND ALL THAT ZANY DIALOGUE--- IT JUST SPILLS OUT OF ME IN AN ENDLESS TORRENT!
YOU'RE CRUISING FOR TH' BIG NERVOUS, AREN'T YOU, NOSE-BOY?
©2008 Bill Griffith. World rights reserved. Distributed by King Features Syndicate
NO, NO!! NOT AT ALL! THIS IS WHAT MAKES ME HAPPY! DRAWING PINHEADS & CARS & FURNITURE & BOWLING BALLS & WASHING MACHINES & POINDEXTER BARBATS, DAY AFTER DAY!!
AND WHAT ABOUT ME, NOSE-BOY? WHERE DO I FIT IN?
YOU? I PUT YOU IN EVERY SO OFTEN JUST TO BREAK UP TH' NUTTINESS, SEE? HERE, YOU'RE IN THIS ONE! YOU KNOW.. TO BREAK UP TH FUN-.. ..SEE? YOU'RE IN THIS ONE....
FINALLY.. ..HE'S GONE INSANE! ...HEH- HEH.. NOW IT'S MY TURN!
GRIFFY 7·10
WHERE'S GRIFFY, MR. TOAD? AND WHERE ARE YOU TAKING US?
ODD, BUT SUDDENLY, I CAN'T THINK OF ANYTHING ZANY TO SAY...
PLEASE, GOD.... DON'T EVER LET ME WAKE UP FROM THIS WONDERFUL NIGHTMARE!

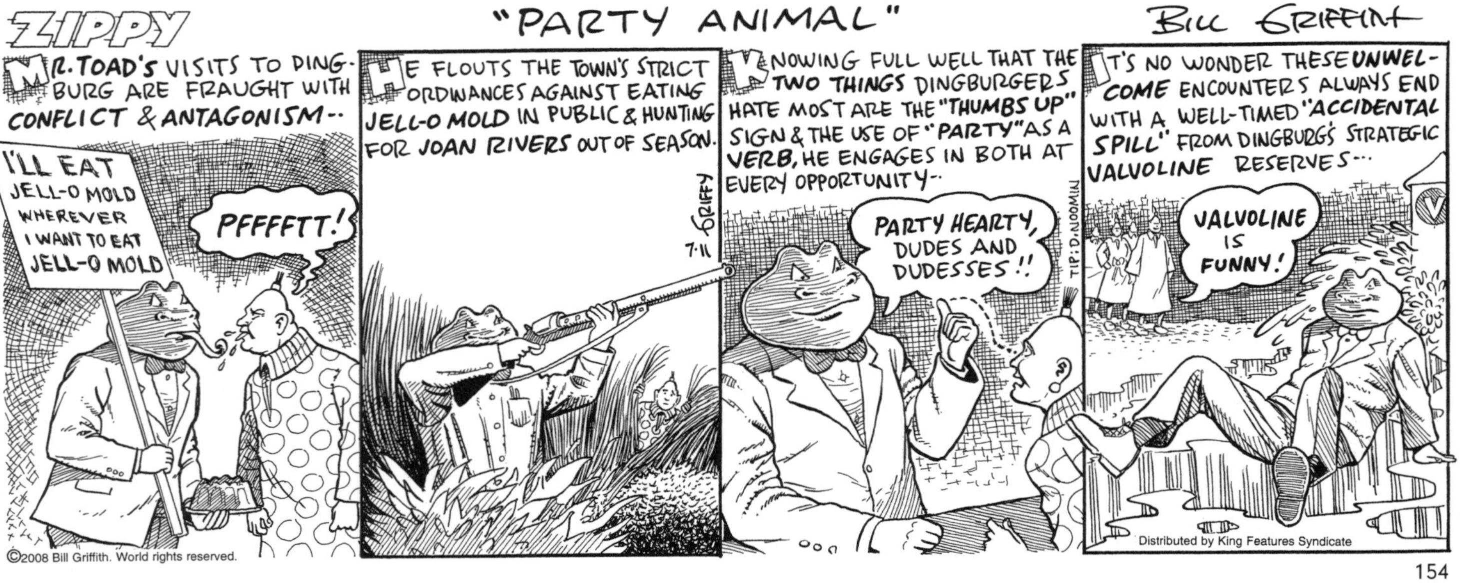
ZIPPY
"PARTY ANIMAL"
BILL GRIFFITH
MR. TOAD'S VISITS TO DINGBURG ARE FRAUGHT WITH CONFLICT & ANTAGONISM--
I'LL EAT JELL-O MOLD WHEREVER I WANT TO EAT JELL-O MOLD
PFFFFTT!
HE FLOUTS THE TOWN'S STRICT ORDINANCES AGAINST EATING JELL-O MOLD IN PUBLIC & HUNTING FOR JOAN RIVERS OUT OF SEASON.
7·11 GRIFFY
KNOWING FULL WELL THAT THE TWO THINGS DINGBURGERS HATE MOST ARE THE "THUMBS UP" SIGN & THE USE OF "PARTY" AS A VERB, HE ENGAGES IN BOTH AT EVERY OPPORTUNITY--
PARTY HEARTY, DUDES AND DUDESSES!!
TIP: D. NOOMIN
IT'S NO WONDER THESE UNWELCOME ENCOUNTERS ALWAYS END WITH A WELL-TIMED "ACCIDENTAL SPILL" FROM DINGBURG'S STRATEGIC VALVOLINE RESERVES...
VALVOLINE IS FUNNY!
©2008 Bill Griffith. World rights reserved.
Distributed by King Features Syndicate
154

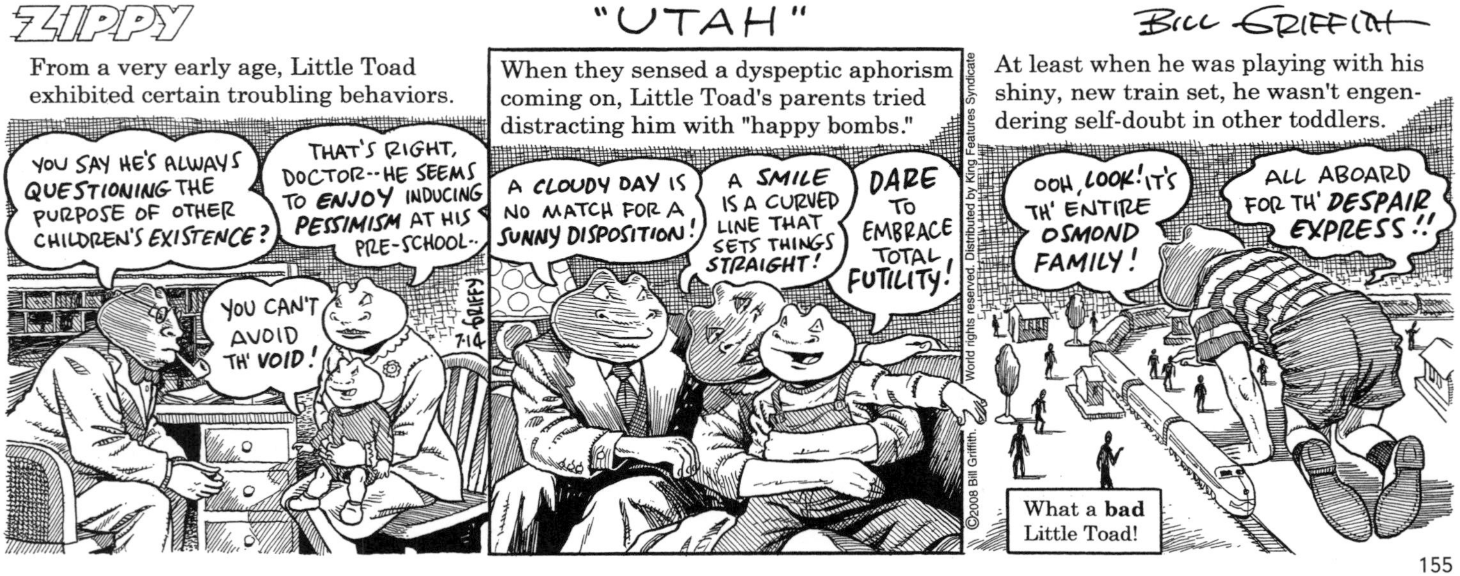
ZIPPY
"UTAH"
BILL GRIFFITH
From a very early age, Little Toad exhibited certain troubling behaviors.
YOU SAY HE'S ALWAYS QUESTIONING THE PURPOSE OF OTHER CHILDREN'S EXISTENCE?
THAT'S RIGHT, DOCTOR--HE SEEMS TO ENJOY INDUCING PESSIMISM AT HIS PRE-SCHOOL..
YOU CAN'T AVOID TH' VOID!
7·14 GRIFFY
When they sensed a dyspeptic aphorism coming on, Little Toad's parents tried distracting him with "happy bombs."
A CLOUDY DAY IS NO MATCH FOR A SUNNY DISPOSITION!
A SMILE IS A CURVED LINE THAT SETS THINGS STRAIGHT!
DARE TO EMBRACE TOTAL FUTILITY!
©2008 Bill Griffith. World rights reserved. Distributed by King Features Syndicate
At least when he was playing with his shiny, new train set, he wasn't engendering self-doubt in other toddlers.
OOH, LOOK! IT'S TH' ENTIRE OSMOND FAMILY!
ALL ABOARD FOR TH' DESPAIR EXPRESS!!
What a bad Little Toad!
155

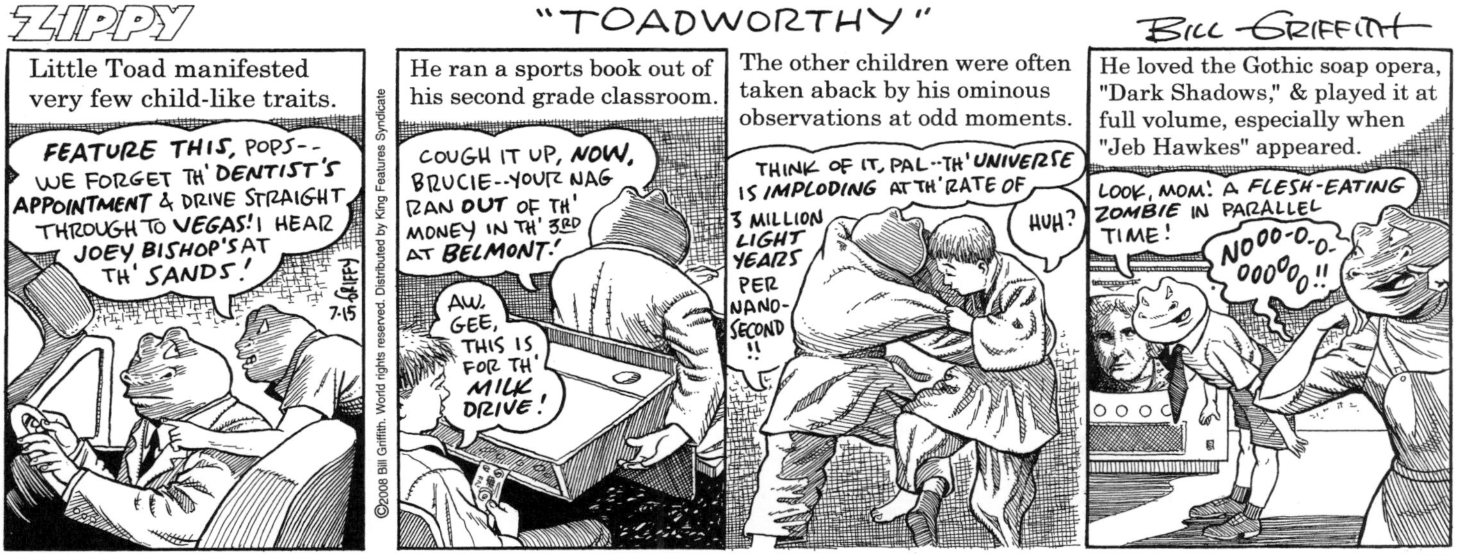
ZIPPY
"TOADWORTHY"
BILL GRIFFITH
Little Toad manifested very few child-like traits.
FEATURE THIS, POPS-- WE FORGET TH' DENTIST'S APPOINTMENT & DRIVE STRAIGHT THROUGH TO VEGAS! I HEAR JOEY BISHOP'S AT TH' SANDS!
GRIFFY 7-15
©2008 Bill Griffith. World rights reserved. Distributed by King Features Syndicate
He ran a sports book out of his second grade classroom.
COUGH IT UP, NOW, BRUCIE--YOUR NAG RAN OUT OF TH' MONEY IN TH' 3RD AT BELMONT!
AW. GEE, THIS IS FOR TH' MILK DRIVE!
The other children were often taken aback by his ominous observations at odd moments.
THINK OF IT, PAL--TH' UNIVERSE IS IMPLODING AT TH' RATE OF 3 MILLION LIGHT YEARS PER NANO-SECOND!!
HUH?
He loved the Gothic soap opera, "Dark Shadows," & played it at full volume, especially when "Jeb Hawkes" appeared.
LOOK, MOM! A FLESH-EATING ZOMBIE IN PARALLEL TIME!
NOOO-O-O-O-OOOOOO!!

156

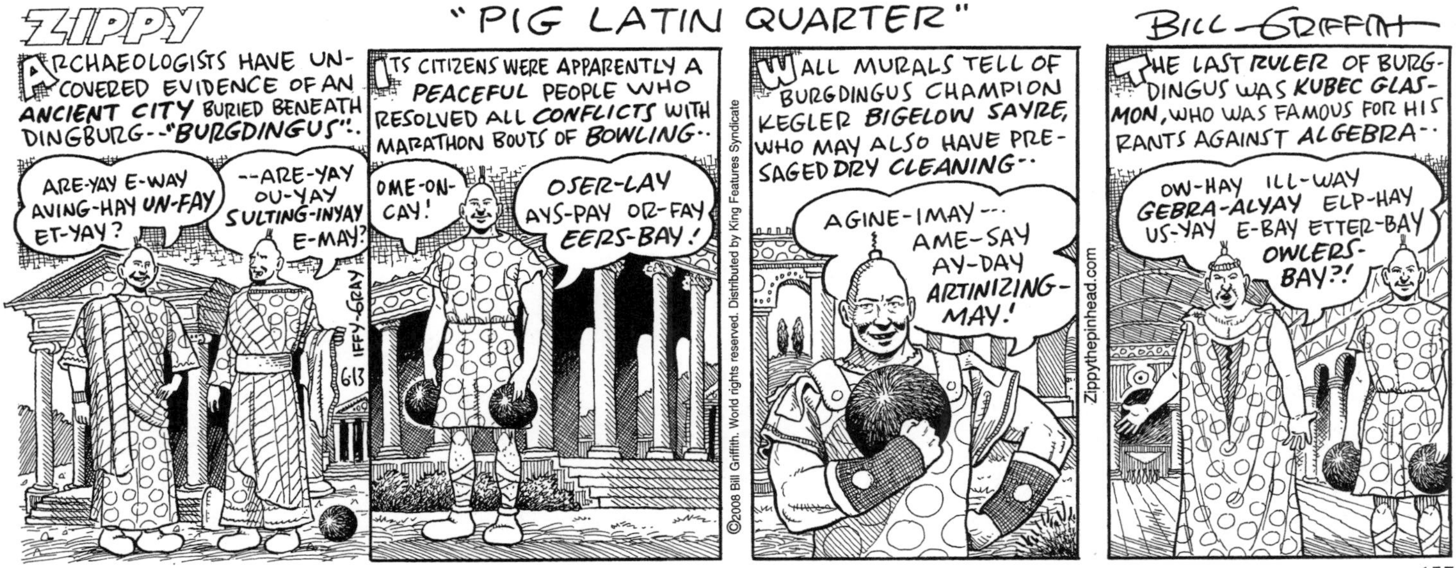
ZIPPY
"PIG LATIN QUARTER"
BILL GRIFFITH
ARCHAEOLOGISTS HAVE UNCOVERED EVIDENCE OF AN ANCIENT CITY BURIED BENEATH DINGBURG--"BURGDINGUS"..
ARE-YAY E-WAY AVING-HAY UN-FAY ET-YAY?
--ARE-YAY OU-YAY SULTING-INYAY E-MAY?
IFFY-GRAY 6-13
ITS CITIZENS WERE APPARENTLY A PEACEFUL PEOPLE WHO RESOLVED ALL CONFLICTS WITH MARATHON BOUTS OF BOWLING..
OME-ON-CAY!
OSER-LAY AYS-PAY OR-FAY EERS-BAY!
©2008 Bill Griffith. World rights reserved. Distributed by King Features Syndicate
WALL MURALS TELL OF BURGDINGUS CHAMPION KEGLER BIGELOW SAYRE, WHO MAY ALSO HAVE PRESAGED DRY CLEANING..
AGINE-IMAY--- AME-SAY AY-DAY ARTINIZING-MAY!
Zippythepinhead.com
THE LAST RULER OF BURGDINGUS WAS KUBEC GLASMON, WHO WAS FAMOUS FOR HIS RANTS AGAINST ALGEBRA..
OW-HAY ILL-WAY GEBRA-ALYAY ELP-HAY US-YAY E-BAY ETTER-BAY OWLERS-BAY?!

157

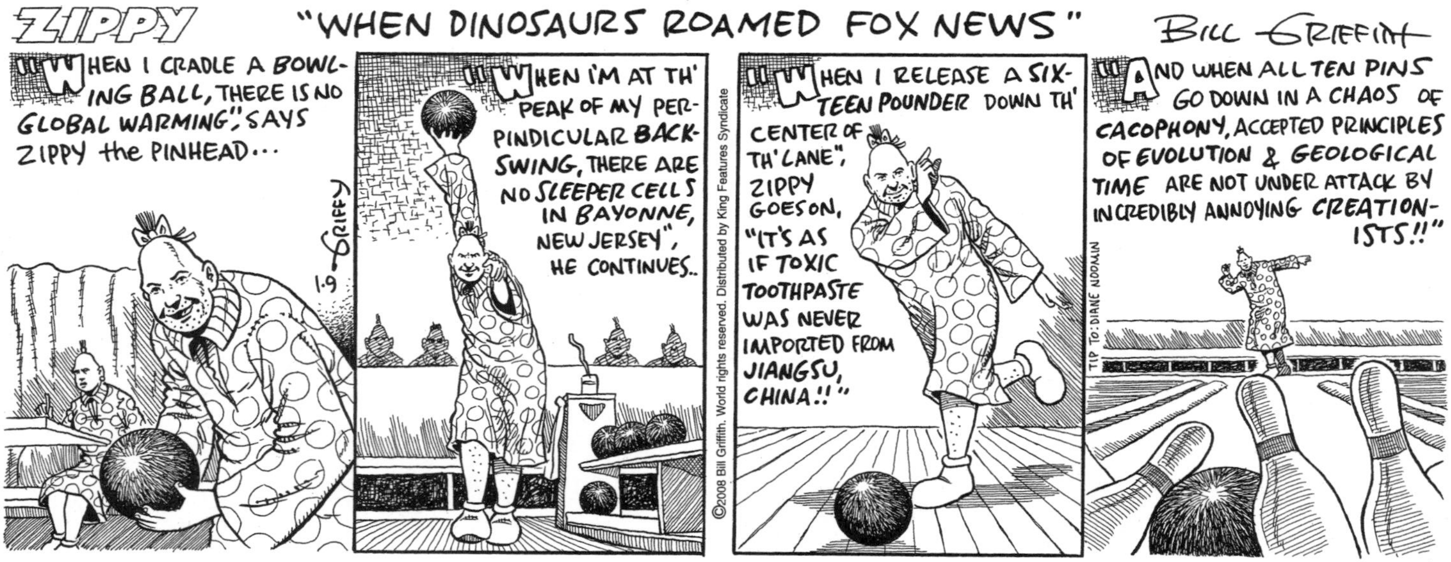
ZIPPY
"WHEN DINOSAURS ROAMED FOX NEWS"
BILL GRIFFITH
"WHEN I CRADLE A BOWLING BALL, THERE IS NO GLOBAL WARMING", SAYS ZIPPY the PINHEAD...
GRIFFY 1.9
"WHEN I'M AT TH' PEAK OF MY PERPINDICULAR BACKSWING, THERE ARE NO SLEEPER CELLS IN BAYONNE, NEW JERSEY", HE CONTINUES..
©2008 Bill Griffith. World rights reserved. Distributed by King Features Syndicate
"WHEN I RELEASE A SIXTEEN POUNDER DOWN TH' CENTER OF TH' LANE", ZIPPY GOES ON, "IT'S AS IF TOXIC TOOTHPASTE WAS NEVER IMPORTED FROM JIANGSU, CHINA!!"
"AND WHEN ALL TEN PINS GO DOWN IN A CHAOS OF CACOPHONY, ACCEPTED PRINCIPLES OF EVOLUTION & GEOLOGICAL TIME ARE NOT UNDER ATTACK BY INCREDIBLY ANNOYING CREATIONISTS!!"
TIP TO: DIANE NOOMIN

158

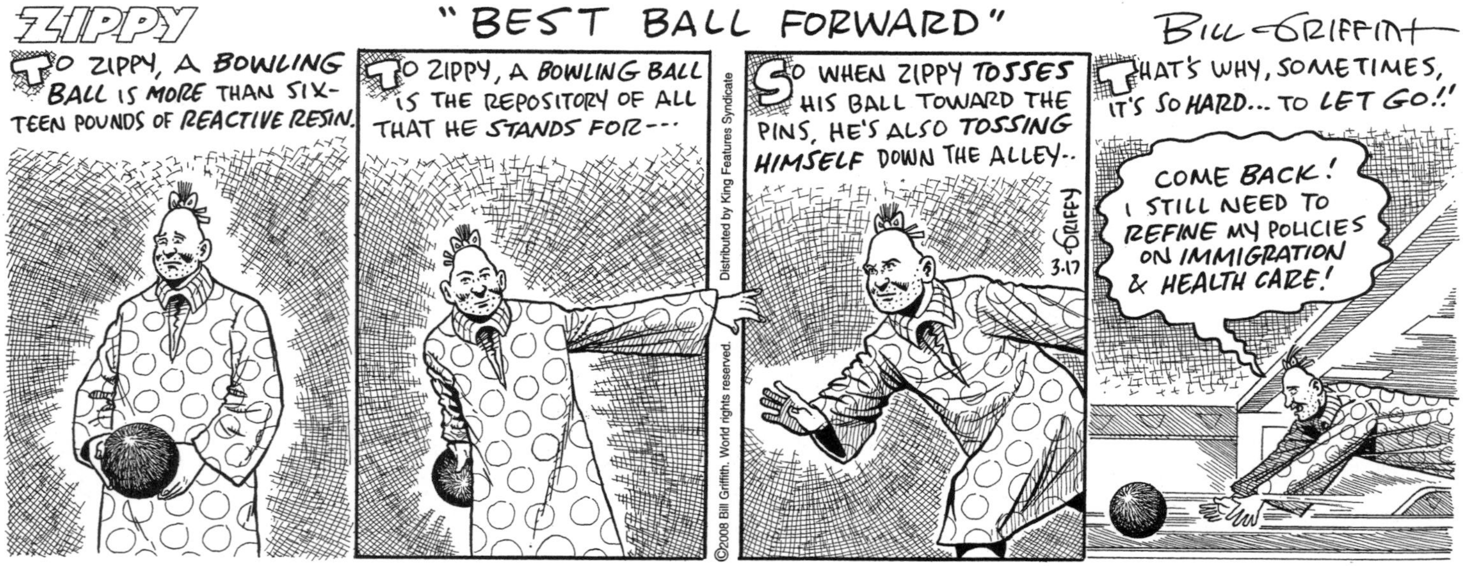
ZIPPY
"BEST BALL FORWARD"
BILL GRIFFITH
TO ZIPPY, A BOWLING BALL IS MORE THAN SIXTEEN POUNDS OF REACTIVE RESIN.
TO ZIPPY, A BOWLING BALL IS THE REPOSITORY OF ALL THAT HE STANDS FOR---
©2008 Bill Griffith. World rights reserved. Distributed by King Features Syndicate
SO WHEN ZIPPY TOSSES HIS BALL TOWARD THE PINS, HE'S ALSO TOSSING HIMSELF DOWN THE ALLEY..
GRIFFY 3.17
THAT'S WHY, SOMETIMES, IT'S SO HARD... TO LET GO!!"
COME BACK! I STILL NEED TO REFINE MY POLICIES ON IMMIGRATION & HEALTH CARE!

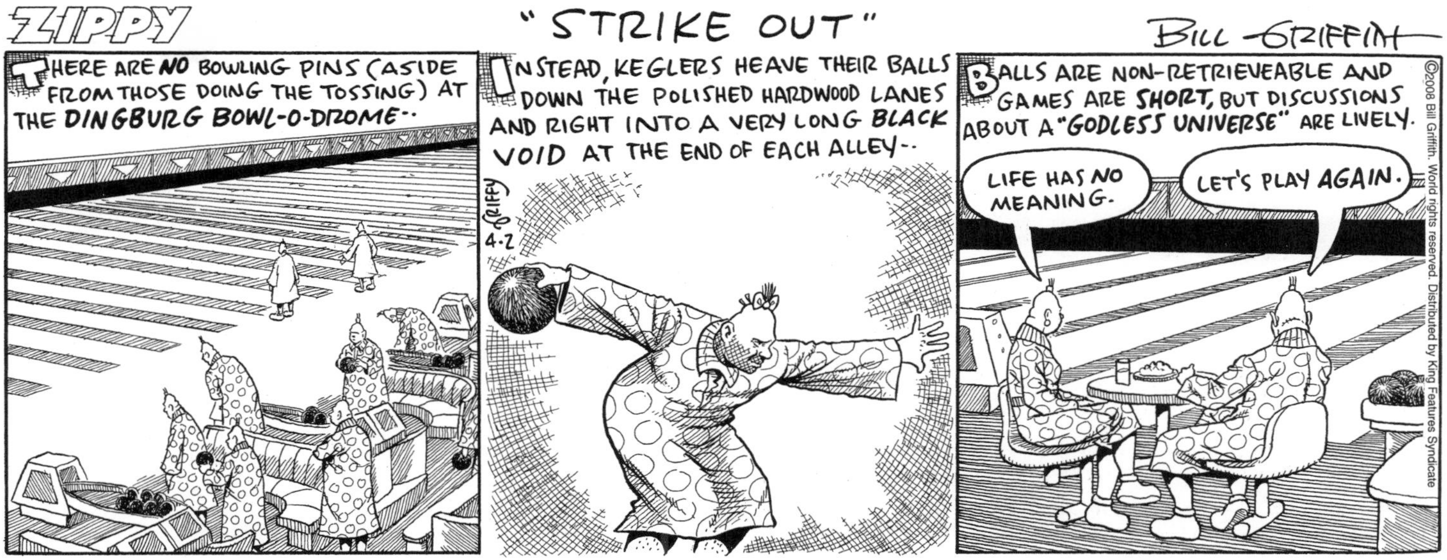
ZIPPY
"STRIKE OUT"
BILL GRIFFITH
THERE ARE NO BOWLING PINS (ASIDE FROM THOSE DOING THE TOSSING) AT THE DINGBURG BOWL-O-DROME..
INSTEAD, KEGLERS HEAVE THEIR BALLS DOWN THE POLISHED HARDWOOD LANES AND RIGHT INTO A VERY LONG BLACK VOID AT THE END OF EACH ALLEY..
GRIFFY 4-2
BALLS ARE NON-RETRIEVEABLE AND GAMES ARE SHORT, BUT DISCUSSIONS ABOUT A "GODLESS UNIVERSE" ARE LIVELY.
LIFE HAS NO MEANING.
LET'S PLAY AGAIN.
©2008 Bill Griffith. World rights reserved. Distributed by King Features Syndicate

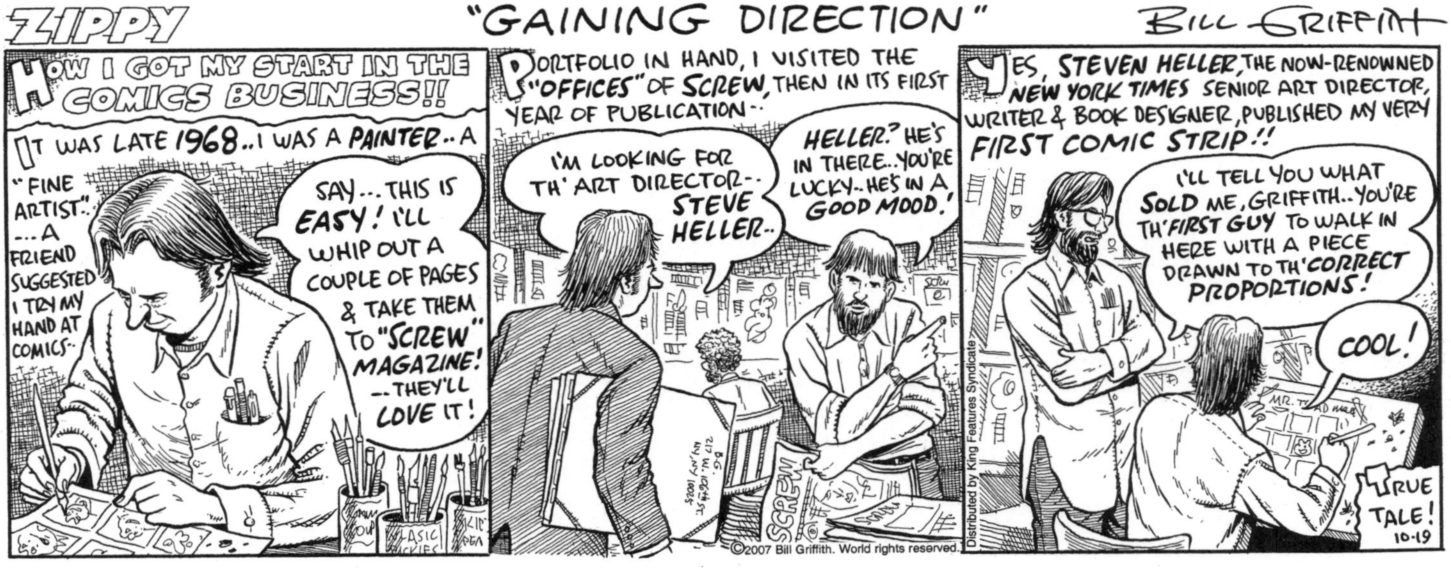
ZIPPY
"GAINING DIRECTION"
BILL GRIFFITH
HOW I GOT MY START IN THE COMICS BUSINESS!!
IT WAS LATE 1968.. I WAS A PAINTER.. A "FINE ARTIST".. ...A FRIEND SUGGESTED I TRY MY HAND AT COMICS..
SAY... THIS IS EASY! I'LL WHIP OUT A COUPLE OF PAGES & TAKE THEM TO "SCREW" MAGAZINE! --THEY'LL LOVE IT!
PORTFOLIO IN HAND, I VISITED THE "OFFICES" OF SCREW, THEN IN ITS FIRST YEAR OF PUBLICATION..
I'M LOOKING FOR TH' ART DIRECTOR.. STEVE HELLER..
HELLER? HE'S IN THERE.. YOU'RE LUCKY.. HE'S IN A GOOD MOOD.
SCREW
©2007 Bill Griffith. World rights reserved.
YES, STEVEN HELLER, THE NOW-RENOWNED NEW YORK TIMES SENIOR ART DIRECTOR, WRITER & BOOK DESIGNER, PUBLISHED MY VERY FIRST COMIC STRIP!!
I'LL TELL YOU WHAT SOLD ME, GRIFFITH.. YOU'RE TH' FIRST GUY TO WALK IN HERE WITH A PIECE DRAWN TO TH' CORRECT PROPORTIONS!
COOL!
TRUE TALE!
10-19
Distributed by King Features Syndicate

# THE PINDEX

## DINGBURG, U.S.A. / Chapter 1

1. Disclaimer: Dingburg is fictional. It is not 17 miles west of Baltimore. It is a state of mind (17 miles west of Baltimore). [pg. 7]

2. Snickerdoodles are sugar cookies rolled in cinnamon sugar. The name may be derived from the German word Schneckennudeln (cinnamon-dusted sweet roll). "Come Fly With Me" was written and composed by Jimmy Van Heusen and Sammy Kahn in 1958. Mr. Clean also made his debut in 1958 as the name of the popular cleaning product. In the mid 1960s, he became Mean Mr. Clean because he "hates dirt." [pg. 7]

3. Actor Broderick Crawford (1911-1986) played tough guys in many Hollywood films, but may be best known for his portrayal of Chief Dan Mathews in the TV police drama, *Highway Patrol* (1955-1959). [pg. 8]

4. Lycra is a brand name of spandex or elastane, invented in 1959 by chemist Joseph Shivers. [pg. 9]

5. Depicted is the High Restaurant, Mt. Vernon OH. Mel Gibson (b. 1958) directed *Apocalypto* in 2006. In the film, a solar eclipse is shown to take only a few seconds. In reality, a solar eclipse occurs over a period of several hours. [pg. 9]

6. Krazy Glue is the trade name for cyanoacrylate. It made its first commercial appearance in 1955 as "Flash Glue." (See also "THE BIG THREE," pg. 17) [pg. 10]

7. The epitaph on singer/politician Sonny Bono's (1935-1998) headstone reads: "And the beat goes on." Woolite is a cold water woolen clothing cleanser created by the Boyle-Midway Company in 1953. [pg. 10]

8. Estonians once worshipped the pagan god Tharapita, which translates as "Thor, help!" [pg. 11]

9. The Clark Bar was created by David L. Clark in 1915. He also created the Zagnut bar (See also "IN A BALTIC STATE," pg. 14 and pg. 82). Head cheese is not a cheese, but a terrine of meat made from the head of a calf or pig. It may also include meat from the feet and the heart. It is also called luncheon meat. [pg. 11]

10. Bulldog statue, Rochester, MA. [pg. 13]

11. Cartoonist Morty Mishkin is fictional, as is Atomic Duck, but a Dr. Morton MIshkin presented a paper titled "On the Neural Basis of Visual Awareness" in Tucson, Arizona, in 1997. [pg. 14]

12. The origins of shuffleboard are not known, but an early version of the game was played by King Henry VIII (1491-1547). (See also "BACK TO ABNORMAL AGAIN," pg. 25) [pg. 15]

13. The first rollerball pen was introduced in 1984 by the Sakura Color Products Corporation (Japan) as the Gelly Roll Pen. [pg. 16]

14. Upon her death, billionaire hotel operator Leona Helmsley (1920-2007) left $12 million to her Maltese dog, Trouble. In 2008, the courts reduced Trouble's inheritance to $2 million. (See also "PINHEAD PRIDE," pg. 57, pg. 96, "END OF THE LINE," pg. 113 and "SQUAWK BOX," pg. 115.) [pg. 17]

15. The web-based open content encyclopedia Wikipedia was launched in 2001 by Jimmy Wales and Larry Sanger. When Wales broke up with his girlfriend, Rachel Marsden, in 2008, he ordered changes to her Wikipedia biography entry. [pg. 19]

16. Comedian Allan Sherman (1924-1973) memorialized the Nauga in his parody of the song "Chim Chim Cheree" (1964) with the lines "My chair is upholstered in real Naugahyde / When they killed that nauga, I sat down and cried!" *American Idol* judge Paula Abdul (b. 1962) broke her nose and arm in 2007 when she tried to avoid tripping over her pet chihuahua. [pg. 19]

17. The burka is is an enveloping outer garment worn by women in some Islamic traditions for the purpose of cloaking the entire body. Pop singer Justin Timberlake (b. 1981) appeared, along with Britney Spears, on *The New Mickey Mouse Club* in the early 1990s. [pg. 20]

18. Ebb and Flo's home is based on a 1910 postcard of "The Barrel House" in the old mining town of Tonopah, NV. [pg. 22]

19. *Flip This House* is a television series which features the purchase and renovation of a single property in each episode. [pg. 22]

20. Camper spotted in Gloucester, MA. [pg. 23]

21. Wealthy entrepreneur and abolitionist Johns Hopkins (1795-1873) gave his name to Johns Hopkins University in Baltimore, MD, as a result of a bequeathment in his will. He also supplied horseshoes to the Union Army during the American Civil War. [pg. 24]

22. "Big Tex," Texas State Fairgrounds, Dallas, TX. [pg. 26]

23. Orville Redenbacher (1907-1995), whose initial business was in agricultural fertilizer, made his fortune by perfecting a hybrid strain of corn ideal for making popcorn and founded the popcorn company bearing his name. He drowned in his hot tub in Coronado, Colorado. "Male/Female" statue by Jonathan Borofsky (b. 1942). (See also pg. 98, "Walk A Mile In My Muu-Muu" and "ONLY A THEORY," pg. 125) [pg. 26]

24. The 1960 Travel Trailer is a real mobile home. [pg. 27]

25. The Dingburg Holiday Inn is based on a 1930s postcard of the Pasadena Community Church, St. Petersburg, FL. [pg. 28]

26. Last panel: lyrics from Celine Dion's "My Heart Will Go On," 1997. [pg. 29]

27. Ventriloquist Edgar Bergen's (1903-1978) country bumpkin dummy, Mortimer Snerd, originated both the phrase "Who'da thunk it?" and the now overused "Duh," to indicate confusion (now mock confusion). [pg. 30]

28. Ho Hos were created by the Hostess Bakery in San Francisco in 1967. The name is a play on "Hostess" and the laugh sound, "ho." (See also "FOOD TUBES," pg. 70) [pg. 31]

29. Cubism was initially developed in 1908 by Pablo Picasso (1881-1973) and Georges Braque (1882-1963). Artist LeRoy Neiman (b. 1927) adopted his ever-present cigar as a result of advice from Salvador Dali (1904-1989) (Dali: "It's a good idea. Keep it.") According to the *Los Angeles Times*, artist Thomas Kinkade (b. 1958) is prone to mark his territory through urination. [pg. 32]

30. U.S. Congressman Dennis Kucinich (b. 1946) drafted articles of impeachment against both Vice President Dick Cheney (b. 1941) and President George W. Bush (b. 1946). In 1982, he borrowed money from friend Shirley MacLaine in order to pay the mortgage due on his Cleveland home. (See also "BADA BING, BADA BONGO," pg. 34) [pg. 33]

31. Skeet shooting was invented by William Harnden Foster, an avid grouse hunter, in 1915. "Skeet" is also slang for semen. [pg. 33]

32. Novo Nordisk is actually a Danish pharmaceutical company, specializing in diabetes care. (See also "HAPPY NORDISK!," pg. 35) [pg. 34]

33. The term "beatnik" was first coined by *San Francisco Chronicle* columnist Herb Caen (1916-1997) in 1958, inspired by the launch of the first Soviet space satellite, Sputnik. Wonder Bread was originally produced by the Taggart Baking Company of Indianapolis, IN in 1921. (See also "LABOR MOVEMENT," pg. 49 and Dingburg Map) [pg. 34]

34. The marquee of the "Bleaker Cinema" (a parody of Greenwich Village's Bleecker Street Cinema) features the film *Shock Corridor* (1963), directed by Sam Fuller (1912-1997). It starred Constance Towers (b. 1934), who went on to play villainess Helena Cassadine on the TV soap opera *General Hospital* (1963-present). [pg. 35]

35. The Undico Office Complex is based on a 1930s postcard of Knapp's Department Store, Lansing MI. The J. C. Penney department store chain was founded in 1902 by James Cash Penney (1875-1971). [pg. 36]

36. *Startling Terror Tales* was first published in 1952 by Star Publications. Cartoonist Wallace Wood (1927-1981) was best known for his work in EC Comics and *Mad* magazine. Wood is also known as the artist of the x-rated, unsigned Disneyland Memorial poster, which first appeared in Paul Krassner's (b. 1932) magazine *The Realist* (#74, 1967). [pg. 36]

37. Based on the roadside restaurant, Aero Dogs, Tulare, CA. [pg. 37]

38. Milk Duds candy was first manufactured in 1928 by F. Hoffman & Company of Chicago IL. The word "Duds" came about because the original aim of having a perfectly round piece of candy was found to be impossible. (See also "DECANTING A CHEWY AROMA," pg. 123) [pg. 38]

39. English actor Ronald Coleman (1891-1958) also appeared as Jack Benny's (1894-1974) next-door neighbor on the Jack Benny radio show in the 1940s. [pg. 38]

40. English singer-songwriter Amy Winehouse (b. 1983) still struggles with alcohol and drug addiction. Her 2006 hit "Rehab" recounts her refusal to remain at an alcohol rehabilitation center (she stayed for 15 minutes). For much of the 1990s, singer Donny Osmond (b. 1957) suffered from Social Anxiety Disorder, which caused him to feel light-headed during performances. The Osmond Brothers hit "Yo-yo" is from 1971. (See also "UTAH," pg. 154) [pg. 39]

41. "Incense and Peppermints" was a hit for the Strawberry Alarm Clock in 1967. [pg. 41]

42. Rudy Giuliani (b. 1944), former Mayor of New York City and failed Presidential candidate, once said, "I don't agree with myself on everything." [pg. 42]

43. Based on photographs of comedian Jimmy Durante (1893-1980). Claude Monet (1840-1926), Alfred Sisley (1839-1899), Camille Pissarro (1830-1903) and Marty Cassatt (1844-1926) were all Impressionist painters. [pg. 43]

44. From early 20th century circus photos by F.W. Glasier (18??-1954). [pg. 44]

45. Tuxedo Sam, a penguin, is a Sanrio cartoon character associated with Hello Kitty. His original motto was "He wants to help, but is not needed." "Good Humor" ice cream trucks plied the streets of the U.S. from 1920 to 1978. [pg. 44]

46. Massapequa is a town on Long Island, NY. Famous residents include Jerry Seinfeld (b.1944) and Neil Diamond (b. 1941). [pg. 45]

47. Andy Panda appeared in a series of animated cartoons produced by Walter Lantz (1899-1994) from 1939 to 1949. He appeared in comic books from 1941 to 1978. One early Andy Panda story from *New Funnies* #76 (1943) was drawn by Uncle Scrooge cartoonist Carl Barks (1901-2000). [pg. 46]

48. The Dingburg Fairy is eerily similar to "Psyche," the White Rock Club Soda fairy, which is based on a late 19th century painting by German artist Paul Thumann (1834-1908). (See also "PING, MEET PONG," pg. 51) [pg. 47]

49. Actor/comedian Phil Silvers (1911-1985) is best known for his TV series *The Phil Silvers Show* (1955-1959) in which he played fast-talking, conniving Army sergeant, Ernie Bilko. [pg. 47]

50. "Martinizing" is a non-flammable chemical-based dry cleaning system developed by chemist Henry Martin in 1949. (See also "LAUNDRY LIST," pg. 114, and "PIG LATIN QUARTER," pg. 155) [pg. 49]

51. The Carvel soft serve ice cream company was founded in 1929 by Tom Carvel (1906-1990). The Beastie Boys song "Cooky Puss" (1983), their first rap recording, is a reference to the Carvel cake Cookie Puss. [pg. 50]

52. This strip ran on Earth Day, April 22, 2008, as part of a similar effort by most daily newspaper cartoonists on that day. [pg. 54]

53. There is a website featuring Garfield strips without Garfield. Garfield's image and dialogue have been deleted. Visit "Garfield minus Garfield" at http://garfieldminusgarfield.net [pg. 55]

54. The "giant ball of oil" Seinfeld episode referred to is titled "The Voice," episode #158, first broadcast on October 2, 1997. [pg. 56]

55. Actress Tuesday Weld (b. 1943) played the unobtainable Thalia Menninger on *The Many Loves of Dobie Gillis* TV series (1959-1963). She is distantly related to Charles J. Guiteau (1841-1882), who assassinated President James A. Garfield (1831-1881). [pg. 57]

56. Neither Thomas Edison, Regis Philbin nor Jay Leno are actually pinheads. [pg. 57]

57. Desenex is an anti-fungal powder that helps combat athlete's foot. [pg. 58]

58. *The Circle of Life* is a short film shown at Disneyworld's Epcot Center featuring characters from the film *The Lion King* (1994). The song Lippy is singing in the last panel is a version of "The Ding Dong Blues," featured in "Are We Having Fun Yet?" by Bill Griffith (1985), pg. 84. [pg. 59]

59. Zippy's autobiography is titled "Lucien Freud and Me." Painter Lucien Freud (b. 1922) is the grandson of Sigmund Freud. Lucien Freud once said, "The longer you look at an object, the more abstract it becomes, and, ironically, the more real." [pg. 59]

60 A-B. The first mention of Zippy's "fur-lined fallout shelter" is in a one-page strip strip titled "The House of His Dreams" (1979), reprinted in the Zippy comic book, *Zippy #3* (1980). [pgs. 60-61]

61. Actor Troy Donahue (1937-2001) starred in the TV series *Surfside 6* (1960-1962). He also had leads in the 1958 film *Monster on the Campus* and the 1957 sci-fi film *The Monolith Monsters*. [pg. 62]

62. Polysorbate 80, also known as Tween 80, is a nonionic surfactant and emulsifier derived from polyoxylated sorbitan and oleic acid. It is often used in Zippy's favorite foods, or as a condiment. Soraya Sarhaddi Nelson is an NPR foreign correspondent currently stationed in Afghanistan. [pg. 63]

63. Sheboygan is a Wisconsin city about 50 miles north of Milwaukee and is famous for its bratwurst. [pg. 63]

64. Actor Vincent D'Onofrio (b. 1959) is now primarily known for his portrayal of Detective Robert Goren on TV's *Law & Order: Criminal Intent* (2001-present). He also played Abbie Hoffman (1936-1989) in the bio-pic *Steal This Movie* (2000). [pg. 65]

65. Devo songs: "Mongoloid" from *Are We Not Men?*, 1978. "Beautiful World" from *New Traditionalists*, 1981. "Space Junk," from *Are We Not Men?*, 1978. [pg. 65]

66. Hall & Oates is a duo made up of singers Daryl Hall (b. 1946) and John Oates (b. 1949). They achieved their greatest fame from 1975 to 1985. Daryl Hall was featured in a 1980s issue of *People* magazine wearing a Zippy t-shirt. [pg. 66]

67. *Little Dot* comics were published from 1948 to 1982, and then occasionally until 1994. Little Dot was created by Vic Herman (1919-1999), who also created Reddy Kilowatt and Elsie the Cow advertisements. *Sad Sack* comics were created by George Baker (1915-1975). [pg. 68]

68. *Boy's Life* is a magazine published by the Boy Scouts of America since 1911. "Skeezix" (slang for "motherless calf") is the adopted child of Walt Wallet from the long-running daily comic strip, *Gasoline Alley*, first created by Frank King (1883-1969). King drew the strip from 1918 to 1956, though it continues to the present time. Tabloid personality Lindsay Lohan (b. 1986) emailed the TV show *Access Hollywood* in 2007 saying, "I appreciate everyone giving me my privacy." (See also "OFF TO THE RACES," pg. 73 and "DEEP COVER," pg. 77) [pg. 70]

69. "Row, Row, Row Your Boat" is an English nursery rhyme, put to music by Eliphalet Oram Lyte in 1881. [pg. 71]

70. The "Hokey Pokey" song and dance may have originated in England in 1942 as the "Cokey Cokey," composed by Jimmy Kennedy (1902-1984). As "The Hokey Pokey," the song was a hit for the Ray Anthony (b. 1922) Orchestra in 1952. [pg. 71]

71. British cartoonist Harry Hanan (? -1982) created the silent daily comic strip, *Louie* (1947-1976). Louie himself appears in the second panel. "Louie, Louie" was originally written by Richard Berry in 1955 and was a hit for The Kingsmen in 1963. The lyrics here are verbatim from their recording. [pg. 72]

72. All George W. Bush quotes authentic and verbatim. [pg. 72]

73. Zerbina refers to Sarah Jessica Parker (b. 1965) in the first panel. Parker played director Ed Wood's girlfriend, Dolores Fuller, in *Ed Wood* (1924-1978), the 1994 bio-pic directed by Tim Burton (b. 1958). [pg. 74]

74. Barack Obama's (b. 1961) father was an atheist. He chews Nicorette regularly and is a good poker player. [pg. 74]

75. Actor/comedian Howie Mandel (b. 1955) has obsessive-compulsive disorder and mysophobia (fear of germs) and, as a result, will not shake hands with contestants on the TV game show he hosts, *Deal or No Deal*. Former CIA Operations Officer Valerie Plame's (b. 1963) great-grandfather was a Ukrainian Rabbi. Her original family name was Plamevotski. TV journalist Katie Couric (b. 1957) underwent an on-air colonoscopy in 2000. TV game show host Pat Sajak (b. 1946) was a major donor to the Ronald Reagan Presidential Library. [pg. 76]

76. Conservative political commentator Ann Coulter (b. 1961) once said, "I'm a Christian first and a mean-spirited, bigoted conservative second, and don't you ever forget it." [pg. 76]

77. On the official Warner Brothers Harry Potter online shop, one can purchase a "Harry Potter Adult Deluxe Death Eater" costume for $44.95. [pg. 78]

78. As previously stated, "Poindexter bar bats" are entirely fictional. [pg. 79]

79. Little Lulu was created by Marjorie Henderson Buell in 1935 and popularized in comic book form (1945-1984) by John Stanley (1914-1993) and Irving Tripp (1921-). Zippy's favorite Little Lulu villain is Clarence McNabbem, truant officer. [pg. 80]

## SUNDAY COLOR/ Chapter 2

80. An isosceles triangle has two sides of equal length. (Note: Zippy's head is an equilateral triangle in shape.) The hypotenuse is the longest side of a right triangle, opposite the right angle. [pg. 82]

81. Based on streets as shown in 1920s and 1930s postcards of 1) Provincetown, MA 2) Westbrook, ME 3) Portland, OR [pg. 82]

82. Mariska Hargitay (b. 1964) stars in the TV cop show, *Law & Order: SVU*. She is the daughter of actress Jayne Mansfield (1933-1967) and Mr. Universe 1955 Mickey Hargitay (1926-2006). Governor Arnold Schwarzenegger (b. 1947) played Mickey Hargitay in the 1982 TV movie, *The Jayne Mansfield Story*. Actor and Senator Fred Thompson (b. 1942) famously bowed out of the 2008 Presidential race on January 22, 2008. TV police detective Brenda Johnson of *The Closer* is portrayed by Kyra Sedgwick (b. 1965), first cousin once removed of Andy Warhol film actress Edie Sedgwick (1943-1971). Ed Green and Lieutenant Van Buren are fictional detectives on the original *Law & Order* TV series. [pg. 83]

83. William Howard Taft (1857-1930) was the twenty-seventh President of the United States. Wassailing is the practice of going door-to-door singing Christmas carols. [pg. 84]

84. The "Magic Marker" was invented in 1952 by Sidney Rosenthal. They are not of alien origin. [pg. 85]

85. Radial tires were first developed by the Michelin tire company in 1946. Comedian Henny Youngman (1906-1998), famous for his one-liners, also starred in the 1972 horror film *The Gore-Gore Girls*, about a string of murdered strippers. [pg. 85]

86. Singer John Denver (1943-1997) entertained both Richard Nixon (1913-1994) and Chinese Premier Zhou Enlai (1898-1976) at a Washington, D.C., concert in 1972. After the performance, Zhou Enlai purchased 500 cassette tapes of Denver's "Take Me Home, Country Roads." The Hale-Bopp Comet was discovered in 1995 by astronomers Alan Hale (b. 1958) and Thomas Bopp (b. 1949). [pg. 86]

87. *The Lone Ranger* TV series (1949-1957) starred Clayton Moore (1914-1999) and Jay Silverheels (1912-1980) as his companion, Tonto, and was assumed to take place in the American West of the 19th century, although *The Lone Ranger* radio show (1933-1954) once anachronistically offered a free premium to listeners called "The Lone Ranger Atom Bomb Ring." [pg. 86]

88. The Cheesecake Factory chain of restaurants started in Beverly Hills, CA in 1978. They are famous for their cheesecake — and their very long wait times. Italian actor Domenico Nesci (b. 1982) co-starred with Tila Nguyen (b. 1981) on the TV series *A Shot At Love with Tila Tequila* (2007). Mike Huckabee (b. 1955), former Governor of Arkansas, after losing 110 pounds and the Republican Presidential nomination in 2008, once said, "I may not be the expert that some people are on foreign policy, but I did stay in a Holiday Inn Express last night." [pg. 87]

89. French playwright Alfred Jarry (1873-1907), creator of the infamous absurdist play *Ubu Roi* (1896), called the bicycle that he rode everywhere "that which rolls." His drink of choice was absinthe, not Extreme Taco Sauce. "Merdre" is Jarry's intentional misspelling of merde, French for "shit." The Hush Puppies shoes brand was founded in 1958 by the Wolverine Company. The name refers to the practice of farmers throwing hush puppies (fried cornballs) to barking dogs to quiet them. [pg. 87]

90. From Henry David Thoreau's (1817-1862) Walden, 1854. Thoreau's last words were "...moose...indian..." [pg. 88]

91. The "Zippy Pledge" first appeared on page 3 of the Zippy paperback book, *Nation of Pinheads*, 1982. [pg. 90]

92. Gertrude Stein (1874-1946) and Alice B. Toklas (1877-1967) lived together in Paris until Stein's death. Stein once said, "I really do not know that anything has been more exciting than diagramming sentences." [pg. 91]

93. Pictured in the last panel is circus clown Emmett Kelly (1898-1979) in his "Weary Willie" persona. In 1956, he performed as the mascot of the Brooklyn Dodgers baseball team. (See also "HOBOPHOBIA," pg. 119) [pg. 93]

94. Animated cartoon character Betty Boop made her first appearance in *Dizzy Dishes*, 1930. She was designed by Grim Natwick (1890-1990) who also helped animate Mickey Mouse, Mr. Magoo and Popeye. [pg. 94]

95. Ivanka Trump (b. 1981) once said, "I've never lived in a building without my name on it." [pg. 95]

96. J. Edgar Hoover (1895-1972) was the director of the FBI from 1924 until 1972. Since his death, there have been several Congressional attempts to remove his name from the FBI building in Washington, DC. (See also pg. 101) [pg. 95]

97. Based on photos of Mark Twain (1835-1910) on the porch of his home in Hartford CT. [pg. 96]

98. Hellboy, created by Mike Mignola (b. 1960), is fireproof. [pg. 99]

99. The flamboyant American actress Tallulah Bankhead (1902-1968) is said to have inspired the personality of Cruella De Vil in the Disney animated feature *One Hundred and One Dalmatians* (1961). [pg. 101]

100. See Pindex #96. [pg. 101]

101. Ice cream store, Las Vegas, NV. [pg. 103]

102. The Pod vehicle shown was designed and built by Geoffrey Conklin and Jon Buller in 1989 in Lyme, CT. (See also "Z-POD," pg. 135) [pg. 103]

103. Lone Pine, CA. [pg. 104]

104. Advertising lines clipped and pasted from early 1950s issues of *Popular Mechanics* magazine. [pg. 105]

105. The HMS Beagle was a survey barque, first launched as a 10-gun brig-sloop of the British Royal Navy in 1820. The ship took naturalist Charles Darwin (1809-1882) on the historic expedition to chart the coastline of South America in 1831. Czech composer Antonin Dvorak (1841-1904) spent the summer of 1893 in Spillville, Iowa. [pg. 106]

106 A-B. The "Fletcher and Tanya" look is a take-off on the daily comic strip *Morty Meekle* by Dick Cavali (b. 1923). All dialog is clipped from 1940s-50s magazine advertisements and other similar sources. (See also "FLETCHER & TANYA/ Chapter 5, pg. 140) [pg. 107]

## LITTLE ZIPPY/ Chapter 3

107. In the last panel. Little Zippy drives a "Wienermobile," first created in 1936 by Carl G. Meyer. [pg. 109]

108. Emmentaler cheese comes from the valley of Emmental, Switzerland. [pg. 110]

109. Mallomars were introduced in 1913 by Nabisco. In Canada, they are known as "Dream Puffs." [pg. 111]

110. Panel 1) Meriden, MS. Panels 2 & 3) Shreveport, LA. [pg. 111]

111. The *Dennis the Menace* daily comic strip was created by Hank Ketcham (1920-2001) in 1951. The strip was said to be set in Wichita, Kansas, where Ketcham was made honorary mayor in 1953. [pg. 113]

112. Dark matter is matter that does not interact with the electromagnetic force, but whose presence can be inferred by gravitational effects on visible matter. The universe is composed mostly of dark matter. [pg. 113]

113. Noted residents of Nutley, New Jersey, include sharpshooter Annie Oakley (1860-1926), artist Reginald Marsh (1898-1954) and wrestler Balls Mahoney (b. 1972). [pg. 115]

114. The symbol Little Zippy is pointing to is that of the Bell (telephone) System, named for telephone inventor Alexander Graham Bell (1847-1922). The Japanese film monster Godzilla debuted in 1954. In Japan, Godzilla is generally seen as a metaphor for the United States. [pg. 116]

115. "Ike" is the nickname of Dwight D. Eisenhower (1890-1969), thirty-fourth President of the United States. Singer and teen idol Ricky Nelson (1940-1985) had thirty Top-40 hits from 1957 to 1962. The Contras were rebel groups opposing Nicaragua's Sandinista government following the 1979 overthrow of Anastasio Somoza Debayle. [pg. 117]

116. Massachusetts State Senator Jarrrett Barrios proposed in 2006 that there be a restriction on the number of servings of Marshmallow Fluff ("Fluffernutter") sandwiches in public schools. He was ridiculed and soon dropped the idea. Later that year, State Representative Kathie-Anne Reinstein proposed that the Fluffernutter be the state sandwich of Massachusetts. [pg. 117]

117. The TV series *My Mother the Car* ran for a single season from 1965 to 1966. It starred Jerry Van Dyke (b. 1931) as the owner of a 1928 automobile which was possessed by the spirit of his dead mother, voiced by actress Ann Sothern (1909-2001). In panel 2, Little Zippy is spouting the ideas of philosopher Georg Friedrich Hegel (1770-1831). *McHale's Navy* was a TV sitcom (1962-1966) starring Ernest Borgnine (b. 1917) in the title role. [pg. 119]

118. As previously stated, "Poindexter Bar Bats" are fictional. Only Zippy knows what they are used for. [pg. 119]

119. Translation from the Latvian: Panel 1) Dad: "How much is this?" Zippy: "My hovercraft is full of eels!" Panel 2) Mom: "Please say that again." Zippy: "Call the police!" Panel 3) Zippy: "One language is never enough!" *True Crime Comics* were published from 1947 to 1949 by Magazine Village, Inc. "Sea Monkeys" were actually a variety of brine shrimp marketed first as "Instant Life" in comic book ads from 1957 through the 1970s. A disclaimer below the drawing of the anthropomorphic Sea Monkey family stated, "Illustration is fanciful." [pg. 121]

120. This strip's title, "SIEGEL, SHUSTER & Z-MAN," refers to Jerry Siegel (1914-1996) and Joe Shuster (1914-1992), who created the original Superman character in 1938. They were paid a total of $130.00 at that time, parodied in panel 3 and 4. [pg. 123]

121. New York City's Art Deco-style Chrysler Building was erected in 1929. It is the world's tallest brick building. [pg. 123]

## ROADSIDE/ Chapter 4

122. Frost Diner, Warrenton, VA. [pg. 125]

123. Blue and White restaurant, Alexandria, VA. [pg. 125]

124. USA Country Diner, Windsor, NJ. [pg. 126]

125. Red Apple Rest, Tuxedo, NY. *The Funky Winkerbean* daily comic strip by Tom Batiuk (b. 1947) debuted in 1972. (See also "FUNKY," pg. 131) [pg. 126]

126. Panels 1 & 4) El Vado Motel, Albuquerque, NM. Panels 2 & 3) Owasso, OK. Piggly Wiggly was the first self-service grocery store, founded in Memphis, Tenn., in 1916. [pg. 127]

127. Vista, CA. [pg. 127]

128. Elmsford, NY. [pg. 128]

129. Gloucester Township, NJ. [pg. 128]

130. Russell Speeder Car Wash, Omaha, NB. [pg. 129]

131. Anchorage, AK. Actually, David Maisel is Chairman of Marvel Studios. Marvel Comics founder Stan Lee (b. 1922), calls him "Greed-for-brains."[pg. 129]

132. New York, NY. [pg. 130]

133. Calgary, Saskatchewan, Canada. [pg. 130]

134. Calgary, Saskatchewan, Canada. [pg. 131]

135. Staten Island, NY. Stephen Hawking (b. 1942) has played himself in several episodes of *The Simpsons* TV series. [pg. 131]

136. Mama's Used Cars, Charleston, SC. [pg. 132]

137. Berwyn, IL. [pg. 132]

138. Hobo Joe restaurant, formerly of Phoenix, AZ. [pg. 133]

139. Better Packages, Shelton, CT. In October 2007, the author accompanied Robert and Aline Crumb on a tour of the Better Packages factory. Later, a piece by both Crumbs appeared in the *New Yorker* magazine of November 26, 2007, titled "Our Beloved Tape Dispenser." This strip was published on December 11, 2007, with the Crumbs' knowledge and approval. [pg. 133]

140. Zippy is driving the 1965 "Peel Trident," manufactured on the Isle of Man, Great Britain. Nouri al-Maliki (b. 1950) is the Prime Minister of Iraq. He once said, "I'm not America's man in Iraq." [pg. 134.]

141A-B. The A&W Root Beer Family in the back yard of a private home, Portland, OR. [pg. 136]

142. Lone Pine, CA. Among other things, architect Frank Gehry (born Ephraim Owen Goldberg, 1929) designed the World Cup of Hockey trophy. [pg. 137]

143. Toad rock, Freedom, NH. [pg. 137]

144. *Judge Parker* was created by Nicholas P. Dallis (1911-1991) in 1952. *Mary Worth* was created by Allen Saunders (1899-1986) and Dale Conner in 1940. *Apartment 3-G* was created by Nicholas P. Dallis and Alex Kotzky (1923-1996) in 1961. [pg. 138]

145. Weenie Beenie restaurant, Arlington, VA. Zippy refers to *God Is Not Great: How Religion Poisons Everything* (2007) by Christopher Hitchens (b. 1949). [pg. 139]

146. Pensionnat Maintenon, Sommieres, France. [pg. 139]

## FLETCHER & TANYA/ Chapter 5

147. NOTE: As previously stated, the "Fletcher & Tanya" look is a take-off on the daily comic strip *Morty Meekle* (1956-1967) by Dick Cavali. All dialog is clipped and pasted from the author's own files in 1940s-1950s magazines and other sources. None of it is written by the author. [pgs. 141-149]

148A-B. The animal characters in these two strips are based on secondary characters featured in *Felix the Cat* comic book #40, 1953. (See also "STRIP SHOW," pg. 148) [pgs. 142-143]

149A-B. Big Head Eddie is a take-off on the Harvey Comics character Richie Rich (1953-present). [pg. 145]

150. Dialog clipped and pasted from 1940s-1950s magazine ads. [pg. 148]

## TOAD ET ALIA/ Chapter 6

151. Actor Kirk Douglas (b. 1916) changed his name from Izzy Demsky just before he entered the U.S. Navy in World War II. [pg. 151]

152. Pith helmets are made of cork or pith, the spongy material found in the stems of vascular plants like the Indian sola. [pg. 152.]

153. Before he founded psychoanalysis, Sigmund Freud (1856-1939) briefly conducted medical research into the location of the sexual organs of the eel, in which he was unsuccessful. [pg. 153.]

154. Jell-o brand gelatin first made its appearance in 1902 as a product of the Genesee Pure Food Company. It was based on a formula developed by Peter Cooper (1791-1883) in 1845, who also built the first American steam-powered locomotive, the Tom Thumb. [pg. 154]

155. The Osmonds originally consisted of Alan, Wayne, Merrill, Jay, Donny, Marie and Jimmy Osmond. Older brothers George and Thomas were born deaf and did not appear on any recordings, though they did make occasional public appearances with the group. Jimmy Osmond (b. 1963) was a big star in Great Britain and Japan, most notably with his hit single, "Long Haired Lover From Liverpool" (1972). [pg. 154]

156. Comedian and actor Joey Bishop (1918-2007) was best-known for being a member of Hollywood's "Rat Pack." He played a TV telethon emcee in the film *Valley of the Dolls* (1967). [pg. 155]

157. The earliest form of bowling dates back to ancient Egypt. Other early instances of the sport appeared in Finland, Yemen and later in Germany, in 300 A.D. [pg. 155]

158. Bayonne, New Jersey, was founded as a township in 1862. Boxer Chuck Wepner (b. 1939), known as the "Bayonne Bleeder," was the inspiration for the *Rocky* films. He went 15 rounds against Muhammad Ali (b. 1942) in 1975. [pg. 156]